WILLIAM DEAN HOWELLS

William Dean Howells

REPRESENTATIVE SELECTIONS, WITH

INTRODUCTION, BIBLIOGRAPHY,

AND NOTES BY

CLARA MARBURG KIRK

and

RUDOLF KIRK

Revised Edition

American Century Series

HILL AND WANG — NEW YORK

FIRST AMERICAN CENTURY SERIES EDITION OCTOBER 1961

Grateful acknowledgment is made to Miss Mildred Howells and Mr. John Mead Howells for permission to reprint the following selections: From *Years of My Youth* (I, iv; II, iv; III, viii), copyright 1916 by Harper and Brothers, copyright 1944 by Mildred Howells and John Mead Howells; from *Literary Friends and Acquaintance* ("My First Visit to New England"), copyright 1900 by Harper and Brothers, copyright 1928 by Mildred Howells and John Mead Howells; the articles on Emile Zola and Frank Norris, by William Dean Howells, from the *North American Review* (1902); and for numerous brief quotations in the Introduction and notes (the sources of which are specifically given in footnotes on the pages on which they occur) from the following: *Years of My Youth,* copyright 1916 by Harper and Brothers, copyright 1944 by Mildred Howells and John Mead Howells; *Literary Friends and Acquaintance,* copyright 1900 by Harper and Brothers, copyright 1928 by Mildred Howells and John Mead Howells; *My Literary Passions,* copyright 1895 by Harper and Brothers, copyright 1922 by Mildred Howells and John Mead Howells; *My Mark Twain,* copyright 1910 by Harper and Brothers, copyright 1938 by Mildred Howells and John Mead Howells; *Life in Letters of William Dean Howells,* by Mildred Howells, copyright 1928 by Doubleday, Doran and Company; and from unpublished letters of William Dean Howells.

The American Century edition of this volume is a reprinting of the American Writers Series *Howells.* Harry Hayden Clark was the General Editor of the original series.

Manufactured in the United States of America

to

FANNY MONCURE MARBURG

PREFACE

Howells is known today as a novelist. But he began and ended his literary career as a journalist, and, though his novels appeared almost every year, and frequently twice a year, from 1872 to 1921, he managed to write half a dozen autobiographical studies, four volumes of poetry, over thirty plays, a dozen or more travel books, uncounted memoirs, biographies, and reviews. The introductory critical study in this volume attempts to relate Howells' multifarious literary expression to his work as a novelist. Since practically all of Howells' writing is ultimately autobiographical, our study must be biographical in order to be properly critical.

To choose "representative selections" from more than a hundred bound volumes of Howells' works, not to mention the uncollected reviews, stories, and essays in magazines, might well baffle the boldest editor, especially since Howells' writing maintained a uniformly high standard. We have attempted to solve the problem by keeping in mind the fact that Howells should be studied first of all as a novelist. What selections we have chosen from his memoirs and his critical essays are designed to throw light on his attitude toward realism as a technique, and his use of his own experience in novel writing. We have included two narrative poems and one play from his many comedies as examples of Howells' search for his novel form. The novels from which we have chosen selections are discussed at length in our Introduction, for, since Howells was essentially an autobiographical novelist, they are only to be understood against the background of his life. *Indian Summer,* for instance, is to be read as a reflection of Howells' stay in Italy in 1882 and as the culmination of a series of Italian novels in which Howells made use of his enriching European experiences; *Annie Kilburn* not only reflects Howells' fine sense of New England small-town life, but also shows the effect of his reading of Tolstoy on his awakening social conscience, which had become articulate in *A Modern Instance* and *The Rise of Silas Lapham* and reached its strongest expression in *A Hazard of New Fortunes.* Howells' concern for society, clearly set forth in *A Traveler from Altruria,* for a time interrupted his novel writing. If space permitted, we should like to include selections from his later novels, such as *The Kentons* and *The Vacation of the Kelwyns,* to show that he at last gave up the social novel, convinced that "the phenomena of our enormous enterprise . . . are the stuff for newspapers, but not for the novel, except as such wonders of the outer world can be related to the miracles of the inner world." The excerpts from Howells' critical comments indicate why he ventured into the wider social fields, and why he returned to more restrained literary expression. The chapters from *Years of My Youth* and *Literary Friends and Acquaintance* are chosen to help the reader understand both the surroundings in which Howells grew up in Ohio and the early associations he formed in Boston and New York. Only from this basis can one appraise his critical position as a writer of realistic novels. The selections in this volume are arranged, therefore, not in order of publication, but in a sequence which will show the development of Howells the novelist. The reader will find few notes to the individual selections, since all the relevant material is included in the introductory critical remarks, where it may be considered in proper relation to Howells' life and writing.

The editors have leaned heavily on the bibliographical knowledge of Dr. George Arms and Dr. William M. Gibson, whose *Bibliography* of Howells is a model of its kind. These scholars prepared the Selected Bibliography for the first edition of this book, but they could not find time to revise it for the present volume. Professor Harry Hayden Clark and Professor Arms read our Introduction and offered many suggestions for improvements.

In preparing the Introduction we have consulted several hundred unpublished letters of Howells, to be found in libraries from the Pacific to the Atlantic. Original letters were lent us by Mr.

Cecil Piatt of Glen Ridge, New Jersey; by Mrs. Frederick W. McReynolds of Washington, D. C.; and by Mr. William Howells of Youngstown, Ohio; and we wish to thank these friends. Miss Mildred Howells has kindly granted us permission to use sentences from these letters. We wish to thank also the New York Public Library, the Ashtabula Public Library, the Huntington Library, and the libraries of the University of Southern California, Ohio State University, and Harvard and Yale Universities for their unfailing courtesy and kindness.

For a note on minor text errata, see page 395.

CONTENTS

Contents

INTRODUCTION

I. THE HOWELLS LEGEND

In 1850, when William Dean Howells was thirteen years of age, he set up his own poems and stories on his father's printing press; essays, reviews, novels were still pouring from his pen when he died in 1920. As a man of seventy, Howells wrote wearily to his brother, "I . . . feel as if it must have been done by a trust named after me."[1]

Between 1860, the date of his first published book, and 1921, over a hundred volumes of poems, plays, short stories, essays, novels, travel sketches, biographies, and autobiographies had accumulated on the Howells shelf. They are now a formidable barrier to an understanding of Howells' mind. Yet Howells' contribution to our culture is of especial interest to students of American literature. Not only did Howells give us the finest examples of the realistic novel written in the nineteenth century, but he also presented, through his novels and his critical essays, the whole problem of realism. Perhaps of still more lasting significance is the fact that Howells' writing reflects more than sixty years of our social history. "They make a great array, a literature in themselves, your studies of American life,"[2] wrote Henry James to Howells on the occasion of his seventy-fifth birthday. Howells was, in fact, the reporter of his age, from the days when, as a nineteen-year-old boy in Ohio, he wrote his own column for the *Cincinnati Gazette*, through his consular term in Venice, when he described the life around him for the *Boston Daily Advertiser*, to the year of his death, when, as Editor of the "Easy Chair" of *Harper's*, he set the standard of taste for

[1] *Life in Letters of William Dean Howells*, ed. by Mildred Howells (New York, 1928), II, 231.
[2] *The Letters of Henry James* (2 vols.), ed. by Percy Lubbock (New York, 1920), II, 224.

cultured America. Born in the Ohio of small towns and open farmland before the Civil War, living for twenty years in the twilight glow of literary Cambridge and Boston, moving to New York at the time when the country was stirred by the Chicago anarchists and a New York traction strike, Howells reflects, at every move, the thought and feeling of America. His poetry, his autobiographical essays, his novels, mirror the culture of pioneering America dominated by the thought of New England, as it gradually moved into the more complex, industrial society of the twentieth century.

But Howells did not remain merely the reporter of his world; twenty-five years of journalistic experience turned the literary youth from Ohio into a novelist who not only discovered for himself the new technique of realism, but also formulated a critical theory in its defence. One has only to compare *Their Wedding Journey* (1872) with *The Rise of Silas Lapham* (1885) to realize the extraordinary evolution of a sensitive, poetic mind, schooled and disciplined by the reporter's habit of observation and respect for fact. The transformation of the youthful writer of heroic couplets and travel essays into the mature novelist can only be explained by the fact that Howells was, through all these years, under the practical necessity of earning his living by means of journalism. The merging of these two aspects of Howells' mind brought him at last to a concept of the novel as an art form dependent on a love of the commonplace which has left its imprint on the development of the novels of Dreiser, Atherton, Lewis, and all the other ungrateful moderns who fail to recognize their debt to the man who, from the "Editor's Study" of *Harper's Magazine*, successfully waged the battle for realism.

The voice of the great "Dean" might have been listened to with more attention had he not lived for thirty years after the enunciation of his theory of realism into the beginning of the nineteen-twenties, when, though the principle remained the same, the method of expression had changed. Howells himself knew that he belonged to another day. "Well, we lived in a great time," he wrote to an old friend, "If we have outlived it, so much the worse for this time." Perhaps Howells' fine sense of irony enabled him to read with composure H. L. Mencken's picture of him as "an Agnes Repplier in pantaloons," "a contriver of pretty things," "the author of a long row of uninspired and hollow books, with no more ideas in them than so many volumes of *The Ladies Home Journal*."[3]

Though it was perhaps necessary for writers whose "realism" reflected the mood of a later, war-shocked generation to overthrow the more tempered, the more subtle realism of Howells, it is now possible, a generation after Howells' death, to arrive at a more just appraisal of his contribution to our culture. Delmar Gross Cooke[4] and Oscar W. Firkins,[5] who wrote of

[3]*Prejudices: First Series* (New York: 1919), p. 56. Though this Howells legend was expressed in lively terms by Mencken, other critics popularized it further. It was revived by Sinclair Lewis, who, in his Stockholm address on the occasion of receiving the Nobel Prize in 1930, put Howells at the head of the timid Victorians from whom the bolder realists of the twenties were revolting; by Lewis Mumford, who relegated him to the Gilded Age in his book entitled *The Golden Day* (1926); by Ludwig Lewisohn, who presented Howells, in his *Expression in America* (1932), as a squeamish, inhibited individual, "as obsessed by sex as a fighting prohibitionist is by alcohol," p. 244. See also: Hartley Grattan, "Howells, Ten Years After," *American Mercury*, XX (May, 1930), 42–50; Matthew Josephson, "Those Who Stayed," *Portrait of the Artist as American* (New York, 1930), pp. 161–166; V. F. Calverton, in *The Liberation of American Literature* (New York, 1932), p. 381; Granville Hicks, in *The Great Tradition* (New York, 1933), pp. 98–99. For a more just appraisal of Howells as a significant novelist, see Carl Van Doren, *The American Novel* (New York, 1940), pp. 115–136; Van Wyck Brooks, *New England: Indian Summer* (New York, 1940), pp. 204–249, 373–394; Walter F. Taylor, *The Economic Novel in America* (Chapel Hill, 1942), pp. 214–281; Alfred Kazin, *On Native Ground* (New York, 1942), pp. 38–44. Such students of American literature as Herbert Edwards, Bernard Smith, Newton Arvin, J. W. Getzels, George Arms, William Gibson, and Edwin H. Cady are doing much to break down the legend which called Howells an idolater of decadent Boston with a vision limited by all the pruderies and conventions of the summer hotel of the nineties, and to present him to the present generation as one of the important figures in the social development of American literary culture. See the Selected Bibliography in this volume.

[4]D. G. Cooke, *William Dean Howells, a Critical Study* (New York, 1922).

[5]O. W. Firkins, *William Dean Howells, a Study* (Cambridge, 1924).

Howells soon after his death, and who must have been lifelong readers of his volumes year by year as they appeared, spoke more sympathetically of the body of his work than the critics who used him merely as a symbol of the "genteel tradition." Necessary as these two writers are to our understanding of Howells, their studies alone could not turn the tide of reaction against him. Vernon Louis Parrington's insistence that Howells was "never a child of the Gilded Age. . . . Neither at heart was he a child of Brahmin culture," but an important "reporter of his generation,"[6] who grew and developed with the times and left his imprint on his age, has made it incumbent on all serious critics to pause to consider the meaning of Howells' life and writing. Brander Matthews' words to Howells, written in 1893, remain true for the reader of today, "From no American author have I learned so much as from you of the ways, customs, traditions, thoughts and characters of my fellow citizens."[7] Thirty years after Howells' death, this reporter of another generation is being heard again.

A reading of the Howells shelf for purposes of reappraisal is, in fact, an education in nineteenth-century American social and literary history. Such a reading takes one back to the Western Reserve of the fifties, to a frontier where life was simple indeed, but where the culture was deeply rooted in New England tradition; and through the eyes of the observant reporter, steeped in the literature of several civilizations, it shows one New England, Venice, Boston, and, finally, New York. We watch the journalist turn novelist, and at last the novelist turn critic, not only of literature, but also of the society in which he had lived and worked. First from the "Editor's Study," and then from the "Editor's Easy Chair," Howells dominated the literary thought of his day for more than a generation. His

[6] *The Beginnings of Critical Realism in America, 1860–1920* (New York, 1930), III, 242–243, 252.
[7] Unpublished letter to Howells, dated December 25, 1893. The Houghton Library, Harvard University.

grasp of the so-called commonplaces of daily life, his democratic, humanitarian spirit, made him the interpreter of his countrymen to themselves in more than thirty-five novels, which take their place to-day in the long tradition of satiric realism. Moreover, his wide reading, shrewd common-sense, and habit of analysis made it possible for him to give expression to the theory of realism, which, in spite of changing fashions, has remained the basis of all novel writing in this country since his day, for realism is, as Howells said, "so largely of the future as well as the present."[8]

II. EDUCATION OF A POET-JOURNALIST

"I supposed myself a poet, and I knew myself a journalist."

Howells spent a lifetime digesting his own experiences. He grew through and by means of his writing. His experiences as a small boy in frontier Ohio towns, his boyhood affection for his large family, the long hours of work at his father's printing press, the talk he heard there and the romps he had with the other boys, the books he read in his "study" under the stairs—all is told and retold in half a dozen autobiographical books, the earliest, *A Boy's Town*, published in 1890, when Howells was 53 years old, and the last, *Years of My Youth*, written when he was an old man in his late seventies.[9]

One may properly ask what Howells carried through later life from this farm and village civilization of the years of his youth, which he never ceased trying to assimilate and under-

---

[8]*Century Magazine*, XXV (Nov., 1882), 28.

[9]In an unpublished letter written by Howells to his cousin Paul Kester, on March 28, 1914, he wrote that he was working too hard at remembering his life at Columbus, and that the effort was painful to him. Howells—Kester Letters, MS Room, New York Public Library. See also *My Literary Passions* (1895), *My Year in a Log Cabin* (1893), *Impressions and Experiences* (1896), *Literary Friends and Acquaintance* (1900), *The Flight of Pony Baker* (1902), *New Leaf Mills* (1913).

stand.[10]   Though Howells supplies the answer to this question
with fullness and seeming candor, one must remember that the
views we get of his early life are always retrospective, and have
the elusive "quality of things dreamt,"[11] and, further, that
Howells was not temperamentally able to be direct in his statements about himself.[12]   The fact that he was small in size as a
boy and never grew taller than five feet four inches, that he was
deeply humiliated by the presence of a mentally retarded
brother[13] in the group of eight Howells children, that he had
contracted the habit, while still a very small boy, of escaping

[10]That Howells as a novelist felt his view of the world was different
because he was the young man from Ohio with his wares, as it were, in his
pocket, is borne out by a dozen of his novels. Bartley Hubbard, in *A
Modern Instance* (1882), trying to establish himself on a Boston newspaper
is Howells; Percy Ray, in *The World of Chance* (1893), adrift in New York,
carrying the MS of his novel from publisher to publisher, is Howells; the
clever Mr. Ardith of *Letters Home* (1903), writing special articles for his
small town paper, is Howells again; the disillusioned Mr. Colville of *Indian
Summer* (1886), leaning over the bridge in Florence and thinking of the
editorial office of Prairie de Vaches in Indiana, is Howells, and so, in part,
is Professor Elmore, who, in *A Fearful Responsibility* (1881), is busily
compiling his history of Venice in a decaying palace on the Grand Canal.
See also various aspects of Howells' *alter ego* in *A Chance Acquaintance*
(1873), *The Shadow of a Dream* (1890), *An Imperative Duty* (1892), *The
Kentons* (1902), *The Leatherwood God* (1916). The life of Altruria, described in *A Traveler from Altruria* (1894), and *Through the Eye of a
Needle* (1907) is, in many important respects, the life Howells knew as a
boy in Ohio. For a discussion of the effect of this early environment on
Howells as a mature man, see Edwin H. Cady, "The Neuroticism of William Dean Howells," *PMLA*, LXI, 229–238 (March, 1946).

[11]*Years of My Youth*, p. 3.

[12]As a man of seventy, Howells wrote to Charles Eliot Norton, "With
whom is one really and truly intimate? I am pretty frank, and I seem to say
myself out to more than one, now and again, but only in this sort to one,
and that sort to another." *Life in Letters*, II, 242. In 1914, when engaged
in writing *Years of My Youth*, he wrote to his son, "I find largely that Tolstoy was right when in trying to furnish reminiscences for his biographer
he declared that remembering was Hell: with the little brave and good you
recall so much bad and base." However, he was determined to write his
reminiscences down and "then cut, cut, cut, until I make myself a respectable figure—somebody that the boys won't want to ignore when people
speak of him." *Life in Letters*, II, 331.

[13]It is significant that nowhere throughout Howells' numerous autobiographical books is this brother mentioned directly. Friends of the
Howells family now living in Jefferson, Ohio, say that the lives of Howells'

into the world of books, all probably contributed to an aloofness—amused, critical, or meditative—which keeps the reader at a certain distance. But in spite of Howells' indirections of style, the main facts of his life are reported by him. The emphasis he himself puts on the kind of family he emerged from, the hard work to which he was born and bred, the reading and studying he set for himself during those barefoot days in the Western Reserve, indicate the importance of an under standing of his Ohio background in a study of his mature mind.

1. Early Ohio Background

Howells' great-grandfather was a prosperous manufacturer of woolens, a Welshman and a Quaker, who loved "equality and fraternity"[14] and came to this country in 1793 to prospect for them as much as for a site for his wool factory. The old gentleman returned to Wales in 1797 with a good deal of money—so the Howells tradition goes—and never came out again. Howells' grandfather inherited his father's radicalism rather than his money and migrated to this country in 1808, when Howells' father was one year old. He landed in Boston and moved from

---

mother and older sisters, first Victoria, and then Aurelia, were, in fact, sacrificed to the care of Henry, who was struck in the head by a baseball at the age of four, and never developed mentally though he lived to be an old man. See *Life in Letters*, I, 111–113, 122. In his letters to Aurelia, Howells frequently sends "Love to Henry," or hopes "that Henry does not grow more troublesome." In a letter of February 24, 1901, he writes, "I wish I could walk out with you and the poor silent father-boy, and look at the quiet fields of snow." *Ibid.*, II, 142. See also *ibid.*, 268.

[14] *A Boy's Town*, p. 10. In 1883 Howells made a visit to Wales to look up the home of his great-grandfather, which was in the town of Hay, on the river Wye. At that time he wrote home to his father, "So far, our ancestry does not impress me as so splendid as our posterity will probably be. It seems to have been a plain, decent, religious-minded ancestry enough, and I wish its memory well, but I'm glad on the whole not to be part of it—in fact to be above ground in America." *Life in Letters*, I, 344. See the two long letters Howells wrote at this time to his father, *ibid*, I, 343–347. Howells visited Hay, Wales, again in 1909, *ibid*, II, 273. For a further account of this trip see an unpublished letter to Miss Bertha Howells, of January 18, 1914, in the Berg Collection of the New York Public Library.

one Quaker neighborhood to another in New York, Virginia, and Ohio, attempting, never successfully, to set up a woolen mill. He came to rest for a while in Wheeling, West Virginia, and here Howells' father and mother met and were married. The grandfather at last established himself at Hamilton, Ohio, in the drug and book business, and Howells remembered him as a small, bright-eyed man in a black Quaker hat. Though he ceased to be a Friend and turned fervent Methodist, he nevertheless remained "a Friend to every righteous cause; and brought shame to his grandson's soul by being an abolitionist in days when it was infamy to wish the slaves set free."[15] Wherever they moved, the Howells family were known for liberal social ideas, and Howells himself never lost the imprint of this early influence.

From the time when William Dean[16] was three years old until he was eleven, his father, William Cooper Howells, owned and edited *The Intelligencer*, the Whig newspaper of Hamilton, then a small village twenty miles north of Cincinnati. Though the family was poor and all the children were put to work as soon as they were able to do their share, none of them actually felt poor. "I suppose that as the world goes now we were poor. [My father's] . . . income was never above twelve hundred a year, and his family was large; but nobody was rich there or then; we lived in the simple abundance of that time and place, and we did not know that we were poor."[17] The family belonged to the employing class, in as much as the father had men to work for him. He also worked with the men and, in fact, put his small boy to setting type before he was ten years old. William's mother did her own housework except for the occasional help of a "hired girl," which was the custom of "that time and place." During these nine happy years in Hamilton, the children at-

[15]*A Boy's Town*, p. 11.
[16]Joseph, four years older than William, was the eldest child. William was followed by Victoria, Samuel, Aurelia, Anne, John, and Henry.
[17]*My Literary Passions*, p. 9.

tended the local school; they swam, hunted, fished, and played games with the village children.[18]

Though William Cooper[19] was never able to remove his family from the fear of poverty, he nevertheless provided a rich cultural experience for his children, which separated them somewhat from the other village children. His idealism expressed itself in his religious, as well as in his poetic nature. After many years of doubt in his youth, he had become a Swedenborgian, and he brought up his children in this faith, which tended further to mark the Howells family as "different." William says of the religion of his family, "It was not only their faith, but their life, and I may say that in this sense they were a very religious household, though they never went to church, because it was the Old Church."[20] The fact that the Howells children were taught that "in every thought and in every deed they were choosing their portion with the devils or the angels, and that God himself could not save them against themselves"[21] may well have been responsible for the fine, unfaltering ethical line that runs through all of Howells' writing. Certainly the strain of mysticism that one is aware of in his mature mind can be traced to the fervent teaching of his father.[22]

---

[18]For a full description of these years in Hamilton, see *A Boy's Town* (1890). That this story actually is an account of Howells' own youth is vouched for by an unpublished letter, in the Huntington Library, to C. W. Stoddard, written January 15, 1893. In this letter Howells is amused that Stoddard should find it necessary to ask him whether the boy in the book was the young Howells. Who else could it possibly be?

[19]For a more detailed analysis of William Cooper Howells' political and religious views, see George Arms, *The Social Criticism of William Dean Howells.* Unpublished thesis, New York University (1939), pp. 52–60.

[20]*A Boy's Town*, p. 11.

[21]*Ibid*, p. 14. William Cooper Howells was the author of two Swedenborgian tracts, *The Science of Correspondence* and *The Freewill of Man.*

[22]For a study of Howells' religion, see Hannah Graham Belcher, "Howells' Opinions on Religious Conflicts of His Age as Exhibited in Magazine Articles." *American Literature*, XV (Nov., 1943), 262–278. She points out that Howells never lost the imprint of his early mysticism, though it was later shaken by science and transmuted to a social philosophy. As he grew older, his early faith tended to return. A later expression

But the father "loved a joke almost as much as he loved a truth," "despised austerity as something owlish," and "set [the children] the example of getting all the harmless fun they could out of experience."[23] He had a decided literary bent, and was as glad to read aloud in the evenings from Thomson's *Seasons* or Pope's translation of the *Iliad* as from Swedenborg's *Heavenly Arcana*. Poor though he was, the father kept his son supplied with Goldsmith, Irving, Cervantes, and listened with pride to the verses William wrote in imitation of Moore or Scott.

If Howells' father was "the soul" of the family, his mother was "the heart."[24] Her name was Mary Dean; her mother, Elizabeth Dock, was German and her father an Irishman who was known chiefly for having won his bride away from the loving arms of her family, established "in great Pennsylvania-German comfort and prosperity on their farm near Harrisburg, to share with him the hardships of the wild country over the westward mountains."[25] The aging grandmother, who always spoke with a German accent, Howells "tenderly loved" as a

of Howells' attitude toward immortality is found in a volume of collected essays on the subject, entitled *In After Days* (1910). "There are many things that I doubt, but few that I deny; where I cannot believe, there I often trust." p. 5. Howells frequently expressed this mild scepticism, tinged with hope. See *Life in Letters*, II, 71–72; *Mark Twain's Letters*, II, 510; *My Mark Twain*, pp. 31–32. For Howells' later comment on Swendenborg, see *Life in Letters*, I, 165–167; II 332–333. See *Stops of Various Quills* (1895) for an expression in poetry of Howells' later religious attitude. See also *The Shadow of a Dream* (1890); *Questionable Shapes* (1903); *Between the Dark and the Daylight* (1907), *A Traveler from Altruria* (1894), Chap. XII. When Howells was eighty years old, he wrote to Mrs. John J. Piatt on July 10, 1917, a letter of consolation after the death of her husband, John J. Piatt, who was Howells' lifelong friend. His words are worth quoting as an indication of Howells' later thought on death and immortality. "In my age I dream more than I read and hardly a night, never a week passes, but I dream of my lost wife. It doesn't matter whether the dreams are kind or unkind, they bring her back. . . . I know how it is with you now while your sorrow is still so new; but after long unbelief I am getting back some hope again and I am at last getting back peace, which seemed gone forever." Unpublished letter in the possession of Cecil Piatt.

[23] *A Boy's Town*, p. 14.
[24] *Years of My Youth*, p. 97.
[25] *Ibid.*, pp. 3–4.

child.[26] Through all of Howells' memoirs, Mary Howells appears as the loving, anxious, hard-working mother, who followed the visionary father from town to town, though she longed for a permanent home of her own. "She was always working for us, and yet, as I so tardily perceived, living for my father anxiously, fearfully, bravely, with absolute trust in his goodness and righteousness. While she listened to his reading at night, she sewed or knitted for us, or darned or mended the day's ravages in our clothes, till, as a great indulgence, we fell asleep on the floor. . . . She was not only the center of home to me; she was home itself."[27]

This much-loved, "earth-bound" mother had herself "an innate love of poetry," and sang the songs of Burns and Moore, then known in every household. Though "her intellectual and spiritual life was in and from"[28] her husband, her sensitive, rather melancholy temperament became a part of the little boy, who was later to show such a peculiar understanding of women in their daily lives.

[26]Mrs. Howells' homesickness for her mother "mounted from time to time to an insupportable crisis," and then she and a child or two—frequently the child was William—went "up-the-River" for a visit. *Ibid.*, p. 29.

[27]*Ibid.*, p. 23. Howells' lifelong devotion to his mother is apparent in many of his poems and letters written many years later. "Respite," from *Stops of Various Quills* (1895), for example, shows how present to him his mother remained:

> ". . . My mother, who has been
> Dead almost half my life, appeared to lean
> Above me; a boy in a house far away,
> That once was home, and all the troubled years
> That have been since were as if they were not."

See also "The Mysteries," in *Poems* (1873). Howells wrote to his brother Joseph in 1911, when he was working on *Years of My Youth*, "Father was what God made him, and he was on the whole the best man I have known, but of course he was trying. . . . I mean to deal more and more tenderly with his character in shading it and rounding it out. Mother was splendid too; how my child's heart used to cling to her, and how her heart clung to each of us! . . . I suppose a woman is always bewildered when a man comes short of that perfection which would be the logic of him in her mind." *Life in Letters*, II, 298. See also *Ibid.*, II, 139–140; 212.

[28]*Years of My Youth*, p. 29.

2. The Printing Office

The happiest period of Howells' boyhood came to an end in 1849 when the father sold his paper in Hamilton and moved to Dayton, where he bought shares in the *Transcript*, for which he never succeeded in paying. William was twelve when the move was made, and school was permanently over for him. Howells tells us, rather wistfully, that "the printing office was my school from a very early date,"[29] for now he was working on his father's paper, setting the telegraphic dispatches into type until eleven o'clock at night, and getting up in the morning between four and five to deliver the papers to the subscribers. The period in Dayton was "a long period of defeat"; William and his older brother, Joseph, were both aware of the "hopeless burden of debt" under which their father was staggering, and which their mother "was carrying on her heart."[30] For a short period William gave up his too arduous work in the printing office, and clerked in a drug store, until it became clear that the owner of the store had no intention of paying him. The bitterness of the struggle carried on by the "duteous children," as well as by the parents, made Howells while still a boy, aware of "the wide-spread, never-ending struggle for life which it was and is the type of."[31] He never lost sight of the social injustice implicit in our civilization. Howells wrote as an old man, "I cannot but abhor the economic conditions which we still suppose an essential of civilization."[32]

The protracted struggle of the Dayton *Transcript*, which the

[29] *My Literary Passions*, p. 8.

[30] *Years of My Youth*, p. 41.

[31] A pleasant memory from the two years spent in Dayton is of a company of travelling players who spent a summer in the town, and for doing their printing, paid the elder Howells in tickets to the evening performances of *Macbeth*, *Othello*, and *Richard III*. "As nearly as I can make out," writes Howells, "I was thus enabled to go every night to the theater, in a passion for it which remains with me ardent still." *Ibid*, p. 36. See also *My Literary Passions*, p. 36.

[32] *Years of My Youth*, p. 41.

elder Howells had unwisely changed from a tri-weekly to a daily, came to an end at last when the father with his brothers evolved a plan for founding a communal settlement on a milling privilege which they had bought near Xenia, Greene County, on the Little Miami River. Here the families of the four brothers were to be settled, together with such friends as might prove cooperative. One of the brothers was to supply the capital, while William Cooper, who knew nothing of mills of any description, was to have charge of a grist mill and sawmill on the property until they could be converted into a paper mill. Such communities, tinged with social idealism, were familiar enough to the brothers, who had long known and discussed the ideas of Fourier and Robert Owen. Moreover, something must be done at once to help the brother whose paper was failing because his delicacy did not permit him to collect the money owed him by subscribers and advertisers.[33] In *My Year in a Log Cabin*, Howells tells of the autumn evenings in their home, when the aunt played the piano and the uncle the fife, and when the talk came round again and again to the log cabin on the river.

Finally words turned into deeds, and the family moved out to the one-room cabin, which the father and the sons had tried to make habitable. The year in the log cabin was a failure from the point of view of all concerned except the Howells boys.[34] Mrs. Howells hated the loneliness of the woods and the rudeness of her few neighbors, nor could she reconcile herself to the companionship of the pigs who nestled comfortably every night outside the house by the warm chimney. Their grunts could be heard while her husband read aloud to the family circling the fire. William Cooper, for all of his trust in the goodness of human nature, could not soften the resentment of the previous tenant miller, who somehow thought he still owned the prop-

[33]*Ibid.*, p. 28.
[34]Howells tells the tale again in *New Leaf Mills* (1913), and once more in *Years of My Youth* (1916). He made further use of the primitive frontier experience of this year in *A Leatherwood God* (1916).

erty. Moreover, the uncle who was to join the family in the spring died of tuberculosis and the other brothers could not make up their minds to give up their shops. William and Joseph, age thirteen and seventeen, worked by the side of their father like full-grown men, clearing the trees for a garden patch, driving to neighboring farms for provisions, and hunting game in the surrounding woods. In spite of the privations and final failure of "New Leaf Mills"—to use the title of a later novel that expresses so well the idealistic hope behind the experiment —Howells always dreamed of some such utopia where all should share equally the labor and the leisure. Altruria is the dream which began in a log cabin in Ohio.[35]

During this year in the woods Howells kept a diary, now lost, in which he continued to write for many years. "I wrote a diary,"[36] he tells us in *My Literary Passions*, "and tried to give its record form and style, but mostly failed. The versifying which I was always at was easier, and yielded itself more to my hand. I should be very glad to know at present what it dealt with." Moreover, Howells discovered a barrel of books in the attic, the overflow from the shelves in the room below, and these he read by candle light as the snow drifted through the holes in the roof. Longfellow and Scott, Whittier and Burns were ever after associated with this year, which came to an abrupt close in the early part of the following winter, when "it was justly thought fit" by the parents, who were again faced with financial ruin, that the young Howellses should "go to earn some money in a printing-office in X———."[37] The foreman

[35]It was this hope of finding an answer to the economic struggle other than that of a competitive, moneyed society that made Howells pause to consider the Shaker communities he later came to know in Massachusetts and New York. His thoughts on the success and failure of Shakerism are reflected in *The Undiscovered Country* (1880), *The Day of Their Wedding*, *A Parting and A Meeting* (1896), and in *The Vacation of the Kelwyns* (1920).

[36]*My Literary Passions*, p. 43.

[37]*Years of My Youth*, p. 61.

of the printing office appeared one day in the cabin and wished to take William back with him that morning in his buggy. A "frenzy of homesickness" fell instantly upon him, and, in fact, never left him until the printer, at the end of the week, found a substitute for the boy and sent him home. But not for long; he was soon sent off to Dayton to work in another printing office, this time to live with an uncle and aunt of whom he was very fond. By drinking a great deal of water with his meals he found he could keep down the sobs and in part conceal his suffering. One evening he returned from his day's work and found his brother waiting for him; the two rode home together on "the italic-footed mare" the next morning "in the keen, silent dark before the November dawn." "The homesick will understand how it was that I was as if saved from death."[38] Howells' extremely sensitive, affectionate nature, as revealed by these passages and many others, must be taken into account in one's final appraisal of him as a proponent of realism. Inured as he was to poverty and hard work, he was as a boy, and also as a mature man, unable to face the intenser forms of emotional suffering which seem to be a part of the "real" world.

By the time William returned to his family in the woods, they had moved to the new house, which father and sons had been building for many months when there was time to spare from more pressing duties. But the "changes of business which had been taking place without the knowledge of us children called us away from that roof, too, and we left the mills and the pleasant country that had grown so dear, to take up our abode in city streets again."[39] The elder Howells was, at this time, scheming in vain to get hold of this paper or that; finally, in 1851, he found work as a reporter of legislative proceedings for the *Ohio State Journal* of Columbus at ten dollars a week, and his son was taken into the office as compositor, for which he

[38]*Ibid., p.* 63.
[39]*Ibid.,* p. 64.

received four dollars a week. With the help of three dollars a week which Joseph was able to earn at a near-by grocery store, the family rented a small brick house for ten dollars a month.[40]

Though William was now one of the main supporters of the large family in the small brick house, he nevertheless had time to daydream over "the familiar cases of type." A "definite literary ambition" grew in him and "in the long reveries of the afternoon," when he was distributing his case, he "fashioned a future of overpowering magnificence and undying celebrity."[41] His day at the press began at seven in the morning and ended at six in the evening, with an hour off for lunch. As soon as the supper was cleared away, he got out his papers and "hammered away" at his Popean heroics until nine, when he promptly went to bed, for he had to rise again in the morning at five. "After my day's work at the case I toiled the evening away at my boyish literary attempts, forcing my poor invention in that unnatural kind, and rubbing and polishing at my wretched verses till they did sometimes take on an effect, which, if it was not like Pope's, was like none of mine. . . ." The severe schooling Howells gave himself taught him how to choose the most suitable words, which he often employed "decoratively and with no vital sense of their qualities." But he "could not imitate Pope without imitating his method, and his method was to the last degree intelligent."[42]

The young Howells' "long subjection to Pope," as he called it, was forming not only the style of the boy poring over his manuscripts, but also his mind. "My reading from the first was such as to enamour me of clearness, of definiteness; anything left in the vague was intolerable to me; but my long subjection to Pope, while it was useful in other ways, made me so strictly literary in my point of view."[43] What he liked, then, was

[40] *Years of My Youth*, p. 69.
[41] *My Literary Passions*, pp. 44–45.
[42] *Ibid.*, pp. 49–50.
[43] *Ibid.*, pp. 58–59.

"regularity, uniformity, exactness." He did not think of literature as "the expression of life," and he could not imagine that
"it ought to be desultory, mutable and unfixed, even if at the
risk of some vagueness."[44] Howells began his apprenticeship to
literature as a follower of Pope, whose "intelligence" the boy
felt to be the source of the regularity of his verse. Howells' own
writing was formed by the great classical tradition, which he
knew and loved through Addison, Goldsmith, and Jane Austen,
as well as through Pope. To conceive of literature as the expression of life was possible to Howells only after an impassioned
reading of the French and Russian authors, Zola, Dostoevsky,
Turgenev, and especially Tolstoy, and after a long and varied
career in the journalistic world of Boston and New York.

Though Howells himself was never satisfied with the pastorals
he laboriously penned, his father was so proud of his son that
he took one of the poems to the editor of the *Ohio State Journal*,
where it was published, to the confusion of the author, who was,
nevertheless, soon emboldened to offer another and another
contribution to the editor.[45]

[44]*Ibid. My Literary Passions*, p. 59.
[45]Howells tells us that some of his verses had been printed in 1850. See
Years of My Youth, p. 79. But his first known contribution to a newspaper
was the poem "Old Winter, loose thy hold on us," published in the *Ohio
State Journal* (March 23, 1852), when its author was just fifteen. *Years of
My Youth*, p. 74.

> Old Winter, loose thy hold on us
>   And let the Spring come forth;
> And take thy frost and ice and snow
>   Back to the frozen North.
>
> The gentle, warm, and blooming Spring,
>   We thought had come at last;
> And then, with all thy cold and woe,
>   Dost for a season past;—
>
> The blackbird on his glossy wing,
>   Was soaring in the sky;
> And pretty red breast robin, too,
>   Was caroling on high . . .
>   Signed V.M.H.

This poem was reprinted in the Cincinnati *Commercial* and in a New York
paper. *Years of My Youth*, p. 74. In *My Literary Passions*, (p. 45),

3. *"The Village Limits"*

But soon the legislature had adjourned and the father's and son's engagement was over. The family now turned eagerly to the new home the father had found for them in the Western Reserve, where, he felt, his anti-slavery opinions[46] would agree better with the Ohio New Englanders than with the Ohio Virginians and Kentuckians among whom they had been living. In 1852 the elder Howells bought a share in the Ashtabula *Sentinel*, the Freesoil newspaper of Ashtabula. Both William Dean and Joseph had resolved to avoid forever any association with a printing press, but now they joined their father gladly because of the chance it held out to their father "at a time when there seemed no other chance in the world for him."[47] The paper was published in Ashtabula, but it was soon transferred some ten miles inland to Jefferson, where it long represented the Freesoil views of the county. Here the two older Howells boys worked on the paper with their father until the family was able to buy the paper in 1854[48] and to establish a home.

Jefferson, the county seat of 400 inhabitants, welcomed the Howellses to "its young gaieties," to "parties, and sleigh rides, and walks, and drives, and picnics, and dances."[49] More impor-

---

Howells tells us: "One of my pieces, which fell so far short of my visionary performances as to treat of the lowly and familiar theme of Spring, was the first thing I ever had in print." This statement seems to refer to the poem above, printed in 1852, and to contradict the first statement cited in this note from *Years of My Youth*. It would seem probable that Howells was writing verses at thirteen but did not get them into print until 1852 when he was fifteen years of age.

[46] A statement of the editorial policy of the Ashtabula *Sentinel* appeared in the paper on January 8, 1853. It is quoted in full by Edwin Cady, "William Dean Howells and the Ashtabula Sentinel", *Ohio Archaeological and Historical Quarterly*, LIII (Jan.-Mar., 1944), 40.

[47] *Years of My Youth*, pp. 81, 115. See "The Country Printer," *Impressions and Experiences* (1896), pp. 4 ff.

[48] The Howells family owned and published the Ashtabula *Sentinel* for more than forty years. Bound files may be found in the Ashtabula Public Library, Ashtabula, Ohio.

[49] *My Literary Passions*, p. 69.

tant still, the little village introduced Howells to "a social liberty and equality which [he] ... long hoped some day to paint as a phase of American civilization worthy the most literal fidelity of fiction."[50] The tree-shaded streets of Jefferson, lined on either side with comfortable nineteenth-century homes, looked in Howells' day—and indeed still do—more like those of an established New England village than like the roads of a frontier town. What Howells found in the hospitable homes of Jefferson, and what he thought he found later in Cambridge, became the utopian dream which he finally expressed in his picture of Altruria, where the village is the economic and social unit and where all who live there do the chores of the day and also enjoy the pleasures of music and books and conversation, where "all had enough and none too much." Like the people of Altruria, the men and women of the Western Reserve of the fifties were farmers and dairymen. They were almost entirely New England in origin, and though blunt in their manners, were open to new ideas. Little money passed through their hands during the year, and "every sort of farm produce was legal tender at the printing office" of the Ashtabula *Sentinel.* Wood was always welcome in exchange for the paper, for the winters along that northern lake were cold and windy and the houses were almost "as flimsy as tents." Often the type in Howells' case froze solid, and the boy's fingers became so stiff that he had to make frequent trips between his table and the stove. He probably forgot the temperature, however, as he set the type for his own stories, which began to appear in the family paper in 1853.[51]

[50]*Years of My Youth,* p. 81.
[51]*Ibid.,* 83. "A Tale of Love and Politics, Adventures of a Printer Boy," Ashtabula *Sentinel,* XXII (Sept. 1, 1853), 1. Unsigned: attribution made through background and narrator. "The Journeyman's Secret, Stray Leaves from the Diary of a Journeyman Printer," Ashtabula *Sentinel,* XXII (Nov. 3, 1853), 1. Unsigned: attribution made through background and approach. Howells' contributions to the Ashtabula *Sentinel* were all unsigned until May 20, 1858. Cady identifies "The Independent Candidate" as a story by Howells, which ran from November 23, 1854 to January

These contributions were two short prose stories having to do with the life of a boy printer. Already Howells was writing stories in which he was personally closely concerned. In 1854 he published a poem in the *Ohio Farmer* and in the *Sentinel* both poems and stories, the latter again seeming to grow out of his own background of Western and printing-house experience; the following year he was sending poems off to the *National Era* and the *Ohio Farmer* and translating Spanish stories for the *Sentinel* and the *Ohio State Journal*. Having served his apprenticeship in the print shop, he was learning to combine poetry and journalism.

Though William and Joseph shared the responsibility of the paper with their father, their daily routine was pleasantly broken by the numerous young visitors who came to the office, some to help fold and address the papers, others to enjoy the general excitement of a newspaper office. "The printing-office was the center of civic and social interest; it was frequented by visitors at all times, and on publication day it was a scene of gaiety that looks a little incredible in retrospect. The place was as bare and rude as a printing-office seems always to be: the walls were splotched with ink and the floor littered with refuse newspapers; but, lured by the novelty of the affair, and perhaps attracted by a natural curiosity to see what manner of strange men the printers were, the school-girls and young ladies of the village flocked in and made it like a scene of comic opera, with their pretty dresses and faces, their eager chatter and lively energy in folding the papers and addressing them to the subscribers, while our fellow-citizens of the place, like the bassos and barytones and tenors of the chorus, stood about and looked on with faintly sarcastic faces."[52]

These temperate, hard-working, anti-slavery Yankees were

11, 1855. "William Dean Howells and the Ashtabula *Sentinel*," *Ohio State Arch. and Histor. Quar.*, LIII (Jan.-March, 1944), 45–51.

[52]*Years of My Youth*, pp. 84–85. See "The Country Printer," *Impressions and Experiences*, pp. 3–34.

ardently political in their thinking, but their talk was not entirely of politics. "When it was not mere banter, it was mostly literary," Howells recalls in *Years of My Youth*, "we disputed about authors among ourselves and with the village wits who dropped in, and liked to stand with their backs to our stove and challenge opinions concerning Holmes and Poe, Irving and Macaulay, Pope and Byron, Dickens and Shakespeare."[53] "Printers in the old-time offices were always spouting Shakespeare more or less,"[54] Howells tells us. Soon the boy had made friends with one of the older men and, as they worked, the two recited speeches from *Hamlet*, *The Tempest*, and *Macbeth*.[55] They took their Shakespeare "into the woods at the ends of the long summer afternoons that remained to us when we had finished our work, and on the shining Sundays of the warm, late spring, the early, warm autumn, and we read it there on grassy slopes or heaps of fallen leaves."[56]

Howells grew to know all those in the village with special interest in literature. He took long rambling walks with "a certain Englishman," an organ mender, three times his age, and talked with him of Dickens. His friend would snatch a volume of *Martin Chuzzlewit* or *Old Curiosity Shop* out of his pocket, and begin to read to him "at the book-store, or the harness-shop, or the law-office,"[57] and on one Christmas eve, still referred to by the old inhabitants of Jefferson, the Englishman read the *Christmas Carol* in the Court House to people who came from the countryside to hear him. Then there was the young poet who was in charge of the books in the drug and book store and who introduced Howells to De Quincey and to Thackeray; the machinist in the shop below the printing office who "swam vividly into [Howells'] ken, with a volume of Macaulay's essays

[53] *Years of My Youth*, p. 89.
[54] *My Literary Passions*, p. 71.
[55] *Ibid*. See "The Country Printer," *Impressions and Experiences*, 1896.
[56] *My Literary Passions*, pp. 78–79.
[57] *Ibid*, p. 102.

in his hand, one day";[58] the eccentric doctor who lent him the
works of Edgar Allan Poe; the young people in the comfortable
houses along the wide village streets with whom he read Tennyson and George Eliot. "Old and young, . . . [the villagers] read
and talked about books."[59] Literature was so generally accepted as a real interest that the bookish young Howells was not
considered queer in his devotion to it.

Yet Howells' extensive reading did, indeed, set him apart
from his family and his neighbors. For after the walks and
talks with his friends in the drugstore and the printing office, he
pored too late over his books "in the narrow little space which
I had for my study, under the stairs at home. There was a desk
pushed back against the wall, which the irregular ceiling sloped
down to meet behind it, and at my left was a window, which
gave a good light on the writing-leaf of my desk."[60] This was
his work-shop for six or seven years. He was "fierce to shut
out" of his study the voices and faces of his family in "pursuit
of the end" which he "sought gropingly, blindly and with very
little hope but with an intense ambition, and a courage that gave
way under no burden, before no obstacles."

During these years Howells, with a young printer friend,
Jim Williams,[61] then living with the family, attempted the study
of four languages, Latin, Greek, German, and Spanish, with
little help other than that which the boys could dig out of the
grammars and dictionaries that fell into their hands. Howells
read "right and left in every direction but chiefly in that of
poetry, criticism and fiction" in all of these languages. The be-
dazed boy would sometimes come from his study to meet a
silent question in his mother's eye, for she was forbidden to ask

[58]*Ibid.*, p. 115.
[59]*Years of My Youth*, p. 106.
[60]*My Literary Passions*, pp. 79–80.
[61]Jim Williams had an ambition to become a professor "in a Western
college," which he realized before he was killed in the Civil War. *Years of
My Youth*, pp. 100–104.

him what he had been doing. Looking back over his youthful "literary passions" as an elderly man, Howells regretted the time he had spent in that little study and wished he had seen "more of the actual world, and had learned to know my brethren in it better."[62] But the love of literature and the hope of doing something in it had become Howells' "passion" to the exclusion of all other interests.

Howells' father was no longer able to guide the reading of his son, who was blindly pushing on to a goal he himself did not understand. Nor was he happy in the pursuit. "This was in a season of great depression, when I began to feel in broken health the effect of trying to burn my candle at both ends." For a while it seemed simple to come home after the work was over at the press, and to work in his study until the family had gone to bed, but his health and spirits flagged. As far as Howells remembers, he was not fond of study, and only thought of it as a means to an end, but what that end was he did not know. "As far as my pleasure went, or my natural bent was concerned, I would rather have been wandering through the woods with a gun on my shoulder, or lying under a tree, or reading some book that cost me no sort of effort. But there was much more than my pleasure involved; there was a hope to fulfil, an aim to achieve." What this hope and this aim were, Howells could not have said; the blind struggle, however, was the very center of his life. "As I look back at the endeavor of those days much of it seems mere purblind groping, wilful and wandering."[63] It ended, at last, in a kind of breakdown, during which he could neither sleep nor work. Having been bitten by a dog as a child, the boy developed an unreasoning dread of hydrophobia, which caused him months of suffering.[64] He was forced to spend days in the

[62]*My Literary Passions*, p. 80.
[63]*My Literary Passions*, pp. 88–90. See also *Years of My Youth*, pp. 90–91.
[64]Howells continued to suffer from what he called hypochondria through his early twenties, after which we hear no more of this difficulty. "For two months," he wrote to his brother Joseph on August 14, 1859, "my familiar

fields and woods now, carrying a gun; actually he passed his time picking blackberries, and reading the book in his pocket.

When Howells' recovery was complete, a family council was held to consider whether or not to send him to an academy in a near-by town. But the boy's labor was worth that of a journeyman compositor, and his father decided that he could not be spared. A Scotch farmer, having heard of this unusual son of his neighbor offered, with several others, to send Howells to Harvard, but again the father decided that the boy was needed at home.[65] For a brief period Howells, in his restlessness, left the printing office and read law with Senator Wade, who lived on the same street with the Howells family. He tried Blackstone for a month and then returned to the printing office as the lesser of two evils, for after his day of work at the press he at least could pursue his own studies.

The energy and determination of Joseph finally established the family fortunes securely; all the notes on the printing office and on the home were at last paid off, and Joseph and his father became joint owners of the Ashtabula *Sentinel*. But security was not purchased without self-denials of every sort. "I think we denied ourselves too much," said Howells in retrospect, though he rejoiced that his hard-working mother at last had her home. Perhaps it was during these difficult years that Howells made

---

devil, Hypochondria, had tormented me, so that I sometimes thought that death would be a relief. Yesterday, I could bear it no longer, and went to Dr. Smith, telling him my trouble, and receiving for answer that there was nothing the matter with me." *Life in Letters*, I, 22. See also *Years of My Youth*, pp. 91–93; 230–231.

[65]Howells always missed "the stamp of the schools," and urged his family to provide a college education for the younger brother, John Butler Howells: "Why not send Johnny to College, and let one Howells have the stamp of the schools? I remember how I longed to go, and I lost much by not going. You couldn't afford it when I was seventeen. You can now when Johnny is the same age." *Life in Letters*, I, 73. As an old man he wrote, "While I live I must regret that want of instruction, and the discipline which would have come with it—though Fortune . . . bore me the offer of professorships in three of our greatest universities." *Years of My Youth*, pp. 110–111.

up his mind that he himself would not be so improvident as his father. His awareness of money and his shrewdness in later years in making his writing pay, in spite of all he said against a money-making society, are understandable in the light of the early struggles of his family for security.

In the winter of 1855–1856 the elder Howells went to Columbus as one of the House clerks in the State Legislature, leaving Joseph and William to manage the newspaper. But "the village limits" were becoming burdensome to William at least, and not entirely because Jefferson did not offer scope to his literary ambitions. William and his older sister Victoria spent many hours in the evenings poring over illustrated magazines. Both of them agreed that Jefferson was to be scorned, "because it did not realize the impossible dreams of that great world of wealth, of fashion, of haughtily and dazzlingly, blindingly brilliant society, which we did not inconveniently consider we were altogether unfit for,"[66] and both of them returned to Columbus with their father when the legislature convened the following year, in January, 1857.

4. *The "Jeffersonian" in Columbus*

Though the elder Howells held the clerkship, the younger Howells was soon doing most of the work. William had been contributing to his father's paper since the age of thirteen;[67] now as a young reporter of nineteen he was a fairly mature journalist quite capable of supporting himself. He tells in *My Literary Passions* the tale of his first independent steps in his writing career, which was to continue for the next sixty-four years:

My father had got one of those legislative clerkships which used to fall sometimes to deserving country editors when their party was in power, and we together imagined and carried out a scheme for corresponding with some city newspapers. We

[66]*Years of My Youth*, p. 124.
[67]*Ibid.*, p. 70. See note 51 on p. xxxiii of this Introduction.

were to furnish a daily letter giving an account of the legislative proceedings, which I was mainly to write up from material he helped me to get together. The letters at once found favor with the editors who agreed to take them, and my father then withdrew from the work altogether, after telling them who was doing it.[68]

The early months of the winter of 1857 passed "quickly and happily" enough for the Howellses in Columbus, which was then a town of 12,000 and as friendly as the village society they had left behind. The reading went on late into the night here as at home. Howells and his sister read Percy's *Reliques* that winter and Shakespeare and Tennyson. Longfellow's *Hiawatha* led Howells to borrow an Icelandic grammar from the State Library to pore over at night. During the day Howells sat at his own desk on the floor of the Senate, "as good as any Senator's,"[69] and took the notes which he later turned into a "Letter from Columbus," over the signature "Jeffersonian,"[70] for the Cincinnati *Gazette*. His reports, in which he "spared no severity" in his censure of senators he found "misguided," met with such favor that by the following April he was asked to be night editor of the Cincinnati *Gazette*.

Howells made the trip to Cincinnati, determined to learn the job by trying himself out as a reporter. But one night's round of the police stations was enough to convince him that he was not meant for the work. "My longing was for the cleanly respectabilities."[71] Looking back in 1916 at his too sensitive twenty-year-old self, he observed, "I have often been sorry

[68] *My Literary Passions*, pp. 160–161.
[69] *Years of My Youth*, p. 132.
[70] Howells wrote for the *Cincinnati Gazette* in 1857 under the pseudonym "Jeffersonian," which was borrowed from his father. The following year he used his own pseudonym "Chispa," which was, in turn, occasionally borrowed by his father. Arms and Gibson are not able in every instance to determine the authorship of the *Letter from Columbus*. See *A Bibliography of William Dean Howells* (New York, 1948), p. 7.
[71] *Years of My Youth*, p. 142.

since, for it would have made known to me many phases of life that I have always been ignorant of, but I did not know then that life was supremely interesting and important. I fancied that literature, that poetry was so; and it was humiliation and anguish indescribable to think of myself torn from my high ideals by labors like those of the reporter."[72] The fact that Howells was at the time, suffering from extreme loneliness, and that his health, not fully restored after the breakdown of the previous year, was now failing him again, may in part explain the withdrawal of this literary youth from "real life." In any case, the bookish young Howells, with his blue and gold Tennyson in his pocket, would not even consent to do the office work of the department dealing with the daily happenings of an American city. After a few weeks of "suffering and sufferance," he turned down a thousand dollars a year and returned to the printing office in Jefferson, broken in health as well as in spirits.[73] The initial bout between Howells, the poet, and Howells, the journalist, left the young man spent and discouraged.

Determined not to be a disappointment to himself and his father, Howells soon returned to Columbus to report the 1858 legislative session not only for the Cincinnati *Gazette*, but also for the Cleveland *Herald*. But he was suffering from rheumatic fever now, and his father had to complete the correspondence that year for him.[74] Howells, home again in Jefferson, resumed the study of the German language, with the sole purpose of reading the poetry of Heine, who had seized his fancy from

[72]Howells further observed, "I think that if I had been wiser than I was then I would have remained in the employ offered me, and learned in the school of reality the many lessons of human nature which it could have taught me. I did not remain, and perhaps I could not; it might have been the necessity of my morbid nerves to save themselves from abhorrent contacts; in any case, I renounced the opportunity offered me by that university of the streets and police-stations, with its faculty of patrolmen and ward politicians and saloon-keepers." *Years of My Youth*, p. 141.

[73]For a reflection of Howells' state of mind during this period, see his letter to his sister Victoria, *Life in Letters*, I, 13–15.

[74]*My Literary Passions*, pp. 177–178.

the first line of his he had seen. Howells and an elderly German bookbinder[75] living in the village, used to meet in the evenings in the editorial room of the Ashtabula *Sentinel*, and with several candles on the table between them, and Heine and a dictionary before them, they worked until they were both exhausted. What the police court of Cincinnati was unable to do for Howells in relating literature to life, Heine seems to have accomplished. Howells tells us that, before reading Heine, he had supposed "that the expression of literature must be different from the expression of life; that it must be an attitude, a pose, with something of state or at least of formality in it; . . . But Heine at once showed me that this ideal of literature was false; that the life of literature was from the springs of the best common speech, and that the nearer it could be made to conform, in voice, look and gait, to graceful, easy, picturesque and humorous or impassioned talk, the better it was."[76] It is to be noticed, that Howells, the realist, learned to appreciate the commonplace not directly from life itself, but from literature. Heine became for the young writer a model to be copied; but before he was able to take experience itself for his model, he had to follow the advice of Lowell, who wrote to him of something he had been writing, "You must sweat the Heine out of your bones as men do mercury." Lowell, Howells tells us, "would not be content with less than the entire expulsion of the poison that had in its good time saved my life."[77]

5. *The Poet-Journalist*

Though Howells was writing poetry during this summer in imitation of Heine, and though his health was improving, the situation was not cheerful for him, and he was glad enough to

[75]As Howells tells us in *Years of My Youth*, (p. 135) this old German appears in *A Hazard of New Fortunes* as Lindau.

[76]*My Literary Passions*, pp. 171–172.

[77]*Ibid.*, pp. 172–173.

escape again from the village in the fall[78] when he was asked to return to Columbus as news editor. His chief duty was that of book reviewer and writer of literary notices for the *Ohio State Journal*, now under a new management. Though Howells wrote a column called "News and Humors of the Mail", and many reviews, translations and articles for his paper, he seems to have had much time for his own reading and writing—and also for the round of dances and suppers which now claimed him. "All the young ladies were beautiful,"[79] Howells reports. Charades and dancing, cards and talk about the latest novel were enough for Howells, in those days when nothing seemed more natural or more delightful than to discuss *Adam Bede* with the ladies with whom one danced the quadrille and the lancers.

Just before Christmas, in 1859, Howells and his friend John J. Piatt made their "first literary venture" together in *Poems of Two Friends*[80] and four of Howells' poems appeared in Lowell's *Atlantic Monthly* in 1860.[81] It was a period of "high literary exaltation" for the young poet, whose head was full of such romantic conceits as "The Yellow Leaf in the Poet's

[78]The memory of that unhappy period in Jefferson perhaps explains Howells' dread of returning there as a man. At a time when Howells thought his father might need his help on the paper, he wrote to him from Venice, offering to return to Jefferson in case of real need, and added, "At the same time, I do not conceal from you that I have not yet in three years shaken off my old morbid horror of going back to live in a place where I have been so wretched. ... It cannot change so much but I shall always hate it." *Life in Letters*, I, 89. See Edwin H. Cady, "The Neuroticism of William Dean Howells," *PMLA*, LXI (1946), 229–238.

[79]*Years of My Youth*, p. 174.

[80]*My Literary Passions*, p. 191. See Rudolf and Clara Kirk, "Poems of Two Friends," *Journal of the Rutgers University Library*, IV (June, 1941), 33–44. Howells and Piatt remained friends throughout their lives. See the unpublished letters of Howells to Piatt in the Rutgers University Library. For Howells' comment on Piatt after his death, see *Harper's Magazine*, CXXXV (July, 1917), 291–293.

[81]"Andenken" (January, 1860), "The Poet's Friends" (February, 1860), "Pleasure-Pain" (April, 1860), "Lost Beliefs" (April, 1860). "Summer Dead" appeared also in 1860, in *Poets and Poetry of the West*.

Book," and "The Letter with a Rose Leaf."[82] "I walked the
street of the friendly little city by day and by night with my
head so full of rhymes and poetic phrases that it seemed as if
their buzzing might have been heard several yards away; and I
do not yet see quite how I contrived to keep their music out of
my newspaper paragraphs." Nor did he, in fact, quite succeed,
for to the amusement of the editor, Henry D. Cooke, he
frequently burst into verse in the paper. But the kindly editor
who gave Howells the freedom he needed,[83] also inspired him
with a passion for his work as a journalist. "I could find time for
poetry only in my brief noonings, and at night after the last
proofs had gone to the composing room, or I had come home
from the theater or from an evening party, but the long day was
a long delight to me over my desk in the room next my senior."[84]
The two winters that Howells spent in Columbus, from 1857
to 1860, were, he afterwards said, "the heyday of life" for him—
perhaps because, while he was supporting himself by his journalism, he was also finding time to write the poems which were
filling his head. It was at this time that Moncure D. Conway,
editor of the short-lived *Dial*, introduced Howells to the Rev.
O. B. Frothingham, with the following remark, "W. D.
Howells, a poet if God ever made one. You will find him skill-

[82]A sense of the "high literary exaltation" experienced by Howells at
this time may be derived from a long letter from Howells to Piatt, written
on September 10, 1859, which is in the Rutgers University Library. In
this letter Howells tells his friend that he has been reading widely and
refers gayly to Tennyson, Heine, Montaigne, de Quincey, Thackeray,
and George Eliot, all in a sentence. He has also, he adds, been doing
a great deal of scribbling; he has, in fact, had a poem accepted by the
Atlantic. Published in Chicago *Midland*, III (June, 1909), 9–13.

[83]*My Literary Passions*, pp. 191–192. The editor let Howells publish
what he pleased, until Howells described a murder done by an injured
husband. Then Cooke turned on the young reporter with words which he
never forgot. "Never, *never* write anything you would be ashamed to read
to a woman." Howells adds, he "made me lastingly ashamed of what I
had done, and fearful of ever doing the like again, even in writing fiction."
Years of My Youth, p. 145.

[84]*Years of My Youth*, p. 152. For a description of how Howells spent his
time, see "Journal to Vic," *Life in Letters*, I, 18–20.

ful in German studies and alive to all that is about. He was *the* poet of the Dial as you were its theologian."[85]

But much as Howells enjoyed his work on the *Ohio State Journal,* much as he appreciated the sociable life in "the amiable little town" of Columbus, a restless urge kept him tirelessly writing and reading and studying, hoping finally to escape from journalism altogether. In 1860 he published a campaign life of Lincoln,[86] and with the money advanced to him on this book he made his famous pilgrimage to New England. He belonged to the larger world, but whether as a newspaper man or poet, he himself could not venture to guess. Though he earned his living as news editor of the *Ohio State Journal,* he was, as he said, "always trying to make my writing literature;"[87] his interests in the political events of the day were, in fact, "mainly literary," and his heart was more in the poems which he was sending off to the *Saturday Press* and *The Atlantic Monthly.* "What I wished to do always and evermore was to think and dream and talk literature, and literature only, whether in its form of prose or of verse, in fiction, or poetry, or criticism."[88] "If there was anyone

[85]Undated manuscript letter in the Houghton Library, Harvard. The *Dial* appeared in Jan.-Dec., 1860.

[86]Follett, Foster, and Company commissioned Howells to write *The Life of Lincoln.* Howells' industry at this time might well have been caused by the fact that the *Journal,* then on an insecure financial basis, had been unable to pay him more than two-thirds of his salary for 1856–1860. See *Life in Letters,* I, 25, and *Years of My Youth,* p. 198. When Howells gave up his job in 1860, he was employed for a while by Follett, Foster, and Company as their reader. Howells was at that time too shy to interview Lincoln personally; in his place a young law student, James Quay Howard, went to Springfield and gathered material later used by Howells. *Life in Letters,* I, 36–37. Once Howells was launched on the *Life,* it ceased to appear to him a mere publisher's job, for he felt "the charm of the material" relating to Lincoln's early life. Furthermore, Howells, like Lincoln, was a member of the new Republican Party and opposed to the Mexican War and to slavery. See the facsimile edition of the book, issued in 1938 by the Abraham Lincoln Association, Springfield, Illinois. Abraham Lincoln's marginal corrections are reproduced.

[87]*Years of My Youth,* p. 159. The John Brown episode at Harpers Ferry in 1859 moved Howells to write "Old Brown." See *Life in Letters,* I, 26.

[88]*Years of My Youth,* p. 163.

in the world who had his being more wholly in literature than
I had in 1860, I am sure I should not have known where to
find him," Howells wrote at this time. "I had been for three
years a writer of news paragraphs, book notices, and political
leaders on a daily paper in an inland city, and I do not know that
my life differed outwardly from that of any other young journalist . . . But inwardly it was altogether different with me. Inwardly I was a poet, with no wish to be anything else, unless in
a moment of careless affluence I might so far forget myself as to
be a novelist."[89]

By trade a journalist, by inclination a poet, Howells turned
toward the East to become one of the greatest novelists this
country has produced. He carried with him a tradition of liberal
thought, inherited from his Quaker ancestors, a democratic outlook, learned from the Western Reserve of his day, and a passion
for the "literary," nourished by the best of five European cul-
tures. More immediately useful than any of these was his practical
knowledge of printing and journalism, by means of which Howells
was to gain a foothold in the literary world of Boston and New
York. His power as a novelist was to develop more slowly.

III. JOURNALIST TO NOVELIST

"He was a journalist before he let it be known that he was an author."

From 1860, when Howells made his literary pilgrimage to
Boston, to 1881, when he gave up the editorship of *The Atlantic
Monthly* in order to devote himself more entirely to his writing,
Howells changed from the young reporter from the West, who
thought of himself as a poet, to the mature novelist, with a series
of successful novels to his credit. The school through which
Howells passed was that of journalism, and the education he re-
ceived is outlined in his own novel, *The World of Chance* (1893).

Like the youthful Howells, the hero of this novel, Percy

[89] *Literary Friends and Acquaintance*, p. 1.

Bysshe Shelley Ray, arrived from the West with a manuscript
under his arm and an ardent wish to mingle in the literary circles
of the East. Howells describes himself when he pictures Ray's
"neat, slight, rather undersized person; his regular face, with its
dark eyes and marked brows; his straight fine nose and pleasant
mouth; his sprouting black moustache, and his brown tint, flecked
with a few browner freckles."[90] Both of these young men nursed
a secret hope that they might prove to be authors; meanwhile
they knew that they could, with proper care, tide themselves over
for a few weeks until their newsletters home to their local papers
should bring them an income. Ray, like Howells, "meant to
let it be known that he was a journalist before he let it be known
that he was an author."[91]

When Howells tells us that young Ray "was fond of adventure and hungry for experience, but he wished all his adventures
to be respectable,"[92] we do not have to be told that he is speaking
ironically of himself, for "the two strains of prudence and of
poetry were strongly blended"[93] in both young men. Ray's
ideas of novel writing are romantic and conventional; they are
fully expressed in *A Modern Romeo*, which, to the publishers
to whom he tries to sell it, he describes as "a love story with a
psychological interest." Into the poetic atmosphere of Ray's
love story very little realism is infused. Nor is Ray able at first to
understand, or indeed quite to see, the daily life of New York.
When Ray heard the tragic story of a man in the room next to
his in the cheap hotel where he is staying, "he felt sorry for the
unhappy man shut in there; but he perceived no special significance in what he had overheard."[94] But the weekly letter
home to the *Midland Echo* taught Ray, as it did Howells, to
sieze these sudden glimpses into "real life" and to make use of

[90] *The World of Chance*, p. 14.
[91] *Ibid*, pp. 30–31.
[92] *Ibid.*, p. 93.
[93] *Ibid.*, p. 27.
[94] *Ibid.*, p. 23.

them for newspaper copy. Ray is shocked when he sees a young thief caught and handcuffed on Broadway, until he considers what good use he can make of the episode in his newsletter.

The intrusion of such a brutal fact of life into the tragic atmosphere of his revery made the young poet a little sick, but the young journalist avidly seized upon it. The poet would not have dreamed of using such an incident, but the journalist saw how well it would work into the scheme of that first letter he was writing home to the *Echo*.[95]

The actual experiences which, as a newspaper man, Howells was forced to face transformed the dreamy literary youth from Ohio into the defender of realism in the novel, who was able to illustrate his theory by a series of novels which reflect the social scene of this country more adequately than any novels before his time. How these twenty years of varied and successful newspaper work educated Howells and prepared him for his great decade of novel writing, which began in 1882 with *A Modern Instance*, becomes clear if one traces his journalistic career through the *Atlantic Monthly* period, noticing at the same time the evolution of his early novels as they appeared from 1872 to 1881 in the pages of the *Atlantic*. It is to be observed that Howells did not produce his first essay toward a novel, *Their Wedding Journey*, until he had completed twelve years as a mature journalist, and, further, that he did not make use of the newspaper world at all in his novels until after he had resigned from the *Atlantic* and digested his experiences. Then, through a series of characters, the most notable of whom are Bartley Hubbard (*A Modern Instance*), Maxwell Brice (*The Quality of Mercy* and *The Story of a Play*), and Percy Bysshe Shelley Ray, Howells' attitude toward journalism becomes abundantly clear.[96] It is essentially that of Ray, who never fully

[95]*Ibid.*, p. 35.
[96]In *Years of My Youth* Howells tries to express the relationship at that time between Howells, the journalist, and Howells, the author. "Journal-

accepted the newspaper work by which he earned a living until he won recognition as a novelist. The superior journalists, such as Maxwell Brice, found that their writing was too good to be altogether acceptable to their editors, who preferred the aggressive vulgarity of the Pinneys and the Fulkersons. Bartley Hubbard, with his flair for the feature story no matter how he got it, reflected the unethical methods of the newspaper world in which Howells did not feel at home, though it was this very world of newspaper men which had contributed so much to the education of the ambitious young reporter from Columbus.

2. Pilgrimage to Boston

Resolved to devote his entire life to the highest and best in literature, Howells set out in July, 1860, on a trip to Boston and Cambridge to seek out those whom he regarded as the literary leaders of his day. Though this trip was paid for by the money his publishers advanced him on his *Life of Lincoln*,[97] he had planned before he left home to increase his increment by writing up his contacts with the literary men he was to meet. Moreover, in order to supplement his funds, this thrifty young poet wrote a series of articles as he travelled along on his journey, "En Passant" for the *Ohio State Journal* and "Glimpses of Summer Travel" for the Cincinnati *Gazette*.[98] The publishers of the

---

ism was not my ideal, but it was my passion, and I was passionately a journalist well after I began author. I tried to make my newspaper work literary, to give it form and distinction, and it seems to me that I did not always try in vain, but I had also the instinct of actuality, of trying to make my poetry speak for its time and place." p. 178.

[97] *Years of My Youth*, p. 207. For a description of the same transaction, see *The Niagara Book* (Buffalo, 1893), pp. 1–2. In this account of the episode, Howells raises the amount of money advanced to him by the publishers of his *Life of Lincoln*.

[98] In the year 1860 Howells was achieving considerable success both as poet and journalist. Not only had *Poems of Two Friends* appeared, but in January came his first poem in the *Atlantic*, followed by others in this same year, and as the year advanced his poems and articles appeared in Moncure D. Conway's *Dial* and the *Ohio Farmer*, as well as in his own *Ohio State Journal* and Ashtabula *Sentinel*. A number of poems and reviews

Life of Lincoln, in fact, made an arrangement whereby Howells was to visit a number of manufacturing establishments and describe the wonders of American industry. This assignment was never really completed, for, in spite of his years of experience as a reporter, Howells was too shy at that time to interview people, least of all manufacturers.[99]

Though Howells was unable to meet the managers of factories, he seems to have been undaunted by the great literary figures of his day. When he reached Cambridge he first sought out Lowell, with whom he had corresponded in his capacity as editor of the *Atlantic*, and "found him at last in a little study at the rear of a pleasant, old-fashioned house near the Delta."[100] Their meeting was a memorably happy one, for as Howells revered the older Lowell as the most gifted American man of letters of the day, so Lowell saw in Howells a young peer. At once the editor of the *Atlantic* set about to introduce his new friend to the literary circle of Cambridge, Boston, and Concord. To Hawthorne he wrote of "the young man who brings this,"[101]

---

were published in the New York *Saturday Press*, and one poem in *Echoes of Harper's Ferry*.

[99] The managers of the factories which he entered were far from friendly, for they suspected Howells of trying to pry into their secrets. "I could not tell the managers that I was both morally and mentally incapable of this," he writes, "that they might have explained and demonstrated the properties and functions of their most recondite machinery, and upon examination afterwards found me guiltless of having anything but a few verses of Heine or Tennyson or Longfellow in my head." *Literary Friends and Acquaintance*, p. 19. However, when *A Traveler from Altruria* appeared in *The Cosmopolitan*, (Nov. 1892–Oct. 1893) we note that the Altrurian finds in the shoe industry one of his best examples of cheap and tawdry production. *The Cosmopolitan*, XV (Oct. 1893), 640.

[100] *Literary Friends and Acquaintance*, p. 23. In 1871, when Howells was editor of *The Atlantic Monthly*, he was asked by "Mr. Carter" "to write of Mr. Lowell." With characteristic delicacy he refused, saying that Providence had protected him from ever writing personally of his literary friends. Unpublished letter of Howells to "Mr. Carter," Boston, December 30, 1871. The Berg Collection, New York Public Library.

[101] *Letters of James Russell Lowell*, ed. by Charles Eliot Norton, (New York, 1894), I, 305–306.

His name is Howells, and he is a fine young fellow, and has
written several *poems* in the *Atlantic*, which of course you have
never read, because you don't do such things yourself, and are
old enough to know better . . . If my judgment is good for anything, this youth has more in him than any of our younger
fellows in the way of rhyme . . . let him look at you and charge it

To yours always,

J. R. Lowell

When he reached home, Howells wrote to Lowell that he "came
nearer" to Hawthorne than he "at first believed possible." Indeed the inmate of the Old Manse seems to have warmed to
Howells; at least he passed him on to Emerson with the note on
the back of his card, "I find this young man worthy."[102]

But the great thing that Lowell did for Howells was to invite
him to dinner at the Parker House.[103] James T. Fields and Dr.
Holmes, the other guests, were evidently as pleased with the
young Westerner as he was with the older men whom he so
revered, for the party lasted four hours. As the Autocrat looked
around the table, at their host, the first editor of the *Atlantic*,
and Fields, its publisher and soon to become the second editor,
and at the eager Howells, who was in the course of years to be
the third editor, he leaned forward and said to Lowell, "Well,
James, this is something like the apostolic succession; this is the
laying on of hands."[104] We are not told more of the conversation, but we know that Dr. Holmes invited Howells to tea, and
that James T. Fields, the editor of the *Atlantic* immediately
after Lowell, invited him to his home for breakfast.[105]

[102] *Life in Letters*, I, 30.

[103] Howells never forgot this occasion. Five years later, in a letter to
Lowell, he refers to the "cordial and flattering reception you both [Lowell
and Holmes] gave a certain raw youngster who visited you in Boston five
years ago—you old ones who *might* have put me off with a little chilly
patronage." *Life in Letters*, I, 84.

[104] *Literary Friends and Acquaintance*, p. 37. See also *Life in Letters*, I,
28–29.

[105] Howells did not hesitate to further his own cause. A few days after
this meeting with Fields, he tells us, "I thought it a favorable moment to

If Howells found in the *Atlantic* group the type of literary men with whom he wished to be associated, when he continued his trip to New York and visited the office of the *Saturday Press* he discovered in Henry Clapp, Jr., and those connected with the *Press* precisely the sort of men of letters whom he most detested. As an ambitious young reporter in Columbus, he had looked upon the *Press*, for which he had written poems, sketches, and criticism,[106] as "the wittiest and sauciest paper in this country,"[107] and many years later he wrote, "It is not too much to say that it was very nearly as well for one to be accepted by the *Press* as to be accepted by the *Atlantic*, and for the time there was no other literary comparison."[108]   Howells tells us that he approached its office "with much the same sort of feeling" that he had on going to the office of the *Atlantic* in Boston, but he went away with "a very different feeling."[109] Clapp, who had lived in Paris for a time, was the center of a Bohemian group which smoked and drank beer at Pfaff's Restaurant at 647 Broadway. He must have enjoyed embarrassing the diffident Ohioan by his banter. When Clapp learned that Howells had met Hawthorne on his trip to Concord, he asked him how they got on together. The youth tried, somewhat hesitantly, to explain that both of them

---

propose myself as the assistant editor of the *Atlantic Monthly*, which I had the belief I could very well become, with advantage to myself if not to the magazine." Fields laughed, asked him how old he was, and said he would have given him the position had it not been filled. *Literary Friends and Acquaintance*, pp. 65–66. Fields offered the position to Howells several years later, and Howells gladly accepted. Meanwhile, he recognized Howells' journalistic capacity at that time and tried to secure for the young man a position with the New York *Evening Post*. The kindly effort failed, for, as Howells wrote to Fields on his return to Ohio, the editor "objected to my youth, and rather deferred the decision." *Life in Letters*, I, 29.

[106]*Literary Friends and Acquaintance*, p. 2.

[107]*Ohio State Journal*, April 20, 1859. Forty-six years later, Howells, as editor of the "Easy Chair" of *Harper's Magazine*, picked up an issue of the New York *Saturday Press* of 1860, and wrote an "Easy Chair" editorial about it. His views remained unchanged. *Harper's*, CXII (March, 1906), 631.

[108]*Literary Friends and Acquaintance*, p. 70.

[109]*Ibid.*, p. 71.

were shy; whereupon "the king of Bohemia" broke in upon him
with, "Oh, a couple of shysters!"[110] Howells was thoroughly
abashed.

A result of this visit, probably unnoticed by Clapp, was that
Howells never again wrote for the *Press*, though he did in the
following autumn express regret at the demise of that paper. For,
in spite of the superficial Bohemianism carefully cultivated by
Clapp and his group, a number of the most talented writers of
the generation, including James, Clemens, and Whitman, were
contributors to this enterprising periodical.[111] But Howells,
at this time, met only Walt Whitman, though many of the
others later became his friends. According to William Winter,
Howells, "a respectable youth in black raiment," made quite as
poor an impression on those he did meet as they made on him.
"They thought him a prig."[112]

Howells returned to Columbus determined to prepare himself
for the best that the future might hold for him, to persevere in
his pursuit of the literary ideals of Boston, rather than those of
New York, and, to these ends, to keep himself "in cotton." "In
fact," he wrote forty years later,

it can do no harm at this distance of time to confess that it
seemed to me then, and for a good while afterwards, that a person who had seen the men and had the things said before him
that I had in Boston, could not keep himself too carefully in
cotton; and this is what I did all the following winter, though
of course it was a secret between me and me. I dare say it was
not the worst thing I could have done, in some respects."[113]

---

[110]*Ibid.*, p. 71.

[111]*Ibid.*, p. 74.

[112]William Winter, *Old Friends* (1909), pp. 89–92. Lowell looked upon
Howells as a promising poet at that time. See two letters to Howells
written in 1860, in which Lowell gives the younger poet advice. "Read
what will make you *think*, not *dream*," he writes, "hold yourself dear, and
more power to your elbow! God bless you." *The Letters of James Russell
Lowell*, 2 vols. (New York, 1894), I, 305.

[113]*Literary Friends and Acquaintance*, p. 76.

Back in Columbus in the difficult winter of 1860–61, while he sought out the next turn in his fortunes, Howells continued to write for the *Ohio State Journal*, for which he conducted one of his favorite "Literary Gossip" columns,[114] and to send off poems to the *Atlantic*,[115] not all of which were accepted.[116] But now there began to show "shadows in the picture otherwise too bright."[117] In November, 1860, Lincoln was elected to the Presidency; in December, South Carolina seceded from the Union; in April, war broke out. "The country was drawing nearer and nearer the abyss where it plunged so soon."[118] Howells, like the other young journalists of his circle, did not think that the Union would be dissolved, or, if it should be, that that was the worst thing that could happen.[119] In a round of social gaieties, neither Howells nor his friends were interested in war. Howells' mood is partly accounted for by the fact that he met his future wife, Elinor G. Mead, at this time. "In that gayest time when we met it did not seem as if there could be an end of time for us, or any time less radiant." "Very likely those dances lasted through the winter, but I cannot be sure; I can only

[114]For a reflection of Howells' state of discouragement about his job at this time, see his letter to his mother, May 5, 1861. *Life in Letters*, I, 34.

[115]On April 4, 1860, Howells wrote gaily to Thomas Fullerton, a youthful fellow poet, about his poem in the April *Atlantic* which he hoped was creating a stir in Peoria. Unpublished letter in the Berg Collection, New York Public Library.

[116]See an unpublished letter to James T. Fields, editor of the *Atlantic*, in the Huntington Library, dated September 29, 1861, in which Howells regrets that his poem "Bereft" is rejected, and wonders whether he will dare to submit poems to the *Atlantic* again.

[117]*Years of My Youth*, p. 169.

[118]*Ibid.*, p. 226.

[119]See "Letter from Columbus" (*Cincinnati Gazette*, Jan.–Apr., 1857; Jan.–Apr., 1858); "News and Humors of the Mails" (*Ohio State Journal*, Nov., 1858–Feb., 1860). In these columns Howells frequently expressed his anti-slavery sentiments. In 1861, Howells wrote a series of letters for the New York *World*, with the title "From Ohio," describing the war activities in that state (New York *World*, I, p. 3, Apr. 22, 1861; p. 4, May 21, 1861; p. 6, May 15, 1861; p. 8, July 17, 1861. William M. Gibson, "Materials and Form in Howells's First Novels." *American Literature*, XIX (1947), 158–166.

be sure that they summed up the raptures of the time, which was the most memorable of my whole life; for now I met her who was to be my wife."[120]

As spring advanced the finances of the *Ohio State Journal* became less and less secure. By May, Howells wrote home to his mother, "I was in extremely low spirits about money matters and about what I was to do in the future . . .Cooke owes me something over two hundred dollars, and I have had doubts whether I shall be able to get the money."[121] A plan to tour the Western cities and write them up for the *Atlantic* had to be cancelled for "want of means."[122] Casting about for some way of escape from his difficulties, it occured to Howells that, as the author of a life of Lincoln, he was a candidate for some kind of political reward. His mastery of German gave him hope for a consulship in Munich, but, after a long wait, he finally received one in Rome. Since this position paid only in fees, he soon exchanged it for a more lucrative post in Venice.[123] Howells sailed for Italy, as consul to Venice, in November, 1861,[124] where he stayed for the duration of the Civil War, glad to escape from the necessity of participating in a war for which he had no enthusiasm.[125] "If I hoped to serve my country there," he wrote

[120] *Years of My Youth*, p. 225. For a further account of the meeting of Howells and Elinor Mead, see *Life in Letters*, I, 24; II, 333. For an account of the family of Miss Mead and a brief analysis of her character, see *ibid.*, I, 10–12.

[121] *Life in Letters*, I, 34.

[122] *Ibid.*, p. 35.

[123] Howells earned $1,500 a year while in Venice. The salary was raised from $750 to $1,500 for the duration of the Civil War. *Life in Letters*, I, 58. In an unpublished letter to John Piatt written from Venice on February 15, 1865, Howells writes, "I suppose you understand that the salary at Venice falls to $750 as soon as peace is made." In the possession of Cecil Piatt.

[124] For an account of Howells' entrance into Venice, see *Life in Letters*, I, 43–44.

[125] Unpublished letter to John Piatt, dated August 4, 1861: "Aren't you sorry the Atlantic goes so gun-powerfully into the war? It's patriotic; but do we not get enough [blot] in the newspapers? I would rather have the honey of Attic bees." See also an unpublished letter of Howells to Holmes, dated May 22, 1861, in which Howells asks Holmes whether he has enlisted in the army, as he has heard. As for himself, Howells writes,

quite frankly, "and sweep the Confederate cruisers from the Adriatic, I am afraid my prime intent was to add to her literature and to my own credit."[126]

2. Consul in Venice

Since the duties of a consul at Venice in the eighteen-sixties were not onerous, Howells may have counted on having a good deal of time for writing, but for the first year and more he published only three installments of a "Letter from Europe" in the *Ohio State Journal*, and one poem. Perhaps the loneliness of his first year in Venice,[127] which he sought to counteract by wide reading,[128] and plans for his approaching marriage,[129] made writing impossible. By the winter of 1863, however, probably in part impelled by the need of money to support the new household installed in an apartment on the Grand Canal, he began to write letters to the *Boston Advertiser*. This venture turned out to be very important in the life of the young journalist-novelist, for it was to lead to a timely recognition of his extraordinary powers as a writer of travel books, which in turn was to bring him to his particular type of realistic fiction. In *My Literary Passions*, Howells tells us that this first stay in romantic Venice changed the whole course of his literary life and turned him into a realist.[130] Since Venice was at that time occupied by the

he has been contemplating joining a local troop with his friends; but then the weather is too hot for drilling, and, moreover, since he has become a thinker he is no longer so interested in deeds of valor. The Houghton Library, Harvard.

[126] *My Literary Passions*, (New York, 1891) p. 195.

[127] For an account of Howells' first winter in Venice, see *Life in Letters*, I, 47–50; 53–54; 58–59.

[128] In 1887 Howells published *Modern Italian Poets*. In his introduction he wrote: "This book has grown out of studies begun twenty years ago in Italy, and continued fitfully, as I found the mood and time for them, long after their original circumstance had become a pleasant memory." P. 1.

[129] Howells and Elinor Mead were married in Paris, on December 24, 1862. See *Life in Letters*, I, 61–62.

[130] "My literary life, almost without my willing it, had taken the course of critical observance of books and men in their actuality." *My Literary Passions*, p. 206. See also *Venetian Life*, p. 94.

Austrians, and the United States was in the midst of war, there were no parties to attend and few visitors to entertain.[131] Howells and Elinor had plenty of time to walk by the side of the canals and to linger on Saint Mark's Square, she with her sketch-book and paints, and he with his note-book.[132] They had time, too, to read and profit by the plays of Goldoni, who, though a writer of the eighteenth century, seemed to Howells to present a more realistic picture of Venice than any later writer.[133]

Although *Venetian Life*, the outcome of these pleasant strolls, was supposedly the work of a "foreign correspondent," the sketches had little or nothing to do with politics and nearly all were concerned with the comings and goings of daily life. "I was studying manners, in the elder sense of the word, wherever I could get at them in the frank life of the people about me,"[134] he writes, not realizing, as we do in re-reading this early book, that his feeling for Venice was that of a novelist rather than that of a journalist.

I was resolved in writing this book to tell what I had found most books of travel very slow to tell,—as much as possible of the everyday life of a people whose habits are so different from our own; endeavoring to develop a just notion of their character, not only from the show-traits which strangers are most likely to see, but also from experience of such things as strangers are most likely to miss.[135]

It is the novelist, rather than the journalist, who delights "in the

[131]*Life in Letters*, I, 12. Visitors were a welcome relief. Moncure D. Conway, Charles Hale, Henry Ward Beecher, and John Motley all came and sat for a while in the Howells' parlor. In an unpublished letter to Moncure D. Conway, written from Venice on January 26, 1864, Howells describes very charmingly the Howells' Saturday evenings at home, when friends dropped in for conversation and cards and Elinor served coffee and cakes. Berg Collection, New York Public Library.

[132]"I have bought Elinor a sketch-book and she proposes to unite sketching with boating." *Life in Letters*, p. 66. I "keep a journal from which I hope to make a book about Venice." *Ibid.*, p. 57.

[133]*My Literary Passions*, p. 207, ff.

[134]*Ibid.*, p. 206.

[135]*Venetian Life*, p. 94.

intricacies of the narrowest, crookedest, and most inconsequent little streets in the world,"[136] and who often pauses in these streets to observe the "young girls steal to their balconies, and linger there for hours, subtly conscious of the young men sauntering to and fro, and looking up at them from beneath."[137] It is the future writer of realistic novels, moreover, who notes the cold winter, the frugal meals, and the thieving servants, facts as important for the notebook of the novelist as are the lovers and the gondolas.

Howells' first thought as he planned this series of articles on Italy was of publication in the *Atlantic*, but, curiously enough, his efforts were rejected. "The editors refused them as they refused everything else in prose or verse I sent them,"[138] he wrote in distress to Lowell. If the most literary magazine in the country would not take his articles, he could at least turn to the newspapers; he remembered a "half promise" he had made to Charles Hale to write for the Boston *Daily Advertiser*,[139] and on March 27, 1863, the first installment of more than thirty "Letters from Venice" made its appearance in this paper. He was disappointed by his failure to find a better outlet for his Italian sketches than a newspaper, but Lowell praised them, and others assured him they were being widely read.[140] Thus encouraged, Howells conceived the idea of collecting all of the articles in a volume. But, as an ambitious young man who knew what it was to have material rejected, he could not afford to publish an unsuccessful book. "The truth is I have worked under great discouragement since I've been in Venice," he wrote to Lowell, in the summer of 1864, "I've got to that point in life where I cannot afford to fail any more."

[136] *Ibid.*, p. 32.
[137] *Ibid.*, p. 63.
[138] *Life in Letters*, I, 85.
[139] *Ibid.*, p. 77.
[140] *Ibid.*, p. 84–85.

He shrewdly planned, therefore, to have the book published abroad, for "a first appearance in England will brighten my prospects in America."[141]

Meanwhile, Howells was restless to return to the United States, for he had "seen enough of uncountreyed Americans in Europe" to disgust him "with voluntary exile, and its effects upon character."[142] He was, moreover, trying to become a writer, and his lack of success in achieving recognition even as a journalist was exceedingly vexing. "The Novel is not written; the Great Poem is hardly dreamed of," he wrote to Stedman[143] in August, 1863; and to Piatt:[144]

I am not myself so lucky as some men I know, and am at the throatcutting level most of the time. If any one, in the fall of 1861 had predicted that I should have advanced no farther than I have by 1865, I would have laughed that prophetic ass to scorn. And yet, here I am.

In July, 1865, Howells secured a leave of absence from his post[145] and set out for the United States, journeying home by

[141]*Ibid.*, p. 85. Many letters, written at this time, in the unpublished correspondence between Howells and Moncure D. Conway attest Conway's efforts to find a publisher for Howells' poems in London. Though Browning read the poems and praised them, they were finally returned to Howells. This experience seems to have made Howells turn from poetry writing. A further spur to Howells' determination to establish himself was the birth of his first child, Winifred, on December 17, 1863. The Houghton Library, Harvard.

[142]*Life in Letters*, I, p. 85.

[143]*Ibid.*, p. 70.

[144]Letter to John Piatt, owned by Cecil Piatt.

[145]Before quitting Italy, Howells and his wife took several weeks' vacation, visiting Rome, Naples, Genoa, Mantua, and other cities, leaving Mrs. Howells' brother, Larkin D. Mead, as Vice-consul in Howells' absence. This trip formed the basis of Howells' second book of travels, *Italian Journeys* (1867). *Life in Letters*, I, 131; 192. In an unpublished letter to John Piatt, written from Venice, February 15, 1865, in the possession of Cecil Piatt, Howell writes, "You know we have been recently to Rome and Naples. The ruins and things are much better as you suppose them to be, than as you find them. On the whole, I was disappointed with Rome; but so I was with Niagara. Pompeii is the only town worth seeing."

way of England, where he made tentative arrangements for his book, *Venetian Life*, to be published.[146] This volume, which appeared in 1866, consisted of the papers from the *Daily Advertiser*. Some of the essays were inserted with little change and others with alterations, some were omitted entirely, and a few new chapters were added—little enough showing for a young man of soaring literary ambitions. He could not have realized that he carried away with him from Italy the material for half a dozen novels, and, what was still more important, the habit of noting down the daily happenings on Italian streets.

3. *Journalist, Novelist, or Poet?*

When Howells first returned to New York, after an absence of nearly four years, he at once sought journalistic employment. "Few men live by making books, and I must look to some position as editor to assist me in my career."[147] No matter what he might write in the future, he must earn his living by journalism if he wished to make a home for his wife and little daughter, who had, for the present, gone to Brattleboro, Vermont, to stay with Mrs. Howells' parents. His letters for the *Daily Advertiser* and "Recent Italian Comedy," which he had contributed to the *North American Review*[148], gave him the introduction which he needed, and we soon find him writing for several New York

---

[146]For plans for the publication of the book, see *Life in Letters*, I, 84; 95–98. For an account of the reception of the book, see *Life in Letters* I, 113–114; 115; 153.

[147]*Life in Letters*, I, 90. Howells was at this time disturbed by the news of the death of his younger brother John, the illness of his brother Sam, and Joseph's enlistment in the Union Army. He assured his father that he would return to Jefferson to take Joseph's place on the Ashtabula *Sentinel* if necessary, but added that his aim was literary, and that he "must seek [his] fortune at the great literary centres." *Ibid.* An unpublished letter in the Huntington Library to J. T. Fields, editor of the *Atlantic*, indicates that Howells was disappointed by the reception of poems sent to the *Atlantic* at that time. The letter is written from New York City, and is dated September 18, 1865.

[148]*The North American Review*, XCIX (Oct., 1864), 304–401.

papers, including the *Times* and the *Tribune*. The *Round Table* seemed for a while interested in giving him a position, but the hope evaporated.[149] Meantime, he wrote a number of articles for this paper, including a review of Walt Whitman's *Drum Taps*, which his poetic nature enjoyed so much and his critical training forced him to condemn.[150] Such work was scattering, however; if he must earn his living as a journalist, he wished at least to secure a more permanent position, and one which would make wider use of his talents. The chance was soon to come. Beginning October 5, 1865, Howells made his first contribution to the *Nation*, newly established by E. L. Godkin. By the 27th of that month, he was able to write his wife that when he took Godkin a review of a new play, the editor had said, "How would you like to write exclusively for the *Nation*, and what will you take to do it?" Howells named $50 a week as a suitable figure, and Godkin replied that he would think it over.[151] But it was agreed, apparently during the same conversation, that Howells should give this magazine a page of "philosophized foreign gossip" each week "for $15 which is $5 more than usually paid." "Minor Topics,"[152] another gossip column of the type which Howells had already so frequently edited, appeared, accordingly, from November 30, 1865, to April 26, 1866. On December 17 he wrote his wife that he was engaged to write for the *Nation* at $40 a week, and that this did not count whatever he was able to earn by writing for other magazines, nor did it include "articles on Italian subjects, and poems, which will be paid for

---

[149]*Life in Letters*, I, 98.

[150]*Round Table*, November 11, 1865. See also Howells' remarks about Whitman as a poet, *Life in Letters*, I, 116. See also Howells' review of *November Boughs*, *Harper's*, LXXVIII (Feb., 1889), 488. See also an interesting unpublished letter concerning the poetry of Whitman written to Howells by Edmund Stedman on December 2, 1866. Stedman again consults Howells concerning an article he proposes to write about Whitman. The Houghton Library, Harvard.

[151]*Life in Letters*, I, 102.

[152]George Arms, *The Social Criticism of William Dean Howells*, p. 392, (unpublished thesis, New York University, 1939).

extra."[153] Though his salary was small, Howells was delighted
to be able to summon his family to New York, and to be working for such a chief as E. L. Godkin. "I worked with joy, with
ardor, and I liked so much to be there, in that place and in that
company, that I hated to have each day come to an end."[154]

But before Howells was fairly settled into his new position in
New York, the great journalistic opportunity of his life came to
him. At a New Year's party he again met James T. Fields, and
a few days later Fields offered him the assistant editorship of the
Atlantic, of which he was editor in succession to Lowell. The
offer was a good one, as Howells stated it in his letter of acceptance to Fields. His work included the

"examination of mss. offered to the *Atlantic*; correspondence
with contributors; reading proof for the magazine after its
revisal by the printers; and writing the *Reviews and Literary
Notices*, for which I am to receive fifty dollars a week, while
I am to be paid extra for anything I may contribute to the
body of the magazine."[155]

Howells was made aware that the experience he had "as practical printer for the work was most valued, if not the most valued,
and that as a proof-reader, [he] was expected to make it avail on the
side of economy."[156] On his twenty-ninth birthday, March 1,
1866, Howells began work on the *Atlantic*. Two months later
he moved his family into "Cottage Quiet,"[157] on Sacramento

---

[153]*Life in Letters*, I, 104. In an unpublished letter in the Huntington
Library, addressed to J. T. Fields, on January 14, 1866, Howells wrote that
his income was about fifty dollars a week, nearly all of it from *The Nation*,
for which Howells wrote articles and reviews and was himself allowed to
choose his subjects.

[154]*Literary Friends and Acquaintance*, p. 106. See also "A Great New
York Journalist," *The North American Review*, CLXXXV (May 1907), 44–
53.

[155]*Life in Letters*, I, 105.

[156]*Literary Friends and Acquaintance*, p. 112.

[157]Later called "the carpenter box". In 1919 Howells wrote down a few
notes for a book which he never completed. The book was to be entitled
Years of My Middle Life; in it Howells referred to several of his homes of
this period: "Settlement in Cambridge, where no suitable house was to be

Street, Cambridge, where the young couple soon began to participate in "this life so refined, so intelligent, so gracefully simple"[158] that Howells doubted whether the world could offer anything more desirable.

Almost as soon as Howells moved into the *Atlantic* office he became the active head of the magazine, for Fields was growing weary of the routine of editorship.[159] The task of forming the policies of the magazine and dealing with the striving young authors who sought recognition through its pages was soon shifted to Howells' willing shoulders. Partly in this way, and partly as a resident of Cambridge, which was a natural resort of writers, Howells soon came to know most of the interesting writers of the day, E. C. Stedman, T. B. Aldrich, S. O. Jewett, H. H. Boyesen, and dozens of other literary people.[160] The

---

found, or rooms, because of leftover war conditions—Charles Eliot Norton joining with my wife's father in buying us a little house in Sacramento Street—I sell this house after four years at a profit of $40." He then moved to Berkeley Street where he lived two years. "Buy land from Professor Parsons on Concord Avenue and build a house where we meant to spend our lives, but spent six years . . . Removal to Belmont in a house built for us by McKim, Mead and White." *Life in Letters*, II, 388. These moves were made necessary by a growing family. John Mead Howells was born in 1868, and Mildred Howells in 1872. For further description of the house of Sacramento Street, see *Suburban Sketches* p. 1 ff.; *Life in Letters*, I, 107–108; 112; *Literary Friends and Acquaintance*, pp. 178–179.

[158]*Literary Friends and Acquaintance*, p. 179. For the pleasure Howells took in his early life in Cambridge, see *Life in Letters*, I, 141–142. See also the "Easy Chair," *Harper's*, CXXXVIII (May 1919), 854–856. See also Hamlin Garland, "Howells' Early Life in Cambridge," *My Friendly Contemporaries* (New York, 1932), 298.

[159]Howells became actual editor of the *Atlantic* in July, 1871. But the Fields Collection of Howells letters in the Huntington Library indicates that from the beginning of his association with the magazine he was influential in selecting material, and in forming policies. On Dec. 24, 1869, in fact, Howells wrote to T. W. Higginson, in answer to his question as to the policy of the *Atlantic* in selecting books for review, and told him that the choice of books was left almost wholly to him. He attempted, he said, not to overlook any important book, and also to choose those interesting to himself, since he did nearly all the reviewing. Unpublished letter in the Berg Collection, New York Public Library.

[160]During the winter of 1869–1870 Howells became a University Lecturer on "New Italian Literature" at Harvard University, which increased his prestige in the literary circles of Cambridge and Boston. *Life in*

young editor, so recently returned from Italy, was invited by
Longfellow to a meeting of the Dante Club at Craigie House.
"During a whole winter of Wednesday evenings," Howells followed, in an Italian text, Longfellow's reading of his translation of the *Paradiso*, and, at the supper parties which ensued, he
grew to know more personally such men as Lowell, Holmes, and
Norton.[161] Through the Contributors' Club, which Howells
inaugurated in 1877,[162] he not only attracted well-known names to
the *Atlantic*, but elicited the fresh talent of Mark Twain and
Bret Harte. Howells became, indeed, the literary mentor for
many of these unknown writers,[163] and through his kindly, firm

---

Letters, I, 139; 144–145. In 1870, Howells delivered lectures on
"Italian Poets of Our Century" before the Lowell Institute. *Life in
Letters*, I, 156–157. These lectures contributed to Howells' later study,
Modern Italian Poets (1887).

[161] *Literary Friends and Acquaintance*, pp. 181–194.

[162] *Life in Letters*, I, 228.

[163] Fresh evidence of Howells' kindness to young writers is constantly
turning up. Mr. R. L. E. Paulin, of Boulder, Colorado, writes to us of
his meeting with Howells at the home of the Hallowells of West Medford,
when Mr. Paulin was a senior at Harvard. There lived three families, all
Quakers, originally from Philadelphia. The three brothers had been
active abolitionists, and had fought in the Northern army, for which they
had been read out of Meeting. Living as close neighbors, the Hallowell
families had made it their practice to gather regularly Sunday evenings
at one home or another for what they called "Coffee." At one house in
particular it was not unusual to meet a well-known artist, or writer, or
celebrity of the day:
    "One evening when all of us young people had come in from playing
tennis I found a rather pudgy, pleasant looking man of perhaps forty
sitting in front of the wood fire. We were introduced to him. He turned
out to be William Dean Howells, the novelist, then editor of the Atlantic
Monthly. While supper was being brought in, he motioned to me to take a
vacant chair at his side. He wanted to know what I was doing in college.
Mostly Greek and German, and Shakespeare with Prof. Child. 'What else?'
He drew out of me that I had been one of the founders of the Harvard
Daily Herald, was on the staff of the Lampoon, and had sold some verses
and prose pieces to Life, the New York weekly. 'So you write?' he went on.
'I would like to see some of your work.' Naturally I was flattered and
puzzled that an author of Howells' standing should care to look at under-
graduate stuff like mine. 'I mean it,' he added. 'Send me some of it; what
you choose. To the office of the Atlantic.' Others came up to take his
attention. When it came time to take leave I went up to thank Howells and
say goodbye. 'Remember what I said,' he added as he shook my hand. I

direction, the *Atlantic* continued, as it had begun, the foremost periodical on this side of the ocean.[164]

As editor of the *Atlantic*, Howells was both influencing others and himself learning from his friends and contributors. It was in the office of James T. Fields, Howells tells us, that he first met Mark Twain in 1866. Howells had recently written a review of *Innocents Abroad*, in which, though he had "intimated" his "reservations" of the book, he had had "the luck, if not the sense, to recognize that it was such fun as we had not had before."[165] Howells' immediate appreciation of the originality of Mark Twain's genius led to an intimate friendship between the two men which lasted through innumerable adventures, both personal and literary, until Mark Twain's death in 1910.[166] In the biography of his friend, *My Mark Twain*, written immediately after his death, Howells delicately describes the nature of their relationship. Though Mark Twain's "graphic touch was always allowing itself a freedom" which Howells could not bring his "fainter pencil to illustrate,"[167] Howells, however, "was always very glad of him and proud of him as a contributor" to the *Atlantic*.[168] When Howells visited Mark Twain in Hartford

---

sent him some verses I had had printed in the Lampoon and in Life. In time came a note of thanks without further comment. That was reward enough. There was nothing of condescension, or even amused curiosity in Howells' manner."

[164]See an unpublished letter to T. W. Higginson, October 18, 1873. The Berg Collection, New York Public Library.

[165]*My Mark Twain*, p. 3. See also *Mark Twain's Letters*, ed. by Albert Bigelow Paine, (New York, 1917), 166.

[166]Paine points out that Mark Twain wrote more letters, and more characteristic ones, to Howells than to any other person. *Mark Twain's Letters*, I, 166.

[167]*My Mark Twain*, p. 3.

[168]*Ibid.*, p. 19. Howells undoubtedly curbed Mark Twain's literary expression, though he was unfailingly cordial to him in the editor-contributor relationship, and as the enthusiastic reviewer of his books. See *Life in Letters*, I, 191; 302. See also Mark Twain's *Autobiography*, I, 178. See also *Mark Twain's Letters*, I, 223–224; 229–230; 249; 259; 263; 266; 272; 512. Howells was the friend who stood by Mark Twain even after the "hideous mistake" of Mark Twain's speech at the Whittier birthday party. *Life in Letters*, I, 241–244. *Mark Twain's Letters*, I, 315–318.

in 1874, *Innocents Abroad* and *Roughing It* were being sold by subscription throughout the country, and Mark Twain was beginning to glimpse the possibility of great money returns from his writing.[169] Though Howells collaborated with Mark Twain on his *Library of Humor*,[170] wrote with him an unsuccessful play, *Colonel Sellers*,[171] joined with him in a collection of stories entitled *Their Husbands' Wives*,[172] he never subscribed to Twain's grandiose literary plans,[173] nor does he seem to have been influenced by Mark Twain either in his thought or style. Howells loved him for his boundless humanity, and perhaps helped his friend translate his violent social indignations to articulate expression in *A Connecticut Yankee in King Arthur's Court:* "He never went so far in socialism as I have gone, if he went that way at all," wrote Howells in *My Mark Twain*, "but he was fascinated with *Looking Backward* and had Bellamy to visit him; and from the first he had a luminous vision of organized labor as the only present help for working-men . . . There was a time when I was afraid that his eyes were a little holden from the truth; but in the very last talk I heard from him I found that I was wrong, and that this great humorist was as great a humanist as ever. I wish that all the work-folk could know this, and could know him their friend in life as he was in literature; as he was in such a glorious gospel of equality as the *Connecticut Yankee in King*

[169] *My Mark Twain*, p. 8. See also *Mark Twain's Letters*, I, 195.

[170] *Life in Letters*, I, 295. *Mark Twain's Letters*, II, 462–464; 484–485.

[171] *Life in Letters*, I, 354; 359; 382–383. *My Mark Twain*, pp. 27–28.

[172] *Life in Letters*, II, 215.

[173] Mark Twain seldom encountered Howells without throwing out a suggestion for a literary collaboration, most of which Howells smilingly refused. Mark Twain suggested, for example, that he and Howells write a play based on *Tom Sawyer*, (see *Life in Letters*, I, 207–208. See also *Mark Twain's Letters*, I, 260–261); that they assemble twelve authors to write stories on a given plot, the collection to be published under the title *Blindfold Novelettes*, (*Life in Letters*, I, 227–228; *Mark Twain's Letters*, I, 275–279); that they dramatize the life of Mark Twain's brother, Orion, (*Life in Letters*, I, 276–277; *Mark Twain's Letters*, I, 352–358; 362–364); that he, Aldrich, Cable and Howells should form a "circus" and tour the country together in a private car, lecturing as they travelled, (*Life in Letters*, I, 364–65; *Mark Twain's Letters*, II, 440–441).

Arthur's Court."[174] Though Howells praised the basic "sense and truth" of the writing of Mark Twain,[175] whom he called "the Lincoln of our literature,"[176] he had nothing to learn from his much-loved friend concerning the problems of authorship.[177]

The friendship formed with Henry James at this time,[178] however, did much to clarify Howells' literary aims, for the two young writers never tired of settling "the true principle of literary art"[179] on their "nocturnal rambles" through the streets of Cambridge. "We seemed presently to be always meeting, at his father's house and at mine, but in the kind Cambridge streets rather than those kind Cambridge houses which it seems to me

[174] *My Mark Twain*, pp. 43–44. See also *ibid.*, pp. 80–81.

[175] *Harper's*, LXXIV (May, 1887), 987.

[176] *My Mark Twain*, p. 101. See also Howells' praise, *Mark Twain's Letters*, II, 657.

[177] Mark Twain's essay on Howells indicates how enthusiastic, though limited, his appreciation of Howells' writing was. *Harper's*, CXIII (July, 1906), 221–225. An unpublished letter from Howells to Francis A. Duneka, written on October 23, 1912, reflects Howells' life-long affection for Mark Twain. The Berg Collection, New York Public Library.

[178] James had already reviewed *Italian Journeys*, in 1868, and had at once shown his appreciation of the story-writer talent of Howells. "Mr. Howells has an eye for the small things of nature, of art, and of human life, which enables him to extract sweetness and profit from adventures the most prosaic, and which prove him a very worthy successor of the author of the 'Sentimental Journey'." He saw, too, that Howells' two books on Italy were definitely "literature". "They belong to literature and to the centre and core of it,—the region where men think and feel, and one may almost say breathe, in good prose, and where the classics stand on guard." But, for James, the insight Howells shows in his comment on the people he meets in his travels is what makes him original among writers of travel books. "Many of the best passages in his book, and the most delicate touches, bear upon the common roadside figures which he met, and upon the manners and morals of the populace." *North American Review*, CVI (Jan., 1868), 336–339. See *My Literary Passions*, p. 224, for a description of Howells' early meeting with James, and his mature critical comment on his writing. See also *Life in Letters*, I, 137. For an analysis of the relation of James and Howells at this time see Cornelia Kelly, *The Early Development of Henry James*, (Urbana, 1930), pp. 73–80. See also Van Wyck Brooks, "Howells and James," *New England: Indian Summer*, (New York, 1940), pp. 224–249.

[179] "Talking of talks: young Harry James and I had a famous one last evening, two or three hours long, in which we settled the true principles of literary art. He is a very earnest fellow, and I think extremely gifted." *Life in Letters*, I, 116.

I frequented more than he," Howells remembered. "We seem to have been presently always together, and always talking methods of fiction, whether we walked the streets by day or night, or we sat together reading our stuff to each other; his stuff which we both hoped might make itself into matter for the *Atlantic Monthly*."[180] Though James was seven years younger than Howells, he was Howells' senior "in the art we both adored." Not only did James direct Howells' attention to the French novelist Balzac, who was a formative influence on both young writers, but, "around the airtight stove which no doubt overheated our little parlor,"[181] they read to each other their own writing. "I could scarcely exaggerate the intensity of our literary association."[182] "Perhaps I did not yet feel my fiction definitely in me," writes Howells, looking back on those long-ago evenings. "I supposed myself a poet, and I knew myself a journalist and a traveller in such books as *Venetian Life* and *Italian Journeys*, and the volume of *Suburban Sketches* where I was beginning to study our American life as I have ever since studied it."[183]

As Howells walked down Sacramento Street to the crowded horse-car which took him from Cambridge to his office in Boston, he must frequently have observed places and people and episodes in the light of recent conversations with James. With the instinct of the practiced journalist on the look-out for copy and with the delicacy of the impressionistic novelist, he turned these street-scenes into essays for the *Atlantic*—"little,

---

[180]*Life in Letters*, II, 397.

[181]*Ibid.*, p. 398.

[182]*The Letters of Henry James*, ed. by Percy Lubbock, (New York, 1920), I, 10.

[183]*Ibid.*, II, 397. Though James was Howells' guide in literary questions, Howells was of great aid to James in getting his early stories before the public. Howells' own account of his relation to James as an editor is to be found in his essay, "Henry James, Jr.," which appeared in *The Century Magazine*, November, 1882. This essay is included in the Selections which follow. See Kelley, "The Early Development of Henry James," footnote, p. 75. See also *The Letters of Henry James*, I, 10–11; 230–32.

short, lively, sketchy things,"—many of which were in 1871
republished as *Suburban Sketches*.[184] As Howells wrote to James,
then in England, about his new book, it "is nothing but an
impudent attempt to interest people in a stroll I take from
Sacramento Street up through the Brickyards and the Irish village of Dublin near by, and so down through North Avenue.
If the public will stand this, I shall consider my fortune made."[185]
And so, indeed, it was. For in describing his quest for a new
maid, his conversation with an Italian beggar on his back door-
step, a walk around the Irish slums of Cambridge, Howells is
more than a mere journalist; he is exploring the possibilities of
real life as stuff for fiction.[186]

Inspired by his talks and his correspondence with James,[187]
by his own reading not only of the French impressionists, but
also of the new Norwegian writer of pastoral romances, Björnson,[188] whose stories he had recently reviewed for the *Atlantic*,

---

[184]A further encouragement came to Howells in 1868, when his salary
on the *Atlantic* was raised from $2,500 to $3,500. His proof-reading
burdens were then lightened, "because they all feel . . . that my value to
the *Atlantic* is in my writing." *Life in Letters*, I, 126.

[185]*Life in Letters*, I, 144.

[186]Howells' happy success in combining novel writing and editing is
attested by a letter of C. E. Norton to James, written February 23, 1874.
"I thought Howells would be here to-night to read a part of the new novel
he has just finished . . . It is a pleasure to see him nowadays, he looks so
much at ease, and his old sweet humor becomes ever more genial and comprehensive. He is in just such relations to the public that he makes the
very editor needed for the 'Atlantic.'" *The Letters of Charles Eliot Norton*,
II (Boston, 1913), 35–36.

[187]James lived in Europe during 1869–1870; 1872–1874; 1879–1881.
His literary conversations with Howells were carried on by mail until
Howells went abroad in July, 1882.

[188]In "The Literary Background of Howells's Social Criticism," *American
Literature*, XIV (Nov., 1942), 271, Arms points out, "In 1870 Howells had
read three of Björnson's pastoral romances in translation; in a long review
he commented most favorably upon the simplicity, the humbleness of the
characters, and their decency (although portions he quoted were concerned with illegitimacy, drunkenness, and attempted murder). Of the
works and the author he concluded: 'From him we can learn . . . that the
lives of men and women, if they be honestly studied, can, without surprising incident or advantageous circumstance, be made as interesting in
literature as are the smallest private affairs of the men and women in one's

Howells was soon to write his first novel, if we may call *Their Wedding Journey*, half travel-book and half character-sketch, by such a term. This so-called novel, which appeared in the latter half of 1871 in the *Atlantic*, at once struck the note which the whole country immediately recognized as finely, humorously American; when the story appeared in book form the following year, the first edition was immediately bought up and another demanded.[189] Like *Suburban Sketches*, it was based on Howells' own experience, as all of Howells' writing, both essays and novels, prove to be. As *Their Wedding Journey* was appearing in the *Atlantic* Howells wrote jubilantly to his father, "At last I am fairly launched upon the story of our last summer's travels, which I am giving the form of fiction so far as the characters are concerned."[190] To throw a thin veil of fiction over his own experience and call it "realism" was the literary program which Howells adopted early in his career, and held to for the next fifty years. "If I succeed in this—and I believe I shall—I see clear before me a path in literature which no one else has tried, and which I believe I can make most distinctly my own,"[191] Howells wrote with prophetic clarity to his father, as he turned with more confidence away from journalism toward the new possibilities apparent to him in the writing of novels, based on experience.[192]

---

own neighborhood; that telling a thing is enough, and explaining it too much.' (*Atlantic Monthly*, XXV, 512)." See also *Life in Letters*, I, 289; the "Editor's Study," *Harper's*, LXXVIII (Feb., 1889), 490–491; *My Literary Passions*, p. 225; and an unpublished letter from Björnson, March 13, 1884, in the Houghton Library, Harvard.

[189] *Life in Letters*, I, 163.

[190] *Ibid.*, p. 162.

[191] *Ibid.*

[192] The picture of American life which Howells drew in *Their Wedding Journey* was so accurate that Henry Adams wondered whether it might be one of the lasting novels of the generation because a student of some future time could find in it a more exact account of the life of the country than in any other book. *North American Review*, CXIV (April, 1872), 444. In less elegant language, Theodore Dreiser was to express his appreciation of the actuality of *Their Wedding Journey*, "Yes, I know his books are pewky

That Howells was at the same time bidding a sentimental farewell to himself as a poet is evident from several autobiographical hints put into the mouth of Basil March, the young husband in *Their Wedding Journey*, who had once aspired to poetry. When his wife fondly tells him that he could have written poetry as good as that which he happened to be reading to her, he replied, as Howells himself might have on a similar occasion:

"O no, I couldn't, dear. It's very difficult being any poet at all, though it's easy to be like one. But I've done with it; I broke with the Muse the day you accepted me. She came into my office, looking so shabby,—not unlike one of those poor shop-girls; and as I was very well dressed from having just been to see you, why, you know, I felt the difference. 'Well, my dear?' said I, not quite liking the look of reproach she was giving me. 'You are going to leave me,' she answered sadly. 'Well, yes; I suppose I must. You see the insurance business is very absorbing; and besides, it has a bad appearance, your coming about so in office hours, and in those clothes.' "[193]

Poems by William Dean Howells appeared, nevertheless, in 1873, and the Muse that strays through the slender green volume of 172 pages does look a little shabby.[194] A new house in Cambridge, a new job, and a very promising one, and, finally, a new baby, the third child in the family, all seemed more substantial to Howells than his nostalgic poems about red roses and autumn

---

and damn-fool enough, but he did one fine piece of work, *Their Wedding Journey*, not a sentimental passage in it, quarrels from beginning to end, just the way it would be, don't you know, quite beautiful and true." Dorothy Dudley, *Forgotten Frontiers: Dreiser and the Land of the Free*, (New York: 1932), p. 197.

[193] *Their Wedding Journey*, p. 24.

[194] *Poems* was not received very cordially, though probably on Howells' reputation as a novelist, it was republished in 1886. In an unpublished letter in the Huntington Library, written to James T. Fields on October 6, 1873, Howells thanks Fields for receiving his little book kindly, and humorously adds that he is able to remain cheerful in spite of unenthusiastic reviews.

sunsets. A casual description of Howells by a friend with whom
he dined at this time does not suggest the poet. Howells seemed
to C. E. Norton "plump and with ease shining out from his eyes.
He has passed his poetic stage and bids fair to be a popular
American author."[195] Verses such as the following were characteristic of the Muse of his youth who preferred not to remain
with Howells in the days of his prosperity.

> And under these December skies
> As bland as May's in other climes
> I move and muse my idle rhymes
> And subtly sentimentalize.

One is sometimes surprised, in the midst of his subtle senti-
mentalizing, by Howells' simple realistic descriptions of his
early life in Ohio, as in "The Mulberries," or in "Louis Lebeau's
Conversion." But the effective melodrama of "The Pilot's
Story," "The Royal Portraits," and other poems reminds us
that Howells is essentially the novelist, though he is gifted in
many directions. It is not surprising that he himself at this time
did not know whether his power lay in novel writing, journalism, or poetry. Though his fame today undoubtedly rests on
his novels, he remained faithful to journalism and poetry, as well
as to novels, for the rest of his life.[196] That he was under no

---

[195]February 6, 1874. *The Letters of Charles Eliot Norton*, II, 33.

[196]In an interesting unpublished letter written to T. R. Lounsbury on
April 5, 1883, Howells refers wistfully to the time when he thought himself
a poet, and expresses the hope that he might return to poetry again when he
is more securely established financially. Yale University Library. In
1895 appeared *Stops of Various Quills*.

> How passionately I will my life away
> Which I would give all that I have to stay;
> How wildly I hurry, for the change I crave,
> To hurl myself into the changeless grave!

Such a poem tells us something of Howells' state of mind in 1895; it makes
us realize, too, that his youthful poetic gift had left him. *The Mother and
the Father* (1909), three "dramatic passages" depicting the feelings of two
parents at the time of the birth, the marriage, and the death of a daughter,
show how naturally Howells moved from prose to poetry, and also how
much more conventional in thought and feeling he was when writing
poetry. The habit of turning from one form to another never left him.

illusion as to his poetic powers at this time is clear from a letter he wrote to James, who had favorably reviewed *Poems*, "The leaf that has commonly been bestowed upon my poetical works by the critics of this continent has not been the laurel leaf—rather rue or cypress."[197] Thomas Hardy, writing to him at the time of his seventy-fifth birthday, on February 16, 1912, perceived the important fact that Howells would have been less of a novelist, had he not begun his career as a poet.[198]

4. The Psychological Romance

In the light and delicate account of *Their Wedding Journey*, Howells travels backwards over the route from Ohio to Boston, which he had made as a pilgrim to the shrine of literature some ten years earlier. In spite of his wide experience as a journalist, both at home and abroad, Howells was still the romantic young reporter, Percy Bysshe Shelley Ray, with *A Modern Romeo*, "a psychological romance," under his arm. Ray, like Howells, noticed that

the difference of things was the source of his romance, as it is with all of us, and he looked in at the window of this French restaurant with the feelings he would have had in the presence

---

The humorous poems in *The Daughter of the Storage* (1916) take their place among the prose sketches, and prove conclusively that Basil was right, "It's very difficult being a poet at all, though it's easy to be like one." Under the guise of the uncle in "A Niece's Literary Advice to Her Uncle" (*Imaginary Interviews*, 1910) Howells says of himself as a poet, "When I was a boy I had a knack at versing, which came rather in anticipation of the subjects to use it on. I exhausted Spring and Morning and Snow and Memory, and the whole range of mythological topics, and then I had my knack lying idle." p. 180. However, Howells found more to talk of than Spring and Morning and Snow and Memory as he grew older. See his bitter poem entitled "The Little Children," *The Book of the Homeless*, edited by Edith Wharton (New York, 1916).

[197]*Life in Letters*, I, 181.

[198]Hardy's manuscript letter is in the Houghton Library, Harvard. After praising Howells' novels, he writes, "You have, too, always upheld the truth that poetry is the heart of literature, and done much to counteract the suicidal opinion held, I am told, by young contemporary journalists, that the times have so advanced as to render poetry nowadays a negligible tract of letters."

of such a restaurant in Paris, and he began to imagine gay, light-minded pictures about it.[199]

Basil and Isabel March,[200] too, find romance in the "difference of things." They joke and quarrel and dream their way through the journey, enjoying the round of hotels, dining cars, carriages, and excursion-boats, which never fail to charm the young man from Ohio and his Bostonian wife, both of whom are well aware of the true source of romance. A trip in a "drawing room car," for instance, gives them endless material for the half-playful meditations of which this book is composed:

They reclined in luxury upon the easy-cushioned, revolving chairs; they surveyed with infinite satisfaction the elegance of the flying-parlor in which they sat, or turned their contented regard through the broad plate-glass windows upon the landscape without. They said that none but Americans or enchanted princes in the "Arabian Nights" ever travelled in such state; and when the stewards of the car came round successively with tropical fruits, ice-creams, and claret-punches, they felt a heightened assurance that they were either enchanted princes— or Americans.[201]

There is no story to be told, and yet there *is* a story too,[202]

[199] *The World of Chance*, p. 25.

[200] Howells' relationship to Basil and Isabel March was a life-long affair, because the Marches were, in fact, the Howellses. One never knows them intimately, yet after associating with them in *Niagara Revisited Twelve Years After* (1884); *A Hazard of New Fortunes* (1890); *The Shadow of a Dream* (1890); *An Open-Eyed Conspiracy* (1897); *Their Silver Wedding Journey* (1899); *A Pair of Patient Lovers* (1901); *A Circle in the Water* (1901); *Hither and Thither in Germany* (1920) one knows them as one knows people in "real life." Francis A. March, Professor of Philology at Lafayette College, and a friend of the Howellses, supplied the name of "March" to Basil and Isabel. Professor March's wife was Mildred Stone Conway, sister of Moncure D. Conway. Howells named his younger daughter, Mildred, after Mrs. March. MS. letter received from Mildred Howells, in possession of the editors.

[201] *Their Wedding Journey*, pp. 95–96.

[202] "Why it [the engagement of Basil and Isabel] was broken off, and why it was renewed after a lapse of years, is part of quite a long love-story, which I do not think myself qualified to rehearse, distrusting my fitness for a sustained or involved narrative." p. 1.

says the author, if only he could bring himself to tell of how Basil and Isabel had been engaged in Europe years before, and how that engagement had been broken and how it had all ended at last in marriage. Thus Howells wistfully glances at the novel latent in these travel-sketches, but turns aside, contenting himself with a description of the bluff Colonel Ellison, his languishing wife, and her niece, Kitty, whom the Marches meet at Niagara. The fact that Kitty, who was invited simply to accompany her uncle and aunt to Niagara, and then on the spur of the moment decides to accept their urgent invitation to go with them to Montreal and Quebec, itself suggests another story. But again Howells glances away and describes instead Isabel March's shopping expedition, and a tour of the cathedrals of Quebec. The essence of Howells is all here—the light humor, the double-edged dialogues, the sense of the romance of "real life." But plot is yet unborn, for Howells still thinks of himself as the reporter writing letters to his home paper treating "of the surface contrasts of life . . . as they present themselves to the stranger."[203] One moves from chapter to chapter, sufficiently sustained by the ironic contrasts noted by our travellers—such, for instance, as that between the character of men and women, as exemplified by Isabel and Basil, or as that between the New England character and that of the Middle Westerner, or between the rich and the poor in our country.

"Good heavens! Isabel, does it take all this to get us plain republicans to Albany in comfort and safety, or are we really a nation of princes in disguise? . . ." Since they could not help it, they mocked the public provision which, leaving no interval between disgraceful squalor and ludicrous splendor, accommodates our democratic *ménage* to the taste of the richest and most extravagant plebian amongst us.[204]

One musingly turns the last page of *Their Wedding Journey*, won-

[203]*A World of Chance*, p. 35.
[204]*Their Wedding Journey*, p. 58.

dering whether one has read a travel book, or a collection of character sketches, or, in fact, a novel of a particularly subtle kind.[205]

With *A Chance Acquaintance* (1873) there can be no doubt in one's mind—here is the typical Howells novel, complete and whole. It is Percy Ray's "psychological romance," only mildly concerned with economic and social ideas, which deepened and at the same time confused Howells' later novels. Here we have the same simple trio we met in *Their Wedding Journey*—Colonel Ellison, or Uncle Dick, an honest, hearty and downright citizen of Milwaukee; his wife, Fanny, who proves to be a romantic lady of the match-making variety; and Kitty, her charming eighteen-year-old niece, an unspoiled and warm-hearted individual straight from a free-thinking, anti-slavery, book-reading western New York home, like that of Howells' youth. Kitty, while standing by the rail of the Saguenay boat, unconsciously slips her hand under the arm of Mr. Miles Arburton, from Boston, mistaking him for her uncle. Here the "novel" begins, for Mr. Arburton, buttoned up in his well-tailored coat, is a Boston snob. All unwittingly he succumbs to the irrepressible charm of Kitty, as they continue their study of the churches of Quebec for a week together while Aunt Fanny recovers from a twisted ankle. The contrast Howells draws between the cold but very knowing comments of the young man from Boston, as he surveys the cathedral, and the more original outbursts of the untutored girl from the New York village, indicate that Howells himself had, during his seven years in Boston, reappraised the Boston culture, to which he had at first so completely succumbed.

Howells' skillful manipulation of the psychological novel is clearly seen as the story unfolds. Kitty almost accepts the proposal of marriage which Arburton utters in spite of his better

[205]See also W. M. Gibson, "The Materials and Form in Howells's First Novels," *American Literature* XIX (1947), 158–166.

judgment, but even while she hesitates two old Boston friends of Arburton, an effusive society lady and her sophisticated daughter, walk across the hotel porch with hands extended to Arburton—who fails to introduce Kitty to them, he hardly knows why. So genuine is his humiliation and distress after his Boston friends have left and so urgent his pleas to Kitty, that the reader almost hopes that Kitty will relent. But Kitty, like Howells, repudiates the Boston snob, with thoughts of her own on the qualities of a true gentleman.[206] *A Chance Acquaintance* is a perfect illustration of what Howells meant by the "psychological romance." Through a small but significant episode, something of the inner nature of his characters has been revealed, and one lays the book aside, both amused and enlightened by this swift, sure study of the motives of men and women. "I've learned a great deal in writing the story," Howells wrote to James, who understood better than anyone else the nature of the experiment in novel writing that Howells was carrying on, "and if it does not destroy my public, I shall be weaponed better than ever for the field of romance. And I'm already thirty pages advanced on a new story."[207]

[206]Though Howells loved Cambridge and Boston, he never failed to attack the Boston snob. See *The Lady of the Aroostook*, *A Woman's Reason*, *Silas Lapham*, *The Minister's Charge*, and *April Hopes*. For Howells' further comment on the "inconclusive conclusion" of the love affair of Kitty and Arburton, see *Niagara Revisited Twelve Years After*, pp. 11–12.

[207]Howells modified his description of his heroine somewhat between the appearance of the story in the *Atlantic* and its publication in book form, because of the criticism of Henry James, who objected to Kitty's "pertness." "Her pertness was but another proof of the contrariness of her sex. I meant her to be everything that was lovely, and went on protesting that she was so, but she preferred being saucy to the young man." *Life in Letters*, I, 174. See also *Ibid.*, I, 181. In his next letter to Howells, James expresses his appreciation of the book: "But your work is a success and Kitty a creation. I have envied you greatly, as I read, the delight of feeling her grow so real and complete, so true and charming. I think, in bringing her through with such unerring felicity, your imagination has *fait ses preuves*." *The Letters of Henry James*, I, 34.

5. The Italian Novels, "An Experiment Upon
My Public"

The new story on which Howells was working when he wrote
to James was *A Foregone Conclusion* (1875). Encouraged to
think of himself as a novelist as well as a journalist,[208] Howells
glances back over his rich and varied experiences as a consul in
Venice ten years earlier and writes the first of his Italian novels.
That Howells considered *A Foregone Conclusion* a new venture
is clear from a letter to Fields, who spoke appreciatively of the
story as it appeared in the *Atlantic*. The novel, Howells wrote,
was the most venturesome experiment he had so far risked, and
he would not dare to consider it a success until he had public
approval of it after its appearance in book form.[209] Evidently
Howells was satisfied with the public response to this venture,
for three more novels with an Italian background appeared during
the next ten years, *The Lady of the Aroostook* (1879), *A Fearful
Responsibility* (1881), and finally the novel Howells himself considered his best, *Indian Summer* (1886).[210] Through these four

[208]In 1871 James had written to their mutual friend, Charles Eliot Norton,
"Howells edits, and observes and produces—the latter in his own particular line with more and more perfection. His recent sketches in the *Atlantic*,
collected into a volume, belong, I think, by the wondrous cunning of their
manner, to very good literature. He seems to have resolved himself,
however [into] one who can write solely of what his fleshly eyes have seen;
and for this reason I wish he were 'located' where they would rest upon
richer and fairer things than his immediate landscape." *The Letters of
Henry James*, I, 30. Might not some such words as these have passed
between James and Howells on their "nocturnal rambles" at this time?
And might not Howells' Venetian novels be a reflection of his effort to
"locate" in a "richer and fairer" environment than that which Cambridge
offered?

[209]Unpublished letter to James T. Fields, dated November 22, 1875.
The Huntington Library.

[210]Two unpublished letters from Howells in the Yale University Library
reflect Howells' affection for *Indian Summer*. The first is dated November
22, 1885, and is addressed to T. R. Lounsbury, who evidently had written
an appreciative letter to Howells. Howells replies that he enjoyed writing
Indian Summer more than he had enjoyed the writing of any novel since *A
Foregone Conclusion*. It is convenient, he adds, to make use of a European

stories Howells digests the impression made by a beautiful and dying civilization on a young American from the West. Again, it is by a delicate sense of contrast that Howells brings out the "psychological" point in his "romances." In the case of these four novels it is the contrast between an old and a new culture.

Howells himself is in and out of all of these novels, for Howells' realism is always basically autobiographical. Mr. Ferris, the consul in *A Foregone Conclusion*, who, Howells tells us, is one of his many predecessors as consul at Venice, seems to be, in fact, the young author of *Venetian Life*. Ferris is an interested, somewhat skeptical observer of the loveliness and the corruption of Venice; like Howells, he is only by chance a consul for his heart is really in his painting.[211] Mr. Ferris, an American grown accustomed to interpreting the Italian to his countrymen, is in a position to sense better than Mrs. Vervain and her daughter could, the misunderstanding which develops between Florida and the Italian priest whom Mr. Ferris had engaged to teach Florida Italian in the ruined little garden of the

background, for the author can then easily divide his characters into two groups; however, the public now no longer wishes to read the novel set on foreign soil, and Howells does not expect to venture in that direction again. William Lyon Phelps gives us the following anecdote, which explains the second letter at Yale: "I once asked him which of all his stories he liked the best, and he replied with an interrogation point. I therefore named *A Modern Instance*. He reflected for a moment and then said with deliberation, 'That is undoubtedly my strongest work; but of all the books I have ever written, I most enjoyed writing *Indian Summer*, which is perhaps my favorite.'" *North American Review*, CCXII (July, 1920), 19. Howells' letter to Phelps is dated April 1, 1906. In this letter Howells welcomes Phelps and his wife to the small group who know how good *Indian Summer* is. An unpublished letter to the same effect is in the Rutgers University Library. See also "The Rambler," *Bookbuyer*, XIV (July, 1897), 559. See also letter from Edmund Gosse, Jan. 8, 1890. Houghton Library, Harvard. For Mark Twain's enjoyment of *Indian Summer* see *Mark Twain's Letters*, II, 454-455.

[211]Though Howells himself did not paint, his wife did. For a description of their excursions along the canals, when Howells took notes for *Venetian Life*, and Elinor sketched, see *Life in Letters*, I, 66. For an illustration by Elinor Howells of a poem by Howells, "Saint Christopher," see *Harper's*, XXVIII (Dec. 1863), 1-2; Elinor Howells also illustrated *No Love Lost*, which appeared in a separate volume in 1869. See *Life in Letters*, I, 136.

Vervain's palace apartment. Florida, the serious, inexperienced and rather inarticulate daughter of an ill, yet frivolous mother, becomes romantically interested in helping Don Ippolito,[212] the priest, leave the church and come to America where his many ingenious inventions, in which he is futilely absorbed, might be appreciated. Don Ippolito, who does not understand Florida's American candor and sincerity, day by day falls more completely in love with her—as does also the well-meaning consul who tries to extricate Florida from her dilemma. The misunderstandings which arise between these charming, intelligent, high-minded people are those which lie in the contrast between American and Italian civilization. Tragedy appears when Don Ippolito tries to convince Ferris, as the priest lies on his death bed, that Florida really loves Ferris. Ferris' habit of skepticism, the critical attitude he had assumed toward the headstrong Florida, made it impossible for him to understand himself or Don Ippolito or Florida until several years later, after the death of the effervescent Mrs. Vervain, when he meets Florida, by chance, in the plain light of a New York exhibition of painting. James takes Howells to task, and rightly, for the final scene between Florida and Ferris. The story, he points out, really ends with the death of Don Ippolito.[213] But he welcomes with enthusiasm Howells' use of the Italian scene, and hails "this little masterpiece" as a "singularly perfect production."[214] That Howells was moving away from the observation of men and manners, as

[212]The prototype of this character may be found in "The Armenians," *Venetian Life*, pp. 195–200. Howells tells us that this character is based on Padre Giacome Issaverdanz, a brother in the American Convent of San Lazzaro at Venice, who often breakfasted with the Howellses. *Life in Letters*, I, 192. The Houghton Library, Harvard, has a photograph album of the Venetian friends of the Howellses.

[213]Howells, it appears, tagged on the inappropriate ending at the request of Fields, who did not think the *Atlantic* readers could stand a tragic ending. To Charles Eliot Norton he wrote, "If I had been perfectly my own master—it's a little droll, but true, that even in such a matter one isn't—the story would have ended with Don Ippolito's rejection." *Life in Letters*, I, 198.

[214]*North American Review*, CXX (Jan. 1875), 214.

reflected in *Venetian Life*, on toward the novel, is not lost on James. "Mr. Howells has already shown that he lacked nothing that art can give in the way of finish and ingenuity of manner," he writes, "but he has now proved he can embrace a dramatic situation with the true imaginative force—give us not only its mechanical structure, but its atmosphere, its meaning, its poetry."[215]

To add to the subtlety of his "psychological romance," Howells doubles and triples his contrasts in *The Lady of the Aroostook* (1879), in the true Jamesian manner.[216] The "lady" is Lydia Blood, the adopted child of her uncle and aunt, who are plain honest villagers living in northern Massachusetts.[217] After consulting the minister, they at last agree that Lydia shall accept the invitation of her dead father's sister, Mrs. Erwin, to spend a year with her and her English husband in Venice, and decide to send her off on Captain Jenness' sailing vessel, never suspecting that she would be the only woman on board. Captain Jenness

[215]*The Nation*, XX (Jan. 1875), 12.

[216]Compare *Daisy Miller*. James' story had completed its serialization four months before Howells' began to go through the *Atlantic*. Did *Daisy Miller* influence *The Lady of the Aroostook*? In spite of the similarity of theme and setting, there is no evidence that there was any direct relation between the two books. Howells tells us that the suggestion for his story came from Samuel P. Langley, the inventor of the heavier-than-air flying machines, who, with his brother, made a similar voyage as a young man and reported his experience to Howells when he was consul. See *Life in Letters*, I, 265.

[217]Mildred Howells tells us that there was little social life in Venice when Howells and his wife lived there, so they were left much to themselves. Mrs. Howells told her husband about life in Brattleboro. "It was this intensive view of New England that made Howells able to understand it so clearly when he went there to live, and it was his wife's vivid powers of observation and her gift for criticism that made her such a great help to him in his work." *Life in Letters*, I, 12. Among the newspaper clippings in the Howells material in the Houghton Library of Harvard is one from the *New York Tribune*, September 29, [1880?] in which a correspondent of the *Syracuse Journal* quotes a friend to the effect that Howells was overheard in a New England inn reading aloud the manuscript of *A Chance Acquaintance* to his wife, chapter by chapter, as he wrote it. She interrupted the reading with frequent comment and suggestion. John Mead Howells reports that his father always read his novels aloud to his wife as he wrote them.

is a bluff and honest fellow, with two daughters of his own, who makes every effort to conceal from Lydia the unconventionality of her position. Lydia is beautiful, quiet, dignified; though intelligent, she is simple, and can only meet the banter of the two smart young Bostonians on the ship with a candid literalness. Staniford and Dunham begin the voyage with supercilious disdain of the plain little country girl, but they both succumb to her goodness and charm before they reach Venice. Dunham properly suppresses his emotions because he is even then on his way to his exacting fiancée, who is travelling in Germany. But the proud and brilliant Staniford goes through the throes of an inner purification, which involves jumping overboard to rescue Mr. Hicks, "the cad," whom he accidentally knocked over the railing in a quarrel—Lydia, of course, being the unconscious cause. To witness the Boston snob brought low by the naïve but ladylike Lydia is a satisfaction only surpassed, in the latter portion of the story, by the soul-searching to which Lydia, all unknowingly, reduces her sophisticated aunt, as she sits with quiet serenity in Mrs. Erwin's little Venetian drawing room, hoping, and not in vain, for a letter from Staniford. The idea of opera on Sunday is horrifying enough to Lydia, but her mounting scorn as she begins to realize the nature of the private lives of the dazzling men and women around her is so unconcealed that the aunt herself is moved to sigh over her own lost American innocence. When Lydia and Staniford are married and return to live on Staniford's western ranch, we are asked to believe that the differences in cultural standards of these two lovers will be of no importance in the great open spaces of our democratic land.

American and European manners are again the backdrop against which Howells views his characters in *A Fearful Responsibility* (1881). Professor and Mrs. Elmore go to Venice at the outbreak of the Civil War, when there are no more students for Professor Elmore to teach. Like Howells, Elmore is interested in writing a history of Venice, but unlike Howells, he is a scholar and a gatherer of notes, rather than a writer.[218] The history languishes and so does his wife, until she is brightened one morning by a letter saying that Lily Mayhew,[219] the younger sister of a friend, is "coming out" to visit them. This beautiful young girl proves to be the "fearful responsibility" which the professor dreads—and with some reason. Before she arrives in Venice, Captain Ehrhardt, a handsome Austrian officer, has already fallen in love with her and presents himself in due form to Elmore to make his "offer." Professor Elmore, looking at him through his American spectacles, is quite unable to understand or appraise the Austrian, and abruptly refuses to encourage him. Three other offers come to Lily during her visit,[220] all of them acceptable, but none move her as did that of the handsome, romantic, unknown Austrian. She refuses them all and sadly

[218]As early as 1874, Howells was interested in writing a history of Venice. In an unpublished letter to C. E. Norton, dated December 28, 1874, he speaks of such a project, and adds that he is eager to return to Venice. In another unpublished letter, this one addressed to W. H. Riding, November 5, 1882, Howells refers to the same desire to write a short history of Venice. The Huntington Library. In 1900, Howells drew up a scheme for a history of Venice, and submitted it to H. M. Alden, the editor of *Harper's*. The history was never written. *Life in Letters*, II, 122–124.

[219]The prototype of this character was Mary Mead, the younger sister of Elinor Mead Howells, who visited the Howellses in Venice in 1863. See also an unpublished letter from Howells to Moncure D. Conway, January 26, 1869, in which Howells reports the presence of Mary Mead and tells something of their life in Venice. The Berg Collection, New York Public Library. In an unpublished letter to John Piatt written from Venice on February 15, 1865, Howells refers to "a grand masked-ball" similar to one described in *A Fearful Responsibility:* "The other week there was a grand masked-ball given by a Russian princess, to which Elinor and I were asked; but being too old to go, we sent Elinor's sister with the Russian consul's wife. Mary went as 'Folly', and I should have made verses at seeing her in cap and bells if I had been six years younger. Ma!—This is the first masquerade in Venice for a great while—since 1859, and no Italians took part in it." In the possession of Cecil Piatt.

[220]Mrs. Howells sketched a picture of her sister and one of her lovers standing on the balcony of the Palazzo Giustinian. It was afterwards discovered that the picture was drawn at the moment when the young man was rejected, and the sketch became for the family a reminder of "the fearfulness of the responsibility." *Life in Letters*, I, 75.

returns home. When Elmore and his wife see her later in America she has grown pale and spiritless. After a few years they hear that she has married a clergyman from Omaha, and has opened a kindergarten with a friend. The kindly professor wonders the rest of his days whether he blasted the lives of Lily and the handsome captain by his American commonsense.

In these three delicately tinted Venetian novels, Howells catches the contrast between the romantic glow of an older, more sophisticated civilization, and the freshness and simplicity of a younger culture. Within this frame, one sees transparently true pictures of the people Howells himself must have known in Ohio, Boston, and Venice, and, by flashes of insight, one is made to understand the motives behind their refusal or acceptance of the lovers' proffered hands. Though these "psychological romances" are slight, their truth makes them among the most artistically perfect on the long Howells shelf of novels.

In 1886 Howells returned once more to the Italian-American scene in *Indian Summer*. The title has a nostalgic overtone, and that was indeed Howells' mood as he summoned up the romantic Italian setting for the last time. Howells had already written *A Modern Instance* and *The Rise of Silas Lapham*; he had resigned from the *Atlantic* and assumed his position on *Harper's*; in his reading he was turning more and more to the Russians. "Italian I care nothing for," he wrote Aldrich in 1885, "but my Russian I am proud of, and I think I know my Tourguenieff."[221] *Indian Summer* was hardly in print before Howells discovered Tolstoy, who was to affect so profoundly his view of the world

[221]The seemingly simple art of Turgenev, in which three or four characters work out the plot themselves while the author stands aside and observes them, must have been the subject of many of the conversations of Howells and James. In 1873, James published an essay on Turgenev, in which he pointed out the Russian's love of fact, his profound understanding of his characters, on whom he does not comment. *The North American Review*, CXVIII (April, 1874), 326–356. Howells tells us he began to appreciate the greatness of Turgenev "about the middle of the seventies." *My Literary Passions*, p. 229. In 1872 Howells reviewed *Smoke* for the *Atlantic*, XXX (August, 1872), 234.

for the next decade. Tolstoy made Howells less interested in the supreme art of Turgenev, he tells us, and gave him a passionate concern for man in society, which made him "impatient even of the artifice that hid itself."[222] In the summer of 1882 James was back from Europe, and lived only a few doors from Howells, who was recovering at that time from a serious illness. The art of the novel and Turgenev's influence on it[223] were eagerly discussed by the two novelists. The upshot of these talks was an essay on James by Howells which appeared in the November issue of *Century Magazine*, for that year.[224] It is James, he declared, "who is shaping and directing" American novelists toward an interest in character rather than plot and a reliance on relevant detail rather than philosophic comment. It is under the influence of James and Turgenev then, that Howells turns once more to the Italian setting in *Indian Summer*, though his thoughts have already begun to move away from the psychological romance to the social novel.

As Howells, in writing *Indian Summer*, takes a vacation from his more serious social novels,[225] so Colville, in the story, takes a vacation from the stress of journalism and returns again to his beloved Florence, with the unfulfilled hope of at last writing a history of the city of his youth. Here, seventeen years earlier, Colville had failed to win the lady of his choice, but had gained an undying love of the city of Florence. As he, handsome, begloved, and forty, stands upon a bridge, gazing into the Arno and contemplating his missed opportunities, he hears a crisp,

[222] *My Literary Passions*, p. 233.

[223] Henry James wrote to Howells in 1876 of his meeting with Turgenev, to whom Howells had sent a personal greeting. Turgenev "bade me to thank you very kindly and to say that he had the most agreeable memory of your two books." *The Letters of Henry James*, I, 49.

[224] "Henry James, Jr." *Century Magazine*, XXV (November, 1882), 27.

[225] The critic writing for *The Literary World* welcomed Howells' return to his earlier style with these words, "If our leading American novelist be wise he will not wander often away to those rude, raw scenes nearer home which have sometimes tempted his pen ... Mr. Howells' arena is the parlor." *The Literary World*, XVII (March 20, 1886), 103.

familiar voice at his elbow and recognizes the chic form of Mrs. Bowen, "best friend" of the Miss Wheelwright of his twenties, and now a widow. One takes in, almost at once, that Mrs. Bowen, and not Miss Wheelwright, is the lady Colville should have proposed to in the lost days of their youth. Before our perfectly polite, perfectly polished hero and heroine discover that they still love each other, Colville is doomed to repeat his earlier error and succumb to the beautiful blonde protégée of Mrs. Bowen, Imogen Graham, who romantically wishes to comfort Colville for his unhappy love affair. The contrast between age twenty and age forty in love is the theme on which Howells hangs his tale. Colville is unable to be amused by "the Englehardt boys," with whom he finds himself standing at the receptions and dances to which Imogen drags him night after weary night; Imogen is hurt by the blankness with which Colville greets her proffered sympathy for the long-forgotten love affair; Mrs. Bowen, perfectly controlled person though she is, is given to unexpected moments of rage at Imogen, of whom she had supposed herself fond. Little Ellie, the eleven-year-old daughter of Mrs. Bowen, is the only one who maintains the clarity of her view. She knows she loves Colville, and is only sad when the complexity of the situation makes it impossible for him to call at the comfortable little apartment for an afternoon cup of tea. The masquerading of the Lenten fête, the brilliant Florentine ball, the salons of the Italianate Americans, all serve further to confuse our Americans, who, one feels, could never so hopelessly have lost their path had they been safely at home, moving among the conventions known to them all. When the glamorous but dull Imogen finally accepts the patient Mr. Morton, who had been wistfully waiting in the background all during this unhappy love affair, and when Colville and Mrs. Bowen are at last able to enjoy their interrupted conversations, we sigh our satisfaction at belated but appropriate marriages.

That James was actually in Howells' mind as he wrote *Indian*

Summer is clear from a whimsical little passage embedded in the novel. A distinguished elderly lady puts up her glasses and surveys a group of characters, observing,

"I feel that we are a very interesting group—almost dramatic." [To which Colville responds], "Oh, call us a passage from a modern novel, if you're in the romantic mood. One of Mr. James's." "Don't you think we ought to be rather more of the great world for that? I hardly feel up to Mr. James. I should have said Howells. Only nothing happens in that case!" "Oh, very well; that's the most comfortable way. If it's only Howells, there's no reason why I should'nt go with Miss Graham to show her the view of Florence from the cypress grove up yonder."[226]

So Howells leaves to James the great romantic world of Europe, and accepts for himself, after writing this last of his Venetian novels, the simpler American setting.[227] James made the other choice, and Howells never ceases to reflect on what he felt to be James' tragic mistake.[228] Though James and Howells continue to write to each other and to visit one another whenever possible, the period of their apprenticeship is over. Now James, bent on other game, hails Howells as the great American naturalist, and urges him to be faithful to the American scene and to widen and deepen the social implications of his novels. "I don't think you go far enough, and you are haunted with romantic phantoms and a tendency to factitious glosses," writes James to Howells in 1884.[229] In 1886, in *Harper's Weekly*, James congratulates Howells for deserting his Italian setting and return-

[226]p. 243.

[227]Howells, on his first stay in Venice, looked toward his own country with longing. "But exile is so sad, and my foolish heart yearns for America. Ah! come abroad, anybody that wants to know what a dear country Americans have." *Life in Letters*, I, 44. In 1876, Howells wrote to his father, "But one at my time of life loses a vast deal of indefinable, essential something, by living out of one's own country, and I'm afraid to risk it." *Life in Letters*, I, 217. See also, *ibid.*, 58–59; 85; 91; 338.

[228]See the last two essays Howells wrote, the first a review of *The Letters of Henry James*, ed. by Percy Lubbock, (New York, 1920), and the second "The American James," *Life in Letters*, II, 394–399.

[229]*The Letters of Henry James*, I, 105.

ing to America and a more serious interest in "common things and unheroic lives."[230] As for himself, James will be faithful to the belief "that it takes an old civilization to set a novelist in motion—a proposition that seems to me so true as to be a truism."[231]

To understand why Howells turned from the psychological romances, which he wrote with such consummate skill, to the social novel, one must look once more to *A World of Chance*, written in 1893, seven years after *Indian Summer* appeared. Ray, as he peddles *A Modern Romeo* from publisher to publisher, becomes less satisfied with his romance, for, having been forced to turn to journalism in order to support himself, he has not been able to disregard the hard terms of the "real life" about him. An older author friend, Mr. Kane, takes him to the noisy, crowded apartment of David Hughes, a noble old socialist and reader of Tolstoy, and the father of two working girls Ray had "by chance" encountered on the train. Hughes welcomes the young man, lends him his Tolstoy to read, but does not hesitate to ask him, in the course of one of the Sunday morning discussions of the comrades in his tenement close by the elevated train, what kind of novel Ray had written. When Ray confesses that his novel is merely a love story with a "psychological interest," Hughes scoffs at the idea of wasting one's powers in such a way when human beings on every side are being exploited by a cruel industrial system. Ray is silently resentful and resolves never again to become involved with that little group of radicals. Not the words of Hughes so much as the actual suffering of the members of Hughes' family finally make Ray think less well of *A Modern Romeo*, though by this time the book has found a publisher and has become a best seller. One tragedy after another befalls his friends until finally old David Hughes himself, about to die, begs Ray to find a publisher for his socio-

[230]"William Dean Howells," *Harper's Weekly*, XXX (June 19, 1886), 394.
[231]*The Letters of Henry James*, I, 72.

logical study, which has been the work of many years. He pathetically remarks that perhaps if he had time to do it again he could cast his ideas into the form of a novel and thus find a publisher. Ray promises to do his best for his dying friend, knowing very well that no publisher would be interested in such a book.

One cannot fail to see through this picture of a developing novelist a reflection of Howells himself, who, in *Their Wedding Journey*, *A Chance Acquaintance*, *A Foregone Conclusion*, *The Lady of the Aroostook*, and *Indian Summer*, charmed his readers with his perfectly executed psychological studies of people falling in and out of love. Both Howells and Ray were broadened by their journalistic experience; both of them became enthusiastic readers of Tolstoy, and both grew less sure that a love story, even if it were true to real life, was sufficiently wide to express their enlarged sense of the harsher aspects of living. Howells, even while absorbed in his more lyric novels, had given proof of his growing concern for the problems of society in such novels as *The Undiscovered Country* (1880), and *Dr. Breen's Practice* (1881).[232] His power to express his conception of the wider relation of the individual to society came to its full maturity, however, only after he resigned from *The Atlantic Monthly* in 1881,[233] in order to give his whole time to creative writing.[234] Encouraged by James, who saw in *Venetian Life* the germ of Howells' Italian novels, Howells knew at last that he was a novel-

[232]Howells was also growing weary of the social rounds of Cambridge. He wrote to his father in 1876, "We have both gone out a great deal more this winter than ever before, and though it is all very pleasant, it is distinctly unprofitable. For a social animal it is amusing to observe how little man can see of his fellows without being demoralized by it." *Life in Letters*, I, 217.

[233]The partners of the publishing firm of Houghton and Osgood, publishers of *The Atlantic Monthly* and of Howells' novels, separated in 1880, and differed in their interpretation of their agreement of separation. Howells wrote identical letters to both men telling them that he did not wish to become the "battle ground in fighting out your different interpretations," and took this occasion to resign. *Life in Letters*, I, 293–295.

[234]*Ibid.*, p. 304.

ist even more than he was a journalist. He had grown "terribly, miserably tired of editing,"[235] and was determined to go abroad for a rest. Perhaps the struggle between the journalist and the novelist in Howells had been too much for his health. Successful as he seemed to others in both realms, he himself did not feel successful. "I think my nerves have given way under the fifteen years' fret and substantial unsuccess," he wrote to H. E. Scudder, "At any rate the MSS., the proofs, the books, the letters have become insupportable. Many a time in the past four years I have been minded to jump out and take the consequences— to throw myself upon the market as you did . . . . The chance came to *light soft* and I jumped out."[236]

Before Howells finally sailed for Europe in July, 1882, the

---

[235]*Ibid.*, p. 294.

[236]*Ibid.*, pp. 294–295. During Howells' fifteen years on *The Atlantic Monthly* he had prospered financially and could well afford to throw himself upon the market, as he wished to do. According to the *Critic*, (June 28, 1884), p. 307, he received $5,000 for his novels serially and probably $3,000 more when they appeared as books. To these sums for a single title must be added what he received from editions subsequent to the first, as well as his salary from the *Atlantic*. Howells contributed to the *Atlantic* "Their Wedding Journey" (1871), "A Chance Acquaintance" (1873), "A Foregone Conclusion" (1874), "Private Theatricals" (1875), "The Lady of the Aroostook" (1878), "The Undiscovered Country" (1880), and "Dr. Breen's Practice" (1881). "Indian Summer" appeared serially in *Harper's* in 1885. All but one of these novels were immediately republished as separate volumes. "Private Theatricals" was published in book form as *Mrs. Farrel* (1921) after Howells' death. In addition to these novels, Howells was constantly writing shorter pieces for the *Atlantic* and for other magazines, and then getting them out in book form. Thus, his *Poems* of 1873 was made up of poetry contributed to newspapers and magazines during the preceding fifteen or more years, *No Love Lost, a Romance of Travel* (1869) had originally come out in *Putnam's*, *A Fearful Responsibility and Other Stories* was composed of stories which had been published here and there, and the comedy *A Counterfeit Presentment* had first run through three numbers of the *Atlantic*. During these same years of his *Atlantic* editorship, Howells also took on outside tasks of a journalistic character. When approached by Houghton, who wished to publish a life of Rutherford B. Hayes during the presidential campaign of 1876, Howells undertook to go through a mass of MSS and write the book, which he did in three weeks (*Life in Letters*, I, 226). He also edited in 1878 a series of short autobiographies, prefaced with introductory essays, some of which he also published in the *Atlantic*.

first installment of *A Modern Instance* appeared in *Century Magazine*, ushering in Howells' brilliant decade of social novels, which began with *A Modern Instance* (1882), and ended with *A Hazard of New Fortunes*, (1890). It is well to remember that the "psychological romance" is the basis of all of his social novels, that during the period of his greatest interest in "society" he wrote such romances as *April Hopes*, and that, after his interest in the problems of society had waned, he returned to this form in such novels as *The Kentons* (1902) and *The Vacation of the Kelwyns* (1920). During these twenty-two years, from 1860 to 1882, Howells had turned from journalism to novel writing. More important still, he had discovered, through his contributions to newspapers and magazines, his own particular approach to the writing of novels, that of the quiet observer of ordinary life who felt, as James said, "the romance of the real and the interest and the thrill and the charm of the common."[237] Now, like Percy Ray, he was ready to put aside the psychological romance for a while and to experiment with the social novel.

IV. NOVELIST TO SOCIAL CRITIC

"I am reading and thinking about questions that carry me beyond myself and my miserable literary idolatries of the past."

"Coming back to Boston in 1883, after a year in Europe," writes Howells' daughter in her Foreword to the 1937 edition of *Silas Lapham*, "my father took a house at 4 Louisburg Square while he searched for the permanent home he always hoped to find, but which always proved, in the end, impermanent. He thought he had found it in a small house on the water side of Beacon Street that he bought in 1884, and as there were various alterations to be made in it, he spent most of the summer overseeing them, while he sent the rest of the family to the coun-

[237] *The Letters of Henry James*, II, 224.

try."[238] Howells' search for the permanent home which in the end always proved impermanent, the interest he took in various alterations of the old house, is symbolic of his search for a new, more modern technique of novel writing, and his way of making old forms his own. He found a convenient home in the "social novel" where he lived for about ten years, writing the novels on which his fame largely rests. Here _The Rise of Silas Lapham_ (1885), _Annie Kilburn_ (1889), and _A Hazard of New Fortunes_ (1890) were written. By the end of this decade he again abandoned this home for a much less lasting abode, borrowed from Bellamy, in which he housed _A Traveler from Altruria_ (1894), and _Through the Eye of a Needle_ (1907). Having expressed in these two "romances," as he carefully subtitles them, his ideas of social right and wrong as completely as he was ever to express them, Howells moved back into the home which he had enjoyed in his first days of novel writing, that of the psychological novel, and here, in fact, he lived very comfortably until his death in 1920.[239]

The contrasts to be noticed in the minor experiences of daily living never ceased to amuse and sadden Howells, quite apart from the larger social problems involved, and it is these subtly analysed contrasts that form the basis of the true Howells novel. For a sense of the range of thought which Howells entertained

---

[238]Howells moved to 302 Beacon Street in August, 1884. _Life in Letters_, I, 363. See also Hamlin Garland, "Howells' Early Life in Cambridge," _My Friendly Contemporaries_, (New York, 1932), p. 301.

[239]In 1899 Howells wrote a paper in _Literature_, entitled "Problems of Existence in Fiction," in which he explained what he considered to be the true subjects of the novelist. It is clear from his essay that he had returned to his earlier conception of the novel. The most important problem of life with which the novelist has to deal is "economical," and by this term he means "pecuniary." Other problems are "social"—in the strictly limited sense—"as, whom shall one ask to dinner"; "domestic," such as "a nagging wife or brutal husband . . . a daughter's wishing in her innocent heart to marry a fool . . . a lingering, hopeless sickness;" and civil, moral, and religious questions, such as "to side with your country when your country is wrong . . . to profess openly a creed which you secretly deny." _Literature_, New Series, I (March 10, 1899), 193–194.

on the irreconcilable natures of the sexes, for instance, one has only to consider the lightness of *April Hopes* (1888) and *An Open-Eyed Conspiracy* (1897), in comparison with the tragic implications of *The Shadow of a Dream* (1890) and *Miss Bellard's Inspiration* (1905). The amusing and also tragic contrasts to be found in class distinctions, Howells plays with again and again—in the gloomy and violent *Landlord at Lion's Head* (1897); in *Ragged Lady* (1899), with its Cinderella charm; in the native realism of backwoods Ohio in *The Leatherwood God* (1916); and in the capricious summer idyll, *The Vacation of the Kelwyns* (1920). The endlessly fascinating contrasts latent in West and East, in Ohio, Boston, and New York, Howells muses upon with a freshness equal to that of his early Boston days. In *Letters Home* (1903) all of these groups meet—the young author-journalist from Ohio, and the wealthy western family; the elderly Boston aristocrat, the New York hostess, as well as the New York tenement dweller. In *The Kentons*[240] (1902) people from Ohio, New York, and Europe come together, misunderstand one another, and quarrel or smile their way to the end of a novel as absorbing as any Howells was able to write in the full flush of the novel writing of the eighties. "You have done nothing more true and complete," wrote James to Howells from England, marvelling at this "demonstration of the freshness, within you still, of the spirit of evocation."[241]

Howells' "spirit of evocation" is apparent in all of his novels, even those most freighted with social implications. This skill he discovered for himself in the seventies; his friendship with James, who was himself engaged in a similar quest, served to encourage him in his own characteristic style. The ambitious social novel, with which he experimented in the eighties and nineties, proved finally too large for him, and he was right to

---

[240]In this novel Howells created the boy which inspired Booth Tarkington's *Penrod*.

[241]*The Letters of Henry James*, I, 398. See also *ibid*, II, **225.**

return to his earlier form of writing. In 1877, Howells wrote to his fellow-novelist, Charles Dudley Warner, who was urging him to broaden his social scene:

Very likely I don't want much world, or effect of it, in my fictions. Not that I could compel it if I did want it; but I find that on taking stock, at forty years, of my experiences, and likes and dislikes, that I don't care for society, and that I do care intensely for people. I suppose therefore my tendency would always be to get any characters away from their belongings, and let four or five people act upon each other. I hate to read stories in which I have to drop the thread of one person's fate and take up that of another; so I suppose I shall always have my people so few that their fates can be interwoven and kept constantly in common before the reader.[242]

This is the essential Howells, though his contact with a larger world through his journalistic experiences, which brought to his attention such authors as Bellamy, Gronlund, George, Tolstoy and others, made him for a time move into a more imposing home, that of the social novel.

1. Dramatic Interlude

It is significant that throughout these strenuous novel-writing days, when Howells was thinking most seriously on social problems, he amused himself by writing thirty-three plays, farces, dramatic sketches and comic operas.[243] "I would ten times rather write plays than anything else,"[244] he wrote Mark Twain, who encouraged him in this departure. From 1876, the date of _The Parlor Car_, to 1911, the date of _Parting Friends_, these little comedies of manners appeared from time to time in _The Atlantic Monthly_, _Harper's Weekly_ and _Harper's Magazine_. Though some of them did find their way to the stages of Boston,

---

[242]_Life in Letters_, I, 233. See also _ibid._, 210.
[243]For a list of Howells' plays, see Arthur Hobson Quinn, _A History of the American Drama_ (New York, 1937), II, 364-365.
[244]_Life in Letters_, I, 255-256.

New York and London,[245] they seem to have been written, for the most part, to be read rather than to be acted. Concerning *Out of the Question*, for example, Howells writes, "The play is too short to have any strong effect, I suppose, but it seems to me to prove that there is a middle form between narrative and drama, which may be developed into something very pleasant to the reader, and convenient to the fictionist."[246] That this "new drama" meant a real break with the old was recognised by William Archer, who wrote to Howells on October 13, 1890, about "the remarks in your *Harper* article."[247] The comments, he said, "apply to the English stage quite as much as to the American . . . our dramatists are all sunk in the old rut." He urged Howells to turn his attention to the new drama, "which

[245]Quinn, *A History of the American Drama*, II, (68–69). See also *Life in Letters*, I, 221–222; 237; 239; 245–246; 249; 251; II, 237–238. *A Counterfeit Presentment*, for example, has quite an extensive stage history, which may be studied in some detail in the Houghton Library of Harvard University. The play was published in *The Atlantic Monthly* in August and October of 1877; it was purchased by the actor Lawrence Barrett, and appeared for the first time on the stage in Cincinnati on the evening of October 11, 1877, after which it toured the East, playing for a night or two in Pittsburgh, Philadelphia, Hartford, and many smaller towns, and finally in Boston on April 1, 1878. Lengthy reviews announced the important dramatic event in words such as the following from *The Golden Rule* of April 17, 1878: "The presentation of Mr. Howells' comedy 'A Counterfeit Presentment' at the Boston Museum, may be said to have marked a positive advance, if not a new era, in a distinctly American drama." However, the consensus of critical opinion was that, though Howells was subtle in his presentation of character, his plot was too tenuous to hold the interest of any but the most educated audience. Though the play received much acclaim, the experiment was not repeated.

Howells, however, never gave up his wish to make the legitimate stage. His correspondence (now in the New York Public Library) with his cousin Paul Kester, reflects his unsuccessful effort to dramatize *Silas Lapham* for the stage. The play was turned down several times by New York producers until the dramatization by Lillian Sabine was produced by the Actors' Guild at the Garrick Theater, on November 25, 1919, where it enjoyed a short run. For the story of the attempted dramatization of *A Hazard of New Fortunes* in collaboration with Frank E. Drake, see the Howells-Drake Letters. MS Room, New York Public Library. Frank Drake himself published an account of the affair in the *Literary Digest*, June 19, 1920.
[246]*Life in Letters*, I, 230.
[247]"Editor's Study," *Harper's*, LXXIX (July, 1889), 314–19.

you and I (I take it) foresee and hope for . . . Why do you not, either in theory or still better in practice, give us some guidance towards the new technique? I have not read your pieces in dramatic form, but I take it they are not intended for the stage."[248] Howells, however, never developed his comedies beyond the level of "mere sketches," wisely realizing that his "farces" were directed to a reading public, interested in amateur theatricals. Edmund Gosse reflected the appreciation of many readers when he wrote to Howells from London on October 12, 1882. "We are all talking about you," he said, "I see ladies giggling over little books in the train, and then I know they must be reading 'The Parlor Car.' "[249] On November 30, 1886, he wrote again to Howells in gratitude for *The Mouse Trap*, which his sister-in-law had read aloud to the Gosse household the evening before. Gosse reported, they "laughed so much that we voted the performance incomplete, and I had to read it, as gravely as I could, right through a second time. I assure you I never read anything more laughable in my life. I congratulate you on a success of the very freshest and most sprightly kind."[250]

By 1906 Howells had sufficiently established his relationship with the readers, as well as the directors of plays, to call forth the following comment from Henry Arthur Jones. "It seems to me," he wrote, "you have hit on the exact form of stage direction which will make a play readable, and also convey to a practical stagemanager the necessary suggestion for business . . . Shaw has adopted something like it in his plays."[251] Howells replied to this letter saying that his pieces "have been done

[248]MS. letter in the Houghton Library, Harvard University.
[249]*The Life and Letters of Sir Edmund Gosse*, by the Hon. Evan Charteris, K. C. (New York, 1931), p. 152.
[250]*Ibid.*, p. 202.
[251]MS. letter in the Houghton Library, Harvard University. The letter is dated December 17, 1906.

everywhere in private theatricals,"[252] but that he still longs for success on the legitimate stage.

In his dramatic *jeux d'esprit* Howells gives himself the pleasure of letting "four or five people act upon each other," with very little serious reference to the social environment in which they live. The settings are those familiar to the reader of Howells' novels, the summer hotel, the New York apartment, the parlor car of a train; the issues are those of drawing room comedy, and depend for their effect on the subtle contrast of social values; the language is the casual, natural talk of every day. Though the writing of these plays covers the period in which Howells was most concerned with the injustices of the world around him, no questions of the sort ever intrude upon these little interludes, so delightfully characteristic of Howells' sense of the irony in the intimate scene around him.

That Howells' plays were not presented professionally more often is not surprising, for the best of them are trial sheets of a novelist rather than serious plays. He, in fact, calls *Out of the Question*, "a long story in dramatic form."[253] In *The Story of a Play* (1898), a novel "founded, as far as the theatrical vicissitudes of the imaginary play are concerned, upon several experiences of my own,"[254] he states clearly the various reasons why the play form was unsatisfactory to him, especially after the manuscript had found its way into the hands of a famous actor and a producer. One can only conclude that Howells was a novelist and not a dramatist, and that he never seriously mistook his vocation.[255] His plays are brief and witty scenes which

[252]Howells' letter is dated December 30, 1906. *The Life and Letters of Henry Arthur Jones*, ed. by Doris Arthur Jones, (London, 1930), p. 238.
[253]*Life in Letters*, I, 227.
[254]"Howells' Unpublished Prefaces," edited by George Arms, *New England Quarterly*, XVII (December 19, 1944), 588.
[255]In a letter to Paul Kester, October 6, 1896, Howells says that he has little faith in himself as far as the theater goes. MS. Room, New York Public Library. The idea of an author talking over a play with a famous

could be inserted into any of his stories. Consider, for instance, this opening of *A Counterfeit Presentment:*

On a lovely day in September, at that season when the most sentimental of the young maples have begun to redden along the hidden courses of the meadow stream, and the elms, with a sudden impression of despair in their langour, betray flocks of yellow on the green of their pendulous boughs—on such a day at noon, two young men enter the parlor of the Ponkwasset Hotel, and deposit about the legs of the piano the burdens they have been carrying: a camp-stool, namely, a field easel, a closed box of colors, and a canvas to which, apparently, some portion of reluctant nature has just been transferred.[256]

Here, surely, is the casual, genial atmosphere of the Howells' novels. In a letter to Henry Arthur Jones, Howells admits as much: "The full stage direction was meant for part of the literature in things to be read rather than seen."[257]

That Howells used the play form as exercise sheets for longer narratives is further borne out by the fact that, having once assembled a group of characters congenial to him, he is loath to let them go. In the course of seventeen years, from 1883 to 1900, he wrote no less than twelve plays about the Robertses and the Campbells, who in their day delighted the readers of *Harper's* and the *Atlantic*, much as we are pleased to-day by familiar figures who appear again and again in *The New Yorker*. Our characters are the talkative Agnes Roberts, her absent-minded husband, Edward, her brother, Willis Campbell from

---

actor before writing it had been suggested to Howells in 1875 by Clemens, when the well-known actor Haskins was looking for a playwright to put into words a plot of his. Howells wrote, "Thank you for thinking of me for Mr. Haskins's play. I should certainly like to talk with him, for I believe I could write a play in that way—by having an actor give me his notion." *Life in Letters,* I, 204. Several months later he wrote, "I have seen Haskins. His *plot* was a series of *stage situations,* which no mortal ingenuity could harness together." *Ibid.,* 207. Howells made a similar effort for the actor Laurence Barrett. *Ibid.,* 257-258.

[256]Edition of 1877, p. 7.
[257]*Life in Letters,* II, 232.

California, who in the course of these scenes falls in love with and marries the clever Amy Somers. They meet in *The Sleeping Car* (1883); they appear in *The Elevator* (1885), suspended between two floors; Willis and Amy fall in love at *Five O'Clock Tea* (1889); they stand on chairs for want of *A Mouse Trap* (1889), and greet *The Unexpected Guests* (1893) for dinner, attempting in vain to carry off the situation.[258] In these comedies of manners, which, if they were gathered together in one volume, would form a short novel, Howells amused his generation by playing finger exercises for his novels. More than that, he gave his readers a humorous insight into the scenes and situations around them. Never once through all these years of play writing, did Howells insert a scene involving "society" in the larger sense. "They will do," he wrote to Henry Arthur Jones, "to amuse the idleness and the intolerable leisure of young people of good society, or young people who wish to be of it, and fancy that my plays will help them."[259]

2. The Shaker Novels

As a young boy Howells had ample opportunity to consider the "social problems" of life, but, as he tells us over and over again, it did not occur to him that these problems should find their place in literature. His work with his brother and his father in the printing office of the *Ohio State Journal*, their heartbreaking effort to buy the home in Jefferson that his mother longed for, talks with the fugitive slaves who passed through Jefferson on their way to Canada, his experiences as night editor of the Cincinnati *Gazette*, might have turned Howells' mind from his Spanish grammar and his translations of Heine to the social problems at hand.[260] But years of slow maturing seem to

---

[258]See also *The Garroters* (1886), *A Likely Story* (1889), *The Albany Depot* (1892), *A Letter of Introduction* (1892), *Evening Dress* (1893), *A Masterpiece of Diplomacy* (1894), *The Smoking Car* (1900).

[259]*Life in Letters*, II, 238.

[260]Howells' unwillingness to look at the harsh side of life was evident

have been necessary to make Howells aware of the story material latent in the economic struggle around him. When he made his famous pilgrimage to Boston, he tells us that he watched the girls pouring out of a shoe factory in Massachusetts, with no particular curiosity or interest. His comments on the beggars and cripples of Venice in *Venetian Life* are those of a clever young journalist. On a later visit to this city in 1883, he writes, looking back on his earlier self, "I don't think I began to see the misery of it when I lived here. The rags and dirt I witnessed in a walk this morning sickened me."[261] In *Their Wedding Journey* he scarcely notices the social panorama through which the Marches travelled, so interested is he in the comments of Basil and Isabel as they gaze upon the churches and forts of Quebec and Montreal. "I do not defend the feeble sentimentality," he writes, "but I understand it, and I forgive it from my soul."[262]

Though Howells' youthful experiences in Ohio provided him with no key to the sordid scenes of big cities, it nevertheless did leave with him a picture of community life, which is reflected in all of his social thinking. From the log-cabin days of the Howells family on Little Miami River, William Dean had been attracted by the notion of a group of mutually helpful people living together, sharing their work and their pleasures, freed from the slavery of a competitive society.[263] In 1876 he wrote a description of "A Shaker Village," which appeared in *The Atlantic Monthly*, for he saw among the Shakers some of these same familiar ideals of social living. The Shakers, Howells ob-

---

as a boy. When he was about twelve years old a young seamstress was employed to help his mother. The seamstress was unmarried and pregnant; Howells refused to speak to the girl, and, in fact, treated her so unkindly that the girl herself was reduced to tears, and Howells reprimanded by his parents. *Years of My Youth*, p. 42.

[261]*Life in Letters* I, 340.

[262]*Their Wedding Journey*, p. 197.

[263]Mrs. Howells' uncle, John Humphrey Noyes, was one of the founders of the Oneida Community in New York. See *Life in Letters*, I, 11.

served, "present great temptations to the fictionist."[264] Howells used this setting in *The Undiscovered Country* (1880), and he returned to it again in two later novels, or long short stories, both published in 1896, *The Day of Their Wedding* and *A Parting and A Meeting*.[265] He is charmed by the cool, plain interiors of the large, barn-like Shaker dwellings, their homespun rugs, the simple furniture, the bountiful meals so generously served to strangers. He watches these grey-clad men and women move about their acres of rich farm land, prune their laden orchard trees, join in their strange communal dances, and he wonders whether they might have the answers to such harassing questions as money, sex, and God. What he discovered interested him, but did not convince him that the Shakers held the key to Utopia. In each of his books on the subject, he tries to explain their inadequacy as well as their wisdom.

The Undiscovered Country, in fact, is more concerned with the country of the spirit after death than with Utopia on earth, and his conclusion is stated in the title. Howells' puppets, for they are hardly more, are a "Dr." Boynton, and his daughter Egeria. The "doctor" is an honest and mistaken spiritualist with hypnotic control of Egeria, who, he thinks, is in touch with the spirits beyond the "veil." A plain and downright journalist, Mr. Ford, who attends one of the seances, tries to free the girl, with whom he is in love, by exposing the father, who he at first thinks is merely a charlatan. Dr. Boynton, fearing an exposure in the papers, flees from Boston with his daughter, who almost dies in a snowstorm on a country road near the Shaker village of Yardley.[266] The Shakers kindly tend this strange pair, and eagerly look forward to the "demonstration" which Dr. Boynton promises them. But when Egeria recovers from her illness, she seems

---

[264]*Ibid.*, 209. See also *Ibid.*, 225.
[265]The Shakers form part of the general background of several of the novels not primarily concerned with Shakerism. See *A World of Chance, The Vacation of the Kelwyns*, and *Mrs. Farrel*.
[266]From the names of two Shaker villages, Shirley and Harvard.

no longer willing to act as a medium for her father, who finally
dies of the disappointment. Egeria is free to marry Ford, and
he easily convinces her that "the undiscovered country" will
always remain undiscovered. Howells, rational as he was, inherited a strain of mysticism from his Swedenborgian father
which made it necessary for him to go through this rather prolonged discussion of spiritualism in order to come out with a
repudiation both of spiritualism and of the Shaker belief that
we must live as saints in order to prepare to join the saints after
death.[267] Egeria chooses marriage in spite of the gentle urgings
of the Sisters and the Brothers that she should join their Heavenly Order and leave marriage to those of the Worldly Order.[268]
The most important contribution to Howells' thinking at this
time was not mysticism or marriage, but rather communal living, which he now is able to study at first hand, and which he
makes use of in his later social novels.

3. Toward the Social Novel

Dr. Breen's Practice (1881), *A Modern Instance* (1882), and
A Woman's Reason (1883) bring Howells closer to the genuine
social novel. All three of these novels are concerned with problems faced by women; two of them deal with women's effort to
earn a living, and one with divorce. In *Dr. Breen's Practice* and
A Woman's Reason, Howells points out that professional women
are not successful because the people around them assume that
they cannot succeed. Dr. Breen, or Grace Breen, is the kind of
woman who goes in for a doctor's career not because of an
ardent interest in medicine or the human race, but because of a

[267]For references to Howells' religious views see note 22 on page xxiii of
this Introduction. Howells was inclined toward mysticism all of his life,
but his Christianity was also strongly social in its bent. See Howells' review of Richard Ely's *Social Aspects of Christianity*, *Harper's*, LXXX,
(Feb., 1890) 484–485.
[268]This same aspect of Shakerism is treated again in the two rather
melancholy long short-stories, *A Parting and a Meeting*, and *The Day of
Their Wedding* (1896).

disappointment in love.[269] She finds herself in a large and drafty summer hotel on an isolated point of the Maine coast with her moralizing, puritanic mother, who disapproves of her daughter's profession, an old school friend, Mrs. Maynard, and Mrs. Maynard's child, Bella. Mrs. Maynard not only has tuberculosis, but is also getting a divorce from her husband, who is somewhere in the West. The conscientious Dr. Breen follows her about with shawls and good advice, but nothing can protect Mrs. Maynard from her own foolishness, especially when Mr. Libby, an old friend of her husband's, turns up and invites her for a run in his sailboat. When Mr. Libby, who is, in fact, rapidly falling in love with Grace Breen, tries to take back the invitation because of a threatening storm, Dr. Breen urges her to go, not being altogether sure of her own motives in advising Mrs. Maynard not to take the sail—for the doctor herself is succumbing to Mr. Libby and knows it.

The storm does break; the boat is badly damaged. As a result, Mrs. Maynard is critically ill, but not so ill as to keep her from stating her distrust of a female physician at a moment of crisis. Dr. Breen swallows her pride and goes for the doctor of a near-by village, a gruff and virile middle-aged bachelor, Dr. Mulbridge, who at first refuses to help, ostensibly because Dr. Breen is a homeopath, but actually because she is a woman. He agrees to take the case if Dr. Breen promises to be entirely under his direction. Dr. Breen accepts the position, but at least is able to say "no" very primly and firmly when he proposes marriage to her after Mrs. Maynard's recovery. The combined effect of the tart remarks of her mother, the weak and foolish lack of confidence shown by Mrs. Maynard, and the bullying of Dr. Mulbridge, make Grace glad to give up her plans to become a doctor

---

[269]The popularity of the theme at that time is suggested by the fact that a Miss Phelps submitted a novel, *Doctor Zay*, to the *Atlantic* at the time when Howells' story was appearing. Another "younger and less well-known authoress" at about the same time sent him the outline of a novel similar to that of *Dr. Breen's Practice*. *Life in Letters* I, 299–300.

in favor of becoming the simple wife of Mr. Libby, whose lightness and sweetness, one supposes, is to be strengthened by his strong-minded wife. A woman can be a doctor, Howells seems to say, but only if she is willing to put up with the disapproval of society and also steel herself against the weakness of love.

But if a woman has no professional training at all, as in the case of Helen Harkness in *A Woman's Reason*,[270] and is suddenly left penniless by the death of a father, her chances of earning a respectable living are slim indeed. Helen Harkness, just before the death of her father, tells her literal-minded fiancé, Robert Fenton, that she is not at all sure she loves him, and that he had better seize the first opportunity to join his ship. To her consternation, he promptly signs up for a three-year term at the Naval Station in Hong Kong,[271] knowing nothing of the death of Mr. Harkness. In spite of the affectionate solicitude of a whole family of Butlers, Helen prefers to move to a Boston boarding house after the sale of her home and her possessions, and try to support herself in the various ways open to genteel ladies of the nineteenth century—by painting flowers on pottery vases, by writing reviews for a newspaper, which are secretly re-written by a friendly editor, and finally and most successfully, by making hats for servant girls. But Helen "was, as the sum of it, merely and entirely a lady, the most charming thing in the

[270]The novel was begun in 1878. See *Life in Letters*, I, 255; 319; 324. It was completed in Switzerland in 1882. Here Howells fled from the sociability of London, where he was unable to work on this novel, which he considered "a most difficult and delicate thing to handle." *Life in Letters*, I, 329. See George Arms, "A Novel and Two Letters," *Journal of the Rutgers University Library*, VIII (Dec., 1944), 9–13, which shows Howells' painstaking effort to be accurate in the details of a rather fantastic story.

[271]Edmund Gosse sent Howells a pamphlet on night life in Hong Kong. Howells was so shocked by what he read that he destroyed the pamphlet. See Edmund Gosse, *Living Age*, CCCVI (July 10, 1920), 99. See also a letter from Gosse to Howells, dated October 12, 1882, in which Gosse offers to send Howells "some blue-books lately published here" on the "life in the low quarter of the town." But perhaps, he adds, "your hero is careful not to get into bad company." *The Life and Letters of Sir Edmund Gosse*, by Evan Charteris, (London, 1931), 155.

world, and as regards anything but a lady's destiny the most helpless."[272] All of her elegant education in dancing, music, and art proves useless, so also do the friends of her aristocratic Boston world, most of whom silently fall away, except for the jolly Butler girls, who are romantically impressed by poor Helen's painful effort to be independent, and Mrs. Atherton, a kind-hearted society matron.[273] More useful to Helen is the curt, practical Cornelia Root, who rooms across the hall from her in her boarding house, and the clever Mr. Evans,[274] of *Saturday Afternoon*, who lives on the floor below with his wife and child. Both of these characters know how useless Helen's efforts are and are amused or sardonic, according to their natures, at her young-ladyish attempts in art and journalism.

Not only does Helen's education leave her totally unprepared to earn her living, but she, like Grace Breen, has her difficulties with inappropriate suitors, both high and low. While her own unfortunate fiancé, in an attempt to return to her, is tossed ashore with one companion on an atoll in the Pacific,[275] a plain young English nobleman, Lord Rainford, falls in love with Helen, whom he quite mistakenly admires for her feminism. Lord Rainford is a Liberal who hopes to find advanced social ideas in this country, but habitually misinterprets what he sees. He is, in fact, too good for Helen, who, confused by the Butler sisters, is unable to say no to him until he is deeply in love with her. A still more difficult lover is the old widower who bought her father's house and terrifies Helen by attempting to restore her to her home as his wife. When Robert does return he finds a paler, thinner Helen, busily making hats for servant girls in the

---

[272]*A Woman's Reason*, p. 137.

[273]She appears in *A Modern Instance* as Clara Kingsbury, who in that novel marries lawyer Atherton. Mrs. Atherton re-appears in *Silas Lapham*, *A Minister's Charge*, and *An Imperative Duty*.

[274]See also *The Minister's Charge* and *The Quality of Mercy*.

[275]"Think of so domestic a man as I wrecking his hero on a coral island—an uninhabited *atoll*—in the South Pacific! There's courage for you!" *Life in Letters*, I, 255.

hot little hall bedroom of her former servant. She marries him and slips back into her niche in society, no wiser than she was before. But the reader, if not Helen, has shared many reflections with Howells on the futility and snobbery of the education given to the protected young lady of the nineteenth century.

Although *A Modern Instance* deals with another phase of nineteenth century miseducation, it takes one into the wider field of divorce as well. With the publication of this novel, Howells began serializing his novels in the *Century Magazine* rather than in *The Atlantic Monthly*.[276] As we have seen, Howells' social conscience was already alive before he left the *Atlantic*;[277] the move does, however, mark a real growth in Howells' social outlook.

When Marcia Gaylord, the impetuous, romantic, willful daughter of a stern old lawyer-father in Equity, Maine, elopes with Bartley Hubbard, the clever young scapegrace journalist of the town, real issues are raised, not all of which have been answered today. From the finely-drawn opening scene in a snow-covered New England village, the long tale of misery unwinds. Soon after the elopement, Bartley Hubbard is looking for a job on a Boston paper, while his bored wife watches for him from a lodging-house window. Bartley exploits his old college friend, Ben Halleck, for the sake of a "special story" about his wealthy father, an injury to which Ben, for Marcia's sake, closes his eyes. Marcia, who smothers Bartley with her affection, is more and more frequently left alone while Bartley finishes his stories in the saloons frequented by his fellow journalists. Nor does their child, whom Bartley loves too, really bring this ill-mated pair together, for the misunderstanding between the materialistic, practical Hubbard, and the willfully blind, emotional Marcia is too complex.

[276]*Century* offered $5,000 for each novel serialized.
[277]See George Arms, "The Literary Background of Howells's Social Criticism," *American Literature*, XIV (Nov., 1942), 267–271.

Ben Halleck, who sees the tragedy growing and generously attempts to help, is unable to avert the final catastrophe. Hubbard deserts Marcia, and is not heard of again until a newspaper notice, stating his desire for a divorce, appears in a western paper. The old judge, Ben, and Marcia, together with the child, make a melancholy trip west to protect the name of Marcia.[278] Hubbard now has degenerated into a fat, red-faced small-town editor, but Marcia is still romantically devoted to her old illusion and refuses to understand Ben Halleck's love for her, which Ben never allows himself to put into words. Mr. Atherton, the sardonic lawyer who befriends Marcia throughout, agrees with Ben that, since he loved Marcia before she was divorced from Hubbard, he has forfeited his right to declare his love now that she is free. Howells made his great break with the code of his day when he wrote a novel in which divorce is frankly considered; he could not allow Ben to marry Marcia.[279] Marcia and her child fade away to a quiet life in Equity; the beautiful, domineering girl becomes a colorless, purposeless, middle-aged woman, and stands as a symbol of the futility of the romantic pursuit of love.

4. The Social Novel

The romantic attitude toward love and marriage is treated with the same sad irony in *The Rise of Silas Lapham*, though the difference in cultural outlook between Marcia Gaylord and Bartley Hubbard is more fraught with tragedy than that be-

[278]In April, 1881, Howells made a trip to Crawfordsville, Indiana, to observe a Western divorce case trial, and thus to make more accurate the details of his description in *A Modern Instance*. See *Life in Letters*, I, 297.

[279]In 1882 Robert Louis Stevenson read this novel as an attack on divorce and, since his wife had divorced her husband to marry him, withdrew his invitation to Howells to visit him while Howells was in England. *Life in Letters*, I, 332–333. In 1893 Stevenson apologized to Howells. *Ibid.*, II, 37–38. Edmund Gosse, on August 30, 1882, expressed his appreciation of the novel, "The end of A Modern Instance is superb. You draw your threads together with extraordinary skill. The old Judge remains the most striking character all through, but all is strong and consistent." Unpublished letter in the Houghton Library, Harvard.

tween Irene Lapham and young Tom Corey, whose mismar-
riage is averted by the good sense of the Rev. Mr. Sewell.[280]

Whereas the Lapham family is growing richer each year, the
old, aristocratic Corey family stands every year more in need of
money.[281] Howells makes the most of the contrast of the
Laphams, plain, good-hearted, loving, and intelligent, with the
Coreys, equally good-hearted, loving and intelligent, but not in
the least plain. When it becomes clear that Tom loves, not the
beautiful domestic Irene, but the dark and humorous Penelope,
one shares Howells' hopes for a happy marriage, beneficial to
both families. All of his life, Howells remained loyal to the
staunch qualities of the village American, though he liked the
breed all the better for the addition of Boston culture. One sees
in *Silas Lapham* as good a statement as possible of the respect
Howells always held for the simple environment of his youth,
which was no stronger than his love for the civilization of Boston. A marriage between the two groups promised, in this case,
the happiest outcome. For Silas Lapham, who is symbolic of
the aggressive, inventive business man of the post Civil War
period, was crude in his ruthless business ethics, as his treatment

---

[280]The Rev. Mr. Sewell re-appears in *The Minister's Charge* and *The
Story of a Play*. The novel inspired Lowell to write to Howells, on July 1,
1885, "I have just been reading 'Silas Lapham' with great interest and admiration. 'Tis the most wonderful bit of *realism* (isn't that what you call
it?) I ever saw, and Henry James is of the same opinion. Zola is nowhere."
The Letters of James Russell Lowell, II, 297.

[281]The move of the Lapham family to the "new house" reflects Howells'
move from Louisburg Square to Beacon Street. That Howells was mindful
of the social implications of this move is clear. While his family was still
in the country, he spent weeks alone in the new house arranging his books.
To his father he wrote, "And how unequally things are divided in this
world. While these beautiful, airy, wholesome houses are uninhabited,
thousands upon thousands of poor creatures are stifling in wretched barracks in the city here, whole families in one room. I wonder that men are
so patient with society as they are." *Life in Letters*, I, 364. Similar
words are used in *Silas Lapham*, p. 273. Howells was consciously using
his own experience in this novel. To James he wrote on August 22, 1884,
"Drolly enough, I am writing a story in which the chief personage builds a
house 'on the water side of Beacon,' and I shall be able to use all my experience, down to the quick." *Life in Letters*, I, 366.

of his partner, Rogers, proved; and the Coreys, in their way reflect the sin of their group—they had forgotten how to work. Silas Lapham's "rise" in the end of the story above his earlier self, when he allows his business to fail in order to repay Rogers, reflects Howells' belief in the spiritual integrity of the American business man; Tom Corey's desire to work in the Lapham Paint Factory, as well as to marry Silas' daughter,[282] seems to suggest Howells' belief in the soundness of American democracy, so long as class distinctions are not allowed to crystallize. By the marriage of Penelope and Tom, Howells brings together the two plots, and, what is still more important, suggests the interdependence of social classes in a democracy.

That Howells' real interest in the first of his great social novels was centered on Silas himself rather than on the love-story is clear from an unpublished synopsis of *The Rise of Silas Needham*,[283] as the novel was first entitled, which Howells presumably sent to the editor of *Century*, before the serial began to appear in November, 1884. In the opening interview with Bartley Hubbard, Howells wrote, Needham's career will be traced from his squalid youth to the time of his prosperity. His character will then be analysed; his love affair told; the episodes marking his rise will be presented; his unjust treatment of his partner will be portrayed, as well as the fact that his conscience never ceased troubling him after he succeeded in edging his partner out of the business. The subordinate plot of the proposed novel Howells summarized in two sentences in which he indicated that the social position of the Needhams in Boston would be studied and Penelope's romance reported. Evidently the intricacies of the three-cornered love affair were not in Howells' mind when he

---

[282]See *A Minister's Charge*, p. 382, for further news of Tom and Penelope.
[283]In the Huntington Library. The manuscript, which is undated, is in Howells' handwriting. Mildred Howells tells us that "Howells would not submit his work to editors but offered them an outline of his idea for a story or article, for them to accept or decline on the strength of his other writings, usually before the thing was written." *Life in Letters*, I, 355.

worked out the synopsis of his story. After this passing reference to a subplot Howells' thought returned to Silas Needham's character, in the portrayal of which, he tells the editor, neither the good nor the bad aspects are to be spared. His low motives are to be presented unsparingly, his family troubles revealed, while the underlying moral strength of the hero is, at first, to be only suggested. According to the original plan Silas abandoned the paint business after he had amassed a fortune, and turned to speculation. Later, in a railroad deal, the choice is once more presented to him of squeezing another man or getting squeezed himself. Now Silas is weakened by the wrong he committed earlier in life, but finally he does resist the temptation and accept financial ruin. The reader is made to feel that this deliberately chosen failure marks the rise of Silas Needham. In *The Rise of Silas Lapham* Howells toned down the stark tale, though he held in all essentials to his outline, the "other man" becoming, first, two Englishmen, intent on their commissions for a wealthy English charitable foundation, who wish to buy from Silas property which Silas warns them the railroad has the right to purchase at any time at a much lower figure, and, second, an unwary purchaser of the Lapham Paint Works, who, when Silas tells him the truth about the financial condition of the company, withdraws his offer. Silas Lapham, like Silas Needham, resists temptation and is financially ruined, though morally he "rises" superior to his former blustering and bullying self.

In this story of the moral struggles of Silas Lapham, Howells is clearly reaching out for the idea that one cannot wrong a fellow man without suffering wrong oneself. Silas' final conversation with the Rev. Mr. Sewell, who, throughout the book is the voice of wisdom, expresses the meaning of the tale.[284]

[284]See also an unpublished letter to Mrs. J. T. Fields, of July 19, 1885, in which Howells writes that he is glad *Silas Lapham* still pleases her, and that he hopes it will continue to do so to the end, for there the true meaning of the lesson is to be found. The Huntington Library.

"'Sometimes,' Silas said to Sewell, 'I get to thinking it all over, and it seems to me I done wrong about Rogers in the first place; that the whole trouble came from that. It was just like starting a row of bricks.' . . . 'We can trace the operation of evil in the physical world,' replied the minister, 'but I'm more and more puzzled about it in the moral world.'"[285]

As we shall see, this same thought, which in his next novel, *The Minister's Charge*, Howells calls "complicity," is developed and illustrated in the three social novels we are about to discuss. The deftly handled love story of Irene, Penelope and Tom, added to the stark story of Silas, reflects the Howells we have come to know as the writer of "psychological romances." The more tragic tale of Silas, as originally planned, suggests Howells' deepening sense of the moral questions implicit in society. Perhaps the greatness of *The Rise of Silas Lapham* lies in the fact that it was written just at the moment when Howells was turning from his earlier love stories to his later social novels. In the finished novel, considered by many to be his masterpiece, the psychological and the social interests are happily blended in the two interweaving plots.

The same group of Bostonians, whom we have met in *A Woman's Reason* and in *The Rise of Silas Lapham*, re-appear in *The Minister's Charge* (1887), the most penetrating criticism of stratified Boston which Howells had yet written.[286] Bromfield Corey, Mrs. Atherton, the Rev. Mr. Sewell, all consider the problem of Lemuel Barker, the gifted young country boy adrift in Boston, and they all give the wrong answers. Mr. Sewell,

---

[285] *The Rise of Silas Lapham*, pp. 513–514.

[286] In 1883 Henry Alden, to whom Howells had submitted an outline of his story, asked him to modify his plan. Howells refused. See *Life in Letters*, I, 356. Evidently Alden had wanted "a more considerable hero." See *ibid.*, p. 361. But Howells insisted that he wished "to make a simple, earnest, and often very pathetic figure of my country boy." (*Ibid.*) "I believe in this story, and am not afraid of its effect before the public." (*Ibid.*, p. 362). Perhaps this discussion delayed the novel; in 1886 it was serialized in *Century*.

in fact, was the summer visitor at Willoughby Pastures, who first in a generous but casual mood praised Lemuel's poetry. To his embarrassment, Lemuel sent some of his effusions to him in Boston, and, when the minister failed to comment on them, came himself to ask him whether he thought he would succeed in a literary career in Boston.

Faced with the necessity for honesty, the minister tells him that his poetry is not good, and that he had better go home to the farm. But Lemuel had secretly hoped to rescue his destitute mother and sister in the country by his poetry. He listens to the minister's words in silence, stumbles out of the house, goes to sleep on a bench in the Common, wakes up to find his money stolen. He pursues the boys he thinks have stolen it, but is himself arrested as the thief who had made off with a shop girl's bag, and spends his first night in Boston in jail. "The minister's charge" is given work in a flop house, when he is freed from jail, and here the Rev. Mr. Sewell finds him several days later, having read an account of the episode in the morning paper over his comfortable cup of coffee. The kindly-disposed minister temporarily rescues him by getting him a job as furnace man in the home of Miss Vance, one of his society parishoners, but his position is soon made impossible by Miss Vance's niece, Sybil, who resents Lemuel's dignified aloofness. Lemuel himself secures a job as clerk in The St. Alban Family Hotel, where he meets a charming young art student, Miss Carver, and her friend, Madeline Swan.

This relationship would have been consoling to Lemuel, had it not been for the fact that he had already become involved with the tubercular Statira Dudley and her protective friend, Wanda Grier, two illiterate little shop girls, one of whose pocket-books he had been accused of stealing on the first eventful evening in Boston. In short, Lemuel falls into all the snares awaiting the country boy adrift in the big city, most of which can be traced back to the bland and irresponsible encouragement given to

Lemuel by the society minister, the Rev. Mr. Sewell, who finds himself beyond his depths as he tries vainly to swim after his charge. Howells' description of the street on which the little shop girls live, their room, their clothes, and the peculiar vulgarity of their language, and their feelings, show that he is perfectly familiar with the scenes and the people he looked at so unwillingly as a young reporter on the Cincinnati *Gazette*. Howells does not sentimentalize these two young women, who, once they have their hands on Lemuel, do not intend to give him up to any Miss Carver—nor do they do so until Statira herself grows bored with Lemuel. The thought which the minister extracts, with the help of Mr. Evans,[287] from the whole disturbing experience, is one of Howells' favorite ideas, which he here calls for the first time, "complicity". By this term he means that all lives are involved with all others, the sum total of which is God.

This thought of complicity, basically social, is the one he half humorously, half ironically illustrated in his next novel, *Annie Kilburn* (1889), which again shows the futility of the helping hand held out to the poor and unfortunate, whom we are not willing to accept, in all simplicity, as equals. Howells, who in 1860 watched the girls pouring out of a shoe factory with no feeling for the possible novel material to be found in such a scene, is, in 1888, fully aware of all the tales a factory might tell.[288]

Before our social thought had become tinged with economic and psychological implications, Howells conceived the theory of "complicity", which for him served to carry the social meaning for which a later generation coined a new vocabulary. How-

[287]We have already met Mr. Evans in *A Woman's Reason*. See Sewell's Sermon on Complicity. *The Minister's Charge;* pp. 457-459.
[288]"Mr. W. D. Howells, the novelist, has been in Lowell for three days this week, inspecting local manufacturing establishments, to obtain material for a new novel." *The Critic,* New Series, VII (February 26, 1887), 103.

ells' thought is basically Christian, in the Tolstoyan sense,[289] and its meaning is essentially social.

Annie Kilburn herself reminds one of the younger Howells, in her kindly but mistaken attitude toward the poor. She returns to her large, old, empty mansion in the small town of Hatboro, Massachusetts, after the death of her father, Judge Kilburn, with whom she had lived for many years in Rome. When the women of the town call on her to ask her to help establish a "Social Union" for the factory workers of this industrial town, she accepts, thinking that she might thus somehow "do good" to those less fortunate than herself. The ladies are planning an evening lawn-fete, to which all but the workers themselves are to be invited.

Mr. Peck, the radical young widower-minister, shocks Annie by pricking her bubble of philanthropy. He points out to her, in clear and unadorned terms, that no one who is not willing actually to share the poverty of the poor can do them good. Mr. Peck becomes the mouthpiece for Howells' theory of "complicity." But he is a peculiarly unmagnetic personality and has absent-mindedly neglected his perverse little daughter, Idella. Annie persuades him to let her take the child into her house, in her general effort to do good to someone.

Annie attempts to help further by providing summer outings

[289]Howells tells us that he had "turned the corner of [his] fiftieth year" when he first knew Tolstoy. The influence of Tolstoy must have been with him, then, when he was writing *Annie Kilburn*, (1888). Compare Howells' review of Tolstoy's *Que Faire?* (1886), for *Harper's*, July 1887, included in this volume, pp. 367-368. See *My Literary Passions*, p. 258. Howells says further that Tolstoy "has not influenced me in aesthetics only, but in ethics, too, so that I can never again see life in the way I saw it before I knew him . . . Tolstoy gave me heart to hope that the world may yet be made over in the image of Him who died for it." *Ibid.*, pp. 250-251. To T. W. Higginson, Howells wrote on September 28, 1888, that Tolstoy teaches men to live as Christ did, individually and collectively, and that that is Tolstoy's entire message, which is less simple than it sounds. Unpublished letter in the Berg Collection, New York Public Library. Howells wrote to Hamlin Garland in 1888, "*Annie Kilburn* is from first to last a cry for *justice*, not *alms*." *Life in Letters*, I, 419.

for the patients of her comfortable, sceptical friend, Dr. Morrell. After the tragic death of one of these children, Annie is still further disheartened. Nor are her confused ideas of social right and wrong clarified by one of the most engaging and distressing of Howells' characters, Mr. Putney, who sees through the whole social structure maintained by the leading citizens of Hatboro, but is himself so hopelessly lost in drink that his wisdom avails him not at all. When Annie finally marries Dr. Morrell, we feel that at least society is protected from her good works, for actually she herself has learned little from her experiences. Howells himself, however, through the serious Mr. Peck and the ironic Mr. Putney, has mocked at our smug, stratified society, which tries to quiet its conscience by charitable lawn parties, but only succeeds in making still more obvious the division between the classes. "Social Union" is still further from attainment, after the club room for the workers of Hatboro is opened, than it was before.

In seven crowded years, from 1881 to 1888, Howells moved from the generalized interest in communal living, which we saw in *The Undiscovered Country*, to the more specific criticism of society in *The Minister's Charge* and *Annie Kilburn*. What turn would his thought now take? Both Johns Hopkins and Harvard offered Howells professorships during this period of his greatest power.[290] But he refused these opportunities, flattering as they were to a "self-lettered man," because he fully realized that his approach to literature was not the traditional one. "I am reading and thinking about questions that carry me beyond myself and my miserable literary idolatries of the past,"[291] he wrote to Garland in 1888. Ten years later, Howells attempted to account for the change of outlook which took place in the '80s:

"It was ten years ago," said Howells, "that I first became interested in the creed of Socialism. I was in Buffalo when

[290]*Life in Letters*, I, 330–332; 386. For an interesting discussion of what Howells would like to teach if he should accept the professorship at Johns Hopkins, see *ibid*, I, 331.

[291]*Ibid.*, 408.

Laurence Gronlund lectured there before the Fortnightly Club. Through this address I was led to read his book 'The Co-operative Commonwealth,' and Kirkup's article in the Encyclopedia Britannica. Afterward I read the 'Fabian Essays;' I was greatly influenced also by a number of William Morris's tracts. The greatest influence, however, came to me through reading Tolstoi. Both as an artist and as a moralist I must acknowledge my deep indebtedness to him."[292]

Howells may have attended the convention of the Socialist Labor Party, which met in Buffalo, in September, 1887; he certainly read Gronlund's *Co-operative Commonwealth*[293] (1884), which is a modified interpretation of Marx's *Das Kapital*.[294] Henry George,[295] Edward Bellamy,[296] T. W. Higginson, and other socialistic writers of the period, contributed to what Howells called a real renaissance in his social thinking. Garland, looking back as an elderly man to his early meetings with Howells, wrote, "He was at this time deeply moved by the social injustice which we had all recently discovered, and often as we walked and talked he spoke of Bellamy's delineation of the growing contrasts between the rich and the poor."[297]

[292]*The American Fabian*, IV, No. 2, (Feb., 1898), 2. See also J. W. Getzels, "William Dean Howells and Socialism," *Science and Society*, II 376–386 (Summer, 1938), and Conrad Wright, "The Sources of Mr. Howells' Socialism," *Science and Society*, II (Fall, 1938), 514–517.

[293]*Harper's*, LXXVI (April, 1888), 801–804; LXXVII (June, 1888), 154.

[294]There is no evidence that Howells read *Das Kapital*, though the 1889 translation must have reached his desk.

[295]Hamlin Garland believed in the single tax idea of George, and talked about it with Howells, but Howells did not agree with Garland on the question. See *Life in Letters*, I, 407–408. See also Garland, "Meetings With Howells", *The Bookman*, XLV (March, 1917), 6. Howells visited George in 1892 and wrote to his father, "He believes his doctrine is gaining ground, though I don't see the proofs." *Life in Letters*, 11, 21. Putney, in *The Quality of Mercy*, is converted to the single tax idea.

[296]Howells reviewed *Looking Backward* in the "Editor's Study," *Harper's*, LXXVII (June, 1888), 154–155. Bellamy wrote to Howells, on October 17, 1888, "I cannot refrain from congratulating you upon the Hazard of New Fortunes, I have read the last numbers with enthusiasm. You are writing of what everybody is thinking and all the rest will have to follow your example or lose their readers." The Houghton Library, Harvard.

[297]"Meetings With Howells," *The Bookman*, XLV, (March, 1917). 6.

Furthermore, Howells' early religious faith was, during this decade, shaken by the current controversy between science and religion. The mysticism of his youth was translated into a social religion.[298] The novels of Tolstoy became to Howells that "final consciousness" through which, he said, "I came ... to the knowledge of myself in ways I had not dreamt of before, and began at least to discern my relations to the race, without which we are each nothing."[299] The idea of "complicity," which Howells first consciously articulated in *The Minister's Charge*, and again in *Annie Kilburn*, is strengthened and enlarged by his reading of Tolstoy, who taught him to "see life not as a chase of a forever impossible personal happiness, but as a field for endeavor toward the happiness of the whole human family."[300] Two years later Howells published *A Hazard of New Fortunes*, (1890), which, through the complex interrelations of its several plots, illustrates the interdependence of the "whole human family," as Howells had come to understand it.[301]

5. Novelist Turned Critic

In order to feel his way into the new and broader New York scene, which reflected his own change from *The Atlantic Monthly* to *Harper's Magazine* in 1885, Howells made use of his old friends, the Marches. "I used my own transition to the com-

[298] See H. G. Belcher, "Howells's Opinions on the Religious Conflicts of his Age", *American Literature*, XV (Nov. 1943), 262–278.

[299] *My Literary Passions*, p. 258.

[300] *Ibid.*, p. 251.

[301] *A Hazard* was begun in 1887, soon after the Chicago anarchists had been condemned to die. The fact that Howells identified himself with their cause sufficiently to write an impassioned letter to the New York *Tribune* (Nov. 6, 1887), urging that they be freed, no doubt added depth to this most ambitious of all of Howells' novels. *Life in Letters*, I, 398. See also a letter Howells wrote at this time to his sister, "Elinor and I both no longer care for the world's life, and would like to be settled somewhere very humbly and simply, where we could be socially identified with the principles of progress and sympathy for the struggling mass ... The last two months have been full of heartache and horror for me, on account of the civic murder committed last Friday at Chicago." *Ibid.*, 404.

mercial metropolis in framing the experience which was wholly that of my supposititious literary adventures," Howells tells us in his Introduction to *A Hazard of New Fortunes* written twenty years later. The first six chapters of the book are taken up entirely with house hunting in New York, after Basil March decides to give up his position in a life-insurance office in Boston and accept Fulkerson's[302] offer of the editorship of *Every Other Week*. "There is nothing in the book with which I amused myself more than the house hunting of the Marches," writes Howells, and the reader shares his pleasure. These delightful chapters, quite out of harmony with the rest of the novel, remind one of the best of the earlier, simpler novels, which were content with an unhurried account of commonplace experience; they give no hint of the darker tale about to be unfolded, which was not, after all, the kind of story Howells enjoyed telling. In a letter to T. W. Higginson, Howells admits the structural weakness of the novel with disarming candor, assuring Higginson that he was entirely right in his comment on the opening chapters, where, for all his hammering, Howells did not begin to construct the real edifice of the book.[303]

After March has irrevocably cut himself off from his Boston position, Fulkerson lets him know that the real owner of *Every Other Week* is a certain Dryfoos, who proves to be an utterly ignorant Pennsylvania farmer, suddenly possessed of a fortune

---

[302]"Fulkerson was imagined from an old friend of mine, Ralph Keeler." *Life in Letters*, II, 38. Ralph Keeler was an operator of showboats on the Missouri and the Ohio Rivers. Van Wyck Brooks, *The Times of Melville and Whitman*, (New York, 1947), p. 88.

[303]Howells adds in the same letter to Higginson of January 30, 1891, that he was writing the opening passages of the novel when his daughter Winifred was stricken, and that after her death he could not change them. Winifred Howells died on March 3, 1889. See Howells' Introduction to the Library Edition of *A Hazard of New Fortunes*, (New York, 1911). See *The Explicator*, I, No. 14 (Nov., 1942) for an analysis of the opening chapters of *A Hazard* as a part of the structural whole. Thomas Hardy particularly admired the opening of *A Hazard*, which he says, in an unpublished letter written on May 10, 1892, he has just been reading. "I like the opening; one seems to see New York, and hear it, and smell it." The Houghton Library, Harvard.

from the oil which was discovered on his farm. Dryfoos, with his fat and confused old wife, his two crude and violent daughters, Mela and Christine, and his misunderstood son, Conrad, moves to New York. There he buys a marble mansion, and also a magazine, which it is March's ill fortune to edit.

For a while Dryfoos is too occupied with spending money in New York to bother the staff of *Every Other Week*, but he at last begins to visit the office, and soon arranges a large dinner party at his palace for the editors. Among the many reporters, art editors, translators, editorial writers, who work for the paper, and whose personal stories we are told in detail, there is one, a gifted old German named Lindau,[304] who, at the splendid dinner sent in from Sherry's, by accident calls down the personal insult of Dryfoos, who instinctively objects to Lindau's radical ideas. Lindau was an old friend and teacher of March's, a good socialist, and a man gifted in languages. To rescue him from utter poverty, March had found occasional translating for him to do on *Every Other Week*. When Dryfoos demands his resignation, March offers his own instead, and succeeds in out-bullying the enraged old man.

Meanwhile Conrad, who hates his father's bigoted ignorance, has taken a minor position on the paper, and, through Lindau, has become interested in a street car strike then in progress in New York. In the violence of the strike the young boy is killed, and his father, who has completely failed to understand his son, is broken with grief. The two daughters, whose vulgarity and insolence have kept them apart from the finer-grained Conrad, are crushed by the blow and are glad to move away from the marble mansion in which they have always been unhappy.

[304]The original of this character was an old German teacher under whom Howells studied in Columbus and whose name he forgot. "He was a political refugee, of those German revolutionists who came to us after the revolts of 1848, and he still dwells venerable in my memory, with his noble, patriarchally bearded head." *Years of My Youth*, p. 135. Compare David Hughes, in *A World of Chance*, who seems also to be based on the same character.

The fact that Lindau, the very person whom Dryfoos had not hesitated to insult and bully from the heights of his wealth, should be the perfectly innocent means by which Conrad should be killed, illustrates Howells idea of "complicity" in human relations.[305] Our lives are inextricably bound together. Wealth, unaccompanied by understanding, brings only unhappiness. Lindau, who lives in a sordid little room among the poor, represents the Tolstoyan disregard of possessions. Basil March, who always reflects Howells' viewpoint, scorns Dryfoos, and befriends Lindau, though he himself, like Howells, steers a middle course between the two and manages to keep his job. The violence of the tragedy of Dryfoos' whole millionaire career, the loneliness and illness and pride of Lindau, the cheerful vulgarity of Fulkerson, who acts as a general promoter of *Every Other Week*, combine to crowd out any interest in the various love affairs, most of them unhappy, which make their way into the story. Howells is not able, in the end, to draw together his scattered plots, and come to a satisfying conclusion. Perhaps he himself realized the structural weakness of his novel. In any case, he never again attempted to bring together such widely disparate groups of people as a means of finding the answer to the problems of a competitive society.

Basil and Isabel March, whose experiences in New York bring them in contact with important people and events, slip back into their kindly personal lives after this plunge into tragedy. They meditate upon the love affairs of their friends in *The Shadow of a Dream* (1890), and go off to Saratoga in *An*

[305]For another example of Howells' idea of "complicity," see *The Quality of Mercy* (1892). Though not distinctly a "social novel," it does show the terrific temptation under which men in a moneyed society struggle. When one of them succumbs to temptation, as Mr. Northwick does, and embezzles $50,000, the fault lies as much with society as with the individual, Howells points out. The right and wrong of the case cannot be determined, but the suffering inflicted on the two daughters Northwick deserts is obvious enough. Maxwell, the young reporter for *The Abstract*, editorializes the case for Howells in terms of "social complicity."

Howells did "trust pen and ink with all the audacity of his social ideas" in *A Traveler from Altruria* (1894) and *Through the Eye of a Needle* (1907).[312] In these two companion volumes,[313] he throws aside all but the bare semblance of a novel and tells us what he thinks of the capitalistic society in which he himself had

[312]In "A Christmas Dream," which appeared in the "Editor's Study" in 1890, we have the first reference to Altruria. *Harper's*, LXXXII (Dec., 1890), 152–156. In this essay Howells wrote, "The change which had passed upon the world was tacit, but no less millennial. It was plainly obvious that the old order was succeeded by the new; that the former imperfect republic of the United States of America had given place to the ideal commonwealth, the Synthetized Sympathies of Altruria. The spectacle was all the more interesting because this was clearly the first Christmas since the establishment of the new status." In the Christmas, 1891, issue, Howells, under the protection of "The Christmas Boy," expressed his indignation at the cruelties of capitalistic society. Again he stated his belief that from our present imperfect system a new order will evolve in which the relationship between property and work is more equable, and the equilibrium between the two is maintained by the state. *Harper's*, LXXXIV (Dec., 1891), 153–156.

[313]See Arms, *The Social Criticism of William Dean Howells*, unpublished thesis, New York University (1939), p. 166. Arms points out that immediately after the serializing of *A Traveler from Altruria* in the Cosmopolitan (Nov., 1892-Oct., 1893), "The Letters of an Altrurian Traveler" ran in the same magazine until September, 1894. The last five installments of the "Letters" were used in 1907 as the first part of *Through the Eye of the Needle*. The thought of the two books is, therefore, more closely connected than critics have sometimes supposed. Howells planned to publish both romances in one volume in the Library Edition of his works. George Arms, "Howells' Unpublished Prefaces," *New England Quarterly*, XVII (Dec., 1944), 589–590. An unpublished letter to Sylvester Baxter, March 8, 1895, indicates that Howells was meditating his second book on Altruria as early as 1895. He asks Baxter in this letter to let him know how he thinks *A Visit to Altruria* would go, after commenting on a new book by Edward Bellamy, [*Miss Ludington's Sister*]. Huntington Library. Several unpublished letters exchanged between Howells and Bellamy show that these two social thinkers were in active correspondence during this fruitful decade. On June 17, 1888, for example, Bellamy wrote to Howells concerning a name for a new party "aiming at a national control of industry" and discussed at length the dissimilarity between *Looking Backward* and Gronlund's *Cooperative Society*. Before the appearance of *A Traveler from Altruria*, on August 14, 1893, Bellamy wrote, "I am awaiting the September Cosmopolitan with impatience. Yours in the sympathy of a common aspiration," and after the romance had appeared, he wrote, on November 7, 1893, "The responsibility upon us who have won the ear of the public, to plead the cause of the voiceless masses, is beyond limit. You have stood up to it nobly in your Altruria." The Houghton Library, Harvard.

been so successful. Making use of a hollow novel form popularized by Edward Bellamy's *Looking Backward* (1888), and bor-
rowing many of the ideas he had found in Gronlund's *Co-operative Commonwealth*,[314] Howells gives final expression to all the
social ideas which had been brewing in his mind during these
ten most significant years of his intellectual life. These social
ideas were never again incorporated in a genuine novel, for they
proved too complex for the typical Howells story to which he
remained loyal for the rest of his life. Published thirteen years
apart, these two Altrurian "romances" actually reflect the
thought of the '90s and mark the height of Howells' dissatisfac-
tion with American society. Like Percy Ray, of *A World of
Chance*, who promised to put into novel form all the sociological
ideas of David Hughes, Howells attempted to make palatable to
the reader of his day the burden of social thought which had
come to him from others.

At the time when Howells was contemplating and writing his
two Altrurian tales he was also serializing reminiscent accounts
of his childhood and youth,[315] which were collected under the
following titles: *A Boy's Town* (1890), *My Year in a Log Cabin*
(1893), *My Literary Passions* (1895), *Literary Friends and Ac-*

---

[314]For a more detailed account of Howells' debt to Gronlund in the
writing of these two books, see Arms, "The Literary Background of
Howells's Social Criticism," *American Literature*, XIV, (Nov., 1942) 260–
276. Howells, in his preface to the 1911 edition of *A Hazard of New
Fortunes*, does not refer to Gronlund, though his influence on Howells was
undoubtedly strong. He writes in 1911, of his feelings twenty-five years
earlier, "We had passed through a period of strong emotioning in the
direction of the humaner economics, if I may phrase it so; the rich seemed
not so much to despise the poor, the poor did not so hopelessly repine.
The solution of the riddle of the painful earth through the dreams of
Henry George, through the dreams of Edward Bellamy, through the
dreams of all generous visionaries of the past, seemed not impossibly
far off." See also the "Editor's Study," *Harper's*, LXXVII (June, 1888),
154. For a contemporary account of the "splendid aim of Howells,
who attacks the whole economic framework of modern society," see *The
American Fabian*, IV, No. 2 (Feb., 1928), p. 2.

[315]"In these days I seem to be all autobiography." *Life in Letters*,
II, 129.

quaintance (1900), and *The Flight of Pony Baker* (1902).[316] The democratic society of Ohio, which he pictures in these books, where as a boy he had read and worked and played in an almost classless society, must have been constantly before him as he wrote his descriptions of an ideal community. Between those early Western Reserve years and the New York of the nineties lay the vast accumulation of American wealth, which changed the whole nature of our society from that of a democracy to that of a plutocracy. Howells did not forget the lessons of his youth; the relationship between money, work, and democracy were never overlooked through the days of his own prosperity and success.[317]

Howells' trip to Europe, in 1882–1883, served to reinforce these social lessons. Switzerland, where Howells and his family passed two peaceful months in the autumn of 1882, is the country in Europe which pleased him the most. "I found Switzerland immensely to my liking,"[318] he wrote. Again from Lake Geneva he said, "It is a distinct pleasure to be in a Republic again; the manners are simple and unceremonious as our own, and people stand upright in all respects. The many resemblances to America constantly strike me; and if I must ever be banished, I hope

[316]In an unpublished letter to W. W. Riding, March 30, 1898, Howells says that the episodes in this story are real. When Howells' brother was 11 years old he was asked to carry the sum of $2,000 from Cincinnati to Hamilton. The thunderstorm and the runaway were episodes of other adventures of this brother. Huntington Library.

[317]In a letter to Charles Eliot Norton, written on March 19, 1902, Howells describes a boat trip on the Ohio River from Pittsburgh to Cincinnati and back: "Through the veils of coal smoke I saw the little ugly house, in the little ugly town, where I was born, the steamboat not staying for me to visit it. The boat did, however, let me visit a vanished epoch in the life of the shores, where the type of Americanism, for good and for bad, of fifty years ago, still prevails." It is marred by hideous industrialism "but thousands of comfortable farmsteads line the banks which the river is always eating away (to its own hurt), and the diabolical contrasts of riches and poverty are almost effaced. I should like to write a book about it. I went because I had pretty much stopped sleeping." *Life in Letters*, II, 154.

[318]*Life in Letters*, I, 335.

it may be to Switzerland."[319] He took great interest in trying out his French on his fellow boarders, on the peasant who raked the garden, on the village *pasteur*, "who lives nearby on the mountain side." "I am perpetually interested," he wrote, "in the life of a foreign community, which is yet so kindred in ideas and principles to ours."[320]

Howells at this period felt that men without the control of social legislation become selfish, that they quickly create a class society, holding property, but not assuming responsibility. He saw, too, that work should earn for itself, not opprobrium, but the right to enjoy property. Howells had been born and bred in a slavery-hating group; the inequalities of an industrial society seemed to him simply another form of slavery, the new industrial slavery, endangering our democracy,[321] and the remedy for the situation, he thought, was not revolution, but the vote.[322] These are the basic ideas which Howells, as a critic of our society,[323] expressed in his two studies of Altruria. He derived

[319]*Ibid*, p. 322.

[320]*Ibid.*, p. 326. See *A Little Swiss Sojourn* (1892), written from a notebook kept at this period.

[321]See Howells' address at the dinner given him on his 75th birthday. *North American Review*, CCXII (July, 1920), 11. See also Howells' discussion of Whittier in *Literary Friends and Acquaintance*, pp. 134–136.

[322]In two unpublished letters of Howells to Sylvester Baxter, the first dated July 4, 1897, and the second, May 11, 1898, Howells expresses his faith in the vote as a means of changing society for the better. Huntington Library. See also *Life in Letters*, II, 26.

[323]Howells avoided identification of himself with the Socialist Party. "People say that you are a Socialist," remarked a young reporter in an interview with Howells. "I should not care to wear a label," Howells replied. "I do not study the question—the question studies me. In great cities one does not easily avoid it. But socialism is not imminent. If the people wanted it they would have it, and without any revolution." This incident is reported by Francis W. Halsey, ed., *American Authors and Their Homes* (New York, 1901), p. 109. In 1894 Howells became a member of the advisory board of The Social Reform Club of New York, the purpose of which was to improve social and industrial conditions in New York. But Howells was never willing to take up the cause of one class against another. For a description of Howells delivering a lecture on Socialism before The Social Reform Club, see Hamlin Garland, *Roadside Meetings*, (New York, 1903), pp. 411–412. In justifying his approval of *The Bread-*

them from his contact with such men as Henry George, Edward Bellamy, and others, and from his wide reading, from his observation of the social unrest around him, from his never-forgotten memories of a simpler, better society in the Western Reserve, and from his European travels. The deepening of his social awareness can be traced in his novels, for he, like all true novelists, evolved his thoughts by means of novel writing.

Howells, the critic, temporarily silenced Howells, the novelist—but only temporarily, for Howells is often the Mr. Twelvemough of *A Traveler from Altruria*, the writer of popular novels,[324] who cannot be silenced, even by Mr. Homos, the large-minded Altrurian. The Traveler moves with disquieting composure among the guests of a New England summer hotel, and stands perhaps for Howells' more critical self, in constant debate with Mr. Twelvemough, who reflects his lighter nature. Mr. Homos, who points the way to the democratic America of an enlightened future, shocks and embarrasses his host, Mr. Twelvemough, on his arrival at the station by attempting to help the baggage man with his trunk. Mr. Twelvemough is overwhelmed with confusion, later in the evening, when Mr. Homos rises to relieve the waitress bearing in his dinner on a heavy tray. Mr. Homos cannot, or will not, understand why a social stigma should be attached to work, in spite of the efforts made to explain our class distinctions by the banker, the professor, the minister, the doctor, the society woman, and the other guests, who gather on the hotel porch to talk with the new arrival. They cannot explain, because, in fact, there is no adequate explanation of the inequalities of a democratic society.

"I wish—I wish," said the minister, gently, "it could be otherwise." "Well, I wish so, too," returned the banker, "But it

---

winners, by John Hay, he wrote, "the working men *as* working men are no better or wiser than the rich *as* the rich, and are quite as likely to be false and foolish." *Life in Letters*, I, 357–358.

[324] See *A Traveler From Altruria* (1894), p. 44.

isn't. Am I right or am I wrong?"[325] he demanded of the manufacturer, who laughed.

The talk on the hotel porch remains politely evasive. Howells' real attack on the industrial system is expressed by a young
farmer, with whom Mr. Homos talks:

"If you want to see American individuality," he explains, "the
real, simon-pure article, you ought to go down to one of our
big factory towns, and look at the mill-hands coming home in
droves after a day's work, young girls and old women, boys and
men, all fluffed over with cotton, and so dead-tired that they can
hardly walk. They come shambling along with all the individuality of a flock of sheep."[326]

Mr. Homos listens to the young farmer sympathetically, for
Altruria, like the United States, had also passed through the
Age of Accumulation.[327] But the people of Altruria had, finally,
by the simple device of the vote, gained control of the state and
resolved to form a society based on the idea of the good of all
rather than the good of the individual. In expressing this
forward-looking idea of the relation of the state and the individual, Howells was also expressing, through Mr. Homos, a
belief in the traditional social concepts of Christianity:

"I do not see why the Alturian system should be considered so
very un-American. Then, as to whether there is or ever was
really a practical altruism, a civic expression of it, I think it
cannot be denied that among the first Christians, those who immediately followed Christ, and might be supposed to be directly influenced by his life, there was an altruism practiced as
radical as that which we have organized into a national policy
and a working economy in Altruria."[328]

[325]*Ibid.*, p. 202.
[326]*Ibid.*, p. 161.
[327]"I imagine that the difference between your civilization and ours is
only one of degree, after all, and that America and Altruria are really one at
heart." *A Traveler from Altruria*, p. 31.
[328]*Ibid.*, pp. 160–161; see also p. 48. Howells' Altrurians were very good
Christians. They declared, "We believe ourselves the true followers of

The Judge, smoking his cigar on the hotel porch, made the most adequate comment on another occasion, when he said, "Remember that wherever life is simplest and purest and kindest, that is the highest civilization."[329]

Howells gives us a glimpse of this highest civilization, in contrast with the confused, moneyed, undemocratic society of New York, in *Through the Eye of the Needle*. In this book, Mr. Homos meets the charming and wealthy Eveleth Strange, and, with some difficulty, persuades her to relinquish her fortune in favor of marrying him. Her letters back to this country, describing the life in her adopted land, make up the second part of this book. We hear of the clothes of the Altrurians, their games, their schools—and we are bored. For this Utopia is no more interesting than any other, though the ideas expressed are the best. Howells, too, was bored, and, like the unredeemed Mr. Twelvemough that he was, after writing these two descriptions of his dream republic, he returned to his novel writing.

The novels which came from Howells' pen with undiminished regularity the rest of his life are singularly untouched by the social thought of the nineties. For it was the earlier novels which he really loved. As an old man of seventy-three he writes, "In going over my books I find that 18 or 20 volumes have been written since I came to Harpers in 1886, and 10 or 12 before that. Of course, my meat went into the earlier ones, and yet there are three or four of the later novels which are as good as any."[330] For a time it seemed to Howells that there might be "a vital promise" in the novel written for social rather than aesthetic ends. "Ten or fifteen years ago," he wrote in 1902, "when fiction was at its highest mark, there seemed a vital

---

Christ, whose doctrine we seek to make our life, as He made His." Pp. 299–300. See also *Life in Letters*, II, 266.

[329]*The Kentons*, p. 144. The judge of *A Traveler from Altruria* appears in *The Kentons*. As late as 1918 Howells was still referring to Altruria in the "Easy Chair." See *Harper's*, CXXXVII (Sept., 1918), 589–592.

[330]*Life in Letters*, II, 268.

promise in its masterpieces besides and beyond their aesthetic value." "The phenomena of our enormous enterprise" now no longer appeared to Howells "as the best material for fiction, as the material with which art would prosper most. That material is the stuff for the newspapers, but not for the novel, except as such wonders of the outer world can be related to the miracles of the inner world. Fiction can deal with the facts of finance and industry and invention only as the expression of character; otherwise these things are wholly dead. Nobody really lives in them, though for the most part we live among them."[331] Thus ended Howells' experiment with the social novel; his interest in social problems, however, he never lost. As late as 1914, Howells wrote to his cousin, Bertha Howells, thanking her for the political "literature" she had sent him and assuring her of his sympathy. He added that he would not set his civic ideals lower than the millennium.[332]

Though Howells, from the eminence of "The Editor's Study," and then "The Editor's Easy Chair," became the Dean of American Letters, and as such, our leading critic, he never again seriously attempted to write a social criticism of our country; his real interest lay more strictly in the realm of literature. In *Silas Lapham*, *The Minister's Charge*, *Annie Kilburn*, *A Hazard of New Fortunes*, Howells had realized the "vital promise" to be found in the social novel through the formulation of his theory of the "complicity," or the interrelation of human affairs. "The phenomena of our enormous enterprise" seemed to him at last too large for the novel; he returned once more to the story written for aesthetic ends, and concerned with "the miracles of the inner world."

[331]The "Easy Chair," *Harper's*, CXXIV (March, 1912), 636.
[332]See unpublished letter to Bertha Howells, January 18, 1914. The Berg Collection, New York Public Library. See also an account of Howells' address to The Twentieth Century Club, in *The Boston Journal*, March 1, 1900. Howells spoke on the subject of Liberty and Equality in the hall of the Boston University Law School, which was filled to overflowing.

V. THE CRITIC

"Essaying has been the enemy of the novelist that was in me."

For almost thirty-five years, from 1885[333] to 1920, Howells was associated with *Harper's Magazine*. His critical thought in this period may be divided neatly into two phases, which are distinguished by the two names of the departments for which he wrote—the "Editor's Study" and the "Editor's Easy Chair." "The Study," wrote Howells in retrospect, as he left it in 1892,[334] "opened its doors (with something too much of a bang)" when he entered it determined to fight for "the cause of Common Honesty in Literature ... The spectacle has not been seemly; the passions of the followers of fraud and humbug were aroused; they returned blow for blow, and much mud from afar."[335] After the vigorous battle for realism which Howells carried on in "The Study," he was ready to recline in the "Easy Chair." For when Howells returned to *Harper's* in 1900, the battle had been won, or, rather, had passed to other fields, leaving the "Easy Chair" untroubled—and unread.

In 1888, several years after he had joined *Harper's*,[336]

---

[333]Howells' connection with *Harper and Brothers* began in the autumn of 1885. He did not undertake "The Study" until January, 1886. Howells' social connections with *Harper's* began earlier. See *Life in Letters*, I, 168–169; 253. For Howells' own account of his long association with *Harper's*, See *The Literary Digest* (June 12, 1920), 54.

[334]Howells left *Harper's* temporarily in 1892 to become an editor of the *Cosmopolitan*.

[335]*Harper's*, LXXXIV (March, 1892), 640–642.

[336]For a year after Howells left Boston and before he settled in New York, he lived with his family near the Sanatorium in Dansville, New York, where his daughter, Winifred, had been taken. Howells made frequent moves during this period. In February, 1888, he lived in an apartment at 46 West 9th Street; for the summer of 1888, he occupied a small house in Little Nahant, near Boston; in the following autumn he moved to a house in New York, east of Stuyvesant Square. Howells always preserved a sentimental preference for Boston. See an unpublished letter to Mrs. J. T. Fields, December 13, 1896, in which he speaks of the years of exile in New York, and of the happy times in Cambridge. Huntington Library.

Howells moved his home to New York. A month later he wrote to his friend, Thomas S. Perry:

I have been trying to catch on to the bigger life of the place. It's immensely interesting, but I don't know whether I shall manage it; I'm now fifty-one, you know. There are lots of interesting young painting and writing fellows, and the place is lordly free, with foreign touches of all kinds all thro' its abounding Americanism: Boston seems of another planet.[337]

In this stirring atmosphere of New York, Howells not only wrote his most powerful social novels, but also, from the "Editor's Study" of *Harper's Magazine*, presented the problem of realism in fiction and defended his ideas with patience and resourcefulness. Howells' defence of his literary theories was the more potent, because during these six years, from 1885 to 1891, the greatest of his novels, *Silas Lapham*, *Indian Summer*, *The Minister's Charge*, *Annie Kilburn*, and *A Hazard of New Fortunes*, were illustrating his conception of realism. When some of the famous *Harper's* essays were gathered together and published under the title of *Criticism and Fiction* in 1891, Howells had made his critical contribution to the art of novel-writing. He had defined precisely what he meant by "realism," and in doing so he had indicated clearly the range and the limitations of his thinking. His defence of such men as Mark Twain, Henry James, Hamlin Garland, Stephen Crane, Frank Norris, and many others, made him the spokesman of the "new school" of writers of his day. Though Howells talked from his "Easy Chair" in his unfailingly amiable way from 1900 to 1920,[338] he had little of importance to add to what he had already said.

---

[337]*Life in Letters*, I, 413. For a full account of the literary friendship of Thomas Sergeant Perry and William Dean Howells see *Thomas Sergeant Perry (1845–1928), A Biographical Study*, unpublished thesis by Agnes Virginia Harlow. Duke University, Durham, North Carolina, 1946.

[338]Many of these essays were collected in *Literature and Life* (1902), and in *Imaginary Interviews* (1910).

1. First Principles

"Commonly," wrote Howells, our critics have "no principles, but only an assortment of prepossessions for and against"[339] the unfortunate authors who fall into their hands. No such accusation could ever be made against Howells; the principle to which he returned in all of his comments on novels was that of "truth and sanity in fiction." In the first review to issue from "The Study," Howells praises a pile of new novels, for "we find in nearly every one of them a disposition to regard our life without the literary glasses so long thought desirable, and to see character, not as it is in other fiction, but as it abounds outside of all fiction."[340] "Let fiction cease to lie about life; let it portray man and women as they are, actuated by the motives and the passions in the measure we all know," he writes in an essay on Mark Twain.[341] To young novel writers he says, "Do not trouble yourselves about standards or contempts or passions; but try to be faithful and natural; and remember that there is no greatness, no beauty, which does not come from truth to your own knowledge of things."[342] Howells boldly ridicules the popular novelist of his day, and, incidentally, the novel reader:

The kind of novels he likes, and likes to write, are intended to take his reader's mind, or what that reader would probably call his mind, off himself; they make one forget life and all its cares and duties; they are not in the least like the novels which make you think of these, and shame you into at least wishing to be a helpfuler and wholesomer creature than you are. No sordid details of verity here, if you please; no wretched being humbly and weakly struggling to do right and to be true, suffering for his follies and his sins, tasting joy only through the mortification of self, and in the help of others; nothing of all this, but a great

[339]*Harper's*, LXXV (June, 1887), 156.
[340]*Ibid.*, LXXII (January, 1886), 322.
[341]*Ibid.*, LXXIV (May, 1887), 987.
[342]*Ibid.*, LXXV (September, 1887), 641.

whirling splendor of peril and achievement, a wild scene of heroic adventure . . . with a stage 'picture' at the fall of the curtain, and all the good characters in a row, their left hands pressed upon their hearts, and kissing their right hands to the audience in the good old way that has always charmed and always will charm, Heaven bless it![343]

Almost every issue of *Harper's*, between the time when Howells entered "The Study," and the time when he closed its door, brought forth another defence of realism, which was often accompanied by a denunciation of the romantic attitude. "The talent that is robust enough to front the everyday world and catch the charm of its work-worn, care-worn, brave, kindly face, need not fear the encounter, though it seems terrible to the sort nurtured in the superstition of the romantic, the bizarre, the heroic, the distinguished, as the thing alone worthy of painting or carving or writing."[344] The novel reader is in part to blame for this attitude, Howells says, for he must have the problem of a novel solved for him "by a marriage or a murder," and must be "spoon-victualled" with a "moral minced small and then thinned with milk and water, and familiarly flavored with sentimentality or religiosity."[345]

Articles soon appeared in all the leading magazines of the times, in *The Atlantic Monthly, The Nation, The Dial, The Forum*, in defence of the romantic and the idealistic.[346] A critic of *The Chicago Sunday Times* insisted that Howells had said that "mediocrity is all of human life that is interesting— that a mild sort of vulgarity is the one living truth in the character of men and women." All realists, complained this critic, deal with the faults of human nature instead of attempting to find in American life subjects "fit for heroic treatment."[347]

[343]*Ibid.*, LXXV (July, 1887), 318.

[344]*Ibid.*, LXXVII (July, 1888), 317–318.

[345]*Ibid.*, LXXXI (September, 1890), 640.

[346]See Herbert Edwards, "Howells and the Controversy over Realism," *American Literature*, III (Nov., 1931), 239–248.

[347]*The Literary World*, XVIII (Sept. 3, 1887), 281. It is appropriate to quote here a letter written by James P. Stabler, an uncle of one of the

The battle between the romantics and the realists was sufficiently important to move *The Daily Tribune* to send a young reporter up to Lake George from New York City in July, 1887, to interview this outspoken critic and novelist. The interview appeared in the Sunday edition of the *Tribune*, on July 10; in it Howells makes a simple statement of his position, which seems to a later generation unassailable. After a description of Howells' "long, low, rambling cottage, on the side of the lake," and of Howells himself, "in a soft felt hat, a white flannel shirt, and a large, easy pair of corduroy trousers," the reporter begins his pre-arranged remarks:

"There are very many beautiful Indian romances relating to the mountain and islands and inlets all about here, Mr. Howells," he ventured to suggest. "True," replied Howells, "the history of Lake George is full of romance, but, then, you know, I look

---

editors of this volume, to Howells, and Howells' reply. The Stabler letter is dated March 14, 1879. It is in the possession of Mrs. Frederick W. McReynolds, of Washington, D.C.

"Dear Sir: In the last serial number of 'The Lady of the Aroostook' occurs this passage—'Women are never blinded by romance, however much they like it in the abstract.'

"The statement made thus broadly cannot be true it seems to me, whether applied to man or woman, and it occurred to me that it was probably intended especially for Lydia, & was through an oversight put in the form of a generality.

"I should be very glad to know whether the conjecture is right; and if at the same time you could justify yourself in the eyes of several ladies of my acquaintance by giving a sufficient reason for inflicting such a name as Lydia Blood upon such a lovely character as the heroine. I should be much pleased to be able to appease their just indignation—In the absence of a good reason, an abject apology might possibly answer. Very truly, Yours &c. James P. Stabler."

Howells replied on March 17, 1879, from the office of *The Atlantic Monthly*:

"Dear Sir: I'm afraid that I can't explain or excuse my heroine's name, which seemed to me from the first an essential part of her.

"I still think I am right on the point you allege against me. Women worth thinking and writing about are never blinded by romance, though they are often blinded by affection."

On the reverse of Howells' letter J. P. Stabler has written the following comment: "Mr. Howells begs the question by limiting the application of a broad statement which included all women to 'women worth thinking or writing about.' He attempts to justify himself by qualifying the phrase without admitting that he was in error—I do not think that candid or very manly & will always think less of Howells for it. J.P.S."

upon that as the province of poetry rather than of prose narrative. I think that it is asking a good deal of people in these busy, practical times, to go back with you for a half a dozen or more generations, and to lose themselves among strange customs and among strange people in a strange land . . . The real sentiment of to-day requires that the novelist shall portray a section of real life, that has in it a useful and animating purpose. All the good work of our times is being done on this theory." "How do you answer the charge that real life is commonplace?" pursued the catechizing reporter. "By asserting that the very things that are not commonplace are those commonly called commonplace. All the rest has long since become hackneyed. In the preposterous what is there to invent? Nothing, except what is so preposterous as to be ludicrous."

Protests against Howells' defence of "the commonplace" as a fit subject for the novelist did not cease to appear as long as Howells occupied "The Study." Charles Dudley Warner, in the *Atlantic*, voiced the feeling of many readers when he declared that the novel should "lighten the burdens of life by taking us for a time out of our humdrum and perhaps sordid conditions, so that we can see familiar life somewhat idealised."[348] *The Literary World* pointed out that "the world is tired of Kodak pictures of the dreary commonplaces of life;"[349] *The Critic* came out for "happy endings" as "healthful and sane," and stated that "a taste for disappointing conclusions is an artificial one, acquired at the expense of much that is necessary to perfect moral sanity."[350]

But there were other writers, besides Howells, interested in realism; his defence of Mark Twain, Henry James, Hamlin Garland, Stephen Crane, Frank Norris, as well as many minor realists,[351] forms an important part of Howells' ammunition.

[348]*The Atlantic Monthly*, LI (April, 1883), 469.
[349]*The Literary World*, XXVIII (Sept. 3, 1887), 281.
[350]*The Critic*, VI, *New Series*, (July 10, 1886), 20.
[351]From the list of writers whom Howells encouraged and commended for their realism one might also mention George W. Cable, Joel

When Mark Twain shocked literary Boston more by his manners than by his ideas, Howells never lost faith in him as the most original of American writers. He published his stories and essays, edited his manuscripts, and finally, after Mark Twain's death, wrote up this unbroken literary friendship in *My Mark Twain*. As we have seen, James and Howells, in the course of long walks and talks through the streets of Cambridge, had developed their ideas of realism; Howells' defence of James in his famous *Century* essay of November, 1882, was a defence of his own beliefs as well. James, like Howells, was accused of lack of "pathos and power," "passion and emotion," for which he substituted, said his critics, immorality and dullness.[352] When Garland's *Main Travelled Roads* appeared in 1891, Howells wrote at once in the "Editor's Study":

The type caught in Mr. Garland's book is not pretty; it is ugly and often ridiculous; but it is heart-breaking in its rude despair ... he has a fine courage to leave a fact with the reader, ungarnished and unvarnished, which is almost the rarest trait in an Anglo-Saxon writer, so infantile and feeble is the custom of our art.[353]

In *Roadside Meetings* (1930) Garland tells of the unfailing encouragement he received as a young writer from Howells, then in a position of eminence among American writers. Garland introduced Stephen Crane to Howells, and immediately Howells befriended the struggling young journalist by writing an introduction to *Maggie, a Girl of the Streets*, and by attempting, in vain, to find a publisher for the book.[354] Reviewing for one of

---

Chandler Harris, Madison Cawein, James Whitcomb Riley, Sarah Orne Jewett, Mary E. Wilkins, Edith Wharton, Mrs. Humphry Ward, and Booth Tarkington. Houghton Library, Harvard.

[352]Herbert Edwards, "Howells and the Controversy over Realism," *American Literature*, III (Nov. 1931), 246.

[353]The "Editor's Study," *Harper's*, LXXXIII (Sept., 1891), 639–640. See also Hamlin Garland, *The Bookman*, XLV (March, 1917), 1–7, and *My Friendly Contemporaries*, (New York, 1932), 294–296.

[354]*The Bookman*, I (May, 1895), 229–230. On August 15, Stephen Crane

Harper's short-lived magazines, *Literature*, Howells was one of the first to recognize and publically praise the power in Frank Norris' *McTeague*. After Norris' sudden death in 1902, Howells wrote the first appraisal to appear in print; here he pointed out that the author had not been sufficiently appreciated in America.[355] Howells' articles on these writers were important not only in themselves, but as a part of his patient and independent defence of realism.

Howells' novels and his critical essays together reflect the first major battle to take place in this country over the novelist's right and duty to tell the truth. Howells, Garland tells us, had become an issue in the literary movement of the day; his utterances from the "Editor's Study" had the effect of dividing the public into two opposing camps. Howells' novels were "being read aloud in thousands of home circles, and clubs and social gatherings rang with argument . . . He was not only admittedly a great novelist but the most talked about critic in all America. His utterances on the side of the realists had made him hated as well as loved."[356]

2. *Theory of Realism*

The five component parts of Howells' theory of realism,[357] each of which became a point of attack for his adversaries, are

wrote to Howells, "I am grateful to you in a way that is hard for me to say. In truth you have always been so generous with me that grace departs at once from my pen when I attempt to tell you of my appreciation." Unpublished letter to Howells in the Houghton Library, Harvard.

[355]"Frank Norris," *The North American Review*, CLXXV(Dec., 1902), 769–778. Reprinted in this book, pp. 384–394.

[356]*Roadside Meetings* (New York, 1930), 55–56.

[357]Arms points out that Howells was moving toward a formulation of a critical theory of realism while still associated with the *Atlantic*. "The Literary Background of Howells's Social Criticism," *American Literature*, XIV (Nov., 1942), 264–271. Howells' analytical mind was definitely interested at this time in discussing and disputing the basic principles of writing and criticism. Perhaps that is why he was tempted to accept President Gilman's offer of a professorship at Johns Hopkins in 1882. See Howells' long letter on how he would handle a class in literature or in writing were he to become a college professor. *Life in Letters*, I, 330–331.

his defence of the commonplace as the source of novel material, his insistence that character is more important than plot, his attack on the romantic writers, his attitude towards idealism and morals, his belief in realism as the expression of democracy. It is important to realize that the ideas set down in "The Study" were not mere theories devised by an editor in need of copy; they were the outgrowth of many years of novel reading and novel writing.

Howells had been consciously seeking the real in human experience as far back as 1872, when *Their Wedding Journey* appeared; his search was the same when he wrote his last novel, *The Vacation of the Kelwyns*. It was, in fact, the commonplace, the average, which supplied Howells throughout his life with sufficient material for amused, as well as serious, meditation. "Nothing in a story can be better than life."[358] Howells, glancing over the shoulders of the Marches, on *Their Wedding Journey*, surveys the carful of people bound for Montreal, and observes:

It was in all respects an ordinary carful of human beings, and it was perhaps the more worthy to be studied on that account. As in literature the true artist will shun the use even of real events if they are of an improbable character, so the sincere observer of man will not desire to look upon his heroic or occasional phases, but will seek him in his habitual moods of vacancy and tiresomeness. To me, at any rate, he is at such times very precious; and I never perceive him to be so much a man and a brother as when I feel the pressure of his vast, natural, unaffected dullness. Then I am able to enter confidently into his life and inhabit there, to think his shallow and feeble thoughts, to be moved by his dumb, stupid desires, to be dimly illumed by his stinted inspirations, to share his foolish prejudices, to practice his obtuse selfishness. Yes, it is a very amusing world, if you do not refuse to be amused.[359]

[358] *Life in Letters*, I, 361.
[359] Pp. 86–87. For further references to realism in fiction in Howells' novels, see *Their Wedding Journey*, p. 110; *Suburban Sketches*, pp. 66, 84,

This appreciation of "the commonplace" as material for
the novel is repeated in *The Rise of Silas Lapham*. It is comparatively simple to paint a young man dying for his country,
observed one of the guests at the Latham dinner party; how
much more difficult to show him fulfilling the duties of a good
citizen—and this is what the speaker would attempt were he a
novelist. "What? the commonplace?" echoed another guest,
"Commonplace? The commonplace is just that light, impal-
pable, aërial essence which they've never got into their confounded books yet. The novelist who could interpret the common feelings of commonplace people would have the answer
to 'the riddle of the painful earth' on his tongue."[360]

The romantically inclined heroine of *The Vacation of the
Kelwyns* finds it at first difficult to reconcile herself to marrying
an average man. Thinking over her recent engagement to
Emerance, she is struck by the fact that

It was not at all the exaltation she had expected in her love for
the hero of her dreams, and, in fact, Emerance was not that hero,
though she found that she liked him better than if he had been.
In derivation and education he was entirely middle-class, as far
removed from what was plebeian as what was patrician. He had
not come out of the new earth, which would have been heroic;
he had sprung from soil wrought for generations, on the common level, which was average.[361]

Emerance was, therefore, according to Howells, the kind of
young man worth studying—and marrying—who would finally
teach Parthenope to look with more understanding on what she
called "the commonplace."

It is perhaps Howells' love of the average human being, who
might, by the exertion of his will, develop into a very unusual

---

92, 172–173, 181, 186, 191; *A Chance Acquaintance*, p. 164; *Dr. Breen's
Profession*, pp. 187–188; *Silas Lapham*, pp. 277–280; *The Minister's Charge*,
pp. 434, 450, 457.
[360] *The Rise of Silas Lapham*, pp. 284–285.
[361] P. 247.

individual, which most sharply differentiates Howells from the later naturalists who accepted the scientists' picture of man in a pre-destined universe in which his will-power could not avail. Howells reflected the scientific atmosphere of his day in his study of the average man in his natural environment; in his insistence on the power of men to improve, he remained in opposition to the deterministic philosophy of such later writers as Dreiser and Farrell.[362]

Contemplation of the daily round of most people had taught Howells the further lesson that, much as we yearn for incident or plot in our experiences, we must reconcile ourselves to the fact that life is usually dull, and that our pleasure must come from ordinary day-to-day adventures. "The want of incident for the most part of the time" was what the Marches found most surprising on their Wedding Journey. Howells comments,

and I who write their history might also sink under it, but that I am supported by the fact that it is so typical in this respect. I even imagine that ideal reader for whom one writes as yawning over these barren details with the life-like weariness of an actual travelling companion of theirs.[363]

The lesson of the relation of plot to character Howells had learned many years before, when as a boy in Ohio he had pored over *Don Quixote*. "I believe that its free and simple design," he wrote in *My Literary Passions*, "where event follows event without the fettering control of intrigue, but where all grows naturally out of character and conditions, is the supreme form of fiction."[364] Howells describes the "joyful astonishment" with

[362]In spite of the fact that Henry James wrote to Howells, "I regard you as the great American naturalist" (*Letters of Henry James*, I, 105), Howells does not discuss the distinction between realism and naturalism, which he leaves for a later generation to quarrel over. The opposition, in Howells' mind, was rather between realism and romance. See Howells' two essays on the death of Zola and the death of Norris reprinted on pp. 372–383 and 384–394 of this book. *North American Review*, CLXXV (Nov., 1902), 587–596; (Dec., 1902) 769–778.

[363]Pp. 94–95.

[364]p. 26.

which, years later, he discovered Turgenev's art of subordinating plot to character. "Here was a master who was apparently not trying to work out a plot, who was not even trying to work out a character, but was standing aside from the whole affair, and letting the characters work the plot out." The story flows naturally from their characters, and when they have said or done something, you understand why "as unerringly as you would if they were people whom you knew outside of a book."[365] The art of Turgenev was, in short, the art of realism. In his essay on Henry James, Howells sums up his attitude toward dramatic incident in stories, when he defines the "new school," of which he says he is a member. "It studies human nature much more in its wonted aspects, and finds its ethical and dramatic examples in the operation of lighter but not less vital motives. The moving accident is certainly not its trade; and it prefers to avoid all manner of dire catastrophes."[366]

Perhaps Howells' attack on the romantic classics, popular in his day, brought down more wrath upon his head than any other aspect of his defence of realism.[367] He did not hesitate to say to the lovers of Scott, Thackeray, and Dickens, that "at least three-fifths of the literature called classic, in all languages, no more lives than the poems and stories that perish monthly in our magazines. It is all printed and reprinted, generation after generation, century after century; but it is not alive; it is as dead as the people who wrote it and read it . . . A superstitious piety preserves it . . . but nobody really enjoys it."[368]

In admiring the art of Jane Austen, Trollope, Turgenev,

---

[365]*Ibid.*, p. 230.

[366]*Century Magazine*, XXV (Nov., 1882), 28. Henry James was in Boston in 1882 for the winter. During the early months of 1882 they had many conversations together, the result of which was the *Century* article. "Harry James is spending the winter only a few doors from us . . . I see him constantly, and we talk literature perpetually, as we used to do in our walks ten years ago." *Life in Letters*, I, 311.

[367]See *Life in Letters*, I, 336–338.

[368]*Harper's*, LXXV (Sept., 1887), 641.

Tolstoy, and other great realists, Howells shocked his generation by pointing out the lack of truth, hence of art, in the great romantics of classical literature, who pretend to be telling us the truth. "The absolutely unreal, the purely fanciful in all the arts" Howells insists he always loved as well as "the absolutely real." What he objected to "is the romantic thing which asks to be accepted with all its fantasticality on the ground of reality; that seems to me hopelessly bad."[369] Discussion of the realists and the romantics of established reputations made more clear to his readers exactly what Howells meant by his use of the terms. Realism is nothing more nor less than "the truthful treatment of material, and Jane Austen was the first and last of the English novelists to treat material with entire truthfulness." "The art of fiction, as Jane Austen knew it, declined from her through Scott, and Bulwer, and Dickens, and Charlotte Bronte, and Thackeray, and even George Eliot, because the mania of romanticism had seized upon all Europe, and these great writers could not escape the taint of their time." Anthony Trollope most resembles Jane Austen, Howells points out, "in simple honesty and instinctive truth, as unphilosophized as the light of common day."[370] In *My Literary Passions*, Howells speaks of "the gross darkness of English fiction" from which Turgenev roused him, Turgenev, who "was of that great race which has more than any other fully and freely uttered human nature, without either false pride or false shame in its nakedness."[371] Turgenev had set a standard of truth for the novel of the future.[372]

4 Not only does the romantic view of life distort events in in-

[369] *My Literary Passions*, pp. 216–217.

[370] *Criticism and Fiction*, pp. 73–75. Howells called on Trollope when he first visited England in 1865. *Life in Letters*, I, 93. Howells dined with Hardy when he was in England in 1893. *Ibid*, 349. In 1867 Howells met Dickens at the home of Longfellow. *Ibid.*, 122–124; 126–127.

[371] pp. 230–231. For further discussion of the romantic English novel as compared with those of the Russians, see the "Editor's Study" in the following numbers of *Harper's*: LXXII (Feb., 1886), 486; LXXIII (Sept., 1886), 639; LXXVIII (May, 1889), 982–983.

[372] *Life in Letters*, I, 232.

sisting on the importance of plot, but it also blurs one's view of truth by an appeal to the idealistic. Howells never misses a chance to enveigh against the noble attitudes which his characters assume.[373] As the Rev. Mr. Sewell says for Howells in *Silas Lapham*, when Pen tries to renounce Tom Corey because her sister romantically desires him, "We somehow think it must be wrong to use our common-sense. I don't know where this false ideal comes from, unless it comes from the novels that befool and debauch almost every intelligence in some degree."[374]

False heroines and heroes are to blame, says Howells, for a great deal of harm in the world, because they exaggerate the importance of passion and consider love "altogether a finer thing than prudence, obedience, reason."[375] Marcia Gaylord, in *A Modern Instance*, who placed love above reason, is such "a false heroine" and is punished, not by Howells, but by life itself for her waywardness. Much as Howells liked his heroine, he was bound, as a conscientious novelist of the "new school," to depict her downfall, for "if a novel flatters the passions, and exalts them above the principles, it is poisonous."[376] The hero, too, of popular novels, so loved by the sentimental reader, is devoted to the "old romantic phase of chivalrous achievement or manifold suffering for love's sake, or its more recent development of the 'virile,' the bullying, and the brutal, or its still more recent agonies of self-sacrifice, as idle and useless as the moral experiences of the insane asylum."[377] Thus it became the "Fearful Responsibility" of Mr. Elmore to protect his young guest from the charms of the "virile" Captain Ehrhardt. "I don't

---

[373]See also *April Hopes, Indian Summer, An Imperative Duty, The Shadow of a Dream, The Son of Royal Langbrith, A Modern Instance, The Vacation of the Kelwyns* for the dilemmas into which false idealism leads people.

[374]p. 339; see also p. 306.

[375]*Criticism and Fiction*, p. 96.

[376]*Criticism and Fiction*, p. 95. See also *Harper's*, LXXIV (April, 1887), 825 and "A Niece's Literary Advice to her Uncle," *Imaginary Interviews* (1910), p. 176.

[377]*Ibid.*, 97.

believe in heroes and heroines, and willingly avoid the heroic,"[378] wrote Howells.

Mrs. Farrell, the only woman in all of Howells' novels of genuinely evil influence, is harmful precisely because she is always playing her "Private Theatricals" and making a false appeal to the romantic idealism of her lover. Rachel Woodward, a foil for the alluring Mrs. Farrell, is the character blessed with common-sense, humor, and downrightness. "Private Theatricals," which came out in the *Atlantic* in serial form in 1875–1876, was not published in book form until 1921, when it appeared under the title *Mrs. Farrell*, because the people of the village did not like to see themselves depicted so realistically. Yet Mrs. Farrell's summer flirtation in a New Hampshire boarding house of the seventies always managed to remain on the decorous side of an illicit love affair. Readers of a later day are inclined to point to this novel as typical of Howells' tiresome insistence on the decorums of social life no matter what the actual situation was. It is worth noticing that the relation between Mrs. Farrell and William Gilbert need not go further than a flirtation to make clear the devastating effects of such a woman on the people around her. "Your Mrs. Farrell is terrific—do for pity's sake give her the Small Pox—she deserves it—"[379]writes Mrs. Fanny Kemble to Howells in 1875, expressing, very probably, the opinion of the general reader of the *Atlantic* at that time.

The following passage from the "Editor's Study" presents Howells' belief that the moral atmosphere of a generation is an aspect of the "reality" to be described, and with this view one can hardly take issue:

Sometimes a novel which has this shuffling air, this effect of truckling to propriety, might defend itself, if it could speak for

---

[378]*Life in Letters*, I, 361; see also the discussion of the novel at the Corey dinner table, *The Rise of Silas Lapham*, pp. 277–280.

[379]*Life in Letters*, I, 205.

itself, by saying that such experiences happened not to come within its scheme, and that, so far from maiming or mutilating itself in ignoring them, it was all the more faithfully representative of the tone of modern life in dealing with love that was chaste, and with passion so honest that it could be openly spoken of before the tenderest bud at dinner. It might say that the guilty intrigue, the betrayal, the extreme flirtation even, was the exceptional thing in life, and unless the scheme of the story necessarily involved it, that it would be bad art to lug it in, and as bad taste as to introduce such topics in a mixed company, and that the vast majority of the company are ladies.[380]

Though one recognizes that Howells, as a realist, must remain faithful to "the tone of modern life," one cannot escape the realization that to accept "the tenderest bud at dinner" as the arbiter of morals is fatal to a novelist of any period, even the 1880's. The inadequacy of Howells' novel *The Coast of Bohemia* (1893), is proof of a certain moral squeamishness in Howells which sometimes lessened his power as a novelist.[381] Though dealing with artists, Howells says in his Introduction that he must remain on the coast of Bohemia, and not penetrate that dangerous

---

[380]*Criticism in Fiction*, pp. 148–149. See also *ibid.* p. 152. See also the "Editor's Study," *Harper's*, LXXIX (June, 1889), 151.

[381]In 1884 Edmund Gosse, through Howells' efforts, was invited to lecture by the Lowell Institute. Mr. and Mrs. Gosse stayed with the Howellses. Edmund Gosse tells of walking with Howells "in the dingier part of Boston, when he stopped and looked up at a very ordinary little house. 'How happy I should be,' he said, 'if I could see everything that is done and hear everything that is said in such a house as that for a week!' I made a rude suggestion about what might possibly be going on behind those dull windows. Howells did not laugh; but he put up his hand as if to ward off a blow. 'Oh! don't say that!' he cried, 'I couldn't bear it; I couldn't write a line if I thought such things were happening.'" *Living Age*, CCCVI (July 10, 1920), 99–100. In a letter to John Hay, of March 18, 1882, Howells writes of his son "John is at this moment curled up on the lounge reading *Doctor Breen's Practice*. For this reason, if for no other, I could not have palpitating divans in my stories; my children are my censors, and if I wished to be wicked, I hope they would be my safe-guards. . . . I am a great admirer of French workmanship, and I read everything of Zola's that I can lay hands on. But I have to hide the books from the children!" *Life in Letters*, I, 311.

territory, because we would not wish "our girls" to make such a perilous trip. We can only conclude that realism is a term relative to the period in which the author lives and to his own way of seeing the life around him.[382]

Howells' "reticent realism," as he himself terms it, is opposed to the romantic in that it attempts to "portray men and women as they are, actuated by the motives and the passions in the measure we all know;" it should "forbear to preach pride and revenge, folly and insanity, egotism and prejudice;" it should "not put on fine literary airs," but should "speak the dialect, the language, that most Americans know—the language of unaffected people everywhere."[383] Howells' realism, as illustrated by his novels and as explained in the "Editor's Study," is in the tradition of Jane Austen, Anthony Trollope, Turgenev, and Tolstoy, who are, says Howells, the greatest novelists, because the most truthful. He took up arms against the classical romanticists, such as Scott and Dickens, as well as their followers in his day, F. Marion Crawford, Kipling, and others, who falsify the real, and thus depart from the truth of ordinary, com-

---

[382]For further discussion of Howells' "reticent realism," see Edwin H. Cady,"The Neuroticism of William Dean Howells," *PMLA*, LXI (March, 1946), 229–238; see also George Arms, *The Social Criticism of William Dean Howells*, Unpublished thesis, New York University (1939), pp. 276–283.

[383]*Criticism and Fiction*, p. 104. Howells enjoyed what seemed to him natural American talk in his own writing and in the writing of others. In reviewing a group of novels for "The Study," he wrote that he was glad "of every tint any of them [the novelists] gets from the parlance he hears; it is much better than the tint he will get from the parlance he reads . . . For our novelists to try to write Americanly, from any motive, would be a dismal error, but being born Americans, we would have them use 'Americanisms' whenever these serve their turn; and when their characters speak, we should like to hear them speak true American, with all the varying Tennesseean, Philadelphian, Bostonian, and New York accents." *Harper's*, LXXII (Jan. 1886), 325. For an interesting discussion of elocution versus a boy's natural talk, see *The Vacation of the Kelwyns*, pp. 116–118. "My idea is that the sum of this art is to speak and to write simply and clearly," for this is "also to write beautifully and strongly." *Life in Letters*, I, 331. See also letters of Nov. 5, 1891, and May 20, 1894, to T. W. Higginson. Berg Collection, New York Public Library.

monplace experience. His own practice as a novelist made clear the critical position he defined in the "Editor's Study,"[384] and now reminds us that, though writing in the larger tradition of realism, he was himself a nineteenth century American, with that century's view of "the proprieties."[385]

Howells' moral provincialism was corrected to some extent by his wide reading of the novelists of Europe, then practically unknown to American readers. Through the columns of *Harper's* he upbraided his fellow critics for not being familiar with "the universal impulse" felt by nineteenth century Europe, "which has given us the work not only of Zola, but of Tourguéneff and Tolstoï in Russia, of Björnson and Ibsen in Norway, of Valdés and Galdós in Spain, of Verga in Italy."[386] This "universal impulse" was the impulse toward brotherhood; Tolstoy, more than any other writer, was "a revelation and a delight" to Howells during the six years that he was speaking to

[384]For further references to realism in the "Editor's Study," see *Harper's*, LXXIV (April, 1887), 827–829; LXXV (July, 1887), 318; LXXVIII (Dec., 1888), 159; LXXXIII (July, 1891), 317.

[385]An incident which indicates Howells' reading of the "proprieties" occurred when Gorky came to this country in 1906, with a woman who was not his wife. Howells' own description of the episode, written to his brother, shows his kindly personal attitude toward Gorky, and also his sense of the impossibility of going against the conventions of his day. "Mark Twain and I have been having a lively time about the Russian novelist and revolutionist, Maxim Gorky; we were going to give him a great literary dinner, but he has been put out of 3 hotels with the lady who was not his wife, and M. T. has been swamped with reporters wanting to know 'how about it.' . . . He is wrong, but I feel sorry for him; he has suffered enough in his own country, except for the false relations which cannot be tolerated here. He is a simple soul and a great writer, but he cannot do impossible things." *Life in Letters*, II, 219–220. See also *My Mark Twain*, pp. 93–95. See also *The Letters and Journal of Brand Whitlock*, by Allan Nevins (New York, 1936), I, 111.

[386]*Criticism and Fiction*, p. 28. In 1887, Howells wrote an introduction for an edition of Tolstoy's *Sebastopol*, in which he expressed Tolstoy's ideas which he later repeated in *My Literary Passions*. Howells used every opportunity to educate his readers on the subject of Tolstoy through the "Editor's Study." See *Harper's*, LXXV (July, 1887), 316; *ibid.*, (Aug., 1887), 478; *ibid.*, (Sept., 1887), 638–640; LXXXI (Sept., 1890), 642; LXXXI (Oct., 1890), 802; LXXXIV (Jan., 1892), 318; LXXXII (April, 1891), 806; "The Easy Chair," *Harper's*, CXIV (Feb., 1907), 479–482.

the reading world from the "Editor's Study" precisely because he reinforced Howells' belief that behind the technique of realism lay a social philosophy of brotherhood or democracy.

Howells lifted *The Cossacks* from his shelves where it had been lying for the past five or six years, he tells us, when he had "turned the corner" of his fiftieth year—when, in fact, he had just taken over "The Study." "I did not know even Tolstoy's name when I opened it, and it was with a kind of amaze that I read it, and felt word by word, and line by line, the truth of a new art in it."[387] After reading him, Howells felt he could "never look at life in the mean and sordid way"[388] that he did before he read Tolstoy. Turgenev, Howells had formerly looked upon as the last word in literary art; now he seemed to him the first, for the lesson he had to teach was aesthetic, whereas Tolstoy's lesson was ethical. "Tolstoy awakens in his reader the will to be a man; not effectively, not spectacularly, but simply, really."[389] By pursuing not personal happiness but the happiness of the whole human family, one achieves the ethical end of man, which is more important than the aesthetic. "The supreme art in literature had its highest effect in making me set art forever below humanity."[390]

With Tolstoy fresh in his mind, Howells was not able to be silent when the Chicago anarchists were executed in 1887; he viewed with concern the telegraph strike of 1883, the engineers' strike of 1888, the Homestead strike of 1892 and the Brooklyn street car strike of 1895.[391] The purpose of art, Howells came to believe, is to lighten the burden of the people. It is not produced for artists themselves, nor even, surprising as it may seem, for the art collectors; it is produced for the masses. Moreover, writers should realize their true position in society, since "the

[387] *My Literary Passions*, p. 253.
[388] *Ibid.*, p. 257.
[389] *Ibid.*, p. 250.
[390] *Ibid.*, p. 258.
[391] *Life in Letters*, II, 24–26; 58.

author is, in the last analysis, merely a working-man." "I wish
that I could make all my fellow-artists realize that economically
they are the same as mechanics, farmers, day-laborers."[392] Perhaps, says Howells, neither the writer nor the artist of the world
will ever come into his own "as long as there are masses whom
he ought to consort with, and classes whom he cannot consort
with." The writers of the future should be instrumental in
bringing about that "human equality of which the instinct has
been divinely implanted in the human soul."[393]

In a magnificent blast from the "Editor's Study," Howells
brings into harmony all that he had for years been preaching
on the subject of realism with all that he had come to believe
on the subject of social democracy:

The pride of caste is becoming the pride of taste; but as before,
it is averse to the mass of men; it consents to know them only in
some conventionalized and artificial guise. It seeks to withdraw
itself, to stand aloof; to be distinguished and not to be identified. Democracy in literature is the reverse of all this. It wishes
to know and to tell the truth, confident that consolation and
delight are there; it does not care to paint the marvelous and
impossible for the vulgar many, or to sentimentalize and falsify
the actual for the vulgar few. Men are more like than unlike one
another; let us make them know one another better, that they
may be all humbled and strengthened with a sense of their fraternity. Neither arts, nor letters, nor sciences, except as they
somehow, clearly or obscurely, tend to make the race better and
kinder, are to be regarded as serious interests; they are all lower
than the rudest crafts that feed and house and clothe, for except
they do this office they are idle; and they cannot do this except
from and through the truth.[394]

[392]"The Man of Letters as a Man of Business," *Literature and Life*, pp. 33-34.
[393]*Ibid.*, p. 35. Arms points out that the "equality" Howells most trusted
was that of the middle class. He grew more and more distrustful of the
laboring class as believers in equality. George Arms, *The Social Criticism
of William Dean Howells*, unpublished thesis, New York University
(1939), 253-56.
[394]The "Editor's Study," *Harper's*, LXXV (Sept., 1887), 639. See also
Howells' address on the occasion of the dinner given in his honor on
his seventy-fifth birthday, *North American Review*, CCXII (July, 1920), 11,

Realism, then, grows from a genuine respect for the common man, and is therefore the basis of a democratic literature; the romantic grows from the aristocratic and the desire for the unusual; it is essentially undemocratic.

From an appreciation of the commonplace in fiction as a limitless source of interest and amusement, Howells developed a belief in the necessity for such an appreciation on the part of critics and novelists as well, if we are ever to have a truly democratic, hence truly American, literature. He came to believe that it is "quite impossible for criticism in sympathy only with class interests, growing out of class education, and admitting only class claims to the finer regard and respect of readers, to do justice to the American school of fiction."[395] In a penetrating discussion of Matthew Arnold's criticism of American society, that we have no "distinction," Howells pointed out that the idea of distinction is essentially a snobbish one. "Such beauty and such grandeur as we have is common beauty, common grandeur . . . It seems to us that these conditions invite the artist to the study and the appreciation of the common, and to the portrayal in every art of those finer and higher aspects which unite rather than sever humanity, if he would thrive in our new order of things . . . The arts must become democratic, and then we shall have the expression of America in art."[396] At the time that Howells was moving rapidly in his social thought toward socialism, in his thought as a critic he was more and more closely identified with democracy.

3. *The Easy Chair*

In March, 1892, Howells left "The Study," convinced that

---

in which Howells' anti-slavery doctrines are expanded to include anti-wage-slavery beliefs. See also H. G. Belcher, "Howells's Opinions on the Religious Conflicts of His Age," *American Literature*, XV (Nov., 1943), 274. Here the writer points out that Howells, as early as 1866, saw the relationship between democracy and Christianity, which seemed to him "the vital force in American democracy."

[395]The "Editor's Study," *Harper's*, LXXXI (July, 1890), 317.
[396]*Ibid.*, LXXVII (July, 1888), 317–318.

nothing more was to be gained by his arguments for realism. He packed up his pictures and busts of "canonized realists," "not, indeed, with the intention of setting them up in another place, but chiefly to save them from the derision and dishonor of the street."[397] For six unhappy months he became editor of the *Cosmopolitan*, in the hope, he said, of "freedom from the anxiety of placing [his] stories and chaffering about prices, and relief from the necessity of making quantity," and also with the hope that he could "do something for humanity as well as the humanities."[398] Howells' work on the *Cosmopolitan* began with the May, 1892, issue, but from the start the association was unhappy, and on June 30 he wrote his father that his name would come off the title-page after August. The reason he gave for the break was "hopeless incompatibility."[399]

Howells' association with Harper did not altogether lapse, however, during the eight years after he left "The Study" and before he took over the "Easy Chair," for, from 1895 to 1898, he undertook to conduct a regular department for *Harper's Weekly*, called "Life and Letters"[400] and contributed to *Literature*, another Harper publication. But he did gain freedom from arduous editorial duties, and enjoyed a period of amazing activity. Howells published a dozen or more plays during these years, eleven novels, two volumes of short stories, four or five volumes of reminiscences or memoirs, a book of poetry, and a book of travel. He sailed to France to visit his son in 1894;[401] he took a trip to Germany for three months to profit by the

---

[397]*Ibid.*, LXXXIV (March, 1892), 643.

[398]*Life in Letters*, II, 19.

[399]*Ibid.*, p. 24.

[400]The department continued for eighty-eight numbers. Many of the papers were later collected in book form, and published under the title *Literature and Life* (1902). Howells contributed to *Literature* from May, 1898, to November, 1899.

[401]Howells was in Paris for only a week when a cable reporting that his father had had a stroke made him return at once to this country. Howells visited his father for two weeks in Jefferson on his return. William Cooper Howells died August 28, 1894. *Life in Letters*, II, 52-53.

waters of Carlsbad in 1897; he undertook in 1899 a lecture tour which extended into the West as far as Kansas and Nebraska. Though financially successful in the venture, Howells suffered under the necessity of facing large and unfamiliar audiences. "Read *Heroes and Heroines* last night to 450 refrigerators," he wrote from Grinnell, Iowa. Lecturing, he said, "would be pleasant if I liked it, and if it did not kill me; but I don't, and it does."[402] "I look back on my lecturing with terror!" he wrote to his daughter after it was over, "What a hideous trade!" And the worst of it was, he complained to Mark Twain, he was successful.[403]

When Howells returned to Franklin Square,[404] full of plans for a history of Venice,[405] he found his relationship to the house of Harper and Brothers distinctly altered. In the first place Harper had recently been rescued from failure by J. P. Morgan, who took it over and put in Colonel George Harvey as manager. "Harpers seems to be on their feet—or *somebody's* feet again, and to be moving forward. But it is all still very strange and sad, down at Franklin Square. I am doing a series of papers for the Bazar on *Heroines of Fiction*, that interests me. But my papers are reportorially spoken of as 'stories,' and I am hurried on proofs, as once I was Not."[406] The old atmosphere was gone;

[402] *Life in Letters*, II, 111–112. "Heroes and Heroines" was a paper Howells had prepared for his lecture tour. Two other lectures were "Novels" and "Heroines of Fiction." See unpublished letter to W. H. Bishop of December 25, 1899, in the Huntington Library.

[403] *Ibid.*, p. 127. See also Howells' letter to Mark Twain on the subject of lecturing, *ibid.*, pp. 119–120. Mark Twain and Howells had, at various times in this busy decade, given "readings" together. See *Mark Twain's Letters*, p. 453.

[404] The year after Winifred's death Howells moved to an apartment in Boston to be near his son John, then a student at Harvard, and to allow his daughter Mildred to make her debut in Boston. In November of 1891, the family returned to New York.

[405] The history was never written, though Howells sent a fairly detailed outline of the book to Alden at this time. See *Life in Letters*, II, 122–124. The idea had been in Howells' mind for many years. See p. lxxxiii, note 218. Compare Professor Elmore in *A Fearful Responsibility*, who also wished to write a history of Venice, and Theodore Colville of *Indian Summer*, who planned a history of Florence.

[406] *Life in Letters*, II, 125.

Howells, moreover, found his own business relation to the House quite different from the loose understanding of the days of "The Study." In December, 1900, he took over the "Easy Chair," and in a letter to his sister, he reported, "I am very happy . . . in a new relation I have formed with Harpers which . . . includes taking all I write at a fixed price, and making me literary adviser of the house. It relieves me of all anxiety about marketing my wares."[407]

By May of the following year, however, Howells is beginning to find his editorial duties irksome. "I have done no fiction since last spring,"[408] he writes to his old friend and fellow novelist-journalist, Thomas Bailey Aldrich, "except a short story—The Easy Chair, and the *N. A. Review* papers[409] having been quite enough for me. I hate criticism; I suppose my feeling must be much like your own. I never did a piece of it that satisfied me; and to write fiction, on the other hand, is a delight. Yet in my old age I seem doomed (on a fat salary) to do criticism and essays. I am ending where I began, in a sort of journalism." Though Howells continued to earn his living, and a very comfortable one it was, by journalism, he remained at heart the novelist. In spite of the very advantageous business arrangement Howells made with Harper, the "Easy Chair" often became for him the "Uneasy Chair," as he called it in a letter to Aldrich, in which he laments, "It might have been wiser for me to keep out of that place, but at 63 one likes a fixed income, even when the unfixed is not bad. Essaying has been the enemy of the novelist that was in me. One cannot do both kinds without hurt to both. If I could have held out fifteen years ago in my

---

[407]*Life in Letters*, II, 137. As editor of the "Study," Howells had earned $10,000 a year, and had engaged to bring out all his works under Harper's imprint, but at no fixed price.

[408]*Ibid.*, p. 144.

[409]Howells at that time was writing regular monthly articles for the *North American Review* as well as for *Harper's*. For a list of his contributions to the *North American Review*, see that magazine, CCXII (July, 1920), 14–16.

refusal of the Study, when Alden tempted me, I might have gone on and beat *Silas Lapham*. Now I can only dream of some leisure day doing better."[410] In an essay for *Scribner's* (1893) concerning the man of letters as a man of business,[411] Howells describes the business of writing as it was practiced in his day. All young journalists, he says, wish to turn novelists: they must be business men as well as literary men, however, and are often forced to make compromises.[412]

Some such compromise between literature and business Howells had been making ever since his arrival in New England in 1860, ostensibly to investigate the shoe factories, but actually to meet the literary men of Boston. Now, as then, he managed to maintain the compromise. One cannot escape the thought, however, that had Howells died in 1900, and never occupied the "Easy Chair" at all, his most significant critical ideas on literature and life would have been expressed. For twenty years he mailed his copy to Franklin Square, sometimes from his cottage at Kittery Point, Maine,[413] sometimes from a London hotel, sometimes from a retreat in Florida. With unfailing reg-

---

[410] *Life in Letters*, II, 138. See also "A Search for Celebrity," *Imaginary Interviews*, pp. 184–192. See also the "Editor's Study," *Harper's*, LXXX (March, 1890), 644–645.

[411] "The Man of Letters as a Man of Business," *Literature and Life*, (1902). The business of writing, as Howells saw it, is reflected in many of Howells' novels, *A Modern Instance*, *A Hazard of New Fortunes*, *The World of Chance*, *The Quality of Mercy*, and others.

[412] One is reminded of a letter written to his sister Victoria in 1856, when Howells was 19 years old, "I want to make money, and be rich and grand." *Life in Letters*, I, 14. To President Gilman Howells wrote when he was offered a professorship at Johns Hopkins, "I am by trade and by affection a writer of novels, and I cannot give up my trade, because, for one reason, I earn nearly twice as much money by it as you offer me for salary." *Life in Letters*, I, 331. When Howells died he left an estate of well over $150,000. See undated, uncaptioned newspaper clipping in the Howells-Kester letters, MS. Room, New York Public Library.

[413] Howells bought a summer house at Kittery Point, Maine, in 1902. For many years this was home to the family. In 1910, after the death of Mrs. Howells, Howells turned it over to his son, John Mead Howells, and purchased a house at York Harbor. For a description of this house, see Hamlin Garland, "Howells' Home at York Harbor," *My Friendly Contemporaries* (1932), 118–119.

ularity he managed to fill his monthly columns with pleasant,
easy essays, such as "Around a Rainy-Day Fire," and "A Day
at Bronx Park."[414] Harmless as these titles sound, one must
observe that in commenting on the pile of novels, poetry, essays
which covered his desk, Howells never missed an opportunity to
preach "that sermon which we are always preaching, in season
and out of season," the sermon on realism. "Only the steady
and steadily stirring narrative of every-day facts"[415] is interesting, he reminds the reader again and again. In 1901 Howells
reviewed with enthusiasm the first of Frank Norris's trilogy,
The Octopus—thus the old realist greeted the young naturalist.[416]
As late as 1910 Mark Twain, expressing the thought of his generation, called Howells "the first critic of the day."[417]

But Howells had no intention of battling for "truth in literature," as he did in the old days of "The Study." When asked
by one of his readers to write an article on "the function of the
critic," he replied, was not "The Study" "perpetually thunder-
ing at the gates of Fiction in Error, and no more sparing the
dead than the quick?" Did not "The Study" offend the feelings
of "that large class of dotards who believed that they read Walter
Scott all through once a year?" Did it not horrify the worshippers at the shrines of Thackeray, Dickens and Balzac? "Did not
it preach Hardy and George Eliot and Jane Austen, Valdés and
Galdós and Pardo-Bazán, Verga and Serao, Flaubert and the
Goncourts and Zola, Björnson and Ibsen, Tourguénief and

[414]These titles were given the essays when they were reprinted in
Imaginary Interviews in 1910.

[415]The "Easy Chair," *Harper's*, CXXII (April, 1911), 795.

[416]The "Easy Chair," *Harper's*, CIII (Oct., 1901), 822–827.

[417]Written in the hand of Mark Twain on the margin of the letter from
Howells to Mark Twain, which is published in *Life in Letters*, II, 278.
The manuscript letter is in the Huntington Library. The note reads, "I
reckon this spontaneous outburst from the first critic of the day is good to
keep, ain't it, Paine?" Mark Twain was evidently sorting his letters for
Paine, who was then preparing material for his life of Mark Twain. Letters
of appreciation poured in to Howells from such people as Thomas Hardy,
Arnold Bennett, William and Henry James, to mention but a few names.
The Houghton Library, Harvard.

Dostoevsky and Tolstoy, and Tolstoy, and even more Tolstoy, till its hearers slumbered in their pews? The tumult of those strenuous days yet fills our soul, and shall we again unseal their noises?" The answer is undoubtedly "No." No more "stormy reverberations from that sulphurous past, no echoes of that fierce intolerance, that tempestuous propaganda which left the apostle without a friend or follower in the aesthetic world"[418] are ever again heard from the urbane and kindly occupant of the "Easy Chair,"[419] who became in 1908 the first president of the American Academy of Arts and Letters.

Just as Howells never failed to put in a word for realism, though a milder word than we heard from "The Study," and to encourage serious young writers, such as Brand Whitlock,[420] so he continued to lift a voice of protest against the social ills of the world. In 1896, Howells wrote to a friend, "I am rather quiescent in my social thinking, just now."[421] In 1905, however, when he must have been at work on *Through the Eye of the Needle*,[422] he devoted an "Easy Chair" to a mildly satiric essay on the rich man in our society. Why should the world unite to deride him, he innocently asks, when the rich man at least returns a portion of his gains in art galleries, libraries, and fellowships. Do we, who are fortunate enough to be poor, do so well? "It could almost be desired that every man were rich, so that in some such equality we who at present are poor might not look too self-righteously on our opulent neighbors; but since this is not practicable, it behooves us, who enjoy the advantage of a comparative poverty, not to deal harshly with our less fortunate

[418]The "Easy Chair," *Harper's*, CXXII (May, 1911), 957.

[419]For further references to realism see the "Easy Chair," *Harper's*, CXXVI (March, 1913), 634–637; CXXXI (July, 1915) 310–313; CXXXIX (Nov., 1919), 925–928.

[420]See George Arms, "'Ever Devotedly Yours'" in the *Journal of the Rutgers University Library*, X (Dec., 1946), 1–19. See also unpublished letters from Brand Whitlock to Howells, in the Houghton Library, Harvard.

[421]*Life in Letters*, II, 70.

[422]See note 313 in this Introduction, on p. cxxiii.

fellows."[423] In spite of the watering down of his more radical social views, Howells spoke from the "Easy Chair" for prison reform,[424] for woman suffrage,[425] for the brotherhood of man.[426] In 1916, when the English government put to death four Irish rebels, Howells wrote a long letter of protest to the *Evening Post*;[427] in 1918, when we had entered the World War, Howells reverted to the Altrurians to explain his attitude toward war. When invasion threatened, he explained, the Altrurians did not remain neutral but adopted conscription, built a hospital for the wounded and launched a Liberty Loan.[428] "Certain hopes of truer and better conditions on which my heart was fixed twenty years ago are not less dear," he wrote in the Introduction to the Library Edition of his works. Though Howells grew old and tired, he never gave up his socialistic beliefs. When Brand Whitlock came to tea with Howells in his "cooperative, if not quite Altrurian" apartment on 57th Street, they talked of "sociology, and the Socialists." Whitlock expressed his faith in the "philosophic anarchists like Emerson and Tolstoy and Whitman and our Sam Jones," but added that he thought "we'd have

[423]*Harper's*, CXII (Dec., 1905), 151.

[424]*Ibid.*, CXX (March, 1910), 633–636. Compare Howells' comments on prisons in *A Traveler from Altruria* and in his short story "A Circle in the Water," in *A Pair of Patient Lovers* (1901).

[425]*Ibid.*, CXXI (Oct., 1910), 795–798. See also *Harper's*, CXXIV (Feb., 1912), 471–474 and CXXVII (June, 1913), 148–151: CXXXVI (Feb., 1918), 450–453. Howells marched in the Suffrage Parade of May, 1912, in New York.

[426]*Ibid.*, CXXIV (April, 1912), 796–799; CXXIV (Jan. 1912), 309–312; CXXIX (Nov., 1914), 958–961. Howells' encouragement of Paul Lawrence Dunbar should be noted here. He had already reviewed Dunbar's poetry in *Harper's Weekly*, and in 1896 wrote an introduction to his book of poetry, *Lyrics of Lowly Life*. See Dunbar's letter of appreciation in the Houghton Library, Harvard.

[427]*Life in Letters*, II, 359.

[428]The "Easy Chair," *Harper's*, CXXXVII (Sept., 1918), 589–592. See an unpublished letter to Sylvester Baxter, dated May 30, 1915, in the Huntington Library, protesting German despotism and expressing the hope that the German people may outlive it. On January 2, 1900, Howells accepted an invitation from E. W. Ordway, to become one of the vice-presidents of the Anti-Imperialist League. MS. Room, New York Public Library.

to go through Socialism to get to it." Howells replied, "That's just what I am—we'll have to pass under the yoke."[429] "But one is so limp and helpless in the presence of the injustice which underlies society, and I am getting so old,"[430] he wrote in a moment of sadness to his old friend, Mark Twain.

4. Travelling Critic

Travel books seemed to the aging Howells a form of comment, or social criticism, if you will, more attractive than diatribes on realism or blasts against the capitalistic system. "I will confess here that I have always loved the world and the pleasures which other sages pretend are so vapid."[431] He writes genially from his "Easy Chair," "It is now the May of the year that is past, and everybody is beginning to go to Europe, and in the apt disguise of a steamer-chair, got from the deck steward for a dollar, the Easy Chair is beginning to go too." He adds characteristically, "There may be a topic over there, but it is doubtful if the Easy Chair has any motive so distinct."[432] But Howells always did find a topic over there which he never failed to turn to good use, either in the form of articles or another travel book, or both.

The travel books which Howells wrote during the years he occupied the "Easy Chair" might be considered an aspect of his work as a critic—or a journalist—satisfactory to the man of business, as well as to the man of letters.[433] The extraordinary

[429] *The Letters and Journal of Brand Whitlock*, ed. by Allan Nevins, I (New York, 1936), 110–111.

[430] *Life in Letters*, II, 175. In an unpublished letter to Albert B. Paine, dated May 30, 1910, Howells discusses the speakers he would like to invite to address the "Commemorative meeting" to be held after the death of Mark Twain, suggesting that a Labor man be included. Huntington Library.

[431] *Years of My Youth*, pp. 168–169.

[432] The "Easy Chair," Harper's, CXXVIII (April, 1914), 796.

[433] In *London Films* (1906), p. 2, Howells reminds us of the many trips to England he had enjoyed before he offered his "films" to his readers: "One could have used the authority of a profound observer after the first few days in 1861 and 1865, but the experience of weeks stretching to months in

success of *Venetian Life*, republished many times since its first
appearance in 1866,[434] and of *Italian Journeys*, which as late as
1901 was reprinted in a de luxe edition with illustrations by
Joseph Pennell,[435] assured the tired editor of eager readers,
among his still untravelled American public, for the easy, unhurried words which flowed so endlessly from his pen. When
Howells returned from Europe in 1882, he had notes for two
travel books in his bag, *Tuscan Cities* (1886), and *A Little Swiss
Sojourn* (1892). From the observations,—inconclusive, amused,
critical, anecdotal,—of visits in 1904 and 1908, came not only
London Films (1906), but also *Certain Delightful English Towns*
(1906), and *Seven English Cities* (1909); from his winter in
Rome in 1908 came *Roman Holidays* (1908);[436] *Familiar Spanish
Travels* (1913) appeared after a three months visit to Spain in
1911.

"Travel is still an unexplored realm compared with that of
fiction," wrote Howells, delighted that he could thus easily
capitalize his trips abroad, "the smallest occurrence on the highway of land or sea will always command breathless attention
if properly worked up. The tragical moments of a delayed lunch
are full of fascination for any one whose train has broken down
or been snowed up short of the station where the dining car was
to have been put on."[437] Much of the material for these travel

---

1882 and 1883, clouded rather than cleared the air through which one
earliest saw one's London; and the successive pauses in 1894 and 1897, with
the longest and latest stays in 1904, have but served to confirm one in the
diffident inconclusion on all important points to which I hope the pages
following will bear witness."

[434]H. H. Boyesen reports that 40,000 copies sold by 1893. George Arms
and William M. Gibson, "Five Interviews with William Dean Howells,"
Americana, XXXVII (April 1943), 266.

[435]An enlarged edition was published in 1872 and two illustrated trade
editions in 1901.

[436]On this visit to Italy, Howells had an interview with the king of Italy,
which lasted half an hour. See letter to Paul Kester from John Mead
Howells among the unpublished letters of the Howells-Kester collection in
the MS. Room of the New York Public Library.

[437]The "Easy Chair," *Harper's*, CXXVI (March, 1913), 637.

books was, in fact, a redoing of his letters home. "He jotted down his English impressions and experiences in note form in letters to his wife," his daughter Mildred tells us, "and much that he wrote her he afterwards used in writing *Certain Delightful Towns* and *London Films*."[438] Nor did Howells intend to penetrate far beneath the surface in his role of observer. "If any one shall say that my little pictures are superficial, I shall not be able to gainsay him. I can only answer that most pictures represent the surface of things."[439] Talk of weather, of London lodging houses, the American tourist abroad, the Englishman's love of royalty, St. James Park on a Bank Holiday, flowed month by month through *Harper's Magazine*, and then was turned into handsomely illustrated books. Never is the even tenor of the familiar prose broken by a melodramatic incident, or by a disturbingly critical remark, "So very mild are the excitements, so slight the incidents, so safe and tame the adventures of modern travel!"[440]

Occasionally one is reminded of the more vigorous Howells as one reads these quietly flowing pages. When he visits the House of Commons, for example, Howells pauses to consider "how far socialism had got itself realized in London through the activities of the County Council, which are so largely in the direction of municipal control."[441] If one hears little of socialism in London, he says, "that is because it has so effectually passed from the debated principle to the accomplished fact." It has become incorporated in so many established institutions that it is accepted as something truly conservative. "It is not, as with us, still under the ban of a prejudice too ignorant to know in how many things it is already effective; but this is, of course, mainly because English administration is so much honester than

[438]*Life in Letters*, II, 186–187.
[439]*London Films*, pp. 1–2.
[440]*Ibid.*, p. 102. See also "Luxuries of Travel," *Imaginary Interviews*, p. 146.
[441]*Ibid.*, p. 69.

ours."[442] And again, Howells glances across at the women visitors in the gallery of Parliament, discretely placed behind a grille which made them look like "frescoed figures done very flat," and expresses his thoughts on the question of women in politics in England and in the United States, coming to the sensible conclusion that when women really want the vote they will have it. But for the most part, these travel essays are more concerned with tea on the terrace with Lloyd George and his wife[443] than with more serious thoughts. "I find a sort of fuzzy-mindedness very prevalent with me, here," he writes his wife, "and it seems as if clear-thinking must cost more effort than it does in America."[444]

For all Howells' "fuzzy-mindedness," and his willingness to be pleased by the English, he never quite succumbs to them, nor loses the critical smile that lights the pages of his essays. "I don't believe the English half know what they're doing things for; certainly the kinder sort don't. That's why they're able to put up with royalty and nobility; they've not thought it out; they are of the same mental texture as Jimmy Ford's basement-diners. [Henry] James says he has not known above two women who were not snobs; but there are several more men, though they are very rare, too. Monarchy is a fairy tale that grown people believe in and pay for. They speak quite awedly of royalties and titles, and won't join in the slightest smile about them."[445] Unlike Henry James, Howells never lost his American viewpoint. Strolling with his daughter through the lovely English countryside around Plymouth, he pauses to muse upon an Elizabethan mansion, set in an extensive deer park, and points out that an alien, "if he has a heart to which the ideal of human equality is dear, . . . must shrink with certain withering doubts

[442]*London Films*, pp. 69–70.
[443]Unpublished letter of Howells to Paul Kester, January 8, 1911. The MS. Room of the New York Public Library.
[444]*Life in Letters*, II, 193.
[445]*Ibid.*

as he looks on the lovely landscapes everywhere in which those who till the fields and keep the woods have no ownership, in severalty or in common." However, Howells concludes, the system works, and the landscape is serene and beautiful. "I do not say that any such anxieties spoiled the pleasure of my afternoon,"[446] he wrote, as he turned to thoughts more acceptable to the readers of *Harper's*.

On his next trip abroad, in 1908, Howells and his daughter joined Mrs. Howells and John in Rome, where the family passed the winter. Though the readers of *Harper's* now hear more of beggars, priests, and archeologists, the essays which trickle through the magazine and are finally gathered up under the title of *Roman Holidays* have much the same pleasant, instructive, anecdotal quality that one finds in the English essays. Howells' Italian is not so good as it was almost fifty years ago when he was consul in Venice, and he very soon "fell luxuriously into the habit of speaking English like a native of Rome."[447] The Howells family lived comfortably in the modern section of Rome, drove from church to art gallery to Forum accompanied by the voluble guides whom Howells overtipped, and saw no more nor less than the Italy familiar to pre-war tourists.

But the Italian essays were sufficiently read, presumably by thousands of Americans planning similar tours, to encourage Howells, several years later, to offer his *Harper's* readers his impressions of Spain, where he journeyed in 1911 with his daughter.[448] We are again mildly interested in the adventures

[446]*Certain Delightful English Towns*, p. 20. See also p. 233 for further comment of the same sort.

[447]*Roman Holidays*, p. 100.

[448]In 1909 Howells made a brief trip to Carlsbad, Germany, with his daughter, and then visited England and Wales, where he looked up the home of his ancestors, which he had previously visited in 1883. See *Life in Letters*, I, 343–45. After the death of his wife in 1910, Howells and his daughter were again in England. See an unpublished letter to W. H. Riding, dated July 4, 1910. Huntington Library. Howells writes again of the death of his wife in another unpublished letter dated July 14, 1910, addressed to Howells' old friend John Piatt, and lent to the editors by

with cab drivers, descriptions of hotels and foods, and train compartments with which *Familiar Spanish Travels* (1913) abound. Since Howells as a boy in Ohio had taught himself the Spanish language, and pored over the pages of the great Spanish authors, a certain sadness for the lost enthusiasms of his youth creeps into his mood.

All appeared fair and noble in that Spain of his which shone with such allure far across the snows through which he trudged morning and evening with his father to and from the printing-office, and made his dream of that great work [*Don Quixote*] the common theme of their talk. Now the boy is as utterly gone as the father, who was a boy too at heart, but who died a very old man many years ago; and in the place of both is another old man trammeled in his tangled memories of Spain visited and unvisited.[449]

5. The Dean Installed

The boy who had read Dante and Cervantes in the original in Ohio, lived long enough to see all that Europe had to offer him; he wished now to find a permanent home. After one last visit to England in 1913, Howells returned to New York and moved into an apartment at 130 West 57th Street, which was to be his home until his death. "I am aware of being physically weaker than I once was, and my work, which has always been so dear to me, is not so satisfactory, though it comes easier. I rattle it off at a great rate, but it does not delight me as it used to do, though now and then a little paper seems just as good as anything I ever did."[450] But often the "Easy Chairs creak along

---

Cecil Piatt. Further in the same letter Howells writes, "We are having a most interesting time, such as I would once have written her about. Well!" Howells was, on this trip, lunching and dining and talking with Galsworthy, Hewlett, Gosse, Barrie, and James.

[449]*Familiar Spanish Travels*, pp. 74–75.

[450]*Life in Letters*, II, 240. See also the unpublished letter of Howells to Paul Kester, February 25, 1913, in which Howells speaks of his weariness. The MS. Room, New York Public Library.

so heavily and slowly."[451] An added discouragement came in 1911, when Harper's attempt to launch a Library Edition of Howells' complete works failed. In spite of Harper's proud statement, in the issue of August 1911, that "perhaps no literary announcement ever made quite takes rank with this one," no more than six volumes of this edition ever appeared.

For many years before Howells' death he felt himself outmoded in the literary world in which he had been a leader. "I am comparatively a dead cult with my statues cut down and the grass growing over them in the pale moonlight,"[452] he wrote to his friend Henry James. When he turned to the current books on his desk his judgment was often unsure. Howells had stubbornly disregarded Sidney Lanier; Booth Tarkington he welcomed; about Theodore Dreiser he was silent; to Robert Herrick he wrote that he could not review his novel until he straightened him out on some of the moral questions raised by the book;[453] Joyce Kilmer he greeted in these terms, "I like you, my dear young brother, not only because you love beauty, but love decency also. There are so many of our brood I could willingly take out and step on."[454] In a long review of poetry by Frost, Lindsay, Fletcher, Aiken, Masters, Lowell, and others Howells showed sympathy for what seemed to him real and natural. But his attack on *vers libre* in this article suggests that his taste in poetry was outmoded.[455]

Howells knew, however, that the young writers would win and that he was on the way out. In 1915 he wrote to Henry James, "A change has passed upon things, we can't deny it; I

[451]*Ibid.*, 371.
[452]*Ibid.*, 350.
[453]*Ibid.*, 262.
[454]*Ibid.*, 352–353
[455]*Harper's*, CXXXI (Sept., 1915), 634–637. Compare Howells' insistence as a young critic that Whitman was not a poet. *Life in Letters*, I, 116. Howells' review of Whitman's *November Boughs* is written in the same spirit as his review of *Drum Taps* in 1866. See the "Editor's Study," *Harper's*, LXXVIII (Feb., 1889), 488.

could not 'serialize' a story of mine now in any American magazines, thousands of them as there are."[456] The following November, for the first time in fifty years, a manuscript of Howells was rejected, and by *Harper's*, to whom he was obligated to submit all his material before marketing it elsewhere. "In fifty years the inevitable acceptance of my work everywhere had perhaps spoiled me for refusal; but the first thing I offered *Harper's*, some months ago, was unconditionally refused."[457] Only temporarily daunted by the rebuffs of a changing world, Howells continued to find happiness in writing as he travelled back and forth from New York to Florida, from Boston to North Carolina, in quest of warmth and health. With his old power to adjust to the times, he wrote in 1916 from Kittery Point, where he was visiting his son's family, that he was "hoping to finish the scenario of my next novel, *The Home-Towners*. I bring moving-picture folks into it; you know they abound in St. Augustine, where I have put the scene of the story. It will be quite different from all my other things."[458] The novel was never finished, nor was the autobiographical volume, *Years of My Middle Life*, pushed beyond the preliminary jottings.[459] On his death bed, in the spring of 1920, Howells began his unfinished essay on Henry James,[460] the friend and critic who had encouraged him in his best work, and to whom his thoughts reverted in the end.

One of the fruits of the friendship between Howells and James was that each made a final critical appraisal of the other before his death. On February 19, 1912, Henry James wrote an "open letter" from England to be read at the dinner held in New York in honor of Howells' seventy-fifth birthday.[461] For almost fifty

[456]*Life in Letters*, II, 349.
[457]*Ibid.*, 365.
[458]*Ibid.*, 363.
[459]*Ibid.*, 387.
[460]*Ibid.*, 394–399.
[461]*The Letters of Henry James*, II, 224–226.

years these two leading novelists of their day had conversed and corresponded with each other; James was, therefore, peculiarly able to understand the lasting qualities of this many-sided writer, who began his career as a poet, ended it as a critic, touched greatness as a novelist and never ceased to be a journalist. Of Howells' books, he wrote:

They make a great array, a literature in themselves, your studies of American life, so acute, so direct, so disinterested, so preoccupied but with the fine truth of the case . . . The *real* affair of the American case and character, as it met your view and brushed your sensibility, that was what inspired and attached you . . . you gave yourself to it with an incorruptible faith. You saw your field with a rare lucidity; you saw all it had to give in the way of the romance of the real and the interest and the thrill and the charm of the common, as one may put it; the character and the comedy, the point, the pathos, the tragedy, the particular home-grown humanity under your eyes and your hand and with which the life all about you was closely interknitted. Your hand reached out to these things with a fondness that was in itself a literary gift, and played with them as the artist only and always can play: freely, quaintly, incalculably, with all the assurance of his fancy and his irony, and yet with that fine taste for the truth and the pity and the meaning of the matter which keeps the temper of observation both sharp and sweet . . . what I wished mainly to put on record is my sense of that unfailing, testifying truth in you which will keep you from ever being neglected. The critical intelligence . . . has not at all begun to render you its tribute . . . your really beautiful time will come."

SELECTED BIBLIOGRAPHY

The present editors have compiled this Bibliography from the one made by George Arms and William M. Gibson for the first edition of *Representative Selections* in 1950. Critical comments on the entries have been eliminated to make room for as many items as possible from the Bibliographies compiled by the same two scholars for *The Howells Sentinel*. A number of titles which have appeared since September, 1960, have been added. We are indebted, as are all scholars in American literature, to the bibliographical staffs of *American Literature, Publications of the Modern Language Association,* and *Abstracts of English Studies.*

I. *Bibliographies*

Arms, George, and Gibson, William M. Bibliographies in *The Howells Sentinel*. See listing below.

Cooke, D. G. "Bibliography," in *William Dean Howells, A Critical Study*. New York: [1922], pp. 257–72.

Elliott, F. M., and Lucy Clark. *The Barrett Library: William Dean Howells*. Charlottesville: University of Virginia Press, 1959.

Firkins, O. W. "Bibliography," in *William Dean Howells, A Study*. Cambridge, Mass.: 1924, pp. 339–46.

Gibson, W. M., and Arms, George. *A Bibliography of William Dean Howells*. New York: 1948. First published in the *Bulletin of the New York Public Library*, L-LI (Sept., 1946–August, 1947). (Check lists, collations, annual register, selected critical writings, and name index. The section, "Selected Critical Writings," forms the basis of the bibliography hereinunder, but frequent additions to it have been made.)

Graham, Philip. "American First Editions" at TxU: XI. William Dean Howells (1837–1920). *The Library Chronicle of the University of Texas*, VI (Spring, 1958), 17–21.

Hartwick, Harry. "William Dean Howells," in *A History of American Letters,* by W. F. Taylor. New York: [1936], pp. 559–62.

Johnson, Merle. "William Dean Howells," in *American First Editions,* Fourth Edition. Revised and enlarged by Jacob Blanck. New York: 1942, pp. 268–73.

[Johnson, T. H.] "William Dean Howells," in *Literary History of the United States.* New York: 1948, III, pp. 571–76.

Kohn, J. S. Van E., and Michael Papantonio. *William Dean Howells 1837–1920.* (Sales catalogue). New York: Seven Gables Bookshop, 1956.

Leary, Lewis. *Articles on American Literature Appearing in Current Periodicals,* 1920–1945. Durham, N.C.: 1947, pp. 149–50.

Leary, Lewis. "Doctoral Dissertations in American Literature, 1933–1948." *American Literature,* XX (May, 1948), 184–85. (Lists 15 dissertations. For earlier work, see *ibid.,* IV, 439 [Jan., 1933]. For later dissertations and research, see "Research in Progress," *PMLA* and *American Literature.*)

Lee, Albert. "A Bibliography of the First Editions of the Writings of William Dean Howells." *Book Buyer,* XIV (March, April, 1897), 143–47, 269–74.

Lydenberg, John, and Cady, Edwin. "The Howells Revival: Rounds Two and Three." *New England Quarterly* XXXII (Sept., 1959), 394–407.

Quinn, A. H. "Bibliography and Play-List," in *A History of the American Drama from the Civil War to the Present Day.* New York: 1943, I, 364–66. (Best list of plays and productions. Supplementary material is in G. C. D. Odell's *Annals of the New York Stage* [New York, 1927–49].)

Reeves, J. K. "Howells Divided." *Autograph Collectors' Journal,* V (Winter, 1953), 55–56.

Reeves, J. K. "The Literary Manuscripts of W. D. Howells: A Descriptive Finding List." *Bulletin of the New York Public*

Library, LXII (June and July, 1958), 267–78, 350–63. Also reprinted separately under the same title. Supplement to appear in 1961.

[Van Doren, Carl.] "William Dean Howells," in *Cambridge History of American Literature.* New York: 1921, IV, pp. 663–66.

Woodress, James. "The Dean's Comeback: Four Decades of Howells Scholarship." *Studies in Language and Literature* (University of Texas), II (Spring, 1960), 115–23.

Woodress, James. *Howells and Italy.* Durham, N.C.: Duke University Press, 1952.

II. *Texts*

"The Writings of William Dean Howells, Library Edition." New York: [1911]. 6 volumes. *My Literary Passions* and *Criticism & Fiction, The Landlord at Lion's Head, Literature and Life, London Films* and *Certain Delightful English Towns, Literary Friends and Acquaintance* [with *My Mark Twain*], *A Hazard of New Fortunes.*

Contributions to newspapers and periodicals. Much remains uncollected. The major *regular* appearances (itemized in Gibson and Arms, *A Bibliography of William Dean Howells*) are cited below:

Critical articles, *North American Review* (1864–69, 1872, 1888, 1894, 1899–1916). See *ibid.,* CCXII, (July, 1920), 14–16 for list.

Reviews, *Atlantic Monthly* (1866–81). See *Atlantic Index* for those ascribed to Howells.

"Editor's Study." *Harper's Magazine* (1886–92).

"Life and Letters." *Harper's Weekly* (1895–98).

"American Letter." *Literature* (1898).

"Editor's Easy Chair." *Harper's Magazine* (1900–20).

Adrian, A. A. "Augustus Hoppin to William Dean Howells." *New England Quarterly*, XXIV (March, 1951), 84–89.

Arms, George, and Gibson, W. M., eds. "Five Interviews with William Dean Howells." *Americana*, XXXVII (April, 1943), 257–95. (With Boyesen, Crane, Dreiser, Brooks, and Kilmer.)

Arms, George, ed. "Howells's Unpublished Prefaces." *New England Quarterly*, XVII (Dec. 1944), 580–91.

Arms, George. " 'Ever Devotedly Yours'—the Whitlock-Howells Correspondence." *Journal of the Rutgers University Library*, X (Dec., 1946), 1–19.

Arms, George, ed. *The Rise of Silas Lapham*. Rinehart Editions. New York: Rinehart & Company, 1949.

Arms, George, ed. *A Hazard of New Fortunes*. American Everyman's Library. New York: E. P. Dutton and Co., 1952.

Arms, George, W. M. Gibson, and Frederic C. Marston, Jr., eds. *Prefaces to Contemporaries* (1882–1920). Gainesville, Fla.: Scholars' Facsimiles & Reprints, 1957.

Ayers, R. W. "W. D. Howells and Stephen Crane: Some Unpublished Letters." *American Literature*, XXVIII, no. 4 (Jan., 1957), 469–77.

Baum, J. H., ed. *Stephen Crane (1871–1900): An Exhibition*. New York: Columbia University Libraries, 1956, pp. 14–15. (Letters by Howells to Cora and Stephen Crane.)

Brooks, Van Wyck, ed. *A Hazard of New Fortunes*. New York: Bantam Books, 1960.

Brooks, Van Wyck. "Introduction," *Their Wedding Journey*. Greenwich, Conn.: Fawcett Publications, Inc., 1960.

Cady, E. H., ed. *The Rise of Silas Lapham*. Boston: Houghton Mifflin Company, 1957.

Cady, E. H. "Howells Bibliography: A 'Find' and a Clarification." *Studies in Bibliography*, XII (1959), 230–33.

Cairns, W. B. *Annie Kilburn*. New York: [1919].

Carter, Everett, ed. *The Rise of Silas Lapham.* New York: Harper & Brothers, 1958.

Clark, H. H., ed. *The Rise of Silas Lapham.* Modern Library College Editions. New York: The Modern Library, 1951.

Commager, H. S., ed. *Selected Writings of William Dean Howells.* New York: Random House, 1950. (*The Rise of Silas Lapham, A Modern Instance, A Boy's Town, My Mark Twain.*)

Coyle, L. P. "Howells' Campaign Biography of Rutherford B. Hayes: A Series of Letters." *Ohio Historical Quarterly,* LXVI (Oct., 1957), 391–406.

Coyle, L. P. "Restoration of a Howells Letter." *Mark Twain Journal,* XI, 12, 15 (Summer, 1960).

Crowder, Richard. "American Nestor: Six Unpublished Letters from Howells to Ade." *Bucknell Review,* VII (March, 1958), 144–49.

Duffy, Charles. "An Unpublished Letter: Howells to Stedman." *American Literature,* XXX (Nov., 1958), 369–70.

Gibson, W. M., ed. *A Modern Instance.* Boston: Houghton Mifflin Company, 1957.

Gibson, W. M., ed. "Novel-Writing and Novel Reading: An Impersonal Explanation." *Bulletin of the New York Public Library,* LXII (Jan., 1958), 15–34. Reprinted in *Howells and James: A Double Billing.* New York: The New York Public Library, 1958, pp. 5–24.

Gibson, W. M., ed. *Indian Summer.* American Everyman's Library. New York: E. P. Dutton and Co., 1951.

Hellman, G. S., ed. "The Letters of Howells to Higginson," in *Twenty-Seventh Annual Report of the Bibliophile Society,* 1901–29. Boston: 1929, pp. 17–56.

Howells, Mildred, ed. *Life in Letters of William Dean Howells.* Garden City, N.Y.: 1928, 2 volumes.

Jones, H. M. "Introduction," in *The Rise of Silas Lapham.* "The World's Classics," London: [1948].

Jones, H. M., ed. *A Traveler from Altruria.* New York: Sagamore Press, 1957.

Kirk, Rudolf, and Clara Kirk. *Criticism and Fiction and Other Essays.* New York: New York University Press, 1959.

Kirk, Clara, and Rudolf Kirk. "Two Howells Letters." *Journal of the Rutgers University Library,* XXI (1957), 1–7.

Kirk, Clara, and Rudolf Kirk. "Letters to an 'Enchanted Guest': W. D. Howells to Edmund Gosse." *Journal of the Rutgers University Library,* XXII (June, 1959), 1–25.

Kirk, Clara, and Rudolf Kirk. "*Niagara Revisited,* by W. D. Howells, The Story of Its Publication and Suppresesion." *Essays in Literary History presented to J. Milton French,* ed. by Rudolf Kirk and C. F. Main. (New Brunswick, New Jersey, 1960.)

Kirk, Clara, and Rudolf Kirk. *Letters Of An Altrurian Traveller* (*1893–94*). A Facsimile Reproduction with an Introduction. (Scholars' Facsimiles & Reprints: Gainesville, Fla., 1961.)

Marston, F. C., Jr. "An Early Howells Letter." *American Literature,* XVIII (May, 1946), 163–65. (A letter to his brother, dated April 10, 1857.)

Meserve, W. J., ed. *The Complete Plays of W. D. Howells.* New York: New York University Press, 1960.

Richardson, L. N. "Men of Letters and the Hayes Administration." *New England Quarterly,* XV (March, 1942), 117–27. (Contains about ten Howells letters.)

Sabine, Lillian. *The Rise of Silas Lapham.* New York: 1927. (Based upon Howells' novel, this play was first produced by the Theatre Guild in 1919.)

Schiffman, Joseph. "Mutual Indebtedness: Unpublished Letters of Edward Bellamy to William Dean Howells." *Harvard Library Bulletin,* XII (Autumn, 1958), 363–74.

Shuman, R. B. "The Howells-Lowell Correspondence: A New Item." *American Literature,* XXXI (Nov., 1959), 338–40.

Smith, H. N., and William M. Gibson, eds. *Mark Twain-Howells Letters: The Correspondence of Samuel L. Clemens and William D. Howells, 1872–1910.* 2 volumes. Cambridge: The Belknap Press of Harvard University Press, 1960.

Stronks, J. B. "An Early Autobiographical Letter by William Dean Howells." *New England Quarterly,* XXXIII (June, 1960), 240–42.

Uncollected letters. Numerous autobiographies and biographies contain one or several letters by Howells. For additional letters, see especially the articles cited under "Biography and Criticism" by Arms, Cady, Drake, Ferguson, Kirk, Richardson, Starke, and others.

Walton, C. C., ed. *Life of Abraham Lincoln.* Bloomington: Indiana University Press, 1960.

Ward, J. W. "Another Howells Anarchist Letter." *American Literature,* XXII (Jan., 1951), 489–90.

Woodress, James. "The Lowell-Howells Friendship: Some Unpublished Letters." *New England Quarterly,* XXVI (Dec., 1953), 523–28.

III. *Biography and Criticism*

A. *Books about Howells*

Bennett, G. N. *William Dean Howells: The Development of a Novelist.* Norman: University of Oklahoma Press, 1959.

Brooks, V. W. *Howells: His Life and World.* New York: E. P. Dutton and Co., 1959.

Cady, E. H. *The Road to Realism: The Early Years, 1837–1885, of William Dean Howells.* Syracuse: Syracuse University Press, 1956.

Cady, E. H. *The Realist at War.* Syracuse, N.Y.: Syracuse University Press, 1958.

Carter, Everett. *Howells and the Age of Realism.* Philadelphia: J. B. Lippincott Co., 1954.

Cooke, D. G. *William Dean Howells, A Critical Study.* New York: [1922].

Firkins, O. W. *William Dean Howells, A Study.* Cambridge, Mass.: 1924.

Fryckstedt, O. W. *In Quest of America: A Study of Howells' Early Development as a Novelist.* Upsala, 1958. Cambridge: Harvard University Press, 1959.

Harvey, Alexander. *William Dean Howells, A Study of the Achievement of a Literary Artist.* New York: 1917.

Hough, R. L. *The Quiet Rebel: William Dean Howells as Social Commentator.* Lincoln: University of Nebraska Press, 1959.

Kirk, Clara, and Rudolf Kirk. *William Dean Howells.* New York: Twayne Publishers, 1962.

Kirk, Clara. *W. D. Howells, Traveler From Altruria.* Rutgers University Press, 1962.

B. *Books Containing Comment on Howells.*

Ahnebrink, Lars. *The Beginnings of Naturalism in American Fiction.* Cambridge, Mass.: Harvard University Press, 1950, pp. 129–35 and *passim.*

Austin, J. C. *Fields of the Atlantic Monthly: Letters to an Editor, 1861–1870.* San Marino, California: The Huntington Library, 1953, pp. 139–63.

Boynton, P. H. "Howells," in *Literature and American Life.* Boston: 1936, pp. 743–48. Cf. *A History of American Literature* (1919).

Brooks, V. W. "Howells in Cambridge," "Howells and James," "Howells in New York," in *New England, Indian Summer, 1865–1915.* New York: 1940, pp. 204–23, 224–49, 373–94.

Brooks, Van Wyck. *The Confident Years, 1885–1915.* New York: E. P. Dutton and Co., 1952, pp. 141–46.

Calverton, V. F. "From Sectionalism to Nationalism," in *The Liberation of American Literature*. New York: 1932, pp. 375–82.

Cargill, Oscar. *The Novels of Henry James*. New York: Macmillan, 1961.

Chase, Richard. *The American Novel and Its Tradition*. Garden City: Doubleday Anchor Books, 1957, pp. 177–84. (On *The Vacation of the Kelwyns*.)

Clark, H. H. "Howells," in *Literary Criticism, Pope to Croce*, ed. G. W. Allen and H. H. Clark. New York: [1941], pp. 562–65.

Cowie, Alexander. "William Dean Howells," in *The Rise of the American Novel*. New York: [1948], pp. 653–701.

Falk, R. P. "The Literary Criticism of the Genteel Decades, 1870–1900," *The Development of American Literary Criticism*. Chapel Hill: The University of North Carolina Press, 1955, pp. 113–57, *passim*.

Garland, Hamlin. "Howells," in *American Writers on American Literature*, ed. John Macy. New York: 1931, pp. 285–97.

Gettman, R. A. "Turgenev in England and America." *University of Illinois Studies in Language and Literature*, XXVII (1941), 51–63.

Gohdes, Clarence. *The Literature of the American People*. New York: Appleton-Century-Crofts, 1951, pp. 665–80.

Gosse, E. W. "To W. D. Howells," in *From Shakespeare to Pope*. New York: 1885, p. iii. Reprinted *Critic*, n.s. IV (Sept. 19, 1885), 139. (Dedicatory poem.)

Harlow, Virginia. *Thomas Sargeant Perry*. Durham, N.C.: Duke University Press, 1950, *passim*.

[Haight, G. S.] "Realism Defined: William Dean Howells," in *Literary History of the United States*, ed. Robert E. Spiller, *et al*. New York: 1948, II, pp. 885–98.

Hartwick, Harry. "Sweetness and Light," in *The Foreground of American Fiction*. New York: [1934], pp. 315–40.

Hearn, Lafcadio. *Essays on American Literature,* eds. Albert Mordell and Sanki Ichikawa. Tokyo: 1929, pp. 189–93, 238–44, 248–50. First printed New Orleans *Times-Democrat* (June 6, 1886, April 12, 1887, May 29, 1887).

Hicks, Granville. "William Dean Howells," in *The Great Tradition*. New York: 1933, pp. 84–99.

Hoffman, F. J. "Henry James, William D. Howells and the Art of Fiction," *The Modern Novel in America 1900–1950*. Chicago: Regnery, 1951, pp. 1–27.

Josephson, Matthew. "Those Who Stayed," in *Portrait of the Artist as American*. New York: [1930], pp. 161–66.

Kazin, Alfred. "The Opening Struggle for Realism," in *On Native Ground*. New York: [1942], pp. 3–50.

Knight, G. C. *The Critical Period in American Literature*. Chapel Hill: University of North Carolina Press, 1951, *passim*.

Lewis, Sinclair. "The American Fear of Literature," in E. A. Karlfeldt's *Why Sinclair Lewis Got the Nobel Prize*. New York: [1931], pp. 20–22.

McMahon, Helen. *Criticism of Fiction: A Study of Trends in the Atlantic Monthly 1857–1898*. New York: Bookman Associates, 1952, p. 189.

Macy, John. "Howells," in *The Spirit of American Literature*. Garden City: 1913, pp. 278–95.

Mencken, H. L. "The Dean," in *Prejudices, First Series*. New York: 1919, pp. 52–58.

Mencken, H. L. *American Language*, Fourth Edition. New York: 1938, p. 168 n.

Mott, F. L. *A History of American Magazines*. Cambridge, Mass.: 1938, II, III, *passim*.

Orcutt, W. D. "Italian Dividends," in *Celebrities off Parade*. Chicago: 1935, pp. 121–28.

Parrington, V. L. "William Dean Howells and the Realism of the Commonplace," in *Main Currents in American Thought*. New York: 1930, III, 241–53.

Pattee, F. L. "The Classical Reaction," in *A History of American Literature Since 1870*. New York: 1915, pp. 197–217.

Pattee, F. L. "Following the Civil War," in *The Development of the American Short Story*. New York: 1923, pp. 208–11.

Phelps, W. L. "William Dean Howells," in *Essays on Modern Novelists*. New York: 1910, pp. 56–81.

Pizer, Donald. *Hamlin Garland's Early Work and Career*. Berkeley: University of California, 1960.

Pritchard, J. P. "William Dean Howells," in *Return to the Fountains*. Durham: 1942, pp. 135–47.

Pritchard, John Paul. *Criticism in America*. Norman: University of Oklahoma Press, 1956, pp. 163–75.

Smith, Bernard. "Democracy and Realism, III," in *Forces in American Criticism*. New York: [1939], pp. 158–75.

Spiller, R. E. *The Cycle of American Literature*. New York: The Macmillan Company, 1955, pp. 113–119.

Stallman, R. W., and Lillian Gilkes, eds. *Stephen Crane: Letters*. New York: New York University Press, 1960, *passim*.

Stoddard, R. H., ed. "W. D. Howells," in *Poet's Homes*. Boston: [1877], pp. 119–38.

Taylor, W. F. "Comedy, Ethics, and Economics: William Dean Howells," in *A History of American Letters*. New York: [1936], pp. 295–303.

Trent, W. P. "Mr. Howells and Romanticism," in *The Authority of Criticism and Other Essays*. New York: 1899, pp. 259–67.

Underwood, J. C. "William Dean Howells and Altruria," in *Literature and Insurgency*. New York: 1914, pp. 87–129.

Vanderbilt, Kermit. *Charles Eliot Norton: Apostle of Culture in a Democracy.* Cambridge: The Belknap Press of Harvard University Press, 1959, pp. 150–58 *et passim.*

Van Doren, Carl. "Howells, May, 1920, Eulogium," in *The Roving Critic.* New York: 1923, pp. 69–80.

Van Doren, Carl. "Howells and Realism," in *The American Novel, 1789–1939.* New York: 1940, pp. 120–36.

Wagenknecht, Edward. *Cavalcade of the American Novel.* New York: Henry Holt and Co., 1952, pp. 127–44.

Wasserstom, William. *Heiress of All the Ages.* Minneapolis: University of Minnesota Press, 1959, pp. 36–37, 84–87, *et passim.*

Weber, Carl J. *The Rise and Fall of James Ripley Osgood.* Waterville: The Colby College Press, 1959, *passim.*

Williams, S. T. "Literature of the New America," in *The American Spirit in Letters,* volume XI of *The Pageant of America.* New Haven: 1926, pp. 257–60. (Illustrations with text.)

Williams, S. T. *The Spanish Background of American Literature.* New Haven: Yale University Press, 1955. II, pp. 240–67.

Winter, William. "Vagrant Comrades," in *Old Friends.* New York: 1909, pp. 89–92.

C. *Articles and Reviews.*

Abel, Darrel, ed. " 'Howells or James?'–An Essay by Henry Blake Fuller." *Modern Fiction Studies,* III (Summer, 1957), 159–64.

Adams, Brooks. "The Undiscovered Country." *International Review.* IX (Aug., 1880), 149–54.

[Adams, Henry.] Review of *Their Wedding Journey. North American Review,* CXIV (April, 1872), 444–45.

Alden, H. M. "Editor's Study." *Harper's Monthly*, CXXXIV (May, 1917), 903–04. (At his eightieth birthday.)

[Aldrich, T. B.] "Mr. Howells's New Book." *Atlantic Monthly*, XLVIII (Sept., 1881), 402–05. (Review of *A Fearful Responsibility*.)

Amacher, A. W. "The Genteel Primitivist and the Semi-Tragic Octoroon." *New England Quarterly*, XXIX (June, 1956), 216–27. (On An *Imperative Duty*.)

American Academy of Arts and Letters. "Public Meeting Held at the Stuart Gallery, New York Public Library, New York, March 1st, 1921, in Memory of William D. Howells." *American Academy Proceedings*, II, 1–21 (July 1, 1921). Reprinted as *Public Meeting . . . in Honor of William Dean Howells*. New York: 1922. (Tributes by W. M. Sloane, Juan Riaño, A. M. Huntington, Roland Ricci, Giovanni Verga, Ciro Trabalza, R. U. Johnson, H. C. de Wiart, Brand Whitlock, Stephen Leacock, J. J. Jusserand, Rudyard Kipling, John Burroughs, Robert Grant, Augustus Thomas, J. L. Williams, Brander Matthews, and Henry Van Dyke.)

Anicetti, Luigi. "William Dean Howells, Console a Venezia (1861–1865)." *Nuova Rivista Storica*, XLI (1957), 87–106.

Anon. "The Earlier and Later Work of Mr. Howells." *Lippincott's*, XXX (Dec., 1882), 604–08. (Review of *A Modern Instance*.)

Anon. "Novels of American Life," *Edinburgh Review*, CLXXXVII (April, 1898), 386–414. Reprinted in *Literary Digest*, XVI (June 25, 1898), 761–62.

Anon. "Mr. Howells." *Literary Digest*, LXV (May 29, 1920), 34–35. (Abstracts of tributes.)

Anon. "William Dean Howells, Printer, Journalist, Poet, Novelist." *Literary Digest*, LXV (June 12, 1920), 53–4, 57. (Abstracts of biographical accounts.)

Anon. "Mr. Howells in England." *Literary Digest*, LXV (June 19, 1920), 37. (Abstracts of British tributes.)

Anon. "Mr. Howells's Latest Novel." *Nation,* L (June 5, 1890), 454–55. (Review of *A Hazard of New Fortunes.*)

Anon. "Smiling Aspects of Life." *Times Literary Supplement* (Oct. 9, 1948), 568. (Review of *The Rise of Silas Lapham,* ed. H. M. Jones.)

Anon. "Howells at Home." New York *Tribune* (Jan. 25, 1880), 3. First printed Boston *Herald.* (Descriptive.)

Anon. Review of *Poems of Two Friends. Saturday Press,* III (Jan. 28, 1860), 1.

Anon. "Scott's Latest Critics." *Saturday Review,* LXVII (May 4, 1889), 521–22.

Anon. "William Dean Howells." *Saturday Review of Literature,* XV (March 13, 1937), 8. (Assays reputation.)

Archer, William. "The Novelist as Critic." *Illustrated London News,* XCIX (Aug. 8, 1891), 175.

Arms, George. "Further Inquiry into Howells's Socialism. *Science and Society,* III (Spring, 1939), 245–48.

[Arms, George.] "Howells' *A Hazard of New Fortunes.*" *Explicator,* I (Nov., 1942), 14.

Arms, George. "The Literary Background of Howells's Social Criticism." *American Literature,* XIV (Nov., 1942), 260–76.

Arms, George, and Gibson, W. M. " 'Silas Lapham,' 'Daisy Miller,' and the Jews." *New England Quarterly,* XVI (March, 1943), 118–22.

Arms, George. "Howells' New York Novel: Comedy and Belief." *New England Quarterly,* XXI (Sept., 1948), 313–25.

Arms, George, and Wasserstrom, William, "That Psychological Stain and a Rejoinder." *New England Quarterly,* XXXIII (June, 1960), 243–245.

Atherton, Gertrude. "Why is American Literature Bourgeois?" *North American Review,* CLXXVIII (May, 1904), 771–81.

Atherton, Gertrude. "Gertrude Atherton Assails 'The Powers.' "

New York *Times,* V (Dec. 29, 1907), 2. Reprinted *Current Literature,* XLIV (Feb., 1908), 158–60.

Bass, A. L. "The Social Consciousness of William Dean Howells." *New Republic,* XXVI (April 13, 1921), 192–94.

Baxter, Sylvester. "Howells and Aldrich." Boston *Sunday Herald* (July 11, 1880), p. 10.

Baxter, Sylvester. "Howells's Latest Novel" *A Hazard of New Fortunes.* Boston *Herald* (December 26, 1889), p. 4.

Beach, J. W. Review of Cooke's *Howells. Journal of English and Germanic Philology,* XXII (July, 1923), 451–54.

Beach, J. W. "An American Master." *Yale Review,* n.s. XV (Jan., 1926), 399–401. (Reviews of Firkins' *Howells* and Phelps' *Howells, James, Bryant.*)

Becker, George J. "William Dean Howells: The Awakening of Conscience." *College English,* XIX (April, 1958), 283–91.

Behrens, Ralph. "Howells' 'A Hazard of New Fortunes.'" *Explicator,* XVIII (June, 1960), item 52.

Belcher, H. G. "Howells's Opinions on the Religious Conflicts of His Age As Exhibited in Magazine Articles." *American Literature,* XV (Nov., 1943), 262–78.

Berti, Luigi. "Saggio su William Dean Howells." *Inventorio,* V (Jan.-Sept., 1953), 49–62.

Betts, W. W., Jr. "The Relations of William Dean Howells to German Life and Letters." *Anglo-German and American-German Crosscurrents.* Chapel Hill: University of North Carolina Press, 1957. I, 189–239.

Bishop, W. H. "Mr. Howells in Beacon Street, Boston," *Critic,* n.s. VI (Nov. 27, 1886), 259–61. Reprinted in *Authors at Home,* eds. L. and J. B. Gilder. New York: [1888], pp. 193–210.

[Blanc, M. T.] "William D. Howells," in *Les Nouveaux Romanciers Américains* par "Th. Bentzon." Paris: 1885, pp. 7–

70. (On *The Undiscovered Country, A Modern Instance, The Lady of the Aroostook, et al.*)

Book News Monthly, XXVI (June, 1908). (A "Howells number" with articles by H. M. Alden, H. W. Mabie, P. Maxwell, and W. de Wagstaff.)

Boston *Evening Transcript*. "William Dean Howells at 75, Tributes from Eminent Americans to Our Foremost Man of Letters," III (Feb. 24, 1912), 2. (W. S. Braithwaite, J. D. Long, M. E. W. Freeman [q.v.], H. M. Alden, F. E. Coates [poem], G. W. Cable, Henry Van Dyke, R. U. Underwood, Robert Herrick ["A Warm Champion of the Truth"], G. E. Woodberry, Alice Brown, Bliss Perry, J. B. Esenwein, W. E. B. DuBois ["As a Friend of the Colored Man"].)

Boyesen, H. H. "Mr. Howells and His Work," *Cosmopolitan*, XII (Feb., 1892), 502–03.

Boyesen, H. H. "Mr. Howells at Close Range." *Ladies' Home Journal*, X (Nov., 1893), 7–8. (Biographical.)

Boynton, P. H. "William Dean Howells." *Literary Review* (New York *Evening Post*), I (April 23, 1921), 22.

Braly, E. B. "William Dean Howells, Author and Journalist." *Journalism Quarterly*, XXXII (Fall, 1955), 456–562.

[Brownell, W. C.] "The Novels of Mr. Howells." *Nation* XXXI (July 15, 1880), 49–51. (Review of *The Undiscovered Country*.)

Bryan, C. W. "The Literature of the Household, A Sketch of America's Leading Writer of Fiction, W. D. Howells," *Good Housekeeping*, I (July 11, 1885), 2–3. Reprinted XII (June, 1891), 293–95. (Biographical sketch endorsed by Howells.)

Budd, L. J. "William Dean Howells' Debt to Tolstoy." *American Slavic and East European Review*, IX (Dec., 1950), 292–301.

Budd, L. J. "W. D. Howells' Defense of the Romance." *PMLA*, LXVII (March, 1952), 32–42.

Budd, L. J. "Howells, the *Atlantic Monthly,* and Republican-
ism." *American Literature,* XXIV (May, 1952), 139–56.

Budd, L. J. "Howells' 'Blistering and Cauterizing.' " *Ohio State
Archaeological and Historical Quarterly,* LXII (Oct., 1953),
334–47.

Budd, L. J. "Altruism Arrives in America," *American Quarterly,* VIII (Spring, 1956), 40–52.

Budd, L. J. "Twain, Howells, and the Boston Nihilists." *New
England Quarterly,* XXXII (Sept., 1959), 351–71.

Burroughs, John. "Mr. Howells's Agreements with Whitman."
Critic, n.s. XVII (Feb. 6, 1892), 85–86.

Cady, E. H. "William Dean Howells and the Ashtabula *Sentinel."* *Ohio State Archaeological and Historical Quarterly,*
LIII (Jan.–March, 1944), 39–51.

Cady, E. H. "A Note on Howells and 'the Smiling Aspects of
Life.' " *American Literature,* XVII (May, 1945), 175–78.

Cady, E. H. "The Neuroticism of William Dean Howells."
PMLA, LXI (March, 1946), 229–38.

Cady, E. H. "Armando Palacio Valdés writes to William Dean
Howells." *Symposium,* II (May, 1948), 19–37.

Cady, E. H. "Howells in 1948." *University of Kansas City Review,* XV (Winter, 1948), 83–91.

Cady, E. H. "The Gentleman as Socialist: William Dean Howells," in *The Gentleman in America.* Syracuse: Syracuse University. [1949].

Cady, E. H. "William Dean Howells in Italy: Some Bibliographical Notes." *Symposium,* VII (May, 1953), 147–53.

Cargill, Oscar. "Henry James's 'Moral Policeman': William
Dean Howells." *American Literature,* XXIX (Jan., 1958),
371–98.

Carter, Everett. "William Dean Howells' Theory of Critical

Realism." *ELH: A Journal of English Literary History*, XVI (June, 1949), 151–66.

Carter, Everett. "The Palpitating Divan." *College English*, XI (May, 1950), 423–28.

Carter, Everett. "The Haymarket Affair in Literature." *American Quarterly*, II (Fall, 1950), 270–78.

Carter, P. J., Jr. "The Influence of William Dean Howells upon Mark Twain's Social Satire." *University of Colorado Studies, Series in Language and Literature*, 4 (July, 1953), 93–100.

Carter, P. J., Jr. "A Howells Letter." *New England Quarterly*, XXVIII (March, 1955), 93–96. (To William Strunk, 1911, on *The Rise of Silas Lapham*.)

Clark, H. H. "The Role of Science in the Thought of W. D. Howells." *Transactions of the Wisconsin Academy of Sciences, Arts and Letters*, XLII (1953), 263–303.

Clemens, S. L. "William Dean Howells." *Harper's Monthly*, CXIII (July, 1906), 221–25. Reprinted in *What Is Man? and Other Essays*. New York: [1917], pp. 228–39.

Commager, H. S. "The Return to Howells." *Spectator*, CLXXX (May 28, 1948), 642–43. (Review of *The Rise of Silas Lapham*, ed. H. M. Jones.)

Commager, H. S. "Business of America: Rise of Silas Lapham." *Scholastic*, LVIII (Feb. 7, 1951), 18–19.

[Conway, M. D.] "Three American Poets," *Broadway*, n.s. I (Oct., 1868), 246–48.

Cooper, J. A. "Bellamy and Howells." *Canadian Magazine*, IX (Aug., 1897), 344–46.

Coyle, L. P. "Mark Twain and William Dean Howells." *The Georgia Review*, X (Fall, 1956), 3–12.

Cronkhite, G. F. "Howells Turns to the Inner Life." *New England Quarterly*, XXX (Dec., 1957), 474–85.

[Curtis, G. W.] "Editor's Easy Chair." *Harper's Monthly,* LXVI (April, 1883), 791–93.

Dawes, A. L. "The Moral Purpose in Howells's Novels." *Andover Review,* XI (Jan., 1889), 23–36.

DeMille, G. E. "The Infallible Dean." *Sewanee Review,* XXXVI (April, 1928), 148–56. Reprinted in *Literary Criticism in America.* New York: [1931], pp. 182–205.

Dove, J. R. "Howells' Irrational Heroines." *The University of Texas Studies in English,* XXXV (1956), 64–80.

Eble, K. E. "The Western Ideals of William Dean Howells." *Western Humanities Review,* XI (Autumn, 1957), 331–38.

Eble, K. E. "Howells' Kisses." *American Quarterly,* IX (Winter, 1957), 441–47.

Edwards, Herbert. "Howells and the Controversy over Realism in American Fiction." *American Literature,* III (Nov., 1931), 237–48.

Edwards, Herbert. "Howells and Herne." *American Literature,* XXII (Jan., 1951), 432–41.

Edwards, Herbert. "The Dramatization of *The Rise of Silas Lapham.*" *New England Quarterly,* XXX (June, 1957), 235–43.

Ekstrom, Kjell. "The Cable-Howells Correspondence." *Studia Neophilologica,* XXII (1950), 48–61.

Ekstrom, W. F. "Equalitarian Principle in the Fiction of W. D. Howells." *American Literature,* XXIV (March, 1952), 40–50.

Elkins, K. C. "Eliot, Howells, and the Courses of Graduate Instruction, 1869–1871." *Harvard Library Bulletin,* X (Winter, 1956), 141–46.

Erskine, John. "William Dean Howells." *Bookman,* LI (June, 1920), 385–89.

Fawcett, Waldon. "Mr. Howells and His Brother." *Critic,* XXXV (Nov., 1899), 1026–28.

Ferguson, Delancy. "The Legacy of Letters." *The American Scholar*, XXIX (Summer, 1960), 406–18. (Discussion of recent editions of letters by Mark Twain, Howells, Melville, and Stephen Crane.)

Firkins, O. W. "Last of the Mountaineers." *Saturday Review of Literature*, V (March 16, 1929), 774–75. Reprinted in *Selected Essays*. Minneapolis: [1933], pp. 94–108. (Review of *Life in Letters*.)

Firkins, O. W. "William Dean Howells." *Dictionary of American Biography*. New York: 1932, IX, 306–11.

Follett, Helen T. and Wilson. "Contemporary Novelists: William Dean Howells." *Atlantic Monthly*, CXIX (March, 1917), 362–72.

Foster, Richard. "The Contemporaneity of Howells." *New England Quarterly*, XXXII (March, 1959), 54–78.

Fox, A. B. "Howells' Doctrine of Complicity." *Modern Language Quarterly*, XIII (March, 1952), 56–60.

Fox, A. B. "Howells as a Religious Critic." *New England Quarterly*, XXV (June, 1952), 199–216.

Frazier, D. L. "Time and the Theme of Indian Summer." *Arizona Quarterly*, XVI (Autumn, 1960), 260–67.

Fréchette, A. H. "William Dean Howells." *Canadian Bookman*, II (July, 1920), 9–12. (Reminiscence by Howells' sister.)

Freeman, M. W. "A Woman's Tribute to Mr. Howells." *Literary Digest*, XLIV (March 9, 1912), 485.

Fryckstedt, O. W. "Howells and Conway in Venice." *Studia Neophilologica*, XXX (1958), 165–74.

Garland, Hamlin. "Mr. Howells's Latest Novels." *New England Magazine*, n.s. II (May, 1890), 243–50.

Garland, Hamlin. "Sanity in Fiction." *North American Review*, CLXXVI (March, 1903), 336–48.

Garland, Hamlin. "Meetings with Howells." *Bookman*, XLV

(March, 1917), 1–7. With changes reprinted in *A Son of the Middle Border*. New York: 1917, pp. 383–90.

Garland, Hamlin. "William Dean Howells, Master Craftsman." *Art World*, I (March, 1917), 411–12.

Garland, Hamlin. "A Great American." *Literary Review* (New) York *Evening Post*), I (March 5, 1921), 1–2. (See P. H. Boynton for reply.)

Garland, Hamlin. "Roadside Meetings of a Literary Nomad, II, William Dean Howells and Other Memories of Boston." *Bookman*, LXX (Nov., 1929), 246–50. Reprinted in *Roadside Meetings*. New York: 1930, pp. 55–65.

Getzels, J. W. "William Dean Howells and Socialism." *Science and Society*, II (Summer, 1938), 376–86.

Gibson, W. M. "Materials and Form in Howells's First Novels." *American Literature*, XIX (May, 1947), 158–66.

Gibson, W. M. "Mark Twain and Howells, Anti-Imperialists." *New England Quarterly*, XX (Dec., 1947), 435–70.

Gifford, Henry. "W. D. Howells: His Moral Conservatism." *Kenyon Review*, XX (Winter, 1958), 124–33.

Gilman, Lawrence. "Dean of American Letters." New York *Times*, V (May 16, 1920), 254–55.

Gorlier, Claudio. "William Dean Howells e le definizioni del realismo." *Studi Americani*, No. 2 (1956), 83–125.

Gosse, E. W. "The Passing of William Dean Howells." *Living Age*, CCCVI (July 10, 1920), 98–100.

Gosse, E. W. "The World of Books, W. D. Howells." *Sunday Times* (London) (March 8, 1925), 8. Reprinted in *Silhouettes*. New York: [1925], pp. 191–99.

Grattan, C. H. "Howells, Ten Years After." *American Mercury*, XX (May, 1930), 42–50.

Gullason, T. A. "New Light on the Crane-Howells Relationship." *New England Quarterly*, XXX (Sept., 1957), 389–92.

Hackett, Francis. "William Dean Howells." *New Republic,* X, supplement (April 21, 1917), 3–5. Reprinted in *Horizons, A Book of Criticism.* New York: 1918, pp. 21–30.

Harlow, Virginia. "William Dean Howells and Thomas Sergeant Perry." *Boston Public Library Quarterly,* I (Oct., 1949), 135–50.

Harper's Weekly. "A Tribute to William Dean Howells, Souvenir of a Dinner Given to the Eminent Author in Celebration of His Seventy-Fifth Birthday," LVI (March 9, 1912), 27–34. (Speeches by George Harvey, Taft, Howells, James Barnes [verses], Winston Churchill, H. W. Mabie, W. A. White, Basil King. Letters by Arnold Bennett, T. W. Dunton, Arthur Pinero, Thomas Hardy, J. M. Barrie, A. T. Ritchie, H. G. Wells, Israel Zangwill, Anthony Hope, W. J. Locke, Andrew Lang, Curzon of Kedleston, Mrs. Humphrey Ward, L. M. Sill [verses], Henry Van Dyke, G. W. Cable, John Burroughs, S. W. Mitchell, H. H. Furness. See also Henry James and F. B. Sanborn.)

Hazard, L. L. "Howells a Hundred Years Later." *Mills Quarterly,* XX (Feb., 1938), 167–72.

Hellman, G. S. "The Reminiscences of Mr. Howells." *Bookman,* XIII (March, 1901), 67–71. (Review of *Literary Friends and Acquaintance.*)

Herford, Oliver. "Celebrities I Have Not Met." *American Magazine,* LXXV (March, 1913), 95. (Satiric poem and drawing.) Reprinted in *Confessions of a Caricaturist,* 1917, which is dedicated to Howells.

Hicks, Granville. "A Grasping Imagination." *Sewanee Review,* LIX (Summer, 1951), 505–17.

Hicks, Granville. "Howells in Our Time." *Saturday Review,* XLII (April 18, 1959), 18. Review article on Bennett's and the Kirks' books.

Higginson, T. W. "Howells." *Literary World,* X (Aug. 2, 1879),

249–50. Reprinted in *Short Studies of American Authors*. Boston: [1879], pp. 32–39.

The Howells Sentinel, published in mimeographed form at irregular intervals from 8 March 1951 and still in progress. Edited by Rudolf Kirk and Clara M. Kirk. Five numbers and a single-sheet supplement have appeared so far. (Contains current bibliographies of latest Howells books, articles, and reviews, and a good many notes about Howells.)

[James, Henry.] Review of *Italian Journeys*. *North American Review*, CVI (Jan., 1868), 336–39.

James, Henry. "Howells's Poems." *Independent*, XXVI (Jan. 8, 1874), 9.

[James, Henry.] Review of *A Foregone Conclusion*. *North American Review*, CXX (Jan., 1875), 207–14.

[James, Henry.] "Howells's *Foregone Conclusion*." *Nation*, XX (Jan. 7, 1875), 12–13.

James, Henry. "William Dean Howells." *Harper's Weekly*, XXX (June 19, 1886), 394–95.

James, Henry. "American Letter." *Literature*, III (July 9, 1898), 18. (Review of *The Story of a Play*.)

James, Henry. "ALetter to Mr. Howells." *North American Review*, CXCV (April, 1912), 558–62.

Kar, Annette. "Archetypes of American Innocence: Lydia Blood and Daisy Miller." *American Quarterly* (Spring, 1953), 31–38.

Kelley, C. P. "The Early Development of Henry James." *University of Illinois Studies in Language and Literature*, XV (1930), 73–80 *et passim*.

Kirk, C. M. "Niagara Revisited." *Columbia Library Columns*, VII (Feb., 1958), 4–12.

Kirk, C. M. "Reality and Actuality in the March Family Narratives of W. D. Howells." *PMLA*, LXXIV (March, 1959), 137–52.

Kirk, Clara, and Rudolf Kirk. "Howells in Caricature." *The Journal of the Rutgers University Library*, XXI (June, 1958), 69–70 and plate.

Kirk, Clara, and Rudolf Kirk. "Howells and the Church of the Carpenter." *New England Quarterly*, XXXII (June, 1959), 185–206.

Kirk, Rudolf, and Clara Kirk. "Howells' Guidebook to Venice." *American Literature*, XXX (May, 1961), 221–224.

Kirk, Rudolf, and Clara Kirk. " 'Poems of Two Friends.' " *Journal of the Rutgers University Library*, IV (June, 1941), 33–44.

Kirk, Clara, and Rudolf Kirk. "William Dean Howells." *Collier's Encyclopedia*, 1962.

Kirk, Clara, and Rudolf Kirk, eds. " 'The Howells Family,' by Richard J. Hinton." *Journal of the Rutgers University Library*, XIV (Dec., 1950), 14–23. (A reprint of an article from the New York *Voice*, 1897.)

[Kirk, S.] "America, Altruria, and the Coast of Bohemia." *Atlantic Monthly*, LXXIV (Nov., 1894), 701–04.

Königsberger, Suzanne. *Die Romantechnik von William Dean Howells*. Düsseldorf, 1933.

Lang, Andrew. "At the Sign of the Ship." *Longman's*, XIX (April, 1892), 682–84. Reprinted *Critic*, XX (April 16, 1892), 233.

Lang, Andrew. "The New Fiction." *Illustrated London News*, CVII (Aug. 3, 1895), 141.

Lathrop, George Parsons. "W. D. Howells. His Career and His Home." *New York Tribune*, November 8, 1885, 3.

Lessing, O. E. "William Dean Howells." *Das Literarische Echo*, XV (Nov. 1, 1912), 155–61. Reprinted in *Brücken über den Atlantik*. Berlin: 1927, pp. 139–49.

[Lowell, J. R.] Review of *Poems by* [sic] *Two Friends*. *Atlantic Monthly*, V (April, 1860), 510–11.

[Lowell, J. R.] Review of *Venetian Life*. *North American Review*, CIII (Oct., 1866), 610–13. Reprinted in J. R. Lowell's *The Function of the Poet,* ed. Albert Mordell. Boston: 1920, pp. 146–52.

[Lowell, J. R.] Review of *Suburban Sketches*. *North American Review,* CXII (Jan., 1871), 236–37.

Lutwack, Leonard. "William Dean Howells and the 'Editor's Study.' " *American Literature,* XXIV (March, 1952), 195–207.

Lydenberg, John, and Cady, E. H. "Essay Review. The Howells Revival: Rounds two and three." *New England Quarterly,* XXXII (Sept., 1959), 394–407. (On books by Cary, Bennett, Fryckstedt, and the Kirks.)

Mabie, H. W. "William Dean Howells." *Outlook,* CXI (Dec., 1915), 786–87. Reprinted in *American Academy Proceedings,* II (Nov., 1916), 51–52.

McCabe, L. R. "Literary and Social Recollections of William Dean Howells." *Lippincott's,* XL (Oct., 1887), 547–52.

McCabe, L. R. "One Never Can Tell." *Outlook,* LIX (May 14, 1898), 131–32. (On *Poems of Two Friends.*)

McElderry, B. R., Jr. "Henry James and 'The Whole Family.' " *Pacific Spectator,* IV (Summer, 1950), 352–60.

Malone, Clifton. "The Realism of William Dean Howells." *Quarterly Bulletin of Oklahoma Baptist University (Faculty Studies, No. 2),* XXXIV (Feb., 1949), 3–22.

Martin, E. S. "W. D. Howells." *Harper's Monthly,* CXLI (July, 1920), 265–66.

Matthews, Brander. "Bret Harte and Mr. Howells as Dramatists." *Library Table,* III (Sept. 13, 1877), 174–75. Reprinted in *American Theatre As Seen by Its Critics,* 1752–1934, eds. M. J. Moses and J. M. Brown. New York: [1934], pp. 147–48.

Matthews, Brander. "Mr. Howells as a Critic." *Forum,* XXXII (Jan., 1902), 629–38.

Matthews, Brander. "American Character in American Fiction." *Munsey's*, XLIX (Aug., 1913), 794–97. (Review of *New Leaf Mills*.)

Matthiessen, F. O. "A Monument to Howells." *New Republic*, LVIII (April 24, 1929), 284–85. (Review of *Life in Letters*.)

Medrano, H. J. "William Dean Howells." *Cuba Contemporánea*, XXIII (July, 1920), 252–56.

Meserole, H. T. "The Dean in Person: Howells' Lecture Tour." *Western Humanities Review*, X (Autumn, 1956), 337–47. (Lecture mentioned by Meserole is in Hayes Memorial Library, Fremont, Ohio.)

Meserve, W. J. "Truth, Morality, and Swedenborg in Howells' Theory of Realism." *New England Quarterly*, XXVII (June, 1954), 252–57.

Meserve, W. J. "Colonel Sellers as a Scientist: A Play by S. L. Clemens and W. D. Howells." *Modern Drama*, I (Dec., 1958), 151–56.

Miller, F. DeW. "Identification of Contributors to the *North American Review* Under Lowell." *Studies in Bibliography*, VI (1954), 225. (Reviews of Howells' books, 1866–1872.)

Millgate, Michael. "The Emotional Commitment of William Dean Howells." *Neophilologus*, XLIV (Jan., 1960), 48–54.

Morby, E. S. "William Dean Howells and Spain." *Hispanic Review*, XIV (July, 1946), 187–212. (Howells' literary relations with Cervantes, Tamayo y Baus ["Estébanez"], Valdés, Valera, Galdós, Pardo Bazán, and Ibáñez.)

Mordell, Albert. "William Dean Howells and the Classics." *Stratford Monthly*, n.s. II (Sept., 1924), 199–205.

Morris, Lloyd. "Conscience in the Parlor: William Dean Howells." *American Scholar*, XVIII (Autumn, 1949), 407–16.

Muirhead, J. F. "W. D. Howells, the American Trollope." *Landmark*, II-III (Dec., 1920–Jan., 1921), 53–56, 812–16. Reprinted *Living Age*, CCCVIII (Jan. 29, 1921), 304–09.

Munford, H. M. "The Disciple Proves Independent: Howells and Lowell." *PMLA*, LXIV (Sept., 1959), 484–87.

Murray, D. M. "Henry B. Fuller: Friend of Howells." *South Atlantic Quarterly*, LII (July, 1953), 431–44.

New York *Sun*. "His Friends Greet William Dean Howells at Eighty." V (Feb. 25, 1917), 10. (Comment by M. B. Mullett, Booth Tarkington, D. Z. Doty, Hamlin Garland; reminiscence by C. H. Towne and T. S. Perry.)

Orr, A. [Mrs. Sutherland.] "International Novelists and Mr. Howells." *Contemporary Review*, XXXVII (May, 1880), 741–65. Reprinted *Living Age*, CXLV (June 5, 1880), 599–615.

Parks, E. W. "Howells and the Gentle Reader." *South Atlantic Quarterly*, L (April, 1951), 239–47.

Parks, E. W. "A Realist Avoids Reality: W. D. Howells and the Civil War Years." *South Atlantic Quarterly*, LII (Jan., 1953), 93–97.

Pearce, R. H. "Adams, Howells, and Their Advocates." *Virginia Quarterly Review*, XXXV (Winter, 1959), 149–53. Review article on Cady's biography.

Pennell, Joseph. "Adventures of an Illustrator, with Howells in Italy." *Century*, CIV (May, 1922), 135–41.

Perkins, George. "Howells and Hawthorne." *Nineteenth-Century Fiction*, XV, No. 3 (Dec., 1960), 259–62.

[Perry, T. S.] "William Dean Howells." *Century*, XXIII (March, 1882), 680–85.

Phelps, W. L. "Howells," in *Howells, James, Bryant, and Other Essays*. New York: 1924, pp. 156–80. In part first printed as "An Appreciation," *North American Review*, CCXII (July, 1920), 17–20, and "William Dean Howells as a Novelist," *Yale Review*, n.s. X (Oct., 1920), 99–109.

Pizer, Donald. "The Ethical Unity of *The Rise of Silas Lapham*." *Language Notes*, LXX (Jan., 1955), 37–39.

Pizer, Donald. "The Ethical Unity of *The Rise of Silas Lapham*." *American Literature,* XXXII (Nov., 1960), 322–27.

Powys, Llewelyn. "The Style of Howells." *Nation,* CXX (June 17, 1925), 694. (Review of Firkins' *Howells*.)

Quinn, A. H. "The Art of William Dean Howells." *Century,* C (Sept., 1920), 675–81.

Quinn, A. H. "William Dean Howells and the Establishment of Realism," in *American Fiction*. New York: 1936, pp. 257–78.

Reeves, J. K. "The Way of a Realist: A Study of Howells' Use of the Saratoga Scene." *PMLA,* LXV (Dec., 1950), 1035–52.

Reeves, J. K. "The Case of the Dead-Pan Scholar." *Prism: Bulletin of the Friends of the Skidmore College Library,* I (1951), 7–15.

Reid, Forrest. "W. D. Howells." *Irish Statesman,* I (Sept. 27, Oct. 4, 1919), 333–34, 359–60.

Rein, D. M. "Howells and the *Cosmopolitan*." *American Literature,* XXI (March, 1949), 49–55.

Rood, Henry. "William Dean Howells, Some Notes of a Literary Acquaintance." *Ladies' Home Journal,* XXXVII (Sept., 1920), 42, 154, 157. (Biographical.)

Sanborn, F. B. "A Letter to the Chairman." *North American Review,* CXCV (April, 1912), 562–66. (Reminiscent letter at birthday.)

Shaw, G. B. "Told You So." *Saturday Review,* LXXX (Dec. 7, 1895), 761–62. Reprinted in *Dramatic Opinions and Essays*. New York: 1906, I, pp. 265–66.

Sinclair, R. B. "Howells in the Ohio Valley." *Saturday Review of Literature,* XXXVIII (Jan. 6, 1945), 22–23.

Sinnott, J. E. "The Nabob and Silas Lapham." *Harvard Monthly,* I (Jan., 1886), 164–68.

Sirluck, Ernest. "Howells' 'A Modern Instance': Title and Theme." *Manitoba Arts Review,* X (Winter, 1956), 66–72.

Smith, Bernard. "Howells, the Genteel Radical." *Saturday Review of Literature,* XI (Aug. 11, 1934), 41–42.

Smith, H. N. " 'That Hideous Mistake of Poor Clemens.' " *Harvard Library Bulletin,* IX (Spring, 1955), 145–80. (The Whittier birthday speech.)

Snell, George. "Howells' Grasshopper." *College English,* VII (May, 1946), 444–52.

Sokoloff, B. A. "Printing and Journalism in the Novels of William Dean Howells." *Transactions of the Wisconsin Academy of Sciences, Arts, and Letters,* XLVI (1957), 165–78.

Sokoloff, B. A. "William Dean Howells and the Ohio Village: A Study of Environment and Art." *American Quarterly,* XI (Spring, 1959), 58–75.

Spiller, R. E. "Father of Modern American Realism." *Saturday Review,* XXXIII (Sept., 1950), 10–11.

Stafford, W. T. "The Two Henry Jameses and Howells: A Bibliographical Mix-Up." *Bulletin of Bibliography,* XXI (Jan.–April, 1955), 135.

Starke, A. H. "William Dean Howells and Sidney Lanier." *American Literature,* III (March, 1931), 79–82.

Stronks, J. B. "William Dean Howells, Ed Howe, and *The Story of a Country Town.*" *American Literature,* XXIX (Jan., 1958), 473–78.

Stronks, J. B. "Paul Laurence Dunbar and William Dean Howells." *Ohio Historical Quarterly,* LXVII (April, 1958), 95–108.

Stronks, J. B. "The Howells Revival." *Commonweal,* LXXI (Jan. 15, 1960), 445–47.

Tarkington, Booth. "Mr. Howells." *Harper's Monthly,* CXLI (Aug., 1920), 346–50. Reprinted with revisions and additions as "Introduction," *The Rise of Silas Lapham* (Boston: 1937), pp. v-xv, and *ibid.* (Riverside Literature Series; Boston: [1937]), pp. xiii-xxi.

Taylor, W. F. "On the Origin of Howells' Interest in Economic Reform." *American Literature,* II (March, 1930), 1–14.

Taylor, W. F. "William Dean Howells and the Economic Novel." *American Literature,* IV (May, 1932), 103–13.

Taylor, W. F. "William Dean Howells, Artist and American." *Sewanee Review,* XLVI (July–Sept., 1938), 288–303.

Taylor, W. F. "William Dean Howells," in *The Economic Novel in America.* Chapel Hill: 1942, pp. 214–81.

Thane, Adele. "Christmas Everyday: A Dramatization of Story by William Dean Howells." *Plays,* XIX (Dec., 1959), 57–65.

Thomas, B. P. "A Unique Biography of Lincoln." *Bulletin of the Abraham Lincoln Association,* No. 35 (June, 1934), 3–8.

Thomas, E. M. "Mr. Howells's Way of Saying Things." *Putnam's,* IV (July, 1908), 443–47.

Thompson, Maurice. "The Analyst, Analyzed." *Critic,* n.s. VI (July 10, 1886), 19–22. (Report of Indianapolis address.)

Thompson, Maurice. "Mr. Maurice Thompson on Mr. Howells." *Literary World,* XVIII (Sept. 3, 1887), 281–82.

Thompson, Maurice. "Studies of Prominent Novelists, No. 3. —William Dean Howells." *Book News,* VI (Nov., 1887), 93–94.

Towne, C. H. "The Kindly Howells." *Touchstone,* VII (July, 1920), 280–82.

Trilling, Lionel. "W. D. Howells and the Roots of Modern Taste." *Partisan Review,* XVIII (Sept.–Oct., 1951), 516–36. Reprinted in *The Opposing Self: Nine Essays in Criticism.* New York: The Viking Press, 1955, pp. 76–103.

Trites, W. B. "William Dean Howells." *Forum,* XLIX (Feb., 1913), 217–40.

Trittschub, Travis. "The Ballad-Seller and His Kind." *Journal of American Folklore,* LXXIII (Jan., 1960), 54–56.

Utley, Francis Lee. "Howells' New York City Ballad Seller."

Journal of American Folklore, LXX (Oct.–Dec., 1957), 361–62.

Van Westrum, A. S. "Mr. Howells and American Aristocracies." *Bookman,* XXV (March, 1907), 67–73.

Walts, R. W. "William Dean Howells and His 'Library Edition.'" *Papers of the Bibliographical Society of America,* LII (1958), 283–94.

[Warner, C. D.] "Editor's Study." *Harper's Monthly,* LXXXIV (April, 1892), 802–03.

Wasserstrom, William. "William Dean Howells: The Indelible Stain." *New England Quarterly,* XXXII (Dec. 1959), 486–95.

Westbrook, Max. "The Critical Implications of Howells' Realism." *Texas Studies in English,* XXXVI (1957), 71–79.

Whiting, L. "W. D. Howells at Home." *Author,* III (Sept. 15, 1891), 130–31. (Biographical.)

Wilcox, Marrion. "W. D. Howells's First Romance." *Harper's Bazar,* XXVII (June 16, 1894), 475. (Review of *A Traveler from Altruria.*)

Wilson, C. D., and Fitzgerald, D. B. "A Day in Howells's 'Boy's Town.'" *New England Magazine,* XXXVI (May, 1907), 289–97.

Wister, Owen. "William Dean Howells." *Atlantic Monthly,* CLX (Dec., 1937), 704–13.

[Woodberry, G. E.] "Howells's Modern Italian Poets." *Atlantic Monthly,* LXI (Jan., 1888), 130–33. (Review.)

Woodress, J. L., Jr. "Howells's Venetian Priest." *Modern Language Notes,* LXVI (April, 1951), 266–67.

Wright, Conrad. "The Sources of Mr. Howells's Socialism." *Science and Society,* II (Fall, 1938), 514–17.

Wyatt, Edith. "A National Contribution." *North American*

Review, CXCVI (Sept., 1912), 339–52. Reprinted in *Great Companions.* New York: 1917, pp. 113–42.

For articles on Howells published after 1949 one should consult especially the current bibliographies in *American Literature, Publications of the Modern Language Association, Annual Bibliography* (Modern Humanities Research Association), Grace G. Griffin's *Writings on American History,* and *The Howells Sentinel.*

CHRONOLOGICAL TABLE AND SELECTED BIBLIOGRAPHY OF THE WORKS OF WILLIAM DEAN HOWELLS

1837 March 1, born, Martin's Ferry, Belmont County, Ohio.

1840 Howells' father bought Hamilton (Ohio) *Intelligencer,* a Whig paper.

1846 At age of nine Howells set type on his father's paper.

1849 Howells' father left Hamilton and bought Dayton *Transcript.*

1850 Beginning in the fall the Howells family spent a year in a log cabin near Xenia, Greene County, Ohio.

1851 When his father took a position as clerk of the House of the Ohio Legislature, Howells became a compositor on *Ohio State Journal.*

1852 William Cooper Howells moved his family to Ashtabula in order that he might become editor of *Sentinel.* Six months later the office was moved to Jefferson, where it remained and where the Howells family lived for many years, Howells contributing to *Ohio State Journal.* July 10, Ashtabula *Sentinel* announced that H. Fassett and W. C. Howells were co-owners of the paper.

1853 January 1, Fassett resigned from Ashtabula *Sentinel,* and W. C. Howells became a partner with J. L. Oliver. Howells begins contributing to *Sentinel.*

1855 Contributed to *Sentinel, Ohio Farmer, Ohio State Journal,* and *National Era.*

1857 Lived in Columbus and became correspondent for Cincinnati *Gazette, a*nd continued contributions to other papers.

1858 Reporter, news editor, and editorial writer of *Ohio State Journal.* Contributed to many papers.

1859 Contributed to *Odd-Fellows' Casket and Review, Saturday*

Press. Collaborated with John James Piatt on *Poems of Two Friends* (1860), which appeared December 23.

1860 Published poems in *Atlantic Monthly* and Cincinnati *Dial.* Wrote the campaign life of Lincoln in *Lives and Speeches of Abraham Lincoln and Hannibal Hamlin.* Poems and a biographical sketch of Howells were included by William T. Coggeshall in *The Poets and Poetry of the West.* Made his first trip to New England. Returned to Columbus, where he met Elinor Mead.

1861 September, appointed United States consul at Venice. Sailed for Italy in November.

1862 December 24, married Elinor Gertrude Mead of Brattleboro, Vermont, in Paris.

1863 March 27, articles on Venice began to appear in Boston *Daily Advertiser.* December 17, Winifred Howells born.

1864 First *North American Review* article. "The Battle in the Clouds" (sheet music).

1865 Returned to the United States from Venice. Writing for *New York Times,* and other papers. Engaged to write for the *Nation,* newly founded by E. L. Godkin.

1866 Assistant editor of *Atlantic Monthly.* Moved to "Cottage Quiet," Sacramento Street, Cambridge, Massachusetts, where he first met Henry James. Contributed to *Galaxy. Venetian Life* published.

1867 *Italian Journeys.* M.A. from Harvard.

1868 Offered professorship at Union College to teach rhetoric. August 14, John Mead Howells born. Howells' mother, Mary Dean Howells, died.

1869 *No Love Lost.* University lecturer at Harvard, 1869–71.

1870 Lowell Institute lecturer at Harvard.

1871 July, editor-in-chief of *Atlantic. Suburban Sketches.*

1872 *Their Wedding Journey.* Built new house, 37 Concord

Avenue, Cambridge. September 26, Mildred Howells born. *Jubilee Days* written and edited with T. B. Aldrich, with illustrations by Augustus Hoppin.

1873 *A Chance Acquaintance. Poems.*

1874 *A Foregone Conclusion.*

1876 *Sketch of the Life and Character of Rutherford B. Hayes. The Parlor Car.*

1877 *Out of the Question. A Counterfeit Presentment.* Memoirs of Vittorio Alfieri, Lord Herbert of Cherbury, Thomas Ellwood, Carlo Goldoni, Frederica S. Wilhelmina, Jean François Marmontel (published 1878), Edward Gibbon.

1879 *The Lady of the Aroostook.*

1880 *The Undiscovered Country.*

1881 Resigned editorship of *Atlantic.* A. M. degree from Yale. Ill with a fever for many weeks, the result of overwork. *A Fearful Responsibility, and Other Stories. Doctor Breen's Practice. A Day's Pleasure and Other Sketches.* Offered literary editorship of New York *Tribune.*

1882 Trip to Europe. Offered professorship of Literature at the Johns Hopkins University. *A Modern Instance.*

1883 Returned from Europe. *The Sleeping Car. A Woman's Reason.* Lived at 4 Louisburg Square, Boston.

1884 Bought house, 302 Beacon Street, Boston. Chosen first president of Tavern Club. *A Little Girl Among the Old Masters. The Register. Three Villages. Niagara Revisited 12 Years after Their Wedding Journey by the Hoosac Tunnel Route,* published without permission and suppressed.

1885 *The Elevator. The Rise of Silas Lapham.* Contract with Harper and Brothers.

1886 January, began "Editor's Study" in *Harper's. Tuscan Cities. The Garroters. Indian Summer.* Refused Smith professorship at Harvard.

1887 November 6, letter to New York *Tribune* asking clemency for the Chicago Anarchists. *The Minister's Charge. Modern Italian Poets.*

1888 Moved to New York. *April Hopes. A Sea Change.*

1889 March 3, Winifred Howells died. *Annie Kilburn. The Mouse Trap, and Other Farces.*

1890 Moved to Boston for the year, 184 Commonwealth Avenue, Boston. *A Hazard of New Fortunes. The Shadow of a Dream. A Boy's Town.*

1891 *Winifred Howells. Criticism and Fiction.* Returned to New York.

1892 March, resigned from "The Editor's Study." Co-editor of *Cosmopolitan* from March, 1892 to June 30, 1892. "Excited" about the steel strike at Homestead, Pennsylvania. *The Albany Depot. An Imperative Duty. The Quality of Mercy. A Letter of Introduction. A Little Swiss Sojourn.*

1893 *Christmas Every Day and Other Stories. The World of Chance. The Unexpected Guests. My Year in a Log Cabin. Evening Dress. The Coast of Bohemia. The Niagara Book.*

1894 Trip to France to visit his son in Paris. Death of William Cooper Howells. Refused editorship of Sunday edition of Chicago *Inter-Ocean. A Likely Story. A Traveler from Altruria. Five O'Clock Tea.*

1895 *My Literary Passions. Stops of Various Quills.* Began regular contributions to *Harper's Weekly.*

1896 Bought house at Far Rockaway, Long Island, but only kept it for one summer. *The Day of Their Wedding. A Parting and a Meeting. Impressions and Experiences.*

1897 Went on a lecture tour. *A Previous Engagement. The Landlord at Lion's Head. An Open-Eyed Conspiracy. Stories of Ohio.* Trip to Carlsbad, Germany.

1898 *The Story of a Play.* Contributed to *Literature,* May, 1898, to November, 1899.

1899 *Ragged Lady. Their Silver Wedding Journey.* Lecture tour in the West.

1900 December, began "Editor's Easy Chair" for *Harper's. Bride Roses. Room Forty-five. An Indian Giver. The Smoking Car. Literary Friends and Acquaintance.*

1901 Received Litt. D. from Yale. *A Pair of Patient Lovers. Heroines of Fiction.*

1902 Bought home at Kittery Point, Maine. *The Kentons. The Flight of Pony Baker. Literature and Life.*

1903 *Questionable Shapes. Letters Home.*

1904 Received Litt. D. from Oxford. *The Son of Royal Langbrith.*

1905 Received Litt. D. from Columbia. *Miss Bellard's Inspiration.*

1906 *London Films. Certain Delightful English Towns.*

1907 *Through the Eye of the Needle. Between the Dark and the Daylight. Minor Dramas. Mulberries in Pay's Garden.*

1908 Elected first president of the American Academy of Arts and Letters, and continued in this office till his death. *Fennel and Rue. Roman Holidays and Others.* Trip to Italy.

1909 Elected Honorary Foreign Fellow of the Royal Society of Literature. Trip to Italy, Spain, Germany, England, and Wales. *The Mother and the Father. Seven English Cities.*

1910 May 6, Mrs. Howells died. Trip to England. *My Mark Twain. Imaginary Interviews.*

1911 Trip to Bermuda. Trip to Spain. *Parting Friends.* Harper begins "Library Edition" of Howells' works, but only six volumes published.

1912 Bought house at York Harbor, Maine. Received L. H. D. from Princeton. Seventy-fifth birthday dinner.

1913 English visit. *New Leaf Mills. Familiar Spanish Travels.* Returned to apartment at 130 W. 57th Street, where he lived for the rest of his life.

1914 *The Seen and Unseen at Stratford-on-Avon.*

1915 Academy of Arts and Letters awarded Howells gold medal for fiction.

1916 *The Daughter of the Storage. The Leatherwood God. Years of My Youth.*

1920 May 10, died in New York City. *Hither and Thither in Germany. Immortality and Sir Oliver Lodge. The Vacation of the Kelwyns.*

1921 *Eighty Years and After. Mrs. Farrell,* which first appeared as "Private Theatricals" in the *Atlantic,* 1875–76.

1928 *Life in Letters of William Dean Howells,* edited by Mildred Howells.

*

Selections from

WILLIAM DEAN HOWELLS

*

AUTOBIOGRAPHY

YEARS OF MY YOUTH

[Howells wrote his autobiography again and again during his long writing career. But nowhere do we find a more delightful description of his printer-father and his own introduction to literature through the printing press, than in Years of My Youth, *written in retrospect by an aging man of 79. At the time to which Howells refers in the following passage, his father was owner and editor of the* Intelligencer, *the Whig paper of Hamilton, Ohio. See Introduction, pp. xxii ff.]*

Part I

Chapter IV

Throughout those years at Hamilton I think of my father as absorbed in the mechanical and intellectual work of his newspaper. My earliest sense of him relates him as much to the types and the press as to the table where he wrote his editorials amidst the talk of the printers, or of the politicians who came to discuss public affairs with him. From a quaint pride, he did not like his printer's craft to be called a trade; he contended that it was a profession; he was interested in it, as the expression of his taste, and the exercise of his ingenuity and invention, and he could supply many deficiencies in its means and processes. He cut fonts of large type for job-work out of apple-wood in default of box or olive; he even made the graver's tools for carving the letters. Nothing pleased him better than to contrive a thing out of something it was not meant for, as making a penknife blade out of an old razor, or the like. He could do almost anything with his ready hand and his ingenious brain, while I have never been able to do anything with mine but write a few score books. But as for the printer's craft with me, it was simply my joy and

pride from the first things I knew of it. I know when I could
not read, for I recall supplying the text from my imagination for
the pictures I found in books, but I do not know when I could
not set type. My first attempt at literature was not written, but
put up in type, and printed off by me. My father praised it, and
this made me so proud that I showed it to one of those eminent
Whig politicians always haunting the office. He made no comment on it, but asked me if I could spell baker. I spelled the
word simple-heartedly, and it was years before I realized that he
meant a hurt to my poor little childish vanity.

Very soon I could set type very well, and at ten years and
onward till journalism became my university, the printing-
office was mainly my school. Of course, like every sort of work
with a boy, the work became irksome to me, and I would gladly
have escaped from it to every sort of play, but it never ceased to
have the charm it first had. Every part of the trade became familiar to me, and if I had not been so little I could at once have
worked not only at case, but at press, as my brother did. I had
my favorites among the printers, who knew me as the Old Man,
because of the habitual gravity which was apt to be broken in
me by bursts of wild hilarity; but I am not sure whether I liked
better the conscience of the young journeyman who wished to
hold me in the leash of his moral convictions, or the nature of
my companion in laughter which seemed to have selected for
him the fit name of Sim Haggett. This merrymaker was married, but so very presently in our acquaintance was widowed,
that I can scarcely put any space between his mourning for his
loss and his rejoicing in the first joke that followed it. There
were three or four of the journeymen, with an apprentice, to do
the work now reduced by many facilities to the competence of
one or two. Some of them slept in a den opening from the
printing-office, where I envied them the wild freedom unham-
pered by the conventions of sweeping, dusting, or bedmaking;
it was next to camping out.

The range of that young experience of mine transcends telling, but the bizarre mixture was pure delight to the boy I was,
already beginning to take the impress of events and characters.

Though I loved the art of printing so much, though my pride even more than my love was taken with it, as something beyond other boys, yet I loved my schools too. In their succession there seem to have been a good many of them, with a variety of teachers, whom I tried to make like me because I liked them. I was gifted in spelling, geography, and reading, but arithmetic was not for me. I could declaim long passages from the speeches of Corwin against the Mexican War, and of Chatham against the American War, and poems from our school readers, or from Campbell or Moore or Byron: but at the blackboard I was dumb. I bore fairly well the mockeries of boys, boldly bad, who played upon a certain simplicity of soul in me, and pretended, for instance, when I came out one night saying I was six years old, that I was a shameless boaster and liar. Swimming, hunting, fishing, foraging at every season, with the skating which the waters of the rivers and canals afforded, were my joy; I took my part in the races and the games, in football and in baseball, then in its feline infancy of Three Corner Cat, and though there was a family rule against fighting, I fought like the rest of the boys and took my defeats as heroically as I knew how; they were mostly defeats.

My world was full of boys, but it was also much haunted by ghosts or the fear of them. Death came early into it, the visible image in a negro babe, with the large red copper cents on its eyelids, which older boys brought me to see, then in the funeral of the dearly loved mate whom we school-fellows followed to his grave. I learned many things in my irregular schooling, and at home I was always reading when I was not playing. I will not pretend that I did not love playing best; life was an experiment which had to be tried in every way that presented itself, but outside of these practical requisitions there was a constant demand upon me from literature. As to the playing I will not speak at large here, for I have already said enough of it in *A Boy's Town*; and as to the reading, the curious must go for it to another book of mine called *My Literary Passions*. Perhaps there was already in my early literary preferences a bent toward the reality which my gift, if I may call it so, has since taken.

I did not willingly read poetry, except such pieces as I mem-
orized: little tragedies of the sad fate of orphan children, and the
cruelties of large birds to small ones, which brought the lump
into my throat, or the moralized song of didactic English
writers of the eighteenth century, such as "Pity the sorrows of
a poor old man." That piece I still partly know by heart; but
history was what I liked best, and if I finally turned to fiction it
seems to have been in the dearth of histories that merited reading
after Goldsmith's *Greece and Rome*[1]*; except Irving's *Conquest of
Granada*, I found none that I could read; but I had then read
Don Quixote and *Gulliver's Travels*, and had heard my father
reading aloud to my mother the poems of Scott and Moore.
Since he seems not to have thought of any histories that would
meet my taste, I fancy that I must have been mainly left to my
own choice in that sort, though he told me of the other sorts of
books which I read.

I should be interested to know now how the notion of authorship first crept into my mind, but I do not in the least know.
I made verses, I even wrote plays in rhyme, but until I attempted
an historical romance I had no sense of literature as an art. As an
art which one might live by, as by a trade or a business, I had
not the slightest conception of it. When I began my first and
last historical romance, I did not imagine it as something to be
read by others; and when the first chapters were shown without
my knowing, I was angry and ashamed. If my father thought
there was anything uncommon in my small performances, he
did nothing to let me guess it unless I must count the instance
of declaiming Halleck's *Marco Bozzaris* before a Swedenborgian
minister who was passing the night at our house. Neither did
my mother do anything to make me conscious, if she was herself conscious of anything out of the common in what I was
trying. It was her sacred instinct to show no partiality among
her children; my father's notion was of the use that could be
combined with the pleasure of life, and perhaps if there had been
anything different in my life, it would not have tended more to
that union of use and pleasure which was his ideal.

[1]*A Boy's Town* (1890), p 172.

Much in the environment was abhorrent to him, and he fought the local iniquities in his paper, the gambling, the drunkenness that marred the mainly moral and religious complexion of the place. In *A Boy's Town* I have studied with a fidelity which I could not emulate here the whole life of it as a boy sees life, and I must leave the reader who cares for such detail to find it there. But I wish again to declare the almost unrivaled fitness of the place to be the home of a boy, with its two branches of the Great Miami River and their freshets in spring, and their witchery at all seasons; with its Hydraulic Channels and Reservoirs, its stretch of the Miami Canal and the Canal Basin so fit for swimming in summer and skating in winter. The mills and factories which harnessed the Hydraulic to their industries were of resistless allure for the boys who frequented them when they could pass the guard of "No Admittance" on their doors, or when they were not foraging among the fields and woods in the endless vacations of the schools. Some boys left school to work in the mills, and when they could show the loss of a finger-joint from the machinery they were prized as heroes. The Fourths of July, the Christmases and Easters and May-Days, which were apparently of greater frequency there and then than they apparently are anywhere now, seemed to alternate with each other through the year, and the Saturdays spread over half the week.

PART II

Chapter IV

[*For two difficult years (1849-1850), the elder Howells attempted, unsuccessfully, to edit the Dayton* Transcript. *The "year of release in the country," which followed this failure, ended when the father became a reporter of the legislature for* The Ohio State Journal. *In 1852 William Cooper Howells became editor of the Ashtabula* Sentinel, *which was soon thereafter moved from Ashtabula to Jefferson, Ohio. Here the Howells family finally became established, through the efforts of the father and his two eldest sons, Joseph ana William. Though both of the sons expressed their dislike of journalism, they were fated to be associated with newspapers and magazines for the rest of their lives. Joseph, after the death of his father, became editor and owner of the* Sentinel; *William soon moved on to the larger journalistic world of Boston.*]

My elder brother and I had several ideals in common quite apart from my own literary ideals. One of these was life in a village, as differenced from life in the country, or in any city, large or little; another was the lasting renunciation of the printing-business in every form. The last was an effect from the anxiety which we had shared with our father and mother in the long adversity, ending in the failure of his newspaper, from which we had escaped to the country. Once clear of that disaster, we meant never to see a press or a case of types again; and after our year of release from them in the country my brother had his hopes of learning the river and becoming a steamboat pilot, but failed in these, and so joined us in Columbus, where he had put off the evil day of his return to the printing-business a little longer. Meanwhile I had yielded to my fate and spent the whole winter in a printing-office; and now we were both going to take up our trade, so abhorrent in its memories, but going gladly because of the chances which it held out to my father at a time when there seemed no other chance in the world for him.

Yet we were about to fulfil our other ideal by going to live in a village. The paper which we were to help make my father make his by our work—for he had no money to buy it—was published in Ashtabula, now a rather obstreperous little city, full of industrial noise and grime, with a harbor emulous of the gigantic activities of the Cleveland lakefront, but it must even then have had a thousand people. Our ideal, therefore, was not perfectly realized till our office was transferred some ten miles inland to the county-seat, for whatever business and political reasons of the joint stock company which had now taken over the paper, with my father as editor. With its four hundred inhabitants less, Jefferson was so much more than Ashtabula a village; and its young gaieties welcomed us and our little force of printers to a social liberty and equality which I long hoped some day to paint as a phase of American civilization worthy the most literal fidelity of fiction. But I shall now never do that, and I must be content to borrow from an earlier page some passages which uninventively record the real events and conditions of our enterprise.

In politics, the county was always overwhelmingly Freesoil, as the forerunner of the Republican party was then called; the Whigs had hardly gathered themselves together since the defeat of General Scott for the Presidency; the Democrats, though dominant in state and nation, and faithful to slavery at every election, did not greatly outnumber among us the zealots called Comeouters, who would not vote at all under a Constitution recognizing the right of men to own men. Our paper was Freesoil, and its field was large among that vast majority of the people who believed that slavery would finally perish if kept out of the territories and confined to the old Slave States.

The people of the county were mostly farmers, and of these nearly all were dairymen. The few manufactures were on a small scale, except perhaps the making of oars, which were shipped all over the world from the heart of the primeval forests densely wooding the vast levels of the region. The portable steam-sawmills dropped down on the borders of the woods have long since eaten their way through and through them, and devoured every stick of timber in most places, and drunk up the water-courses that the woods once kept full; but at that time half the land was in the shadow of those mighty poplars and hickories, elms and chestnuts, ashes and hemlocks; and the meadows that pastured the herds of red cattle were dotted with stumps as thick as harvest stubble. Now there are not even stumps; the woods are gone, and the watercourses are torrents in spring and beds of dry clay in summer. The meadows themselves have vanished, for it has been found that the strong yellow soil will produce more in grain than in milk. There is more money in the hands of the farmers there now, but half a century ago there was so much less that fifty dollars seldom passed through a farmer's hands in a year. Payment was made us in kind rather than in coin, and every sort of farm produce was legal tender at the printing-office. Wood was welcome in any quantity, for our huge box-stove consumed it with inappeasable voracity, and even then did not heat the wide, low room which was at once editorial-room, composing-room, and press-room. Perhaps this was not so much the fault of the stove as of the

building. In that cold, lake-shore country the people dwelt in
wooden structures almost as thin and flimsy as tents; and often
in the first winter of our sojourn the type froze solid with the
water which the compositor put on it when he wished to distribute his case, placed near the window so as to get all the light
there was, but getting all the cold there was, too. From time
to time the compositor's fingers became so stiff that blowing
on them would not avail; he made many excursions between his
stand and the stove; in severe weather he practised the device of
warming his whole case of types by the fire, and, when they
lost heat, warming it again.

The first floor of our office-building was used by a sash-and-
blind factory; there was a machine-shop somewhere in it, and a
mill for sawing out shingles; and it was better fitted to the exercise of these robust industries than to the requirements of our
more delicate craft. Later, we had a more comfortable place, in
a new wooden "business block," and for several years before I
left it the office was domiciled in an old dwelling-house, which
we bought, and which we used without much change. It could
never have been a very comfortable dwelling, and my associations with it are of a wintry cold, scarcely less polar than that
we were inured to elsewhere. In fact, the climate of that region
is rough and fierce; I know that there were lovely summers and
lovelier autumns in my time there, full of sunsets of a strange,
wild, melancholy splendor, I suppose from some atmospheric
influence of the lake; but I think chiefly of the winters, so awful
to us after the mild seasons of southern Ohio; the frosts of ten
and twenty below; the village streets and the country roads
drowned in snow, the consumptives in the thin houses, and the
"slippin'," as the sleighing was called, that lasted from December to April with hardly a break. At first our family was housed
on a farm a little way out, because there was no tenement to be
had in the village, and my father and I used to walk to and from
the office together in the morning and evening. I had taught
myself to read Spanish, in my passion for *Don Quixote*, and I
was now, at the age of fifteen, intending to write a life of Cervantes. The scheme occupied me a good deal in those bleak

walks, and perhaps it was because my head was so hot with it that my feet were always very cold; but my father assured me that they would get warm as soon as my boots froze. If I have never yet written that life of Cervantes, on the other hand I have never been quite able to make it clear to myself why my feet should have got warm when my boots froze.

Part III

Chapter VIII

[*Howells at the age of* 21, *became reporter, news-editor, and editorial writer of the* Ohio State Journal, *of which Henry David Cooke was "our chief" and Samuel R. Reed a beloved elder member of the staff. By* 1860 *Howells felt at home in the sociable little city of Columbus, Ohio. Governor Salmon B. Chase, to whom Howells refers in the following selection, had welcomed the editorial board of the paper to his house, and it is not surprising to find that the* Journal *was supporting Chase's nomination for Presiden on the Republican ticket. More interesting to Howells at this time, however, were the beautiful daughter of the Governor; the evening parties of pre-Civil War Columbus; ana the appearance in* 1860 *of* Poems of Two Friends, *in the writing of which John J. Piatt and Howells collaborated.*]

Chase was of course *our* man for the 1860 nomination, and the political relations between him and our chief were close; but somehow I went more to other houses than to his, though I found myself apparently launched from it upon a social tide that bore me through all the doors of the amiable little city. I was often at the evening parties (we called them evening parties then) which his daughter gave, and one day the Governor himself, as we met in the street, invited me to luncheon with him. I duly went and passed the shining butler's misgiving into the dining-room, where I found the family at table with no vacant place among them. The Governor had forgotten me! That was clear enough, but he was at once repentant, and I lunched with him, outwardly forgiving, but inwardly resolved that it should be the last time I would come at his informal bidding. I have since forgotten much more serious engagements myself; I have not gone to dinners where I have promised over my own signature to go; but at twenty-one men are proud, and

I was prouder then than I can yet find any reason for having been.

In our capital at that day we had rather the social facts than the social forms. We were invited to parties ceremoniously enough, but we did not find it necessary to answer whether we would come or not. Our hostess remained in doubt of us till we came or did not come; at least that was the case with young men; we never inquired whether it was so with young girls or not. But sometimes when a certain youth wished to go with a certain maiden he found out as delicately as he could whether she was invited, and if she was he begged her to let him go with her, and arrived with her in one of the lumbering two-horse hacks which supplied our cab-service, and which I see still bulking in the far perspective of the State Street corner of the State House yard. If you had courage so high or purse so full you had sent the young lady a flower which she wore to the party, preferably a white camellia which the German florist, known to our young world only as Joe, grew very successfully, and allowed you to choose from the tree. Why preferably a camellia I could not say after this lapse of time; perhaps because its cold, odorless purity expressed the unimpassioned emotion which oftenest inspired the gift and its acceptance. It was very simple, very pastoral; I do not know when Columbus outgrew this custom, which of course it did long ago.

Bringing a young lady to a party necessarily meant nothing but that you enjoyed the pleasure of bringing her. Very likely she found her mother there when she came with you, unmindful, the one and the other, that there was such a thing as chaperonage in a more fastidious or censorious world. It seems to me, indeed, that parties at the Columbus houses were never wanting in the elders whom our American society of girls and boys used to be accused of ignoring. They superabounded at the legislative receptions, but even at the affairs which my sophistication early distinguished from those perfunctory hospitalities there were mature people enough, both married and unmarried, who, though they had felt no charge concerning their daughters or nieces, found it agreeable to remain till the young ladies were ready to be seen home by their self-chosen escorts. A youth who

danced so reluctantly as I, was rather often thrown upon these
charitable elders for his entertainment, and I cannot remember
ever failing of it. People, and by people I do not mean women
only, read a good deal in that idyllic Columbus, and it was my
delight to talk with any one who would about the new books or
the old. The old books were known mostly to that number of
professional men—lawyers, doctors, divines, and scientists—
which was disproportionately large in our capital; they were each
cultivated in his own way, and in mine, too, or the better part of
it, as I found. The young and the younger women read the
current fiction and poetry at least enough to be asked whether
they had read this thing or that; and there was a group of young
men with whom I could share my sometimes aggressive interest
in our favorite authors. I put the scale purposely low; I think
that I could truthfully say that there was then no American community west of the Alleghanies which surpassed ours in the
taste for such things. At the same time I must confess that it
would be easy for such an exclusively literary spirit as I was to
deceive himself, and to think that he always found what he may
have oftener brought.

For a long time after the advent of our new journalism, the
kind of writing which we practised—light, sarcastic, a little
cruel, with a preference for the foibles of our political enemies as
themes—seemed to be the pleasure of good society, which in
that serious yet hopeful time did not object to such conscience
as we put into our mocking. Some who possibly trembled at
our boldness darklingly comforted themselves for our persiflage
by the good cause in which it frisked. When anything very
daring came out in the afternoon the young news-editor in his
round of calls could hear the praise of it from charming readers
in the evening, or he might be stopped in the street next day and
told how good it was by the fathers, or brothers, or brothers-in-
law, of those charming readers. It was more like the prompt
acclaim the drama enjoys than the slow recognition of literature;
but I, at least, was always trying to make my writing literature,
and after fifty-odd years it may perhaps be safely owned that I
had mainly a literary interest in the political aspects and events

which I treated. I felt the ethical quality of the slavery question, and I had genuine convictions about it; but for practical politics I did not care; I wished only to understand enough of them to seize any chance for a shot at the other side which they might give. I had been in the midst of practical politics almost from my childhood; through my whole youth the din of meetings, of rallies, of conventions had been in my ears; but I was never at a meeting, a rally, or a convention; I have never yet heard a political speech to the end. For a future novelist, a realist, that was a pity, I think, but so it was.

In that day of lingering intolerance, intolerance which can scarcely be imagined in this day, and which scarcely stopped short of condemning the mild latitudinarianism of the *Autocrat of the Breakfast Table* as infidelity, every one but a few outright atheists was more or less devout. In Columbus everybody went to church; the different forms of Calvinism drew the most worshippers; our chief was decorously constant with his family at the Episcopal service; but Reed was frankly outside of all ecclesiastical allegiance, and I who, no more than he, attended any religious service, believed myself of my father's Swedenborgian faith; at any rate, I could make it my excuse for staying away from other churches, since there were none of mine. While I am about these possibly needless confidences I will own that sermons and lectures as well as speeches have mostly been wearisome to me, and that I have heard only as many of them as I must. Of the three, I prefer sermons; they interest me, they seem really to concern me; but I have been apt to get a suggestive thought from them and hide away with it in a corner of my consciousness and lose the rest. My absences under the few sermons which I then heard must have ended chiefly in the construction or the reconstruction of some scene in my fiction, or some turn of phrase in my verse.

Naturally, under these circumstances, the maturer men whom I knew were oftener doctors of medicine than doctors of divinity; in fact, I do not think I knew one clergyman. This was not because I was oftener sick than sorry; I was often sorry enough, and very sensible of my sins, though I took no established means of repenting them; but I have always found the conversation of physicians more interesting than that of most other men, even authors. I have known myself in times past to say that they were the saints of the earth, as far as we then had saints, but that was in the later Victorian period when people allowed themselves to say anything in honor of science. Now it is already different; we have begun to have our doubts of doubt and to believe that there is much more in faith than we once did; and I, within the present year, my seventy-ninth, have begun to go to church and to follow the sermon with much greater, or more unbroken, attention than I once could, perhaps because I no longer think so much in the terms of fiction or meditate the muse as I much more used to do.

LITERARY FRIENDS AND ACQUAINTANCE

[Literary Friends and Acquaintance *was written in 1900, many years after Howells undertook his editorial duties on* Harper's. *Howells' removal from Boston to New York in 1888 has often been said to mark the ascendency of New York over Boston as the literary center of the country. Though Howells, with his subtle literary sensitivity, moved a little ahead of public tastes, and accepted with eager appreciation the more strident tones of the newer culture, he nevertheless always looked back on New England as the literary source of our national genius. In* Literary Friends and Acquaintance, *Howells gives us an unforgettable picture of his first visit to New England, when the young reporter of 23, from the* Ohio State Journal, *was recognized by Lowell as the heir to the great tradition. See Introduction pp. xlix–li.*]

PART I
My First Visit to New England

I

If there was any one in the world who had his being more wholly in literature than I had in 1860, I am sure I should not have known where to find him, and I doubt if he could have been found nearer the centres of literary activity than I then was, or among those more purely devoted to literature than myself. I had been for three years a writer of news paragraphs, book notices, and political leaders on a daily paper in an inland city, and I do not know that my life differed outwardly from that of any other young journalist, who had begun as I had in a country printing-office, and might be supposed to be looking forward to advancement in his profession or in public affairs. But inwardly it was altogether different with me. Inwardly I was a poet, with no wish to be anything else, unless in a moment of careless affluence I might so far forget myself as to be a novelist. I was, with my friend J. J. Piatt, the half-author of a little volume of very unknown verse,[1] and Mr. Lowell had lately accepted and had begun to print in the *Atlantic Monthly* five or six poems of mine.[2] Besides this I had written poems, and sketches, and criticisms for the *Saturday Press* of New York, a long-forgotten but once very lively expression of literary intention in an extinct bohemia of that city; and I was always writing poems, and sketches, and criticisms in our own paper. These, as well as my feats in the renowned periodicals of the East, met with kindness, if not honor, in my own city which ought to have given me grave doubts whether I was any real prophet. But it only intensified my literary ambition, already so strong that my veins might well have run ink rather than blood, and gave me a higher opinion of my fellow-citizens, if such a thing could be. They were indeed very charming people, and such of them as I mostly saw were readers and lovers of books. Society in Columbus at that day had a pleasant refinement which I think I do not exaggerate in the fond retrospect. It had the finality which it seems to have had nowhere since the war; it had certain fixed ideals, which were none the less graceful and becoming because they were the simple old American ideals, now vanished, or fast vanishing, before the knowledge of good and evil as they have it in Europe, and as it has imparted itself to American travel and sojourn. There was a mixture of many strains in the capital of Ohio, as there was throughout the State. Virginia, Kentucky, Pennsylvania, New York, and New England all joined to characterize the manners and customs. I suppose it was the South which gave the social tone; the intellectual taste among the elders was the Southern taste for the classic and the standard in literature; but we who were younger preferred the modern authors: we read Thackeray, and George Eliot, and Hawthorne, and Charles Reade, and De Quincey, and Tennyson, and Browning,

---

[1] *Poems of Two Friends*, 1860.

[2] "Andenken," *Atlantic*, V (January, 1860), 100–102, "The Poet's Friends," V (February, 1860), 185, "Pleasure-pain," V (April, 1860), 468–470, "Lost Beliefs," V (April, 1860), 486, "The Pilot's ¦Story," VI (September, 1860), 323–325, "The Old Homestead," VII (February, 1861), 213. For titles in the *Saturday Press* and elsewhere, see Gibson and Arms, *A Bibliography of William Dean Howells* (New York, 1948).

and Emerson, and Longfellow; and I—I read Heine, and evermore Heine, when there was not some new thing from the
others. Now and then an immediate French book penetrated to
us: we read Michelet and About, I remember. We looked to
England and the East largely for our literary opinions; we
accepted the *Saturday Review* as law if we could not quite receive
it as gospel. One of us took the *Cornhill Magazine*, because
Thackeray was the editor; the *Atlantic Monthly* counted many
readers among us; and a visiting young lady from New England[1],
who screamed at sight of the periodical in one of our houses,
"Why, have you got the *Atlantic Monthly out here?*" could be
answered, with cold superiority, "There are several *contributors*
to the *Atlantic* in Columbus." There were in fact two: my roommate,[2] who wrote Browning for it, while I wrote Heine and
Longfellow. But I suppose two are as rightfully several as
twenty are.

II

That was the heyday of lecturing, and now and then a literary
light from the East swam into our skies. I heard and saw Emerson, and I once met Bayard Taylor socially, at the hospitable
house where he was a guest after his lecture. Heaven knows
how I got through the evening. I do not think I opened my
mouth to address him a word; it was as much as I could do to sit
and look at him, while he tranquilly smoked, and chatted with
our host, and quaffed the beer which we had very good in the
West. All the while I did him homage as the first author by
calling whom I had met. I longed to tell him how much I liked
his poems, which we used to get by heart in those days, and I
longed (how much more I longed!) to have him know that—

"Auch ich war in Arkadien geboren,"[3]

that I had printed poems in the *Atlantic Monthly* and the *Saturday Press*, and was the potential author of things destined to

[1]Elinor G. Mead, whom Howells married in 1862.
[2]Thomas Fullerton. *Life in Letters*, I, 15.
[3]Goethe, *Travels in Italy* (Motto).

eclipse all literature hitherto attempted. But I could not tell him; and there was no one else who thought to tell him. Perhaps it was as well so; I might have perished of his recognition, for my modesty was equal to my merit.

In fact I think we were all rather modest young fellows, we who formed the group wont to spend some part of every evening at that house, where there was always music, or whist, or gay talk, or all three. We had our opinions of literary matters, but (perhaps because we had mostly accepted them from England or New England, as I have said) we were not vain of them; and we would by no means have urged them before a living literary man like that. I believe none of us ventured to speak, except the poet, my roommate, who said, He believed so and so was the original of so and so; and was promptly told, He had no right to say such a thing. Naturally, we came away rather critical of our host's guest, whom I afterwards knew as the kindliest heart in the world. But we had not shone in his presence, and that galled us; and we chose to think that he had not shone in ours.

III

At that time he was filling a large space in the thoughts of the young people who had any thoughts about literature. He had come to his full repute as an agreeable and intelligent traveller, and he still wore the halo of his early adventures afoot in foreign lands when they were yet really foreign. He had not written his novels of American life, once so welcomed, and now so forgotten; it was very long before he had achieved that incomparable translation of Faust which must always remain the finest and best, and which would keep his name alive with Goethe's, if he had done nothing else worthy of remembrance. But what then most commended to the regard of us star-eyed youth (now blinking sadly toward our seventies) was the poetry which he printed in the magazines from time to time: in the first *Putnam's* (where there was a dashing picture of him in an Arab burnoose and a turban), and in *Harper's*, and in the *Atlantic*. It was often very lovely poetry, I thought, and I still think so; and

it was rightfully his, though it paid the inevitable allegiance to
the manner of the great masters of the day. It was graced for us
by the pathetic romance of his early love, which some of its
sweetest and saddest numbers confessed, for the young girl he
married almost in her death hour; and we who were hoping to
have our hearts broken, or already had them so, would have been
glad of something more of the obvious poet in the popular
lecturer we had seen refreshing himself after his hour on the
platform.

He remained for nearly a year the only author I had seen, and
I met him once again before I saw any other. Our second
meeting was far from Columbus, as far as remote Quebec, when
I was on my way to New England by way of Niagara and the
Canadian rivers and cities. I stopped in Toronto, and realized
myself abroad without any signal adventures; but at Montreal
something very pretty happened to me. I came into the hotel
office, the evening of a first day's lonely sight-seeing, and vainly
explored the register for the name of some acquaintance; as I
turned from it two smartly dressed young fellows embraced it,
and I heard one of them say, to my great amaze and happiness,
"Hello, here's Howells!"

"Oh," I broke out upon him, "I was just looking for some
one *I* knew. I hope you are some one who knows *me*!"

"Only through your contributions to the *Saturday Press*,"
said the young fellow, and with these golden words, the precious
first personal recognition of my authorship I had ever received
from a stranger, and the rich reward of all my literary endeavor,
he introduced himself and his friend. I do not know what
became of this friend, or where or how he eliminated himself;
but we two others were inseparable from that moment. He was
a young lawyer from New York, and when I came back from
Italy, four or five years later, I used to see his sign in Wall
Street, with a never-fulfilled intention of going in to see him.
In whatever world he happens now to be, I should like to send
him my greetings, and confess to him that my art has never
since brought me so sweet a recompense, and nothing a thousandth part so much like Fame, as that outcry of his over the

hotel register in Montreal. We were comrades for four or five rich days, and shared our pleasures and expenses in viewing the monuments of those ancient Canadian capitals, which I think we valued at all their picturesque worth. We made jokes to mask our emotions; we giggled and made giggle, in the right way; we fell in and out of love with all the pretty faces and dresses we saw; and we talked evermore about literature and literary people. He had more acquaintance with the one, and more passion for the other, but he could tell me of Pfaff's lager-beer cellar on Broadway[1], where the *Saturday Press* fellows and the other bohemians met; and this, for the time, was enough: I resolved to visit it as soon as I reached New York, in spite of the tobacco and beer (which I was given to understand were *de rigueur*), though they both, so far as I had known them, were apt to make me sick.

I was very desolate after I parted from this good fellow, who returned to Montreal on his way to New York, while I remained in Quebec to continue later on mine to New England. When I came in from seeing him off in a calash for the boat, I discovered Bayard Taylor in the reading-room, where he sat sunken in what seemed a somewhat weary muse. He did not know me, or even notice me, though I made several errands in and out of the reading-room in the vain hope that he might do so: doubly vain, for I am aware now that I was still flown with the pride of that pretty experience in Montreal, and trusted in a repetition of something like it. At last, as no chance volunteered to help me, I mustered courage to go up to him and name myself, and say I had once had the pleasure of meeting him at Doctor ————'s in Columbus. The poet gave no sign of consciousness at the sound of a name which I had fondly begun to think might not be so all unknown. He looked up with an unkindling eye, and asked, Ah, how was the Doctor? and when I had reported favorably of the Doctor, our conversation ended.

He was probably as tired as he looked, and he must have

---

[1] *Trow's New York City Directory*, 1859–60, lists "Pfaff Charles, liquors, h[ouse] 647 B'way." The *Directory* for the next year substitutes the word "restaurant" for "liquors."

classed me with that multitude all over the country who had shared the pleasure I professed in meeting him before; it was surely my fault that I did not speak my name loud enough to be recognized, if I spoke it at all; but the courage I had mustered did not quite suffice for that. In after years he assured me, first by letter and then by word, of his grief for an incident which I can only recall now as the untoward beginning of a cordial friendship. It was often my privilege, in those days, as reviewer and editor, to testify my sense of the beautiful things he did in so many kinds of literature, but I never liked any of them better than I liked him. He had a fervent devotion to his art, and he was always going to do the greatest things in it, with an expectation of effect that never failed him. The things he actually did were none of them mean, or wanting in quality, and some of them are of a lasting charm that any one may feel who will turn to his poems; but no doubt many of them fell short of his hopes of them with the reader. It was fine to meet him when he was full of a new scheme; he talked of it with a single-hearted joy, and tried to make you see it of the same colors and proportions it wore to his eyes. He spared no toil to make it the perfect thing he dreamed it, and he was not discouraged by any disappointment he suffered with the critic or the public.

He was a tireless worker, and at last his health failed under his labors at the newspaper desk, beneath the midnight gas, when he should long have rested from such labors. I believe he was obliged to do them through one of those business fortuities which deform and embitter all our lives; but he was not the man to spare himself in any case. He was always attempting new things, and he never ceased endeavoring to make his scholarship reparation for the want of earlier opportunity and training. I remember that I met him once in a Cambridge street with a book in his hand which he let me take in mine. It was a Greek author, and he said he was just beginning to read the language at fifty: a patriarchal age to me of the early thirties! I suppose I intimated the surprise I felt at his taking it up so late in the day, for he said, with charming seriousness, "Oh, but you know, I expect to use it in the other world." Yes, that made it worth while, I consented; but was he sure of the other world? "As sure as I am of this," he said; and I have always kept the impression of the young faith which spoke in his voice and was more than his words.

I saw him last in the hour of those tremendous adieux which were paid him in New York before he sailed to be minister in Germany. It was one of the most graceful things done by President Hayes, who, most of all our Presidents after Lincoln, honored himself in honoring literature by his appointments, to give that place to Bayard Taylor. There was no one more fit for it, and it was peculiarly fit that he should be so distinguished to a people who knew and valued his scholarship and the service he had done German letters. He was as happy in it, apparently, as a man could be in anything here below, and he enjoyed to the last drop the many cups of kindness pressed to his lips in parting; though I believe these farewells, at a time when he was already fagged with work and excitement, were notably harmful to him, and helped to hasten his end. Some of us who were near of friendship went down to see him off when he sailed, as the dismal and futile wont of friends is; and I recall the kind, great fellow standing in the cabin, amid those sad flowers that heaped the tables, saying good-by to one after another, and smiling fondly, smiling wearily, upon all. There was champagne, of course, and an odious hilarity, without meaning and without remission, till the warning bell chased us ashore, and our brave poet escaped with what was left of his life.

IV

I have followed him far from the moment of our first meeting; but even on my way to venerate those New England luminaries, which chiefly drew my eyes, I could not pay a less devoir to an author who, if Curtis[1] was not, was chief of the New York group of authors in that day. I distinguished between the New-Englanders and the New-Yorkers, and I suppose there is no question but our literary centre was then in Boston, wherever it is, or is

[1]George William Curtis (1824–1892).

not, at present. But I thought Taylor then, and I think him now, one of the first in our whole American province of the republic of letters, in a day when it was in a recognizably flourishing state, whether we regard quantity or quality in the names that gave it lustre. Lowell was then in perfect command of those varied forces which will long, if not lastingly, keep him in memory as first among our literary men, and master in more kinds than any other American. Longfellow was in the fulness of his world-wide fame, and in the ripeness of the beautiful genius which was not to know decay while life endured. Emerson had emerged from the popular darkness which had so long held him a hopeless mystic, and was shining a lambent star of poesy and prophecy at the zenith. Hawthorne, the exquisite artist, the unrivalled dreamer, whom we still always liken this one and that one to, whenever this one or that one promises greatly to please us, and still leave without a rival, without a companion, had lately returned from his long sojourn abroad, and had given us the last of the incomparable romances which the world was to have perfect from his hand. Doctor Holmes had surpassed all expectations in those who most admired his brilliant humor and charming poetry by the invention of a new attitude if not a new sort in literature. The turn that civic affairs had taken was favorable to the widest recognition of Whittier's splendid lyrical gift; and that heart of fire, doubly snow-bound by Quaker tradition and Puritan environment, was penetrating every generous breast with its flamy impulses, and fusing all wills in its noble purpose. Mrs. Stowe, who far outfamed the rest as the author of the most renowned novel ever written, was proving it no accident or miracle by the fiction she was still writing.

This great New England group might be enlarged perhaps without loss of quality by the inclusion of Thoreau, who came somewhat before his time, and whose drastic criticism of our expediential and mainly futile civilization would find more intelligent acceptance now than it did then, when all resentment of its defects was specialized in enmity to Southern slavery. Doctor Edward Everett Hale belonged in this group too, by virtue of that humor, the most inventive and the most fantastic, the sanest, the sweetest, the truest, which had begun to find expression in the *Atlantic Monthly*; and there a wonderful young girl had written a series of vivid sketches and taken the heart of youth everywhere with amaze and joy, so that I thought it would be no less an event to meet Harriet Prescott than to meet any of those I have named.

I expected somehow to meet them all, and I imagined them all easily accessible in the office of the *Atlantic Monthly*, which had lately adventured in the fine air of high literature where so many other periodicals had gasped and died before it. The best of these, hitherto, and better even than the *Atlantic* for some reasons, the lamented *Putnam's Magazine*, had perished of inanition at New York, and the claim of the commercial capital to the literary primacy had passed with that brilliant venture. New York had nothing distinctive to show for American literature but the decrepit and doting *Knickerbocker Magazine*. *Harper's New Monthly*, though Curtis had already come to it from the wreck of *Putnam's*, and it had long ceased to be eclectic in material, and had begun to stand for native work in the allied arts which it has since so magnificently advanced, was not distinctively literary, and the *Weekly* had just begun to make itself known. The *Century*, *Scribner's*, the *Cosmopolitan*, *McClure's*, and I know not what others, were still unimagined by five, and ten, and twenty years, and the *Galaxy* was to flash and fade before any of them should kindle its more effectual fires. The *Nation*, which was destined to chastise rather than nurture our young literature, had still six years of dreamless potentiality before it; and the *Nation* was always more Bostonian than New-Yorkish by nature, whatever it was by nativity.

Philadelphia had long counted for nothing in the literary field. *Graham's Magazine* at one time showed a certain critical force, but it seemed to perish of this expression of vitality; and there remained *Godey's Lady's Book* and *Peterson's Magazine*, publications really incredible in their insipidity. In the South there was nothing but a mistaken social ideal, with the moral principles all standing on their heads in defence of slavery; and in the West there was a feeble and foolish notion that Western talent was repressed by Eastern jealousy. At Boston chiefly, if not at Boston alone, was there a vigorous intellectual life among such authors as I have named. Every young writer was ambitious to join his name with theirs in the *Atlantic Monthly*, and in the lists of Ticknor & Fields, who were literary publishers in a sense such as the business world has known nowhere else before or since. Their imprint was a warrant of quality to the reader and of immortality to the author, so that if I could have had a book issued by them at that day I should now be in the full enjoyment of an undying fame.

v

Such was the literary situation as the passionate pilgrim from the West approached his holy land at Boston, by way of the Grand Trunk Railway from Quebec to Portland. I have no recollection of a sleeping-car, and I suppose I waked and watched during the whole of that long, rough journey; but I should hardly have slept if there had been a car for the purpose. I was too eager to see what New England was like, and too anxious not to lose the least glimpse of it, to close my eyes after I crossed the border at Island Pond. I found that in the elm-dotted levels of Maine it was very like the Western Reserve in northern Ohio, which is, indeed, a portion of New England transferred with all its characteristic features, and flattened out along the lake shore. It was not till I began to run southward into the older regions of the country that it lost this look, and became gratefully strange to me. It never had the effect of hoary antiquity which I had expected of a country settled more than two centuries; with its wood-built farms and villages it looked newer than the coal-smoked brick of southern Ohio. I had pre-figured the New England landscape bare of forests, relieved here and there with the trees of orchards or plantations; but I found apparently as much woodland as at home.

At Portland I first saw the ocean, and this was a sort of dis-appointment. Tides and salt water I had already had at Quebec, so that I was no longer on the alert for them; but the color and the vastness of the sea I was still to try upon my vision. When I stood on the Promenade at Portland with the kind young Unitarian minister whom I had brought a letter to, and who led me there for a most impressive first view of the ocean, I could not make more of it than there was of Lake Erie; and I have never thought the color of the sea comparable to the tender blue of the lake. I did not hint my disappointment to my friend; I had too much regard for the feelings of an Eastern man to decry his ocean to his face, and I felt besides that it would be vulgar and provincial to make comparisons. I am glad now that I held my tongue, for that kind soul is no longer in this world, and I should not like to think he knew how far short of my expectations the sea he was so proud of had fallen. I went up with him into a tower or belvedere there was at hand; and when he pointed to the eastern horizon and said, Now there was nothing but sea between us and Africa, I pretended to expand with the thought, and began to sound myself for the emotions which I ought to have felt at such a sight. But in my heart I was empty, and heaven knows whether I saw the steamer which the ancient mariner in charge of that tower invited me to look at through his telescope. I never could see anything but a vitreous glare through a telescope, which has a vicious habit of dodging about through space, and failing to bring down anything of less than planetary magnitude.

But there was something at Portland vastly more to me than seas or continents, and that was the house where Longfellow was born. I believe, now, I did not get the right house, but only the house he went to live in later; but it served, and I rejoiced in it with a rapture that could not have been more genuine if it had been the real birthplace of the poet. I got my friend to show me

> "—the breezy dome of groves,
> The shadows of Deering's woods,"[1]

because they were in one of Longfellow's loveliest and tenderest poems; and I made an errand to the docks, for the sake of the

---

[1] This quotation and the three that follow are all taken from "My Lost Youth," by H. W. Longfellow.

> "—black wharves and the slips,
>   And the sea-tides tossing free,
> And Spanish sailors with bearded lips,
> And the beauty and mystery of the ships,
>   And the magic of the sea,"

mainly for the reason that these were colors and shapes of the
fond vision of the poet's past. I am in doubt whether it was at
this time or a later time that I went to revere

> "—the dead captains as they lay
> In their graves o'erlooking the tranquil bay,
>   Where they in battle died,"

but I am quite sure it was now that I wandered under

> "—the trees which shadow each well-known street,
> As they balance up and down,"

for when I was next in Portland the great fire had swept the city
avenues bare of most of those beautiful elms, whose Gothic
arches and traceries I well remember.

The fact is that in those days I was bursting with the most
romantic expectations of life in every way, and I looked at the
whole world as material that might be turned into literature, or
that might be associated with it somehow. I do not know how
I managed to keep these preposterous hopes within me, but
perhaps the trick of satirizing them, which I had early learnt,
helped me to do it. I was at that particular moment resolved
above all things to see things as Heinrich Heine saw them, or
at least to report them as he did, no matter how I saw them; and
I went about framing phrases to this end, and trying to match
the objects of interest to them whenever there was the least
chance of getting them together.

VI

I do not know how I first arrived in Boston, or whether it
was before or after I had passed a day or two in Salem. As
Salem is on the way from Portland, I will suppose that I stopped

there first, and explored the quaint old town (quainter then than now, but still quaint enough) for the memorials of Hawthorne and of the witches which united to form the Salem I cared for. I went and looked up the House of Seven Gables, and suffered an unreasonable disappointment that it had not a great many more of them; but there was no loss in the death-warrant of Bridget Bishop,[1] with the sheriff's return of execution upon it, which I found at the Court-house; if anything, the pathos of that witness of one of the cruelest delusions in the world was rather in excess of my needs; I could have got on with less. I saw the pins which the witches were sworn to have thrust into the afflicted children, and I saw Gallows Hill, where the hapless victims of the perjury were hanged. But that death-warrant remained the most vivid color of my experience of the tragedy; I had no need to invite myself to a sense of it, and it is still like a stain of red in my memory.

The kind old ship's captain whose guest I was, and who was transfigured to poetry in my sense by the fact that he used to voyage to the African coast for palm-oil in former days, led me all about the town, and showed me the Custom-house, which I desired to see because it was in the preface to the *Scarlet Letter*. But I perceived that he did not share my enthusiasm for the author, and I became more and more sensible that in Salem air there was a cool undercurrent of feeling about him. No doubt the place was not altogether grateful for the celebrity his romance had given it, and would have valued more the uninterrupted quiet of its own flattering thoughts of itself; but when it came to hearing a young lady say she knew a girl who said she would like to poison Hawthorne, it seemed to the devout young pilgrim from the West that something more of love for the great romancer would not have been too much for him. Hawthorne had already had his say, however, and he had not used his native town with any great tenderness. Indeed, the advantages to any place of having a great genius born and reared in its midst are so doubtful that it might be well for

[1]The first person to be hanged as a witch in Salem, June, 1692. Charles W. Upham, *Salem Witchcraft* (1867), II, 266.

localities designing to become the birthplaces of distinguished
authors to think twice about it. Perhaps only the largest capitals, like London and Paris, and New York and Chicago, ought
to risk it. But the authors have an unaccountable perversity,
and will seldom come into the world in the large cities, which
are alone without the sense of neighborhood, and the personal
susceptibilities so unfavorable to the practice of the literary art.

I dare say that it was owing to the local indifference to her
greatest name, or her reluctance from it, that I got a clearer
impression of Salem in some other respects than I should have
had if I had been invited there to devote myself solely to the
associations of Hawthorne. For the first time I saw an old New
England town, I do not know but the most characteristic, and
took into my young Western consciousness the fact of a more
complex civilization than I had yet known. My whole life had
been passed in a region where men were just beginning ancestors, and the conception of family was very imperfect. Literature of course was full of it, and it was not for a devotee of
Thackeray to be theoretically ignorant of its manifestations; but
I had hitherto carelessly supposed that family was nowhere
regarded seriously in America except in Virginia, where it furnished a joke for the rest of the nation. But now I found myself
confronted with it in its ancient houses, and heard its names
pronounced with a certain consideration, which I dare say was
as much their due in Salem as it could be anywhere. The names
were all strange, and all indifferent to me, but those fine square
wooden mansions, of a tasteful architecture, and a pale buff-
color, withdrawing themselves in quiet reserve from the quiet
street, gave me an impression of family as an actuality and a
force which I had never had before, but which no Westerner
can yet understand the East without taking into account. I do
not suppose that I conceived of family as a fact of vital import
then; I think I rather regarded it as a color to be used in any
aesthetic study of the local conditions. I am not sure that I
valued it more even for literary purposes, than the steeple which
the captain pointed out as the first and last thing he saw when he
came and went on his long voyages, or than the great palm-oil

casks, which he showed me, and which I related to the tree that stood

"Auf brennender Felsenwand."[1]

Whether that was the kind of palm that gives the oil, or was a sort only suitable to be the dream of a lonely fir-tree in the North on a cold height, I am in doubt to this day.

I heard, not without concern, that the neighboring industry of Lynn was penetrating Salem, and that the ancient haunt of the witches and the birthplace of our subtlest and somberest wizard was becoming a great shoetown; but my concern was less for its memories and sensibilities than for an odious duty which I owed that industry, together with all the others in New England. Before I left home I had promised my earliest publisher that I would undertake to edit, or compile, or do something literary to, a work on the operation of the more distinctive mechanical inventions of our country, which he had conceived the notion of publishing by subscription. He had furnished me, the most immechanical of humankind, with a letter addressed generally to the great mills and factories of the East, entreating their managers to unfold their mysteries to me for the purposes of this volume. His letter had the effect of shutting up some of them like clams, and others it put upon their guard against my researches, lest I should seize the secret of their special inventions and publish it to the world. I could not tell the managers that I was both morally and mentally incapable of this; that they might have explained and demonstrated the properties and functions of their most recondite machinery, and upon examination afterwards found me guiltless of having anything but a few verses of Heine or Tennyson or Longfellow in my head. So I had to suffer in several places from their unjust anxieties, and from my own weariness of their ingenious engines, or else endure the pangs of a bad conscience from ignoring them. As long as I was in Canada I was happy, for there was no industry in Canada that I saw, except that of the peasant girls, in their Evangeline hats and kirtles, tossing the hay in the way-side fields; but when I reached Portland my troubles began. I went

[1] Heinrich Heine, "Der Fichtenbaum."

with that young minister of whom I have spoken to a large foundry, where they were casting some sort of ironmongery, and inspected the process from a distance beyond any chance spurt of the molten metal, and came away sadly uncertain of putting the rather fine spectacle to any practical use. A manufactory where they did something with coal-oil (which I now heard for the first time called kerosene) refused itself to me, and I said to myself that probably all the other industries of Portland were as reserved, and I would not seek to explore them; but when I got to Salem, my conscience stirred again. If I knew that there were shoe-shops in Salem, ought not I to go and inspect their processes? This was a question which would not answer itself to my satisfaction, and I had no peace till I learned that I could see shoemaking much better at Lynn, and that Lynn was such a little way from Boston that I could readily run up there, if I did not wish to examine the shoe machinery at once. I promised myself that I would run up from Boston, but in order to do this I must first go to Boston.

VII

I am supposing still that I saw Salem before I saw Boston, but however the fact may be, I am sure that I decided it would be better to see shoemaking in Lynn, where I really did see it, thirty years later. For the purposes of the present visit, I contented myself with looking at a machine in Haverhill, which chewed a shoe sole full of pegs, and dropped it out of its iron jaws with an indifference as great as my own, and probably as little sense of how it had done its work. I may be unjust to that machine; heaven knows I would not wrong it; and I must confess that my head had no room in it for the conception of any machinery but the mythological, which also I despised, in my revulsion from the eighteenth-century poets to those of my own day.

I cannot quite make out after the lapse of so many years just how or when I got to Haverhill, or whether it was before or after I had been in Salem. There is an apparitional quality in my presences, at this point or that, in the dim past; but I hope that, for the credit of their order, ghosts are not commonly taken with such trivial things as I was. For instance, in Haverhill I was much interested by the sight of a young man, coming gayly down the steps of the hotel where I lodged, in peg-top trousers so much more peg-top than my own that I seemed to be wearing mere spring-bottoms in comparison; and in a day when every one who respected himself had a necktie as narrow as he could get, this youth had one no wider than a shoestring, and red at that, while mine measured almost an inch, and was black. To be sure, he was one of a band of Negro minstrels, who were to give a concert that night, and he had a right to excel in fashion.

I will suppose, for convenience' sake, that I visited Haverhill, too, before I reached Boston: somehow that shoe-pegging machine must come in, and it may as well come in here. When I actually found myself in Boston, there were perhaps industries which it would have been well for me to celebrate, but I either made believe there were none, or else I honestly forgot all about them. In either case I released myself altogether to the literary and historical associations of the place. I need not say that I gave myself first to the first, and it rather surprised me to find that the literary associations of Boston referred so largely to Cambridge. I did not know much about Cambridge, except that it was the seat of the university where Lowell was, and Longfellow had been, professor; and somehow I had not realized it as the home of these poets. That was rather stupid of me, but it is best to own the truth, and afterward I came to know the place so well that I may safely confess my earlier ignorance.

I had stopped in Boston at the Tremont House, which was still one of the first hostelries of the country, and I must have inquired my way to Cambridge there; but I was sceptical of the direction the Cambridge horsecar took when I found it, and I hinted to the driver my anxieties as to why he should be starting east when I had been told that Cambridge was west of Boston. He reassured me in the laconic and sarcastic manner of his kind, and we really reached Cambridge by the route he had taken.

The beautiful elms that shaded great part of the way massed

themselves in the "groves of academe" at the Square, and showed pleasant glimpses of "Old Harvard's scholar factories red," then far fewer than now. It must have been in vacation, for I met no one as I wandered through the college yard, trying to make up my mind as to how I should learn where Lowell lived; for it was he whom I had come to find. He had not only taken the poems I sent him, but he had printed two of them in a single number of the *Atlantic*,[1] and had even written me a little note about them, which I wore next to my heart in my breast pocket till I almost wore it out; and so I thought I might fitly report myself to him. But I have always been helpless in finding my way, and I was still depressed by my failure to convince the horse-car driver that he had taken the wrong road. I let several people go by without questioning them, and those I did ask abashed me farther by not knowing what I wanted to know. When I had remitted my search for the moment, an ancient man, with an open mouth and an inquiring eye, whom I never afterwards made out in Cambridge, addressed me with a hospitable offer to show me the Washington Elm. I thought this would give me time to embolden myself for the meeting with the editor of the *Atlantic* if I should ever find him, and I went with that kind old man, who when he had shown me the tree, and the spot where Washington stood when he took command of the Continental forces, said that he had a branch of it, and that if I would come to his house with him he would give me a piece. In the end, I meant merely to flatter him into telling me where I could find Lowell, but I dissembled my purpose and pretended a passion for a piece of the historic elm, and the old man led me not only to his house but his wood-house, where he sawed me off a block so generous that I could not get it into my pocket. I feigned the gratitude which I could see that he expected, and then I took courage to put my question to him. Perhaps that patriarch lived only in the past, and cared for history and not literature. He confessed that he could not tell me where to find Lowell; but he did not forsake me; he set forth

[1] "Pleasure-pain," *Atlantic*, V (April, 1860), pp. 468–470, and "Lost Beliefs," *ibid.*, p. 486.

with me upon the street again, and let no man pass without asking him. In the end we met one who was able to say where Mr. Lowell was, and I found him at last in a little study at the rear of a pleasant, old-fashioned house near the Delta.

Lowell was not then at the height of his fame; he had just reached this thirty years after, when he died; but I doubt if he was ever after a greater power in his own country, or more completely embodied the literary aspiration which would not and could not part itself from the love of freedom and the hope of justice. For the sake of these he had been willing to suffer the reproach which followed their friends in the earlier days of the anti-slavery struggle. He had outlived the reproach long before; but the fear of his strength remained with those who had felt it, and he had not made himself more generally loved by the *Fable for Critics* than by the *Biglow Papers*, probably. But in the *Vision of Sir Launfal* and the *Legend of Brittany* he had won a liking if not a listening far wider than his humor and his wit had got him; and in his lectures on the English poets, given not many years before he came to the charge of the *Atlantic*, he had proved himself easily the wisest and finest critic in our language. He was already more than any American poet,

> "Dowered with the hate of hate, the scorn of scorn,
> The love of love."[1]

and he held a place in the public sense which no other author among us has held. I had myself never been a great reader of his poetry, when I met him, though when I was a boy of ten years I had heard my father repeat passages from the *Biglow Papers* against war and slavery and the war for slavery upon Mexico, and later I had read those criticisms of English poetry, and I knew Sir Launfal must be Lowell in some sort; but my love for him as a poet was chiefly centred in my love for his tender rhyme, *Auf Wiedersehen*, which I cannot yet read without something of the young pathos it first stirred in me. I knew and felt his greatness somehow apart from the literary proofs of it; he ruled my fancy and held my allegiance as a character, as a man; and I am neither sorry nor ashamed that I was abashed when I

[1]Alfred, Lord Tennyson, "The Poet," stanza 1.

first came into his presence; and that in spite of his words of welcome I sat inwardly quaking before him. He was then forty-one years old, and nineteen my senior, and if there had been nothing else to awe me, I might well have been quelled by the disparity of our ages. But I have always been willing and even eager to do homage to men who have done something, and notably to men who have done something in the sort I wished to do something in, myself. I could never recognize any other sort of superiority; but that I am proud to recognize; and I had before Lowell some such feeling as an obscure subaltern might have before his general. He was by nature a bit of a disciplinarian, and the effect was from him as well as in me; I dare say he let me feel whatever difference there was, as helplessly as I felt it. At the first encounter with people he always was apt to have a certain frosty shyness, a smiling cold, as from the long, high-sunned winters of his Puritan race; he was not quite himself till he had made you aware of his quality: then no one could be sweeter, tenderer, warmer than he; then he made you free of his whole heart; but you must be his captive before he could do that. His whole personality had now an instant charm for me; I could not keep my eyes from those beautiful eyes of his, which had a certain starry serenity, and looked out so purely from under his white forehead, shadowed with auburn hair untouched by age; or from the smile that shaped the auburn beard, and gave the face in its form and color the Christ-look which Page's portrait has flattered in it.

His voice had as great a fascination for me as his face. The vibrant tenderness and the crisp clearness of the tones, the perfect modulation, the clear enunciation, the exquisite accent, the elect diction—I did not know enough then to know that these were the gifts, these were the graces, of one from whose tongue our rough English came music such as I should never hear from any other. In this speech there was nothing of our slipshod American slovenliness, but a truly Italian conscience and an artistic sense of beauty in the instrument.

I saw, before he sat down across his writing-table from me, that he was not far from the medium height; but his erect carriage made the most of his five feet and odd inches. He had been smoking the pipe he loved, and he put it back in his mouth, presently, as if he found himself at greater ease with it, when he began to chat, or rather to let me show what manner of young man I was by giving me the first word. I told him of the trouble I had in finding him, and I could not help dragging in something about Heine's search for Börne, when he went to see him in Frankfort; but I felt at once this was a false start, for Lowell was such an impassioned lover of Cambridge, which was truly his *patria*, in the Italian sense, that it must have hurt him to be unknown to any one in it; he said, a little dryly, that he should not have thought I would have so much difficulty; but he added, forgivingly, that this was not his own house, which he was out of for the time. Then he spoke to me of Heine, and when I showed my ardor for him, he sought to temper it with some judicious criticisms, and told me that he had kept the first poem I sent him, for the long time it had been unacknowledged, to make sure that it was not a translation. He asked me about myself, and my name, and its Welsh origin, and seemed to find the vanity I had in this harmless enough. When I said I had tried hard to believe that I was at least the literary descendant of Sir James Howels, he corrected me gently with "James Howel," and took down a volume of the *Familiar Letters* from the shelves behind him to prove me wrong. This was always his habit, as I found afterwards: when he quoted anything from a book he liked to get it and read the passage over, as if he tasted a kind of hoarded sweetness in the words. It visibly vexed him if they showed him in the least mistaken; but

"The love he bore to learning was at fault"[1]

for this foible, and that other of setting people right if he thought them wrong. I could not assert myself against his version of Howel's name, for my edition of his letters was far away in Ohio, and I was obliged to own that the name was spelt in several different ways in it. He perceived, no doubt, why I had chosen the form likest my own, with the title which the pleasant old turncoat ought to have had from the many masters he served

[1] Oliver Goldsmith, "The Deserted Village," line 197.

according to their many minds, but never had except from that
erring edition. He did not afflict me for it, though; probably it
amused him too much; he asked me about the West, and when
he found that I was as proud of the West as I was of Wales, he
seemed even better pleased, and said he had always fancied that
human nature was laid out on rather a larger scale there than in
the East, but he had seen very little of the West. In my heart
I did not think this then, and I do not think it now; human nature has had more ground to spread over in the West; that is all;
but "it was not for me to bandy words with my sovereign."
He said he liked to hear of the differences between the different
sections, for what we had most to fear in our country was a
wearisome sameness of type.

He did not say now, or at any other time during the many
years I knew him, any of those slighting things of the West
which I had so often to suffer from Eastern people, but suffered
me to praise it all I would. He asked me what way I had taken
in coming to New England, and when I told him, and began to
rave of the beauty and quaintness of French Canada, and to pour
out my joy in Quebec, he said, with a smile that had now lost all
its frost, Yes, Quebec was a bit of the seventeenth century;
it was in many ways more French than France, and its people
spoke the language of Voltaire, with the accent of Voltaire's time.

I do not remember what else he talked of, though once I
remembered it with what I believed an ineffaceable distinctness.
I set nothing of it down at the time; I was too busy with the letters I was writing for a Cincinnati paper; and I was severely
bent upon keeping all personalities out of them. This was very
well, but I could wish now that I had transgressed at least so
far as to report some of the things that Lowell said; for the
paper did not print my letters, and it would have been perfectly
safe, and very useful for the present purpose. But perhaps he did
not say anything very memorable; to do that you must have
something positive in your listener; and I was the mere response,
the hollow echo, that youth must be in like circumstances. I
was all the time afraid of wearing my welcome out, and I hurried
to go when I would so gladly have staid. I do not remember

where I meant to go, or why he should have undertaken to show me the way across-lots, but this was what he did; and when we came to a fence, which I clambered gracelessly over, he put his hands on the top, and tried to take it at a bound. He tried twice, and then laughed at his failure, but not with any great pleasure, and he was not content till a third trial carried him across. Then he said, "I commonly do that the first time," as if it were a frequent habit with him, while I remained discreetly silent, and for that moment at least felt myself the elder of the man who had so much of the boy in him. He had, indeed, much of the boy in him to the last, and he parted with each hour of his youth reluctantly, pathetically.

VIII

We walked across what must have been Jarvis Field to what must have been North Avenue, and there he left me. But before he let me go he held my hand while he could say that he wished me to dine with him; only, he was not in his own house, and he would ask me to dine with him at the Parker House in Boston, and would send me word of the time later.

I suppose I may have spent part of the intervening time in viewing the wonders of Boston, and visiting the historic scenes and places in it and about it. I certainly went over to Charlestown, and ascended Bunker Hill Monument, and explored the navy-yard, where the immemorial man-of-war begun in Jackson's time was then silently stretching itself under its long shed in a poetic arrest, as if the failure of the appropriation for its completion had been some kind of enchantment. In Boston, I early presented my letter of credit to the publisher it was drawn upon, not that I needed money at the moment, but from a young eagerness to see if it would be honored; and a literary attaché of the house kindly went about with me, and showed me the life of the city. A great city it seemed to me then, and a seething vortex of business as well as a whirl of gayety, as I saw it in Washington Street, and in a promenade concert at Copeland's restaurant in Tremont Row. Probably I brought some idealizing force to bear upon it, for I was not all so strange to the world as I must seem; perhaps I accounted for quality as well as quantity in my impressions of the New England metropolis, and aggrandized it in the ratio of its literary importance. It seemed to me old, even after Quebec, and very likely I credited the actual town with all the dead and gone Bostonians in my sentimental census. If I did not, it was no fault of my cicerone, who thought even more of the city he showed me than I did. I do not know now who he was, and I never saw him after I came to live there, with any certainty that it was he, though I was often tormented with the vision of a spectacled face like his, but not like enough to warrant me in addressing him.

He became part of that ghostly Boston of my first visit, which would sometimes return and possess again the city I came to know so familiarly in later years, and to be so passionately interested in. Some color of my prime impressions has tinged the fictitious experiences of people in my books, but I find very little of it in my memory. This is like a web of frayed old lace, which I have to take carefully into my hold for fear of its fragility, and make out as best I can the figure once so distinct in it. There are the narrow streets, stretching saltwards to the docks, which I haunted for their quaintness, and there is Faneuil Hall, which I cared to see so much more because Wendell Phillips had spoken in it than because Otis and Adams[1] had. There is the old Colonial House, and there is the State House, which I dare say I explored, with the Common sloping before it. There is Beacon Street, with the Hancock House where it is incredibly no more, and there are the beginnings of Commonwealth Avenue, and the other streets of the Back Bay, laid out with their basements left hollowed in the made land, which the gravel trains were yet making out of the westward hills. There is the Public Garden, newly planned and planted, but without the massive bridge destined to make so ungratefully little of the lake that occasioned it. But it is all very vague, and I could easily believe now that it was some one else who saw it then in my place.

I think that I did not try to see Cambridge the same day that
[1]James Otis (1725–1783) and Samuel Adams (1722–1803).

I saw Lowell, but wisely came back to my hotel in Boston, and tried to realize the fact. I went out another day, with an acquaintance from Ohio, whom I ran upon in the street. We went to Mount Auburn together, and I viewed its monuments with a reverence which I dare say their artistic quality did not merit. But I am not sorry for this, for perhaps they are not quite so bad as some people pretend. The Gothic chapel of the cemetery, unstoried as it was, gave me, with its half-dozen statues standing or sitting about an emotion such as I am afraid I could not receive now from the Acropolis, Westminster Abbey, and Santa Croce in one. I tried hard for some aesthetic sense of it, and I made believe that I thought this thing and that thing in the place moved me with its fitness or beauty; but the truth is that I had no taste in anything but literature, and did not feel the effect I would so willingly have experienced.

I did genuinely love the elmy quiet of the dear old Cambridge streets, though, and I had a real and instant pleasure in the yellow colonial houses, with their white corners and casements and their green blinds, that lurked behind the shrubbery of the avenue I passed through to Mount Auburn. The most beautiful among them was the most interesting for me, for it was the house of Longfellow; my companion, who had seen it before, pointed it out to me with an air of custom, and I would not let him see that I valued the first sight of it as I did. I had hoped that somehow I might be so favored as to see Longfellow himself, but when I asked about him of those who knew, they said, "Oh, he is at Nahant," and I thought that Nahant must be a great way off, and at any rate I did not feel authorized to go to him there. Neither did I go to see the author[1] of *The Amber Gods*, who lived at Newburyport, I was told, as if I should know where Newburyport was; I did not know, and I hated to ask. Besides, it did not seem so simple as it had seemed in Ohio, to go and see a young lady simply because I was infatuated with her literature; even as the envoy of all the infatuated young people of Columbus, I could not quite do this; and when I got

[1] Harriet Elizabeth Prescott Spofford (1835–1921). See an earlier reference to her on page 25.

home, I had to account for my failure as best I could. Another
failure of mine was the sight of Whittier, which I then very
much longed to have. They said, "Oh, Whittier lives at Ames-
bury," but that put him at an indefinite distance, and without
the introduction I never would ask for, I found it impossible to
set out in quest of him. In the end, I saw no one in New England whom I was not presented to in the regular way, except
Lowell, whom I thought I had a right to call upon in my quality
of contributor, and from the acquaintance I had with him by
letter. I neither praise nor blame myself for this; it was my shyness that withheld me rather than my merit. There is really no
harm in seeking the presence of a famous man, and I doubt if the
famous man resents the wish of people to look upon him without some measure, great or little, of affectation. There are bores
everywhere, but he is likelier to find them in the wonted figures
of society than in those young people, or old people, who come
to him in the love of what he has done. I am well aware how
furiously Tennyson sometimes met his worshippers, and how
insolently Carlyle, but I think these facts are little specks in their
sincerity. Our own gentler and honester celebrities did not forbid approach, and I have known some of them caress adorers
who seemed hardly worthy of their kindness; but that was better
than to have hurt any sensitive spirit who had ventured too far,
by the rules that govern us with common men.

IX

My business relations were with the house that so promptly
honored my letter of credit. This house had published in the
East the campaign life of Lincoln which I had lately written, and
I dare say would have published the volume of poems I had
written earlier with my friend Piatt, if there had been any public
for it; at least, I saw large numbers of the book on the counters.
But all my literary affiliations were with Ticknor & Fields, and
it was the Old Corner Book-Store on Washington Street that
drew my heart as soon as I had replenished my pocket in Cornhill. After verifying the editor of the *Atlantic Monthly* I wished

to verify its publishers, and it very fitly happened that when I was shown into Mr. Fields's little room at the back of the store, with its window looking upon School Street, and its scholarly keeping in books and prints, he had just got the magazine sheets of a poem of mine from the Cambridge printers. He was then lately from abroad, and he had the zest for American things which a foreign sojourn is apt to renew in us, though I did not know this then, and could not account for it in the kindness he expressed for my poem. He introduced me to Mr. Ticknor, who I fancied had not read my poem; but he seemed to know what it was from the junior partner, and he asked me whether I had been paid for it. I confessed that I had not, and then he got out a chamois-leather bag, and took from it five half-eagles in gold and laid them on the green cloth top of the desk, in much the shape and of much the size of the Great Bear. I have never since felt myself paid so lavishly for any literary work, though I have had more for a single piece than the twenty-five dollars that dazzled me in this constellation. The publisher seemed aware of the poetic character of the transaction; he let the pieces lie a moment, before he gathered them up and put them into my hand, and said, "I always think it is pleasant to have it in gold."

But a terrible experience with the poem awaited me, and quenched for the moment all my pleasure and pride. It was *The Pilot's Story*, which I suppose has had as much acceptance as anything of mine in verse (I do not boast of a vast acceptance for it), and I had attempted to treat in it a phase of the national tragedy of slavery, as I had imagined it on a Mississippi steamboat. A young planter has gambled away the slave-girl who is the mother of his child, and when he tells her, she breaks out upon him with the demand:

"What will you say to our boy when he cries for me,
there in Saint Louis?"

I had thought this very well, and natural and simple, but a fatal proof-reader had not thought it well enough, or simple and natural enough, and he had made the line read:

"What will you say to our boy when he cries for '*Ma*,'
there in Saint Louis?"

He had even had the inspiration to quote the word he preferred to the one I had written, so that there was no merciful
possibility of mistaking it for a misprint, and my blood froze
in my veins at sight of it. Mr. Fields had given me the sheets to
read while he looked over some letters, and he either felt the chill
of my horror, or I made some sign or sound of dismay that
caught his notice, for he looked round at me. I could only show
him the passage with a gasp. I dare say he might have liked to
laugh, for it was cruelly funny, but he did not; he was concerned
for the magazine as well as for me. He declared that when he
first read the line he had thought I could not have written it so,
and he agreed with me that it would kill the poem if it came out
in that shape. He instantly set about repairing the mischief, so
far as could be. He found that the whole edition of that sheet
had been printed, and the air blackened round me again, lighted
up here and there with baleful flashes of the newspaper wit at my
cost, which I previsioned in my misery; I knew what I should
have said of such a thing myself, if it had been another's. But
the publisher at once decided that the sheet must be reprinted,
and I went away weak as if in the escape from some deadly peril.
Afterwards it appeared that the line had passed the first proof-
reader as I wrote it, but that the final reader had entered so
sympathetically into the realistic intention of my poem as to
contribute the modification which had nearly been my end.

X

As it fell out, I lived without farther difficulty to the day and
hour of the dinner Lowell made for me; and I really think, looking at myself impersonally, and remembering the sort of young
fellow I was, that it would have been a great pity if I had not.
The dinner was at the old-fashioned Boston hour of two, and the
table was laid for four people in some little upper room at
Parker's, which I was never afterwards able to make sure of.
Lowell was already there when I came, and he presented me, to
my inexpressible delight and surprise, to Dr. Holmes, who was
there with him.

Holmes was in the most brilliant hour of that wonderful second youth which his fame flowered into long after the world thought he had completed the cycle of his literary life. He had already received full recognition as a poet of delicate wit, nimble humor, airy imagination, and exquisite grace, when the Autocrat papers advanced his name indefinitely beyond the bounds which most immortals would have found range enough. The marvel of his invention was still fresh in the minds of men, and time had not dulled in any measure the sense of its novelty. His readers all fondly identified him with his work; and I fully expected to find myself in the Autocrat's presence when I met Dr. Holmes. But the fascination was none the less for that reason; and the winning smile, the wise and humorous glance, the whole genial manner was as important to me as if I had foreboded something altogether different. I found him physically of the Napoleonic height which spiritually overtops the Alps, and I could look into his face without that unpleasant effort which giants of inferior mind so often cost the man of five feet four.

A little while after, Fields came in, and then our number and my pleasure were complete.

Nothing else so richly satisfactory, indeed, as the whole affair could have happened to a like youth at such a point in his career; and when I sat down with Doctor Holmes and Mr. Fields, on Lowell's right, I felt through and through the dramatic perfection of the event. The kindly Autocrat recognized some such quality of it in terms which were not the less precious and gracious for their humorous excess. I have no reason to think that he had yet read any of my poor verses, or had me otherwise than wholly on trust from Lowell; but he leaned over towards his host, and said, with a laughing look at me, "Well, James, this is something like the apostolic succession; this is the laying on of hands." I took his sweet and caressing irony as he meant it; but the charm of it went to my head long before any drop of wine, together with the charm of hearing him and Lowell calling each other James and Wendell, and of finding them still cordially boys together.

I would gladly have glimmered before those great lights in the

talk that followed, if I could have thought of anything brilliant
to say, but I could not, and so I let them shine without a ray of
reflected splendor from me. It was such talk as I had, of course,
never heard before, and it is not saying enough to say that I have
never heard such talk since except from these two men. It was
as light and kind as it was deep and true, and it ranged over a
hundred things, with a perpetual sparkle of Doctor Holmes's
wit, and the constant glow of Lowell's incandescent sense. From
time to time Fields came in with one of his delightful stories
(sketches of character they were, which he sometimes did not
mind caricaturing), or with some criticism of the literary situation from his stand-point of both lover and publisher of books.
I heard fames that I had accepted as proofs of power treated as
factitious, and witnessed a frankness concerning authorship, far
and near, that I had not dreamed of authors using. When Doctor Holmes understood that I wrote for the *Saturday Press*,
which was running amuck among some Bostonian immortalities
of the day, he seemed willing that I should know they were not
thought so very undying in Boston, and that I should not take
the notion of a Mutual Admiration Society too seriously, or
accept the New York bohemian view of Boston as true. For the
most part the talk did not address itself to me, but became an exchange of thoughts and fancies between himself and Lowell.
They touched, I remember, on certain matters of technique, and
the doctor confessed that he had a prejudice against some words
that he could not overcome; for instance, he said, nothing could
induce him to use *'neath* for *beneath*, no exigency of versification
or stress of rhyme. Lowell contended that he would use any
word that carried his meaning; and I think he did this to the
hurt of some of his earlier things. He was then probably in the
revolt against too much literature in literature, which every one
is destined sooner or later to share; there was a certain roughness,
very like crudeness, which he indulged before his thought and
phrase mellowed to one music in his later work. I tacitly agreed
rather with the doctor, though I did not swerve from my allegiance to Lowell, and if I had spoken I should have sided with
him; I would have given that or any other proof of my devotion.

Fields casually mentioned that he thought "The Dandelion" was the most popularly liked of Lowell's briefer poems, and I made haste to say that I thought so too, though I did not really think anything about it; and then I was sorry, for I could see that the poet did not like it, quite; and I felt that I was duly punished for my dishonesty.

Hawthorne was named among other authors, probably by Fields, whose house had just published his "Marble Faun," and who had recently come home on the same steamer with him. Doctor Holmes asked if I had met Hawthorne yet, and when I confessed that I had hardly yet even hoped for such a thing, he smiled his winning smile, and said: "Ah, well! I don't know that you will ever feel you have really met him. He is like a dim room with a little taper of personality burning on the corner of the mantel."

They all spoke of Hawthorne, and with the same affection, but the same sense of something mystical and remote in him; and every word was priceless to me. But these masters of the craft I was 'prentice to probably could not have said anything that I should not have found wise and well, and I am sure now I should have been the loser if the talk had shunned any of the phases of human nature which it touched. It is best to find that all men are of the same make, and that there are certain universal things which interest them as much as the supernal things, and amuse them even more. There was a saying of Lowell's which he was fond of repeating at the menace of any form of the transcendental, and he liked to warn himself and others with his homely, "Remember the dinner-bell." What I recall of the whole effect of a time so happy for me is that in all that was said, however high, however fine, we were never out of hearing of the dinner-bell; and perhaps this is the best effect I can leave with the reader. It was the first dinner served in courses that I had sat down to, and I felt that this service gave it a romantic importance which the older fashion of the West still wanted. Even at Governor Chase's table in Columbus the Governor carved; I knew of the dinner *à la Russe*, as it was then called, only from books; and it was a sort of literary flavor that I tasted in the successive dishes. When it came to the black coffee, and then to the *petits verres* of cognac, with lumps of sugar set fire to atop, it was something that so far transcended my home-kept experience that it began to seem altogether visionary.

Neither Fields nor Doctor Holmes smoked, and I had to confess that I did not; but Lowell smoked enough for all three, and the spark of his cigar began to show in the waning light before we rose from the table. The time that never had, nor can ever have, its fellow for me had to come to an end, as all times must, and when I shook hands with Lowell in parting, he overwhelmed me by saying that if I thought of going to Concord he would send me a letter to Hawthorne. I was not to see Lowell again during my stay in Boston; but Doctor Holmes asked me to tea for the next evening, and Fields said I must come to breakfast with him in the morning.

XI

I recall with the affection due to his friendly nature, and to the kindness afterwards to pass between us for many years, the whole aspect of the publisher when I first saw him. His abundant hair, and his full "beard as broad as any spade," that flowed from his throat in Homeric curls, were touched with the first frost. He had a fine color, and his eyes, as keen as they were kind, twinkled restlessly above the wholesome russet-red of his cheeks. His portly frame was clad in those Scotch tweeds which had not yet displaced the traditional broadcloth with us in the West, though I had sent to New York for a rough suit, and so felt myself not quite unworthy to meet a man fresh from the hands of the London tailor.

Otherwise I stood as much in awe of him as his jovial soul would let me; and if I might I should like to suggest to the literary youth of this day some notion of the importance of his name to the literary youth of my day. He gave aesthetic character to the house of Ticknor & Fields, but he was by no means a silent partner on the economic side. No one can forecast the fortune of a new book, but he knew as well as any publisher can know not only whether a book was good, but whether the reader would think so; and I suppose that his house made as few bad guesses, along with their good ones, as any house that ever tried the uncertain temper of the public with its ventures. In the minds of all who loved the plain brown cloth and tasteful print of its issues he was more or less intimately associated with their literature; and those who were not mistaken in thinking De Quincey one of the delightfulest authors in the world, were especially grateful to the man who first edited his writings in book form, and proud that this edition was the effect of American sympathy with them. At that day, I believed authorship the noblest calling in the world, and I should still be at a loss to name any nobler. The great authors I had met were to me the sum of greatness, and if I could not rank their publisher with them by virtue of equal achievement, I handsomely brevetted him worthy of their friendship, and honored him in the visible measure of it.

In his house beside the Charles, and in the close neighborhood of Doctor Holmes, I found an odor and an air of books such as I fancied might belong to the famous literary houses of London. It is still there, that friendly home of lettered refinement, and the gracious spirit which knew how to welcome me, and make the least of my shyness and strangeness, and the most of the little else there was in me, illumines it still, though my host of that rapturous moment has many years been of those who are only with us unseen and unheard. I remember his burlesque pretence that morning of an inextinguishable grief when I owned that I had never eaten blueberry cake before, and how he kept returning to the pathos of the fact that there should be a region of the earth where blueberry cake was unknown. We breakfasted in the pretty room whose windows look out through leaves and flowers upon the river's coming and going tides, and whose walls were covered with the faces and the autographs of all the contemporary poets and novelists. The Fieldses had spent some days with Tennyson in their recent English sojourn, and Mrs. Fields had much to tell of him, how he looked, how he smoked, how he read aloud, and how he said, when he asked her to go with him to the tower of his house, "Come up and see the sad

English sunset!" which had an instant value to me such as some rich verse of his might have had. I was very new to it all, how new I could not very well say, but I flattered myself that I breathed in that atmosphere as if in the return from life-long exile. Still I patriotically bragged of the West a little, and I told them proudly that in Columbus no book since *Uncle Tom's Cabin* had sold so well as *The Marble Faun*. This made the effect that I wished, but whether it was true or not, heaven knows; I only know that I heard it from our leading bookseller, and I made no question of it myself.

After breakfast, Fields went away to the office, and I lingered, while Mrs. Fields showed me from shelf to shelf in the library, and dazzled me with the sight of authors' copies, and volumes invaluable with the autographs and the pencilled notes of the men whose names were dear to me from my love of their work. Everywhere was some souvenir of the living celebrities my hosts had met; and whom had they not met in that English sojourn in days before England embittered herself to us during our civil war? Not Tennyson only, but Thackeray, but Dickens, but Charles Reade, but Carlyle, but many a minor fame was in my ears from converse so recent with them that it was as if I heard their voices in their echoed words.

I do not remember how long I stayed; I remember I was afraid of staying too long, and so I am sure I did not stay as long as I should have liked. But I have not the least notion how I got away, and I am not certain where I spent the rest of a day that began in the clouds, but had to be ended on the common earth. I suppose I gave it mostly to wandering about the city, and partly to recording my impressions of it for that newspaper which never published them. The summer weather in Boston, with its sunny heat struck through and through with the coolness of the sea, and its clear air untainted with a breath of smoke, I have always loved, but it had then a zest unknown before; and I should have thought it enough simply to be alive in it. But everywhere I came upon something that fed my famine for the old, the quaint, the picturesque, and however the day passed it was a banquet, a festival. I can only recall my breathless first sight of the Public Library and of the Athenaeum Gallery: great sights then, which the Vatican and the Pitti hardly afterwards eclipsed for mere emotion. In fact I did not see these elder treasuries of literature and art between breakfasting with the Autocrat's publisher in the morning, and taking tea with the Autocrat himself in the evening, and that made a whole world's difference.

XII

The tea of that simpler time is wholly inconceivable to this generation, which knows the thing only as a mild form of afternoon reception; but I suppose that in 1860 very few dined late in our whole pastoral republic. Tea was the meal people asked people to when they wished to sit at long leisure and large ease; it came at the end of the day, at six o'clock, or seven; and one went to it in morning dress. It had an unceremonied domesticity in the abundance of its light dishes, and I fancy these did not vary much from East to West, except that we had a Southern touch in our fried chicken and corn bread; but at the Autocrat's tea table the cheering cup had a flavor unknown to me before that day. He asked me if I knew it, and I said it was English breakfast tea; for I had drunk it at the publisher's in the morning, and was willing not to seem strange to it. "Ah, yes," he said; "but this is the flower of the souchong; it is the blossom, the poetry of tea," and then he told me how it had been given him by a friend, a merchant in the China trade, which used to flourish in Boston, and was the poetry of commerce, as this delicate beverage was of tea. That commerce is long past, and I fancy that the plant ceased to bloom when the traffic fell into decay.

The Autocrat's windows had the same outlook upon the Charles as the publisher's, and after tea we went up into a back parlor of the same orientation, and saw the sunset die over the water, and the westering flats and hills. Nowhere else in the world has the day a lovelier close, and our talk took something of the mystic coloring that the heavens gave those mantling expanses. It was chiefly his talk, but I have always found the

best talkers are willing that you should talk if you like, and a
quick sympathy and a subtle sense met all that I had to say from
him and from the unbroken circle of kindred intelligences about
him. I saw him then in the midst of his family, and perhaps never
afterwards to better advantage, or in a finer mood. We spoke
of the things that people perhaps once liked to deal with more
than they do now; of the intimations of immortality, of the experiences of morbid youth, and of all those messages from the
tremulous nerves which we take for prophecies. I was not
ashamed, before his tolerant wisdom, to acknowledge the effects
that had lingered so long with me in fancy and even in conduct,
from a time of broken health and troubled spirit; and I remember
the exquisite tact in him which recognized them as things common to all, however peculiar in each, which left them mine for
whatever obscure vanity I might have in them, and yet gave me
the companionship of the whole race in their experience. We
spoke of forebodings and presentiments; we approached the
mystic confines of the world from which no traveller has yet
returned with a passport *en règle* and properly *visé;* and he held
his light course through these filmy impalpabilities with a charming sincerity, with the scientific conscience that refuses either to
deny the substance of things unseen, or to affirm it. In the gathering dusk, so weird did my fortune of being there and listening
to him seem, that I might well have been a blessed ghost, for all
the reality I felt in myself.

I tried to tell him how much I had read him from my boyhood, and with what joy and gain; and he was patient of these
futilities, and I have no doubt imagined the love that inspired
them, and accepted that instead of the poor praise. When the
sunset passed, and the lamps were lighted, and we all came back
to our dear little firm-set earth, he began to question me about
my native region of it. From many forgotten inquiries I recall
his asking me what was the fashionable religion in Columbus, or
the Church that socially corresponded to the Unitarian Church
in Boston. He had first to clarify my intelligence as to what
Unitarianism was; we had Universalists but not Unitarians; but
when I understood, I answered from such vantage as my own

wholly outside Swedenborgianism gave me, that I thought most of the most respectable people with us were of the Presbyterian Church; some were certainly Episcopalians, but upon the whole the largest number were Presbyterians. He found that very strange indeed; and said that he did not believe there was a Presbyterian Church in Boston; that the New England Calvinists were all of the Orthodox Church. He had to explain Orthodoxy to me, and then I could confess to one Congregational Church in Columbus.

Probably I failed to give the Autocrat any very clear image of our social frame in the West, but the fault was altogether mine, if I did. Such lecturing tours as he had made had not taken him among us, as those of Emerson and other New-Englanders had, and my report was positive rather than comparative. I was full of pride in journalism at that day, and I dare say that I vaunted the brilliancy and power of our newspapers more than they merited; I should not have been likely to wrong them otherwise. It is strange that in all the talk I had with him and Lowell, or rather heard from them, I can recall nothing said of political affairs, though Lincoln had then been nominated by the Republicans, and the Civil War had practically begun. But we did not imagine such a thing in the North; we rested secure in the belief that if Lincoln were elected the South would eat all its fiery words, perhaps from the mere love and inveterate habit of fire-eating.

I rent myself away from the Autocrat's presence as early as I could, and as my evening had been too full of happiness to sleep upon at once, I spent the rest of the night till two in the morning wandering about the streets and in the Common with a Harvard Senior whom I had met. He was a youth of like literary passions with myself, but of such different traditions in every possible way that his deeply schooled and definitely regulated life seemed as anomalous to me as my own desultory and self-found way must have seemed to him. We passed the time in the delight of trying to make ourselves known to each other, and in a promise to continue by letter the effort, which duly lapsed into silent patience with the necessarily insoluble problem.

XIII

I must have lingered in Boston for the introduction to Hawthorne which Lowell had offered me, for when it came, with a little note of kindness and counsel for myself such as only Lowell had the gift of writing, it was already so near Sunday that I stayed over till Monday before I started. I do not recall what I did with the time, except keep myself from making it a burden to the people I knew, and wandering about the city alone. Nothing of it remains to me except the fortune that favored me that Sunday night with a view of the old Granary Burying-ground on Tremont Street. I found the gates open, and I explored every path in the place, wreaking myself in such meagre emotion as I could get from the tomb of the Franklin family, and rejoicing with the whole soul of my Western modernity in the evidence of a remote antiquity which so many of the dim inscriptions afforded. I do not think that I have ever known anything practically older than these monuments, though I have since supped so full of classic and mediaeval ruin. I am sure that I was more deeply touched by the epitaph of a poor little Puritan maiden who died at sixteen in the early sixteen-thirties than afterwards by the tomb of Caecilia Metella, and that the heartache which I tried to put into verse when I got back to my room in the hotel was none the less genuine because it would not lend itself to my literary purpose, and remains nothing but pathos to this day.

I am not able to say how I reached the town of Lowell, where I went before going to Concord, that I might ease the unhappy conscience I had about those factories which I hated so much to see, and have it clean for the pleasure of meeting the fabricator of visions whom I was authorized to molest in any air-castle where I might find him. I only know that I went to Lowell, and visited one of the great mills, which with their whirring spools, the ceaseless flight of their shuttles, and the bewildering sight and sound of all their mechanism have since seemed to me the death of the joy that ought to come from work, if not the cap-

tivity of those who tended them. But then I thought it right
and well for me to be standing by
"With sick and scornful looks averse,"
while these others toiled; I did not see the tragedy in it, and I got
my pitiful literary antipathy away as soon as I could, no wiser
for the sight of the ingenious contrivances I inspected, and I am
sorry to say no sadder. In the cool of the evening I sat at the
door of my hotel, and watched the long files of the work-worn
factory-girls stream by, with no concern for them but to see
which was pretty and which was plain, and with no dream of a
truer order than that which gave them ten hours' work a day in
those hideous mills and lodged them in the barracks where they
rested from their toil.

XIV

I wonder if there is a stage that still runs between Lowell and
Concord, past meadow walls, and under the caressing boughs of
way-side elms, and through the bird-haunted gloom of woodland roads, in the freshness of the summer morning? By a
blessed chance I found that there was such a stage in 1860, and I
took it from my hotel, instead of going back to Boston and up
to Concord as I must have had to do by train. The journey gave
me the intimacy of the New England country as I could have
had it in no other fashion, and for the first time I saw it in all the
summer sweetness which I have often steeped my soul in since.
The meadows were newly mown, and the air was fragrant with
the grass, stretching in long winrows among the brown bowlders,
or capped with canvas in the little haycocks it had been gathered
into the day before. I was fresh from the affluent farms of the
Western Reserve, and this care of the grass touched me with a
rude pity, which I also bestowed on the meagre fields of corn
and wheat; but still the land was lovelier than any I had ever
seen, with its old farm-houses, and brambled gray stone walls,
its stony hill-sides, its staggering orchards, its wooded tops, and
its thick-brackened valleys. From West to East the difference

was as great as I afterwards found it from America to Europe, and my impression of something quaint and strange was no keener when I saw Old England the next year than when I saw New England now. I had imagined the landscape bare of trees, and I was astonished to find it almost as full of them as at home, though they all looked very little, as they well might to eyes used to the primeval forests of Ohio. The road ran through them from time to time, and took their coolness on its smooth hard reaches, and then issued again in the glisten of the open fields.

I made phrases to myself about the scenery as we drove along; and yes, I suppose I made phrases about the young girl who was one of the inside passengers, and who, when the common strangeness had somewhat worn off, began to sing, and sang most of the way to Concord. Perhaps she was not very sage, and I am sure she was not of the caste of Vere de Vere, but she was pretty enough, and she had a voice of a birdlike tunableness, so that I would not have her out of the memory of that pleasant journey if I could. She was long ago an elderly woman, if she lives, and I suppose she would not now point out her fellow-passenger if he strolled in the evening by the house where she had dismounted, upon her arrival in Concord, and laugh and pull another girl away from the window, in the high excitement of the prodigious adventure.

XV

Her fellow-passenger was in far other excitement; he was to see Hawthorne, and in a manner to meet Priscilla and Zenobia, and Hester Prynne and little Pearl, and Miriam and Hilda, and Hollingsworth and Coverdale, and Chillingworth and Dimmesdale, and Donatello and Kenyon; and he had no heart for any such poor little reality as that, who could not have been got into any story that one could respect, and must have been difficult even in a Heinesque poem.

I wasted that whole evening and the next morning in fond delaying, and it was not until after the indifferent dinner I got at the tavern where I stopped, that I found courage to go and present Lowell's letter to Hawthorne. I would almost have foregone meeting the weird genius only to have kept that letter, for it said certain infinitely precious things of me with such a sweetness, such a grace as Lowell alone could give his praise. Years afterwards, when Hawthorne was dead, I met Mrs. Hawthorne, and told her of the pang I had in parting with it, and she sent it me, doubly enriched by Hawthorne's keeping. But now if I were to see him at all I must give up my letter, and I carried it in my hand to the door of the cottage he called The Wayside. It was never otherwise than a very modest place, but the modesty was greater then than to-day, and there was already some preliminary carpentry at one end of the cottage, which I saw was to result in an addition to it. I recall pleasant fields across the road before it; behind rose a hill wooded with low pines, such as is made in *Septimius Felton* the scene of the involuntary duel between Septimius and the young British officer. I have a sense of the woods coming down to the house, but if this was so I do not know what to do with a grassy slope which seems to have stretched part way up the hill. As I approached, I looked for the tower which the author was fabled to climb into at sight of the coming guest, and pull the ladder up after him; and I wondered whether he would fly before me in that sort, or imagine some easier means of escaping me.

The door was opened to my ring by a tall handsome boy whom I suppose to have been Mr. Julian Hawthorne; and the next moment I found myself in the presence of the romancer, who entered from some room beyond. He advanced carrying his head with a heavy forward droop, and with a pace for which I decided that the word would be *pondering*. It was the pace of a bulky man of fifty, and his head was that beautiful head we all know from the many pictures of it. But Hawthorne's *look* was different from that of any picture of him that I have seen. It was sombre and brooding, as the look of such a poet should have been; it was the look of a man who had dealt faithfully and therefore sorrowfully with that problem of evil which forever attracted, forever evaded Hawthorne. It was by no means troubled; it was full of a dark repose. Others who knew him better and saw him oftener were familiar with other aspects, and I remember that one night at Longfellow's table, when one of the guests happened to speak of the photograph of Hawthorne which hung in a corner of the room, Lowell said, after a glance at it, "yes, it's good; but it hasn't his fine *accipitral* look."

In the face that confronted me, however, there was nothing of keen alertness; but only a sort of quiet, patient intelligence, for which I seek the right word in vain. It was a very regular face, with beautiful eyes; the mustache, still entirely dark, was dense over the fine mouth. Hawthorne was dressed in black, and he had a certain effect which I remember, of seeming to have on a black cravat with no visible collar. He was such a man that if I had ignorantly met him anywhere I should have instantly felt him to be a personage.

I must have given him the letter myself, for I have no recollection of parting with it before, but I only remember his offering me his hand, and making me shyly and tentatively welcome. After a few moments of the demoralization which followed his hospitable attempts in me, he asked if I would not like to go up on his hill with him and sit there, where he smoked in the afternoon. He offered me a cigar, and when I said that I did not smoke, he lighted it for himself, and we climbed the hill together. At the top, where there was an outlook in the pines over the Concord meadows, we found a log, and he invited me to a place on it beside him, and at intervals of a minute or so he talked while he smoked. Heaven preserved me from the folly of trying to tell him how much his books had been to me, and though we got on rapidly at no time, I think we got on better for this interposition. He asked me about Lowell, I dare say, for I told him of my joy in meeting him and Doctor Holmes, and this seemed greatly to interest him. Perhaps because he was so lately from Europe, where our great men are always seen through the wrong end of the telescope, he appeared surprised at my devotion, and asked me whether I cared as much for meeting them as I should care for meeting the famous English authors. I professed that I cared much more, though whether this was true, I now have my doubts, and I think Hawthorne doubted it at the time. But he said nothing in comment, and went on to speak generally of Europe and America. He was curious about the West, which he seemed to fancy much more purely American, and said he would like to see some part of the country on which the shadow (or, if I must be precise, the damned shadow) of Europe had not fallen. I told him I thought the West must finally be characterized by the Germans, whom we had in great numbers, and, purely from my zeal for German poetry, I tried to allege some proofs of their present influence, though I could think of none outside of politics, which I thought they affected wholesomely. I knew Hawthorne was a Democrat, and I felt it well to touch politics lightly, but he had no more to say about the fateful election then pending than Holmes or Lowell had.

With the abrupt transition of his talk throughout, he began somehow to speak of women, and said he had never seen a woman whom he thought quite beautiful. In the same way he spoke of the New England temperament, and suggested that the apparent coldness in it was also real, and that the suppression of emotion for generations would extinguish it at last. Then he questioned me as to my knowledge of Concord, and whether I had seen any of the notable people. I answered that I had met no one but himself, as yet, but I very much wished to see Emerson and Thoreau. I did not think it needful to say that I wished to see Thoreau quite as much because he had suffered in the cause of John Brown as because he had written the books which had taken me; and when he said that Thoreau prided himself on coming nearer the heart of a pine-tree than any other human being, I could say honestly enough that I would rather come near the heart of a man. This visibly pleased him, and I saw that it did not displease him, when he asked whether I was not going to see his next neighbor Mr. Alcott, and I confessed that I had never heard of him. That surprised as well as pleased him; he remarked, with whatever intention, that there was nothing like recognition to make a man modest; and he entered into some account of the philosopher, whom I suppose I need not be ashamed of not knowing then, since his influence was of the immediate sort that makes a man important to his townsmen while he is still strange to his countrymen.

Hawthorne descanted a little upon the landscape, and said certain of the pleasant fields below us belonged to him; but he preferred his hilltop, and if he could have his way those arable fields should be grown up to pines too. He smoked fitfully, and slowly, and in the hour that we spent together, his whiffs were of the desultory and unfinal character of his words. When we went down, he asked me into his house again, and would have me stay to tea, for which we found the table laid. But there was a great deal of silence in it all, and at times, in spite of his shadowy kindness, I felt my spirits sink. After tea, he showed me a bookcase, where there were a few books toppling about on the half-filled shelves, and said, coldly, "This is my library." I knew that men were his books, and though I myself cared for books so much, I found it fit and fine that he should care so little, or seem to care so little. Some of his own romances were among the volumes on these shelves, and when I put my finger on the *Blithedale Romance* and said that I preferred that to the others, his face lighted up, and he said that he believed the Germans liked that best too.

Upon the whole we parted such good friends that when I offered to take leave he asked me how long I was to be in Concord, and not only bade me come to see him again, but said he would give me a card to Emerson, if I liked. I answered, of course, that I should like it beyond all things; and he wrote on the back of his card something which I found, when I got away, to be, "I find this young man worthy." The quaintness, the little stiffness of it, if one pleases to call it so, was amusing to one who was not without his sense of humor, but the kindness filled me to the throat with joy. In fact, I entirely liked Hawthorne. He had been as cordial as so shy a man could show himself; and I perceived, with the repose that nothing else can give, the entire sincerity of his soul.

Nothing could have been further from the behavior of this very great man than any sort of posing, apparently, or a wish to affect me with a sense of his greatness. I saw that he was as much abashed by our encounter as I was; he was visibly shy to the point of discomfort, but in no ignoble sense was he conscious, and as nearly as he could with one so much his younger he made an absolute equality between us. My memory of him is without alloy one of the finest pleasures of my life. In my heart I paid him the same glad homage that I paid Lowell and Holmes, and he did nothing to make me think that I had overpaid him. This seems perhaps very little to say in his praise, but to my mind it is saying everything, for I have known but few great men, especially of those I met in early life, when I wished to lavish my admiration upon them, whom I have not the impression of having left in my debt. Then, a defect of the Puritan quality, which I have found in many New-Englanders, is that, wittingly or unwittingly, they propose themselves to you as an example, or if not quite this, that they surround themselves with a subtle ether of potential disapprobation, in which, at the first sign of unworthiness in you, they helplessly suffer you to gasp and perish; they have good hearts, and they would probably come to your succor out of humanity, if they knew how, but they do not know how. Hawthorne had nothing of this about him; he was no more tacitly than he was explicitly didactic. I thought him as thoroughly in keeping with his romances as Doctor Holmes had seemed with his essays and poems, and I met him as I had met the Autocrat in the supreme hour of his fame. He had just given the world the last of those incomparable works which it was to have finished from his hand; the *Marble Faun* had worthily followed, at a somewhat longer interval than usual, the *Blithedale Romance*, and the *House of Seven Gables*, and the *Scarlet Letter*, and had perhaps carried his name higher than all the rest, and certainly farther. Everybody was reading it, and more or less bewailing its indefinite close, but yielding him that full honor and praise which a writer can hope for but once in his life. Nobody dreamed that thereafter only precious fragments, sketches more or less faltering, though all with the divine touch in them, were further to enrich a legacy which in its kind is the finest the race has received from any mind. As I have said, we are always find-

ing new Hawthornes, but the illusion soon wears away, and then
we perceive that they were not Hawthornes at all; that he had
some peculiar difference from them, which, by-and-by, we shall
no doubt consent must be his difference from all men evermore.

I am painfully aware that I have not summoned before the
reader the image of the man as it has always stood in my memory,
and I feel a sort of shame for my failure. He was so altogether
simple that it seems as if it would be easy to do so; but perhaps a
spirit from the other world would be simple too, and yet would
no more stand at parle, or consent to be sketched, than Hawthorne. In fact, he was always more or less merging into the
shadow, which was in a few years wholly to close over him;
there was nothing uncanny in his presence, there was nothing
even unwilling, but he had that apparitional quality of some
great minds which kept Shakespeare largely unknown to those
who thought themselves his intimates, and has at last left him a
sort of doubt. There was nothing teasing or wilfully elusive in
Hawthorne's impalpability, such as I afterwards felt in Thoreau;
if he was not there to your touch, it was no fault of his; it was
because your touch was dull, and wanted the use of contact with
such natures. The hand passes through the veridical phantom
without a sense of its presence, but the phantom is none the less
veridical for all that.

XVI

I kept the evening of the day I met Hawthorne wholly for the
thoughts of him, or rather for that reverberation which continues in the young sensibilities after some important encounter.
It must have been the next morning that I went to find Thoreau,
and I am dimly aware of making one or two failures to find him,
if I ever really found him at all.

He is an author who has fallen into that abeyance, awaiting
all authors, great or small, at some time or another; but I think
that with him, at least in regard to his most important book, it
can be only transitory. I have not read the story of his hermitage
beside Walden Pond since the year 1858, but I have a fancy that

if I should take it up now, I should think it a wiser and truer conception of the world than I thought it then. It is no solution of the problem; men are not going to answer the riddle of the painful earth by building themselves shanties and living upon beans and watching ant-fights; but I do not believe Tolstoy himself has more clearly shown the hollowness, the hopelessness, the unworthiness of the life of the world than Thoreau did in that book. If it were newly written it could not fail of a far vaster acceptance than it had then, when to those who thought and felt seriously it seemed that if slavery could only be controlled, all things else would come right of themselves with us. Slavery has not only been controlled, but it has been destroyed, and yet things have not begun to come right with us; but it was in the order of Providence that chattel slavery should cease before industrial slavery, and the infinitely crueler and stupider vanity and luxury bred of it, should be attacked. If there was then any prevision of the struggle now at hand, the seers averted their eyes, and strove only to cope with the less evil. Thoreau himself, who had so clear a vision of the falsity and folly of society as we still have it, threw himself into the tide that was already, in Kansas and Virginia, reddened with war; he aided and abetted the John Brown raid, I do not recall how much or in what sort; and he had suffered in prison for his opinions and actions. It was this inevitable heroism of his that, more than his literature even, made me wish to see him and revere him; and I do not believe that I should have found the veneration difficult, when at last I met him in his insufficient person, if he had otherwise been present to my glowing expectation. He came into the room a quaint, stump figure of a man, whose effect of long trunk and short limbs was heightened by his fashionless trousers being let down too low. He had a noble face, with tossed hair, a distraught eye, and a fine aquilinity of profile, which made me think at once of Don Quixote and of Cervantes; but his nose failed to add that foot to his stature which Lamb says a nose of that shape will always give a man. He tried to place me geographically after he had given me a chair not quite so far off as Ohio, though still across the whole room, for he sat against one wall, and I against the other; but apparently he failed to pull himself out of his revery by the effort, for he remained in a dreamy muse, which all my attempts to say something fit about John Brown and Walden Pond seemed only to deepen upon him. I have not the least doubt that I was needless and valueless about both, and that what I said could not well have prompted an important response; but I did my poor best, and I was terribly disappointed in the result. The truth is that in those days I was a helplessly concrete young person, and all forms of the abstract, the air-drawn, afflicted me like physical discomforts. I do not remember that Thoreau spoke of his books or of himself at all, and when he began to speak of John Brown, it was not the warm, palpable, loving, fearful old man of my conception, but a sort of John Brown type, a John Brown ideal, a John Brown principle, which we were somehow (with long pauses between the vague, orphic phrases) to cherish, and to nourish ourselves upon.

It was not merely a defeat of my hopes, it was a rout, and I felt myself so scattered over the field of thought that I could hardly bring my forces together for retreat. I must have made some effort, vain and foolish enough, to rematerialize my old demi-god, but when I came away it was with the feeling that there was very little more left of John Brown than there was of me. His body was not mouldering in the grave, neither was his soul marching on; his ideal, his type, his principle alone existed, and I did not know what to do with it. I am not blaming Thoreau; his words were addressed to a far other understanding than mine, and it was my misfortune if I could not profit by them. I think, or I venture to hope, that I could profit better by them now; but in this record I am trying honestly to report their effect with the sort of youth I was then.

XVII

Such as I was, I rather wonder that I had the courage, after this experiment of Thoreau, to present the card Hawthorne had given me to Emerson. I must have gone to him at once, however, for I cannot make out any interval of time between my

visit to the disciple and my visit to the master. I think it was
Emerson himself who opened his door to me, for I have a vision
of the fine old man standing tall on his threshold, with the card
in his hand, and looking from it to me with a vague serenity,
while I waited a moment on the door-step below him. He must
then have been about sixty, but I remember nothing of age in
his aspect, though I have called him an old man. His hair, I am
sure, was still entirely dark, and his face had a kind of marble
youthfulness, chiselled to a delicate intelligence by the highest and
noblest thinking that any man has done. There was a strange
charm in Emerson's eyes, which I felt then and always, something like that I saw in Lincoln's, but shyer, but sweeter and less
sad. His smile was the very sweetest I have ever beheld, and the
contour of the mask and the line of the profile were in keeping
with this incomparable sweetness of the mouth, at once grave
and quaint, though quaint is not quite the word for it either,
but subtly, not unkindly arch, which again is not the word.

It was his great fortune to have been mostly misunderstood,
and to have reached the dense intelligence of his fellow-men
after a whole lifetime of perfectly simple and lucid appeal, and
his countenance expressed the patience and forbearance of a
wise man content to bide his time. It would be hard to persuade
people now that Emerson once represented to the popular mind
all that was most hopelessly impossible, and that in a certain sort
he was a national joke, the type of the incomprehensible, the
byword of the poor paragrapher. He had perhaps disabused the
community somewhat by presenting himself here and there as a
lecturer, and talking face to face with men in terms which they
could not refuse to find as clear as they were wise; he was more
and more read, by certain persons, here and there; but we are
still so far behind him in the reach of his far-thinking that it
need not be matter of wonder that twenty years before his
death he was the most misunderstood man in America. Yet in
that twilight where he dwelt he loomed large upon the imagination; the minds that could not conceive him were still aware of
his greatness. I myself had not read much of him, but I knew
the essays he had written in the *Atlantic,* and I knew certain of

his poems, though by no means many; yet I had this sense of
him, that he was somehow, beyond and above my ken, a presence of force and beauty and wisdom, uncompanioned in our
literature. He had lately stooped from his ethereal heights to
take part in the battle of humanity, and I suppose that if the
truth were told he was more to my young fervor because he had
said that John Brown had made the gallows glorious like the
cross, than because he had uttered all those truer and wiser
things which will still a hundred years hence be leading the
thought of the world.

I do not know in just what sort he made me welcome, but I
am aware of sitting with him in his study or library, and of his
presently speaking of Hawthorne, whom I probably celebrated
as I best could, and whom he praised for his personal excellence,
and for his fine qualities as a neighbor. "But his last book,"
he added, reflectively, "is a mere mush," and I perceived that
this great man was no better equipped to judge an artistic fiction
than the groundlings who were then crying out upon the indefinite close of the *Marble Faun.* Apparently he had read it,
as they had, for the story, but it seems to me now, if it did not
seem to me then, that as far as the problem of evil was involved,
the book must leave it where it found it. That is forever insoluble, and it was rather with that than with his more or less
shadowy people that the romancer was concerned. Emerson
had, in fact, a defective sense as to specific pieces of literature;
he praised extravagantly, and in the wrong place, especially
among the new things, and he failed to see the worth of much
that was fine and precious beside the line of his fancy.

He began to ask me about the West, and about some unknown
man in Michigan, who had been sending him poems, and whom
he seemed to think very promising, though he has not apparently
kept his word to do great things. I did not find what Emerson
had to say of my section very accurate or important, though it
was kindly enough, and just enough as to what the West ought
to do in literature. He thought it a pity that a literary periodical[1]

---

[1] *The Dial*, which ran for the twelve months of 1860, was founded in
Cincinnati by Moncure D. Conway.

which had lately been started in Cincinnati should be appealing to the East for contributions, instead of relying upon the writers nearer home; and he listened with what patience he could to my modest opinion that we had not the writers nearer home. I never was of those Westerners who believed that the West was kept out of literature by the jealousy of the East, and I tried to explain why we had not the men to write that magazine full in Ohio. He alleged the man in Michigan as one who alone could do much to fill it worthily, and again I had to say that I had never heard of him.

I felt rather guilty in my ignorance, and I had a notion that it did not commend me, but happily at this moment Mr. Emerson was called to dinner, and he asked me to come with him. After dinner we walked about in his "pleached garden" a little, and then we came again into his library, where I meant to linger only till I could fitly get away. He questioned me about what I had seen of Concord, and whom besides Hawthorne I had met, and when I told him only Thoreau, he asked me if I knew the poems of Mr. William Henry Channing. I have known them since, and felt their quality, which I have gladly owned a genuine and original poetry; but I answered then truly that I knew them only from Poe's criticisms: cruel and spiteful things which I should be ashamed of enjoying as I once did.

"Whose criticisms?" asked Emerson.

"Poe's," I said again.

"Oh," he cried out, after a moment, as if he had returned from a far search for my meaning, "*you mean the jingle-man!*"

I do not know why this should have put me to such confusion, but if I had written the criticisms myself I do not think I could have been more abashed. Perhaps I felt an edge of reproof, of admonition, in a characterization of Poe which the world will hardly agree with; though I do not agree with the world about him, myself, in its admiration. At any rate, it made an end of me for the time, and I remained as if already absent, while Emerson questioned me as to what I had written in the *Atlantic Monthly*. He had evidently read none of my contributions, for he looked at them, in the bound volume of the magazine which he got down, with the effect of being wholly strange to them, and then gravely affixed my initials to each. He followed me to the door, still speaking of poetry, and as he took a kindly enough leave of me, he said one might very well give a pleasant hour to it now and then.

A pleasant hour to poetry! I was meaning to give all time and all eternity to poetry, and I should by no means have wished to find pleasure in it; I should have thought that a proof of inferior quality in the work; I should have preferred anxiety, anguish even, to pleasure. But if Emerson thought from the glance he gave my verses that I had better not lavish myself upon that kind of thing, unless there was a great deal more of me than I could have made apparent in our meeting, no doubt he was right. I was only too painfully aware of my shortcoming, but I felt that it was shorter-coming than it need have been. I had somehow not prospered in my visit to Emerson as I had with Hawthorne, and I came away wondering in what sort I had gone wrong. I was not a forth-putting youth, and I could not blame myself for anything in my approaches that merited withholding; indeed, I made no approaches; but as I must needs blame myself for something, I fell upon the fact that in my confused retreat from Emerson's presence I had failed in a certain slight point of ceremony, and I magnified this into an offence of capital importance. I went home to my hotel, and passed the afternoon in pure misery. I had moments of wild question when I debated whether it would be better to go back and own my error, or whether it would be better to write him a note, and try to set myself right in that way. But in the end I did neither, and I have since survived my mortal shame some forty years or more. But at the time it did not seem possible that I should live through the day with it, and I thought that I ought at least to go and confess it to Hawthorne, and let him disown the wretch who had so poorly repaid the kindness of his introduction by such misbehavior. I did indeed walk down by the Wayside, in the cool of the evening, and there I saw Hawthorne for the last time. He was sitting on one of the timbers beside his cottage, and smoking with an air of friendly calm. I had got on very well with him, and I longed to go in, and tell him how ill I had got on with Emerson; I believed that though he cast me off, he would understand me, and would perhaps see some hope for me in another world, though there could be none in this.

But I had not the courage to speak of the affair to any one but Fields, to whom I unpacked my heart when I got back to Boston, and he asked me about my adventures in Concord. By this time I could see it in a humorous light, and I did not much mind his lying back in his chair and laughing and laughing, till I thought he would roll out of it. He perfectly conceived the situation, and got an amusement from it that I could get only through sympathy with him. But I thought it a favorable moment to propose myself as the assistant editor of the *Atlantic Monthly*, which I had the belief I could very well become, with advantage to myself if not to the magazine. He seemed to think so too; he said that if the place had not just been filled, I should certainly have had it; and it was to his recollection of this prompt ambition of mine that I suppose I may have owed my succession to a like vacancy some four years later. He was charmingly kind; he entered with the sweetest interest into the story of my economic life, which had been full of changes and chances already. But when I said very seriously that now I was tired of these fortuities, and would like to be settled in something, he asked, with dancing eyes, "Why, how old are you?"

"I am twenty-three," I answered, and then the laughing fit took him again.

"Well," he said, "you begin young, out there!"

In my heart I did not think that twenty-three was so very young, but perhaps it was; and if any one were to say that I had been portraying here a youth whose aims were certainly beyond his achievements, who was morbidly sensitive, and if not conceited was intolerably conscious, who had met with incredible kindness, and had suffered no more than was good for him, though he might not have merited his pain any more than his joy, I do not know that I should gainsay him, for I am not at all sure that I was not just that kind of youth when I paid my first visit to New England.

POEMS

Howells began his literary career with the high hope of becoming a poet, and, indeed, his first published volume was Poems of Two Friends *(1860), in which he collaborated with John James Piatt. But even in his early poems he displayed something of the narrative power which was to prove his greatest talent. Two of the best of his stories in verse are "The Pilot's Story" and "Louis Lebeau's Confession" in which he employs metrical form to relate tales of his own West. These pieces help one to understand the continuity of Howells' story-telling impulse from the early days when he fancied himself a poet to the years when he knew himself a novelist. They also remind the reader of the truth of Thomas Hardy's comment on Howells, that his poetic impulse is felt in all of his writing.*

THE PILOT'S STORY

I

It was a story the pilot told, with his back to his hearers,—
Keeping his hand on the wheel and his eye on the globe of the
    jack-staff,
Holding the boat to the shore and out of the sweep of the current,
Lightly turning aside for the heavy logs of the drift-wood,
Widely shunning the snags that made us sardonic obeisance.

II

All the soft, damp air was full of delicate perfume
From the young willows in bloom on either bank of the river,—
Faint, delicious fragrance, trancing the indolent senses
In a luxurious dream of the river and land of the lotus.
Not yet out of the west the roses of sunset were withered;
In the deep blue above light clouds of gold and of crimson
Floated in slumber serene; and the restless river beneath them
Rushed away to the sea with a vision of rest in its bosom;
Far on the eastern shore lay dimly the swamps of the cypress;
Dimly before us the islands grew from the river's expanses,—
Beautiful, wood-grown isles, with the gleam of the swart
    inundation

Seen through the swaying boughs and slender trunks of their
 willows;
And on the shore beside us the cotton-trees rose in the evening,
Phantom-like, yearningly, wearily, with the inscrutable sadness
Of the mute races of trees. While hoarsely the steam from her
 'scape-pipes
Shouted, then whispered a moment, then shouted again to the
 silence,
Trembling through all her frame with the mighty pulse of her
 engines,
Slowly the boat ascended the swollen and broad Mississippi,
Bank-full, sweeping on, with tangled masses of drift-wood,
Daintily breathed about with whiffs of silvery vapor,
Where in his arrowy flight the twittering swallow alighted,
And the belated blackbird paused on the way to its nestlings.

III

It was the pilot's story:—"They both came aboard there, at
 Cairo,
From a New Orleans boat, and took passage with us for Saint
 Louis.
She was a beautiful woman, with just enough blood from her
 mother
Darkening her eyes and her hair to make her race known to a
 trader:
You would have thought she was white. The man that was
 with her,—you see such,—
Weakly good-natured and kind, and weakly good-natured and
 vicious,
Slender of body and soul, fit neither for loving nor hating.
I was a youngster then, and only learning the river,—
Not over-fond of the wheel, I used to watch them at monte,
Down in the cabin at night, and learned to know all of the
 gamblers.
So when I saw this weak one staking his money against them,
Betting upon the turn of the cards, I knew what was coming:
They never left their pigeons a single feather to fly with.
Next day I saw them together,—the stranger and one of the
 gamblers:
Picturesque rascal he was, with long black hair and moustaches,

Black slouch hat drawn down to his eyes from his villanous
    forehead.
On together they moved, still earnestly talking in whispers,
On toward the forecastle, where sat the woman alone by the
    gangway.
Roused by the fall of feet, she turned, and, beholding her master,
Greeted him with a smile that was more like a wife's than
    another's,
Rose to meet him fondly, and then, with the dread apprehension
Always haunting the slave, fell her eye on the face of the
    gambler,—
Dark and lustful and fierce and full of merciless cunning.
Something was spoken so low that I could not hear what the
    words were;
Only the woman started, and looked from one to the other,
With imploring eyes, bewildered hands, and a tremor
All through her frame: I saw her from where I was standing, she
    shook so.
'Say! is it so?' she cried. On the weak, white lips of her master
Died a sickly smile, and he said, 'Louise, I have sold you.'
God is my judge! May I never see such a look of despairing,
Desolate anguish, as that which the woman cast on her master,
Griping her breast with her little hands, as if he had stabbed her,
Standing in silence a space, as fixed as the Indian woman
Carved out of wood, on the pilot-house of the old Pocahontas!
Then, with a gurgling moan, like the sound in the throat of the
    dying,
Came back her voice, that, rising, fluttered, through wild
    incoherence,
Into a terrible shriek that stopped my heart while she answered:—
'Sold me? sold me? sold—And you promised to give me my
    freedom!—
Promised me, for the sake of our little boy in Saint Louis!
What will you say to our boy, when he cries for me there in
    Saint Louis?
What will you say to our God?—Ah, you have been joking! I
    see it!—
No? God! God! He shall hear it,—and all of the angels in
    heaven,—
Even the devils in hell!—and none will believe when they hear
    it!

Sold me!'—Her voice died away with a wail, and in silence
Down she sank on the deck, and covered her face with her
fingers."

IV

In his story a moment the pilot paused, while we listened
To the salute of a boat, that, rounding the point of an island,
Flamed toward us with fires that seemed to burn from the
waters,—
Stately and vast and swift, and borne on the heart of the current.
Then, with the mighty voice of a giant challenged to battle,
Rose the responsive whistle, and all the echoes of island,
Swamp-land, glade, and brake replied with a myriad clamor,
Like wild birds that are suddenly startled from slumber at
midnight,
Then were at peace once more; and we heard the harsh cries of
the peacocks
Perched on a tree by a cabin-door, where the white-headed
settler's
White-headed children stood to look at the boat as it passed
them,
Passed them so near that we heard their happy talk and their
laughter.
Softly the sunset had faded, and now on the eastern horizon
Hung, like a tear in the sky, the beautiful star of the evening.

V

Still with his back to us standing, the pilot went on with his
story:—
"All of us flocked round the woman. The children cried, and
their mothers
Hugged them tight to their breasts; but the gambler said to the
captain,—
'Put me off there at the town that lies round the bend of the
river.
Here, you! rise at once, and be ready now to go with me.'
Roughly he seized the woman's arm and strove to uplift her.
She—she seemed not to heed him, but rose like one that is
dreaming,

Slid from his grasp, and fleetly mounted the steps of the gang-
    way,
Up to the hurricane-deck, in silence, without lamentation.
Straight to the stern of the boat, where the wheel was, she ran,
    and the people
Followed her fast till she turned and stood at bay for a moment,
Looking them in the face, and in the face of the gambler.
Not one to save her,—not one of all the compassionate people!
Not one to save her, of all the pitying angels in heaven!
Not one bolt of God to strike him dead there before her!
Wildly she waved him back, we waiting in silence and horror.
Over the swarthy face of the gambler a pallor of passion
Passed, like a gleam of lightning over the west in the night-time.
White, she stood, and mute, till he put forth his hand to secure
    her;
Then she turned and leaped,—in mid-air fluttered a moment,—
Down then, whirling, fell, like a broken-winged bird from a
    tree-top,
Down on the cruel wheel, that caught her, and hurled her, and
    crushed her,
And in the foaming water plunged her, and hid her forever."

VI

Still with his back to us all the pilot stood, but we heard him
Swallowing hard, as he pulled the bell-rope for stopping. Then,
    turning,—
"This is the place where it happened," brokenly whispered the
    pilot.
"Somehow, I never like to go by here alone in the night-time."
Darkly the Mississippi flowed by the town that lay in the star-
    light,
Cheerful with lamps. Below we could hear them reversing the
    engines,
And the great boat glided up to the shore like a giant exhausted.
Heavily sighed her pipes. Broad over the swamps to the east-
    ward
Shone the full moon, and turned our far-trembling wake into
    silver.
All was serene and calm, but the odorous breath of the willows
Smote with a mystical sense of infinite sorrow upon us.

LOUIS LEBEAU'S CONVERSION

Yesterday, while I moved with the languid crowd on the Riva,
Musing with idle eyes on the wide lagoons and the islands,
And on the dim-seen seaward glimmering sails in the distance,
Where the azure haze, like a vision of Indian-Summer,
Haunted the dreamy sky of the soft Venetian December,—
While I moved unwilled in the mellow warmth of the weather,
Breathing air that was full of Old World sadness and beauty
Into my thought came this story of free, wild life in Ohio,
When the land was new, and yet by the Beautiful River
Dwelt the pioneers and Indian hunters and boatmen.

Pealed from the campanili, responding from island to island,
Bells of that ancient faith whose incense and solemn devotions
Rise from a hundred shrines in the broken heart of the city;
But in my revery heard I only the passionate voices
Of the people that sang in the virgin heart of the forest.
Autumn was in the land, and the trees were golden and crimson,
And from the luminous boughs of the over-elms and the maples
Tender and beautiful fell the light in the worshippers' faces,
Softer than lights that stream through the saints on the windows
     of churches,
While the balsamy breath of the hemlocks and pines by the river
Stole on the winds through the woodland aisles like the breath
     of a censer.
Loud the people sang old camp-meeting anthems that quaver
Quaintly yet from lips forgetful of lips that have kissed them;
Loud they sang the songs of the Sacrifice and Atonement,
And of the end of the world, and the infinite terrors of Judg-
     ment:—
Songs of ineffable sorrow, and wailing, compassionate warning
Unto the generations that hardened their hearts to their Savior;
Songs of exultant rapture for them that confessed him and
     followed,
Bearing his burden and yoke, enduring and entering with him
Into the rest of his saints, and the endless reward of the blessed.
Loud the people sang; but through the sound of their singing

Broke inarticulate cries and moans and sobs from the mourners,
As the glory of God, that smote the apostle of Tarsus,
Smote them and strewed them to earth like leaves in the breath of
    the whirlwind.

Hushed at last was the sound of the lamentation and singing;
But from the distant hill the throbbing drum of the pheasant
Shook with its heavy pulses the depths of the listening silence,
When from his place arose a white-haired exhorter, and faltered:
"Brethren and sisters in Jesus! the Lord hath heard our petitions,
So that the hearts of his servants are awed and melted within
    them,—
Even the hearts of the wicked are touched by his infinite mercy.
All my days in this vale of tears the Lord hath been with me,
He hath been good to me, he hath granted me trials and patience;
But this hour hath crowned my knowledge of him and his
    goodness.
Truly, but that it is well this day for me to be with you,
Now might I say to the Lord,—'I know thee, my God, in all
    fulness;
Now let thy servant depart in peace to the rest thou hast
    promised!'"

Faltered and ceased. And now the wild and jubilant music
Of the singing burst from the solemn profound of the silence,
Surged in triumph, and fell, and ebbed again into silence.

Then from the group of the preachers arose the greatest
    among them,—
He whose days were given in youth to the praise of the Savior,
He whose lips seemed touched, like the prophet's of old, from
    the altar,
So that his words were flame, and burned to the hearts of his
    hearers,
Quickening the dead among them, reviving the cold and the
    doubting.
There he charged them pray, and rest not from prayer while a
    sinner
In the sound of their voices denied the Friend of the sinner:
"Pray till the night shall fall,—till the stars are faint in the
    morning,—

Yea, till the sun himself be faint in that glory and brightness,
Faint in the light which shall dawn in mercy for penitent
    sinners."
Kneeling, he led them in prayer; and the quick and sobbing
    responses
Spake how their souls were moved with the might and the grace
    of the Spirit.
Then while the converts recounted how God had chastened and
    saved them,—
Children, whose golden locks yet shone with the lingering
    effulgence
Of the touches of Him who blessed little children forever;
Old men, whose yearning eyes were dimmed with the far-
    streaming brightness
Seen through the opening gates in the heart of the heavenly
    city,—
Stealthily through the harking woods the lengthening shadows
Chased the wild things to their nests, and the twilight died into
    darkness.

  Now the four great pyres that were placed there to light the
    encampment,
High on platforms raised above the people, were kindled.
Flaming aloof, as it were the pillar by night in the Desert
Fell their crimson light on the lifted orbs of the preachers,
Fell on the withered brows of the old men, and Israel's mothers,
Fell on the bloom of youth, and the earnest devotion of man-
    hood,
Fell on the anguish and hope in the tearful eyes of the mourners.
Flaming aloof, it stirred the sleep of the luminous maples
With warm summer-dreams, and faint, luxurious languor.
Near the four great pyres the people closed in a circle,
In their midst the mourners, and, praying with them, the ex-
    horters,
And on the skirts of the circle the unrepentant and scorners,—
Ever fewer and sadder, and drawn to the place of the mourners,
One after one, by the prayers and tears of the brethren and
    sisters,
And by the Spirit of God, that was mightily striving within
    them,
Till at the last alone stood Louis Lebeau, unconverted.

  Louis Lebeau, the boatman, the trapper, the hunter, the
      fighter,
From the unlucky French of Gallipolis he descended,
Heir to Old World want and New World love of adventure.
Vague was the life he led, and vague and grotesque were the
      rumors
Through which he loomed on the people,—the hero of mythical
      hearsay,
Quick of hand and of heart, impatient, generous, Western,
Taking the thought of the young in secret love and in envy.
Not less the elders shook their heads and held him for outcast,
Reprobate, roving, ungodly, infidel, worse than a Papist,
With his whispered fame of lawless exploits at St. Louis,
Wild affrays and loves with the half-breeds out on the Osage,
Brawls at New Orleans, and all the towns on the rivers,
All the godless towns of the many-ruffianed rivers.
Only she who loved him the best of all, in her loving
Knew him the best of all, and other than that of the rumors.
Daily she prayed for him, with conscious and tender effusion,
That the Lord would convert him. But when her father forbade
      him
Unto her thought, she denied him, and likewise held him for
      outcast,
Turned her eyes when they met, and would not speak, though
      her heart broke.

  Bitter and brief his logic that reasoned from wrong unto
      error:
"This is their praying and singing," he said, "that makes you
      reject me,—
You that were kind to me once. But I think my fathers' religion,
With a light heart in the breast and a friendly priest to absolve
      one,
Better than all these conversions that only bewilder and vex me,
And that have made men so hard and women fickle and cruel.
Well, then, pray for my soul, since you would not have spoken
      to save me,—
Yes; for I go from these saints to my brethren and sisters, the
      sinners."
Spoke and went, while her faint lips fashioned unuttered en-
      treaties,—

Went, and came again in a year at the time of the meeting,
Haggard and wan of face, and wasted with passion and sorrow.
Dead in his eyes was the careless smile of old, and its phantom
Haunted his lips in a sneer of restless, incredulous mocking.
Day by day he came to the outer skirts of the circle,
Dwelling on her, where she knelt by the white-haired exhorter,
    her father,
With his hollow looks, and never moved from his silence.

Now, where he stood alone, the last of impenitent sinners,
Weeping, old friends and comrades came to him out of the circle,
And with their tears besought him to hear what the Lord had
    done for them.
Ever he shook them off, not roughly, nor smiled at their
    transports.
Then the preachers spoke and painted the terrors of Judgment,
And of the bottomless pit, and the flames of hell everlasting.
Still and dark he stood, and neither listened nor heeded;
But when the fervent voice of the white-haired exhorter was
    lifted,
Fell his brows in a scowl of fierce and scornful rejection.
"Lord, let this soul be saved!" cried the fervent voice of the old
    man;
"For that the Shepherd rejoiceth more truly for one that hath
    wandered,
And hath been found again, than for all the others that strayed
    not."

Out of the midst of the people, a woman old and decrepit,
Tremulous through the light, and tremulous into the shadow,
Wavered toward him with slow, uncertain paces of palsy,
Laid her quivering hand on his arm and brokenly prayed him:
"Louis Lebeau, I closed in death the eyes of your mother.
On my breast she died, in prayer for her fatherless children,
That they might know the Lord, and follow him always, and
    serve him.
O, I conjure you, my son, by the name of your mother in glory,
Scorn not the grace of the Lord!" As when a summer-noon's
    tempest
Breaks in one swift gush of rain, then ceases and gathers
Darker and gloomier yet on the lowering front of the heavens,

So broke his mood in tears, as he soothed her, and stilled her
 entreaties,
And so he turned again with his clouded looks to the people.

Vibrated then from the hush the accents of mournfullest
 pity,—
His who was gifted in speech, and the glow of the fires illumined
All his pallid aspect with sudden and marvellous splendor:
"Louis Lebeau," he spake, "I have known you and loved you
 from childhood;
Still, when the others blamed you, I took your part, for I knew
 you.
Louis Lebeau, my brother, I thought to meet you in heaven,
Hand in hand with her who is gone to heaven before us,
Brothers through her dear love! I trusted to greet you and lead
 you
Up from the brink of the River unto the gates of the City.
Lo! my years shall be few on the earth. O my brother,
If I should die before you had known the mercy of Jesus,
Yea, I think it would sadden the hope of glory within me!"

Neither yet had the will of the sinner yielded an answer;
But from his lips there broke a cry of unspeakable anguish,
Wild and fierce and shrill, as if some demon within him
Rent his soul with the ultimate pangs of fiendish possession;
And with the outstretched arms of bewildered imploring toward
 them,
Death-white unto the people he turned his face from the dark-
 ness.

Out of the sedge by the creek a flight of clamorous killdees
Rose from their timorous sleep with piercing and iterant
 challenge,
Wheeled in the starlight, and fled away into distance and silence.
White in the vale lay the tents, and beyond them glided the
 river,
Where the broadhorn* drifted slow at the will of the current,
And where the boatman listened, and knew not how, as he
 listened,

*The old-fashioned flatboats were so called. [*Howells' note.*]

Something touched through the years the old lost hopes of his
   childhood,—
Only his sense was filled with low, monotonous murmurs,
As of a faint-heard prayer, that was chorused with deeper
   responses.

   Not with the rest was lifted her voice in the fervent responses,
But in her soul she prayed to Him that heareth in secret,
Asking for light and for strength to learn his will and to do it:
"O, make me clear to know if the hope that rises within me
Be not part of a love unmeet for me here, and forbidden!
So, if it be not that, make me strong for the evil entreaty
Of the days that shall bring me question of self and reproaches,
When the unrighteous shall mock, and my brethren and sisters
   shall doubt me!
Make me worthy to know thy will, my Savior, and do it!"
In her pain she prayed, and at last, through her mute adoration,
Rapt from all mortal presence, and in her rapture uplifted,
Glorified she rose, and stood in the midst of the people,
Looking on all with the still, unseeing eyes of devotion,—
Vague, and tender, and sweet, as the eyes of the dead, when we
   dream them
Living and looking on us, but they cannot speak, and we
   cannot,—
Knowing only the peril that threatened his soul's unrepentance,
Knowing only the fear and error and wrong that withheld him,
Thinking, "In doubt of me, his soul had perished forever!"
Touched with no feeble shame, but trusting her power to save
   him,
Through the circle she passed, and straight to the side of her
   lover,
Took his hand in her own, and mutely implored him an instant,
Answering, giving, forgiving, confessing, beseeching him all
   things;
Drew him then with her, and passed once more through the
   circle
Unto her place, and knelt with him there by the side of her father,
Trembling as women tremble who greatly venture and triumph,—
But in her innocent breast was the saint's sublime exultation.

   So was Louis converted; and though the lips of the scorners
Spared not in after years the subtle taunt and derision

(What time, meeker grown, his heart held his hand from its
    answer),
Not the less lofty and pure her love and her faith that had saved
    him,
Not the less now discerned was her inspiration from heaven
By the people, that rose, and embracing and weeping together,
Poured forth their jubilant songs of victory and of thanksgiving,
Till from the embers leaped the dying flame to behold them,
And the hills of the river were filled with reverberant echoes,—
Echoes that out of the years and the distance stole to me hither,
While I moved unwilled in the mellow warmth of the weather;
Echoes that mingled and fainted and fell with the fluttering
    murmurs
In the hearts of the hushing bells, as from island to island
Swooned the sound on the wide lagoons into palpitant silence.

DRAMA

While Howells was preaching his doctrine of realism in The Atlantic Monthly *and in* Harper's, *he was illustrating his ideas in his novels. He was also practising realism in a series of farces which began with* The Parlor Car *(1876) and ended with* Parting Friends *(1911). Though these amusing little comedies were seldom seen on the professional stage, they were familiar to several generations devoted to amateur theatricals. Henry Arthur Jones wrote to Howells, "I think . . . that these little pieces of yours ought to be constantly played by amateurs,"[1] and, in fact, they were. In 1883* The Sleeping Car *appeared, the first of a series of twelve farces presenting scenes in the lives of the Robertses and the Campbells, which illustrate Howells' pleasure in the comic situations in which ordinary men and women become involved. See Introduction, pp. xciv–xcix.*

THE SLEEPING-CAR

A Farce

I

SCENE: *One side of a sleeping-car on the Boston and Albany Road. The curtains are drawn before most of the berths: from the hooks and rods hang hats, bonnets, bags, bandboxes, umbrellas, and other travelling gear; on the floor are boots of both sexes, set out for* THE PORTER *to black.* THE PORTER *is making up the beds in the upper and lower berths adjoining the seats on which a young mother, slender and pretty, with a baby asleep on the seat beside her, and a stout old lady, sit confronting each other—* MRS. AGNES ROBERTS *and her aunt* MARY.

MRS. ROBERTS. Do you always take down your back hair, aunty?

AUNT MARY. No, never, child; at least not since I had such a fright about it once, coming on from New York. It's all well enough to take down your back hair if it *is* yours; but if it

[1]Letter dated January 29, 1907. The Houghton Library, Harvard.

isn't, your head's the best place for it. Now, as I buy mine of Madame Pierrot—

Mrs. Roberts. Don't you *wish* she wouldn't advertise it as *human* hair? It sounds so pokerish—like human flesh, you know.

Aunt Mary. Why, she couldn't call it *in*human hair, my dear.

Mrs. Roberts (*thoughtfully*). No—just *hair.*

Aunt Mary. Then people might think it was for mattresses. But, as I was saying, I took it off that night, and tucked it safely away, as I supposed, in my pocket, and I slept sweetly till about midnight, when I happened to open my eyes, and saw something long and black crawl off my bed and slip under the berth. *Such* a shriek as I gave, my dear! "A snake! a snake! oh, a snake!" And everybody began talking at once, and some of the gentlemen swearing, and the porter came running with the poker to kill it; and all the while it was that ridiculous switch of mine, that had worked out of my pocket. And glad enough I was to grab it up before anybody saw it, and say I must have been dreaming.

Mrs. Roberts. Why, aunty, how funny! How *could* you suppose a serpent could get on board a sleeping-car, of all places in the world!

Aunt Mary. That was the perfect absurdity of it.

The Porter. Berths are ready now, ladies.

Mrs. Roberts. (*to* The Porter, *who walks away to the end of the car, and sits down near the door*). Oh, thank you. Aunty, do you feel nervous the least bit?

Aunt Mary. Nervous? No. Why?

Mrs. Roberts. Well, I don't know. I suppose I've been worked up a little about meeting Willis, and wondering how he'll look, and all. We can't *know* each other, of course. It doesn't stand to reason that if he's been out there for twelve years, ever since I was a child, though we've corresponded regularly—at least *I* have—that he could recognize me; not at the first glance, you know. He'll have a full beard; and then I've got married, and here's the baby. Oh, *no!* he'll never guess who it is in the world. Photographs really amount to nothing in such a case. I wish we were at home, and it was all over. I wish he had written some particulars, instead of telegraphing from Ogden, "Be with you on the 7 A.M., Wednesday."

AUNT MARY. Californians always telegraph, my dear; they never think of writing. It isn't expensive enough, and it doesn't make your blood run cold enough to get a letter, and so they send you one of those miserable yellow despatches whenever they can—those printed in a long string, if possible, so that you'll be *sure* to die before you get to the end of it. I suppose your brother has fallen into all those ways, and says "reckon" and "ornary" and "which the same," just like one of Mr. Bret Harte's characters.

MRS. ROBERTS. But it isn't exactly our not knowing each other, aunty, that's worrying me; that's something that could be got over in time. What is simply driving me distracted is Willis and Edward meeting there when I'm away from home. Oh, how *could* I be away! and why *couldn't* Willis have given us fair warning? I would have hurried from the ends of the earth to meet him. I don't believe poor Edward ever saw a Californian; and he's so quiet and preoccupied, I'm sure he'd never get on with Willis. And if Willis is the least loud, he wouldn't like Edward. Not that I suppose he *is* loud; but I don't believe he knows anything about literary men. But you can see, aunty, can't you, how very anxious I must be? Don't you see that I ought to have been there when Willis and Edward met, so as to—to—well, to *break* them to each other, don't you know?

AUNT MARY. Oh, you needn't be troubled about that, Agnes. I dare say they've got on perfectly well together. Very likely they're sitting down to the unwholesomest hot supper this instant that the ingenuity of man could invent.

MRS. ROBERTS. Oh, do you *think* they are, aunty? Oh, if I could *only* believe they were sitting down to a hot supper together now, I should be *so* happy! They'd be sure to get on if they were. There's nothing like eating to make men friendly with each other. Don't you know, at receptions,

how they never have anything to say to each other till the
escalloped oysters and the chicken salad appear; and then how
sweet they are as soon as they've helped the ladies to ice? Oh,
thank you, *thank* you, aunty, for thinking of the hot supper.
It's such a relief to my mind! You can understand, can't you,
aunty dear, how anxious I must have been to have my only
brother and my only—my husband—get on nicely together?
My life would be a wreck, simply a wreck, if they didn't. And
Willis and I not having seen each other since I was a child
makes it all the worse. I do *hope* they're sitting down to a hot
supper.

An Angry Voice *from the next berth but one.* I wish people in
sleeping-cars—

A Voice *from the berth beyond that.* You're mistaken in your
premises, sir. This is a waking-car. Ladies, go on, and oblige
an eager listener.

[*Sensation, and smothered laughter from the other berths.*]

Mrs. Roberts (*after a space of terrified silence, in a loud whisper
to her* Aunt). What horrid things! But now we really must
go to bed. It *was* too bad to keep talking. I'd no idea my
voice was getting so loud. Which berth will you have, aunty?
I'd better take the upper one, because—

Aunt Mary (*whispering*). No, no; I must take that, so that you
can be with the baby below.

Mrs. Roberts. Oh, how good you are, Aunt Mary! It's too
bad; it is really. I can't let you.

Aunt Mary. Well then, you must; that's all. You know how
that child tosses and kicks about in the night. You never can
tell where his head's going to be in the morning, but you'll
probably find it at the foot of the bed. I couldn't sleep an
instant, my dear, if I thought that boy was in the upper berth;
for I'd be sure of his tumbling out over you. Here, let me
lay him down. *She lays the baby in the lower berth.* There!
Now get in, Agnes—do, and leave me to my struggle with
the attraction of gravitation.

Mrs. Roberts. Oh, *poor* aunty, how will you ever manage it?
I *must* help you up.

AUNT MARY. No, my dear; don't be foolish. But you may go and call the porter, if you like. I dare say he's used to it.

[MRS. ROBERTS *goes and speaks timidly to* THE PORTER, *who fails at first to understand, then smiles broadly, accepts a quarter with a duck of his head, and comes forward to* AUNT MARY'S *side.*]

MRS. ROBERTS. Had he better give you his hand to rest your foot in, while you spring up as if you were mounting horse-back?

AUNT MARY (*with disdain*). *Spring!* My dear, I haven't *sprung* for a quarter of a century. I shall require every fibre in the man's body. His hand, indeed! You get in first, Agnes.

MRS. ROBERTS. I will, aunty dear; but—

AUNT MARY (*sternly*). Agnes, do as I say. [MRS. ROBERTS *crouches down on the lower berth.*] I don't choose that any member of my family shall witness my contortions. Don't you look.

MRS. ROBERTS. No, no, aunty.

AUNT MARY. Now, porter, are you strong?

PORTER. I used to be porter at a Saratoga hotel, and carried up de ladies' trunks dere.

AUNT MARY. Then you'll do, I think. Now, then, your knee; now your back. There! And very handsomely done. Thanks.

MRS. ROBERTS. Are you really in, Aunt Mary?

AUNT MARY (*dryly*). Yes. Goodnight.

MRS. ROBERTS. Good-night, aunty.

[*After a pause of some minutes.*] Aunty!

AUNT MARY. Well, what?

MRS. ROBERTS. Do you think it's perfectly safe?

[*She rises in her berth, and looks up over the edge of the upper.*]

AUNT MARY. I suppose so. It's a well-managed road. They've got the air-brake, I've heard, and the Miller platform, and all those horrid things. What makes you introduce such unpleasant subjects?

MRS. ROBERTS. Oh, I don't mean accidents. But, you know, when you turn, it does creak so awfully. I shouldn't mind myself; but the baby—

AUNT MARY. Why, child, do you think I'm going to break through? I couldn't. I'm one of the *lightest* sleepers in the world.

MRS. ROBERTS. Yes, I know you're a light sleeper; but—it doesn't seem quite the same thing, somehow.

AUNT MARY. But it is; it's quite the same thing, and you can be perfectly easy in your mind, my dear. I should be quite as loth to break through as you would to have me. Good-night.

MRS. ROBERTS. Yes; good-night. Aunty!

AUNT MARY. Well?

MRS. ROBERTS. You ought to just see him, how he's lying. He's a perfect log. *Couldn't* you just bend over, and peep down at him a moment?

AUNT MARY. Bend over! It would be the death of me. Good-night.

MRS. ROBERTS. Good-night. Did you put the glass into my bag or yours? I feel so very thirsty, and I want to go and get some water. I'm sure I don't know why I should be thirsty. Are you, Aunt Mary? Ah! here it is. Don't disturb yourself, aunty; I've found it. It was in my bag, just where I'd put it myself. But all this trouble about Willis has made me so fidgety that I don't know where anything is. And now I don't know how to manage about the baby while I go after the water. He's sleeping soundly enough now; but if he should happen to get into one of his rolling moods, he might tumble out on to the floor. Never mind, aunty, I've thought of something. I'll just barricade him with these bags and shawls. Now, old fellow, roll as much as you like. If you should happen to hear him stir, aunty, won't you—aunty! Oh, dear! she's asleep already; and what shall I do? [*While Mrs. Roberts continues talking, various notes of protest, profane and otherwise, make themselves heard from different berths.*] I know. I'll make a bold dash for the water, and be back in an instant, baby. Now, don't you move, you little rogue. [*She runs to the water-tank at the end of the car, and then back to her berth.*] Now, baby, here's mamma again. Are you all right, mamma's own?

[*A shaggy head and bearded face are thrust from the curtains of the next berth.*]

THE STRANGER. Look here, ma'am. I don't want to be disagreeable about this thing, and I hope you won't take any offence; but the fact is, I'm half dead for want of sleep, and if you'll only keep quiet now a little while, I'll promise not to speak above my breath if ever I find you on a sleeping-car after you've come straight through from San Francisco, day and night, and not been able to get more than about a quarter of your usual allowance of rest—I will indeed.

MRS. ROBERTS. I'm very sorry that I've disturbed you, and I'll try to be more quiet. I didn't suppose I was speaking so loud; but the cars keep up such a rattling that you never can tell how loud you *are* speaking. Did I understand you to say that you were from California?

THE CALIFORNIAN. Yes, ma'am.

MRS. ROBERTS. San Francisco?

THE CALIFORNIAN. Yes, ma'am.

MRS. ROBERTS. Thanks. It's a terribly long journey, isn't it? I know quite how to feel for you. I've a brother myself coming on. In fact we expected him before this. [*She scans his face as sharply as the lamp-light will allow, and continues, after a brief hesitation.*] It's always such a silly question to ask a person, and I suppose San Francisco is a large place, with a great many people always coming and going, so that it would be only one chance in a thousand if you did.

THE CALIFORNIAN (*patiently*). Did what, ma'am?

MRS. ROBERTS. Oh, I was just wondering if it was possible— but of course it isn't, and it's very flat to ask—that you'd ever happened to meet my brother there. His name is Willis Campbell.

THE CALIFORNIAN (*with more interest*). Campbell? Campbell? Yes, I know a man of that name. But I disremember his first name. Little low fellow—pretty chunky?

MRS. ROBERTS. I don't know. Do you mean short and stout?

THE CALIFORNIAN. Yes, ma'am.

MRS. ROBERTS. I'm sure I can't tell. It's a great many years since he went out there, and I've never seen him in all that time. I thought if you *did* happen to know him— He's a lawyer.

THE CALIFORNIAN. It's quite likely I know him; and in the morning, ma'am—

MRS. ROBERTS. Oh, excuse me. I'm very sorry to have kept you so long awake with my silly questions.

THE MAN IN THE UPPER BERTH. Don't apologize, madam. I'm not a Californian myself, but I'm an orphan, and away from home, and I thank you, on behalf of all our fellow-passengers, for the mental refreshment that your conversation has afforded us. *I* could lie here and listen to it all night; but there are invalids in some of these berths, and perhaps on their account it will be as well to defer everything till the morning, as our friend suggests. Allow me to wish you pleasant dreams, madam.

[THE CALIFORNIAN, *while* MRS. ROBERTS *shrinks back under the curtain of her berth in dismay, and stammers some inaudible excuse, slowly emerges full length from his berth.*]

THE CALIFORNIAN. Don't you mind me, ma'am; I've got everything but my boots and coat on. Now, then [*standing beside the berth, and looking in upon the man in the upper tier*], you, do you know that this is a lady you're talking to?

THE UPPER BERTH. By your voice and your shaggy personal appearance I shouldn't have taken you for a lady—no, sir. But the light is very imperfect; you may be a bearded lady.

THE CALIFORNIAN. You never mind about my looks. The question is, Do you want your head rapped up against the side of this car?

THE UPPER BERTH. With all the frankness of your own Pacific slope, no.

MRS. ROBERTS (*hastily reappearing*). Oh, no, no, don't hurt him. He's not to blame. I was wrong to keep on talking. Oh, please don't hurt him!

THE CALIFORNIAN (*to the Upper Berth*). You hear? Well, now, don't you speak another word to that lady tonight. Just go on, ma'am, and free your mind on any little matter you like.

I don't want any sleep. How long has your brother been in California?

MRS. ROBERTS. Oh, don't let's talk about it now; I don't want to talk about it. I thought—I thought— Goodnight. Oh, dear! I didn't suppose I was making so much trouble. I didn't mean to disturb anybody. I—

[MRS. ROBERTS *gives way to the excess of her confusion and mortification in a little sob, and then hides her grief behind the curtains of her berth.* THE CALIFORNIAN *slowly emerges again from his couch, and stands beside it, looking in upon the man in the berth above.*]

THE CALIFORNIAN. For half a cent I *would* rap your head up against that wall. Making the lady cry, and getting me so mad I can't sleep! Now see here, you just apologize. You beg that lady's pardon, or I'll have you out of there before you know yourself. [*Cries of* "Good!" "That's right!" *and* "Make him show himself!" *hail* MRS. ROBERTS'S *champion, and heads, more or less dishevelled, are thrust from every berth.* MRS. ROBERTS *remains invisible and silent, and the loud and somewhat complicated respiration of her* AUNT *makes itself heard in the general hush of expectancy. A remark to the effect that* "The old lady seems to enjoy her rest" *achieves a facile applause.* THE CALIFORNIAN *again addresses the culprit.*] Come now, what do you say? I'll give you just one-half a minute.

MRS. ROBERTS (*from her shelter*). Oh, please, *please* don't make him say anything. It was very trying in me to keep him awake, and I know he didn't mean any offence. Oh, *do* let him be!

THE CALIFORNIAN. You hear that? You stay quiet the rest of the time; and if that lady chooses to keep us all awake the whole night, don't *you* say a word, or I'll settle with you in the morning.

[*Loud and continued applause, amidst which* THE CALIFORNIAN *turns from the man in the berth before him, and restores order by marching along the aisle of the car in his stocking feet. The heads vanish behind the curtains. As the laughter subsides, he returns to his berth, and after a stare up and down the tranquillized car, he is about to retire.*]

A Voice. Oh, don't just bow. Speak!

[*A fresh burst of laughter greets this sally.* The Californian *erects himself again with an air of baited wrath, and then suddenly breaks into a helpless laugh.*]

The Californian. Gentlemen, you're too many for *me.*

[*He gets into his berth, and after cries of* "Good for California!" "You're all right, William Nye!" *and* "You're several ahead yet!" *the occupants of the different berths gradually relapse into silence, and at last, as the car lunges onward through the darkness, nothing is heard but the rhythmical clank of the machinery, with now and then a burst of audible slumber from* Mrs. Roberts's Aunt Mary.]

II

At Worcester, where the train has made the usual stop, The Porter, *with his lantern on his arm, enters the car, preceding a gentleman somewhat anxiously smiling; his nervous speech contrasts painfully with the business-like impassiveness of* The Porter, *who refuses, with an air of incredulity, to enter into the confidences which the gentleman seems reluctant to bestow.*

Mr. Edward Roberts. This is the Governor Marcy, isn't it?

The Porter. Yes, sah.

Mr. Roberts. Came on from Albany, and not from New York?

The Porter. Yes, sah, it did.

Mr. Roberts. Ah! it must be all right. I—

The Porter. Was your wife expecting you to come on board here?

Mr. Roberts. Well, no, not exactly. She was expecting me to meet her at Boston. But I— [*struggling to give the situation dignity, but failing, and throwing himself, with self-convicted silliness, upon the* Porter's *mercy*]. The fact is, I thought I would surprise her by joining her here.

The Porter (*refusing to have any mercy*). Oh! How did you expect to find her?

Mr. Roberts. Well— well— I don't know. I didn't consider. [*He looks down the aisle in despair at the close-drawn curtains* of the berths, and up at the dangling hats and bags and bonnets, and down at the chaos of boots of both sexes on the floor.] I don't know *how* I expected to find her.

[MR. ROBERTS'S *countenance falls, and he visibly sinks so low in his own esteem and an imaginary public opinion that* THE PORTER *begins to have a little compassion.*]

THE PORTER. Dey's so many ladies on board *I* couldn't find her.

MR. ROBERTS. Oh, no, no, of course not. I didn't expect that.

THE PORTER. Don't like to go routing 'em all up, you know. I wouldn't be allowed to.

MR. ROBERTS. I don't ask it; that would be preposterous.

THE PORTER. What sort of looking lady was she?

MR. ROBERTS. Well, I don't know, really. Not very tall, rather slight, blue eyes. I—I don't know what you'd call her nose. And—stop! Oh yes, she had a child with her, a little boy. Yes!

THE PORTER (*thoughtfully looking down the aisle*). Dey was three ladies had children. I didn't notice whether dey was boys or girls, or *what* dey was. Didn't have anybody with her?

MR. ROBERTS. No, no. Only the child.

THE PORTER. Well, I don't know what you are going to do, sah. It won't be a great while now till morning, you know. Here comes the conductor. Maybe he'll know what to do.

[MR. ROBERTS *makes some futile, inarticulate attempts to prevent* THE PORTER *from laying the case before* THE CONDUCTOR, *and then stands guiltily smiling, overwhelmed with the hopeless absurdity of his position.*]

THE CONDUCTOR (*entering the car, and stopping before* THE PORTER, *and looking at* MR. ROBERTS). Gentleman want a berth?

THE PORTER (*grinning*). Well, no, sah. He's lookin' for his wife.

THE CONDUCTOR (*with suspicion*). Is she aboard this car?

MR. ROBERTS (*striving to propitiate* THE CONDUCTOR *by a dastardly amiability*). Oh, yes, yes. There's no mistake about the car—the Governor Marcy. She telegraphed the name just before you left Albany, so that I could find her at Boston in the morning. Ah!

THE CONDUCTOR. At Boston. [*Sternly.*] Then what are you trying to find her at Worcester in the middle of the night for?

MR. ROBERTS. Why—I— that is—

THE PORTER (*taking compassion on Mr. Robert's inability to continue*). Says he wants to surprise her.

MR. ROBERTS. Ha—yes, exactly. A little caprice, you know.

THE CONDUCTOR. Well, that may all be so. [MR. ROBERTS *continues to smile in agonized helplessness against* THE CONDUCTOR'S *injurious tone, which becomes more and more offensively patronizing.*] But *I* can't do anything for you. Here are all these people asleep in their berths, and I can't go round waking them up because you want to surprise your wife.

MR. ROBERTS. No, no; of course not. I never thought—

THE CONDUCTOR. My advice to *you* is to have a berth made up, and go to bed till we get to Boston, and surprise your wife by telling her what you tried to do.

MR. ROBERTS (*unable to resent the patronage of this suggestion*). Well, I don't know but I will.

THE CONDUCTOR (*going out*). The porter will make up the berth for you.

MR. ROBERTS (*to* THE PORTER, *who is about to pull down the upper berth over a vacant seat*). Ah! Er—I—I don't think I'll trouble you to make it up; it's so near morning now. Just bring me a pillow, and I'll try to get a nap without lying down. [*He takes the vacant seat.*]

THE PORTER. All right, sah.

[*He goes to the end of the car and returns with a pillow.*]

MR. ROBERTS. Ah—porter!

THE PORTER. Yes, sah.

MR. ROBERTS. Of course you didn't notice; but you don't think you *did* notice who was in that berth yonder? [*He indicates a certain berth.*]

THE PORTER. Dat's a gen'leman in dat berth, I think, sah.

MR. ROBERTS (*astutely*). There's a bonnet hanging from the hook at the top. I'm not sure, but it looks like my wife's bonnet.

THE PORTER (*evidently shaken by this reasoning, but recovering his firmness*). Yes, sah. But you can't depend upon de ladies to hang deir bonnets on de right hook. Jes' likely as not dat lady's took de hook at de foot of her berth instead o' de head. Sometimes dey takes both.

MR. ROBERTS. Ah! [*After a pause.*] Porter!

THE PORTER. Yes, sah.

MR. ROBERTS. You wouldn't feel justified in looking?

THE PORTER. I couldn't, sah; I couldn't, indeed.

MR. ROBERTS (*reaching his left hand toward* THE PORTER'S, *and pressing a half dollar into his instantly responsive palm*). But there's nothing to prevent *my* looking if I feel perfectly sure of the bonnet?

THE PORTER. N-no, sah.

MR. ROBERTS. All right.

[THE PORTER *retires to the end of the car, and resumes the work of polishing the passengers' boots. After an interval of quiet,* MR. ROBERTS *rises, and, looking about him with what he feels to be melodramatic stealth, approaches the suspected berth. He unloops the curtain with a trembling hand, and peers ineffectually in; he advances his head further and further into the darkened recess, and then suddenly dodges back again, with* THE CALIFORNIAN *hanging to his neckcloth with one hand.*]

THE CALIFORNIAN (*savagely*). What do you want?

MR. ROBERTS (*struggling and breathless*). I—I—I want my wife.

THE CALIFORNIAN. Want your wife! Have *I* got your wife?

MR. ROBERTS. No—ah—that is—ah, excuse me—I thought you *were* my wife.

THE CALIFORNIAN (*getting out of the berth, but at the same time keeping hold of* MR. ROBERTS). Thought I was your *wife!* Do I look like your wife? You can't play that on me, old man. Porter! conductor!

MR. ROBERTS (*agonized*). Oh, I beseech you, my dear sir, don't —don't! I can explain it—I can indeed. I know it has an ugly look; but if you will allow me two words—only two words—

MRS. ROBERTS (*suddenly parting the curtain of her berth, and*

springing out into the aisle, with her hair wildly dishevelled).
Edward!

MR. ROBERTS. Oh, Agnes, explain to this gentleman! [*Imploringly.*] Don't you know me?

A VOICE. Make him show you the strawberry mark on his left arm.

MRS. ROBERTS. Edward! Edward! [THE CALIFORNIAN *mechanically looses his grip, and they fly into each other's embrace.*] *Where* did you come from?

A VOICE. Centre door, left hand, one back.

THE CONDUCTOR (*returning with his lantern*). Hallo! What's the matter here?

A VOICE. Train robbers! Throw up your hands! Tell the express-messenger to bring his safe.

[*The passengers emerge from their berths in various* deshabille *and bewilderment.*]

THE CONDUCTOR (*to* MR. ROBERTS). Have *you* been making all this row, waking up my passengers?

THE CALIFORNIAN. No, sir, he hasn't. *I've* been making this row. This gentleman was peaceably looking for his wife, and I misunderstood him. You want to say anything to *me?*

THE CONDUCTOR (*silently taking* THE CALIFORNIAN'S *measure with his eye, as he stands six feet in his stockings*). If I did, I'd get the biggest brakeman I could find to do it for me. *I've* got nothing to say except that I think you'd better all go back to bed again.

[*He goes out, and the passengers disappear one by one, leaving the* ROBERTSES *and* THE CALIFORNIAN *alone.*]

THE CALIFORNIAN (*to* MR. ROBERTS). Stranger, I'm sorry I got you into this scrape.

MR. ROBERTS. Oh, don't speak of it, my dear sir. I'm sure we owe you all sorts of apologies, which I shall be most happy to offer you at my house in Boston, with every needful explanation. [*He takes out his card, and gives it to* THE CALIFORNIAN, *who looks at it, and then looks at* MR. ROBERTS *curiously.*] There's my address, and I'm sure we shall both be glad to have you call.

MRS. ROBERTS. Oh, yes, indeed. [THE CALIFORNIAN *parts the curtains of his berth to re-enter it.*] Good-night, sir, and I assure you *we* shall do nothing more to disturb you—shall we, Edward?

MR. ROBERTS. No. And now, dear, I think you'd better go back to your berth.

MRS. ROBERTS. I couldn't sleep, and I shall not go back. Is this your place? I will just rest my head on your shoulder; and we must both be perfectly quiet. You've no idea what a nuisance I have been making of myself. The whole car was perfectly furious at me one time, I kept talking so loud. I don't know how I came to do it, but I suppose it was thinking about you and Willis meeting without knowing each other made me nervous, and I couldn't be still. I woke everybody up with my talking, and some of them were quite outrageous in their remarks; but I didn't blame them the least bit, for I should have been just as bad. That California gentleman was perfectly splendid, though. I can tell you *he* made them stop. We struck up quite a friendship. I told him I had a brother coming on from California, and he's going to try to think whether he knows Willis. [*Groans and inarticulate protests make themselves heard from different berths.*] I declare, I've got to talking again! There, now, I *shall* stop, and they won't hear another squeak from me the rest of the night. [*She lifts her head from her husband's shoulder.*] I wonder if baby will roll out. He *does* kick so! And I just sprang up and left him when I heard your voice, without putting anything to keep him in. I *must* go and have another look at him, or I never can settle down. No, no, don't you go, Edward; you'll be prying into all the wrong berths in the car, you poor thing! You stay here, and I'll be back in half a second. I wonder which is my berth. Ah! that is it; I know the one now. [*She makes a sudden dash at a berth, and pulling open the curtains is confronted by the bearded visage of* THE CALIFORNIAN.] Ah! Ow! ow! Edward! Ah! I—I beg your pardon, sir; excuse me; I didn't know it was you. I came for my baby.

THE CALIFORNIAN (*solemnly*). I haven't got any baby, ma'am.

Mrs. Roberts. No—no—I thought *you* were my baby.

The Californian. Perhaps I am, ma'am; I've lost so much sleep I could cry, anyway. Do I *look* like your baby?

Mrs. Roberts. No, no, you don't. [*In distress that overcomes her mortification.*] Oh, where *is* my baby? I left him all uncovered, and he'll take his death of cold, even if he dosen't roll out. Oh, Edward, Edward, help me to find baby!

Mr. Roberts (*bustling aimlessly about*). Yes, yes; certainly, my dear. But don't be alarmed; we shall find him.

The Californian (*getting out in his stocking feet*). We shall find him, ma'am, if we have to search every berth in this car. Don't you take on. That baby's going to be found if he's aboard the train now, you bet! [*He looks about and then tears open the curtains of a berth at random.*] That your baby, ma'am?

Mrs. Roberts (*flying upon the infant thus exposed*). Oh, *baby*, baby, baby! I thought I had lost you. Um! um! um! [*She clasps him in her arms, and covers his face and neck with kisses.*]

The Californian (*as he gets back into his berth*, sotto voce). I wish I *had* been her baby.

Mrs. Roberts (*returning with her husband to his seat, and bringing the baby with her*). There! Did you ever *see* such a sleeper, Edward? [*In her ecstasy she abandons all control of her voice, and joyfully exclaims.*] He has slept all through this excitement, without a wink.

A solemn Voice from one of the berths. I envy him.
[*A laugh follows, in which all the passengers join.*]

Mrs. Roberts (*in a hoarse whisper, breaking a little with laughter*). Oh, my goodness! there I went again. But how funny! I assure you, Edward, that if their remarks had not been about me, I could have really quite enjoyed some of them. I wish there had been somebody here to take them down. And I hope I shall see some of the speakers in the morning before— Edward. I've got an idea!

Mr. Roberts (*endeavoring to teach his wife by example to lower her voice, which has risen again*). What—what is it, my dear?

Mrs. Roberts. Why, don't you see? How perfectly ridiculous

it was of me not to think of it before! though I did think of it once, and hadn't the courage to insist upon it. But of course it is; and it accounts for his being so polite and kind to me through all, and it's the only thing that can. Yes, yes, it *must* be.

MR. ROBERTS (*mystified*). What?

MRS. ROBERTS. Willis.

MR. ROBERTS. Who?

MRS. ROBERTS. This Californian.

MR. ROBERTS. Oh!

MRS. ROBERTS. No *stranger* could have been so patient and—and—attentive; and I know that he recognized me from the first, and he's just kept it up for a joke, so as to surprise us and have a good laugh at us when we get to Boston. Of *course* it's Willis.

MR. ROBERTS (*doubtfully*). Do you think so, my dear?

MRS. ROBERTS. I *know* it. Didn't you notice how he looked at your card? And I want you to go at once and speak to him, and turn the tables on him.

MR. ROBERTS. I—I'd rather *not*, my dear.

MRS. ROBERTS. Why, Edward, what can you mean?

MR. ROBERTS. He's very violent. Suppose it *shouldn't* be Willis?

MRS. ROBERTS. Nonsense! It *is* Willis. Come, let's both go and just tax him with it. He can't deny it, after all he's done for me. [*She pulls her reluctant husband toward* THE CALIFORNIAN'S *berth, and they each draw a curtain.*] Willis!

THE CALIFORNIAN (*with plaintive endurance*). Well, ma'am?

MRS. ROBERTS (*triumphantly*). There! I knew it was you all along. How could you play such a joke on me?

THE CALIFORNIAN. I didn't know there'd been any joke; but I suppose there must have been, if you say so. Who am I now, ma'am—your husband, or your baby, or your husband's wife, or—

MRS. ROBERTS. How funny you are! You *know* you're Willis Campbell, my only brother. Now *don't* try to keep it up any longer, Willis.

[*Voices from various berths.* "Give us a rest, Willis!" "Joke's too thin, Willis!" "You're played out, Willis!" "Own up, old fellow—own up!"]

THE CALIFORNIAN (*issuing from his berth, and walking up and down the aisle, as before, till quiet is restored*). I haven't got any sister, and my name ain't Willis, and it ain't Campbell. I'm very sorry, because I'd like to oblige you any way I could.

MRS. ROBERTS (*in deep mortification*). It's I who ought to apologize, and I do so most humbly. I don't know what to say; but when I got to thinking about it, and how kind you had been to me, and how sweet you had been under all my—interruptions, I felt perfectly sure that you couldn't be a mere stranger, and then the idea struck me that you must be my brother in disguise; and I was so certain of it that I couldn't help just letting you know that we'd found you out, and—

MR. ROBERTS (*offering a belated and feeble moral support*). Yes.

MRS. ROBERTS (*promptly turning upon him*). And *you* ought to have kept me from making such a simpleton of myself, Edward.

THE CALIFORNIAN (*soothingly*). Well, ma'am, that ain't always so easy. A man may mean well, and yet not be able to carry out his intentions. But it's all right. And I reckon we'd better try to quiet down again, and get what rest we can.

MRS. ROBERTS. Why, yes, certainly, and I will try—oh, I will *try* not to disturb you again. And if there's anything we can do in reparation after we reach Boston, we shall be *so* glad to do it!

[*They bow themselves away, and return to their seat, while* THE CALIFORNIAN *re-enters his berth.*]

III

The train stops at Framingham, and THE PORTER *comes in with a passenger, whom he shows to the seat opposite* MR. AND MRS. ROBERTS.

THE PORTER. You can sit here, sah. We'll be in about an hour from now. Hang up your bag, sah?

THE PASSENGER. No, leave it on the seat here.

[THE PORTER *goes out, and the* ROBERTSES *maintain a dejected* silence. *The bottom of the bag, thrown carelessly on the seat, is toward the Robertses, who regard it listlessly.*]

MRS. ROBERTS (*suddenly clutching her husband's arm, and hissing in his ear*). See! [*She points to the white lettering on the bag, where the name* "Willis Campbell, San Francisco," *is distinctly legible.*] But it can't be; it must be some other Campbell. I can't risk it.

MR. ROBERTS. But there's the name. It would be very strange if there were two people from San Francisco of exactly the same name. *I* will speak.

MRS. ROBERTS (*as wildly as one can in whisper*). No, no, I can't let you. We've made ourselves the laughing-stock of the whole car already with our mistakes, and I can't go on. I would rather perish than ask him. You don't suppose it *could* be? No, it couldn't. There may be twenty Willis Campbells in San Francisco, and there probably are. Do you think he looks like me? He has a straight nose; but you can't tell anything about the lower part of his face, the beard covers it so; and I can't make out the color of his eyes by this light. But of course it's all nonsense. Still if it *should* be! It would be very stupid of us to ride all the way from Framingham to Boston with that name staring one in the eyes. I *wish* he would turn it away. If it really turned out to *be* Willis, he would think we were awfully stiff and cold. But I can't help it; I *can't* go attacking every stranger I see, and accusing him of being my brother. No, no, I can't, and I *won't*, and that's all about it. [*She leans forward and addresses the stranger with sudden sweetness.*] Excuse me, sir, but I *am* very much interested by the name on your bag. Not that I think you are even acquainted with him, and there are probably a great many of them there; but your coming from the same city and all *does* seem a little queer, and I hope you won't think me intrusive in speaking to you, because if you *should* happen, by the thousandth of a chance, to be the right one, I should be *so* happy!

CAMPBELL. The right what, madam?

MRS. ROBERTS. The right Willis Campbell.

CAMPBELL. I hope I'm not the wrong one; though after a week's pull on the railroad it's pretty hard for a man to tell which Willis Campbell he is. May I ask if your Willis Campbell had friends in Boston?

MRS. ROBERTS (*eagerly*). He had a sister and a brother-in-law and a nephew.

CAMPBELL. Name of Roberts?

MRS. ROBERTS. Every one.

CAMPBELL. Then you're—

MRS. ROBERTS (*ecstatically*). Agnes!

CAMPBELL. And he's—

MRS. ROBERTS. Mr. Roberts!

CAMPBELL. And the baby's—

MRS. ROBERTS. Asleep!

CAMPBELL. Then I *am* the right one.

MRS. ROBERTS. Oh, Willis! Willis! Willis! To think of our meeting in this way! [*She kisses and embraces him, while* MR. ROBERTS *shakes one of his hands which he finds disengaged.*] *How* in the world did it happen?

CAMPBELL. Ah, I found myself a little ahead of time, and I stopped off with an old friend of mine at Framingham; I didn't want to disappoint you when you came to meet this train, or get you up last night at midnight.

MRS. ROBERTS. And I was in Albany, and I've been moving heaven and earth to get home before you arrived; and Edward came aboard at Worcester to surprise me, and— Oh, you've never seen the baby! I'll run right and get him this instant, just as he is, and bring him. Edward, you be explaining to Willis— Oh, my goodness! [*Looking wildly about.*] I don't remember the berth, and I shall be sure to wake up that poor California gentleman again. *What* shall I do?

CAMPBELL. What California gentleman?

MRS. ROBERTS. Oh, somebody we've been stirring up the whole blessed night. First I took him for my baby, and then Edward took him for me, and then I took him for my baby again, and then we both took him for you.

CAMPBELL. Did he look like any of us?

MRS. ROBERTS. Like *us?* He's eight feet tall, if he's an inch, in his stockings—and he's always in them—and he has a long black beard and mustaches, and he's very lanky, and stoops over a good deal; but he's just as lovely as he can be and live, and he's been as kind and patient as twenty Jobs.

CAMPBELL. Speaks in a sort of soft, slow grind?

MRS. ROBERTS. Yes.

CAMPBELL. Gentle and deferential to ladies?

MRS. ROBERTS. As pie.

CAMPBELL. It's Tom Goodall. I'll have him out of there in half a second. I want you to take him home with you, Agnes. He's the best fellow in the world. *Which* is his berth?

MRS. ROBERTS. Don't ask me, Willis. But if you'd go for baby, you'll be sure to find *him.*

MR. ROBERTS (*timidly indicating a berth*). I think that's the one.

CAMPBELL (*plunging at it, and pulling the curtains open*). You old Tom Goodall!

THE CALIFORNIAN (*appearing*). I ain't any Tom Goodall. My name's Abram Sawyer.

CAMPBELL (*falling back*). Well, sir, you're right. I'm awfully sorry to disturb you; but, from my sister's description here, I felt certain you must be my old friend Tom Goodall.

THE CALIFORNIAN. I ain't surprised at it. I'm only surprised I *ain't* Tom Goodall. I've been a baby twice, and I've been a man's wife once, and once I've been a long-lost brother.

CAMPBELL (*laughing*). Oh, they've found *him.* *I'm* the long-lost brother.

THE CALIFORNIAN (*sleepily*). Has she found the other one?

CAMPBELL. Yes; we're all together here. [*The Californian makes a movement to get into bed again.*] Oh, don't! You'd better make a night of it now. It's almost morning anyway. We want you to go home with us, and Mrs. Roberts will give you a bed at her house, and let you sleep a week.

THE CALIFORNIAN. Well, I reckon you're right, stranger. I seem to be in the hands of Providence to-night anyhow. [*He pulls on his boots and coat, and takes his seat beside* CAMPBELL.] I reckon there ain't any use in fighting against Providence.

Mrs. Roberts (*briskly, as if she had often tried it and failed*). Oh, not the least in the world. I'm sure it was all intended; and if you had turned out to be Willis at last, I should be *certain* of it. What surprises me is that you shouldn't turn out to be anybody, after all.

The Californian. Yes, it's kind of curious. But I couldn't help it. I did my best.

Mrs. Roberts. Oh, don't speak of it. *We* are the ones who ought to apologize. But if you only had been somebody, it would have been such a good joke! We could always have had such a laugh over it, don't you see?

The Californian. Yes, ma'am, it would have been funny. But I hope you've enjoyed it as it is.

Mrs. Roberts. Oh, very much, thanks to you. Only I can't seem to get reconciled to your not being anybody, after all. You *must* at least be some one we've heard about, don't you think? It's so strange that you and Willis never even met. Don't you think you have some acquaintances in common?

Campbell. Look here, Agnes, do you always shout at the top of your voice in this way when you converse in a sleeping-car?

Mrs. Roberts. Was I talking loud again? Well, you can't help it if you want to make people hear you.

Campbell. But there must be a lot of them who don't want to hear you. I wonder that the passengers who are not blood-relations don't throw things at you—boots and hand-bags and language.

Mrs. Roberts. Why, that's what they've *been* doing—language, at least—and I'm only surprised they're not doing it now.

The Californian (*rising*). They'd better not, ma'am.

[*He patrols the car from end to end, and quells some rising murmurs, halting at the rebellious berths as he passes.*]

Mrs. Roberts (*enraptured by his companionship*). Oh, he *must* be some connection. [*She glances through the window.*] I do believe that was Newton, or Newtonville, or West Newton, or Newton Centre. I must run and wake up baby, and get him dressed. I shan't want to wait an instant after we get in.

Why, we're slowing up! Why, I do believe we're there! Edward, we're there! Only fancy being there already!

MR. ROBERTS. Yes, my dear. Only we're not quite there yet. Hadn't we better call your Aunt Mary?

MRS. ROBERTS. I'd forgotten her.

CAMPBELL. Is Aunt Mary with you?

MRS. ROBERTS. To be sure she is. Didn't I tell you? She came on expressly to meet you.

CAMPBELL (*starting up impetuously*). Which berth is she in?

MRS. ROBERTS. Right over baby.

CAMPBELL. And which berth is baby in?

MRS. ROBERTS (*distractedly*). Why, that's just what I can't *tell*. It was bad enough when they were all filled up, but now since the people have begun to come out of them, and some of them are made into seats I *can't* tell.

THE CALIFORNIAN. I'll look for you, ma'am. I should like to wake up all the wrong passengers on this car. I'd take a pleasure in it. If you could make sure of any berth that *ain't* the one, I'll begin on that.

MRS. ROBERTS. I can't even be sure of the wrong one. No, no; you mustn't—

[THE CALIFORNIAN *moves away, and pauses in front of one of the berths, looking back inquiringly at* MRS. ROBERTS.] Oh, don't ask *me!* *I* can't tell. (*To* CAMPBELL.) *Isn't* he amusing? So like all those Californians that one reads of—so chivalrous and *so* humorous!

AUNT MARY (*thrusting her head from the curtains of the berth before which* THE CALIFORNIAN *is standing*). Go along with you. What do you want?

THE CALIFORNIAN. Aunt Mary.

AUNT MARY. Go away. Aunt Mary, indeed!

MRS. ROBERTS (*running toward her, followed by* CAMPBELL *and* MR. ROBERTS). Why, Aunt Mary, it *is* you! And here's Willis, and here's Edward.

AUNT MARY. Nonsense! How did they get aboard?

MRS. ROBERTS. Edward came on at Worcester and Willis at Framingham, to surprise me.

AUNT MARY. And a very silly performance. Let them wait till I'm dressed, and then I'll talk to them. Send for the porter. [*She withdraws her head behind the curtain, and then thrusts it out again.*] And who, pray, may *this* be?

[*She indicates* THE CALIFORNIAN.]

MRS. ROBERTS. Oh, a friend of ours from California, who's been so kind to us all night, and who's going home with us.

AUNT MARY. Another ridiculous surprise, I suppose. But he shall not surprise *me*. Young man, isn't your name Sawyer?

THE CALIFORNIAN. Yes, ma'am.

AUNT MARY. Abram?

THE CALIFORNIAN. Abram Sawyer. You're right there, ma'am.

MRS. ROBERTS. Oh! oh! I knew it! I knew that he must be somebody belonging to us. Oh, thank you, aunty, for think-ing—

AUNT MARY. Don't be absurd, Agnes. Then you're my—

A VOICE *from one of the berths.* Lost step-son. Found! found at last!

[THE CALIFORNIAN *looks vainly round in an endeavor to identify the speaker, and then turns again to* AUNT MARY.]

AUNT MARY. Weren't your parents from Bath?

THE CALIFORNIAN (*eagerly*). Both of 'em, ma'am—both of 'em.

THE VOICE. O my prophetic soul, my uncle!

AUNT MARY. Then you're my old friend Kate Harris's daughter?

THE CALIFORNIAN. I might be her *son*, ma'am; but *my* mother's name was Susan Wakeman.

AUNT MARY (*in sharp disgust*). Call the porter, please.

[*She withdraws her head and pulls her curtains together; the rest look blankly at one another.*]

CAMPBELL. Another failure, and just when we thought we were sure of you. I don't know what we shall do about you, Mr. Sawyer.

THE VOICE. Adopt him.

CAMPBELL. That's a good idea. We will adopt you. You shall be our adoptive—

THE VOICE. Baby boy.

ANOTHER VOICE. Wife.

A Third Voice. Brother.

A Fourth Voice. Early friend.

A Fifth Voice. Kate Harris's daughter.

Campbell (*laying his hand on* The Californian's *shoulder, and breaking into a laugh*). Don't mind them. They don't mean anything. It's just their way. You come home with my sister, and spend Christmas, and let us devote the rest of our lives to making your declining years happy.

Voices. "Good for you, Willis!" "We'll all come!" "No ceremony!" "Small and early!"

Campbell (*looking round*). We appear to have fallen in with a party of dry-goods drummers. It makes a gentleman feel like an intruder. [*The train stops; he looks out of the window.*] We've arrived. Come, Agnes; come, Roberts; come, Mr. Sawyer—let's be going.

[*They gather up their several wraps and bags, and move with great dignity toward the door.*]

Aunt Mary (*putting out her head*). Agnes! If you must forget your aunt, at least remember your child.

Mrs. Roberts (*running back in an agony of remorse*). Oh, *baby*, did I forget you?

Campbell. Oh, aunty, did she forget you? [*He runs back, and extends his arms to his aunt.*] Let me help you down, Aunt Mary.

Aunt Mary. Nonsense, Willis. Send the porter.

Campbell (*turning round and confronting* The Porter). He was here upon instinct. Shall he fetch a step-ladder?

Aunt Mary. *He* will know what to do. Go away, Willis; go away with that child, Agnes. If I should happen to fall on you—[*They retreat; the curtain drops, and her voice is heard behind it addressing* The Porter.] Give me your hand; now your back; now your knee. So! And very well done. Thanks.

NOVELS

INDIAN SUMMER

Chapter XIV

[Theodore Colville, having sold his newspaper in Prairie Des Vaches, Indiana, returns to Florence to renew the study of architecture, from which he had been diverted twenty years earlier by an unhappy love affair. His friendship with Mrs. Bowen, the widowed friend of the girl who had jilted him, whom he by chance meets again in Florence, prospers more than his studies. But before Colville understands himself sufficiently to realize that it was Evelina Ridgeley (now Mrs. Bowen) and not her friend whom he loved in the first place, he has to repeat his error and propose to Imogene Graham, a young protégée of Mrs. Bowen, who has hopelessly romanticised his former affair, and now wishes "to make it up" to poor Colville.

In the following chapter we encounter our middle-aged hero walking meditatively through the Boboli Garden in Florence, considering his relations with Imogene, with whom Mrs. Bowen has accused him of flirting. Imogene herself suddenly appears around the bend of a path in the company of Effie, Mrs. Bowen's little daughter, and under the chaperonage of Mrs. Amsden, a talkative member of the English-speaking group in Florence. See Introduction, pp. lxxxvii.]

When he entered the beautiful old garden, its benison of peace fell upon his tumult, and he began to breathe a freer air, reverting to his purpose to be gone in the morning and resting in it, as he strolled up the broad curve of its alley from the gate. He had not been there since he walked there with one now more like a ghost to him than any of the dead who had since died. It was there that she had refused him; he recalled with a grim smile the awkwardness of getting back with her to the gate from the point, far within the garden, where he had spoken. Except that this had happened in the fall, and now it was early spring, there seemed no change since then; the long years that had elapsed were like a winter between.

He met people in groups and singly loitering through the paths, and chiefly speaking English; but no one spoke to him,

and no one invaded the solitude in which he walked. But the
garden itself seemed to know him, and to give him a tacit recognition; the great, foolish grotto before the gate, with its statues
by Bandinelli, and the fantastic effects of drapery and flesh in
party-coloured statues lifted high on either side of the avenue;
the vast shoulder of wall, covered thick with ivy and myrtle,
which he passed on his way to the amphitheatre behind the
palace; the alternate figures and urns on their pedestals in the
hemicycle, as if the urns were placed there to receive the ashes
of the figures when they became extinct; the white statues or
the colossal busts set at the ends of the long alleys against black
curtains of foliage; the big fountain, with its group in the centre
of the little lake, and the meadow, quiet and sad, that stretched
away on one side from this; the keen light under the levels of the
dense pines and ilexes; the paths striking straight on either
hand from the avenue through which he sauntered, and the walk
that coiled itself through the depths of the plantations; all knew
him, and from them and from the winter neglect which was upon
the place distilled a subtle influence, a charm, an appeal belonging to that combination of artifice and nature which is perfect
only in an Italian garden under an Italian sky. He was right
in the name which he mockingly gave the effect before he felt it;
it was a debauch, delicate, refined, of unserious pensiveness, a
smiling melancholy, in which he walked emancipated from his
harassing hopes, and keeping only his shadowy regrets.

Colville did not care to scale the easy height from which you
have the magnificent view, conscious of many photographs, of
Florence. He wandered about the skirts of that silent meadow,
and seeing himself unseen, he invaded its borders far enough to
pluck one of those large scarlet anemones, such as he had given
his gentle enemy. It was tilting there in the breeze above the
unkempt grass, and the grass was beginning to feel the spring,
and to stir and stretch itself after its winter sleep; it was sprinkled
with violets, but these he did not molest. He came back to a
stained and mossy stone bench on the avenue, fronting a pair of
rustic youths carved in stone, who had not yet finished some
game in which he remembered seeing them engaged when he

was there before. He had not walked fast, but he had walked far, and was warm enough to like the whiffs of soft wind on his uncovered head. The spring was coming; that was its breath, which you know unmistakably in Italy after all the kisses that winter gives. Some birds were singing in the trees; down an alley into which he could look, between the high walls of green, he could see two people in flirtation: he waited patiently till the young man should put his arm round the girl's waist, for the fleeting embrace from which she pushed it and fled further down the path.

"Yes, it's spring," thought Colville; and then, with the selfishness of the troubled soul, he wished that it might be winter still and indefinitely. It occurred to him now that he should not go back to Des Vaches, for he did not know what he should do there. He would go to New York; though he did not know what he should do in New York, either.

He became tired of looking at the people who passed, and of speculating about them through the second consciousness which enveloped the sad substance of his misgivings like an atmosphere; and he let his eyelids fall, as he leaned his head back against the tree behind his bench. Then their voices pursued him through the twilight that he had made himself, and forced him to the same weary conjecture as if he had seen their faces. He heard gay laughter, and laughter that affected gaiety; the tones of young men in earnest disquisition reached him through the veil, and the talk, falling to whisper, of girls, with the names of men in it; sums of money, a hundred francs, forty thousand francs, came in high tones; a husband and wife went by quarrelling in the false security of English, and snapping at each other as confidingly as if in the sanctuary of home. The man bade the woman not be a fool, and she asked him how she was to endure his company if she was not a fool.

Colville opened his eyes to look after them, when a voice that he knew called out, "Why, it *is* Mr. Colville!"

It was Mrs. Amsden, and pausing with her, as if they had passed in doubt, and arrested themselves when they had got a little way by, were Effie Bowen and Imogene Graham. The old lady had the child by the hand, and the girl stood a few paces apart from them. She was one of those beauties who have the property of looking very plain at times, and Colville, who had seen her in more than one transformation, now beheld her somehow clumsy of feature, and with the youth gone from her aspect. She seemed a woman of thirty, and she wore an unbecoming walking dress of a fashion that contributed to this effect of age. Colville was aware afterward of having wished that she was really as old and plain as she looked.

He had to come forward, and put on the conventional delight of a gentleman meeting lady friends.

"It's remarkable how your having your eyes shut estranged you," said Mrs. Amsden. "Now, if you had let me see you oftener in church, where people close their eyes a good deal for one purpose or another, I should have known you at once."

"I hope you haven't lost a great deal of time, as it is, Mrs. Amsden," said Colville. "Of course I should have had my eyes open if I had known you were going by."

"Oh, don't apologise!" cried the old thing, with ready enjoyment of his tone.

"I don't apologise for not being recognisable; I apologise for being visible," said Colville, with some shapeless impression that he ought to excuse his continued presence in Florence to Imogene, but keeping his eyes upon Mrs. Amsden, to whom what he said could not be intelligible. "I ought to be in Turin to-day."

"In Turin! Are you going away from Florence?"

"I'm going home."

"Why, did *you* know that?" asked the old lady of Imogene, who slightly nodded, and then of Effie, who also assented. "Really, the silence of the Bowen family in regard to the affairs of others is extraordinary. There never was a family more eminently qualified to live in Florence. I dare say that if I saw a little more of them, I might hope to reach the years of discretion myself some day. *Why* are you going away? (You see I haven't reached them yet!) Are you tired of Florence already?"

"No," said Colville passively; "Florence is tired of me."

"You're quite sure?"

"Yes; there's no mistaking one of her sex on such a point."

Mrs. Amsden laughed. "Ah, a great many people mistake us, both ways. And you're really going back to America. What in the world for?"

"I haven't the least idea."

"Is America fonder of you than Florence?"

"She's never told her love. I suspect it's merely that she's more used to me."

They were walking, without any volition of his, down the slope of the broad avenue to the fountain, where he had already been.

"Is your mother well?" he asked of the little girl. It seemed to him that he had better not speak to Imogene, who still kept that little distance from the rest, and get away as soon as he decently could.

"She has a headache," said Effie.

"Oh, I'm sorry," returned Colville.

"Yes, she deputed me to take her young people out for an airing," said Mrs. Amsden; "and Miss Graham decided us for the Boboli, where she hadn't been yet. I've done what I could to make the place attractive. But what is an old woman to do for a girl in a garden? We ought to have brought some other young people—some of the Inglehart boys. But we're respectable, we Americans abroad; we're decorous, above all things; and I don't know about meeting *you* here, Mr. Colville. It has a very bad appearance. Are you sure that you didn't know I was to go by here at exactly half-past four?"

"I was living from breath to breath in the expectation of seeing you. You must have noticed how eagerly I was looking out for you."

"Yes, and with a single red anemone in your hand, so that I should know you without being obliged to put on my spectacles."

"You divine everything, Mrs. Amsden," he said, giving her the flower.

"I shall make my brags to Mrs. Bowen when I see her," said the old lady. "How far into the country did you walk for this?"

"As far as the meadow yonder."

They had got down to the sheet of water from which the sea-horses of the fountain sprang, and the old lady sank upon a bench near it. Colville held out his hand toward Effie. "I saw a lot of violets over there in the grass."

"Did you?" She put her hand eagerly into his, and they strolled off together. After a first motion to accompany them, Imogene sat down beside Mrs. Amsden, answering quietly the talk of the old lady, and seeming in nowise concerned about the expedition for violets. Except for a dull first glance, she did not look that way. Colville stood in the border of the grass, and the child ran quickly hither and thither in it, stooping from time to time upon the flowers. Then she came out to where he stood, and showed her bunch of violets, looking up into the face which he bent upon her, while he trifled with his cane. He had a very fatherly air with her.

"I think I'll go and see what they've found," said Imogene irrelevantly, to a remark of Mrs. Amsden's about the expensiveness of Madame Bossi's bonnets.

"Well," said the old lady. Imogene started, and the little girl ran to meet her. She detained Effie with her admiration of the violets till Colville lounged reluctantly up. "Go and show them to Mrs. Amsden," she said, giving back the violets, which she had been smelling. The child ran on. "Mr. Colville, I want to speak with you."

"Yes," said Colville helplessly.

"Why are you going away?"

"Why? Oh, I've accomplished the objects—or no-objects—I came for," he said, with dreary triviality, "and I must hurry away to other fields of activity." He kept his eyes on her face, which he saw full of a passionate intensity, working to some sort of overflow.

"That is not true, and you needn't say it to spare me. You are going away because Mrs. Bowen said something to you about me."

"Not quite that," returned Colville gently.

"No; it was something that she said to me about you. But it's the same thing. It makes no difference. I ask you not to go for that."

"Do you know what you are saying, Imogene?"

"Yes."

Colville waited a long moment. "Then, I thank you, you dear girl, and I am going to-morrow, all the same. But I shan't forget this; whatever my life is to be, this will make it less unworthy and less unhappy. If it could buy anything to give you joy, to add some little grace to the good that must come to you, I would give it. Some day you'll meet the young fellow whom you're to make immortal, and you must tell him of an old fellow who knew you afar off, and understood how to worship you for an angel of pity and unselfishness. Ah, I hope he'll understand, too! Good-bye." If he was to fly, that was the sole instant. He took her hand, and said again, "Good-bye." And then he suddenly cried, "Imogene, do you wish me to stay?"

"Yes!" said the girl, pouring all the intensity of her face into that whisper.

"Even if there had been nothing said to make me go away—should you still wish me to stay?"

"Yes."

He looked her in the starry, lucid eyes, where a divine fervour deepened. He sighed in nerveless perplexity; it was she who had the courage.

"It's a mistake! You mustn't! I am too old for you! It would be a wrong and a cruelty! Yes, you must let me go, and forget me. I have been to blame. If Mrs. Bowen has blamed me, she was right—I deserved it; I deserved all she could say against me."

"She never said anything against you. Do you think I would have let her? No; it was I that said it, and I blamed you. It was because I thought that you were—you were—"

"Trifling with you? How could you think that?"

"Yes, I know now how it was, and it makes you seem all the grander to me. Did you think I cared for your being older than I was? I never cared for it—I never hardly thought of it after the very first. I tried to make you understand that, and how it hurt me to have you speak of it. Don't you think that I could see how good you were? Do you suppose that all I want is to be happy? I don't care for that—I despise it, and I always hate myself for seeking my own pleasure, if I find myself doing it. I have seen enough of life to know what *that* comes to! And what hurt me worst of all was that you seemed to believe that I cared for nothing but amusing myself, when I wished to be something better, higher! It's nothing whether you are of my age or not, if—if—you care for me."

"Imogene!"

"All that I ask is to be with you, and try to make you forget what's been sad in your life, and try to be of use to you in whatever you are doing, and I shall be prouder and gladder of that than anything that people *call* happiness."

Colville stood holding her hand, while she uttered these ideas and incoherent repetitions of them, with a deep sense of powerlessness. "If I believed that I could keep you from regretting this—"

"What should I regret? I won't let you depreciate yourself—make yourself out not good enough for the best. Oh, I know how it happened! But now you shall never think of it again. No; I will not let you. That is the only way you could make me regret anything."

"I am going to stay," said Colville. "But on my own terms. I will be bound to you, but you shall not be bound to me."

"You doubt me! I would rather have you go! No; stay. And let me prove to you how wrong you are. I mustn't ask more than that. Only give me the chance to show you how different I am from what you think—how different you are, too."

"Yes. But you must be free."

"Well."

"What are they doing so long there?" asked Mrs. Amsden of Effie, putting her glasses to her eyes. "I can't see."

"They are just holding hands," said the child, with an easy satisfaction in the explanation, which perhaps the old lady did not share. "He always holds my hand when he is with me."

"Does he, indeed?" exclaimed Mrs. Amsden, with a cackle. She added, "That's very polite of him, isn't it? You must be a great favourite with Mr. Colville. You will miss him when he's gone."

"Yes. He's very nice."

Colville and Imogene returned, coming slowly across the loose, neglected grass toward the old woman's seat. She rose as they came up.

"You don't seem to have succeeded so well in getting flowers for Miss Graham as for the other ladies. But perhaps you didn't find her favourite over there. What is your favourite flower, Miss Graham? Don't say you have none! I didn't know that I preferred scarlet anemones. Were there no forget-me-nots over there in the grass?"

"There was no occasion for them," answered Colville.

"You always did make such pretty speeches!" said the old lady. "And they have such an orphic character, too; you can interpret them in so many different ways. Should you mind saying just what you meant by that one?"

"Yes, very much," replied Colville.

The old lady laughed with cheerful resignation. She would as lief report that reply of his as another. Even more than a man whom she could entangle in his speech she liked a man who could slip through the toils with unfailing ease. Her talk with such a man was the last consolation which remained to her from a life of harmless coquetries.

"I will refer it to Mrs. Bowen," she said. "She is a very wise woman, and she used to know you a great while ago."

"If you like, I will do it for you, Mrs. Amsden. I'm going to see her."

"To renew your adieux? Well, why not? Parting is such sweet sorrow! And if I were a young man I would go to say good-bye to Mrs. Bowen as often as she would let me. Now tell me honestly, Mr. Colville, did you ever see such an exquisite, perfect *creature?*"

"Oh, that's asking a good deal."

"What?"

"To tell you a thing honestly. How did you come here, Mrs. Amsden?"

"In Mrs. Bowen's carriage. I sent it round from the Pitti entrance to the Porta Romana. It's waiting there now, I suppose."

"I thought you had been corrupted, somehow. Your zeal is

carriage-bought. It *is* a delightful vehicle. Do you think you could give me a lift home in it?"

"Yes, indeed. I've always a seat for you in my carriage. To Hotel d'Atene?"

"No, to Palazzo Pinti."

"This is deliciously mysterious," said Mrs. Amsden, drawing her shawl up about her shoulders, which, if no longer rounded, had still a charming droop. One realises in looking at such old ladies that there are women who could manage their own skeletons winningly. She put up her glasses, which were an old-fashioned sort, held to the nose by a handle, and perused the different persons of the group. "Mr. Colville concealing an inward trepidation under a bold front; Miss Graham agitated but firm; the child as much puzzled as the old woman. I feel that we are a very interesting group—almost dramatic."

"Oh, call us a passage from a modern novel," suggested Colville, "if you're in the romantic mood. One of Mr. James's."

"Don't you think we ought to be rather more of the great world for that? I hardly feel up to Mr. James. I should have said Howells. Only nothing happens in that case!"

"Oh, very well; that's the most comfortable way. If it's only Howells, there's no reason why I shouldn't go with Miss Graham to show her the view of Florence from the cypress grove up yonder."

"No; he's very particular when he's on Italian ground," said Mrs. Amsden, rising. "You must come another time with Miss Graham, and bring Mrs. Bowen. It's quite time we were going home."

The light under the limbs of the trees had begun to grow more liquid. The currents of warm breeze streaming through the cooler body of the air had ceased to ruffle the lakelet round the fountain, and the naiads rode their sea-horses through a perfect calm. A damp, pierced with the fresh odour of the water and of the springing grass, descended upon them. The saunterers through the different paths and alleys were issuing upon the main avenues, and tending in gathering force toward the gate.

They found Mrs. Bowen's carriage there, and drove first to her house, beyond which Mrs. Amsden lived in a direct line. On the way Colville kept up with her the bantering talk that they always carried on together, and found in it a respite from the formless future pressing close upon him. He sat with Effie on the front seat, and he would not look at Imogene's face, which, nevertheless, was present to some inner vision. When the porter opened the iron gate below and rang Mrs. Bowen's bell, and Effie sprang up the stairs before them to give her mother the news of Mr. Colville's coming, the girl stole her hand into his.

"Shall you—tell her?"

"Of course. She must know without an instant's delay."

"Yes, yes; that is right. Oh!— Shall I go with you?"

"Yes; come!"

Chapter xx

[*Colville attempts to play the young lover and to accompany Imogene to the balls and carnivals of Florence. Though he is fond of Imogene, association with "the Inglehardt boys" and other contemporaries of his fiancée becomes unbearable to Colville. Quiet drives in the country with Imogene, Mrs. Bowen, and her little daughter, evenings at the piano in their charming apartment, are too undramatic for Imogene, however, who wishes to take heroic measures to prove her love for Colville. A former lover, Mr. Morton, renews his suit, not knowing of Imogene's understanding with Colville, which cannot be made official until word comes from Mrs. Graham in the United States. Meanwhile, Colville, talking over the affair with Mrs. Bowen on the sofa while Miss Graham and Mr. Morton play together at the piano, unconsciously shows that he is more interested in Mrs. Bowen than in Imogene. In the following chapter we meet our four lovers after they have had time to reconsider their altered relationships.*]

In the morning Mrs. Bowen received a note from her banker covering a despatch by cable from America. It was from Imogene's mother; it acknowledged the letters they had written, and announced that she sailed that day for Liverpool. It was dated at New York, and it was to be inferred that after perhaps writing in answer to their letter, she had suddenly made up her mind to come out.

"Yes, that is it," said Imogene, to whom Mrs. Bowen hastened with the despatch. "Why should she have telegraphed to *you?*"

she asked coldly, but with a latent fire of resentment in her tone.

"You must ask her when she comes," returned Mrs. Bowen, with all her gentleness. "It won't be long now."

They looked as if they had neither of them slept; but the girl's vigil seemed to have made her wild and fierce, like some bird that has beat itself all night against its cage, and still from time to time feebly strikes the bars with its wings. Mrs. Bowen was simply worn to apathy.

"What shall you do about this?" she asked.

"Do about it? Oh, I will think. I will try not to trouble you."

"Imogene!"

"I shall have to tell Mr. Colville. But I don't know that I shall tell him at once. Give me the despatch, please." She possessed herself of it greedily, offensively. "I shall ask you not to speak of it."

"I will do whatever you wish."

"Thank you."

Mrs. Bowen left the room, but she turned immediately to re-open the door she had closed behind her.

"We were to have gone to Fiesole to-morrow," she said inquiringly.

"We can still go if the day is fine," returned the girl. "Nothing is changed. I wish very much to go. Couldn't we go to-day?" she added, with eager defiance.

"It's too late to-day," said Mrs. Bowen quietly. "I will write to remind the gentlemen."

"Thank you. I wish we could have gone to-day."

"You can have the carriage if you wish to drive anywhere," said Mrs. Bowen.

"I will take Effie to see Mrs. Amsden." But Imogene changed her mind, and went to call upon two Misses Guicciardi, the result of an international marriage, whom Mrs. Bowen did not like very well. Imogene drove with them to the Cascine, where they bowed to a numerous military acquaintance, and they asked her if Mrs. Bowen would let her join them in a theatre party that evening: they were New-Yorkers by birth, and it was to be a theatre party in the New York style; they were to be chap-

eroned by a young married lady; two young men cousins of
theirs, just out from America, had taken the box.

When Imogene returned home she told Mrs. Bowen that she
had accepted this invitation. Mrs. Bowen said nothing, but
when one of the young men came up to hand Imogene down to
the carriage, which was waiting with the others at the gate, she
could not have shown a greater tolerance of his second-rate
New Yorkiness if she had been a Boston dowager offering him
the scrupulous hospitalities of her city.

Imogene came in at midnight; she hummed an air of the opera
as she took off her wraps and ornaments in her room, and this
in the quiet of the hour had a terrible, almost profane effect:
it was as if some other kind of girl had whistled. She showed the
same nonchalance at breakfast, where she was prompt, and answered Mrs. Bowen's inquiries about her pleasure the night before with a liveliness that ignored the polite resolution that
prompted them.

Mr. Morton was the first to arrive, and if his discouragement
began at once, the first steps masked themselves in a reckless
welcome, which seemed to fill him with joy, and Mrs. Bowen
with silent perplexity. The girl ran on about her evening at the
opera, and about the weather, and the excursion they were going
to make; and after an apparently needless ado over the bouquet
which he brought her, together with one for Mrs. Bowen, she
put it into her belt, and made Colville notice it when he came:
he had not thought to bring flowers.

He turned from her hilarity with anxious question to Mrs.
Bowen, who did not meet his eye, and who snubbed Effie when
the child found occasion to whisper: "*I* think Imogene is acting
very strangely, for her; don't you, mamma? It seems as if going
with those Guicciardi girls just once had spoiled her."

"Don't make remarks about people, Effie," said her mother
sharply. "It isn't nice in little girls, and I don't want you to do
it. You talk too much lately."

Effie turned grieving away from this rejection, and her face
did not light up even at the whimsical sympathy in Colville's
face, who saw that she had met a check of some sort; he had to

take her on his knee and coax and kiss her before her wounded feelings were visibly healed. He put her down with a sighing wish that some one could take him up and soothe his troubled sensibilities too, and kept her hand in his while he sat waiting for the last of those last moments in which the hurrying delays of ladies preparing for an excursion seem never to end.

When they were ready to get into the carriage, the usual contest of self-sacrifice arose, which Imogene terminated by mounting to the front seat; Mr. Morton hastened to take the seat beside her, and Colville was left to sit with Effie and her mother. "You old people will be safer back there," said Imogene. It was a little joke which she addressed to the child, but a gleam from her eye as she turned to speak to the young man at her side visited Colville in desperate defiance. He wondered what she was about in that allusion to an idea which she had shrunk from so sensitively hitherto. But he found himself in a situation which he could not penetrate at any point. When he spoke with Mrs. Bowen, it was with a dark undercurrent of conjecture as to how and when she expected him to tell Mr. Morton of his relation to Imogene, or whether she still expected him to do it; when his eyes fell upon the face of the young man, he despaired as to the terms in which he should put the fact; any form in which he tacitly dramatised it remained very embarrassing, for he felt bound to say that while he held himself promised in the matter, he did not allow her to feel herself so.

A sky of American blueness and vastness, a mellow sun, and a delicate breeze did all that these things could for them, as they began the long, devious climb of the hills crowned by the ancient Etruscan city. At first they were all in the constraint of their own and one another's moods, known or imagined, and no talk began till the young clergyman turned to Imogene and asked, after a long look at the smiling landscape, "What sort of weather do you suppose they are having at Buffalo to-day?"

"At Buffalo?" she repeated, as if the place had only a dim existence in her remotest consciousness. "Oh! The ice isn't near out of the lake yet. You can't count on it before the first of May."

"And the first of May comes sooner or later, according to the season," said Colville. "I remember coming on once in the middle of the month, and the river was so full of ice between Niagara Falls and Buffalo that I had to shut the car window that I'd kept open all the way through Southern Canada. But we have very little of that local weather at home; our weather is as democratic and continental as our political constitution. Here it's March or May any time from September till June, according as there's snow on the mountains or not."

The young man smiled. "But don't you like," he asked with deference, "this slow, orderly advance of the Italian spring, where the flowers seem to come out one by one, and every blossom has its appointed time?"

"Oh yes, it's very well in its way; but I prefer the rush of the American spring; no thought of mild weather this morning; a warm, gusty rain to-morrow night; day after to-morrow a burst of blossoms and flowers and young leaves and birds. I don't know whether we were made for our climate or our climate was made for us, but its impatience and lavishness seem to answer some inner demand of our go-ahead souls. This happens to be the week of the peach blossoms here, and you see their pink everywhere to-day, and you don't see anything else in the blossom line. But imagine the American spring abandoning a whole week of her precious time to the exclusive use of peach blossoms! She wouldn't do it; she's got too many other things on hand."

Effie had stretched out over Colville's lap, and with her elbow sunk deep in his knee, was resting her chin in her hand and taking the facts of the landscape thoroughly in. "Do they have just a week?" she asked.

"Not an hour more or less," said Colville. "If they found an almond blossom hanging round anywhere after their time came, they would make an awful row; and if any lazy little peach-blow hadn't got out by the time their week was up, it would have to stay in till next year; the pear blossoms wouldn't let it come out."

"Wouldn't they?" murmured the child, in dreamy sympathy with this belated peach-blow.

"Well, that's what people say. In America it would be allowed to come out any time. It's a free country."

Mrs. Bowen offered to draw Effie back to a posture of more decorum, but Colville put his arm round the little girl. "Oh, let her stay! It doesn't incommode me, and she must be getting such a novel effect of the landscape."

The mother fell back into her former attitude of jaded passivity. He wondered whether she had changed her mind about having him speak to Mr. Morton; her quiescence might well have been indifference; one could have said, knowing the whole situation, that she had made up her mind to let things take their course, and struggle with them no longer.

He could not believe that she felt content with him; she must feel far otherwise; and he took refuge, as he had the power of doing, from the discomfort of his own thoughts in jesting with the child, and mocking her with this extravagance and that; the discomfort then became merely a dull ache that insisted upon itself at intervals, like a grumbling tooth.

The prospect was full of that mingled wildness and subordination that gives its supreme charm to the Italian landscape; and without elements of great variety, it combined them in infinite picturesqueness. There were olive orchards and vineyards, and again vineyards and olive orchards. Closer to the farm-houses and cottages there were peaches and other fruit trees and kitchen-gardens; broad ribbons of grain waved between the ranks of trees; around the white villas the spires of the cypresses pierced the blue air. Now and then they came to a villa with weather-beaten statues strutting about its parterres. A mild, pleasant heat brooded upon the fields and roofs, and the city, drooping lower and lower as they mounted, softened and blended its towers and monuments in a sombre mass shot with gleams of white.

Colville spoke to Imogene, who withdrew her eyes from it with a sigh, after long brooding upon the scene. "You can do nothing with it, I see."

"With what?"

"The landscape. It's too full of every possible interest. What a history is written all over it, public and private! If you don't take it simply like any other landscape, it becomes an oppression. It's well that tourists come to Italy so ignorant, and keep so. Otherwise they couldn't live to get home again; the past would crush them."

Imogene scrutinised him as if to extract some personal meaning from his words, and then turned her head away. The clergyman addressed him with what was like a respectful toleration of the drolleries of a gifted but eccentric man, the flavour of whose talk he was beginning to taste.

"You don't really mean that one shouldn't come to Italy as well informed as possible?"

"Well, I did," said Colville, "but I don't."

The young man pondered this, and Imogene started up with an air of rescuing them from each other—as if she would not let Mr. Morton think Colville trivial or Colville consider the clergyman stupid, but would do what she could to take their minds off the whole question. Perhaps she was not very clear as to how this was to be done; at any rate she did not speak, and Mrs. Bowen came to her support, from whatever motive of her own. It might have been from a sense of the injustice of letting Mr. Morton suffer from the complications that involved herself and the others. The affair had been going very hitchily ever since they started, with the burden of the conversation left to the two men and that helpless girl; if it were not to be altogether a failure she must interfere.

"Did you ever hear of Gratiano when you were in Venice?" she asked Mr. Morton.

"Is he one of their new water-colourists?" returned the young man. "I heard they had quite a school there now."

"No," said Mrs. Bowen, ignoring her failure as well as she could; "he was a famous talker; he loved to speak an infinite deal of nothing more than any man in Venice."

"An ancestor of mine, Mr. Morton," said Colville; "a poor, honest man, who did his best to make people forget that the ladies were silent. Thank you, Mrs. Bowen, for mentioning him. I wish he were with us to-day."

The young man laughed. "Oh, in the *Merchant of Venice!*"

"No other," said Colville.

"I confess," said Mrs. Bowen, "that I am rather stupid this morning. I suppose it's the softness of the air; it's been harsh and irritating so long. It makes me drowsy."

"Don't mind *us*," returned Colville. "We will call you at important points." They were driving into a village at which people stop sometimes to admire the works of art in its church. Here, for example, is—What place is this?" he asked of the coachman.

"San Domenico."

"I should know it again by its beggars." Of all ages and sexes they swarmed round the carriage, which the driver had instinctively slowed to oblige them, and thrust forward their hands and hats. Colville gave Effie his small change to distribute among them, at sight of which they streamed down the street from every direction. Those who had received brought forward the halt and blind, and did not scruple to propose being rewarded for this service. At the same time they did not mind his laughing in their faces; they laughed too, and went off content, or as nearly so as beggars ever are. He buttoned up his pocket as they drove on more rapidly. "I am the only person of no principle—except Effie—in the carriage, and yet I am at this moment carrying more blessings out of this village than I shall ever know what to do with. Mrs. Bowen, I know, is regarding me with severe disapproval. She thinks that I ought to have sent the beggars of San Domenico to Florence, where they would all be shut up in the Pia Casa di Ricovero, and taught some useful occupation. It's terrible in Florence. You can walk through Florence now and have no appeal made to your better nature that is not made at the appellant's risk of imprisonment. When I was there before, you had opportunities of giving at every turn."

"You can send a cheque to the Pia Casa," said Mrs. Bowen.

"Ah, but what good would that do me? When I give I want the pleasure of it; I want to see my beneficiary cringe under my bounty. But I've tried in vain to convince you that the world has gone wrong in other ways. Do you remember the one-armed man whom we used to give to on the Lung' Arno? That persevering sufferer has been repeatedly arrested for mendicancy, and obliged to pay a fine out of his hard earnings to escape being sent to your Pia Casa."

Mrs. Bowen smiled, and said, Was he living yet? in a pensive tone of reminiscence. She was even more than patient of Colville's nonsense. It seemed to him that the light under her eyelids was sometimes a grateful light. Confronting Imogene and the young man whose hopes of her he was to destroy at the first opportunity, the lurid moral atmosphere which he breathed seemed threatening to become a thing apparent to sense, and to be about to blot the landscape. He fought it back as best he could, and kept the hovering cloud from touching the earth by incessant effort. At times he looked over the side of the carriage, and drew secretly a long breath of fatigue. It began to be borne in upon him that these ladies were using him ill in leaving him the burden of their entertainment. He became angry, but his heart softened, and he forgave them again, for he conjectured that he was the cause of the cares that kept them silent. He felt certain that the affair had taken some new turn. He wondered if Mrs. Bowen had told Imogene what she had demanded of him. But he could only conjecture and wonder in the dreary undercurrent of thought that flowed evenly and darkly on with the talk he kept going. He made the most he could of the varying views of Florence which the turns and mounting levels of the road gave him. He became affectionately grateful to the young clergyman when he replied promptly and fully, and took an interest in the objects or subjects he brought up.

Neither Mrs. Bowen nor Imogene was altogether silent. The one helped on at times wearily, and the other broke at times from her abstraction. Doubtless the girl had undertaken too much in insisting upon a party of pleasure with her mind full of so many things, and doubtless Mrs. Bowen was sore with a rankling resentment at her insistence, and vexed at herself for having yielded to it. If at her time of life and with all her experience of it, she could not rise under this inner load, Imogene must have been crushed by it.

Her starts from the dreamy oppression, if that were what kept her silent, took the form of aggression, when she disagreed with Colville about things he was saying, or attacked him for this or that thing which he had said in times past. It was an unhappy and unamiable self-assertion, which he was not able to compassionate so much when she resisted or defied Mrs. Bowen, as she seemed seeking to do at every point. Perhaps another would not have felt it so; it must have been largely in his consciousness; the young clergyman seemed not to see anything in these bursts but the indulgence of a gay caprice, though his laughing at them did not alleviate the effect to Colville, who, when he turned to Mrs. Bowen for her alliance, was astonished with a prompt snub, unmistakable to himself, however imperceptible to others.

He found what diversion and comfort he could in the party of children who beset them at a point near the town, and followed the carriage, trying to sell them various light and useless trifles made of straw—fans, baskets, parasols, and the like. He bought recklessly of them and gave them to Effie, whom he assured, without the applause of the ladies, and with the grave question of the young clergyman, that the vendors were little Etruscan girls, all at least twenty-five hundred years old. "It's very hard to find any Etruscans under that age; most of the grown-up people are three thousand."

The child humoured his extravagance with the faith in fable which children are able to command, and said, "Oh, tell me about them!" while she pushed up closer to him, and began to admire her presents, holding them up before her, and dwelling fondly upon them one by one.

"Oh, there's very little to tell," answered Colville. "They're mighty close people, and always keep themselves very much *to* themselves. But wouldn't you like to see a party of Etruscans of all ages, even down to little babies only eleven or twelve hundred years old, come driving into an American town? It would make a great excitement, wouldn't it?"

"It would be splendid."

"Yes; we would give them a collation in the basement of the City Hall, and drive them out to the cemetery. The Americans and Etruscans are very much alike in that—they always show you their tombs."

"Will they in Fiesole?"

"How you always like to burrow into the past!" interrupted Imogene.

"Well, it's rather difficult burrowing into the future," returned Colville defensively. Accepting the challenge, he added: "Yes, I should really like to meet a few Etruscans in Ficsole this morning. I should feel as if I'd got amongst my contemporaries at last; they would understand me."

The girl's face flushed. "Then no one else can understand you?"

"Apparently not. I am the great American *incompris*."

"I'm sorry for you," she returned feebly; and, in fact, sarcasm was not her strong point.

When they entered the town they found the Etruscans preoccupied with other visitors, whom at various points in the quaint little piazza they surrounded in dense groups, to their own disadvantage as guides and beggars and dealers in straw goods. One of the groups reluctantly dispersed to devote itself to the new arrivals, and these then perceived that it was a party of artists, scattered about and sketching, which had absorbed the attention of the population. Colville went to the restaurant to order lunch, leaving the ladies to the care of Mr. Morton. When he came back he found the carriage surrounded by the artists, who had turned out to be the Inglehart boys. They had walked up to Fiesole the afternoon before, and they had been sketching there all the morning. With the artist's indifference to the conventional objects of interest, they were still ignorant of what ought to be seen in Fiesole by tourists, and they accepted Colville's proposition to be of his party in going the rounds of the Cathedral, the Museum, and the view from that point of the wall called the Belvedere. They found that they had been at the Belvedere before without knowing that it merited particular recognition, and some of them had made sketches from it—of bits of architecture and landscape, and of figure amongst the women with straw fans and baskets to sell, who thronged round the whole party again, and interrupted the prospect. In the church they differed amongst themselves as to the best bits for study, and Colville listened in whimsical despair to the enthusiasm of their likings and dislikings. All that was so far from him now; but in the Museum, which had only a thin interest based upon a small collection of art and archaeology, he suffered a real affliction in the presence of a young Italian couple, who were probably plighted lovers. They went before a grey-haired pair, who might have been the girl's father and mother, and they looked at none of the objects, though they regularly stopped before them and waited till their guide had said his say about them. The girl, clinging tight to the young man's arm, knew nothing but him; her mouth and eyes were set in a passionate concentration of her being upon him, and he seemed to walk in a dream of her. From time to time they peered upon each other's faces, and then they paused, rapt and indifferent to all besides.

The young painters had their jokes about it; even Mr. Morton smiled, and Mrs. Bowen recognised it. But Imogene did not smile; she regarded the lovers with an interest in them scarcely less intense than their interest in each other; and a cold perspiration of question broke on Colville's forehead. Was that her ideal of what her own engagement should be? Had she expected him to behave in that way to her, and to accept from her a devotion like that girl's? How bitterly he must have disappointed her! It was so impossible to him that the thought of it made him feel that he must break all ties which bound him to anything like it. And yet he reflected that the time was when he could have been equal to that, and even more.

After lunch the painters joined them again, and they all went together to visit the ruins of the Roman theatre and the stretch of Etruscan wall beyond it. The former seems older than the latter, whose huge blocks of stone lie as firmly and evenly in their courses as if placed there a year ago; the turf creeps to the edge at top, and some small trees nod along the crest of the wall, whose ancient face, clean and bare, looks sternly out over a vast prospect, now young and smiling in the first delight of spring.

The piety or interest of the community, which guards the entrance to the theatre by a fee of certain centesimi, may be concerned in keeping the wall free from the grass and vines which are stealing the half-excavated arena back to forgetfulness and decay; but whatever agency it was, it weakened the appeal that the wall made to the sympathy of the spectators. They could do nothing with it; the artists did not take their sketch-blocks from their pockets. But in the theatre, where a few broken columns marked the place of the stage, and the stone benches of the auditorium were here and there reached by a flight of uncovered steps, the human interest returned.

"I suspect that there is such a thing as a ruin's being too old," said Colville. "Our Etruscan friends made the mistake of building their wall several thousand years too soon for our purpose."

"Yes," consented the young clergyman. "It seems as if our own race became alienated from us through the mere effect of time, don't you think, sir? I mean, of course, terrestrially."

The artists looked uneasy, as if they had not counted upon anything of this kind, and they began to scatter about for points of view. Effie got her mother's leave to run up and down one of the stairways, if she would not fall. Mrs. Bowen sat down on one of the lower steps, and Mr. Morton took his place respectfully near her.

"I wonder how it looks from the top?" Imogene asked this of Colville, with more meaning than seemed to belong to the question properly.

"There is nothing like going to see," he suggested. He helped her up, giving her his hand from one course of seats to another. When they reached the point which commanded the best view of the whole, she sat down, and he sank at her feet, but they did not speak of the view.

"Theodore, I want to tell you something," she said abruptly. "I have heard from home."

"Yes?" he replied, in a tone in which he did his best to express a readiness for any fate.

"Mother has telegraphed. She is coming out. She is on her way now. She will be here very soon."

Colville did not know exactly what to say to these passionately consecutive statements. "Well?" he said at last.

"Well"—she repeated his word—"what do you intend to do?"

"Intend to do in what event?" he asked, lifting his eyes for the first time to the eyes which he felt burning down upon him.

"If she should refuse?"

Again he could not command an instant answer, but when it came it was a fair one. "It isn't for me to say what I shall do," he replied gravely. "Or, if it is, I can only say that I will do whatever you wish."

"Do *you* wish nothing?"

"Nothing but your happiness."

"Nothing but my happiness!" she retorted. "What is my happiness to me? Have I ever sought it?"

"I can't say," he answered; "but if I did not think you would find it—"

"I shall find it, if ever I find it, in yours," she interrupted. "And what shall you do if my mother will not consent to our engagement?"

The experienced and sophisticated man—for that in no ill way was what Colville was—felt himself on trial for his honour and his manhood by this simple girl, this child. He could not endure to fall short of her ideal of him at that moment, no matter what error or calamity the fulfilment involved. "If you feel sure that you love me, Imogene, it will make no difference to me what your mother says. I would be glad of her consent; I should hate to go counter to her will; but I know that I am good enough man to be true and keep you all my life the first in all my thoughts, and that's enough for me. But if you have any fear, any doubt of yourself, now is the time—"

Imogene rose to her feet as in some turmoil of thought or emotion that would not suffer her to remain quiet.

"Oh, keep still!" "Don't get up yet!" "Hold on a minute, please!" came from the artists in different parts of the theatre, and half a dozen imploring pencils were waved in the air.

"They are sketching you," said Colville, and she sank compliantly into her seat again.

"I have no doubt for myself—no," she said, as if there had been no interruption.

"Then we need have no anxiety in meeting your mother," said Colville, with a light sigh, after a moment's pause. "What makes you think she will be unfavourable?"

"I don't think that; but I thought—I didn't know but—"

"What?"

"Nothing, now." Her lips were quivering; he could see her struggle for self-control, but he could not see it unmoved.

"Poor child!" he said, putting out his hand toward her.

"Don't take my hand; they're all looking," she begged.

He forbore, and they remained silent and motionless a little while, before she had recovered herself sufficiently to speak again.

"Then we are promised to each other, whatever happens," she said.

"Yes."

"And we will never speak of this again. But there is one thing. Did Mrs. Bowen ask you to tell Mr. Morton of our engagement?"

"She said that I ought to do so."

"And did you say you would?"

"I don't know. But I suppose I ought to tell him."

"I don't wish you to!" cried the girl.

"You don't wish me to tell him?"

"No; I will not have it!"

"Oh, very well; it's much easier not. But it seems to me that it's only fair to him."

"Did you think of that yourself?" she demanded fiercely.

"No," returned Colville, with sad self-recognition. "I'm afraid I'm not apt to think of the comforts and rights of other people. It was Mrs. Bowen who thought of it."

"I knew it!"

"But I must confess that I agreed with her, though I would have preferred to postpone it till we heard from your family." He was thoughtfully silent a moment; then he said, "But if their decision is to have no weight with us, I think he ought to be told at once."

"Do you think that I am flirting with him?"

"Imogene!" exclaimed Colville reproachfully.

"That's what you imply; that's what she implies."

"You're very unjust to Mrs. Bowen, Imogene."

"Oh, you always defend her! It isn't the first time you've told me I was unjust to her."

"I don't mean that you are willingly unjust, or could be so, to any living creature, least of all to her. But I—we—owe her so much; she has been so patient."

"What do we owe her? How has she been patient?"

"She has overcome her dislike to me."

"Oh, indeed!"

"And—and I feel under obligation to her for—in a thousand little ways; and I should be glad to feel that we were acting with her approval; I should like to please her."

"You wish to tell Mr. Morton?"

"I think I ought."

"To please Mrs. Bowen! Tell him, then! You always cared more to please her than me. Perhaps you stayed in Florence to please her!"

She rose and ran down the broken seats and ruined steps so recklessly and yet so sure-footedly that it seemed more like a flight than a pace to the place where Mrs. Bowen and Mr. Morton were talking together.

Colville followed as he could, slowly and with a heavy heart. A good thing develops itself in infinite and unexpected shapes of good; a bad thing into manifold and astounding evils. This mistake was whirling away beyond his recall in hopeless mazes of error. He saw this generous young spirit betrayed by it to ignoble and unworthy excess, and he knew that he and not she was to blame.

He was helpless to approach her, to speak with her, to set her right, great as the need of that was, and he could see that she avoided him. But their relations remained outwardly undisturbed. The artists brought their sketches for inspection and comment, and, without speaking to each other, he and Imogene discussed them with the rest.

When they started homeward the painters said they were coming a little way with them for a send-off, and then going back to spend the night in Fiesole. They walked beside the carriage, talking with Mrs. Bowen and Imogene, who had taken their places, with Effie between them, on the back seat; and when they took their leave, Colville and the young clergyman, who had politely walked with them, continued on foot a little further, till they came to the place where the highway to Florence divided into the new road and the old. At this point it steeply overtops the fields on one side, which is shored up by a wall some ten or twelve feet deep; and here round a sharp turn of the hill on the other side came a peasant driving a herd of the black pigs of the country.

Mrs. Bowen's horses were, perhaps, pampered beyond the habitual resignation of Florentine horses to all manner of natural phenomena; they reared at sight of the sable crew, and backing violently up-hill, set the carriage across the road, with its hind wheels a few feet from the brink of the wall. The coachman sprang from his seat, the ladies and the child remained in theirs as if paralysed.

Colville ran forward to the side of the carriage. "Jump, Mrs. Bowen! jump, Effie! Imogene—"

The mother and the little one obeyed. He caught them in his arms and set them down. The girl sat still, staring at him with reproachful, with disdainful eyes.

He leaped forward to drag her out; she shrank away, and then he flew to help the coachman, who had the maddened horses by the bit.

"Let go!" he heard the young clergyman calling to him; "she's safe!" He caught a glimpse of Imogene, whom Mr. Morton had pulled from the other side of the carriage. He struggled to free his wrist from the curb-bit chain of the horse, through which he had plunged it in his attempt to seize the bridle. The wheels of the carriage went over the wall; he felt himself whirled into the air, and then swung ruining down into the writhing and crashing heap at the bottom of the wall.

Chapter XXIII

[*Mrs. Graham arrives from America to find Colville in the hospital as a result of a carriage accident. She proves to be a judicial and strong-minded woman, who relieves Colville by explaining to him that her daughter is in love with Morton, but determined to sacrifice herself and marry Colville. Colville releases Imogene, with inner thankfulness, and quietly recovers from the accident in Mrs. Bowen's apartment, which, on his recovery, he reluctantly leaves. Mr. Waters, a kindly old clergyman friend, hints to Colville that he perhaps owes something to Mrs. Bowen. In the following chapter Colville repays his debt, and brings the novel to a conclusion.*]

Colville went back to his own room, and spent a good deal of time in the contemplation of a suit of clothes, adapted to the season, which had been sent home from the tailor's just before Mr. Waters came in. The coat was of the lightest serge, the trousers of a pearly grey tending to lavender, the waistcoat of cool white duck. On his way home from Palazzo Pinti he had stopped in Via Tornabuoni and bought some silk gauze neckties of a tasteful gaiety of tint, which he had at the time thought very well of. But now, as he spread out the whole array on his bed, it seemed too emblematic of a light and blameless spirit for his wear. He ought to put on something as nearly analogous to sackcloth as a modern stock of dry-goods afforded; he ought, at least, to wear the grave materials of his winter costume. But they were really insupportable in this sudden access of summer. Besides, he had grown thin during his sickness, and the things bagged about him. If he were going to see Mrs. Bowen that evening, he ought to go in some decent shape. It was perhaps providential that he had failed to find her at home in the morning, when he had ventured thither in the clumsy attire in which he had been loafing about her drawing-room for the past week. He now owed it to her to appear before her as well as he could. How charmingly punctilious she always was herself!

As he put on his new clothes he felt the moral support which the becomingness of dress alone can give. With the blue silk gauze lightly tied under his collar, and the lapels of his thin coat thrown back to admit his thumbs to his waistcoat pockets, he felt almost cheerful before his glass. Should he shave? As once before, this important question occurred to him. His thinness gave him some advantages of figure, but he thought that it made his face older. What effect would cutting off his beard have upon it? He had not seen the lower part of his face for fifteen years. No one could say what recent ruin of a double chin might not be lurking there. He decided not to shave, at least till after dinner, and after dinner he was too impatient for his visit to brook the necessary delay.

He was shown into the salotto alone, but Effie Bowen came running in to meet him. She stopped suddenly, bridling.

"You never expected to see me looking quite so pretty," said Colville, tracing the cause of her embarrassment to his summer splendour. "Where is your mamma?"

"She is in the dining-room," replied the child, getting hold of his hand. "She wants you to come and have coffee with us."

"By all means—not that I haven't had coffee already, though."

She led the way, looking up at him shyly over her shoulder as they went.

Mrs. Bowen rose, napkin in lap, and gave him a hand of welcome. "How are you feeling to-day?" she asked, politely ignoring his finery.

"Like a new man," he said. And then he added, to relieve the strain of the situation, "Of the best tailor's make in Florence."

"You look very well," she smiled.

"Oh, I always do when I take pains," said Colville. "The trouble is that I don't always take pains. But I thought I would to-night, in calling upon a lady."

"Effie will feel very much flattered," said Mrs. Bowen.

"Don't refuse a portion of the satisfaction," he cried.

"Oh, is it for me too?"

This gave Colville consolation which no religion or philosophy could have brought him, and his pleasure was not marred, but rather heightened, by the little pangs of expectation, bred by long custom, that from moment to moment Imogene would appear. She did not appear, and a thrill of security succeeded upon each alarm. He wished her well with all his heart; such is the human heart that he wished her arrived home the betrothed of that excellent, that wholly unobjectionable young man, Mr. Morton.

"Will you have a little of the ice before your coffee?" asked Mrs. Bowen, proposing one of the moulded creams with her spoon.

"Yes, thank you. Perhaps I will take it in place of the coffee. They forgot to offer us any ice at the *table d'hôte* this evening."

"This is rather luxurious for us," said Mrs. Bowen. "It's a compromise with Effie. She wanted me to take her to Giacosa's this afternoon."

"I *thought* you would come," whispered the child to Colville.

Her mother made a little face of mock surprise at her. "Don't give yourself away, Effie."

"Why, let us go to Giacosa's too," said Colville, taking the ice. "We shall be the only foreigners there, and we shall not even feel ourselves foreign. It's astonishing how the hot weather has dispersed the tourists. I didn't see a Baedeker on the whole way up here, and I walked down Via Tornabuoni across through Porta Rosso and the Piazza della Signoria and the Uffizi. You've no idea how comfortable and home-like it was—all the statues loafing about in their shirt sleeves, and the objects of interest stretching and yawning round, and having a good rest after their winter's work."

Effie understood Colville's way of talking well enough to enjoy this; her mother did not laugh.

"Walked?" she asked.

"Certainly. Why not?"

"You are getting well again. You'll soon be gone too."

"I've *got* well. But as to being gone, there's no hurry. I rather think I shall wait now to see how long you stay."

"We may keep you all summer," said Mrs. Bowen, dropping her eyelids indifferently.

"Oh, very well. All summer it is, then. Mr. Waters is going to stay, and he is such a very cool old gentleman that I don't think one need fear the wildest antics of the mercury where he is."

When Colville had finished his ice, Mrs. Bowen led the way

to the salotto; and they all sat down by the window there and watched the sunset die on San Miniato. The bronze copy of Michelangelo's David, in the Piazzale below the church, blackened in perfect relief against the pink sky and then faded against the grey while they talked. They were so domestic that Colville realised with difficulty that this was an image of what might be rather than what really was; the very ease with which he could apparently close his hand upon the happiness within his grasp unnerved him. The talk strayed hither and thither, and went and came aimlessly. A sound of singing floated in from the kitchen, and Effie eagerly asked her mother if she might go and see Maddalena. Maddalena's mother had come to see her, and she was from the mountains.

"Yes, go," said Mrs. Bowen; "but don't stay too long."

"Oh, I will be back in time," said the child, and Colville remembered that he had proposed going to Giacosa's.

"Yes; don't forget." He had forgotten it himself.

"Maddalena is the cook," explained Mrs. Bowen. "She sings ballads to Effie that she learned from her mother, and I suppose Effie wants to hear them at first hand."

"Oh yes," said Colville dreamily.

They were alone now, and each little silence seemed freighted with a meaning deeper than speech.

"Have you seen Mr. Waters to-day?" asked Mrs. Bowen, after one of these lapses.

"Yes; he came this afternoon."

"He is a very strange old man. I should think he would be lonely here."

"He seems not to be. He says he finds company in the history of the place. And his satisfaction at having got out of Haddam East Village is perennial."

"But he will want to go back there before he dies."

"I don't know. He thinks not. He's a strange old man, as you say. He has the art of putting all sorts of ideas into people's heads. Do you know what we talked about this afternoon?"

"No, I don't," murmured Mrs. Bowen.

"About you. And he encouraged me to believe—imagine—

that I might speak to you—ask—tell you that—I loved you, Lina." He leaned forward and took one of the hands that lay in her lap. It trembled with a violence inconceivable in relation to the perfect quiet of her attitude. But she did not try to take it away. "Could you—do you love me?"

"Yes," she whispered; but here she sprang up and slipped from his hold altogether, as with an inarticulate cry of rapture he released her hand to take her in his arms.

He followed her a pace or two. "And you will—will be my wife?" he pursued eagerly.

"Never!" she answered, and now Colville stopped short, while a cold bewilderment bathed him from head to foot. It must be some sort of jest, though he could not tell where the humour was, and he could not treat it otherwise than seriously.

"Lina, I have loved you from the first moment that I saw you this winter, and Heaven knows how long before!"

"Yes; I know that."

"And every moment."

"Oh, I know that too."

"Even if I had no sort of hope that you cared for me, I loved you so much that I must tell you before we parted—"

"I expected that—I intended it."

"You intended it! and you do love me! And yet you won't —Ah, I don't understand!"

"How could *you* understand? I love you—I blush and burn for shame to think that I love you. But I will never marry you; I can at least help doing that, and I can still keep some little trace of self-respect. How you must really despise me, to think of anything else, after all that has happened! Did you suppose that I was merely waiting till that poor girl's back was turned, as you were? Oh, how can you be yourself, and still be yourself? Yes, Jenny Wheelwright was right. You are too much of a mixture, Theodore Colville"—her calling him so showed how often she had thought of him so—"too much for her, too much for Imogene, too much for me; too much for any woman except some wretched creature who enjoys being trampled on and dragged through the dust, as you have dragged me."

"*I* dragged *you* through the dust? There hasn't been a moment in the past six months when I wouldn't have rolled myself in it to please you."

"Oh, I knew that well enough! And do you think that was flattering to me?"

"That has nothing to do with it. I only know that I love you, and that I couldn't help wishing to show it even when I wouldn't acknowledge it to myself. That is all. And now when I am free to speak, and you own that you love me, you won't—I give it up!" he cried desperately. But in the next breath he implored, "*Why* do you drive me from you, Lina?"

"Because you have humiliated me too much." She was perfectly steady, but he knew her so well that in the twilight he knew what bitterness there must be in the smile which she must be keeping on her lips. "I was here in the place of her mother, her best friend, and you made me treat her like an enemy. You made me betray her and cast her off."

"I?"

"Yes, you! I knew from the very first that you did not really care for her, that you were playing with yourself, as you were playing with her, and I ought to have warned her."

"It appears to me you did warn her," said Colville, with some resentful return of courage.

"I tried," she said simply, "and it made it worse. It made it worse because I knew that I was acting for my own sake more than hers, because I wasn't—disinterested." There was something in this explanation, serious, tragic, as it was to Mrs. Bowen, which made Colville laugh. She might have had some perception of its effect to him, or it may have been merely from a hysterical helplessness, but she laughed too a little.

"But why," he gathered courage to ask, "do you still dwell upon that? Mr. Waters told me that Mr. Morton—that there was—"

"He is mistaken. He offered himself, and she refused him. He told me."

"Oh!"

"Do you think she would do otherwise, with you lying here between life and death? No: you can have no hope from that."

Colville, in fact, had none. This blow crushed and dispersed him. He had not strength enough to feel resentment against Mr. Waters for misleading him with this *ignis fatuus*.

"No one warned him, and it came to that," said Mrs. Bowen. "It was of a piece with the whole affair. I was weak in that too."

Colville did not attempt to reply on this point. He feebly reverted to the inquiry regarding himself, and was far enough from mirth in resuming it.

"I couldn't imagine," he said, "that you cared anything for me when you warned another against me. If I could——"

"You put me in a false position from the beginning. I ought to have sympathised with her and helped her instead of making the poor child feel that somehow I hated her. I couldn't even put her on guard against herself, though I knew all along that she didn't really care for you, but was just in love with her own fancy for you. Even after you were engaged I ought to have broken it off; I ought to have been frank with her; it was my duty; but I couldn't without feeling that I was acting for myself too, and I would not submit to that degradation. No! I would rather have died. I dare say you don't understand. How could you? You are a man, and the kind of man who couldn't. At every point you made me violate every principle that was dear to me. I loathed myself for caring for a man who was in love with me when he was engaged to another. Don't think it was gratifying to me. It was detestable; and yet I did let you see that I cared for you. Yes, I even *tried* to make you care for me —falsely, cruelly, treacherously."

"You didn't have to try very hard," said Colville, with a sort of cold resignation to his fate.

"Oh no; you were quite ready for any hint. I could have told her for her own sake that she didn't love you, but that would have been for my sake too; and I would have told you if I hadn't cared for you and known how you cared for me. I've saved at least the consciousness of this from the wreck."

"I don't think it's a great treasure," said Colville. "I wish that you had saved the consciousness of having been frank even to your own advantage."

"Do you dare to reproach me, Theodore Colville? But perhaps I've deserved this too."

"No, Lina, you certainly don't deserve it, if it's unkindness, from me. I won't afflict you with my presence: but will you listen to me before I go?"

She sank into a chair in sign of assent. He also sat down. He had a dim impression that he could talk better if he took her hand, but he did not venture to ask for it. He contented himself with fixing his eyes upon as much of her face as he could make out in the dusk, a pale blur in a vague outline of dark.

"I want to assure you, Lina—Lina, my love, my dearest, as I shall call you for the first and last time!—that I do understand everything, as delicately and fully as you could wish, all that you have expressed, and all that you have left unsaid. I understand how high and pure your ideals of duty are, and how heroically, angelically, you have struggled to fulfil them, broken and borne down by my clumsy and stupid selfishness from the start. I want you to believe, my dearest love—you must forgive me!— that if I didn't see everything at the time, I do see it now, and that I prize the love you kept from me far more than any love you could have given me to the loss of your self-respect. It isn't logic—it sounds more like nonsense, I am afraid—but you know what I mean by it. You are more perfect, more lovely to me, than any being in the world, and I accept whatever fate you choose for me. I would not win you against your will if I could. You are sacred to me. If you say we must part, I know that you speak from a finer discernment than mine, and I submit. I will try to console myself with the thought of your love, if I may not have you. Yes, I submit."

His instinct of forbearance had served him better than the subtlest art. His submission was the best defence. He rose with a real dignity, and she rose also. "Remember," he said, "that I confess all you accuse me of, and that I acknowledge the justice of what you do—because you do it." He put out his hand and took the hand which hung nerveless at her side. "You are quite right. Good-bye." He hesitated a moment. "May I kiss you, Lina?" He drew her to him, and she let him kiss her on the lips.

"Good-bye," she whispered. "Go—"

"I am going."

Effie Bowen ran into the room from the kitchen. "Aren't you going to take—" She stopped and turned to her mother. She must not remind Mr. Colville of his invitation; that was what her gesture expressed.

Colville would not say anything. He would not seize his advantage, and play upon the mother's heart through the feelings of her child, though there is no doubt that he was tempted to prolong the situation by any means. Perhaps Mrs. Bowen divined both the temptation and the resistance. "Tell her," she said, and turned away.

"I can't go with you to-night, Effie," he said, stooping toward her for the inquiring kiss that she gave him. "I am—going away, and I must say good-bye."

The solemnity of his voice alarmed her. "Going away!" she repeated.

"Yes—away from Florence. I'm afraid I shall not see you again."

The child turned from him to her mother again, who stood motionless. Then, as if the whole calamitous fact had suddenly flashed upon her, she plunged her face against her mother's breast. "I can't *bear* it!" she sobbed out; and the reticence of her lamentation told more than a storm of cries and prayers.

Colville wavered.

"Oh, you must stay!" said Lina, in the self-contemptuous voice of a woman who falls below her ideal of herself.

ANNIE KILBURN

Chapter VI

[*At the death of her father, Judge Kilburn, Annie leaves Rome, where the father and daughter had been living for the past twelve years, and returns to her empty old family mansion in Hatboro', Massachusetts. Annie is imbued with the idea of "doing good" in the little industrial town of her birth. The opportunity of putting her ideas into action soon presents itself. She is waited upon by a committee of local women who wish to raise money to build a club house for the working people of the community, to be called Social Union. The ladies on the committee make it clear to Annie that the workers themselves are not to be invited to the dance following the theatrical performance by means of which the money is to be raised. Annie gladly promises to support the project and is happy in her plans until she meets and talks with the new minister, Mr. Peck, who has occupied her house during her absence. See Introduction, pp. cxiii–cxv.*]

Toward five o'clock Annie was interrupted by a knock at her door, which ought to have prepared her for something unusual, for it was Mrs. Bolton's habit to come and go without knocking. But she called "Come in!" without rising from her letter, and Mrs. Bolton entered with a stranger. The little girl clung to his forefinger, pressing her head against his leg, and glancing shyly up at Annie. She sprang up, and, "This is Mr. Peck, Miss Kilburn," said Mrs. Bolton.

"How do you do?" said Mr. Peck, taking the hand she gave him.

He was gaunt, without being tall, and his clothes hung loosely about him, as if he had fallen away in them since they were made. His face was almost the face of the caricature American: deep, slightly curved vertical lines enclosed his mouth in their parenthesis; a thin, dust-coloured beard fell from his cheeks and chin; his upper lip was shaven. But instead of the slight frown of challenge and self-assertion which marks this face in the type, his large blue eyes, set near together, gazed sadly from under a smooth forehead, extending itself well up toward the crown, where his dry hair dropped over it.

"I am very glad to see you, Mr. Peck," said Annie; "I've wanted to tell you how pleased I am that you found shelter in my old home when you first came to Hatboro'."

Mr. Peck's trousers were short and badly kneed, and his long coat hung formlessly from his shoulders; she involuntarily took a patronising tone toward him which was not habitual with her.

"Thank you," he said, with the dry, serious voice which seemed the fit vocal expression of his presence; "I have been afraid that it seemed like an intrusion to you."

"Oh, not the least," retorted Annie. "You were very welcome. I hope you're comfortably placed where you are now?"

"Quite so," said the minister.

"I'd heard so much of your little girl from Mrs. Bolton, and her attachment to the house, that I ventured to send for her to-day. But I believe I gave her rather a bad quarter of an hour, and that she liked the place better under Mrs. Bolton's *régime*."

She expected some deprecatory expression of gratitude from him, which would relieve her of the lingering shame she felt for having managed so badly, but he made none.

"It was my fault. I'm not used to children, and I hadn't taken the precaution to ask her name—"

"Her name is Idella," said the minister.

Annie thought it very ugly, but, with the intention of saying something kind, she said, "What a quaint name!"

"It was her mother's choice," returned the minister. "Her own name was Ella, and my mother's name was Ida; she combined the two."

"Oh!" said Annie. She abhorred those made-up names in which the New England country people sometimes indulge their fancy, and Idella struck her as a particularly repulsive invention; but she felt that she must not visit the fault upon the little creature. "Don't you think you could give me another trial some time, Idella?" She stooped down and took the child's unoccupied hand, which she let her keep, only twisting her face away to hide it in her father's pantaloon leg. "Come now, won't you give me a forgiving little kiss?" Idella looked round, and Annie made bold to gather her up.

Idella broke into a laugh, and took Annie's cheeks between her hands.

"Well, I declare!" said Mrs. Bolton. "You never can tell what that child will do next."

"I never can tell what I will do next myself," said Annie. She liked the feeling of the little, warm, soft body in her arms, against her breast, and it was flattering to have triumphed where she had seemed to fail so desperately. They had all been standing, and she now said, "Won't you sit down, Mr. Peck?" She added, by an impulse which she instantly thought ill-advised, "There is something I would like to speak to you about."

"Thank you," said Mr. Peck, seating himself beyond the stove. "We must be getting home before a great while. It is nearly tea-time."

"I won't detain you unduly," said Annie.

Mrs. Bolton left him at her hint of something special to say to the minister. Annie could not have had the face to speak of Mr. Brandreth's theatricals in that grim presence; and as it was, she resolved to put forward their serious object. She began abruptly: "Mr. Peck, I've been asked to interest myself for a Social Union which the ladies of South Hatboro' are trying to establish for the operatives. I suppose you haven't heard anything of the scheme?"

"No, I hadn't," said Mr. Peck.

He was one of those people who sit very high, and he now seemed taller and more impressive than when he stood.

"It is certainly a very good object," Annie resumed; and she went on to explain it at second-hand from Mr. Brandreth as well as she could. The little girl was standing in her lap, and got between her and Mr. Peck, so that she had to look first around one side of her and then another to see how he was taking it.

He nodded his head, and said gravely, "Yes," and "Yes," and "Yes," at each significant point of her statement. At the end he asked: "And are the means forthcoming? Have they raised the money for renting and furnishing the rooms?"

"Well, no, they haven't yet, or not quite, as I understand."

"Have they tried to interest the working people themselves in it? If they are to value its benefits, it ought to cost them something—self-denial, privation even."

"Yes, I know," Annie began.

"I'm not satisfied," the minister pursued, "that it is wise to provide people with even harmless amusements that take them much away from their homes. These things are invented by well-to-do people who have no occupation, and think that others want pastimes as much as themselves. But what working people want is rest, and what they need are decent homes where they can take it. Besides, unless they help to support this union out of their own means, the better sort among them will feel wounded by its existence, as a sort of superfluous charity."

"Yes, I see," said Annie. She saw this side of the affair with surprise. The minister seemed to have thought more about such matters than she had, and she insensibly receded from her first hasty generalisation of him, and paused to reapproach him on another level. The little girl began to play with her glasses, and accidentally knocked them from her nose. The minister's face and figure became a blur, and in the purblindness to which she was reduced she had a moment of clouded volition in which she was tempted to renounce, and even oppose, the scheme for a Social Union, in spite of her promise to Mr. Brandreth. But she remembered that she was a consistent and faithful person, and she said: "The ladies have a plan for raising the money, and they've applied to me to second it—to use my influence somehow among the villagers to get them interested; and the working people can help too if they choose. But I'm quite a stranger amongst those I'm expected to influence, and I don't at all know how they will take it." The minister listened, neither prompting nor interrupting. "The ladies' plan is to have an entertainment at one of the cottages, and charge an admission, and devote the proceeds to the union." She paused. Mr. Peck still remained silent, but she knew he was attentive. She pushed on. "They intend to have a—a representation, in the open air, of one of Shakespeare's plays, or scenes from one—"

"Do you wish me," interrupted the minister, "to promote the establishment of this union? Is that why you speak to me of it?"

"Why, I don't know *why* I speak to you of it," she replied with a laugh of embarrassment, to which he was cold, apparently. "I certainly couldn't ask you to take part in an affair that you didn't approve."

"I don't know that I disapprove of it. Properly managed, it might be a good thing."

"Yes, of course. But I understand why you might not sympathise with that part of it, and that is why I told you of it," said Annie.

"What part?"

"The—the—theatricals."

"Why not?" asked the minister.

"I know—Mrs. Bolton told me you were very liberal," Annie faltered on; "but I didn't expect you as a—But of course—"

"I read Shakespeare a great deal," said Mr. Peck. "I have never been in the theatre; but I should like to see one of his plays represented where it could cause no one to offend."

"Yes," said Annie, "and this would be by amateurs, and there could be no *possible* 'offence in it.' I wished to know how the general idea would strike you. Of course the ladies would be only too glad of your advice and co-operation. Their plan is to sell tickets to every one for the theatricals, and to a certain number of invited persons for a supper, and a little dance afterward on the lawn."

"I don't know if I understand exactly," said the minister.

Annie repeated her statement more definitely, and explained, from Mr. Brandreth, as before, that the invitations were to be given so as to eliminate the shop-hand element from the supper and dance.

Mr. Peck listened quietly. "That would prevent my taking part in the affair," he said, as quietly as he had listened.

"Of course—dancing," Annie began.

"It is not that. Many people who hold strictly to the old opinions now allow their children to learn dancing. But I could not join at all with those who were willing to lay the foundations of a Social Union in a social disunion—in the exclusion of its beneficiaries from the society of their benefactors."

He was not sarcastic, but the grotesqueness of the situation as he had sketched it was apparent. She remembered now that she had felt something incongruous in it when Mr. Brandreth exposed it, but not deeply.

The minister continued gently: "The ladies who are trying to get up this Social Union proceed upon the assumption that working people can neither see nor feel a slight; but it is a great mistake to do so."

Annie had the obtuseness about those she fancied below her which is one of the consequences of being brought up in a superior station. She believed that there was something to say on the other side, and she attempted to say it.

"I don't know that you could call it a slight exactly. People can ask those they prefer to a social entertainment."

"Yes—if it is for their own pleasure."

"But even in a public affair like this the work-people would feel uncomfortable and out of place, wouldn't they, if they stayed to the supper and the dance? They might be exposed to greater suffering among those whose manners and breeding were different, and it might be very embarrassing all round. Isn't there that side to be regarded?"

"You beg the question," said the minister, as unsparingly as if she were a man. "The point is whether a Social Union beginning in social exclusion could ever do any good. What part do these ladies expect to take in maintaining it? Do they intend to spend their evenings there, to associate on equal terms with the shoe-shop and straw-shop hands?"

"I don't suppose they do, but I don't know," said Annie dryly; and she replied by helplessly quoting Mr. Brandreth: "They intend to organise a system of lectures, concerts, and readings. They wish to get on common ground with them."

"They can never get on common ground with them in that way," said the minister. "No doubt they think they want to do them good; but good is from the heart, and there is no heart in what they propose. The working people would know that at once."

"Then you mean to say," Annie asked, half alarmed and half

amused, "that there can be no friendly intercourse with the poor and the well-to-do unless it is based upon social equality?"

'I will answer your question by asking another. Suppose you were one of the poor, and the well-to-do offered to be friendly with you on such terms as you have mentioned, how should you feel toward them?"

"If you make it a personal question—"

"It makes itself a personal question," said the minister dispassionately.

"Well, then, I trust I should have the good sense to see that social equality between people who were better dressed, better taught, and better bred than myself was impossible, and that for me to force myself into their company was not only bad taste, but it was foolish. I have often heard my father say that the great superiority of the American practice of democracy over the French ideal was that it didn't involve any assumption of social equality. He said that equality before the law and in politics was sacred, but that the principle could never govern society, and that Americans all instinctively recognised it. And I believe that to try to mix the different classes would be un-American."

Mr. Peck smiled, and this was the first break in his seriousness. "We don't know what is or will be American yet. But we will suppose you are quite right. The question is, how would you feel toward the people whose company you wouldn't force yourself into?"

"Why, of course," Annie was surprised into saying, "I suppose I shouldn't feel very kindly toward them."

"Even if you knew that they felt kindly toward you?"

"I'm afraid that would only make the matter worse," she said, with an uneasy laugh.

The minister was silent on his side of the stove.

"But do I understand you to say," she demanded, "that there can be no love at all, no kindness, between the rich and the poor? God tells us all to love one another."

"Surely," said the minister. "Would you suffer such a slight as your friends propose, to be offered to any one you loved?"

She did not answer, and he continued, thoughtfully: "I suppose that if a poor person could do a rich person a kindness which cost him some sacrifice, he might love him. In that case there could be love between the rich and the poor."

"And there could be no love if a rich man did the same?"

"Oh yes," the minister said—"upon the same ground. Only, the rich man would have to make a sacrifice first that he would really feel."

"Then you mean to say that people can't do any good at all with their money?" Annie asked.

"Money is a palliative, but it can't cure. It can sometimes create a bond of gratitude perhaps, but it can't create sympathy between rich and poor."

"But *why* can't it?"

"Because sympathy—common feeling—the sense of fraternity—can spring only from like experiences, like hopes, like fears. And money cannot buy these."

He rose, and looked a moment about him, as if trying to recall something. Then, with a stiff obeisance, he said, "Good evening," and went out, while she remained daunted and bewildered, with the child in her arms, as unconscious of having kept it as he of having left it with her.

Mrs. Bolton must have reminded him of his oversight, for after being gone so long as it would have taken him to walk to her parlour and back, he returned, and said simply, "I forgot Idella."

He put out his hands to take her, but she turned perversely from him, and hid her face in Annie's neck, pushing his hands away with a backward reach of her little arm.

"Come, Idella!" he said. Idella only snuggled the closer.

Mrs. Bolton came in with the little girl's wraps; they were very common and poor, and the thought of getting her something prettier went through Annie's mind.

At sight of Mrs. Bolton the child turned from Annie to her older friend.

"I'm afraid you have a woman-child for your daughter, Mr. Peck," said Annie, remotely hurt at the little one's fickleness.

Neither Mr. Peck nor Mrs. Bolton smiled, and with some vague intention of showing him that she could meet the poor on common ground by sharing their labours, she knelt down and helped Mrs. Bolton tie on and button on Idella's things.

Chapter VIII

[In the following chapter the members of the local committee for the theatricals meet in Mr. Gerrish's back office and exchange views not only on the enterprise before them, but also on labor conditions in general. Mr. Gerrish is carrying things pretty much his own way until Ralph Putney, the town liberal and the town drunkard, puts in an appearance. Lawyer Putney comes out on Minister Peck's side of the argument and expresses one of Howells' favorite ideas, confidence in the power of the vote, which, properly used, "might make the whole United States of America a Labour Union."]

Mrs. Munger drove across the street, and drew up before a large, handsomely ugly brick dry-goods store, whose showy windows had caught Annie's eye the day she arrived in Hatboro'.

"I see Mrs. Gerrish has got here first," Mrs. Munger said, indicating the perambulator at the door, and she dismounted and fastened her pony with a weight, which she took from the front of the phaeton. On either door jamb of the store was a curved plate of polished metal, with the name GERRISH cut into it in black letters; the sills of the wide windows were of metal, and bore the same legend. At the threshold a very prim, ceremonious little man, spare and straight, met Mrs. Munger with a ceremonious bow, and a solemn "How do you do, ma'am? how do you do? I hope I see you well," and he put a small dry hand into the ample clasp of Mrs. Munger's gauntlet.

"Very well indeed, Mr. Gerrish. Isn't it a lovely morning? You know Miss Kilburn, Mr. Gerrish."

He took Annie's hand into his right and covered it with his left, lifting his eyes to look her in the face with an old-merchant-like cordiality.

"Why, yes, indeed! Delighted to see her. Her father was one of my best friends. I may say that I owe everything that I am to Squire Kilburn; he advised me to stick to commerce when I once thought of studying law. Glad to welcome you back to Hatboro', Miss Kilburn. You see changes on the surface, no doubt, but you'll find the genuine old feeling here. Walk right back, ladies," he continued, releasing Annie's hand to waft them before him toward the rear of the store. "You'll find Mrs. Gerrish in my room there—my Growlery, as *I* call it." He seemed to think he had invented the name. "And Mrs. Gerrish tells me that you've really come back," he said, leaning decorously toward Annie as they walked, "with the intention of taking up your residence permanently among us. You will find very few places like Hatboro'."

As he spoke, walking with his hands clasped behind him, he glanced to right and left at the shop-girls on foot behind the counter, who dropped their eyes under their different bangs as they caught his glance, and bridled nervously. He denied them the use of chewing-gum; he permitted no conversation, as he called it, among them; and he addressed no jokes or idle speeches to them himself. A system of grooves overhead brought to his counting-room the cash from the clerks in wooden balls, and he returned the change, and kept the accounts, with a pitiless eye for errors. The women were afraid of him, and hated him with bitterness, which exploded at crises in excesses of hysterical impudence.

His store was an example of variety, punctuality, and quality. Upon the theory, for which he deserved the credit, of giving to a country place the advantages of one of the great city establishments, he was gradually gathering, in their fashion, the small commerce into his hands. He had already opened his bazaar through into the adjoining store, which he had bought out, and he kept every sort of thing desired or needed in a country town, with a tempting stock of articles before unknown to the shop-keepers of Hatboro'. Everything was of the very quality represented; the prices were low, but inflexible, and cash payments, except in the case of some rich customers of unimpeachable credit, were invariably exacted; at the same time every reasonable facility for the exchange or return of goods was afforded. Nothing could exceed the justice and fidelity of his dealing with the public. He had even some effects of generosity in his dealing with his dependants; he furnished them free seats in the churches of their different persuasions, and he closed every night at six o'clock, except Saturday, when the shop hands were paid off, and made their purchases for the coming week.

He stepped lightly before Annie and Mrs. Munger, and pushed open the ground-glass door of his office for them. It was like a bank parlour, except for Mrs. Gerrish sitting in her husband's leather-cushioned swivel chair, with her last-born in her lap; she greeted the others noisily, without trying to rise.

"You see we are quite at home here," said Mr. Gerrish.

"Yes, and very snug you are, too," said Mrs. Munger, taking one half of the leather lounge, and leaving the other half to Annie. "I don't wonder Mrs. Gerrish likes to visit you here."

Mr. Gerrish laughed, and said to his wife, who moved provisionally in her chair, seeing he had none, "Sit still, my dear; I prefer my usual perch." He took a high stool beside a desk, and gathered a ruler in his hand.

"Well, I may as well begin at the beginning," said Mrs. Munger, "and I'll try to be short, for I know that these are business hours."

"Take all the time you want, Mrs. Munger," said Mr. Gerrish affably. "It's my idea that a good business man's business can go on without him, when necessary."

"Of course!" Mrs. Munger sighed. "If everybody had your *system*, Mr. Gerrish!" She went on and succinctly expounded the scheme of the Social Union. "I suppose I can't deny that the idea occurred to *me*," she concluded, "but we can't hope to develop it without the co-operation of the ladies of Old Hatboro', and I've come, first of all, to Mrs. Gerrish."

Mr. Gerrish bowed his acknowledgments of the honour done his wife, with a gravity which she misinterpreted.

"I think," she began, with her censorious manner and accent, "that these people have too much done for them *now*. They're perfectly spoiled. Don't you, Annie?"

Mr. Gerrish did not give Annie time to answer. "I differ with you, my dear," he cut in. "It is my opinion— Or I don't know but you wish to confine this matter entirely to the ladies?" he suggested to Mrs. Munger.

"Oh, I'm only too proud and glad that you feel interested in the matter!" cried Mrs. Munger. "Without the gentlemen's practical views, we ladies are such feeble folk—mere conies in the rocks."

"I am as much opposed as Mrs. Gerrish—or any one—to acceding to unjust demands on the part of my clerks or other employees," Mr. Gerrish began.

"Yes, that's what I mean," said his wife, and broke down with a giggle.

He went on, without regarding her: "I have always made it a rule, as far as business went, to keep my own affairs entirely in my own hands. I fix the hours, and I fix the wages, and I fix all the other conditions, and I say plainly, 'If you don't like them, 'don't come,' or 'don't stay,' and I never have any difficulty."

"I'm sure," said Mrs. Munger, "that if all the employers in the country would take such a stand, there would soon be an end of labour troubles. I think we're too concessive."

"And I do too, Mrs. Munger!" crid Mrs. Gerrish, glad of the occasion to be censorious and of the finer lady's opinion at the same time. "That's what I meant. Don't you, Annie?"

"I'm afraid I don't understand exactly," Annie replied.

Mr. Gerrish kept his eye on Mrs. Munger's face, now arranged for indefinite photography, as he went on. "That is exactly what I say to them. That is what I said to Mr. Marvin one year ago, when he had that trouble in his shoe shop. I said, 'You're too concessive.' I said, 'Mr. Marvin, if you give those fellows an inch, they'll take an ell. Mr. Marvin,' said I, 'you've got to begin by being your own master, if you want to be master of anybody else. You've got to put your foot down,' as Mr. Lincoln said; and as *I* say, you've got to *keep* it down.' "

Mrs. Gerrish looked at the other ladies for admiration, and Mrs. Munger said, rapidly, without disarranging her face—

"Oh yes. And how much *misery* could be saved in such cases by a little firmness at the outset!"

"Mr. Marvin differed with me," said Mr. Gerrish sorrowfully.

"He agreed with me on the main point, but he said that too many of his hands had been in his regiment, and he couldn't lock them out. He submitted to arbitration. And what is arbitration?" asked Mr. Gerrish, levelling his ruler at Mrs. Munger. "It is postponing the evil day."

"Exactly," said Mrs. Munger, without winking.

"Mr. Marvin," Mr. Gerrish proceeded, "may be running very smoothly now, and sailing before the wind all—all—nicely; but I tell *you* his house is built upon the *sand*." He put his ruler by on the desk very softly, and resumed with impressive quiet: "I never had any trouble but once. I had a porter in this store who wanted his pay raised. I simply said that I made it a rule to propose all advances of salary myself, and I should submit to no dictation from any one. He told me to go to—a place that I will not repeat, and I told him to walk out of my store. He was under the influence of liquor at the time, I suppose. I understand that he is drinking very hard. He does nothing to support his family whatever, and from all that I can gather, he bids fair to fill a drunkard's grave inside of six months."

Mrs. Munger seized her opportunity. "Yes; and it is just such cases as this that the Social Union is designed to meet. If this man had some such place to spend his evenings—and bring his family if he chose—where he could get a cup of good coffee for the same price as a glass of rum— Don't you see?"

She looked round, at the different faces, and Mr. Gerrish slightly frowned, as if the vision of the Social Union interposing between his late porter and a drunkard's grave, with a cup of good coffee, were not to his taste altogether; but he said: "Precisely so! And I was about to make the remark that while I am very strict —and obliged to be—with those under me in business, *no* one is more disposed to promote such objects as this of yours."

"I was *sure* you would approve of it," said Mrs. Munger. "That is why I came to you—to you and Mrs. Gerrish—first," said Mrs. Munger. "I was sure you would see it in the right light." She looked round at Annie for corroboration, and Annie was in the social necessity of making a confirmatory murmur.

Mr. Gerrish ignored them both in the more interesting work of celebrating himself. "I may say that there is not an institution in this town which I have not contributed my humble efforts to—to—establish, from the drinking fountain in front of this store, to the soldiers' monument on the village green."

Annie turned red; Mrs. Munger said shamelessly, "That beautiful monument!" and looked at Annie with eyes full of gratitude to Mr. Gerrish.

"The schools, the sidewalks, the water-works, the free library, the introduction of electricity, the projected system of drainage, and *all* the various religious enterprises at various times, I am proud—I am humbly proud—that I have been allowed to be the means of doing—sustaining—"

He lost himself in the labyrinths of his sentence, and Mrs. Munger came to his rescue: "I fancy Hatboro' wouldn't be Hatboro' without *you*, Mr. Gerrish! And you *don't* think that Mr. Peck's objection will be seriously felt by other leading citizens?"

"*What* is Mr. Peck's objection?" demanded Mr. Gerrish, perceptibly bristling up at the name of his pastor.

"Why, he talked it over with Miss Kilburn last night, and he objected to an entertainment which wouldn't be open to all—to the shop hands and everybody." Mrs. Munger explained the point fully. She repeated some things that Annie had said in ridicule of Mr. Peck's position regarding it. "If you *do* think that part would be bad or impolitic," Mrs. Munger concluded, "we could drop the invited supper and the dance, and simply have the theatricals."

She bent upon Mr. Gerrish a face of candid deference that filled him with self-importance almost to bursting.

"No!" he said, shaking his head, and "No!" closing his lips abruptly, and opening them again to emit a final "No!" with an explosive force which alone seemed to save him. "Not at all, Mrs. Munger; not on any account! I am surprised at Mr. Peck, or rather I am *not* surprised. He is not a practical man—not a man of the world; and I should have much preferred to hear that he objected to the dancing and the play; I could have understood that; I could have gone with him in that to a certain extent, though I can see no harm in such things when properly conducted. I have a great respect for Mr. Peck; I was largely instrumental in getting him here; but he is altogether wrong in this matter. We are not obliged to go out into the highways and the hedges until the bidden guests have—er—declined."

"Exactly," said Mrs. Munger. "I never thought of that."

Mrs. Gerrish shifted her baby to another knee, and followed her husband with her eyes, as he dismounted from his stool and began to pace the room.

"I came into this town a poor boy, without a penny in my pocket, and I have made my own way, every inch of it, unaided and alone. I am a thorough believer in giving every one an equal chance to rise and to—get along; I would not throw an obstacle in anybody's way; but I do not believe—I do *not* believe—in pampering those who have not risen, or have made no effort to rise."

"It's their wastefulness, in nine cases out of ten, that keeps them down," said Mrs. Gerrish.

"I don't care *what* it is, I don't *ask* what it is, that keeps them down. I don't expect to invite my clerks or Mrs. Gerrish's servants into my parlour. I will meet them at the polls, or the communion table, or on any proper occasion; but a man's home is *sacred*. I will not allow my wife or my children to associate with those whose—whose—whose idleness, or vice, or whatever, has kept them down in a country where—where everybody stands on an equality; and what I will not do myself, I will not ask others to do. I make it a rule to do unto others as I would have them do unto me. It is all nonsense to attempt to introduce those one-ideaed notions into—put them in practice."

"Yes," said Mrs. Munger, with deep conviction, "that is my own feeling, Mr. Gerrish, and I'm glad to have it corroborated by your experience. Then you *wouldn't* drop the little invited dance and supper?"

"I will tell you how I feel about it, Mrs. Munger," said Mr. Gerrish, pausing in his walk, and putting on a fine, patronising, gentleman-of-the-old-school smile. "You may put me down for any number of tickets—five, ten, fifteen—and you may command me in anything I can do to further the objects of your enterprise, if you will *keep* the invited supper and dance. But I should not be prepared to do anything if they are dropped."

"What a comfort it is to meet a person who knows his own mind!" exclaimed Mrs. Munger.

"Got company, Billy?" asked a voice at the door; and it added, "Glad to see *you* here, Mrs. Gerrish."

"Ah, Mr. Putney! Come in. Hope I see you well, sir!" cried Mr. Gerrish. "Come in!" he repeated, with jovial frankness. "Nobody but friends here."

"I don't know about that," said Mr. Putney, with whimsical perversity, holding the door ajar. "I see that arch-conspirator from South Hatboro'," he said, looking at Mrs. Munger.

He showed himself, as he stood holding the door ajar, a lank little figure, dressed with reckless slovenliness in a suit of old-fashioned black; a loose neck-cloth fell stringing down his shirt front, which his unbuttoned waistcoat exposed, with its stains from the tobacco upon which his thin little jaws worked mechanically, as he stared into the room with flamy blue eyes; his silk hat was pushed back from a high, clear forehead; he had yesterday's stubble on his beardless cheeks; a heavy moustache and imperial gave dash to a cast of countenance that might otherwise have seemed slight and effeminate.

"Yes; but I'm in charge of Miss Kilburn, and you needn't be afraid of me. Come in. We wish to consult you," cried Mrs. Munger. Mrs. Gerrish cackled some applausive incoherencies.

Putney advanced into the room, and dropped his burlesque air as he approached Annie.

"Miss Kilburn, I must apologise for not having called with Mrs. Putney to pay my respects. I have been away; when I got back I found she had stolen a march on me. But I'm going to make Ellen bring me at once. I don't think I've been in your house since the old Judge's time. Well, he was an able man, and a good man; I was awfully fond of the old Judge, in a boy's way."

"Thank you," said Annie, touched by something gentle and honest in his words.

"He was a Christian gentleman," said Mr. Gerrish, with authority.

Putney said, without noticing Mr. Gerrish, "Well, I'm glad you've come back to the old place, Miss Kilburn—I almost said Annie."

"I shouldn't have minded, Ralph," she retorted.

"Shouldn't you? Well, that's right." Putney continued, ignoring the laugh of the others at Annie's sally: "You'll find Hatboro' pretty exciting, after Rome, for a while, I suppose. But you'll get used to it. It's got more of the modern improvements, I'm told, and it's more public-spirited—more snap to it. I'm told that there's more enterprise in Hatboro', more real *crowd* in South Hatboro' alone, than there is in the Quirinal and the Vatican put together."

"You had better come and live at South Hatboro', Mr. Putney; that would be just the atmosphere for you," said Mrs. Munger, with aimless hospitality. She said this to every one.

"Is it about coming to South Hatboro' you want to consult me?" asked Putney.

"Well, it is, and it isn't," she began.

"Better be honest, Mrs. Munger," said Putney. "You can't do anything for a client who won't be honest with his attorney. That's what I have to continually impress upon the reprobates who come to me. I say, 'It don't matter what you've done; if you expect me to get you off, you've got to make a clean breast of it.' They generally do; they see the sense of it."

They all laughed, and Mr. Gerrish said, "Mr. Putney is one of Hatboro's privileged characters, Miss Kilburn."

"Thank you, Billy," returned the lawyer, with mock-tenderness. "Now Mrs. Munger, out with it!"

"You'll have to tell him sooner or later, Mrs. Munger!" said Mrs. Gerrish, with overweening pleasure in her acquaintance with both of these superior people. "He'll get it out of you anyway." Her husband looked at her, and she fell silent.

Mrs. Munger swept her with a tolerant smile as she looked up at Putney. "Why, it's really Miss Kilburn's affair," she began; and she laid the case before the lawyer with a fulness that made Annie wince.

Putney took a piece of tobacco from his pocket, and tore off a morsel with his teeth. "Excuse me, Annie! It's a beastly habit. But it's saved me from something worse. *You* don't know what I've been; but anybody in Hatboro' can tell you. I made my shame so public that it's no use trying to blink the past. You don't have to be a hypocrite in a place where everybody's seen you in the gutter; that's the only advantage I've got over my fellow-citizens, and of course I abuse it; that's nature, you know. When I began to pull up I found that tobacco helped me; I smoked and chewed both; now I only chew. Well," he said, dropping the pathetic simplicity with which he had spoken, and turning with a fierce jocularity from the shocked and pitying look in Annie's face to Mrs. Munger, "what do you propose to do? Brother Peck's head seems to be pretty level, in the abstract."

"Yes," said Mrs. Munger, willing to put the case impartially; "and I should be perfectly willing to drop the invited dance and supper, if it was thought best, though I must say I don't at all agree with Mr. Peck in principle. I don't see what would become of society."

"You ought to be in politics, Mrs. Munger," said Putney. "Your readiness to sacrifice principle to expediency shows what a reform will be wrought when you ladies get the suffrage. What does Brother Gerrish think?"

"No, no," said Mrs. Munger. "We want an impartial opinion."

"I always think as Brother Gerrish thinks," said Putney. "I guess you better give up the fandango; hey Billy?"

"No, sir; no, Mr. Putney," answered the merchant nervously. "I can't agree with you. And I will tell you why, sir."

He gave his reasons, with some abatement of pomp and detail and with the tremulous eagerness of a solemn man who expects a sarcastic rejoinder. "It would be a bad precedent. This town is full now of a class of persons who are using every opportunity to—to abuse their privileges. And this would be simply adding fuel to the flame."

"Do you really think so, Billy?" asked the lawyer, with cool derision. "Well, we all abuse our privileges at every opportunity, of course; I was just saying that I abused mine; and I suppose those fellows would abuse theirs if you happened to hurt their wives' and daughters' feelings. And how are you going to manage? Aren't you afraid that they will hang around, after the show, indefinitely, unless you ask all those who have not received invitations to the dance and supper to clear the grounds, as they do in the circus when the minstrels are going to give a performance not included in the price of admission? Mind, I don't care anything about your Social Union."

"Oh, but *surely*!" cried Mrs. Munger, "you *must* allow that it's a good object."

"Well, perhaps it is, if it will keep the men away from the rum-holes. Yes, I guess it is. You won't sell liquor?"

"We expect to furnish coffee at cost price," said Mrs. Munger, smiling at Putney's joke.

"And good navy-plug too, I hope. But you see it would be rather awkward, don't you? You see, Annie?"

"Yes, I see," said Annie. "I hadn't thought of that part before."

"And you didn't agree with Brother Peck on general principles? There we see the effect of residence abroad," said Putney. "The uncorrupted—or I will say the uninterrupted—Hatborian has none of those aristocratic predilections of yours, Annie. He grows up in a community where there is neither poverty nor richness, and where political economy can show by the figures that the profligate shop hands get nine-tenths of the profits, and starve on 'em, while the good little company rolls in luxury on the other tenth. But you've got used to something different over there, and of course Brother Peck's ideas startled you. Well, I suppose I should have been just so myself."

"Mr. Putney has never felt just right about the working-men since he lost the boycotters' case," said Mr. Gerrish, with a snicker.

"Oh, come now, Billy, why did you give me away?" said Putney, with mock suffering. "Well, I suppose I might as well own up, Mrs. Munger; it's no use trying to keep it from *you*; you know it already. Yes, Annie, I defended some poor devils here for combining to injure a non-union man—for doing once just what the big manufacturing Trusts do every day of the year with impunity; and I lost the case. I expected to. I told 'em they were wrong, but I did my best for 'em. 'Why, you fools,' said I —that's the way I talk to 'em, Annie; I call 'em pet names; they like it; they're used to 'em; they get 'em every day in the newspapers—'you fools,' said I, 'what do you want to boycott for, when you can *vote*? What do you want to break the laws for, when you can *make* 'em? You idiots, you,' said I, 'what do you putter round for, persecuting non-union men, that have as good a right to earn their bread as you, when you might make the whole United States of America a Labour Union?' Of course I didn't say that in court."

"Oh, how delicious you are, Mr. Putney!" said Mrs. Munger.

"Glad you like me, Mrs. Munger," Putney replied.

"Yes, you're delightful," said the lady, recovering from the effects of the drollery which they had all pretended to enjoy, Mr. Gerrish, and Mrs. Gerrish by his leave, even more than the others. "But you're not candid. All this doesn't help us to a conclusion. Would you give up the invited dance and supper, or wouldn't you? That's the question."

"And no shirking, hey?" asked Putney.

"No shirking."

Putney glanced through a little transparent space in the ground-glass windows framing the room, which Mr. Gerrish used for keeping an eye on his sales-ladies to see that they did not sit down.

"Hello!" he exclaimed. "There's Dr. Morrell. Let's put the case to him." He opened the door and called down the store, "Come in here, Doc!"

"What?" called back an amused voice; and after a moment steps approached, and Dr. Morrell hesitated at the open door. He was a tall man, with a slight stoop; well dressed; full bearded; with kind, boyish blue eyes that twinkled in fascinating friendliness upon the group. "Nobody sick here, I hope?"

"Walk right in, sir! come in, Dr. Morrell," said Mr. Gerrish. "Mrs. Munger and Mrs. Gerrish you know. Present you to

Miss Kilburn, who has come to make her home among us after a prolonged residence abroad. Dr. Morrell, Miss Kilburn."

"No, there's nobody sick here, in one sense," said Putney, when the doctor had greeted the ladies. "But we want your advice all the same. Mrs. Munger is in a pretty bad way morally, Doc."

"Don't you mind Mr. Putney, doctor!" screamed Mrs. Gerrish.

Putney said, with respectful recognition of the poor woman's attempt to be arch, "I'll try to keep within the bounds of truth in stating the case, Mrs. Gerrish."

He went on to state it, with so much gravity and scrupulosity, and with so many appeals to Mrs. Munger to correct him if he were wrong, that the doctor was shaking with laughter when Putney came to an end with unbroken seriousness. At each repetition of the facts, Annie's relation to them grew more intolerable; and she suspected Putney of an intention to punish her. "Well, what do you say?" he demanded of the doctor.

"Ha, ha, ha! ah, ha, ha." laughed the doctor, shutting his eyes and throwing back his head.

"Seems to consider it a *laughing* matter," said Putney to Mrs. Munger.

"Yes; and that is all your fault," said Mrs. Munger, trying, with the ineffectiveness of a large woman, to pout.

"No, no, I'm not laughing," began the doctor.

"Smiling, perhaps," suggested Putney.

The doctor went off again. Then, "I beg—I *beg* your pardon, Mrs. Munger," he resumed. "But it isn't a professional question, you know; and I—I really couldn't judge—have any opinion on such a matter."

"No shirking," said Putney. "That's what Mrs. Munger said to me."

"Of course not," gurgled the doctor. "You ladies will know what to do. I'm sure *I* shouldn't," he added.

"Well, I must be going," said Putney. "Sorry to leave you in this fix, Doc." He flashed out of the door, and suddenly came back to offer Annie his hand. "I beg your pardon, Annie. I'm going to make Ellen bring me round. Good morning." He bowed cursorily to the rest.

"Wait—I'll go with you, Putney," said the doctor.

Mrs. Munger rose, and Annie with her. "We must go too," she said. "We've taken up Mr. Gerrish's time most unconscionably," and now Mr. Gerrish did not urge her to remain.

"Well, good-bye," said Mrs. Gerrish, with a genteel prolongation of the last syllable.

Mr. Gerrish followed his guests down the store, and even out upon the sidewalk, where he presided with unheeded hospitality over the superfluous politeness of Putney and Dr. Morrell in putting Mrs. Munger and Annie into the phaeton. Mrs. Munger attempted to drive away without having taken up her hitching weight.

"I suppose that there isn't a post in this town that my wife hasn't tried to pull up in that way," said Putney gravely.

The doctor doubled himself down with another fit of laughing.

Annie wanted to laugh too, but she did not like his laughing. She questioned if it were not undignified. She felt that it might be disrespectful. Then she asked herself why he should respect her.

Chapter XI

[*Ralph Putney and Annie Kilburn discuss Hatboro', which, like all other towns in the world, is in a "transitory state," symbolized by the character of J. Milton Northwick. Putney's ironic analysis of Peck, for the benefit of Dr. Morrell and Annie, helps to alter Annie's attitude toward Mr. Peck and the Social Union. Dr. Morrell's genial common sense strengthens Annie's waning self-esteem.*]

Putney met Annie at the door, and led her into the parlour beside the hall. He had a little crippled boy on his right arm, and he gave her his left hand. In the parlour he set his burden down in a chair, and the child drew up under his thin arms a pair of crutches that stood beside it. His white face had the eager purity and the waxen translucence which we see in sufferers from hip-disease.

"This is our Winthrop," said his father, beginning to talk at once. "We receive the company and do the honours while mother's looking after the tea. We only keep one undersized girl," he explained more directly to Annie, "and Ellen has to be chief cook and bottlewasher herself. She'll be in directly. Just lay off your bonnet anywhere."

She was taking in the humility of the house and its belongings while she received the impression of an unimagined simplicity in its life from his easy explanations. The furniture was in green terry, the carpet a harsh, brilliant tapestry; on the marble-topped centre table was a big clasp Bible and a basket with a stereoscope and views; the marbleised iron shelf above the stove-pipe hole supported two glass vases and a French clock under a glass bell; through the open door, across the oil-cloth of the hallway, she saw the white-painted pine balusters of the steep, cramped stairs. It was clear that neither Putney nor his wife had been touched by the aesthetic craze; the parlour was in the tastelessness of fifteen years before; but after the decoration of South Hatboro', she found a delicious repose in it. Her eyes dwelt with relief on the wall-paper of French grey, sprigged with small gilt flowers, and broken by a few cold engravings and framed photographs.

Putney himself was as little decorated as the parlour. He had put on a clean shirt, but the bulging bosom had broken away from its single button, and showed two serrated edges of ragged linen; his collar lost itself from time to time under the rise of his plastron scarf band, which kept escaping from the stud that ought to have held it down behind. His hair was brushed smoothly across a forehead which looked as innocent and gentle as the little boy's.

"We don't often give these festivities," he went on, "but you don't come home once in twelve years every day, Annie. I can't tell you how glad I am to see you in our house; and Ellen's just as excited as the rest of us; she was sorry to miss you when she called."

"You're very kind, Ralph. I can't tell *you* what a pleasure it was to come, and I'm not going to let the trouble I'm giving spoil my pleasure."

"Well, that's right," said Putney. "*We* sha'n't either." He took out a cigar and put it into his mouth. "It's only a dry smoke. Ellen makes me let up on my chewing when we have company, and I must have something in my mouth, so I get a cigar. It's a sort of compromise. I'm a terribly nervous man, Annie; you can't imagine. If it wasn't for the grace of God, I think I should fly to pieces sometimes. But I guess that's what holds me together—that and Winthy here. I dropped him on the stairs out there, when I was drunk, one night. I saw you looking at them; I suppose you've been told; it's all right. I presume the Almighty knows what He's about; but sometimes He appears to save at the spigot and waste at the bung-hole, like the rest of us. He let me cripple my boy to reform me."

"Don't, Ralph!" said Annie, with a voice of low entreaty. She turned and spoke to the child, and asked him if he would not come to see her.

"What?" he asked, breaking with a sort of absent-minded start from his intentness upon his father's words.

She repeated her invitation.

"Thanks!" he said, in the prompt, clear little pipe which startles by its distinctness and decision on the lips of crippled children. "I guess father'll bring me some day. Don't you want I should go out and tell mother she's here?" he asked his father.

"Well, if you want to, Winthrop," said his father.

The boy swung himself lightly out of the room on his crutches, and his father turned to her. "Well, how does Hatboro' strike you, anyway, Annie? You needn't mind being honest with me, you know."

He did not give her a chance to say, and she was willing to let him talk on, and tell her what he thought of Hatboro' himself. "Well, it's like every other place in the world, at every moment of history—it's in a transition state. The theory is, you know, that most places are at a standstill the greatest part of the time; they haven't begun to move, or they've stopped moving; but I guess that's a mistake; they're moving all the while. I suppose Rome itself was in a transition state when you left?"

"Oh, very decidedly. It had ceased to be old and was becoming new."

"Well, that's just the way with Hatboro'. There *is* no old Hatboro' any more; and there never was, as your father and mine could tell us if they were here. They lived in a painfully transitional period, poor old fellows! But, for all that, there is a difference. They lived in what was really a New England village, and we live now in a sprawling American town; and by American of course I mean a town where at least one-third of the people are raw foreigners or rawly extracted natives. The old New England ideal characterises them all, up to a certain point, socially; it puts a decent outside on most of 'em; it makes 'em keep Sunday, and drink on the sly. We got in the Irish long ago, and now they're part of the conservative element. We got in the French Canadians, and some of them are our best mechanics and citizens. We're getting in the Italians, and as soon as they want something better than bread and vinegar to eat, they'll begin going to Congress and boycotting and striking and forming pools and trusts just like any other class of law-abiding Americans. There used to be some talk of the Chinese, but I guess they've pretty much blown over. We've got Ah Lee and Sam Lung here, just as they have everywhere, but their laundries don't seem to increase. The Irish are spreading out into the country and scooping in the farms that are not picturesque enough for the summer folks. You can buy a farm anywhere round Hatboro' for less than the buildings on it cost. I'd rather the Irish would have the land than the summer folks. They make an honest living off it, and the other fellows that come out to roost here from June till October simply keep somebody else from making a living off it, and corrupt all the poor people in sight by their idleness and luxury. That's what I tell 'em at South Hatboro'. They don't like it, but I guess they believe it; anyhow they have to hear it. They'll tell you in self-defence that J. Milton Northwick is a practical farmer, and sells his butter for a dollar a pound. He's done more than anybody else to improve the breeds of cattle and horses; and he spends fifteen thousand a year on his place. It can't return him five; and that's the reason he's a curse and a fraud."

"Who *is* Mr. Northwick, Ralph?" Annie interposed. "Everybody at South Hatboro' asked me if I'd met the Northwicks."

"He's a very great and good man," said Putney. "He's worth a million, and he runs a big manufacturing company at Ponkwasset Falls, and he owns a fancy farm just beyond South Hatboro'. He lives in Boston, but he comes out here early enough to dodge his tax there, and let poorer people pay it. He's got miles of cut stone wall round his place, and conservatories and gardens and villas and drives inside of it, and he keeps up the town roads outside at his own expense. Yes, we feel it such an honour and advantage to have J. Milton in Hatboro' that our assessors practically allow him to fix the amount of tax here himself. People who can pay only a little at the highest valuation are assessed to the last dollar of their property and income; but the assessors know that this wouldn't do with Mr. Northwick. They make a guess at his income, and he always pays their bills without asking for abatement; they think themselves wise and public-spirited men for doing it, and most of their fellow-citizens think so too. You see it's not only difficult for a rich man to get into the kingdom of heaven, Annie, but he makes it hard for other people.

"Well, as I was saying, socially the old New England element is at the top of the heap here. That's so everywhere. The people that are on the ground first, it don't matter much who they are, have to manage pretty badly not to leave their descendants in social ascendency over all newer comers for ever. Why, I can see it in my own case. I can see that I was a sort of fetich to the bedevilled fancy of the people here when I was seen drunk in the streets every day, just because I was one of the old Hatboro' Putneys; and when I began to hold up, there wasn't a man in the community that wasn't proud and flattered to help me. Curious, isn't it? It made me sick of myself and ashamed of them, and I just made up my mind, as soon as I got straight again, I'd give all my help to the men that hadn't a tradition. That's what I've done, Annie. There isn't any low, friendless rapscallion in this town that hasn't got me for his friend—and Ellen. We've been in all the strikes with the men, and all their fool boycottings and kicking over the traces generally. Anybody else would have been turned out of respectable society for one-half that I've done, but it tolerates me because I'm one of the old Hatboro' Putneys. You're one of the old Hatboro' Kilburns, and if you want to have a mind of your own and a heart of your own, all you've got to do is to have it. They'll like it; they'll think it's original. That's the reason South Hatboro' got after you with that Social Union scheme. They were right in thinking you would have a great deal of influence. I was sorry you had to throw it against Brother Peck."

Annie felt herself jump at this climax, as if she had been touched on an exposed nerve. She grew red, and tried to be angry, but she was only ashamed and tempted to lie out of the part she had taken. "Mrs. Munger," she said, "gave that a very unfair turn. I didn't mean to ridicule Mr. Peck. I think he was perfectly sincere. The scheme of the invited dance and supper has been entirely given up. And I don't care for the project of the Social Union at all."

"Well, I'm glad to hear it," said Putney, indifferently, and he resumed his analysis of Hatboro'—

"We've got all the modern improvements here, Annie. I suppose you'd find the modern improvements, most of 'em, in Sheol: electric light, Bell telephone, asphalt sidewalks, and city water—though I don't know about the water; and I presume they haven't got a public library or an opera-house—perhaps they *have* got an opera-house in Sheol: you see I use the Revised Version, it don't sound so much like swearing. But, as I was saying—"

Mrs. Putney came in, and he stopped with the laugh of a man who knows that his wife will find it necessary to account for him and apologise for him.

The ladies kissed each other. Mrs. Putney was dressed in the black silk of a woman who has one silk; she was red from the kitchen, but all was neat and orderly in the hasty toilet which she must have made since leaving the cook-stove. A faint, mixed perfume of violet sachet and fricasseed chicken attended her.

"Well, as you were saying, Ralph?" she suggested.

"Oh, I was just tracing a little parallel between Hatboro' and Sheol," replied her husband.

Mrs. Putney made a *tchk* of humorous patience, and laughed toward Annie for sympathy. "Well, then, I guess you needn't go on. Tea's ready. Shall we wait for the doctor?"

"No; doctors are too uncertain. We'll wait for him while we're eating. That's what fetches him the soonest. I'm hungry. Ain't you, Win?"

"Not so very," said the boy, with his queer promptness. He stood resting himself on his crutches at the door, and he now wheeled about, and led the way out to the living-room, swinging himself actively forward. It seemed that his haste was to get to the dumb-waiter in the little china closet opening off the dining-room, which was like the papered inside of a square box. He called to the girl below, and helped pull it up, as Annie could tell by the creaking of the rope, and the light jar of the finally arriving crockery. A half-grown girl then appeared, and put the dishes on at the places indicated with nods and looks by Mrs. Putney, who had taken her place at the table. There was a platter of stewed fowl, and a plate of high-piled waffles, sweltering in successive courses of butter and sugar. In cut-glass dishes, one at each end of the table, there were canned cherries and pine-apple. There was a square of old-fashioned soda biscuit, not broken apart, which sent up a pleasant smell; in the centre of the table was a shallow vase of strawberries.

It was all very good and appetising; but to Annie it was pathetically old-fashioned, and helped her to realise how wholly out of the world was the life which her friends led.

"Winthrop," said Putney, and the father and mother bowed their heads.

The boy dropped his over his folded hands, and piped up clearly: "Our Father, which art in heaven, help us to remember those who have nothing to eat. Amen!"

"That's a grace that Win got up himself," his father explained, beginning to heap a plate with chicken and mashed potato, which he then handed to Annie, passing her the biscuit and the butter. "We think it suits the Almighty about as well as anything."

"I suppose you know Ralph of old, Annie?" said Mrs. Putney. "The only way he keeps within bounds at all is by letting himself perfectly loose."

Putney laughed out his acquiescence, and they began to talk together about old times. Mrs. Putney and Annie recalled the childish plays and adventures they had together, and one dreadful quarrel. Putney told of the first time he saw Annie, when his father took him one day for a call on the old judge, and how the old judge put him through his paces in American history, and would not admit the theory that the battle of Bunker's Hill could have been fought on Breed's Hill. Putney said that it was years before it occurred to him that the judge must have been joking: he had always thought he was simply ignorant.

"I used to set a good deal by the battle of Bunker's Hill," he continued. "I thought the whole Revolution and subsequent history revolved round it, and that it gave us all liberty, equality, and fraternity at a clip. But the Lord always finds some odd jobs to look after next day, and I guess He didn't clear 'em all up at Bunker's Hill."

Putney's irony and piety were very much of a piece apparently, and Annie was not quite sure which this conclusion was. She glanced at his wife, who seemed satisfied with it in either case. She was waiting patiently for him to wake up to the fact that he had not yet given her anything to eat; after helping Annie and the boy, he helped himself, and pending his wife's pre-occupation with the tea, he forgot her.

"Why didn't you throw something at me?" he roared, in grief and self-reproach. "There wouldn't have been a loose piece of crockery on this side of the table if I hadn't got my tea in time."

"Oh, I was listening to Annie's share in the conversation," said Mrs. Putney; and her husband was about to say something in retort of her thrust when a tap on the front door was heard.

"Come in, come in, Doc!" he shouted. "Mrs. Putney's just been helped, and the tea is going to begin."

Dr. Morrell's chuckle made answer for him, and after time enough to put down his hat, he came in, rubbing his hands and smiling, and making short nods round the table. "How d'ye do, Mrs. Putney? How d'ye do, Miss Kilburn? Winthrop?" He passed his hand over the boy's smooth hair and slipped into the chair beside him.

"You see, the reason why we always wait for the doctor in this formal way," said Putney, "is that he isn't in here more than seven nights of the week, and he rather stands on his dignity. Hand round the doctor's plate, my son," he added to the boy, and he took it from Annie, to whom the boy gave it, and began to heap it from the various dishes. "Think you can lift that much back to the doctor, Win?"

"I guess so," said the boy coolly.

"What is flooring Win at present," said his father, "and getting him down and rolling him over, is that problem of the robin that eats half a pint of grass-hoppers and then doesn't weigh a bit more than he did before."

"When he gets a little older," said the doctor, shaking over his plateful, "he'll be interested to trace the processes of his father's thought from a guest and half a peck of stewed chicken, to a robin and half a pint of—"

"Don't, doctor!" pleaded Mrs. Putney. "He won't have the least trouble if he'll keep to the surface."

Putney laughed impartially, and said: "Well, we'll take the doctor out and weigh him when he gets done. We expected Brother Peck here this evening," he explained to Dr. Morrell. "You're our sober second thought—Well," he broke off, looking across the table at his wife with mock anxiety. "Anything wrong about that, Ellen?"

"Not as far as I'm concerned, Mrs. Putney," interposed the doctor. "I'm glad to be here on any terms. Go on, Putney."

"Oh, there isn't anything more. You know how Miss Kilburn here has been round throwing ridicule on Brother Peck, because he wants the shop-hands treated with common decency, and my idea was to get the two together and see how she would feel."

Dr. Morrell laughed at this with what Annie thought was unnecessary malice; but he stopped suddenly, after a glance at her, and Putney went on—

"Brother Peck pleaded another engagement. Said he had to go off into the country to see a sick woman that wasn't expected to live. You don't remember the Merrifields, do you, Annie? Well, it doesn't matter. One of 'em married West, and her husband left her, and she came home here and got a divorce; I got it for her. She's the one. As a consumptive, she had superior attractions for Brother Peck. It isn't a case that admits of jealousy exactly, but it wouldn't matter to Brother Peck anyway. If he saw a chance to do a good action, he'd wade through blood."

"Now look here, Ralph," said Mrs. Putney, "there's such a thing as letting yourself *too* loose."

"Well, *gore*, then," said Putney, buttering himself a biscuit.

The boy, who had kept quiet till now, seemed reached by this last touch, and broke into a high, crowing laugh, in which they all joined except his father.

" 'Gore' suits Winthy, anyway," he said, beginning to eat his biscuit. "I met one of the deacons from Brother Peck's last parish, in Boston, yesterday. He asked me if we considered Brother Peck anyways peculiar in Hatboro', and when I said we thought he was a little too luxurious, the deacon came out with a lot of things. The way Brother Peck behaved toward the needy in that last parish of his made it simply uninhabitable to the standard Christian. They had to get rid of him somehow —send him away or kill him. Of course the deacon said they didn't want to *kill* him."

"Where was his last parish?" asked the doctor.

"Down on the Maine coast somewhere. Penobscotport, I believe."

"And was he indigenous there?"

"No, I believe not; he's from Massachusetts. Farm-boy and then millhand, I understand. Self-helped to an education; divinity student with summer intervals of waiting at table in the mountain hotels probably. Drifted down Maine way on his first call and stuck; but I guess he won't stick here very long. Annie's friend Mr. Gerrish is going to look after Brother Peck before a great while." He laughed to see her blush, and went on. "You see, Brother Gerrish has got a high ideal of what a Christian minister ought to be; he hasn't said much about it, but I can see that Brother Peck doesn't come up to it. Well, Brother Gerrish has got a good many ideals. He likes to get anybody he can by the throat, and squeeze the difference of opinion out of 'em."

"There, now Ralph," his wife interposed, "you let Mr. Gerrish alone. *You* don't like people to differ with you, either. Is your cup out, doctor?"

"Thank you," said the doctor, handing it up to her. "And you mean Mr. Gerrish doesn't like Mr. Peck's doctrine?" he asked of Putney.

"Oh, I don't know that he objects to his doctrine; he can't very well; it's 'between the leds of the Bible,' as the Hard-shell Baptist said. But he objects to Brother Peck's walk and conversation. He thinks he walks too much with the poor, and converses too much with the lowly. He says he thinks that the pew-owners in Mr. Peck's church and the people who pay his salary have some rights to his company that he's bound to respect."

The doctor relished the irony, but he asked, "Isn't there something to say on that side?"

"Oh yes, a good deal. There's always something to say on both sides, even when one's a wrong side. That's what makes it all so tiresome—makes you wish you were dead." He looked up, and caught his boy's eye fixed with melancholy intensity upon him. "I hope you'll never look at both sides when you grow up, Win. It's mighty uncomfortable. You take the right side, and stick to that. Brother Gerrish," he resumed, to the doctor, "goes round taking the credit of Brother Peck's call here; but the fact is he opposed it. He didn't like his being so indifferent about the salary. Brother Gerrish held that the labourer was worthy of his hire, and if he didn't inquire what his wages were going to be, it was a pretty good sign that he wasn't going to earn them."

"Well, there was some logic in that," said the doctor, smiling as before.

"Plenty. And now it worries Brother Gerrish to see Brother Peck going round in the same old suit of clothes he came here in, and dressing his child like a shabby little Irish girl. He says that he who provideth not for those of his own household is worse than a heathen. That's perfectly true. And he would like to know what Brother Peck does with his money, anyway. He would like to insinuate that he loses it at poker, I guess; at any rate, he can't find out whom he gives it to, and he certainly doesn't spend it on himself."

"From your account of Mr. Peck," said the doctor, "I should think Brother Gerrish might safely object to him as a certain kind of sentimentalist."

"Well, yes, he might, looking at him from the outside. But when you come to talk with Brother Peck, you find yourself sort of frozen out with a most unexpected, hard-headed cold-bloodedness. Brother Peck is plain common-sense itself. He seems to be a man without an illusion, without an emotion."

"Oh, not so bad as that!" laughed the doctor.

"Ask Miss Kilburn. She's talked with him, and she hates him."

"No, I don't, Ralph," Annie began.

"Oh, well, then, perhaps he only made you hate yourself," said Putney. There was something charming in his mockery, like the teasing of a brother with a sister; and Annie did not find the atonement to which he brought her altogether painful. It seemed to her really that she was getting off pretty easily, and she laughed with hearty consent at last.

Winthrop asked solemnly, "How did he do that?"

"Oh, I can't tell exactly, Winthrop," she said, touched by the boy's simple interest in this abstruse point. "He made me feel that I had been rather mean and cruel when I thought I had only been practical. I can't explain; but it wasn't a comfortable feeling, my dear."

"I guess that's the trouble with Brother Peck," said Putney. "He doesn't make you feel comfortable. He doesn't flatter you up worth a cent. There was Annie expecting him to take the most fervent interest in her theatricals, and her Social Union, and coo round, and tell her what a noble woman she was, and beg her to consider her health, and not overwork herself in doing good; but instead of that he simply showed her that she was a moral Cave-Dweller, and that she was living in a Stone Age of social brutalities; and of course she hated him."

"Yes, that was the way, Winthrop," said Annie; and they all laughed with her.

"Now you take them into the parlour, Ralph," said his wife, rising, "and tell them how he made *you* hate him."

"I shouldn't like anything better," replied Putney. He lifted the large ugly kerosene lamp that had been set on the table when it grew dark during tea, and carried it into the parlour with him. His wife remained to speak with her little helper, but she sent Annie with the gentlemen.

"Why, there isn't a great deal of it—more spirit than letter, so to speak," said Putney, when he put down the lamp in the parlour. "You know how I like to go on about other people's sins, and the world's wickedness generally; but one day Brother Peck, in that cool, impersonal way of his, suggested that it was not a wholly meritorious thing to hate evil. He went so far as to say that perhaps we could not love them that despitefully used us if we hated their evil so furiously. He said it was a good deal more desirable to understand evil than to hate it, for then we could begin to cure it. Yes, Brother Peck let in a good deal of light on me. He rather insinuated that I must be possessed by the very evils I hated, and that was the reason I was so violent about them. I had always supposed that I hated other people's cruelty because I was merciful, and their meanness because I was magnanimous, and their intolerance because I was generous, and their conceit because I was modest, and their selfishness because I was disinterested; but after listening to Brother Peck a while I came to the conclusion that I hated these things in others because I was cruel myself, and mean, and bigoted, and conceited, and piggish; and that's why I've hated Brother Peck ever since—just like you, Annie. But he didn't reform me, I'm thankful to say, any more than he did you. I've gone on just the same, and I suppose I hate more infernal scoundrels and loathe more infernal idiots today than ever; but I perceive that I'm no part of the power that makes for righteousness as long as I work that racket; and now I sin with light and knowledge, anyway. No, Annie," he went on, "I can understand why Brother Peck is not the success with women, and feminine temperaments like me, that his virtues entitle him to be. What we feminine temperaments want is a prophet, and Brother Peck doesn't prophesy worth a cent. He doesn't pretend to be authorised in any sort of way; he has a sneaking style of being no better than you are, and of being rather stumped by some of the truths he finds out. No, women like a good prophet about as well as they do a good doctor. Now if you, if you could unite the two functions, Doc—"

"Sort of medicine-man?" suggested Morrell.

"Exactly! The aborigines understood the thing. Why, I suppose that a real live medicine-man could go through a community like this and not leave a sinful soul nor a sore body in it among the ladies—perfect faith cure."

"But what did you say to Mr. Peck, Ralph?" asked Annie. "Didn't you attempt any defence?"

"No," said Putney. "He had the advantage of me. You can't talk back at a man in the pulpit."

"Oh, it was a sermon?"

"I suppose the other people thought so. But I knew it was a private conversation that he was publicly holding with me."

Putney and the doctor began to talk of the nature and origin of evil, and Annie and the boy listened. Putney took high ground, and attributed it to Adam. "You know, Annie," he explained, "I don't *believe* this; but I like to get a scientific man that won't quite deny Scripture or the good old Bible premises, and see him suffer. Hello! you up yet, Winthrop? I guess I'll go through the form of carrying you to bed, my son."

When Mrs. Putney rejoined them, Annie said she must go,

and Mrs. Putney went upstairs with her, apparently to help her put on her things, but really to have that talk before parting which guest and hostess value above the whole evening's pleasure. She showed Annie the pictures of the little girls that had died, and talked a great deal about their sickness and their loveliness in death. Then they spoke of others, and Mrs. Putney asked Annie if she had seen Lyra Wilmington lately. Annie told of her call with Mrs. Munger, and Mrs. Putney said: "I *like* Lyra, and I always did. I presume she isn't very happily married; he's too old; there couldn't have been any love on her part. But she would be a better woman than she is if she had children. Ralph says," added Mrs. Putney, smiling, "that he knows she would be a good mother, she's such a good aunt."

Annie put her two hands impressively on the hands of her friend folded at her waist. "Ellen, what *does* it mean?"

"Nothing more than what you saw, Annie. She must have—or she *will* have—some one to amuse her; to be at her beck and call; and it's best to have it all in the family, Ralph says."

"But isn't it—doesn't he think it's—odd?"

"It makes talk."

They moved a little toward the door, holding each other's hands. "Ellen, I've had a *lovely* time!"

"And so have I, Annie. I thought you'd like to meet Dr. Morrell."

"Oh yes, indeed!"

"And I can't tell you what a night this has been for Ralph. He likes you so much, and it isn't often that he has a chance to talk to *two* such people as you and Dr. Morrell."

"How brilliant he is!" Annie sighed.

"Yes, he's a very able man. It's very fortunate for Hatboro' to have such a doctor. He and Ralph are great cronies. I never feel uneasy now when Ralph's out late—I know he's been up at the doctor's office, talking. I—"

Annie broke in with a laugh. "I've no doubt Dr. Morrell is all you say, Ellen, but I meant Ralph when I spoke of brilliancy. He has a great future, I'm sure."

Mrs. Putney was silent for a moment. "I'm satisfied with the present, so long as Ralph—" The tears suddenly gushed out of her eyes and ran down over the fine wrinkles of her plump little cheeks.

"Not quite so much loud talking, please," piped a thin, high voice from a room across the stairs landing.

"Why, dear little soul!" cried Annie. "I forgot he'd gone to bed."

"Would you like to see him?" asked his mother.

She led the way into the room where the boy lay in a low bed near a larger one. His crutches lay beside it. "Win sleeps in our room yet. He can take care of himself quite well. But when he wakes in the night he likes to reach out and touch his father's hand."

The child looked mortified.

"I wish I could reach out and touch *my* father's hand when I wake in the night," said Annie.

The cloud left the boy's face. "I can't remember whether I said my prayers, mother, I've been thinking so."

"Well, say them over again, to me."

The men's voices sounded in the hall below, and the ladies found them there. Dr. Morrell had his hat in his hand.

"Look here, Annie," said Putney, "*I* expected to walk home with you, but Doc Morrell says he's going to cut me out. It looks like a put-up job. I don't know whether you're in it or not, but there's no doubt about Morrell."

Mrs. Putney gave a sort of gasp, and then they all shouted with laughter, and Annie and the doctor went out into the night. In the imperfect light which the electrics of the main street flung afar into the little avenue where Putney lived, and the moon sent through the sidewalk trees, they struck against each other as they walked, and the doctor said, "Hadn't you better take my arm, Miss Kilburn, till we get used to the dark?"

"Yes, I think I had, decidedly," she answered; and she hurried to add: "Dr. Morrell, there is something I want to ask you. You're their physician, aren't you?"

"The Putneys? Yes."

"Well, then, you can tell me—"

"Oh no, I can't, if you ask me as their physician," he interrupted.

"Well, then, as their friend. Mrs. Putney said something to me that makes me very unhappy. I thought Mr. Putney was out of all danger of his—trouble. Hasn't he perfectly reformed? Does he ever—"

She stopped, and Dr. Morrell did not answer at once. Then he said seriously: "It's a continual fight with a man of Putney's temperament, and sometimes he gets beaten. Yes, I guess you'd better know it."

"Poor Ellen!"

"They don't allow themselves to be discouraged. As soon as he's on his feet they begin the fight again. But of course it prevents his success in his profession, and he'll always be a second-rate country lawyer."

"Poor Ralph! And so brilliant as he is! He could be anything."

"We must be glad if he can be something, as it is."

"Yes, and how happy they seem together, all three of them! That child worships his father; and how tender Ralph is of him! How good he is to his wife; and how proud she is of him! And that awful shadow over them all the time! I don't see how they live!"

The doctor was silent for a moment, and finally said: "They have the peace that seems to come to people from the presence of a common peril, and they have the comfort of people who never blink the facts."

"I think Ralph is terrible. I wish he'd let other people blink the facts a little."

"Of course," said the doctor, "it's become a habit with him now, or a mania. He seems to speak of his trouble as if mentioning it were a sort of conjuration to prevent it. I wouldn't venture to check him in his way of talking. He may find strength in it."

"It's all terrible!"

"But it isn't by any means hopeless."

"I'm so glad to hear you say so. You see a great deal of them, I believe?"

"Yes," said the doctor, getting back from their seriousness, with apparent relief. "Pretty nearly every day. Putney and I consider the ways of God to man a good deal together. You can imagine that in a place like Hatboro' one would make the most of such a friend. In fact, anywhere."

"Yes, of course," Annie assented. "Dr. Morrell," she added, in that effect of continuing the subject with which one breaks away from it, "do you know much about South Hatboro'?"

"I have some patients there."

"I was there this morning—"

"I heard of you. They all take a great interest in your theatricals."

"In *my* theatricals? Really this is too much! Who has made them my theatricals, I should like to know? Everybody at South Hatboro' talked as if I had got them up."

"And haven't you?"

"No. I've had nothing to do with them. Mr. Brandreth spoke to me about them a week ago, and I was foolish enough to go round with Mrs. Munger to collect public opinion about her invited dance and supper; and now it appears that I have invented the whole affair."

"I certainly got that impression," said the doctor, with a laugh lurking under his gravity.

"Well, it's simply atrocious," said Annie. "I've nothing at all to do with either. I don't even know that I approve of their object."

"Their object?"

"Yes. The Social Union."

"Oh! Oh yes. I had forgot about the object," and now the doctor laughed outright.

"It seems to have dropped into the background with everybody," said Annie, laughing too.

"You like the unconventionality of South Hatboro'?" suggested the doctor, after a little silence.

"Oh, very much," said Annie. "I was used to the same thing abroad. It might be an American colony anywhere on the Continent."

"I suppose," said the doctor musingly, "that the same conditions of sojourn and disoccupation *would* produce the same social effects anywhere. Then you must feel quite at home in South Hatboro'!"

"Quite! It's what I came back to avoid. I was sick of the life over there, and I wanted to be of some use here, instead of wasting all my days."

She stopped, resolved not to go on if he took this lightly, but the doctor answered her with sufficient gravity: "Well?"

"It seemed to me that if I could be of any use in the world anywhere, I could in the place where I was born, and where my whole childhood was spent. I've been at home a month now, the most useless person in Hatboro'. I did catch at the first thing that offered—at Mr. Brandreth and his ridiculous Social Union and theatricals, and brought all this trouble on myself. I talked to Mr. Peck about them. You know what his views are?"

"Only from Putney's talk," said the doctor.

"He didn't merely disapprove of the dance and supper, but he had some very peculiar notions about the relations of the different classes in general," said Annie; and this was the point she had meant circuitously to lead up to when she began to speak of South Hatboro', though she theoretically despised all sorts of feminine indirectness.

"Yes?" said the doctor. "What notions?"

"Well, he thinks that if you have money, you *can't* do good with it."

"That's rather odd," said Dr. Morrell.

"I don't state it quite fairly. He meant that you can't make any kindness with it between yourself and the—the poor."

"That's odd too."

"Yes," said Annie anxiously. "You can impose an obligation, he says, but you can't create sympathy. Of course Ralph exaggerates what I said about him in connection with the invited dance and supper, though I don't justify what I did say; and if I'd known then, as I do now, what his history had been, I should have been more careful in my talk with him. I should be very sorry to have hurt his feelings, and I suppose people who've come up in that way are sensitive?"

She suggested this, and it was not the reassurance she was seeking to have Dr. Morrell say, "Naturally."

She continued, with an effort: "I'm afraid I didn't respect his sincerity, and I ought to have done that, though I don't at all agree with him on the other points. It seems to me that what he said was shocking, and perfectly—impossible."

"Why, what was it?" asked the doctor.

"He said there could be no real kindness between the rich and poor, because all their experiences of life were different. It amounted to saying that there ought not to *be* any wealth. Don't you think so?"

"Really, I've never thought about it," returned Dr. Morrell. After a moment he asked, "Isn't it rather an abstraction?"

"Don't say that!" said Annie nervously. "It's the *most* concrete thing in the world!"

The doctor laughed with enjoyment of her convulsive emphasis; but she went on: "I don't think life's worth living if you're to be shut up all your days to the intelligence merely of your own class."

"Who said you were?"

"Mr. Peck."

"And what was your inference from the fact? That there oughtn't to be any classes?"

"Of course it won't do to say that. There *must* be social differences. Don't you think so?"

"I don't know," said Dr. Morrell. "I never thought of it in that light before. It's a very curious question." He asked, brightening gaily after a moment of sober pause, "Is that the whole trouble?"

"Isn't it enough?"

"No; I don't think it is. Why didn't you tell him that you didn't want any gratitude?"

"Not *want* any?" she demanded.

"Oh!" said Dr. Morrell, "I didn't know but you thought it was enough to *give*."

Annie believed that he was making fun of her, and she tried to make her resentful silence dignified; but she only answered sadly: "No; it isn't enough for me. Besides, he made me see that you can't give sympathy where you can't receive it."

"Well, that *is* bad," said the doctor, and he laughed again. "Excuse me," he added. "I see the point. But why don't you forget it?"

"Forget it!"

"Yes. If you can't help it, why need you worry about it?"

She gave a kind of gasp of astonishment. "Do you really think that would be right?" She edged a little away from Dr. Morrell, as if with distrust.

"Well, no; I can't say that I do," he returned thoughtfully, without seeming to have noticed her withdrawal. "I don't suppose I was looking at the moral side. It's rather out of my way to do that. If a physician let himself get into the habit of doing that, he might regard nine-tenths of the diseases he has to treat as just penalties, and decline to interfere."

She fancied that he was amused again, rather than deeply concerned, and she determined to make him own his personal complicity in the matter if she could. "Then you *do* feel sympathy with your patients? You find it necessary to do so?"

The doctor thought a moment. "I take an interest in their diseases."

"But you want them to get well?"

"Oh, certainly. I'm bound to do all I can for them as a physician."

"Nothing more?"

"Yes; I'm sorry for them—for their families, if it seems to be going badly with them."

"And—and as—as—Don't you care at all for your work as a part of what every one ought to do for others—as humanity, philan—" She stopped the offensive word.

"Well, I can't say that I've looked at it in that light exactly," he answered. "I suspect I'm not very good at generalising my own relations to others, though I like well enough to speculate in the abstract. But don't you think Mr. Peck has overlooked one important fact in his theory? What about the people who have grown rich from being poor, as most Americans have? They have the same experiences, and why can't they sympathise with those who have remained poor?"

"I never thought of that. Why didn't I ask him that?" She lamented so sincerely that the doctor laughed again. "I think that Mr. Peck—"

"Oh no! oh no!" said the doctor, in an entreating, coaxing tone, expressive of a satiety with the subject that he might very well have felt; and he ended with another laugh, in which, after a moment of indignant self-question, she joined him.

"Isn't that delicious?" he exclaimed; and she involuntarily slowed her pace with his.

The spicy scent of sweet-currant blossoms hung in the dewy air that wrapped one of the darkened village houses. From a syringa bush before another, as they moved on, a denser perfume stole out with the wild song of a cat-bird hidden in it; the music and the odour seemed braided together. The shadows of the trees cast by the electrics on the walks were so thick and black that they looked palpable; it seemed as if she could stoop down and lift them from the ground. A broad bath of moonlight washed one of the house fronts, and the white-painted clapboards looked wet with it.

They talked of these things, of themselves, and of their own traits and peculiarities; and at her door they ended far from Mr. Peck and all the perplexities he had suggested.

She had told Dr. Morrell of some things she had brought home with her, and had said she hoped he would find time to come and see them. It would have been stiff not to do it, and she believed she had done it in a very off-hand, business-like way. But she continued to question whether she had.

Chapter XIV

[In spite of Mr. Peck's views, which she is unable to combat in her own mind, Annie throws herself into plans for the theatricals for the benefit of the Social Union. Her zeal for "doing good" received a rebuff, however, when one of the poor children she sent to the seashore, without Dr. Morrell's recommendation,

died. Because of this unfortunate experience, as well as because of her unre-
solved thoughts on Social Union, Annie, in the following chapter, summons
Peck to her home for a conversation. In his stark way, Peck expresses the
Christian-socialism of Howells himself. Neither the voice of Peck nor that of
Putney is heeded by Annie, however. The former finally drifts away from
Hatboro' and the latter wastes himself in drink. Annie at last gives up "doing
good" beyond the good which she can accomplish as the wife of Dr. Morrell.]

It was in her revulsion from the direct beneficence which had
proved so dangerous that Annie was able to give herself to the
more general interests of the Social Union. She had not the
courage to test her influence for it among the workpeople whom
it was to entertain and elevate, and whose co-operation Mr.
Peck had thought important; but she went about among the
other classes, and found a degree of favour and deference which
surprised her, and an ignorance of what lay so heavy on her
heart which was still more comforting. She was nowhere
treated as the guilty wretch she called herself; some who knew of
the facts had got them wrong; and she discovered what must
always astonish the inquirer below the pretentious surface of our
democracy—an indifference and an incredulity concerning the
feelings of people of lower station which could not be surpassed
in another civilisation. Her concern for Mrs. Savor was treated
as a great trial for Miss Kilburn; but the mother's bereavement
was regarded as something those people were used to, and got
over more easily than one could imagine.

Annie's mission took her to the ministers of the various denominations, and she was able to overcome any scruples they
might have about the theatricals by urging the excellence of
their object. As a Unitarian, she was not prepared for the
liberality with which the matter was considered; the Episcopalians of course were with her; but the Universalist minister
himself was not more friendly than the young Methodist
preacher, who volunteered to call with her on the pastor of the
Baptist church, and help present the affair in the right light; she
had expected a degree of narrow-mindedness, of bigotry, which
her sect learned to attribute to others in the militant period before they had imbibed so much of its own tolerance.

But the recollection of what had passed with Mr. Peck remained a reproach in her mind, and nothing that she accomplished for the Social Union with the other ministers was important. In her vivid reveries she often met him, and combated his peculiar ideas, while she admitted a wrong in her own position, and made every expression of regret, and parted from him on the best terms, esteemed and complimented in high degree; in reality she saw him seldom, and still more rarely spoke to him, and then with a distance and consciousness altogether different from the effects dramatised in her fancy. Sometimes during the period of her interest in the sick children of the hands, she saw him in their houses, or coming and going outside; but she had no chance to speak with him, or else said to herself that she had none, because she was ashamed before him. She thought he avoided her; but this was probably only a phase of the impersonality which seemed characteristic of him in everything. At these times she felt a strange pathos in the lonely man whom she knew to be at odds with many of his own people, and she longed to interpret herself more sympathetically to him, but actually confronted with him she was sensible of something cold and even hard in the nimbus her compassion cast about him. Yet even this added to the mystery that piqued her, and that loosed her fancy to play, as soon as they parted, in conjecture about his past life, his marriage, and the mad wife who had left him with the child he seemed so ill-fitted to care for. Then, the next time they met she was abashed with the recollection of having unwarrantably romanced the plain, simple, homely little man, and she added an embarrassment of her own to that shyness of his which kept them apart.

Except for what she had heard Putney say, and what she learned casually from the people themselves, she could not have believed he ever did anything for them. He came and went so elusively, as far as Annie was concerned, that she knew of his presence in the houses of sickness and death usually by his little girl, whom she found playing about in the street before the door with the children of the hands. She seemed to hold her own among the others in their plays and their squabbles; if she tried to make up to her, Idella smiled, but she would not be approached, and Annie's heart went out to the little mischief in as helpless goodwill as toward the minister himself.

She used to hear his voice through the summer-open windows when he called upon the Boltons, and wondered if some accident would not bring them together, but she had to send for Mrs. Bolton at last, and bid her tell Mr. Peck that she would like to see him before he went away, one night. He came, and then she began a parrying parley of preliminary nothings before she could say that she supposed he knew the ladies were going on with their scheme for the establishment of the Social Union; he admitted vaguely that he had heard something to that effect, and she added that the invited dance and supper had been given up.

He remained apparently indifferent to the fact, and she hurried on: "And I ought to say, Mr. Peck, that nearly every one—every one whose opinion you would value—agreed with you that it would have been extremely ill-advised, and—and shocking. And I'm quite ashamed that I should not have seen it from the beginning; and I hope—I hope you will forgive me if I said things in my—my excitement that must have—I mean not only what I said to you, but what I said to others; and I assure you that I regret them, and—"

She went on and repeated herself at length, and he listened patiently, but as if the matter had not really concerned either of them personally. She had to conclude that what she had said of him had not reached him, and she ended by confessing that she had clung to the Social Union project because it seemed the only thing in which her attempts to do good were not mischievous.

Mr. Peck's thin face kindled with a friendlier interest than it had shown while the question at all related to himself, and a light of something that she took for humorous compassion came into his large, pale blue eyes. At least it was intelligence; and perhaps the woman nature craves this as much as it is supposed to crave sympathy; perhaps the two are finally one.

"I want to tell you something, Mr. Peck—an experience of mine," she said abruptly, and without trying to connect it ob-

viously with what had gone before, she told him the story of her
ill-fated beneficience to the Savors. He listened intently, and at
the end he said: "I understand. But that is sorrow you have
caused, not evil; and what we intend in goodwill must not rest a
burden on the conscience, no matter how it turns out. Otherwise the moral world is no better than a crazy dream, without
plan or sequence. You might as well rejoice in an evil deed because good happened to come of it."

"Oh, I *thank* you!" she gasped. "You don't know what a
load you have lifted from me!"

Her words feebly expressed the sense of deliverance which
overflowed her heart. Her strength failed her like that of a person suddenly relieved from some great physical stress or peril;
but she felt that he had given her the truth, and she held fast by
it while she went on.

"If you knew, or if any one knew, how difficult it is, what a
responsibility, to do the least thing for others! And once it
seemed so simple! And it seems all the more difficult, the more
means you have for doing good. The poor people seem to help
one another without doing any harm, but if *I* try it—"

"Yes," said the minister, "it is difficult to help others when
we cease to need help ourselves. A man begins poor, or his
father or grandfather before him—it doesn't matter how far
back he begins—and then he is in accord and full understanding
with all the other poor in the world; but as he prospers he withdraws from them and loses their point of view. Then when he
offers help, it is not as a brother of those who need it, but a
patron, an agent of the false state of things in which want is
possible; and his help is not an impulse of the love that ought to
bind us all together, but a compromise proposed by iniquitous
social conditions, a peace-offering to his own guilty consciousness of his share in the wrong."

"Yes," said Annie, too grateful for the comfort he had given
her to question words whose full purport had not perhaps
reached her. "And I assure you, Mr. Peck, I feel very differently
about these things since I first talked with you. And I wish to
tell you, in justice to myself, that I had no idea then that—that—

you were speaking from your own experience when you—you said how working people looked at things. I didn't know that you had been—that is, that—"

"Yes," said the minister, coming to her relief, "I once worked in a cotton-mill. Then," he continued, dismissing the personal concern, "it seems to me that I saw things in their right light, as I have never been able to see them since—"

"And how brutal," she broke in, "how cruel and vulgar, what I said must have seemed to you!"

"I fancied," he continued evasively, "that I had authority to set myself apart from my fellow-workmen, to be a teacher and guide to the true life. But it was a great error. The true life was the life of work, and no one ever had authority to turn from it. Christ Himself came as a labouring man."

"That is true," said Annie; and his words transfigured the man who spoke them, so that her heart turned reverently toward him. "But if you had been meant to work in a mill all your life," she pursued, "would you have been given the powers you have, and that you have just used to save me from despair?"

The minister rose, and said, with a sigh: "No one was meant to work in a mill all his life. Good night."

She would have liked to keep him longer, but she could not think how, at once. As he turned to go out through the Boltons' part of the house, "Won't you go out through my door?" she asked, with a helpless effort at hospitality.

"Oh, if you wish," he answered submissively.

When she had closed the door upon him she went to speak with Mrs. Bolton. She was in the kitchen mixing flour to make bread, and Annie traced her by following the lamp-light through the open door. It discovered Bolton sitting in the outer doorway, his back against one jamb and his stocking-feet resting against the base of the other.

"Mrs. Bolton," Annie began at once, making herself free of one of the hard kitchen chairs, "how is Mr. Peck getting on in Hatboro'?"

"I d'know as I know just what you mean, Miss Kilburn," said Mrs. Bolton, on the defensive.

"I mean, is there a party against him in his church? Is he unpopular?"

Mrs. Bolton took some flour and sprinkled it on her bread-board; then she lifted the mass of dough out of the trough before her, and let it sink softly upon the board.

"I d'know as you can say he's unpoplah. He ain't poplah with some. Yes, there's a party—the Gerrish party."

"Is it a strong one?"

"It's pretty strong."

"Do you think it will prevail?"

"Well, most o' folks don't know *what* they want; and if there's some folks that know what they *don't* want, they can generally keep from havin' it."

Bolton made a soft husky prefatory noise of protest in his throat, which seemed to stimulate his wife to a more definite assertion, and she cut in before he could speak—

"*I* should say that unless them that stood Mr. Peck's friends first off, and got him here, done something to keep him, his enemies wa'n't goin' to take up his cause."

Annie divined a personal reproach for Bolton in the apparent abstraction.

"Oh, now, you'll see it'll all come out right in the end, Pauliny," he mildly opposed. "There ain't any such great feelin' about Mr. Peck; nothin' but what'll work itself off perfec'ly natural, give it time. It's goin' to come out all right."

"Yes, at the day o' jedgment," Mrs. Bolton assented, plunging her fists into the dough, and beginning to work a contempt for her husband's optimism into it.

"Yes, an' a good deal before," he returned. "There's always somethin' to objec' to every minister; we ain't any of us perfect, and Mr. Peck's got his failin's; he hain't built up the church quite so much as some on 'em expected but what he would; and there's some that don't like his prayers; and some of 'em thinks he ain't doctrinal enough. But I guess, take it all round, he suits pretty well. It'll come out all right, Pauliny. You'll see."

A pause ensued, of which Annie felt the awfulness. It seemed to her that Mrs. Bolton's impatience with this intolerable hopefulness must burst violently. She hastened to interpose. "I think the trouble is that people don't fully understand Mr. Peck at first. But they do finally."

"Yes; take time," said Bolton.

"Take eternity, I guess, for some," retorted his wife. "If you think William B. Gerrish is goin' to work round with time—" She stopped for want of some sufficiently rejectional phrase, and did not go on.

"The way I look at it," said Bolton, with incorrigible courage, "is like this: When it comes to anything like askin' Mr. Peck to resign, it'll develop his strength. You can't tell how strong he is without you try to git red of him. I 'most wish it would come, once, fair and square."

"I'm sure you're right, Mr. Bolton," said Annie. "I don't believe that your church would let such a man go when it really came to it. Don't they all feel that he has great ability?"

"Oh, I guess they appreciate him as far forth as ability goes. Some of 'em complains that he's a little *too* intellectual, if anything. But I tell 'em it's a good fault; it's a thing that can be got over in time."

Mrs. Bolton had ceased to take part in the discussion. She finished kneading her dough, and having fitted it into two baking-pans and dusted it with flour, she laid a clean towel over both. But when Annie rose she took the lamp from the mantel-shelf, where it stood, and held it up for her to find her way back to her own door.

Annie went to bed with a spirit lightened as well as chastened, and kept saying over the words of Mr. Peck, so as to keep fast hold of the consolation they had given her. They humbled her with a sense of his wisdom and insight; the thought of them kept her awake. She remembered the tonic that Dr. Morrell had left her, and after questioning whether she really needed it now, she made sure by getting up and taking it.

A MODERN INSTANCE

Chapter XVII

[*Marcia Gaylord, having eloped with her father's young law assistant, Bartley Hubbard, now begins her married life in a Boston lodging house. Except for Ben Halleck, Bartley's wealthy college roommate, the Hubbards are without connections in the big city. Bartley has decided to postpone his study of the law in order to support his wife by reporting for the* Chronicle-Abstract, *a job for which he is in fact better suited, though Marcia urges him to return to law. Our romantic heroine, who set aside the village conventions of Equity, New Hampshire, to throw herself into Bartley's arms, is here discovering that her married life is "inevitably tried by the same sordid tests that every married life is put to," that she too has to struggle with pregnancy, inadequate housing, and small income. In the domestic friction which arises, the differences in her values and Bartley's become apparent. In the following chapter Bartley is beginning his work on the* Chronicle. *See Introduction, pp. cvi–cvii.*]

During several months that followed, Bartley's work consisted of interviewing, of special reporting in all its branches, of correspondence by mail and telegraph from points to which he was sent; his leisure he spent in studying subjects which could be treated like that of the boarding-houses. Marcia entered into his affairs with the keen half-intelligence which characterizes a woman's participation in business; whatever could be divined, she was quickly mistress of; she vividly sympathized with his difficulties and his triumphs; she failed to follow him in matters of political detail, or of general effect; she could not be dispassionate or impartial; his relation to any enterprise was always more important than anything else about it. On some of his missions he took her with him, and then they made it a pleasure excursion; and if they came home late with the material still unwritten, she helped him with his notes, wrote from his dictation, and enabled him to give a fuller report than his rivals. She caught up with amusing aptness the technical terms of the profession, and was voluble about getting in ahead of the Events and the other papers; and she was indignant if any part of his report was cut out or garbled, or any feature was spoiled.

He made a "card" of grouping and treating with picturesque freshness the spring openings of the milliners and dry-goods people; and when he brought his article to Ricker, the editor ran it over, and said, "Guess you took your wife with you, Hubbard."

"Yes, I did," Bartley owned. He was always proud of her looks, and it flattered him that Ricker should see the evidences of her feminine taste and knowledge in his account of the bonnets and dress goods. "You don't suppose I could get at all these things by inspiration, do you?"

Marcia was already known to some of his friends whom he had introduced to her in casual encounters. They were mostly unmarried, or if married they lived at a distance, and they did not visit the Hubbards at their lodgings. Marcia was a little shy, and did not quite know whether they ought to call without being asked, or whether she ought to ask them; besides, Mrs. Nash's reception-room was not always at her disposal, and she would not have liked to take them all the way up to her own room. Her social life was therefore confined to the public places where she met these friends of her husband's. They sometimes happened together at a restaurant, or saw one another between the acts at the theatre, or on coming out of a concert. Marcia was not so much admired for her conversation by her acquaintance, as for her beauty and her style; a rustic reluctance still lingered in her; she was thin and dry in her talk with any one but Bartley, and she could not help letting even men perceive that she was uneasy when they interested him in matters foreign to her.

Bartley did not see why they could not have some of these fellows up in their room for tea; but Marcia told him it was impossible. In fact, although she willingly lived this irregular life with him, she was at heart not at all a Bohemian. She did not like being in lodgings or dining at restaurants; on their horse-car excursions into the suburbs, when the spring opened, she was always choosing this or that little house as the place where she would like to live, and wondering if it were within their means. She said she would gladly do all the work herself; she hated to be idle so much as she now must. The city's novelty wore off for her sooner than for him; the concerts, the lectures, the theatres, had already lost their zest for her, and she went because he wished her to go, or in order to be able to help him with what he was always writing about such things.

As the spring advanced, Bartley conceived the plan of a local study, something in the manner of the boarding-house article, but on a much vaster scale: he proposed to Ricker a timely series on the easily accessible hot-weather resorts, to be called "Boston's Breathing-Places," and to relate mainly to the seaside hotels and their surroundings. His idea was encouraged, and he took Marcia with him on most of his expeditions for its realization. These were largely made before the regular season had well begun; but the boats were already running, and the hotels were open, and they were treated with the hospitality which a knowledge of Bartley's mission must invoke. As he said, it was a matter of business, give and take on both sides, and the landlords took more than they gave in any such trade.

On her part Marcia regarded dead-heading as a just and legitimate privilege of the press, if not one of its chief attributes; and these passes on boats and trains, this system of paying hotel-bills by the presentation of a card, constituted distinguished and honorable recognition from the public. To her simple experience, when Bartley told how magnificently the reporters had been accommodated, at some civic or commerical or professional banquet, with a table of their own, where they were served with all the wines and courses, he seemed to have been one of the principal guests, and her fear was that his head should be turned by his honors. But at the bottom of her heart, though she enjoyed the brilliancy of Bartley's present life, she did not think his occupation comparable to the law in dignity. Bartley called himself a journalist now, but his newspaper connection still identified him in her mind with those country editors of whom she had always heard her father speak with such contempt: men dedicated to poverty and the despite of all the local notables who used them. She could not shake off the old feeling of degradation, even when she heard Bartley and some of his fellow-journalists talking in their boastfulest vein of the sovereign character of journalism; and she secretly resolved never to relinquish her purpose of having him a lawyer. Till he was fairly this, in regular and prosperous practice, she knew that she should not have shown her father that she was right in marrying Bartley.

In the mean time their life went ignorantly on in the obscure channels where their isolation from society kept it longer than was natural. Three or four months after they came to Boston, they were still country people, with scarcely any knowledge of the distinctions and differences so important to the various worlds of any city. So far from knowing that they must not walk in the Common, they used to sit down on a bench there, in the pleasant weather, and watch the opening of the spring, among the lovers whose passion had a publicity that neither surprised nor shocked them. After they were a little more enlightened, they resorted to the Public Garden, where they admired the bridge, and the rock-work, and the statues. Bartley, who was already beginning to get up a taste for art, boldly stopped and praised the Venus, in the presence of the gardeners planting tulip-bulbs.

They went sometimes to the Museum of Fine Arts, where they found a pleasure in the worst things which the best never afterwards gave them; and where she became as hungry and tired as if it were the Vatican. They had a pride in taking books out of the Public Library, where they walked about on tiptoe with bated breath; and they thought it a divine treat to hear the Great Organ play at noon. As they sat there in the Music Hall, and let the mighty instrument bellow over their strong young nerves, Bartley whispered Marcia the jokes he had heard about the organ; and then, upon the wave of aristocratic sensation from this experience, they went out and dined at Copeland's, or Weber's, or Fera's, or even at Parker's: they had long since forsaken the humble restaurant with its doilies and its ponderous crockery, and they had so mastered the art of ordering that they

could manage a dinner as cheaply at these finer places as anywhere, especially if Marcia pretended not to care much for her
half of the portion, and connived at its transfer to Bartley's
plate.

In his hours of leisure, they were so perpetually together that
it became a joke with the men who knew them to say, when
asked if Bartley were married, "Very *much* married." It was not
wholly their inseparableness that gave the impression of this
extreme conjugality; as I said, Marcia's uneasiness when others
interested Bartley in things alien to her made itself felt even by
these men. She struggled against it because she did not wish to
put him to shame before them, and often with an aching sense
of desolation she sent him off with them to talk apart, or left
him with them if they met on the street, and walked home
alone, rather than let any one say that she kept her husband
tied to her apron-strings. His club, after the first sense of its
splendor and usefulness wore away, was an ordeal; she had
failed to conceal that she thought the initiation and annual fees
extravagant. She knew no other bliss like having Bartley sit
down in their own room with her; it did not matter whether
they talked; if he were busy, she would as lief sit and sew, or sit
and silently look at him as he wrote. In these moments she
liked to feign that she had lost him, that they had never been
married, and then come back with a rush of joy to the reality.
But on his club nights she heroically sent him off, and spent the
evening with Mrs. Nash. Sometimes she went out by day with
the landlady, who had a passion for auctions and cemeteries,
and who led Marcia to an intimate acquaintance with such
pleasures. At Mount Auburn, Marcia liked the marble lambs,
and the emblematic hands pointing upward with the dexter
finger, and the infants carved in stone, and the angels with
folded wings and lifted eyes, better than the casts which Bartley
said were from the antique, in the Museum; on this side her mind
was as wholly dormant as that of Mrs. Nash herself. She always
came home feeling as if she had not seen Bartley for a year, and
fearful that something had happened to him.

The hardest thing about their irregular life was that he must sometimes be gone two or three days at a time, when he could not take her with him. Then it seemed to her that she could not draw a full breath in his absence; and once he found her almost wild on his return: she had begun to fancy that he was never coming back again. He laughed at her when she betrayed her secret, but she was not ashamed; and when he asked her, "Well, what if I hadn't come back?" she answered passionately, "It wouldn't have made much difference to me: I should not have lived."

The uncertainty of his income was another cause of anguish to her. At times he earned forty or fifty dollars a week; oftener he earned ten; there was now and then a week when everything that he put his hand to failed, and he earned nothing at all. Then Marcia despaired; her frugality became a mania, and they had quarrels about what she called his extravagance. She embittered his daily bread by blaming him for what he spent on it; she wore her oldest dresses, and would have had him go shabby in token of their adversity. Her economies were frantic child's play,— methodless, inexperienced, fitful; and they were apt to be followed by remorse in which she abetted him in some wanton excess.

The future of any heroic action is difficult to manage; and the sublime sacrifice of her pride and all the conventional proprieties which Marcia had made in giving herself to Bartley was inevitably tried by the same sordid tests that every married life is put to.

That salaried place which he was always seeking on the staff of some newspaper, proved not so easy to get as he had imagined in the flush of his first successes. Ricker willingly included him among the Chronicle-Abstract's own correspondents and special reporters; and he held the same off-and-on relation to several other papers; but he remained without a more definite position. He earned perhaps more money than a salary would have given him, and in their way of living he and Marcia laid up something out of what he earned. But it did not seem to her that he exerted himself to get a salaried place; she was sure that, if so many others who could not write half so well had places, he might get one if he only kept trying. Bartley laughed at these business-turns of Marcia's as he called them; but sometimes they enraged him, and he had days of sullen resentment when he resisted all her advances towards reconciliation. But he kept hard at work, and he always owned at last how disinterested her most ridiculous alarm had been.

Once, when they had been talking as usual about that permanent place on some newspaper, she said, "But I should only want that to be temporary, if you got it. I want you should go on with the law, Bartley. I've been thinking about that. I don't want you should always be a journalist."

Bartley smiled. "What could I do for a living, I should like to know, while I was studying law?"

"You could do some newspaper work,—enough to support us,—while you were studying. You said when we first came to Boston that you should settle down to the law."

"I hadn't got my eyes open, then. I've got a good deal longer row to hoe than I supposed, before I can settle down to the law."

"Father said you didn't need to study but a little more."

"Not if I were going into the practice at Equity. But it's a very different thing, I can tell you, in Boston: I should have to go in for a course in the Harvard Law School, just for a little start-off."

Marcia was silenced, but she asked, after a moment, "Then you're going to give up the law, altogether?"

"I don't know what I'm going to do; I'm going to do the best I can for the present, and trust to luck. I don't like special reporting, for a finality; but I shouldn't like shystering, either."

"What's shystering?" asked Marcia.

"It's pettifogging in the city courts. Wait till I can get my basis,—till I have a fixed amount of money for a fixed amount of work,—and then I'll talk to you about taking up the law again. I'm willing to do it whenever it seems the right thing. I guess I should like it, though I don't see why it's any better than journalism, and I don't believe it has any more prizes."

"But you've been a long time trying to get your basis on a newspaper," she reasoned. "Why don't you try to get it in some other way? Why don't you try to get a clerk's place with some lawyer?"

"Well, suppose I was willing to starve along in that way, how should I go about to get such a place?" demanded Bartley, with impatience.

"Why don't you go to that Mr. Halleck you visited here? You used to tell me he was going to be a lawyer."

"Well, if you remember so distinctly what I said about going into the law when I first came to Boston," said her husband angrily, "perhaps you'll remember that I said I shouldn't go to Halleck until I didn't need his help. I shall not go to him *for* his help."

Marcia gave way to spiteful tears. "It seems as if you were ashamed to let them know that you were in town. Are you afraid I shall want to get acquainted with them? Do you suppose I shall want to go to their parties, and disgrace you?"

Bartley took his cigar out of his mouth, and looked blackly at her. "So, that's what you've been thinking, is it?"

She threw herself upon his neck. "No! no, it isn't!" she cried, hysterically. "You know that I never thought it till this instant; you know I didn't think it at all; I just *said* it. My nerves are all gone; I don't know *what* I'm saying half the time, and you're as strict with me as if I were as well as ever! I may as well take off my things,—I'm not well enough to go with you, to-day, Bartley."

She had been dressing while they talked for an entertainment which Bartley was going to report for the Chronicle-Abstract; and now she made a feint of wishing to remove her hat. He would not let her. He said that if she did not go, he should not; he reproached her with not wishing to go with him any more; he coaxed her laughingly and fondly.

"It's only because I'm not so strong, now," she said in a whisper that ended in a kiss on his cheek. "You must walk very slowly, and not hurry me."

The entertainment was to be given in aid of the Indigent Children's Surf-Bathing Society, and it was at the end of June, rather late in the season. But the society itself was an afterthought, not conceived till a great many people had left town on whose assistance such a charity must largely depend. Strenuous appeals had been made, however: it was represented that ten thousand poor children could be transported to Nantasket Beach, and there, as one of the ladies on the committee said, bathed, clam-baked, and lemonaded three times during the summer at a cost so small that it was a saving to spend the money. Class Day falling about the same time, many exiles at Newport and on the North Shore came up and down; and the affair promised to be one of social distinction, if not pecuniary success. The entertainment was to be varied; a distinguished poet was to read an old poem of his, and a distinguished poetess was to read a new poem of hers; some professional people were to follow with comic singing; an elocutionist was to give impressions of noted public speakers; and a number of vocal and instrumental amateurs were to contribute their talent.

Bartley had instructions from Ricker to see that his report was very full socially. "We want something lively, and at the same time nice and tasteful, about the whole thing, and I guess you're the man to do it. Get Mrs. Hubbard to go with you, and keep you from making a fool of yourself about the costumes." He gave Bartley two tickets. "Mighty hard to get, I can tell you, for *love* or money,—especially love," he said; and Bartley made much of this difficulty in impressing Marcia's imagination with the uncommon character of the occasion. She had put on a new dress which she had just finished for herself, and which was a marvel not only of cheapness, but of elegance; she had plagiarized the idea from the costume of a lady with whom she stopped to look in at a milliner's window where she formed the notion of her bonnet. But Marcia had imagined the things anew in relation to herself, and made them her own; when Bartley first saw her in them, though he had witnessed their growth from the germ, he said that he was afraid of her, she was so splendid, and he did not quite know whether he felt acquainted. When they were seated at the concert, and had time to look about them, he whispered, "Well, Marsh, I don't see anything here that comes near you in style," and she flung a little corner of her drapery out over his hand so that she could squeeze it: she was quite happy again.

After the concert, Bartley left her for a moment and went up to a group of the committee near the platform, to get some points for his report. He spoke to one of the gentlemen, note-book and pencil in hand, and the gentleman referred him to one of the ladies of the committee, who, after a moment of hesitation, demanded in a rich tone of injury and surprise, "Why! Isn't this Mr. Hubbard?" and, indignantly answering herself, "Of *course* it is!" gave her hand with a sort of dramatic cordiality, and flooded him with questions: "When did you come to Boston? Are you at the Hallecks'? Did you come— Or no, you're *not* Harvard. You're not *living* in Boston? And what in the world are *you* getting items for? Mr. Hubbard, Mr. Atherton."

She introduced him in a breathless climax to the gentleman to whom he had first spoken, and who had listened to her attack on Bartley with a smile which he was at no trouble to hide from her. "Which question are you going to answer first, Mr. Hubbard?" he asked quietly, while his eyes searched Bartley's for an instant with inquiry which was at once kind and keen. His face had the distinction which comes of being clean-shaven in our bearded times.

"Oh, the last," said Bartley. "I'm reporting the concert for the Chronicle-Abstract, and I want to interview some one in authority about it."

"Then interview *me*, Mr. Hubbard," cried the young lady. "*I'm* in authority about this affair,—it's my own invention, as the White Knight says,—and then I'll interview you afterward. And you've gone into journalism, like all the Harvard men! So glad it's you, for you can be a perfect godsend to the cause if you will. The entertainment hasn't given us all the money we shall want, by any means, and we shall need all the help the press can give us. Ask me any questions you please, Mr. Hubbard: there isn't a soul here that I wouldn't sacrifice to the last personal particular, if the press will only do its duty in return. You've no idea how we've been working during the last fortnight since this Old Man of the Sea-Bathing sprang upon us. I was sitting quietly at home, thinking of anything else in the world, I can assure you, when the atrocious idea occurred to me." She ran on to give a full sketch of the inception and history of the scheme up to the present time. Suddenly she arrested herself and Bartley's flying pencil: "Why, you're not putting all that nonsense down?"

"Certainly I am," said Bartley, while Mr. Atherton, with a laugh, turned and walked away to talk with some other ladies. "It's the very thing I want. I shall get in ahead of all the other papers on this; they haven't had anything like it, yet."

She looked at him for a moment in horror. Then, "Well, go on; I would do anything for the cause!" she cried.

"Tell me who's been here, then," said Bartley.

She recoiled a little. "I don't like giving names."

"But I can't say who the people were, unless you do."

"That's true," said the young lady thoughtfully. She prided herself on her thoughtfulness, which sometimes came before and sometimes after the fact. "You're not obliged to say who told you?"

"Of course not."

She ran over a list of historical and distinguished names, and he slyly asked if this and that lady were not dressed so, and so, and worked in the costumes from her unconsciously elaborate answers; she was afterwards astonished that he should have known what people had on. Lastly, he asked what the committee expected to do next, and was enabled to enrich his report with many authoritative expressions and intimations. The lady became all zeal in these confidences to the public, at last; she told everything she knew, and a great deal that she merely hoped.

"And now come into the committee-room and have a cup of coffee; I know you must be faint with all this talking," she concluded. "I want to ask you something about yourself." She was not older than Bartley, but she addressed him with the freedom we use in encouraging younger people.

"Thank you," he said coolly; "I can't, very well. I must go back to my wife, and hurry up this report."

"Oh! is Mrs. Hubbard here?" asked the young lady with well-controlled surprise. "Present me to her!" she cried, with that fearlessness of social consequences for which she was noted: she believed there were ways of getting rid of undesirable people without treating them rudely.

The audience had got out of the hall, and Marcia stood alone near one of the doors waiting for Bartley. He glanced proudly toward her, and said, "I shall be very glad."

Miss Kingsbury drifted by his side across the intervening space, and was ready to take Marcia impressively by the hand when she reached her; she had promptly decided her to be very beautiful and elegantly simple in dress, but she found her smaller than she had looked at a distance. Miss Kingsbury was herself rather large,—sometimes, she thought, rather too large: certainly too large if she had not had such perfect command of every inch of herself. In complexion she was richly blonde, with beautiful fair hair roughed over her forehead, as if by a breeze, and apt to escape in sunny tendrils over the peachy tints of her temples. Her features were massive rather than fine; and though she thoroughly admired her chin and respected her mouth, she had doubts about her nose, which she frankly referred to friends for solution: had it not *too* much of a knob at the end? She seemed to tower over Marcia as she took her hand at Bartley's introduction, and expressed her pleasure at meeting her.

"I don't know why it need be such a surprise to find one's gentlemen friends married, but it always is, somehow. I don't think Mr. Hubbard would have known me if I hadn't insisted upon his recognizing me; I can't blame him: it's three years since we met. Do you help him with his reports? I know you do! You *must* make him lenient to our entertainment,—the cause is so good! How long have you been in Boston? Though I don't know why I should ask that,—you may have always been in Boston! One used to know everybody; but the place *is* so large, now. I should like to come and see you; but I'm going out of town tomorrow, for the summer. I'm not really here, now, except *ex officio;* I ought to have been away weeks ago, but this Indigent Surf-Bathing has kept me. You've no idea what such an undertaking is. But you *must* let me have your address, and as soon as I get back to town in the fall, I shall insist upon looking you up. *Good* by! I must run away, now, and leave you; there are a thousand things for me to look after yet to-day." She took Marcia again by the hand, and superadded some bows and nods and smiles of parting, after she released her, but she did not ask her to come into the committee-room and have some coffee; and Bartley took his wife's hand under his arm and went out of the hall.

"Well," he said, with a man's simple pleasure in Miss Kingsbury's friendliness to his wife, "that's the girl I used to tell you about,—the rich one with the money in her own right, whom I met at the Hallecks'. She seemed to think you were about the thing, Marsh! I saw her eyes open as she came up, and I felt awfully proud of you; you never looked half so well. But why didn't you *say* something?"

"She didn't give me any chance," said Marcia, "and I had nothing to say, anyway. I thought she was very disagreeable."

"Disagreeable!" repeated Bartley in amaze.

Miss Kingsbury went back to the committee-room, where one of the amateurs had been lecturing upon her: "Clara Kingsbury can say and do, from the best heart in the world, more offensive things in ten minutes than malice could invent in a week. Somebody ought to go out and drag her away from that reporter by main force. But I presume it's too late already; she's had time to destroy us all. You'll see that there won't be a shred left of us in *his* paper at any rate. Really, I wonder that, in a city full of nervous and exasperated people like Boston, Clara Kingsbury has been suffered to live. She throws her whole soul into everything she undertakes, and she has gone so *en masse* into this Indigent Bathing, and splashed about in it so, that *I* can't understand how we got anybody to come to-day. Why, I haven't the least doubt that she's offered that poor man a ticket to go down to Nantasket and bathe with the other Indigents; she's treated *me* as if I ought to be personally surf-bathed for the last fortnight; and if there's any chance for us left by her tactlessness, you may be sure she's gone at it with her conscience and simply swept it off the face of the earth."

Chapter XXIV

[*Bartley Hubbard has now become assistant managing editor of the* Events, *at a salary of thirty dollars a week, having assured the editor, Mr. Witherby, that he concurs with his belief that the interests of advertisers should be supported by the editors. After the birth of Flavia, Bartley and Marcia see less of each other by day, and disagree more openly at home in the evening. The Hallecks, old friends of Bartley whom he now considers bores, become a constant source of argument, for Ben Halleck and his two sisters are the only friends that Marcia has found in her new surroundings. At the opening of the following chapter, Marcia has locked her door, after another family altercation, and Bartley has walked out of their apartment. Bartley's adventures during the night not only show the reader his character but also give a clear interpretation of Howells' own attitude toward newspaper ethics.*]

Bartley walked about the streets for a long time, without purpose or direction, brooding fiercely on his wrongs, and reminding himself how Marcia had determined to have him, and had indeed flung herself upon his mercy, with all sorts of good promises; and had then at once taken the whip-hand, and goaded and tormented him ever since. All the kindness of their common life counted for nothing in this furious reverie, or rather it was never once thought of; he cursed himself for a fool that he had ever asked her to marry him, and for doubly a fool that he had married her when she had as good as asked him. He was glad, now, that he had taunted her with that; he only regretted that he had told her he was sorry. He was presently aware of being so tired that he could scarcely pull one leg after another; and yet he felt hopelessly wide awake. It was in simple despair of anything else to do that he climbed the stairs to Ricker's lofty perch in the Chronicle-Abstract office. Ricker turned about as he entered, and stared up at him from beneath the green pasteboard visor with which he was shielding his eyes from the gas; his hair, which was of the harshness and color of hay, was stiffly poked up and strewn about on his skull, as if it were some foreign product.

"Hello!" he said, "Going to issue a morning edition of the Events?"

"What makes you think so?"

"Oh, I supposed you evening-paper gents went to bed with the hens. What has kept you up, esteemed contemporary?" He went on working over some despatches which lay upon his table.

"Don't you want to come out and have some oysters?" asked Bartley.

"Why this princely hospitality? I'll come with you in half a minute," Ricker said, going to the slide that carried up the copy to the composing-room and thrusting his manuscript into the box.

"Where are you going?" he asked, when they found themselves out in the soft starlit autumnal air; and Bartley answered with the name of an oyster-house, obscure, but of singular excellence.

"Yes, that's the best place," Ricker commented. "What I always wonder at in you is the rapidity with which you've taken on the city. You were quite in the green wood when you came here, and now you know your Boston like a little man. I suppose it's your newspaper work that's familiarized you with the place. Well, how do you like your friend Witherby, as far as you've gone?"

"Oh, we shall get along, I guess," said Bartley. "He still keeps me in the background, and plays at being editor, but he pays me pretty well."

"Not too well, I hope."

"I should like to see him try it."

"I shouldn't," said Ricker. "He'd expect certain things of you, if he did. You'll have to look out for Witherby."

"You mean that he's a scamp?"

"No; there isn't a better conscience than Witherby carries in the whole city. He's perfectly honest. He not only believes that he has a right to run the Events in his way; but he sincerely believes that he is right in doing it. There's where he has the advantage of you, if you doubt him. I don't suppose he ever did a wrong thing in his life; he'd persuade himself that the thing was right before he did it."

"That's a common phenomenon, isn't it?" sneered Bartley. "Nobody sins."

"You're right, partly. But some of us sinners have our misgivings, and Witherby never has. You know he offered me your place?"

"No, I didn't," said Bartley, astonished and not pleased.

"I thought he might have told you. He made me inducements; but I was afraid of him: Witherby is the counting-room incarnate. I talked you into him for some place or other; but he didn't seem to wake up to the value of my advice at once. Then I couldn't tell what he was going to offer you."

"Thank you for letting me in for a thing you were afraid of!"

"I didn't believe he would get you under his thumb, as he would me. You've got more back-bone than I have. I have to keep out of temptation; you have noticed that I never drink, and I would rather not look upon Witherby when he is red and giveth his color in the cup. I'm sorry if I've let you in for anything that you regret. But Witherby's sincerity makes him dangerous,—I own that."

"I think he has some very good ideas about newspapers," said Bartley, rather sulkily.

"Oh, very," assented Ricker. "Some of the very best going. He believes that the press is a great moral engine, and that it ought to be run in the interest of the engineer."

"And I suppose you believe that it ought to be run in the interest of the public?"

"Exactly—after the public has paid."

"Well, I don't; and I never did. A newspaper is a private enterprise."

"It's private property, but it isn't a private enterprise, and in its very nature it can't be. You know I never talk 'journalism' and stuff; it amuses me to hear the young fellows at it, though I think they might be doing something worse than magnifying their office; they might be decrying it. But I've got a few ideas and principles of my own in my back pantaloons pocket."

"Haul them out," said Bartley.

"I don't know that they're very well formulated," returned Ricker, "and I don't contend that they're very new. But I con-

sider a newspaper a public enterprise, with certain distinct duties
to the public. It's sacredly bound not to do anything to deprave
or debauch its readers; and it's sacredly bound not to mislead
or betray them, not merely as to questions of morals and politics,
but as the questions of what we may lump as 'advertising.'
Has friend Witherby developed his great ideas of advertisers'
rights to you?" Bartley did not answer, and Ricker went on:
"Well, then, you can understand my position, when I say it's
exactly the contrary."

"You ought to be on a religious newspaper, Ricker," said
Bartley with a scornful laugh.

"Thank you, a secular paper is bad enough for me."

"Well, I don't pretend that I made the Events just what I
want," said Bartley. "At present, the most I can do is to indulge
in a few cheap dreams of what I should do, if I had a paper of
my own."

"What are your dreams? Haul out, as you say."

"I should make it pay, to begin with; and I should make it pay
by making it such a thorough newspaper that every class of
people *must* have it. I should cater to the lowest class first, and as
long as I was poor I would have the fullest and best reports of
every local accident and crime; that would take all the rabble.
Then, as I could afford it, I'd rise a little, and give first-class
non-partisan reports of local political affairs; that would fetch
the next largest class, the ward politicians of all parties. I'd
lay for the local religious world, after that;—religion comes
right after politics in the popular mind, and it interests the
women like murder: I'd give the minutest religious intelligence,
and not only that, but the religious gossip, and the religious
scandal. Then I'd go in for fashion and society,—that comes
next. I'd have the most reliable and thorough-going financial
reports that money could buy. When I'd got my local ground
perfectly covered, I'd begin to ramify. Every fellow that could
spell, in any part of the country, should understand that, if he
sent me an account of a suicide, or an elopement, or a murder,
or an accident, he should be well paid for it; and I'd rise on the
same scale through all the departments. I'd add art criticisms,

dramatic and sporting news, and book reviews, more for the looks of the thing than for anything else; they don't any of 'em appeal to a large class. I'd get my paper into such a shape that people of every kind and degree would have to say, no matter what particular objection was made to it, 'Yes, that's so; but it's the best *news*paper in the world, *and we can't get along without it.*'"

"And then," said Ricker, "you'd begin to clean up, little by little,—let up on your murders and scandals, and purge and live cleanly like a gentleman? The trick's been tried before."

They had arrived at the oyster-house, and were sitting at their table, waiting for the oysters to be brought to them. Bartley tilted his chair back. "I don't know about the cleaning up. I should want to keep all my audience. If I cleaned up, the dirty fellows would go off to some one else; and the fellows that pretended to be clean would be disappointed."

"Why don't you get Witherby to put your ideas in force?" asked Ricker, dryly.

Bartley dropped his chair to all fours, and said with a smile, "He belongs to church."

"Ah! he has his limitations. What a pity! He has the money to establish this great moral engine of yours, and you haven't. It's a loss to civilization."

"One thing, I know," said Bartley, with a certain effect of virtue, "nobody should buy or sell me; and the advertising element shouldn't spread beyond the advertising page."

"Isn't that rather high ground?" inquired Ricker.

Bartley did not think it worth while to answer. "I don't believe that a newspaper is obliged to be superior in tone to the community," he said.

"I quite agree with you."

"And if the community is full of vice and crime, the newspaper can't do better than reflect its condition."

"Ah! there I should distinguish, esteemed contemporary. There are several tones in every community, and it will keep any newspaper scratching to rise above the highest. But if it keeps out of the mud at all, it can't help rising above the lowest. And

no community is full of vice and crime any more than it is full
of virtue and good works. Why not let your model newspaper
mirror these?"

"They're not snappy."

"No, that's true."

"You must give the people what they want."

"Are you sure of that?"

"Yes, I am."

"Well, it's a beautiful dream," said Ricker, "nourished on a
youth sublime. Why do not these lofty imaginings visit us
later in life? You make me quite ashamed of my own ideal newspaper. Before you began to talk, I had been fancying that the
vice of our journalism was its intense localism. I have doubted
a good while whether a drunken Irishman who breaks his wife's
head, or a child who falls into a tub of hot water, has really established a claim on the public interest. Why should I be told
by telegraph how three Negroes died on the gallows in North
Carolina? Why should an accurate correspondent inform me of
the elopement of a married man with his maid-servant in East
Machias? Why should I sup on all the horrors of a railroad accident, and have the bleeding fragments hashed up for me at
breakfast? Why should my newspaper give a succession
of shocks to my nervous system, as I pass from column to
column, and poultice me between shocks with the nastiness
of a distant or local scandal? You reply, because I like spice.
But I don't. I am sick of spice; and I believe that most of our
readers are."

"Cater to them with milk-toast, then," said Bartley.

Ricker laughed with him, and they fell to upon their
oysters.

When they parted, Bartley still found himself wakeful. He
knew that he should not sleep if he went home, and he said to
himself that he could not walk about all night. He turned into a
gayly-lighted basement, and asked for something in the way of
a night-cap.

The bar-keeper said there was nothing like a hot-scotch to
make you sleep; and a small man with his hat on, who had been

talking with the bar-keeper, and coming up to the counter occasionally to eat a bit of cracker or a bit of cheese out of the two bowls full of such fragments that stood at the end of the counter, said that this was so.

It was very cheerful in the bar-room, with the light glittering on the rows of decanters behind the bar-keeper, a large, stout, clean, pale man in his shirt-sleeves, after the manner of his kind; and Bartley made up his mind to stay there till he was drowsy, and to drink as many hot-scotches as were necessary to the result. He had his drink put on a little table and sat down to it easily, stirring it to cool it a little, and feeling its flattery in his brain from the first sip.

The man who was munching cheese and crackers wore a hat rather large for him, pulled down over his eyes. He now said that he did not care if he took a gin-sling, and the bar-keeper promptly set it before him on the counter, and saluted with "Good evening, Colonel," a large man who came in, carrying a small dog in his arms. Bartley recognized him as the manager of a variety combination playing at one of the theatres, and the manager recognized the little man with the gin-sling as Tommy. He did not return the bar-keeper's salutation, but he asked, as he sat down at a table, "What do I want for supper, Charley?"

The bar-keeper said, oracularly, as he leaned forward to wipe his counter with a napkin, "Fricassee chicken."

"Fricassee devil," returned the manager. "Get me a Welsh rabbit."

The bar-keeper, unperturbed by this rejection, called into the tube behind him, "One Welsh rabbit."

"I want some cold chicken for my dog," said the manager.

"One cold chicken," repeated the bar-keeper, in his tube.

"White meat," said the manager.

"White meat," repeated the bar-keeper.

"I went into the Parker House one night about midnight, and I saw four doctors there eating lobster salad, and devilled crab, and washing it down with champagne; and I made up my mind that the doctors needn't talk to me any more about what was wholesome. I was going in for what was *good*. And there ain't anything better for supper than Welsh rabbit in *this* world."

As the manager addressed this philosophy to the company at large, no one commented upon it, which seemed quite the same to the manager, who hitched one elbow over the back of his chair, and caressed with the other hand the dog lying in his lap.

The little man in the large hat continued to walk up and down, leaving his gin-sling on the counter, and drinking it between his visits to the cracker and cheese.

"What's that new piece of yours, Colonel?" he asked, after a while. "I ain't seen it yet."

"Legs, principally," sighed the manager. "That's what the public wants. I give the public what it wants. I don't pretend to be any better than the public. Nor any worse," he added, stroking his dog.

These ideas struck Bartley in their accordance with his own ideas of journalism, as he had propounded them to Ricker. He had drunk half of his hot-scotch.

"That's what I say," assented the little man. "All that a theatre has got to do is to keep even with the public."

"That's so, Tommy," said the manager of a school of morals, with wisdom that impressed more and more the manager of a great moral engine.

"The same principle runs through everything," observed Bartley, speaking for the first time.

The drink had stiffened his tongue somewhat, but it did not incommode his utterance; it rather gave dignity to it, and his head was singularly clear. He lifted his empty glass from the table, and, catching the bar-keeper's eye, said, "Do it again." The man brought it back full.

"It runs through the churches as well as the theatres. As long as the public wanted hell-fire, the ministers gave them hell-fire. But you couldn't get hell-fire—not the pure, old-fashioned brimstone article—out of a popular preacher now, for love or money."

The little man said, "I guess you've got about the size of it there;" and the manager laughed.

"It's just so with the newspapers, too," said Bartley. "Some newspapers used to stand out against publishing murders, and personal gossip, and divorce trials. There ain't a newspaper that pretends to keep anyways up with the times, now, that don't do it! The public want spice, and they will have it!"

"Well, sir," said the manager, "that's my way of looking at it. I say, if the public don't want Shakespeare, give 'em burlesque till they're sick of it. I believe in what Grant said: 'The quickest way to get rid of a bad law is to enforce it.'"

"That's so," said the little man, "every time." He added, to the bar-keeper, that he guessed he would have some brandy and soda, and Bartley found himself at the bottom of his second tumbler. He ordered it replenished.

The little man seemed to be getting further away. He said, from the distance to which he had withdrawn, "You want to go to bed with three nightcaps on, like an old-clothes man."

Bartley felt like resenting the freedom, but he was anxious to pour his ideas of journalism into the manager's sympathetic ear, and he began to talk, with an impression that it behooved him to talk fast. His brain was still very clear, but his tongue was getting stiffer. The manager now had his Welsh rabbit before him; but Bartley could not make out how it had got there, nor when. He was talking fast, and he knew, by the way everybody was listening, that he was talking well. Sometimes he left his table, glass in hand, and went and laid down the law to the manager, who smilingly assented to all he said. Once he heard a low growling at his feet, and looking down, he saw the dog with his plate of cold chicken, that had also been conjured into the room somehow.

"Look out," said the manager, "he'll nip you in the leg."

"Curse the dog! he seems to be on all sides of you," said Bartley. "I can't stand anywhere."

"Better sit down, then," suggested the manager.

"Good idea," said the little man, who was still walking up and down. It appeared as if he had not spoken for several hours; his hat was further over his eyes. Bartley had thought he was gone.

"What business is it of yours?" he demanded, fiercely, moving towards the little man.

"Come, none of that," said the bar-keeper, steadily. Bartley looked at him in amazement. "Where's your hat?" he asked.

The others laughed; the bar-keeper smiled.

"Are you a married man?"

"Never mind!" said the bar-keeper, severely.

Bartley turned to the little man: "You married?"

"Not *much*," replied the other. He was now topping off with a whiskey-straight.

Bartley referred himself to the manager: "You?"

"*Pas si bête*," said the manager, who did his own adapting from the French.

"Well, you're scholar, and you're gentleman," said Bartley. The indefinite articles would drop out, in spite of all his efforts to keep them in. " 'N' I want ask you do—to—ask—you—what—would—you—do," he repeated, with painful exactness, but he failed to make the rest of the sentence perfect, and he pronounced it all in a word, " 'fyourwifelockyouout?"

"I'd take a walk," said the manager.

"I'd bu'st the door in," said the little man.

Bartley turned and gazed at him as if the little man were a much more estimable person than he had supposed. He passed his arm through the little man's, which the other had just crooked to lift his whiskey to his mouth. "Look here," said Bartley, "tha's jus' what *I* told her. I want you to go home 'th me; I want t' introduce you to my wife."

"All right," answered the little man. "Don't care if I do." He dropped his tumbler to the floor. "Hang it up, Charley, glass and all. Hang up this gentleman's nightcaps—my account. Gentleman asks me home to his house, I'll hang him—I'll get him hung,—well, fix it to suit yourself,—every time!"

They got themselves out of the door, and the manager said to the bar-keeper, who came round to gather up the fragments of the broken tumbler, "Think his wife will be glad to see 'em, Charley?"

"Oh, they'll be taken care of before they reach his house."

Chapter xxx

[*Ben Halleck, respectfully in love with Marcia, brings Bartley home from his night prowlings, while he is still drunk. Marcia, who does not recognize his ailment, is smitten with remorse. But the breach in their marital relations has been made, and can never really be healed. Marcia and Flavia go to Equity for a few weeks in the summer, and are occasionally visited by Bartley, who spoils a picnic for Marcia by openly flirting with a Mrs. McAllister, a former acquaintance of his, now visiting in Equity.*

In the following chapter, Bartley offends in a still more serious way. Against the expressed wishes of Kinney, an old lumber-camp friend, Bartley wrote up the man's experiences in the West and sold them to Ricker, editor of the Chronicle-Abstract, *leaving his old friend to suppose the article written by Ricker himself. As Bartley fell in the estimation of Ricker, he rose in the esteem of the rival editor, Witherby, who offered him $3,000 worth of shares in the stock of his paper, half of which he suggested Hubbard should buy from his salary over three years. How Bartley collects the other half of the sum, as described in this chapter, is evidence of the moral decay of the man and points to the inevitable divorce of Bartley and Marcia, which closes this* Modern Instance, *and shows in realistic terms the outcome of romantic marriages.*]

The Presidential canvas of the summer which followed upon these events in Bartley's career was not very active. Sometimes, in fact, it languished so much that people almost forgot it, and a good field was afforded the Events for the practice of independent journalism. To hold a course of strict impartiality, and yet come out on the winning side was a theory of independent journalism which Bartley illustrated with cynical enjoyment. He developed into something rather artistic the gift which he had always shown in his newspaper work for ironical persiflage. Witherby was not a man to feel this burlesque himself; but when it was pointed out to him by others, he came to Bartley in some alarm from its effect upon the fortunes of the paper. "We can't afford, Mr. Hubbard," he said, with virtuous trepidation, "we can't *afford* to make fun of our friends!"

Bartley laughed at Witherby's anxiety. "They're no more our friends than the other fellows are. We are independent journalists; and this way of treating the thing leaves us perfectly free hereafter to claim, just as we choose, that we were in fun or in earnest on any particular question if we're ever attacked. See?"

"I see," said Witherby, with not wholly subdued misgiving. But after due time for conviction no man enjoyed Bartley's irony more than Witherby when once he had mastered an instance of it. Sometimes it happened that Bartley found him chuckling over a perfectly serious paragraph, but he did not mind that; he enjoyed Witherby's mistake even more than his appreciation.

In these days Bartley was in almost uninterrupted good humor, as he had always expected to be when he became fairly prosperous. He was at no time an unamiable fellow, as he saw it; he had his sulks, he had his moments of anger; but generally he felt good, and he had always believed, and he had promised Marcia, that when he got squarely on his legs he should feel good perpetually. This sensation he now agreeably realized; and he was also now in that position in which he had proposed to himself some little moral reforms. He was not much in the habit of taking stock; but no man wholly escapes the contingencies in which he is confronted with himself, and sees certain habits, traits, tendencies, which he would like to change for the sake of his peace of mind hereafter. To some souls these contingencies are full of anguish, of remorse for the past, of despair; but Bartley had never yet seen the time when he did not feel himself perfectly able to turn over a new leaf and blot the old one. There were not many things in his life which he really cared to have very different; but there were two or three shady little corners which he always intended to clean up. He had meant some time or other to have a religious belief of some sort, he did not much care what; since Marcia had taken to the Hallecks' church, he did not see why he should not go with her, though he had never yet done so. He was not quite sure whether he was always as candid with her as he might be, or as kind; though he maintained against this question that in all their quarrels it was six of one and half a dozen of the other. He had never been tipsy but once in his life, and he considered that he had repented and atoned for that enough, especially as nothing had ever come of it; but sometimes he thought he might be over-doing the beer; yes, he thought he must cut down on the tivoli; he was getting ridiculously fat. If ever he met Kinney again he should tell him that it was he and not Ricker who had appropriated his facts and he intended to make it up with Ricker somehow.

He had not found just the opportunity yet; but in the mean time he did not mind telling the real cause of their alienation to good fellows who could enjoy a joke. He had his following, though so many of his brother journalists had cooled toward him, and those of his following considered him as smart as chain-lightning and bound to rise. These young men and not very wise elders roared over Bartley's frank declaration of the situation between himself and Ricker, and they contended that, if Ricker had taken the article for the Chronicle-Abstract, he ought to take the consequences. Bartley told them that, of course, he should explain the facts to Kinney; but that he meant to let Ricker enjoy his virtuous indignation awhile. Once, after a confidence of this kind at the club, where Ricker had refused to speak to him, he came away with a curious sense of moral decay. It did not pain him a great deal, but it certainly surprised him that now, with all these prosperous conditions, so favorable for cleaning up, he had so little disposition to clean up. He found himself quite willing to let the affair with Ricker go, and he suspected that he had been needlessly virtuous in his intentions concerning church-going and beer. As to Marcia, it appeared to him that he could not treat a woman of her disposition otherwise than as he did. At any rate, if he had not done everything he could to make her happy, she seemed to be getting along well enough, and was probably quite as happy as she deserved to be. They were getting on very quietly now; there had been no violent outbreak between them since the trouble about Kinney, and then she had practically confessed herself in the wrong, as Bartley looked at it. She had appeared contented with his explanation; there was what might be called a perfect business amity between them. If her life with him was no longer an expression of that intense devotion which she used to show him, it was more like what married life generally comes to, and he accepted her tractability and what seemed her common-sense

view of their relations as greatly preferable. With his growth
in flesh, Bartley liked peace more and more.

Marcia had consented to go down to Equity alone, that summer, for he had convinced her that during a heated political
contest it would not do for him to be away from the paper. He
promised to go down for her when she wished to come home;
and it was easily arranged for her to travel as far as the Junction
under Halleck's escort, when he went to join his sisters in the
White Mountains. Bartley missed her and the baby at first.
But he soon began to adjust himself with resignation to his solitude. They had determined to keep their maid over this summer,
for they had so much trouble in replacing her the last time after
their return; and Bartley said he should live very economically.
It was quiet, and the woman kept the house cool and clean; she
was a good cook, and when Bartley brought a man home to
dinner she took an interest in serving it well. Bartley let her
order the things from the grocer and butcher, for she knew what
they were used to getting, and he had heard so much talk from
Marcia about bills since he bought that Events stock that he was
sick of the prices of things. There was no extravagance, and
yet he seemed to live very much better after Marcia went. There
is no doubt but he lived very much more at his ease. One little
restriction after another fell away from him; he went and came
with absolute freedom, not only without having to account for
his movements, but without having a pang for not doing so.
He had the sensation of stretching himself after a cramping
posture; and he wrote Marcia the cheerfulest letters, charging
her not to cut short her visit from anxiety on his account. He
said that he was working hard, but hard work evidently agreed
with him, for he was never better in his life. In this high content he maintained a feeling of loyalty by going to the Hallecks,
where Mrs. Halleck often had him to tea in pity of his loneliness.
They were dull company, certainly; but Marcia liked them, and
the cooking was always good. Other evenings he went to the
theatres, where there were amusing variety bills; and sometimes
he passed the night at Nantasket, or took a run for a day to
Newport; he always reported these excursions to Marcia, with

expressions of regret that Equity was too far away to run down to for a day.

Marcia's letters were longer and more regular than his; but he could have forgiven some want of constancy for the sake of a less searching anxiety on her part. She was anxious not only for his welfare, which was natural and proper, but she was anxious about the housekeeping and the expenses, things Bartley could not afford to let trouble him, though he did what he could in a general way to quiet her mind. She wrote fully of the visit which Olive Halleck had paid her, but said that they had not gone about much, for Ben Halleck had only been able to come for a day. She was very well, and so was Flavia.

Bartley realized Flavia's existence with an effort, and for the rest this letter bored him. What could he care about Olive Halleck's coming, or Ben Halleck's staying away? All that he asked of Ben Halleck was a little extension of time when his interest fell due. The whole thing was disagreeable; and he resented what he considered Marcia's endeavor to clap the domestic harness on him again. His thoughts wandered to conditions, to contingencies, of which a man does not permit himself even to think without a degree of moral disintegration. In these ill-advised reveries he mused upon his life as it might have been if he had never met her, or if they had never met after her dismissal of him. As he recalled the facts, he was at that time in an angry and embittered mood, but he was in a mood of entire acquiescence; and the reconciliation had been of her own seeking. He could not blame her for it; she was very much in love with him, and he had been fond of her. In fact, he was still very fond of her; when he thought of little ways of hers, it filled him with tenderness. He did justice to her fine qualities, too: her generosity, her truthfulness, her entire loyalty to his best interests; he smiled to realize that he himself preferred his second-best interests, and in her absence he remembered that her virtues were tedious, and even painful at times. He had his doubts whether there was sufficient compensation in them. He sometimes questioned whether he had not made a great mistake to get married; he expected now to stick it through; but this doubt occurred to him. A moment came in which he asked himself, What if he had never come back to Marcia that night when she locked him out of her room? Might it not have been better for both of them? She would soon have reconciled herself to the irreparable; he even thought of her happy in a second marriage; and the thought did not enrage him; he generously wished Marcia well. He wished—he hardly knew what he wished. He wished nothing at all but to have his wife and child back again as soon as possible; and he put aside with a laugh the fancies which really found no such distinct formulation as I have given them; which were mere vague impulses, arrested mental tendencies, scraps of undirected revery. Their recurrence had nothing to do with what he felt to be his sane and waking state. But they recurred, and he even amused himself in turning them over.

THE RISE OF SILAS LAPHAM

Chapter XIV

[The Coreys, Boston aristocrats, have asked the Laphams to dinner at the behest of young Corey, who is in love with Penelope Lapham. Colonel Lapham is the owner of a prosperous paint factory in Vermont with offices in Boston, and is, at this point in the story, building a new home on Beacon Street for the sake of his daughters' social careers. Both the Coreys and the Laphams think it is the beautiful daughter, Irene, with whom Tom is in love, and both families are struggling unavailingly to overcome the social differences between them. Penelope, the clever daughter, whom Tom really loves, senses the whole situation, and wisely decides to stay at home from the dinner party. See Introduction, pp. cvii-cxi]

The Coreys were one of the few old families who lingered in Bellingham Place, the handsome, quiet old street which the sympathetic observer must grieve to see abandoned to boarding-houses. The dwellings are stately and tall, and the whole place wears an air of aristocratic seclusion, which Mrs. Corey's father might well have thought assured when he left her his house there at his death. It is one of two evidently designed by the same architect who built some houses in a characteristic taste on Beacon Street opposite the Common. It has a wooden portico, with slender fluted columns, which have always been painted white, and which, with the delicate moldings of the cornice, form the sole and sufficient decoration of the street front; nothing could be simpler, and nothing could be better. Within, the architect has again indulged his preference for the classic; the roof of the vestibule, wide and low, rests on marble columns, slim and fluted like the wooden columns without, and an ample staircase climbs in a graceful, easy curve from the tesselated pavement. Some carved Venetian *scrigni* stretched along the wall; a rug lay at the foot of the stairs; but otherwise the simple adequacy of the architectural intention had been respected, and the place looked bare to the eyes of the Laphams when they entered. The Coreys had once kept a man, but when young

Corey began his retrenchments the man had yielded to the neat maid who showed the Colonel into the reception-room and asked the ladies to walk up two flights.

He had his charges from Irene not to enter the drawing-room without her mother, and he spent five minutes in getting on his gloves, for he had desperately resolved to wear them at last. When he had them on, and let his large fists hang down on either side, they looked, in the saffront tint which the shop-girl said his gloves should be of, like canvassed hams. He perspired with doubt as he climbed the stairs, and while he waited on the landing for Mrs. Lapham and Irene to come down from above before going into the drawing-room, he stood staring at his hands, now open and now shut, and breathing hard. He heard quiet talking beyond the *portière* within, and presently Tom Corey came out.

"Ah, Colonel Lapham! Very glad to see you."

Lapham shook hands with him and gasped, "Waiting for Mis' Lapham," to account for his presence. He had not been able to button his right glove, and he now began, with as much in- difference as he could assume, to pull them both off, for he saw that Corey wore none. By the time he had stuffed them into the pocket of his coat-skirt his wife and daughter descended.

Corey welcomed them very cordially too, but looked a little mystified. Mrs. Lapham knew that he was silently inquiring for Penelope, and she did not know whether she ought to excuse her to him first or not. She said nothing, and after a glance toward the regions where Penelope might conjecturably be lingering, he held aside the *portière* for the Laphams to pass, and entered the room with them.

Mrs. Lapham had decided against low-necks on her own re- sponsibility, and had entrenched herself in the safety of a black silk, in which she looked very handsome. Irene wore a dress of one of those shades which only a woman or an artist can decide to be green or blue, and which to other eyes looks both or neither, according to their degrees of ignorance. If it was more like a ball dress than a dinner dress, that might be excused to the exquisite effect. She trailed, a delicate splendour, across the carpet in her mother's sombre wake, and the consciousness of success brought a vivid smile to her face. Lapham, pallid with anxiety lest he should somehow disgrace himself, giving thanks to God that he should have been spared the shame of wearing gloves where no one else did, but at the same time despairing that Corey should have seen him in them, had an unwonted aspect of almost pathetic refinement.

Mrs. Corey exchanged a quick glance of surprise and relief with her husband as she started across the room to meet her guests, and in her gratitude to them for being so irreproachable, she threw into her manner a warmth that people did not always find there. "General Lapham?" she said, shaking hands in quick succession with Mrs. Lapham and Irene, and now addressing herself to him.

"No, ma'am, only Colonel," said the honest man, but the lady did not hear him. She was introducing her husband to Lapham's wife and daughter, and Bromfield Corey was already shaking his hand and saying he was very glad to see him again, while he kept his artistic eye on Irene, and apparently could not take it off. Lily Corey gave the Lapham ladies a greeting which was physically rather than socially cold, and Nanny stood holding Irene's hand in both of hers a moment, and taking in her beauty and her style with a generous admiration which she could afford, for she was herself faultlessly dressed in the quiet taste of her city, and looking very pretty. The interval was long enough to let every man present confide his sense of Irene's beauty to every other; and then, as the party was small, Mrs. Corey made everybody acquainted. When Lapham had not quite understood, he held the person's hand, and leaning urbanely forward, inquired, "What name?" He did that because a great man to whom he had been presented on the platform at a public meeting had done so to him, and he knew it must be right.

A little lull ensued upon the introductions, and Mrs. Corey said quietly to Mrs. Lapham, "Can I send any one to be of use to Miss Lapham?" as if Penelope must be in the dressing-room.

Mrs. Lapham turned fire-red, and the graceful forms in which she had been intending to excuse her daughter's absence went out of her head. "She isn't upstairs," she said, at her bluntest, as country people are when embarrassed. "She didn't feel just like coming tonight. I don't know as she's feeling very well."

Mrs. Corey emitted a very small "O!"—very small, very cold,—which began to grow larger and hotter and to burn into Mrs. Lapham's soul before Mrs. Corey could add, "I'm very sorry. It's nothing serious, I hope?"

Robert Chase, the painter, had not come, and Mrs. James Bellingham was not there, so that the table really balanced better without Penelope; but Mrs. Lapham could not know this, and did not deserve to know it. Mrs. Corey glanced round the room, as if to take account of her guests, and said to her husband, "I think we are all here, then," and he came forward and gave his arm to Mrs. Lapham. She perceived then that in their determination not to be the first to come they had been the last, and must have kept the others waiting for them.

Lapham had never seen people go down to dinner arm-in-arm before, but he knew that his wife was distinguished in being taken out by the host, and he waited in jealous impatience to see if Tom Corey would offer his arm to Irene. He gave it to that big girl they called Miss Kingsbury, and the handsome old fellow whom Mrs. Corey had introduced as her cousin took Irene out. Lapham was startled from the misgiving in which this left him by Mrs. Corey's passing her hand through his arm, and he made a sudden movement forward, but felt himself gently restrained. They went out the last of all; he did not know why, but he submitted, and when they sat down he saw that Irene, although she had come in with that Mr. Bellingham, was seated beside young Corey, after all.

He fetched a long sigh of relief when he sank into his chair and felt himself safe from error if he kept a sharp lookout and did only what the others did. Bellingham had certain habits which he permitted himself, and one of these was tucking the corner of his napkin into his collar; he confessed himself an uncertain shot with a spoon, and defended his practice on the ground of neatness and common-sense. Lapham put his napkin into his collar too, and then, seeing that no one but Bellingham did it, became alarmed and took it out again slyly. He never had wine on his table at home, and on principle he was a prohibitionist; but now he did not know just what to do about the glasses at the right of his plate. He had a notion to turn them all down, as he had read of a well-known politician's doing at a public dinner, to show that he did not take wine; but, after twiddling with one of them a moment, he let them be, for it seemed to him that would be a little too conspicuous, and he felt that every one was looking. He let the servant fill them all, and he drank out of each, not to appear odd. Later, he observed that the young ladies were not taking wine, and he was glad to see that Irene had refused it, and that Mrs. Lapham was letting it stand untasted. He did not know but he ought to decline some of the dishes, or at least leave most of some on his plate, but he was not able to decide; he took everything and ate everything.

He noticed that Mrs. Corey seemed to take no more trouble about the dinner than anybody, and Mr. Corey rather less; he was talking busily to Mrs. Lapham, and Lapham caught a word here and there that convinced him she was holding her own. He was getting on famously himself with Mrs. Corey, who had begun with him about his new house; he was telling her all about it, and giving her his ideas. Their conversation naturally included his architect across the table; Lapham had been delighted and secretly surprised to find the fellow there; and at something Seymour said the talk spread suddenly, and the pretty house he was building for Colonel Lapham became the general theme. Young Corey testified to its loveliness, and the architect said laughingly that if he had been able to make a nice thing of it, he owed it to the practical sympathy of his client.

"Practical sympathy is good," said Bromfield Corey; and, slanting his head confidentially to Mrs. Lapham, he added, "Does he bleed your husband, Mrs. Lapham? He's a terrible fellow for appropriations!"

Mrs. Lapham laughed, reddening consciously, and said she guessed the Colonel knew how to take care of himself. This struck Lapham, then draining his glass of sauterne, as wonderfully discreet in his wife.

Bromfield Corey leaned back in his chair a moment. "Well, after all, you can't say, with all your modern fuss about it, that you do much better now than the old fellows who built such houses as this."

"Ah," said the architect, "nobody can do better than well. Your house is in perfect taste; you know I've always admired it; and I don't think it's at all the worse for being old-fashioned. What we've done is largely to go back of the hideous style that raged after they forgot how to make this sort of house. But I think we may claim a better feeling for structure. We use better material, and more wisely; and by and by we shall work out something more characteristic and original."

"With your chocolates and olives, and your clutter of bric-a-brac?"

"All that's bad, of course, but I don't mean that. I don't wish to make you envious of Colonel Lapham, and modesty prevents my saying that his house is prettier,—though I may have my convictions,—but it's better built. All the new houses are better built. Now, your house—"

"Mrs. Corey's house," interrupted the host, with a burlesque haste in disclaiming responsibility for it that made them all laugh. "*My* ancestral halls are in Salem, and I'm told you couldn't drive a nail into their timbers; in fact, I don't know that you would want to do it."

"I should consider it a species of sacrilege," answered Seymour, "and I shall be far from pressing the point I was going to make against a house of Mrs. Corey's."

This won Seymour the easy laugh, and Lapham silently wondered that the fellow never got off any of those things to him.

"Well," said Corey, "you architects and the musicians are the true and only artistic creators. All the rest of us, sculptors, painters, novelists, and tailors, deal with forms that we have before us; we try to imitate, we try to represent. But you two sorts of artists create form. If you represent, you fail. Somehow or other you do evolve the camel out of your inner consciousness."

"I will not deny the soft impeachment," said the architect, with a modest air.

"I dare say. And you'll own that it's very handsome of me to say this, after your unjustifiable attack on Mrs. Corey's property."

Bromfield Corey addressed himself again to Mrs. Lapham, and the talk subdivided itself as before. It lapsed so entirely away from the subject just in hand, that Lapham was left with rather a good idea, as he thought it, to perish in his mind, for want of a chance to express it. The only thing like a recurrence to what they had been saying was Bromfield Corey's warning Mrs. Lapham, in some connection that Lapham lost, against Miss Kingsbury. "She's worse," he was saying, "when it comes to appropriations than Seymour himself. Depend upon it, Mrs. Lapham, she will give you no peace of your mind, now she's met you, from this out. Her tender mercies are cruel; and I leave you to supply the context from your own scriptural knowledge. Beware of her, and all her works. She calls them works of charity; but heaven knows whether they are. It don't stand to reason that she gives the poor *all* the money she gets out of people. I have my own belief"—he gave it in a whisper for the whole table to hear—"that she spends it for champagne and cigars."

Lapham did not know about that kind of talking; but Miss Kingsbury seemed to enjoy the fun as much as anybody, and he laughed with the rest.

"You shall be asked to the very next debauch of the committee, Mr. Corey; then you won't dare expose us," said Miss Kingsbury.

"I wonder you haven't been down upon Corey to go to the Chardon Street home and talk with your indigent Italians in their native tongue," said Charles Bellingham. "I saw in the *Transcript* the other night that you wanted some one for the work."

"We did think of Mr. Corey," replied Miss Kingsbury; "but we reflected that he probably wouldn't talk with them at all; he would make them keep still to be sketched, and forget all about their wants."

Upon the theory that this was a fair return for Corey's pleasantry, the others laughed again.

"There is one charity," said Corey, pretending superiority to Miss Kingsbury's point, "that is so difficult, I wonder it hasn't occurred to a lady of your courageous invention."

"Yes?" said Miss Kingsbury. "What is that?"

"The occupation, by deserving poor of neat habits, of all the beautiful, airy, wholesome houses that stand empty the whole summer long, while their owners are away in their lowly cots beside the sea."

"Yes, that is terrible," replied Miss Kingsbury, with quick earnestness, while her eyes grew moist. "I have often thought of our great, cool houses standing useless here, and the thousands of poor creatures stifling in their holes and dens, and the little children dying for wholesome shelter. How cruelly selfish we are!"

"That is a very comfortable sentiment, Miss Kingsbury," said Corey, "and must make you feel almost as if you had thrown open No. 31 to the whole North End. But I am serious about this matter. I spend my summers in town, and I occupy my own house, so that I can speak impartially and intelligently; and I tell you that in some of my walks on the Hill and down on the Back Bay, nothing but the surveillance of the local policeman prevents my offering personal violence to those long rows of close-shuttered, handsome, brutally insensible houses. If I were a poor man, with a sick child pining in some garret or cellar at the North End, I should break into one of them, and camp out on the grand piano."

"Surely, Bromfield," said his wife, "you don't consider what havoc such people would make with the furniture of a nice house!"

"That is true," answered Corey, with meek conviction. "I never thought of that."

"And if you were a poor man with a sick child, I doubt if you'd have so much heart for burglary as you have now," said James Bellingham.

"It's wonderful how patient they are," said the minister. "The spectacle of the hopeless comfort the hard-working poor man sees must be hard to bear."

Lapham wanted to speak up and say that he had been there himself, and knew how such a man felt. He wanted to tell them that generally a poor man was satisfied if he could make both ends meet; that he didn't envy any one his good luck, if he had earned it, so long as he wasn't running under himself. But before he could get the courage to address the whole table, Sewell added, "I suppose he don't always think of it."

"But some day he *will* think about it," said Corey. "In fact, we rather invite him to think about it, in this country."

"My brother-in-law," said Charles Bellingham, with the pride a man feels in a mentionably remarkable brother-in-law, "has no end of fellows at work under him out there at Omaha, and he says it's the fellows from countries where they've been kept from thinking about it that are discontented. The Americans never make any trouble. They seem to understand that so long as we give unlimited opportunity, nobody has a right to complain."

"What do you hear from Leslie?" asked Mrs. Corey, turning from these profitless abstractions to Mrs. Bellingham.

"You know," said the lady in a lower tone, "that there is another baby?"

"No! I hadn't heard of it!"

"Yes; a boy. They have named him after his uncle."

"Yes," said Charles Bellingham, joining in. "He is said to be a noble boy, and to resemble me."

"All boys of that tender age are noble," said Corey, "and look like anybody you wish them to resemble. Is Leslie still homesick for the bean-pots of her native Boston?"

"She is getting over it, I fancy," replied Mrs. Bellingham. "She's very much taken up with Mr. Blake's enterprises, and leads a very exciting life. She says she's like people who have been home from Europe three years; she's past the most poignant stage of regret, and hasn't reached the second, when they feel that they *must* go again."

Lapham leaned a little toward Mrs. Corey, and said of a picture which he saw on the wall opposite, "Picture of your daughter, I presume?"

"No; my daughter's grandmother. It's a Stewart Newton; he painted a great many Salem beauties. She was a Miss Polly Burroughs. My daughter *is* like her, don't you think?" They both looked at Nanny Corey and then at the portrait. "Those pretty old-fashioned dresses are coming in again. I'm not surprised you took it for her. The others"—she referred to the other portraits more or less darkling on the walls—"are my people; mostly Copleys."

These names, unknown to Lapham, went to his head like the wine he was drinking; they seemed to carry light for the moment, but a film of deeper darkness followed. He heard Charles Bellingham telling funny stories to Irene and trying to amuse the girl; she was laughing, and seemed very happy. From time to time Bellingham took part in the general talk between the host and James Bellingham and Miss Kingsbury and that minister, Mr. Sewell. They talked of people mostly; it astonished Lapham to hear with what freedom they talked. They discussed these persons unsparingly; James Bellingham spoke of a man known to Lapham for his business success and great wealth as not a gentleman; his cousin Charles said he was surprised that the fellow had kept from being governor so long.

When the latter turned from Irene to make one of these excursions into the general talk, young Corey talked to her; and Lapham caught some words from with it seemed that they were speaking of Penelope. It vexed him to think she had not come; she could have talked as well as any of them; she was just as bright; and Lapham was aware that Irene was not as bright, though when he looked at her face, triumphant in its young beauty and fondness, he said to himself that it did not make any difference. He felt that he was not holding up his end of the line, however. When some one spoke to him he could only summon a few words of reply, that seemed to lead to nothing; things often came into his mind appropriate to what they were saying, but before he could get them out they were off on something else; they jumped about so, he could not keep up; but he felt, all the same, that he was not doing himself justice.

At one time the talk ran off upon a subject that Lapham had

never heard of before; but again he was vexed that Penelope was not there, to have her say; he believed that her say would have been worth hearing.

Miss Kingsbury leaned forward and asked Charles Bellingham if he had read *Tears, Idle Tears*, the novel that was making such a sensation; and when he said no, she said she wondered at him. "It's perfectly heart-breaking, as you'll imagine from the name; but there's such a dear old-fashioned hero and heroine in it, who keep dying for each other all the way through, and making the most wildly satisfactory and unnecessary sacrifices for each other. You feel as if you'd done them yourself."

"Ah, that's the secret of its success," said Bromfield Corey. "It flatters the reader by painting the characters colossal, but with his limp and stoop, so that he feels himself of their supernatural proportions. You've read it, Nanny?"

"Yes," said his daughter. "It ought to have been called *Slop, Silly Slop*."

"Oh, not quite *slop*, Nanny," pleaded Miss Kingsbury.

"It's astonishing," said Charles Bellingham, "how we do like the books that go for our heart-strings. And I really suppose that you can't put a more popular thing than self-sacrifice into a novel. We do like to see people suffering sublimely."

"There was talk some years ago," said James Bellingham, "about novels going out."

"They're just coming in!" cried Miss Kingsbury.

"Yes," said Mr. Sewell, the minister. "And I don't think there ever was a time when they formed the whole intellectual experience of more people. They do greater mischief than ever."

"Don't be envious, parson," said the host.

"No," answered Sewell. "I should be glad of their help. But those novels with old-fashioned heroes and heroines in them—excuse me, Miss Kingsbury—are ruinous!"

"Don't you feel like a moral wreck, Miss Kingsbury?" asked the host.

But Sewell went on: "The novelists might be the greatest possible help to us if they painted life as it is, and human feelings in their true proportion and relation, but for the most part they have been and are altogether noxious."

This seemed sense to Lapham; but Bromfield Corey asked: "But what if life as it is isn't amusing? Aren't we to be amused?"

"Not to our hurt," sturdily answered the minister. "And the self-sacrifice painted in most novels like this—"

"*Slop, Silly Slop?*" suggested the proud father of the inventor of the phrase.

"Yes—is nothing but psychical suicide, and is as wholly immoral as the spectacle of a man falling upon his sword."

"Well, I don't know but you're right, parson," said the host; and the minister, who had apparently got upon a battle-horse of his, careered onward in spite of some tacit attempts of his wife to seize the bridle.

"Right? To be sure I am right. The whole business of love, and love-making and marrying, is painted by the novelists in a monstrous disproportion to the other relations of life. Love is very sweet, very pretty—"

"Oh, *thank* you, Mr. Sewell," said Nanny Corey, in a way that set them all laughing.

"But it's the affair, commonly, of very young people, who have not yet character and experience enough to make them interesting. In novels it's treated, not only as if it were the chief interest of life, but the sole interest of the lives of two ridiculous young persons; and it is taught that love is perpetual, that the glow of a true passion lasts for ever; and that it is sacrilege to think or act otherwise."

"Well, but isn't that true, Mr. Sewell?" pleaded Miss Kingsbury.

"I have known some most estimable people who had married a second time," said the minister, and then he had the applause with him. Lapham wanted to make some open recognition of his good sense, but could not.

"I suppose the passion itself has been a good deal changed," said Bromfield Corey, "since the poets began to idealise it in the days of chivalry."

"Yes; and it ought to be changed again," said Mr. Sewell.

"What! Back?"

"I don't say that. But it ought to be recognised as something natural and mortal, and divine honours, which belong to righteousness alone, ought not to be paid it."

"Oh, you ask too much, parson," laughed his host, and the talk wandered away to something else.

It was not an elaborate dinner; but Lapham was used to having everything on the table at once, and this succession of dishes bewildered him; he was afraid perhaps he was eating too much. He now no longer made any pretence of not drinking his wine, for he was thirsty, and there was no more water, and he hated to ask for any. The ice-cream came, and then the fruit. Suddenly Mrs. Corey rose, and said across the table to her husband, "I suppose you will want your coffee here." And he replied, "Yes; we'll join you at tea."

The ladies all rose, and the gentlemen got up with them. Lapham started to follow Mrs. Corey, but the other men merely stood in their places, except young Corey, who ran and opened the door for his mother. Lapham thought with shame that it was he who ought to have done that; but no one seemed to notice, and he sat down again gladly, after kicking out one of his legs which had gone to sleep.

They brought in cigars with coffee, and Bromfield Corey advised Lapham to take one that he chose for him. Lapham confessed that he liked a good cigar about as well as anybody, and Corey said: "These are new. I had an Englishman here the other day who was smoking old cigars in the superstition that tobacco improved with age, like wine."

"Ah," said Lapham, "anybody who had ever lived off a tobacco country could tell him better than that." With the fuming cigar between his lips he felt more at home than he had before. He turned sidewise in his chair and, resting one arm on the back, intertwined the fingers of both hands, and smoked at large ease.

James Bellingham came and sat down by him. "Colonel Lapham, weren't you with the 96th Vermont when they charged across the river in front of Pickensburg, and the rebel battery opened fire on them in the water?"

Lapham slowly shut his eyes and slowly dropped his head for assent, letting out a white volume of smoke from the corner of his mouth.

"I thought so," said Bellingham. "I was with the 85th Massachusetts, and I sha'n't forget that slaughter. We were all new to it still. Perhaps that's why it made such an impression."

"I don't know," suggested Charles Bellingham. "Was there anything much more impressive afterward? I read of it out in Missouri, where I was stationed at the time, and I recollect the talk of some old army men about it. They said that death-rate couldn't be beaten. I don't know that it ever was."

"About one in five of us got out safe," said Lapham, breaking his cigar-ash off on the edge of a plate. James Bellingham reached him a bottle of Apollinaris. He drank a glass, and then went on smoking.

They all waited, as if expecting him to speak, and then Corey said: "How incredible those things seem already! You gentlemen *know* that they happened; but are you still able to believe it?"

"Ah, nobody *feels* that anything happened," said Charles Bellingham. "The past of one's experience doesn't differ a great deal from the past of one's knowledge. It isn't more probable; it's really a great deal less vivid than some scenes in a novel that one read when a boy."

"I'm not sure of that," said James Bellingham.

"Well, James, neither am I," consented his cousin, helping himself from Lapham's Apollinaris bottle. "There would be very little talking at dinner if one only said the things that one was sure of."

The others laughed, and Bromfield Corey remarked thoughtfully, "What astonishes the craven civilian in all these things is the abundance—the superabundance—of heroism. The cowards were the exception; the men that were ready to die, the rule."

"The woods were full of them," said Lapham, without taking his cigar from his mouth.

"That's a nice little touch in *School*," interposed Charles Bellingham, "where the girl says to the fellow who was at

Inkerman, 'I should think you would be so proud of it,' and he reflects a while, and says, "Well, the fact is, you know, there were so many of us.'"

"Yes, I remember that," said James Bellingham, smiling for pleasure in it. "But I don't see why you claim the credit of being a craven civilian, Bromfield," he added, with a friendly glance at his brother-in-law, and with the willingness Boston men often show to turn one another's good points to the light in company; bred so intimately together at school and college and in society, they all know these points. "A man who was out with Garibaldi in '48," continued James Bellingham.

"Oh, a little amateur red-shirting," Corey interrupted in deprecation. "But even if you choose to dispute my claim, what has become of all the heroism? Tom, how many club men do you know who would think it sweet and fitting to die for their country?"

"I can't think of a great many at the moment, sir," replied the son, with the modesty of his generation.

"And I couldn't in '61," said his uncle. "Nevertheless they were there."

"Then your theory is that it's the occasion that is wanting," said Bromfield Corey. "But why shouldn't civil service reform, and the resumption of specie payment, and a tariff for revenue only, inspire heroes? They are all good causes."

"It's the occasion that's wanting," said James Bellingham, ignoring the *persiflage*. "And I'm very glad of it."

"So am I," said Lapham, with a depth of feeling that expressed itself in spite of the haze in which his brain seemed to float. There was a great deal of the talk that he could not follow; it was too quick for him; but here was something he was clear of. "I don't want to see any more men killed in my time." Something serious, something sombre must lurk behind these words, and they waited for Lapham to say more; but the haze closed round him again, and he remained silent, drinking Apollinaris.

"We non-combatants were notoriously reluctant to give up fighting," said Mr. Sewell, the minister; "but I incline to think Colonel Lapham and Mr. Bellingham may be right. I dare say

we shall have the heroism again if we have the occasion. Till it
comes, we must content ourselves with the every-day generosi-
ties and sacrifices. They make up in quantity what they lack in
quality, perhaps."

"They're not so picturesque," said Bromfield Corey. "You
can paint a man dying for his country, but you can't express on
canvas a man fulfilling the duties of a good citizen."

"Perhaps the novelists will get at him by and by," suggested
Charles Bellingham. "If I were one of these fellow, I shouldn't
propose to myself anything short of that."

"What? the commonplace?" asked his cousin.

"Commonplace? The commonplace is just that light, im-
palpable, aërial essence which they've never got into their confounded books yet. The novelist who could interpret the common feelings of commonplace people would have the answer to
'the riddle of the painful earth' on his tongue."

"Oh, not so bad as that, I hope," said the host; and Lapham
looked from one to the other, trying to make out what they
were at. He had never been so up a tree before.

"I suppose it isn't well for us to see human nature at white
heat habitually," continued Bromfield Corey, after a while. "It
would make us vain of our species. Many a poor fellow in that
war and in many another has gone into battle simply and purely
for his country's sake, not knowing whether, if he laid down his
life, he should ever find it again, or whether, if he took it up
hereafter, he should take it up in heaven or hell. Come, parson!"
he said, turning to the minister, "what has ever been conceived
of omnipotence, of omniscience, so sublime, so divine as that?"

"Nothing," answered the minister quietly. "God has never
been imagined at all. But if you suppose such a man as that was
Authorised, I think it will help you to imagine what God must
be."

"There's sense in that," said Lapham. He took his cigar out
of his mouth, and pulled his chair a little toward the table, on
which he placed his ponderous fore-arms. "I want to tell you
about a fellow I had in my own company when we first went
out. We were all privates to begin with; after a while they

elected me captain—I'd had the tavern stand, and most of 'em knew me. But Jim Millon never got to be anything more than corporal; corporal when he was killed." The others arrested themselves in various attitudes of attention, and remained listening to Lapham with an interest that profoundly flattered him. Now, at last, he felt that he was holding up his end of the rope. "I can't say he went into the thing from the highest motives, altogether; our motives are always pretty badly mixed, and when there's such a hurrah-boys as there was then, you can't tell which is which. I suppose Jim Millon's wife was enough to account for his going, herself. She was a pretty bad assortment," said Lapham, lowering his voice and glancing round at the door to make sure that it was shut, "and she used to lead Jim *one* kind of life. Well, sir," continued Lapham, synthetising his auditors in that form of address, "that fellow used to save every cent of his pay and send it to that woman. Used to get me to do it for him. I tried to stop him. 'Why, Jim,' said I, 'you know what she'll do with it.' 'That's so, Cap,' says he, 'but I don't know what she'll do without it.' And it did keep her straight—straight as a string—as long as Jim lasted. Seemed as if there was something mysterious about it. They had a little girl,—about as old as my oldest girl,—and Jim used to talk to me about her. Guess he done it as much for her as for the mother; and he said to me before the last action we went into, 'I should like to turn tail and run, Cap. I ain't comin' out o' this one. But I don't suppose it would do.' 'Well, not for you, Jim,' said I. 'I want to live,' he says; and he bust out crying right there in my tent. 'I want to live for poor Molly and Zerrilla'—that's what they called the little one; I dunno where they got the name. 'I ain't ever had half a chance; and now she's doing better, and I believe we should get along after this.' He set there cryin' like a baby. But he wan't no baby when he went into action. I hated to look at him after it was over, not so much because he'd got a ball that was meant for me by a sharpshooter —he saw the devil takin' aim, and he jumped to warn me—as because he didn't look like Jim; he looked like—fun; all desperate and savage. I guess he died hard."

The story made its impression, and Lapham saw it. "Now I say," he resumed, as if he felt that he was going to do himself justice, and say something to heighten the effect his story had produced. At the same time he was aware of a certain want of clearness. He had the idea, but it floated vague, elusive, in his brain. He looked about as if for something to precipitate it in tangible shape.

"Apollinaris?" asked Charles Bellingham, handing the bottle from the other side. He had drawn his chair closer than the rest to Lapham's, and was listening with great interest. When Mrs. Corey asked him to meet Lapham, he accepted gladly. "You know I go in for that sort of thing, Anna. Since Leslie's affair we're rather bound to do it. And I think we meet these practical fellows too little. There's always something original about them." He might naturally have believed that the reward of his faith was coming.

"Thanks, I will take some of this wine," said Lapham, pouring himself a glass of Madeira from a black and dusty bottle caressed by a label bearing the date of the vintage. He tossed off the wine, unconscious of its preciousness, and waited for the result. That cloudiness in his brain disappeared before it, but a mere blank remained. He not only could not remember what he was going to say, but he could not recall what they had been talking about. They waited, looking at him, and he stared at them in return. After a while he heard the host saying, "Shall we join the ladies?"

Lapham went, trying to think what had happened. It seemed to him a long time since he had drunk that wine.

Miss Corey gave him a cup of tea, where he stood aloof from his wife, who was talking with Miss Kingsbury and Mrs. Sewell; Irene was with Miss Nanny Corey. He could not hear what they were talking about; but if Penelope had come, he knew that she would have done them all credit. He meant to let her know how he felt about her behaviour when he got home. It was a shame for her to miss such a chance. Irene was looking beautiful, as pretty as all the rest of them put together, but she was not talking, and Lapham perceived that at a dinner-party you ought to talk. He was himself conscious of having talked very well. He now wore an air of great dignity, and, in conversing with the other gentlemen, he used a grave and weighty deliberation. Some of them wanted him to go into the library. There he gave his ideas of books. He said he had not much time for anything but the papers; but he was going to have a complete library in his new place. He made an elaborate acknowledgment to Bromfield Corey of his son's kindness in suggesting books for his library; he said that he had ordered them all, and that he meant to have pictures. He asked Mr. Corey who was about the best American painter going now. "I don't set up to be a judge of pictures, but I know what I like," he said. He lost the reserve which he had maintained earlier, and began to boast. He himself introduced the subject of his paint, in a natural transition from pictures; he said Mr. Corey must take a run up to Lapham with him some day, and see the Works; they would interest him, and he would drive him round the country; he kept most of his horses up there, and he could show Mr. Corey some of the finest Jersey grades in the country. He told about his brother William, the judge at Dubuque; and a farm he had out there that paid for itself every year in wheat. As he cast off all fear, his voice rose, and he hammered his arm-chair with the thick of his hand for emphasis. Mr. Corey seemed impressed; he sat perfectly quiet, listening, and Lapham saw the other gentlemen stop in their talk every now and then to listen. After this proof of his ability to interest them, he would have liked to have Mrs. Lapham suggest again that he was unequal to their society, or to the society of anybody else. He surprised himself by his ease among men whose names had hitherto overawed him. He got to calling Bromfield Corey by his surname alone. He did not understand why young Corey seemed so preoccupied, and he took occasion to tell the company how he had said to his wife the first time he saw that fellow that he could make a man of him if he had him in the business; and he guessed he was not mistaken. He began to tell stories of the different young men he had in his employ. At last he had the talk altogether to himself; no one else talked, and he talked unceasingly. It was a great time; it was a triumph.

He was in this successful mood when word came to him that Mrs. Lapham was going; Tom Corey seemed to have brought it, but he was not sure. Anyway, he was not going to hurry. He made cordial invitations to each of the gentlemen to drop in and see him at his office, and would not be satisfied till he had exacted a promise from each. He told Charles Bellingham that he liked him, and assured James Bellingham that it had always been his ambition to know him, and that if any one had said when he first came to Boston that in less than ten years he should be hobnobbing with Jim Bellingham, he should have told that person he lied. He would have told anybody he lied that had told him ten years ago that a son of the Bromfield Corey would have come and asked him to take him into the business. Ten years ago he, Silas Lapham, had come to Boston a little worse off than nothing at all, for he was in debt for half the money that he had bought out his partner with, and here he was now worth a million, and meeting you gentlemen like one of you. And every cent of that was honest money,—no speculation,—every copper of it for value received. And here, only the other day, his old partner, who had been going to the dogs ever since he went out of the business, came and borrowed twenty thousand dollars of him! Lapham lent it because his wife wanted him to: she had always felt bad about the fellow's having to go out of the business.

He took leave of Mr. Sewell with patronising affection, and bade him come to him if he ever got into a tight place with his parish work; he would let him have all the money he wanted; he had more money than he knew what to do with. "Why, when your wife sent to mine last fall," he said, turning to Mr. Corey, "I drew my cheque for five hundred dollars, but my wife wouldn't take more than one hundred; said she wasn't going to show off before Mrs. Corey. I call that a pretty good joke on Mrs. Corey. I must tell her how Mrs. Lapham done her out of a cool four hundred dollars."

He started toward the door of the drawing-room to take leave of the ladies; but Tom Corey was at his elbow, saying, "I think Mrs. Lapham is waiting for you below, sir," and in obeying the direction Corey gave him toward another door he forgot all about his purpose, and came away without saying good-night to his hostess.

Mrs. Lapham had not known how soon she ought to go, and had no idea that in her quality of chief guest she was keeping the others. She stayed till eleven o'clock, and was a little frightened when she found what time it was; but Mrs. Corey, without pressing her to stay longer, had said it was not at all late. She and Irene had had a perfect time. Everybody had been very polite; on the way home they celebrated the amiability of both the Miss Coreys and of Miss Kingsbury. Mrs. Lapham thought that Mrs. Bellingham was about the pleasantest person she ever saw; she had told her all about her married daughter who had married an inventor and gone to live in Omaha—a Mrs. Blake.

"If it's that car-wheel Blake," said Lapham proudly, "I know all about him. I've sold him tons of the paint."

"Pooh, papa! How you do smell of smoking!" cried Irene.

"Pretty strong, eh?" laughed Lapham, letting down a window of the carriage. His heart was throbbing wildly in the close air, and he was glad of the rush of cold that came in, though it stopped his tongue, and he listened more and more drowsily to the rejoicings that his wife and daughter exchanged. He meant to have them wake Penelope up and tell her what she had lost; but when he reached home he was too sleepy to suggest it. He fell asleep as soon as his head touched the pillow, full of supreme triumph.

But in the morning his skull was sore with the unconscious, nightlong ache; and he rose cross and taciturn. They had a silent breakfast. In the cold grey light of the morning the glories of the night before showed poorer. Here and there a painful doubt obtruded itself and marred them with its awkward shadow. Penelope sent down word that she was not well, and was not coming to breakfast, and Lapham was glad to go to his office without seeing her.

He was severe and silent all day with his clerks, and peremptory with customers. Of Corey he was slyly observant, and as the day wore away he grew more restively conscious. He sent

out word by his office-boy that he would like to see Mr. Corey
for a few minutes after closing. The type-writer girl had lingered
too, as if she wished to speak with him, and Corey stood in
abeyance as she went toward Lapham's door.

"Can't see you to-night, Zerrilla," he said bluffly, but not
unkindly. "Perhaps I'll call at the house, if it's important."

"It is," said the girl, with a spoiled air of insistence.

"Well," said Lapham, and, nodding to Corey to enter, he
closed the door upon her. Then he turned to the young man
and demanded: "Was I drunk last night?"

Chapter XXI

[*Tom Corey's love for Penelope, rather than Irene, has been declared to the
Laphams, with the result that Irene has gone West to visit an uncle and aunt
for an indefinite stay, and Penelope has refused to see Tom. Corey asks to be
taken into the Lapham paint business, rather to the consternation of his own
family. At this point in the story the Colonel's former partner, Milton K.
Rogers, has turned up again and is attempting to blackmail Lapham, whose
conscience is not altogether clear because he bought up Rogers's share in the
business years ago when he knew the factory was about to boom. Since then his
wife, Persis, has never ceased to remind him that he had not treated Rogers with
candor and generosity. This chapter makes it clear that Rogers was, in fact, a
shady character with whom one could not have business relations.*]

Lapham was gone a fortnight. He was in a sullen humour
when he came back, and kept himself shut close within his own
den at the office the first day. He entered it in the morning without a word to his clerks as he passed through the outer room, and
he made no sign throughout the forenoon, except to strike
savagely on his desk-bell from time to time, and send out to
Walker for some book of accounts or a letter-file. His boy confidentially reported to Walker that the old man seemed to have
got a lot of papers round; and at lunch the bookkeeper said to
Corey, at the little table which they had taken in a corner together, in default of seats at the counter, "Well, sir, I guess
there's a cold wave coming."

Corey looked up innocently, and said, "I haven't read the
weather report."

"Yes, sir," Walker continued, "it's coming. Areas of rain

along the whole coast, and increased pressure in the region of the private office. Storm-signals up at the old man's door now."

Corey perceived that he was speaking figuratively, and that his meteorology was entirely personal to Lapham. "What do you mean?," he asked, without vivid interest in the allegory, his mind being full of his own tragi-comedy.

"Why, just this: I guess the old man's takin' in sail. And I guess he's got to. As I told you the first time we talked about him, there don't any one know one-quarter as much about the old man's business as the old man does himself; and I ain't betraying any confidence when I say that I guess that old partner of his has got pretty deep into his books. I guess he's over head and ears in 'em, and the old man's gone in after him, and he's got a drownin' man's grip round his neck. There seems to be a kind of a lull—kind of a dead calm, *I* call it— in the paint market just now; and then again a ten-hundred-thousand-dollar man don't build a hundred-thousand-dollar house without feeling the drain, unless there's a regular boom. And just now there ain't any boom at all. Oh, I don't say but what the old man's got anchors to windward; guess he *has;* but if he's *goin'* to leave me his money, I wish he'd left it six weeks ago. Yes, sir, I guess there's a cold wave comin'; but you can't generally 'most always tell, as a usual thing, where the old man's concerned, and it's *only* a guess." Walker began to feed in his breaded chop with the same nervous excitement with which he abandoned himself to the slangy and figurative excesses of his talks. Corey had listened with a miserable curiosity and compassion up to a certain moment, when a broad light of hope flashed upon him. It came from Lapham's potential ruin; and the way out of the labyrinth that had hitherto seemed so hopeless was clear enough, if another's disaster would befriend him, and give him the opportunity to prove the unselfishness of his constancy. He thought of the sum of money that was his own, and that he might offer to lend, or practically give, if the time came; and with his crude hopes and purposes formlessly exulting in his heart, he kept on listening with an unchanged countenance.

Walker could not rest till he had developed the whole situation, so far as he knew it. "Look at the stock we've got on hand. There's going to be an awful shrinkage on that, now! And when everybody is shutting down, or running half-time, the works up at Lapham are going full chip, just the same as ever. Well, it's his pride. I don't say but what it's a good sort of pride, but he likes to make his brags that the fire's never been out in the works since they started, and that no man's work or wages has ever been cut down yet at Lapham, it don't matter *what* the times are. Of course," explained Walker, "I shouldn't talk so to everybody; don't know as I should talk so to *any*body but you, Mr. Corey."

"Of course," assented Corey.

"Little off your feed to-day," said Walker, glancing at Corey's plate.

"I got up with a headache."

"Well, sir, if you're like me you'll carry it round all day, then. I don't know a much meaner thing than a headache—unless it's earache, or toothache, or some other kind of ache. I'm pretty hard to suit when it comes to diseases. Notice how yellow the old man looked when he came in this morning? I don't like to see a man of his build look yellow—much."

About the middle of the afternoon the dust-coloured face of Rogers, now familiar to Lapham's clerks, showed itself among them. "Has Colonel Lapham returned yet?" he asked, in his dry, wooden tones, of Lapham's boy.

"Yes, he's in his office," said the boy; and as Rogers advanced, he rose and added, "I don't know as you can see him to-day. His orders are not to let anybody in."

"Oh, indeed!" said Rogers; "I think he will see *me!*" and he pressed forward.

"Well, I'll have to ask," returned the boy; and hastily preceding Rogers, he put his head in at Lapham's door, and then withdrew it. "Please to sit down," he said; "he'll see you pretty soon;" and, with an air of some surprise, Rogers obeyed. His sere, dull-brown whiskers and the moustache closing over both lips were incongruously and illogically clerical in effect, and the effect was heightened for no reason by the parchment texture of his skin; the baldness extending to the crown of his head was like a baldness made up for the stage. What his face expressed chiefly was a bland and beneficent caution. Here, you must have said to yourself, is a man of just, sober, and prudent views, fixed purposes, and the good citizenship that avoids debt and hazard of every kind.

"What do you want?" asked Lapham, wheeling round in his swivel-chair as Rogers entered his room, and pushing the door shut with his foot, without rising.

Rogers took the chair that was not offered him, and sat with his hat-brim on his knees, and its crown pointed towards Lapham. "I want to know what you are going to do," he answered with sufficient self-possession.

"I'll tell you, first, what I've *done*," said Lapham. "I've been to Dubuque, and I've found out all about that milling property you turned in on me. Did you know that the G. L. & P. had leased the P. Y. & X.?"

"I some suspected that it might."

"Did you know it when you turned the property in on me? Did you know that the G. L. & P. wanted to buy the mills?"

"I presumed the road would give a fair price for them," said Rogers, winking his eyes in outward expression of inwardly blinking the point.

"You lie," said Lapham, as quietly as if correcting him in a slight error; and Rogers took the word with equal *sang froid.* "You knew the road wouldn't give a fair price for the mills. You knew it would give what it chose, and that I couldn't help myself, when you let me take them. You're a thief, Milton K. Rogers, and you stole money I lent you." Rogers sat listening, as if respectfully considering the statements. "You knew how I felt about that old matter—or my wife did; and that I wanted to make it up to you, if you felt anyway badly used. And you took advantage of it. You've got money out of me, in the first place, on securities that wan't worth thirty-five cents on the dollar, and you've let me in for this thing, and that thing, and you've bled me every time. And all I've got to show for it is a milling property on a line of road that can squeeze me, whenever it

wants to, as dry as it pleases. And you want to know what I'm
going to do? I'm going to squeeze *you*. I'm going to sell these
collaterals of yours,"—he touched a bundle of papers among
others that littered his desk,—"and I'm going to let the mills go
for what they'll fetch. *I* ain't going to fight the G. L. & P."

Lapham wheeled about in his chair and turned his burly back
on his visitor, who sat wholly unmoved.

"There are some parties," he began, with a dry tranquility
ignoring Lapham's words, as if they had been an outburst
against some third person, who probably merited them, but in
whom he was so little interested that he had been obliged to use
patience in listening to his condemnation,—"there are some
English parties who have been making inquiries in regard to
those mills."

"I guess you're lying, Rogers," said Lapham, without looking
round.

"Well, all that I have to ask is that you will not act hastily."

"I see you don't think I'm in earnest!" cried Lapham, facing
fiercely about. "You think I'm fooling, do you?" He struck his
bell, and "William," he ordered the boy who answered it, and
who stood waiting while he dashed off a note to the brokers and
enclosed it with the bundle of securities in a large envelope,
"take these down to Gallop & Paddock's, in State Street, right
away. Now go!" he said to Rogers, when the boy had closed the
door after him; and he turned once more to his desk.

Rogers rose from his chair, and stood with his hat in his hand.
He was not merely dispassionate in his attitude and expression,
he was impartial. He wore the air of a man who was ready to
return to business whenever the wayward mood of his inter-
locutor permitted. "Then I understand," he said, "that you will
take no action in regard to the mills till I have seen the parties
I speak of."

Lapham faced about once more, and sat looking up into the
visage of Rogers in silence. "I wonder what you're up to," he
said at last; "I *should* like to know." But as Rogers made no sign
of gratifying his curiosity, and treated this last remark of Lapham's as of the irrelevance of all the rest, he said, frowning,

"You bring me a party that will give me enough for those mills to clear me of you, and I'll talk to you. But don't you come here with any man of straw. And I'll give you just twenty-four hours to prove yourself a swindler again."

Once more Lapham turned his back, and Rogers, after looking thoughtfully into his hat a moment, cleared his throat, and quietly withdrew, maintaining to the last his unprejudiced demeanour.

Lapham was not again heard from, as Walker phrased it, during the afternoon, except when the last mail was taken in to him; then the sound of rending envelopes, mixed with that of what seemed suppressed swearing, penetrated to the outer office. Somewhat earlier than the usual hour for closing, he appeared there with his hat on and his overcoat buttoned about him. He said briefly to his boy, "William, I shan't be back again this afternoon," and then went to Miss Dewey and left a number of letters on her table to be copied, and went out. Nothing had been said, but a sense of trouble subtly diffused itself through those who saw him go out.

That evening as he sat down with his wife alone at tea, he asked, "Ain't Pen coming to supper?"

"No, she ain't," said his wife. "I don't know as I like the way she's going on, any too well. I'm afraid, if she keeps on, she'll be down sick. She's got deeper feelings than Irene."

Lapham said nothing, but having helped himself to the abundance of his table in his usual fashion, he sat and looked at his plate with an indifference that did not escape the notice of his wife. "What's the matter with *you?*" she asked.

"Nothing. I haven't got any appetite."

"What's the matter?" she persisted.

"Trouble's the matter; bad luck and lots of it's the matter," said Lapham. "I haven't ever hid anything from you, Persis, when you asked me, and it's too late to begin now. I'm in a fix. I'll tell you what kind of a fix, if you think it'll do you any good; but I guess you'll be satisfied to know that it's a fix."

"How much of a one?" she asked with a look of grave, steady courage in her eyes.

"Well, I don't know as I can tell, just yet," said Lapham, avoiding this look. "Things have been dull all the fall, but I thought they'd brisk up come winter. They haven't. There have been a lot of failures, and some of 'em owed me, and some of 'em had me on their paper; and—" Lapham stopped.

"And what?" prompted his wife.

He hesitated before he added, "And then—Rogers."

"I'm to blame for that," said Mrs. Lapham. "I forced you to it."

"No; I was as willing to go into it as what you were," answered Lapham. "I don't want to blame anybody."

Mrs. Lapham had a woman's passion for fixing responsibility; she could not help saying, as soon as acquitted, "I warned you against him, Silas. I told you not to let him get in any deeper with you."

"Oh yes. I had to help him to try to get my money back. I might as well poured water into a sieve. And now—" Lapham stopped.

"Don't be afraid to speak out to me, Silas Lapham. If it comes to the worst, I want to know it—I've got to know it. What did I ever care for the money? I've had a happy home with you ever since we were married, and I guess I shall have as long as you live, whether we go on to the Back Bay, or go back to the old house at Lapham. I know who's to blame, and I blame myself. It was my forcing Rogers on to you." She came back to this, with her helpless longing, inbred in all Puritan souls, to have some one specifically suffer for the evil in the world, even if it must be herself.

"It hasn't come to the worst yet, Persis," said her husband. "But I shall have to hold up on the new house a little while, till I can see where I am."

"I shouldn't care if we had to sell it," cried his wife, in passionate self-condemnation. "I should be *glad* if we had to, as far as I'm concerned."

"I shouldn't," said Lapham.

"I know!" said his wife; and she remembered ruefully how his heart was set on it.

He sat musing. "Well, I guess it's going to come out all right in the end. Or, if it ain't," he sighed, "we can't help it. May be Pen needn't worry so much about Corey, after all," he continued, with a bitter irony new to him. "It's an ill wind that blows nobody good. And there's a chance," he ended, with a still bitterer laugh, "that Rogers will come to time, after all."

"I don't believe it!" exclaimed Mrs. Lapham, with a gleam of hope in her eyes. "What chance?"

"One in ten million," said Lapham; and her face fell again. "He says there are some English parties after him to buy these mills."

"Well?"

"Well, I gave him twenty-four hours to prove himself a liar."

"You don't believe there are any such parties?"

"Not in *this* world."

"But if there were?"

"Well, if there were, Persis— But pshaw!"

"No, no!" she pleaded eagerly. "It don't seem as if he *could* be such a villain. What would be the use of his pretending? If he brought the parties to you—"

"Well," said Lapham scornfully, "I'd let them have the mills at the price Rogers turned 'em in on me at. *I* don't want to make anything on 'em. But guess I shall hear from the G. L. & P. first. And when they make their offer, I guess I'll have to accept it, whatever it is. I don't think they'll have a great many competitors."

Mrs. Lapham could not give up her hope. "If you could get your price from those English parties before they knew that the G. L. & P. wanted to buy the mills, would it let you out with Rogers?"

"Just about," said Lapham.

"Then I know he'll move heaven and earth to bring it about. I *know* you won't be allowed to suffer for doing him a kindness, Silas. He *can't* be so ungrateful! Why, why *should* he pretend to have any such parties in view when he hasn't? Don't you be down-hearted, Si. You'll see that he'll be round with them to-morrow."

Lapham laughed, but she urged so many reasons for her belief in Rogers that Lapham began to rekindle his own faith a little. He ended by asking for a hot cup of tea; and Mrs. Lapham sent the pot out and had a fresh one steeped for him. After that he made a hearty supper in the revulsion from his entire despair; and they fell asleep that night talking hopefully of his affairs, which he laid before her fully, as he used to do when he first started in business. That brought the old times back, and he said: "If this had happened then, I shouldn't have cared much. I was young then, and I wasn't afraid of anything. But I noticed that after I passed fifty I began to get scared easier. I don't believe I could pick up, now, from a regular knock-down."

"Pshaw! *You* scared, Silas Lapham?" cried his wife proudly. "I should like to see the thing that ever scared you; or the knock-down that *you* couldn't pick up from!"

"Is that so, Persis?" he asked, with the joy her courage gave him.

In the middle of the night she called to him, in a voice which the darkness rendered still more deeply troubled: "Are you awake, Silas?"

"Yes; I'm awake."

"I've been thinking about those English parties, Si—"

"So've I."

"And I can't make it out but what you'd be just as bad as Rogers, every bit and grain, if you were to let them have the mills—"

"And not tell 'em what the chances were with the G. L. & P.? I thought of that, and you needn't be afraid."

She began to bewail herself, and to sob convulsively: "O Silas! O Silas!" Heaven knows in what measure the passion of her soul was mixed with pride in her husband's honesty, relief from an apprehended struggle, and pity for him.

"Hush, hush, Persis!" he besought her. "You'll wake Pen if you keep on that way. Don't cry any more! You mustn't."

"Oh, let me cry, Silas! It'll help me. I shall be all right in a minute. Don't you mind." She sobbed herself quiet. "It does seem too hard," she said, when she could speak again, "that you have to give up this chance when Providence had fairly raised it up for you."

"I guess it wasn't *Providence* raised it up," said Lapham. "Any rate, it's got to go. Most likely Rogers was lyin', and there ain't any such parties; but if there were, they couldn't have the mills from me without the whole story. Don't you be troubled, Persis. I'm going to pull through all right."

"Oh, I ain't afraid. I don't suppose but what there's plenty would help you, if they knew you needed it, Si."

"They would if they knew I *didn't* need it," said Lapham sardonically.

"Did you tell Bill how you stood?"

"No, I couldn't bear to. I've been the rich one so long, that I couldn't bring myself to own up that I was in danger."

"Yes."

"Besides, it didn't look so ugly till to-day. But I guess we shan't let ugly looks scare us."

"No."

Chapter xxv

[*The $100,000 home that Lapham, in his pride, has built, burns to the ground. Lapham, moreover, has just learned of a rival paint company in West Virginia, which he might buy up before the owners realize the true worth of their business. His old lawyer friend, Mr. Bellingham, points out to him the issues involved in this deal. In the following chapter Lapham's various business difficulties close in on him, but he, at the crisis, "rises" above self-interest and even above the now confused conscience of his wife. After his failure in business, Lapham and his wife return to Vermont, where he broods over the ethical values clarified by his choice. In the end, the old couple at least have the satisfaction of seeing Tom and Penelope married, and Irene fully recovered from her disappointment.*]

Lapham awoke confused, and in a kind of remoteness from the loss of the night before, through which it loomed mistily. But before he lifted his head from the pillow, it gathered substance and weight against which it needed all his will to bear up and live. In that moment he wished that he had not wakened, that he might never have wakened; but he rose, and faced the day and its cares.

The morning papers brought the report of the fire, and the conjectured loss. The reporters somehow had found out the fact that the loss fell entirely upon Lapham, they lighted up the hackneyed character of their statements with the picturesque interest of the coincidence that the policy had expired only the week before; heaven knows how they knew it. They said that nothing remained of the building but the walls; and Lapham, on his way to business, walked up past the smoke-stained shell. The windows looked like the eye-sockets of a skull down upon the blackened and trampled snow of the street; the pavement was a sheet of ice, and the water from the engines had frozen, like streams of tears, down the face of the house, and hung in icy tags from the window-sills and copings.

He gathered himself up as well as he could, and went on to his office. The chance of retrieval that had flashed upon him, as he sat smoking by that ruined hearth the evening before, stood him in such stead now as a sole hope may; and he said to himself that, having resolved not to sell his house, he was no more crippled by its loss than he would have been by letting his money lie idle in it; what he might have raised by mortgage on it could be made up in some other way; and if they would sell he could still buy out the whole business of that West Virginia company, mines, plant, stock on hand, good-will, and everything, and unite it with his own. He went early in the afternoon to see Bellingham, whose expressions of condolence for his loss he cut short with as much politeness as he knew how to throw into his impatience. Bellingham seemed at first a little dazzled with the splendid courage of his scheme; it was certainly fine in its way; but then he began to have his misgivings.

"I happen to know that they haven't got much money behind them," urged Lapham. "They'll jump at an offer."

Bellingham shook his head. "If they can show profit on the old manufacture, and prove they can make their paint still cheaper and better hereafter, they can have all the money they want. And it will be very difficult for you to raise it if you're threatened by them. With that competition, you know what your plant at Lapham would be worth, and what the shrinkage

on your manufactured stock would be. Better sell out to them"
he concluded, "if they will buy."

"There ain't money enough in this country to buy out my
paint," said Lapham, buttoning up his coat in a quiver of resentment. "Good afternoon, sir." Men are but grown-up boys
after all. Bellingham watched this perversely proud and ob-
stinate child fling petulantly out of his door, and felt a sympathy
for him which was as truly kind as it was helpless.

But Lapham was beginning to see through Bellingham, as he
believed. Bellingham was, in his way, part of that conspiracy
by which Lapham's creditors were trying to drive him to the
wall. More than ever now he was glad that he had nothing to
do with that cold-hearted, self-conceited race, and that the
favours so far were all from his side. He was more than ever
determined to show them, every one of them, high and low,
that he and his children could get along without them, and
prosper and triumph without them. He said to himself that if
Penelope were engaged to Corey that very minute, he would
make her break with him.

He knew what he should do now, and he was going to do it
without loss of time. He was going on to New York to see
those West Virginia people; they had their principal office there,
and he intended to get at their ideas, and then he intended to
make them an offer. He managed this business better than could
possibly have been expected of a man in his impassioned mood.
But when it came really to business, his practical instincts, alert
and wary, came to his aid against the passions that lay in wait to
betray after they ceased to dominate him. He found the West
Virginians full of zeal and hope, but in ten minutes he knew that
they had not yet tested their strength in the money market, and
had not ascertained how much or how little capital they could
command. Lapham himself, if he had had so much, would not
have hesitated to put a million dollars into their business. He
saw, as they did not see, that they had the game in their own
hands, and that if they could raise the money to extend their
business, they could ruin him. It was only a question of time,
and he was on the ground first. He frankly proposed a union of

their interests. He admitted that they had a good thing, and that he should have to fight them hard; but he meant to fight them to the death unless they could come to some sort of terms. Now, the question was whether they had better go on and make a heavy loss for both sides by competition, or whether they had better form a partnership to run both paints and command the whole market. Lapham made them three propositions, each of which was fair and open: to sell out to them altogether; to buy them out altogether; to join facilities and forces with them, and go on in an invulnerable alliance. Let them name a figure at which they would buy, a figure at which they would sell, a figure at which they would combine,—or, in other words, the amount of capital they needed.

They talked all day, going out to lunch together at the Astor House, and sitting with their knees against the counter on a row of stools before it for fifteen minutes of reflection and deglutition, with their hats on, and then returning to the basement from which they emerged. The West Virginia company's name was lettered in gilt on the wide low window, and its paint, in the form of ore, burnt, and mixed, formed a display on the window shelf. Lapham examined it and praised it; from time to time they all recurred to it together; they sent out for some of Lapham's paint and compared it, the West Virginians admitting its former superiority. They were young fellows, and country persons, like Lapham, by origin, and they looked out with the same amused, undaunted provincial eyes at the myriad metropolitan legs passing on the pavement above the level of their window. He got on well with them. At last, they said what they would do. They said it was nonsense to talk of buying Lapham out, for they had not the money; and as for selling out, they would not do it, for they knew they had a big thing. But they would as soon use his capital to develop it as anybody else's, and if he could put in a certain sum for this purpose, they would go in with him. He should run the works at Lapham and manage the business in Boston, and they would run the works at Kanawha Falls and manage the business in New York. The two brothers with whom Lapham talked named their figure, subject to the approval of another brother at Kanawha Falls, to whom they would write, and who would telegraph his answer, so that Lapham could have it inside of three days. But they felt perfectly sure that he would approve; and Lapham started back on the eleven o'clock train with an elation that gradually left him as he drew near Boston, where the difficulties of raising this sum were to be overcome. It seemed to him, then, that those fellows had put it up on him pretty steep, but he owned to himself that they were right in believing they could raise the same sum elsewhere; it would take all of it, he admitted, to make their paint pay on the scale they had the right to expect. At their age, he would not have done differently; but when he emerged, old, sore, and sleep-broken, from the sleeping-car in the Albany depot at Boston, he wished with a pathetic self-pity that they knew how a man felt at his age. A year ago, six months ago, he would have laughed at the notion that it would be hard to raise the money. But he thought ruefully of that immense stock of paint on hand, which was now a drug in the market, of his losses by Rogers and by the failures of other men, of the fire that had licked up so many thousands in a few hours; he thought with bitterness of the tens of thousands that he had gambled away in stocks, and of the commissions that the brokers had pocketed whether he won or lost; and he could not think of any securities on which he could borrow, except his house in Nankeen Square, or the mine and works at Lapham. He set his teeth in helpless rage when he thought of that property out on the G. L. & P., that ought to be worth so much, and was worth so little if the Road chose to say so.

He did not go home, but spent most of the day shining round, as he would have expressed it, and trying to see if he could raise the money. But he found that people of whom he hoped to get it were in the conspiracy which had been formed to drive him to the wall. Somehow, there seemed a sense of his embarrassments abroad. Nobody wanted to lend money on the plant at Lapham without taking time to look into the state of the business; but Lapham had no time to give, and he knew that the state of the business would not bear looking into. He could raise fifteen thousand on his Nankeen Square house, and another fifteen on his Beacon Street lot, and this was all that a man who was worth a million by rights could do! He said a million, and he said it in defiance of Bellingham, who had subjected his figures to an analysis which wounded Lapham more than he chose to show at the time, for it proved that he was not so rich and not so wise as he had seemed. His hurt vanity forbade him to go to Bellingham now for help or advice; and if he could have brought himself to ask his brothers for money, it would have been useless; they were simply well-to-do Western people, but not capitalists on the scale he required.

Lapham stood in the isolation to which adversity so often seems to bring men. When its test was applied, practically or theoretically, to all those who had seemed his friends, there was none who bore it; and he thought with bitter self-contempt of the people whom he had befriended in their time of need. He said to himself that he had been a fool for that; and he scorned himself for certain acts of scrupulosity by which he had lost money in the past. Seeing the moral forces all arrayed against him, Lapham said that he would like to have the chance offered him to get even with them again; he thought he should know how to look out for himself. As he understood it, he had several days to turn about in, and he did not let one day's failure dishearten him. The morning after his return he had, in fact, a gleam of luck that gave him the greatest encouragement for the moment. A man came in to inquire about one of Rogers's wildcat patents, as Lapham called them, and ended by buying it. He got it, of course, for less than Lapham took it for, but Lapham was glad to be rid of it for something, when he had thought it worth nothing; and when the transaction was closed, he asked the purchaser rather eagerly if he knew where Rogers was; it was Lapham's secret belief that Rogers had found there was money in the thing, and had sent the man to buy it. But it appeared that this was a mistake; the man had not come from Rogers, but had heard of the patent in another way; and Lapham was astonished in the afternoon, when his boy came to tell him that Rogers was in the outer office, and wished to speak with him.

"All right," said Lapham, and he could not command at once the severity for the reception of Rogers which he would have liked to use. He found himself, in fact, so much relaxed towards him by the morning's touch of prosperity that he asked him to sit down, gruffly, of course, but distinctly; and when Rogers said in his lifeless way, and with the effect of keeping his appointment of a month before, "Those English parties are in town, and would like to talk with you in reference to the mills," Lapham did not turn him out-of-doors.

He sat looking at him, and trying to make out what Rogers was after; for he did not believe that the English parties, if they existed, had any notion of buying his mills.

"What if they are not for sale?" he asked. "You know that I've been expecting an offer from the G. L. & P."

"I've kept watch of that. They haven't made you any offer," said Rogers quietly.

"And did you think," demanded Lapham, firing up, "that I would turn them in on somebody else as you turned them in on me, when the chances are that they won't be worth ten cents on the dollar six months from now?"

"I didn't know what you would do," said Rogers non-committally. "I've come here to tell you that these parties stand ready to take the mills off your hands at a fair valuation—at the value I put upon them when I turned them in."

"I don't believe you!" cried Lapham brutally, but a wild predatory hope made his heart leap so that it seemed to turn over in his breast. "I don't believe there are any such parties to begin with; and in the next place, I don't believe they would buy at any such figure; unless—you've lied to them, as you've lied to me. Did you tell them about the G. L. & P.?"

Rogers looked compassionately at him, but he answered, with unvaried dryness, "I did not think that necessary."

Lapham had expected this answer, and he had expected or intended to break out in furious denunciation of Rogers when he got it; but he only found himself saying, in a sort of baffled gasp, "I wonder what your game is!"

Rogers did not reply categorically, but he answered, with his impartial calm, and as if Lapham had said nothing to indicate that he differed at all with him as to disposing of the property in the way he had suggested: "If we should succeed in selling, I should be able to repay you your loans, and should have a little capital for a scheme that I think of going into."

"And do you think that I am going to steal these men's money to help you plunder somebody in a new scheme?" answered Lapham. The sneer was on behalf of virtue, but it was still a sneer.

"I suppose the money would be useful to you too, just now."

"Why?"

"Because I know that you have been trying to borrow."

At this proof of wicked omniscience in Rogers, the question whether he had better not regard the affair as a fatality, and yield to his destiny, flashed upon Lapham; but he answered, "I shall want money a great deal worse than I've ever wanted it yet, before I go into such rascally business with you. Don't you know that we might as well knock these parties down on the street, and take the money out of their pockets?"

"They have come on," answered Rogers, "from Portland to see you. I expected them some weeks ago, but they disappointed me. They arrived on the *Circassian* last night; they expected to have got in five days ago, but the passage was very stormy."

"Where are they?" asked Lapham, with helpless irrelevance, and feeling himself somehow drifted from his moorings by Roger's shipping intelligence.

"They are at Young's. I told them we would call upon them after dinner this evening; they dine late."

"Oh, you did, did you?" asked Lapham, trying to drop another anchor for a fresh clutch on his underlying principles. "Well, now, you go and tell them that I said I wouldn't come."

"Their stay is limited," remarked Rogers. "I mentioned this evening because they were not certain they could remain over another night. But if to-morrow would suit you better—"

"Tell 'em I shan't come at all," roared Lapham, as much in

terror as defiance, for he felt his anchor dragging. "Tell 'em I shan't come at all! Do you understand that?"

"I don't see why you should stickle as to the matter of going to them," said Rogers; "but if you think it will be better to have them approach you, I suppose I can bring them to you."

"No, you can't! I shan't let you! I shan't see them! I shan't have anything to do with them. *Now* do you understand?"

"I inferred from our last interview," persisted Rogers, unmoved by all this violent demonstration of Lapham's, "that you wished to meet these parties. You told me that you would give me time to produce them; and I have promised them that you would meet them; I have committed myself."

It was true that Lapham had defied Rogers to bring on his men, and had implied his willingness to negotiate with them. That was before he had talked the matter over with his wife, and perceived his moral responsibility in it; even she had not seen this at once. He could not enter into this explanation with Rogers; he could only say, "I said I'd give you twenty-four hours to prove yourself a liar, and you did it. I didn't say twenty-four days."

"I don't see the difference," returned Rogers. "The parties are here now, and that proves that I was acting in good faith at the time. There has been no change in the posture of affairs. You don't know now any more than you knew then that the G. L. & P. is going to want the property. If there's any difference, it's in favour of the Road's having changed its mind."

There was some sense in this, and Lapham felt it—felt it only too eagerly, as he recognised the next instant.

Rogers went on quietly: "You're not obliged to sell to these parties when you meet them; but you've allowed me to commit myself to them by the promise that you would talk with them."

"'Twan't a promise," said Lapham.

"It was the same thing; they have come out from England on my guaranty that there was such and such an opening for their capital; and now what am I to say to them? It places me in a ridiculous position." Rogers urged his grievance calmly, almost impersonally, making his appeal to Lapham's sense of justice. "I *can't* go back to those parties and tell them you won't see them. It's no answer to make. They've got a right to know *why* you won't see them."

"Very well, then!" cried Lapham; "I'll come and *tell* them why. Who shall I ask for? When shall I be there?"

"At eight o'clock, please," said Rogers, rising, without apparent alarm at his threat, if it was a threat. "And ask for me; I've taken a room at the hotel for the present."

"I won't keep you five minutes when I get there," said Lapham; but he did not come away till ten o'clock.

It appeared to him as if the very devil was in it. The Englishmen treated his downright refusal to sell as a piece of bluff, and talked on as though it were merely the opening of the negotiation. When he became plain with them in his anger, and told them why he would not sell, they seemed to have been prepared for this as a stroke of business, and were ready to meet it.

"Has this fellow," he demanded, twisting his head in the direction of Rogers, but disdaining to notice him otherwise, "been telling you that it's part of my game to say this? Well, sir, I can tell you, on my side, that there isn't a slipperier rascal unhung in America than Milton K. Rogers!"

The Englishmen treated this as a piece of genuine American humour, and returned to the charge with unabated courage. They owned now, that a person interested with them had been out to look at the property, and that they were satisfied with the appearance of things. They developed further the fact that they were not acting solely, or even principally, in their own behalf, but were the agents of people in England who had projected the colonisation of a sort of community on the spot, somewhat after the plan of other English dreamers, and that they were satisfied, from a careful inspection, that the resources and facilities were those best calculated to develop the energy and enterprise of the proposed community. They were prepared to meet Mr. Lapham—Colonel, they begged his pardon, at the instance of Rogers—at any reasonable figure, and were quite willing to assume the risks he had pointed out. Something in the eyes of these men, something that lurked at an infinite depth below their speech, and was not really in their eyes when Lapham looked again, had flashed through him a sense of treachery in them. He had thought them the dupes of Rogers; but in that brief instant he had seen them—or thought he had seen them—his accomplices, ready to betray the interests of which they went on to speak with a certain comfortable jocosity, and a certain incredulous slight of his show of integrity. It was a deeper game than Lapham was used to, and he sat looking with a sort of admiration from one Englishman to the other, and then to Rogers, who maintained an exterior of modest neutrality, and whose air said, "I have brought you gentlemen together as the friend of all parties, and I now leave you to settle it among yourselves. I ask nothing, and expect nothing, except the small sum which shall accrue to me after the discharge of my obligations to Colonel Lapham."

While Roger's presence expressed this, one of the Englishmen was saying, "And if you have any scruple in allowin' us to assume this risk, Colonel Lapham, perhaps you can console yourself with the fact that the loss, if there is to be any, will fall upon people who are able to bear it—upon an association of rich and charitable people. But we're quite satisfied there will be no loss," he added savingly. "All you have to do is to name your price, and we will do our best to meet it."

There was nothing in the Englishman's sophistry very shocking to Lapham. It addressed itself in him to that easy-going, not evilly intentioned, potential immorality which regards common property as common prey, and gives us the most corrupt municipal governments under the sun—which makes the poorest voter, when he has tricked into place, as unscrupulous in regard to others' money as an hereditary prince. Lapham met the Englishman's eye, and with difficulty kept himself from winking. Then he looked away, and tried to find out where he stood, or what he wanted to do. He could hardly tell. He had expected to come into that room and unmask Rogers, and have it over. But he had unmasked Rogers without any effect whatever, and the play had only begun. He had a whimsical and sarcastic sense of its being very different from the plays at the theatre. He could not get up and go away in silent contempt; he could not tell the Englishmen that he believed them a pair of scoundrels and should have nothing to do with them; he could no longer treat them as innocent dupes. He remained baffled and perplexed, and the one who had not spoken hitherto remarked—

"Of course we shan't 'aggle about a few pound, more or less. If Colonel Lapham's figure should be a little larger than ours, I've no doubt 'e'll not be too 'ard upon us in the end."

Lapham appreciated all the intent of this subtle suggestion, and understood as plainly as if it had been said in so many words, that if they paid him a larger price, it was to be expected that a certain portion of the purchase-money was to return to their own hands. Still he could not move; and it seemed to him that he could not speak.

"Ring that bell, Mr. Rogers," said the Englishman who had last spoken, glancing at the annunciator button in the wall near Rogers's head, "and 'ave up something 'ot, can't you? I should like to wet me w'istle, as you say 'ere, and Colonel Lapham seems to find it rather dry work."

Lapham jumped to his feet, and buttoned his overcoat about him. He remembered with terror the dinner at Corey's where he had disgraced and betrayed himself, and if he went into this thing at all, he was going into it sober. "I can't stop," he said, "I must be going."

"But you haven't given us an answer yet, Mr. Lapham," said the first Englishman with a successful show of dignified surprise.

"The only answer I can give you now is, *No*," said Lapham. "If you want another, you must let me have time to think it over."

"But 'ow much time?" said the other Englishman. "We're pressed for time ourselves, and we hoped for an answer—'oped for a hanswer," he corrected himself, "at once. That was our understandin' with Mr. Rogers."

"I can't let you know till morning, anyway," said Lapham, and he went out, as his custom often was, without any parting salutation. He thought Rogers might try to detain him; but

Rogers had remained seated when the others got to their feet, and paid no attention to his departure.

He walked out into the night air, every pulse throbbing with the strong temptation. He knew very well those men would wait, and gladly wait, till the morning, and that the whole affair was in his hands. It made him groan in spirit to think that it was. If he had hoped that some chance might take the decision from him, there was no such chance, in the present or future, that he could see. It was for him alone to commit this rascality—if it was a rascality—or not.

He walked all the way home, letting one car after another pass him on the street, now so empty of other passing, and it was almost eleven o'clock when he reached home. A carriage stood before his house, and when he let himself in with his key, he heard talking in the family-room. It came into his head that Irene had got back unexpectedly, and that the sight of her was some-how going to make it harder for him; then he thought it might be Corey, come upon some desperate pretext to see Penelope; but when he opened the door he saw, with a certain absence of surprise, that it was Rogers. He was standing with his back to the fireplace, talking to Mrs. Lapham, and he had been shedding tears; dry tears they seemed, and they had left a sort of sandy, glistening trace on his cheeks. Apparently he was not ashamed of them, for the expression with which he met Lapham was that of a man making a desperate appeal in his own cause, which was identical with that of humanity, if not that of justice.

"I some expected," began Rogers, "to find you here—"

"No, you didn't," interrupted Lapham; "you wanted to come here and make a poor mouth to Mrs. Lapham before I got home."

"I knew that Mrs. Lapham would know what was going on," said Rogers more candidly, but not more virtuously, for that he could not, "and I wished her to understand a point that I hadn't put to you at the hotel, and that I want you should consider. And I want you should consider me a little in this business too; you're not the only one that's concerned, I tell you, and I've been telling Mrs. Lapham that it's my one chance; that if you don't meet me on it, my wife and children will be reduced to beggary."

"So will mine," said Lapham, "or the next thing to it."

"Well, then, I want you to give me this chance to get on my feet again. You've no right to deprive me of it; it's unchristian. In our dealings with each other we should be guided by the Golden Rule, as I was saying to Mrs. Lapham before you came in. I told her that if I knew myself, I should in your place consider the circumstances of a man in mine, who had honourably endeavoured to discharge his obligations to me, and had patiently borne my undeserved suspicions. I should consider that man's family, I told Mrs. Lapham."

"Did you tell her that if I went in with you and those fellows, I should be robbing the people who trusted them?"

"I don't see what you've got to do with the people that sent them here. They are rich people, and could bear it if it came to the worst. But there's no likelihood, now, that it will come to the worst; you can see yourself that the Road has changed its mind about buying. And here am I without a cent in the world; and my wife is an invalid. She needs comforts, she needs little luxuries, and she hasn't even the necessaries; and you want to sacrifice her to a mere idea! You don't know in the first place that the Road will ever want to buy; and if it does, the probability is that with a colony like that planted on its line, it would make very different terms from what it would with you or me. These agents are not afraid, and their principals are rich people; and if there was any loss, it would be divided up amongst them so that they wouldn't any of them feel it."

Lapham stole a troubled glance at his wife, and saw that there was no help in her. Whether she was daunted and confused in her own conscience by the outcome, so evil and disastrous, of the reparation to Rogers which she had forced her husband to make, or whether her perceptions had been blunted and darkened by the appeals which Rogers had now used, it would be difficult to say. Probably there was a mixture of both causes in the effect which her husband felt in her, and from which he turned, girding himself anew, to Rogers.

"I have no wish to recur to the past," continued Rogers, with growing superiority. "You have shown a proper spirit in regard to that, and you have done what you could to wipe it out."

"I should think I had," said Lapham. "I've used up about a hundred and fifty thousand dollars trying."

"Some of my enterprises," Rogers admitted, "have been unfortunate, seemingly; but I have hopes that they will yet turn out well—in time. I can't understand why you should be so mindful of others now, when you showed so little regard for me then. I had come to your aid at a time when you needed help, and when you got on your feet you kicked me out of the business. I don't complain, but that is the fact; and I had to begin again, after I had supposed myself settled in life, and establish myself elsewhere."

Lapham glanced again at his wife; her head had fallen; he could see that she was so rooted in her old remorse for that questionable act of his, amply and more than fully atoned for since, that she was helpless, now in the crucial moment, when he had the utmost need of her insight. He had counted upon her; he perceived now that when he had thought it was for him alone to decide, he had counted upon her just spirit to stay his own in its struggle to be just. He had not forgotten how she held out against him only a little while ago, when he asked her whether he might not rightfully sell in some such contingency as this; and it was not now that she said or even looked anything in favour of Rogers, but that she was silent against him, which dismayed Lapham. He swallowed the lump that rose in his throat, the self-pity, the pity for her, the despair, and said gently, "I guess you better go to bed, Persis. It's pretty late."

She turned towards the door, when Rogers said, with the obvious intention of detaining her through her curiosity—

"But I let that pass. And I don't ask now that you should sell to these men."

Mrs. Lapham paused, irresolute.

"What are you making this bother for, then?" demanded Lapham. "What *do* you want?"

"What I've been telling your wife here. I want you should

sell to *me*. I don't say what I'm going to do with the property, and you will not have an iota of responsibility, whatever happens."

Lapham was staggered, and he saw his wife's face light up with eager question.

"I want that property," continued Rogers, "and I've got the money to buy it. What will you take for it? If it's the price you're standing out for—"

"Persis," said Lapham, "go to bed," and he gave her a look that meant obedience for her. She went out of the door, and left him with his tempter.

"If you think I'm going to help you whip the devil round the stump, you're mistaken in your man, Milton Rogers," said Lapham lighting a cigar. "As soon as I sold to you, you would sell to that other pair of rascals. *I* smelt 'em out in half a minute."

"They are Christian gentlemen," said Rogers. "But I don't purpose defending them; and I don't purpose telling you what I shall or shall not do with the property when it is in my hands again. The question is, Will you sell, and, if so, what is your figure? You have got nothing whatever to do with it after you've sold."

It was perfectly true. Any lawyer would have told him the same. He could not help admiring Rogers for his ingenuity, and every selfish interest of his nature joined with many obvious duties to urge him to consent. He did not see why he should refuse. There was no longer a reason. He was standing out alone for nothing, any one else would say. He smoked on as if Rogers were not there, and Rogers remained before the fire as patient as the clock ticking behind his head on the mantel, and showing the gleam of its pendulum beyond his face on either side. But at last he said, "Well?"

"Well," answered Lapham, "you can't expect me to give you an answer to-night, any more than before. You know that what you've said now hasn't changed the thing a bit. I wish it had. The Lord knows, I want to be rid of the property fast enough."

"Then why don't you sell to me? Can't you see that you will not be responsible for what happens after you have sold?"

"No, I *can't* see that; but if I can by morning, I'll sell."

"Why do you expect to know any better by morning? You're wasting time for nothing!" cried Rogers, in his disappointment. "Why are you so particular? When you drove me out of the business you were not so very particular."

Lapham winced. It was certainly ridiculous for a man who had once so selfishly consulted his own interests to be stickling now about the rights of others.

"I guess nothing's going to happen overnight," he answered sullenly. "Anyway, I shan't say what I shall do till morning."

"What time can I see you in the morning?"

"Half-past nine."

Rogers buttoned his coat, and went out of the room without another word. Lapham followed him to close the street-door after him.

His wife called down to him from above as he approached the room again, "Well?"

"I've told him I'd let him know in the morning."

"Want I should come down and talk with you?"

"No," answered Lapham, in the proud bitterness which his isolation brought, "you couldn't do any good." He went in and shut the door, and by and by his wife heard him begin walking up and down; and then the rest of the night she lay awake and listened to him walking up and down. But when the first light whitened the window, the words of the Scripture came into her mind: "And there wrestled a man with him until the breaking of the day ... And he said, Let me go, for the day breaketh. And he said, I will not let thee go, except thou bless me."

She could not ask him anything when they met, but he raised his dull eyes after the first silence, and said, "*I* don't know what I'm going to say to Rogers."

She could not speak; she did not know what to say, and she saw her husband, when she followed him with her eyes from the window, drag heavily down toward the corner, where he was to take the horse-car.

He arrived rather later than usual at his office, and he found his letters already on his table. There was one, long and official-looking, with a printed letter-heading on the outside, and Lapham had no need to open it in order to know that it was the offer of the Great Lacustrine & Polar Railroad for his mills. But he went mechanically through the verification of his prophetic fear, which was also his sole hope, and then sat looking blankly at it.

Rogers came promptly at the appointed time, and Lapham handed him the letter. He must have taken it all in at a glance, and seen the impossibility of negotiating any further now, even with victims so pliant and willing as those Englishmen.

"You've ruined me!" Rogers broke out. "I haven't a cent left in the world! God help my poor wife!"

He went out, and Lapham remained staring at the door which closed upon him. This was his reward for standing firm for right and justice to his own destruction: to feel like a thief and a murderer.

A HAZARD OF NEW FORTUNES

Part First

Chapter VII

[*In a note, entitled "Bibliographical," written for* A Hazard of New Fortunes *when it was reprinted in 1909, Howells tells us that the novel "was the first fruit of my New York life when I began to live it after my quarter of a century in Cambridge and Boston, ending in 1889; and I used my own transition to the commercial metropolis in framing the experience which was wholly that of my suppositious literary adventurer." Basil March, already known to* Harper's *readers from* Their Wedding Journey, *gave up his position in a Boston insurance company, as Howells resigned his as editor of* The Atlantic Monthly, *to try his fortunes in New York. The Marches are here house-hunting. See Introduction, pp. cxvii–cxx.*]

They went to a quiet hotel far down-town, and took a small apartment which they thought they could easily afford for the day or two they need spend in looking up a furnished flat. They were used to staying at this hotel when they came on for a little outing in New York, after some rigid winter in Boston, at the time of the spring exhibitions. They were remembered there from year to year; the colored call-boys, who never seemed to get any older, smiled upon them, and the clerk called March by name even before he registered. He asked if Mrs. March were with him, and said then he supposed they would want their usual quarters; and in a moment they were domesticated in a far interior that seemed to have been waiting for them in a clean, quiet, patient disoccupation ever since they left it two years before. The little parlor, with its gilt paper and ebonized furniture, was the lightest of the rooms, but it was not very light at noonday without the gas, which the bell-boy now flared up for them. The uproar of the city came to it in a soothing murmur, and they took possession of its peace and comfort with open celebration. After all, they agreed, there *was* no place in the world so delightful as a hotel apartment like that; the boasted charms of home were nothing to it; and then the magic of its being always there, ready for any one, every one, just as if it were for some one alone: it was like the experience of an Arabian Nights hero come true for all the race.

"Oh, *why* can't we always stay here, just we two!" Mrs. March sighed to her husband, as he came out of his room rubbing his face red with the towel, while she studied a new arrangement of her bonnet and hand-bag on the mantel.

"And ignore the past? I'm willing. I've no doubt that the children could get on perfectly well without us, and could find some lot in the scheme of Providence that would really be just as well for them."

"Yes; or could contrive somehow never to have existed. I should insist upon that. If they *are*, don't you see that we couldn't wish them *not to be*?"

"Oh yes; I see your point; it's simply incontrovertible."

She laughed and said: "Well, at any rate, if we can't find a flat to suit us we can all crowd into these three rooms somehow, for the winter, and then browse about for meals. By the week we could get them much cheaper; and we could save on the eating, as they do in Europe. Or on something else."

"Something else, probably," said March. "But we won't take this apartment till the ideal furnished flat winks out altogether. We shall not have any trouble. We can easily find some one who is going South for the winter and will be glad to give up their flat 'to the right party' at a nominal rent. That's my notion. That's what the Evanses did one winter when they came on here in February. All but the nominality of the rent."

"Yes, and we could pay a very good rent and still save something on letting our house. You can settle yourselves in a hundred different ways in New York, that *is* one merit of the place. But if everything else fails, we can come back to this. I want you to take the refusal of it, Basil. And we'll commence looking this very evening as soon as we've had dinner. I cut a lot of things out of the *Herald* as we came on. See here!"

She took a long strip of paper out of her hand-bag with minute advertisements pinned transversely upon it, and forming the effect of some glittering nondescript vertebrate.

"Looks something like the sea-serpent," said March, drying his hands on the towel, while he glanced up and down the list. "But we sha'n't have any trouble. I've no doubt there are half a dozen things there that will do. You haven't gone up-town? Because we must be near the *Every Other Week* office."

"No; but I *wish* Mr. Fulkerson hadn't called it that! It always makes one think of 'jam yesterday and jam to-morrow, but never jam to-day,' in *Through the Looking-Glass.* They're all in this region."

They were still at their table, beside a low window, where some sort of never-blooming shrub symmetrically balanced itself in a large pot, with a leaf to the right and a leaf to the left and a spear up the middle, when Fulkerson came stepping square-footedly over the thick dining-room carpet. He wagged in the air a gay hand of salutation at sight of them, and of repression when they offered to rise to meet him; then, with an apparent simultaneity of action he gave a hand to each, pulled up a chair from the next table, put his hat and stick on the floor beside it, and seated himself.

"Well, you've burned your ships behind you, sure enough," he said, beaming upon them from eyes and teeth.

"The ships are burned," said March, "though I'm not sure we alone did it. But here we are, looking for shelter, and a little anxious about the disposition of the natives."

"Oh, they're an awful peaceable lot," said Fulkerson. "I've been round among the caciques a little, and I think I've got two or three places that will just suit you, Mrs. March. How did you leave the children?"

"Oh, how kind of you! Very well, and very proud to be left in charge of the smoking wrecks."

Fulkerson naturally paid no attention to what she said, being but secondarily interested in the children at the best. "Here are some things right in this neighborhood, within gunshot of the office, and if you want you can go and look at them to-night; the agents gave me houses where the people would be in."

"We will go and look at them instantly," said Mrs. March. "Or, as soon as you've had coffee with us."

"Never do," Fulkerson replied. He gathered up his hat and stick. "Just rushed in to say Hello, and got to run right away again. I tell you, March, things are humming. I'm after those fellows with a sharp stick all the while to keep them from loafing on my house, and at the same time I'm just bubbling over with ideas about *The Lone Hand*—wish we *could* call it that!—that I want to talk up with you."

"Well, come to breakfast," said Mrs. March, cordially.

"No; the ideas will keep till you've secured your lodge in this vast wilderness. Good-bye."

"You're as nice as you can be, Mr. Fulkerson," she said, "to keep us in mind when you have so much to occupy you."

"I wouldn't have *any*thing to occupy me if I *hadn't* kept you in mind, Mrs. March," said Fulkerson, going off upon as good a speech as he could apparently hope to make.

"Why, Basil," said Mrs. March, when he was gone, "he's charming! But now we mustn't lose an instant. Let's see where the places are." She ran over the half-dozen agents' permits. "Capital—first-rate—the very thing—every one. Well, I consider ourselves settled! We can go back to the children to-morrow if we like, though I rather think I should like to stay over another day and get a little rested for the final pulling-up that's got to come. But this simplifies everything enormously, and Mr. Fulkerson is as thoughtful and as sweet as he can be. I know you will get on well with him. He has such a good heart. And his attitude toward you, Basil, is beautiful always—so respectful; or not that so much as appreciative. Yes, appreciative—that's the word; I must always keep that in mind."

"It's quite important to do so," said March.

"Yes," she assented, seriously, "and we must not forget just what kind of flat we are going to look for. The *sine qua nons* are an elevator and steam heat, not above the third floor, to begin with. Then we must each have a room, and you must have your study and I must have my parlor; and the two girls must each have a room. With the kitchen and dining-room, how many does that make?"

"Ten."

"I thought eight. Well, no matter. You can work in the parlor, and run into your bedroom when anybody comes; and I can sit in mine, and the girls must put up with one, if it's large and sunny, though I've always given them two at home. And the kitchen must be sunny, so they can sit in it. And the rooms must *all* have outside light. And the rent must not be over eight hundred for the winter. We only get a thousand for our whole house, and we *must* save something out of that, so as to cover the expenses of moving. Now, do you think you can remember all that?"

"Not the half of it," said March. "But *you* can; or if you forget a third of it, I can come in with my partial half and more than make it up."

She had brought her bonnet and sack downstairs with her, and was transferring them from the hat-rack to her person while she talked. The friendly door-boy let them into the street, and the clear October evening air brightened her so that as she tucked her hand under her husband's arm and began to pull him along she said, "If we find something right away—and we're just as likely to get the right flat soon as late; it's all a lottery—we'll go to the theatre somewhere."

She had a moment's panic about having left the agents' permits on the table, and after remembering that she had put them into her little shopping-bag, where she kept her money (each note crushed into a round wad), and had left it on the hat-rack, where it would certainly be stolen, she found it on her wrist. She did not think that very funny; but after a first impulse to inculpate her husband, she let him laugh, while they stopped under a lamp and she held the permits half a yard away to read the numbers on them.

"Where are your glasses, Isabel?"

"On the mantel in our room, of course."

"Then you ought to have brought a pair of tongs."

"I wouldn't get off second-hand jokes, Basil," she said; and "Why, here!" she cried, whirling round to the door before which they had halted, "this is the very number. Well, I do believe it's a sign!"

One of those colored men who soften the trade of janitor in many of the smaller apartment-houses in New York by the sweetness of their race let the Marches in, or rather, welcomed them to the possession of the premises by the bow with which he acknowledged their permit. It was a large, old mansion cut up into five or six dwellings, but it had kept some traits of its former dignity, which pleased people of their sympathetic tastes. The dark-mahogany trim, of sufficiently ugly design, gave a rich gloom to the hallway, which was wide and paved with marble; the carpeted stairs curved aloft through a generous space.

"There is no elevator?" Mrs. March asked of the janitor.

He answered, "No, ma'am; only two flights up," so winningly that she said—"Oh!" in courteous apology, and whispered her husband, as she followed lightly up, "We'll take it, Basil, if it's like the rest."

"If it's like him, you mean."

"I don't wonder they wanted to own them," she hurriedly philosophized. "If I had such a creature, nothing but death should part us, and I should no more think of giving him his *freedom*!"

"No; we couldn't afford it," returned her husband.

The apartment the janitor unlocked for them, and lit up from those chandeliers and brackets of gilt brass in the form of vine bunches, leaves, and tendrils in which the early gas-fitter realized most of his conceptions of beauty, had rather more of the ugliness than the dignity of the hall. But the rooms were large, and they grouped themselves in a reminiscence of the time when they were part of a dwelling that had its charm, its pathos, its impressiveness. Where they were cut up into smaller spaces, it had been done with the frankness with which a proud old family of fallen fortunes practises its economies. The rough pine floors showed a black border of tack-heads where carpets had been lifted and put down for generations; the white paint was yellow with age; the apartment had light at the front and at the back, and two or three rooms had glimpses of the day through small windows let into their corners; another one seemed lifting an appealing eye to heaven through a glass circle in its ceiling; the rest must darkle in perpetual twilight. Yet something pleased in it all, and Mrs. March had gone far to adapt the different rooms to the members of her family, when she suddenly thought (and for her to think was to say), "Why, but there's no steam heat!"

"No, ma'am," the janitor admitted; "but dere's grates in most o' de rooms, and dere's furnace heat in de halls."

"That's true," she admitted, and, having placed her family in the apartments, it was hard to get them out again. "Could we manage?" she referred to her husband.

"Why, *I* shouldn't care for the steam heat if— What is the rent?" he broke off to ask the janitor.

"Nine hundred, sir."

March concluded to his wife, "If it were furnished."

"Why, of course! What could I have been thinking of? We're looking for a furnished flat," she explained to the janitor, "and this was so pleasant and home-like that I never thought whether it was furnished or not."

She smiled upon the janitor, and he entered into the joke and chuckled so amiably at her flattering oversight on the way downstairs that she said, as she pinched her husband's arm, "Now, if you don't give him a quarter, I'll never speak to you again, Basil!"

"I would have given half a dollar willingly to get you beyond his glamour," said March, when they were safely on the pavement outside. "If it hadn't been for my strength of character, you'd have taken an unfurnished flat without heat and with no elevator, at nine hundred a year, when you had just sworn me to steam-heat, an elevator, furniture, and eight hundred."

"Yes! How could I have lost my head so completely?" she said, with a lenient amusement in her aberration which she was not always able to feel in her husband's.

"The next time a colored janitor opens the door to us, I'll tell him the apartment doesn't suit at the threshold. It's the only way to manage you, Isabel."

"It's true. I *am* in love with the whole race. I never saw one of them that didn't have perfectly angelic manners. I think we shall all be black in heaven—that is, black-souled."

"That isn't the usual theory," said March.

"Well, perhaps not," she assented. "Where are we going now. Oh yes, to the Xenophon!"

She pulled him gayly along again, and after they had walked a block down and half a block over they stood before the apartment-house of that name, which was cut on the gas-lamps on either side of the heavily spiked, aesthetic-hinged black door. The titter of an electric-bell brought a large, fat Buttons, with a stage effect of being dressed to look small, who said he would call the janitor, and they waited in the dimly splendid, copper-coloured interior, admiring the whorls and waves into which the wall-paint was combed, till the janitor came in his gold-banded cap, like a continental *portier*. When they said they would like to see Mrs. Grosvenor Green's apartment, he owned his inability to cope with the affair, and said he must send for the Superintendent; he was either in the Herodotus or the Thucydides, and would be there in a minute. The Buttons brought him—a Yankee of browbeating presence in plain clothes—almost before they had time to exchange a frightened whisper in recognition of the fact that there could be no doubt of the steam-heat and elevator in this case. Half stifled in the one, they mounted in the other eight stories, while they tried to keep their self-respect under the gaze of the Superintendent, which they felt was classing and assessing them with unfriendly accuracy. They could not, and they faltered abashed at the threshold of Mrs. Grosvenor Green's apartment, while the Superintendent lit the gas in the gangway that he called a private hall, and in the drawing-room and the succession of chambers stretching rearward to the kitchen. Everything had been done by the architect to save space, and everything to waste it by Mrs. Grosvenor Green. She had conformed to a law for the necessity of turning round in each room, and had folding-beds in the chambers; but there her subordination had ended, and wherever you might have turned round she had put a gimcrack so that you would knock it over if you did turn. The place was rather pretty and even imposing at first glance, and it took several joint ballots for March and his wife to make sure that with the kitchen there were only six rooms. At every door hung a portière from large rings on a brass rod; every shelf and dressing-case and mantel was littered with gimcracks, and the corners of the tiny rooms were curtained off, and behind these portières swarmed more gimcracks. The front of the upright piano had what March called a short-skirted portière on it, and the top was covered with vases, with dragon candlesticks and with Jap fans, which also expanded themselves bat-wise on the walls between the etchings and the water-colors. The floors were covered with filling, and then rugs and then skins; the easy-chairs all had tidies, Armenian and Turkish and Persian; the lounges and sofas had embroidered cushions hidden under tidies. The radiator was concealed by a Jap screen, and over the top of this some Arab scarfs were flung. There was a superabundance of clocks. China pugs guarded the hearth; a brass sunflower smiled from the top of either andiron, and a brass peacock spread its tail before them inside a high filigree fender; on one side was a coal-hod in *repoussé* brass, and on the other a wrought-iron wood-basket. Some red Japanese bird-kites were stuck about in the necks of spelter vases, a crimson Jap umbrella hung opened beneath the chandelier, and each globe had a shade of yellow silk.

March, when he had recovered his self-command a little in the presence of the agglomeration, comforted himself by calling the bric-à-brac James-cracks, as if this was their full name.

The disrespect he was able to show the whole apartment by means of this joke strengthened him to say boldly to the Superintendent that it was altogether too small; then he asked carelessly what the rent was.

"Two hundred and fifty."

The Marches gave a start, and looked at each other.

"Don't you think we could make it do?" she asked him, and he could see that she had mentally saved five hundred dollars as the difference between the rent of their house and that of this flat. "It has some very pretty features, and we could manage to squeeze in, couldn't we?"

"You won't find another furnished flat like it for no two fifty a month in the whole city," the superintendent put in.

They exchanged glances again, and March said, carelessly, "It's too small."

"There's a vacant flat in the Herodotus for eighteen hundred a year, and one in the Thucydides for fifteen," the Superintendent suggested, clicking his keys together as they sank down in the elevator; "seven rooms and bath."

"Thank you," said March; "we're looking for a furnished flat."

They felt that the Superintendent parted from them with repressed sarcasm.

"Oh, Basil, do you think we *really* made him think it was the smallness and not the dearness?"

"No, but we saved our self-respect in the attempt; and that's a great deal."

"Of course, I *wouldn't* have taken it, anyway, with only six rooms, and so high up. But what prices! Now, we must be very circumspect about the next place."

It was a janitress, large, fat, with her arms wound up in her apron, who received them there. Mrs. March gave her a succinct but perfect statement of their needs. She failed to grasp the nature of them, or feigned to do so. She shook her head, and said that her son would show them the flat. There was a radiator visible in the narrow hall, and Isabel tacitly compromised on steam-heat without an elevator, as the flat was only one flight up. When the son appeared from below with a small kerosene hand-lamp, it appeared that the flat was unfurnished, but there was no stopping him till he had shown it in all its impossibility. When they got safely away from it and into the street March said, "Well, have you had enough for to-night, Isabel? Shall we go to the theatre now?"

"Not on any account. I want to see the whole list of flats that Mr. Fulkerson thought would be the very thing for us." She laughed, but with a certain bitterness.

"You'll be calling him my Mr. Fulkerson next, Isabel."

"Oh no!"

The fourth address was a furnished flat without a kitchen, in a house with a general restaurant. The fifth was a furnished house. At the sixth a pathetic widow and her pretty daughter wanted to take a family to board, and would give them a private table at a rate which the Marches would have thought low in Boston.

Mrs. March came away tingling with compassion for their evident anxiety, and this pity naturally soured into a sense of injury. "Well, I must say I have completely lost confidence in Mr. Fulkerson's judgment. Anything more utterly different from what I told him we wanted I couldn't imagine. If he doesn't manage any better about his business than he has done about this, it will be a perfect failure."

"Well, well, let's hope he'll be more circumspect about that," her husband returned, with ironical propitiation. "But I don't think it's Fulkerson's fault altogether. Perhaps it's the house-agents'. They're a very illusory generation. There seems to be something in the human habitation that corrupts the natures of those who deal in it, to buy or sell it, to hire or let it. You go to an agent and tell him what kind of a house you want. He has no such house, and he sends you to look at something altogether different, upon the well-ascertained principle that if you can't get what you want you will take what you can get. You don't suppose the 'party' that took our house in Boston was looking for any such house? He was looking for a totally different kind of house in another part of the town."

"I don't believe that!" his wife broke in.

"Well, no matter. But see what a scandalous rent you asked for it."

"We didn't get much more than half; and, besides, the agent told me to ask fourteen hundred."

"Oh, I'm not blaming you, Isabel. I'm only analyzing the house-agent, and exonerating Fulkerson."

"Well, I don't believe he told them just what we wanted; and, at any rate, I'm done with agents. Tomorrow, I'm going entirely by advertisements."

Chapter XI

[*Howells accepted the editorship of the "Editor's Study" of* Harper's *in 1886; March, his counterpart, occupied the position of literary editor of* Every Other Week. *This paper is owned by an ignorant, opinionated oil magnate, Mr. Dryfoos, and managed by the aggressive but well-intentioned advertiser, Mr. Fulkerson, who had persuaded March to give up his position in Boston and migrate to New York. March's final effort to find an apartment in New York is interrupted by lunch with Fulkerson, who gives March much to think about.*]

Mrs. March was one of those wives who exact a more rigid adherence to their ideals from their husbands than from themselves. Early in their married life she had taken charge of him in all matters which she considered practical. She did not include the business of bread-winning in these; that was an affair that might safely be left to his absent-minded, dreamy inefficiency, and she did not interfere with him there. But in such things as rehanging the pictures, deciding on a summer boarding-place, taking a seaside cottage, repapering rooms, choosing seats at the theatre, seeing what the children ate when she was not at table, shutting the cat out at night, keeping run of calls and invitations, and seeing if the furnace was damped, he had failed her so often that she felt she could not leave him the slightest discretion in regard to a flat. Her total distrust of his judgment in the matters cited and others like them consisted with the greatest admiration of his mind and respect for his character. She often said that if he would only bring these to bear in such exigencies he would be simply perfect; but she had long given up his ever doing so. She subjected him, therefore, to an iron code, but after proclaiming it she was apt to abandon him to the native lawlessness of his temperament. She expected him in this event to do as he pleased, and she resigned herself to it with considerable comfort in holding him accountable. He learned to expect this, and after suffering keenly from her disappointment with whatever he did he waited patiently till she forgot her grievance and began to extract what consolation lurks in the irreparable. She would almost admit at moments that what he had done was a very good thing, but she reserved the right to return in full force to her original condemnation of it; and she accumulated each act of independent volition in witness and warning against him. Their mass oppressed but never deterred him. He expected to do the wrong thing when left to his own devices, and he did it without any apparent recollection of his former misdeeds and their consequences. There was a good deal of comedy in it all, and some tragedy.

He now experienced a certain expansion, such as husbands of his kind will imagine, on going back to his hotel alone. It was, perhaps, a revulsion from the pain of parting; and he toyed with the idea of Mrs. Grosvenor Green's apartment, which, in its preposterous unsuitability, had a strange attraction. He felt that he could take it with less risk than anything else they had seen, but he said he would look at all the other places in town first. He really spent the greater part of the next day in hunting up the owner of an apartment that had neither steam heat nor an elevator, but was otherwise perfect, and trying to get him to take less than the agent asked. By a curious psychical operation he was able, in the transactions, to work himself into quite a passionate desire for the apartment, while he held the Grosvenor Green apartment in the background of his mind as something that he could return to as altogether more suitable. He conducted some simultaneous negotiation for a furnished house, which enhanced still more the desirability of the Grosvenor Green apartment. Toward evening he went off at a tangent far up-town, so as to be able to tell his wife how utterly preposterous the best there would be as compared even with this ridiculous Grosvenor Green gimcrackery. It is hard to report the processes of his sophistication; perhaps this, again, may best be left to the marital imagination.

He rang at the last of these up-town apartments as it was falling dusk, and it was long before the janitor appeared. Then the man was very surly, and said if he looked at the flat now he would say it was too dark, like all the rest. His reluctance irritated March in proportion to his insincerity in proposing to look at it at all. He knew he did not mean to take it under any circumstances; that he was going to use his inspection of it in dishonest justification of his disobedience to his wife; but he put on an air of offended dignity. "If you don't wish to show the apartment," he said, "I don't care to see it."

The man groaned, for he was heavy, and no doubt dreaded the stairs. He scratched a match on his thigh, and led the way up. March was sorry for him, and he put his fingers on a quarter in his waistcoat-pocket to give him at parting. At the same time, he had to trump up an objection to the flat. This was easy, for it was advertised as containing ten rooms, and he found the number eked out with the bath-room and two large closets. "It's light enough," said March, "but I don't see how you make out ten rooms."

"There's ten rooms," said the man, deigning no proof.

March took his fingers off the quarter, and went downstairs and out of the door without another word. It would be wrong, it would be impossible, to give the man anything after such insolence. He reflected, with shame, that it was also cheaper to punish than forgive him.

He returned to his hotel prepared for any desperate measure, and convinced now that the Grosvenor Green apartment was not merely the only thing left for him, but was, on its own merits, the best thing in New York.

Fulkerson was waiting for him in the reading-room, and it gave March the curious thrill with which a man closes with temptation when he said: "Look here! Why don't you take that woman's flat in the Xenophon? She's been at the agents again, and they've been at me. She likes your look—or Mrs. March's —and I guess you can have it at a pretty heavy discount from the original price. I'm authorized to say you can have it for one seventy-five a month, and I don't believe it would be safe for you to offer one fifty."

March shook his head, and dropped a mask of virtuous rejection over his corrupt acquiescence. "It's too small for us—we couldn't squeeze it."

"Why, look here!" Fulkerson persisted. "How many rooms do you want?"

"I've got to have a place to work—"

"Of course! And you've got to have it at the *Fifth Wheel* office."

"I hadn't thought of that," March began. "I suppose I *could* do my work at the office, as there's not much writing—"

"Why, of course you can't do your work at home. You just come round with me now, and look at that flat again."

"No; I can't do it."

"Why?"

"I—I've got to dine."

"All right," said Fulkerson. "Dine with me. I want to take you round to a little Italian place that I know."

One may trace the successive steps of March's descent in this simple matter with the same edification that would attend the study of the self-delusions and obfuscations of a man tempted to crime. The process is probably not at all different, and to the philosophical mind the kind of result is unimportant; the process is everything.

Fulkerson led him down one block and half across another to the steps of a small dwelling-house, transformed, like many others, into a restaurant of the Latin ideal, with little or no structural change from the pattern of the lower middle-class New York home. There were the corroded brown-stone steps, the mean little front door, and the cramped entry with its narrow stairs by which ladies could go up to a dining-room appointed for them on the second floor; the parlours on the first were set about with tables, where men smoked cigarettes between the courses, and a single waiter ran swiftly to and fro with plates and dishes, and exchanged unintelligible outcries with a cook beyond a slide in the back parlor. He rushed at the new-comers, brushed the soiled table-cloth before them with a towel on his arm, covered its worst stains with a napkin, and brought them, in their order, the vermicelli soup, the fried fish, the cheese-strewn spaghetti, the veal cutlets, the tepid roast fowl and salad, and the wizened pear and coffee which form the dinner at such places.

"Ah, this is *nice*!" said Fulkerson, after the laying of the charitable napkin, and he began to recognise acquaintances, some of whom he described to March as young literary men and artists with whom they should probably have to do; others were simply frequenters of the place, and were all nationalities and religions apparently—at least, several were Hebrews and Cubans. "You get a pretty good slice of New York here," he said, "all except the frosting on top. That you won't find much at Maroni's, though you will occasionally. I don't mean the ladies ever, of course." The ladies present seemed harmless and reputable looking people enough, but certainly they were not of the first fashion, and, except in a few instances, not Americans. "It's like cutting straight down through a fruit-cake," Fulkerson went on, "or a mince-pie, when you don't know who made the pie; you get a little of everything." He ordered a small flask of Chianti with the dinner, and it came in its pretty wicker jacket. March smiled upon it with tender reminiscence, and Fulkerson laughed. "Lights you up a little. I brought old Dryfoos here one day, and he thought it was sweet-oil; that's the kind of bottle they used to have it in at the country drug-stores."

"Yes, I remember now; but I'd totally forgotten it," said March. "How far back that goes! Who's Dryfoos?"

"Dryfoos?" Fulkerson, still smiling, tore off a piece of the half-yard of French loaf which had been supplied them, with two pale, thin disks of butter, and fed it into himself. "Old Dryfoos? Well, of course! I call him old, but he ain't so very. About fifty, or along there."

"No," said March, "that isn't very old—or not so old as it used to be."

"Well, I suppose you've got to know about him anyway," said Fulkerson, thoughtfully. "And I've been wondering just how I should tell you. Can't always make out exactly how much of a Bostonian you really *are*! Ever been out in the natural-gas country?"

"No," said March. "I've had a good deal of curiosity about it, but I've never been able to get away except in summer, and then we always preferred to go over the old ground, out to Niagara and back through Canada, the route we took on our wedding journey. The children like it as much as we do."

"Yes, yes," said Fulkerson. "Well, the natural-gas country is worth seeing. I don't mean the Pittsburg gas-fields, but out in Northern Ohio and Indiana around Moffitt—that's the place in the heart of the gas region that they've been booming so. Yes, you ought to see that country. If you haven't been West for a good many years, you haven't got any idea how old the country looks. You remember how the fields used to be all full of stumps?"

"I should think so."

"Well, you won't see any stumps now. All that country out around Moffitt is just as smooth as a checker-board, and looks as old as England. You know how we used to burn the stumps out; and then somebody invented a stump-extractor, and we pulled them out with a yoke of oxen. Now they just touch 'em off with a little dynamite, and they've got a cellar dug and filled up with kindling ready for house-keeping whenever you want it. Only they haven't got any use for kindling in that country—all gas. I rode along on the cars through those level black fields at corn-planting time, and every once in a while I'd come to a place with a piece of ragged old stove-pipe stickin' up out of the ground, and blazing away like forty, and a fellow ploughing all round it and not minding it any more than if it was spring violets. Horses didn't notice it, either. Well, they've always known about the gas out there; they say there are places in the woods where it's been burning ever since the country was settled.

"But when you come in sight of Moffitt—my, oh, my! Well, you come in smell of it about as soon. That gas out there ain't odorless, like the Pittsburg gas, and so it's perfectly safe; but the smell isn't bad—about as bad as the finest kind of benzine. Well, the first thing that strikes you when you come to Moffitt is the notion that there has been a good warm, growing rain, and the town's come up overnight. That's in the suburbs, the annexes, and additions. But it ain't shabby—no shanty-town business; nice brick and frame houses, some of 'em Queen Anne style, and all of 'em looking as if they had come to stay. And when you drive up from the depôt you think everybody's mov-

ing. Everything seems to be piled into the street; old houses
made over, and new ones going up everywhere. You know the
kind of street Main Street always used to be in our section—half
plank-road and turnpike, and the rest mud-hole, and a lot of
stores and doggeries strung along with false fronts a story
higher than the back, and here and there a decent building with
the gable end to the public; and a court-house and jail and two
taverns and three or four churches. Well, they're all there in
Moffitt yet, but architecture has struck it hard, and they've got
a lot of new buildings that needn't be ashamed of themselves
anywhere; the new court-house is as big as St. Peter's, and the
Grand Opera-House is in the highest style of the art. You can't
buy a lot on that street for much less than you can buy a lot in
New York—or you couldn't when the boom was on; I saw the
place just when the boom was in its prime. I went out there to
work the newspapers in the syndicate business, and I got one of
their men to write me a real bright, snappy account of the gas;
and they just took me in their arms and showed me everything.
Well, it *was* wonderful, and it was beautiful, too! To see a whole
community stirred up like that was—just like a big boy, all hope
and high spirits, and no discount on the remotest future; nothing
but perpetual boom to the end of time—I tell you it warmed
your blood. Why, there were some things about it that made
you think what a nice kind of world this would be if people ever
took hold together, instead of each fellow fighting it out on his
own hook, and devil take the hindmost. They made up their
minds at Moffitt that if they wanted their town to grow they'd
got to keep their gas public property. So they extended their
corporation line so as to take in pretty much the whole gas
region round there; and then the city took possession of every
well that was put down, and held it for the common good.
Anybody that's a mind to come to Moffitt and start any kind of
manufacture can have all the gas he wants *free*; and for fifteen
dollars a year you can have all the gas you want to heat and light
your private house. The people hold on to it for themselves,
and, as I say, it's a grand sight to see a whole community hanging
together and working for the good of all, instead of splitting up

into as many different cut-throats as there are able-bodied citizens. See that fellow?" Fulkerson broke off, and indicated with a twirl of his head a short, dark, foreign-looking man going out of the door. "They say that fellow's a Socialist. I think it's a shame they're allowed to come here. If they don't like the way we manage our affairs, let 'em stay at home," Fulkerson continued. "They do a lot of mischief, shooting off their mouths round here. I believe in free speech and all that; but I'd like to see these fellows shut up in jail and left to jaw one another to death. *We* don't want any of their poison."

March did not notice the vanishing Socialist. He was watching, with a teasing sense of familiarity, a tall, shabbily dressed, elderly man, who had just come in. He had the aquiline profile uncommon among Germans, and yet March recognized him at once as German. His long, soft beard and mustache had once been fair, and they kept some tone of their yellow in the gray to which they had turned. His eyes were full, and his lips and chin shaped the beard to the noble outline which shows in the beards the Italian masters liked to paint for their Last Suppers. His carriage was erect and soldierly, and March presently saw that he had lost his left hand. He took his place at a table where the overworked waiter found time to cut up his meat and put everything in easy reach of his right hand.

"Well," Fulkerson resumed, "they took me round everywhere in Moffitt, and showed me their big wells—lit 'em up for a private view, and let me hear them purr with the soft accents of a mass-meeting of locomotives. Why, when they let one of these wells loose in a meadow that they'd piped it into temporarily, it drove the flame away forty feet from the mouth of the pipe and blew it over half an acre of ground. They say when they let one of their big wells burn away all winter before they had learned how to control it, that well kept up a little summer all around it; the grass stayed green, and the flowers bloomed all through the winter. *I* don't know whether it's so or not. But I can believe anything of natural gas. My! but it was beautiful when they turned on the full force of that well and shot a roman candle into the gas—that's the way they light it—and a plume of fire about twenty feet wide and seventy-five feet high, all red and yellow and violet, jumped into the sky, and that big roar shook the ground under your feet! You felt like saying: 'Don't trouble yourself; I'm perfectly convinced. I believe in Moffitt.' We-e-e-ll!" drawled Fulkerson, with a long breath, "that's where I met old Dryfoos."

"Oh yes!—Dryfoos," said March. He observed that the waiter had brought the old one-handed German a towering glass of beer.

"Yes," Fulkerson laughed. "We've got round to Dryfoos again. I thought I could cut a long story short, but I seem to be cutting a short story long. If you're not in a hurry, though—"

"Not in the least. Go on as long as you like."

"I met him there in the office of a real-estate man—speculator, of course; everybody was, in Moffitt; but a first-rate fellow, and public-spirited as all get-out; and when Dryfoos left he told me about him. Dryfoos was an old Pennsylvania Dutch farmer, about three or four miles out of Moffitt, and he'd lived there pretty much all his life; father was one of the first settlers. Everybody knew he had the right stuff in him, but he was slower than molasses in January, like those Pennsylvania Dutch. He'd got together the largest and handsomest farm anywhere around there; and he was making money on it, just like he was in some business somewhere; he was a very intelligent man; he took the papers and kept himself posted; but he was awfully old-fashioned in his ideas. He hung on to the doctrines as well as the dollars of the dads; it was a real thing with him. Well, when the boom began to come he hated it awfully, and he fought it. He used to write communications to the weekly newspaper in Moffitt—they've got three dailies there now—and throw cold water on the boom. He couldn't catch on no way. It made him sick to hear the clack that went on about the gas the whole while, and that stirred up the neighborhood and got into his family. Whenever he'd hear of a man that had been offered a big price of his land and was going to sell out and move into town, he'd go and labor with him and try to talk him out of it, and tell him how long his fifteen or twenty thousand would last him to live on, and shake the Standard Oil Company before him, and try to make him believe it wouldn't be five years before the Standard owned the whole region.

"Of course, he couldn't do anything with them. When a man's offered a big price for his farm, he don't care whether it's by a secret emissary from the Standard Oil or not; he's going to sell and get the better of the other fellow if he can. Dryfoos couldn't keep the boom out of his own family even. His wife was with him. She thought whatever he said and did was just as right as if it had been thundered down from Sinai. But the young folks were sceptical, especially the girls that had been away to school. The boy that had been kept at home because he couldn't be spared from helping his father manage the farm was more like him, but they contrived to stir the boy up with the hot end of the boom, too. So when a fellow came along one day and offered old Dryfoos a cool hundred thousand for his farm, it was all up with Dryfoos. He'd 'a' liked to 'a' kept the offer to himself and not done anything about it, but his vanity wouldn't let him do that; and when he let it out in his family the girls outvoted him. They just *made* him sell.

"He wouldn't sell all. He kept about eighty acres that was off in one piece by itself, but the three hundred that had the old brick house on it, and the big barn—that went, and Dryfoos bought him a place in Moffitt and moved into town to live on the interest of his money. Just what he had scolded and ridiculed everybody else for doing. Well, they say that at first he seemed like he would go crazy. He hadn't anything to do. He took a fancy to that land-agent, and he used to go and set in his office and ask him what he should do. 'I hain't got any horses, I hain't got any cows, I hain't got any pigs, I hain't got any chickens. I hain't got anything to do from sunup to sundown.' The fellow said the tears used to run down the old fellow's cheeks, and if he hadn't been so busy himself he believed he should 'a' cried, too. But most o' people thought old Dryfoos was down in the mouth because he hadn't asked more for his farm, when he wanted to buy it back and found they held it at a hundred and fifty thousand. People couldn't believe he was just homesick and heartsick for the old place. Well, perhaps he *was* sorry he hadn't asked more; that's human nature, *too*.

"After a while something happened. That land-agent used to tell Dryfoos to get out to Europe with his money and see life a little, or go and live in Washington, where he could *be* somebody; but Dryfoos wouldn't, and he kept listening to the talk there, and all of a sudden he caught on. He came into that fellow's one day with a plan for cutting up the eighty acres he'd kept into town lots; and he'd got it all plotted out so well, and had so many practical ideas about it, that the fellow was astonished. He went right in with him, as far as Dryfoos would let him, and glad of the chance; and they were working the thing for all it was worth when I struck Moffitt. Old Dryfoos wanted me to go out and see the Dryfoos & Hendry Addition—guess he thought may be I'd write it up; and he drove me out there himself. Well, it was funny to see a town made: streets driven through; two rows of shade-trees, hard and soft, planted; cellars dug and houses put up—regular Queen Anne style, too, with stained glass—all at once. Dryfoos apologized for the streets because they were hand-made; said they expected their street-making machine Tuesday, and then they intended to *push* things."

Fulkerson enjoyed the effect of his picture on March for a moment, and then went on: "He was mighty intelligent, too, and he questioned me up about my business as sharp as *I* ever was questioned; seemed to kind of strike his fancy; I guess he wanted to find out if there was any money in it. He was making money, hand over hand, then; and he never stopped speculating and improving till he'd scraped together three or four hundred thousand dollars; they said a million, but they like round numbers at Moffitt, and I guess half a million would lay over it comfortably and leave a few thousands to spare, probably. Then he came on to New York."

Fulkerson struck a match against the ribbed side of the porcelain cup that held the matches in the centre of the table, and lit a cigarette, which he began to smoke, throwing his head back with a leisurely effect, as if he had got to the end of at least as much of his story as he meant to tell without prompting.

March asked him the desired question. "What in the world for?"

Fulkerson took out his cigarette and said, with a smile: "To spend his money, and get his daughters into the old Knickerbocker society. May be he thought they were all the same kind of Dutch."

"And has he succeeded?"

"Well, they're not social leaders yet. But it's only a question of time—generation or two—especially if time's money, and if *Every Other Week* is the success it's bound to be."

"You don't mean to say, Fulkerson," said March, with a half-doubting, half-daunted laugh, "that *he's* your Angel?"

"That's what I mean to say," returned Fulkerson. "I ran onto him in Broadway one day last summer. If you ever saw anybody in your life, you're sure to meet him in Broadway again, sooner or later. That's the philosophy of the bunco business; country people from the same neighborhood are sure to run up against each other the first time they come to New York. I put out my hand, and I said, 'Isn't this Mr. Dryfoos from Moffitt?' He didn't seem to have any use for my hand; he let me keep it, and he squared those old lips of his till his imperial stuck straight out. Ever seen Bernhardt in '*L'Étrangère*'? Well, the American husband is old Dryfoos all over; no mustache, and hay-coloured chin-whiskers cut slanting from the corners of his mouth. He cocked his little gray eyes at me, and says he, 'Yes, young man; my name *is* Dryfoos, and I'm from Moffitt. But I don't want no present of Longfellow's Works, illustrated; and I don't want to taste no fine teas; but I know a policeman that does; and if you're the son of my old friend Squire Strohfeldt, you'd better get out.' 'Well, then,' said I, 'how would you like to go into the newspaper syndicate business?' He gave another look at me, and then he burst out laughing, and he grabbed my hand, and he just froze to it. I never saw anybody so glad.

"Well, the long and the short of it was that I asked him round here to Maroni's to dinner; and before we broke up for the night we had settled the financial side of the plan that's brought you to New York. I can see," said Fulkerson, who had kept his eyes fast on March's face, "that you don't more than half like the idea of Dryfoos. It ought to give you more confidence in the thing than you ever had. You needn't be afraid," he added, with some feeling, "that I talked Dryfoos into the thing for my own advantage."

"Oh, my dear Fulkerson!" March protested, all the more fervently because he was really a little guilty.

"Well, of course not! I didn't mean you were. But I just happened to tell him what I wanted to go into when I could see my way to it, and he caught on of his own accord. The fact is," said Fulkerson, "I guess I'd better make a clean breast of it, now I'm at it. Dryfoos wanted to get something for that boy of his to do. He's in railroads himself, and he's in mines and other things, and he keeps busy, and he can't bear to have his boy hanging round the house doing nothing, like as if he was a girl. I told him that the great object of a rich man was to get his son into just that fix, but he couldn't seem to see it, and the boy hated it himself. He's got a good head, and he wanted to study for the ministry when they were all living together out on the farm; but his father had the old-fashioned ideas about that. You know they used to think that any sort of stuff was good enough to make a preacher out of; but they wanted the good timber for business; and so the old man wouldn't let him. You'll see the fellow; you'll like him; he's no fool, I can tell you; and he's going to be our publisher, nominally at first and actually when I've taught him the ropes a little."

PART FOURTH

Chapter III

[*Though Howells disavows the actual experiences of the Marches as his own, the reader, nevertheless, is aware of the pleasant fact that Basil and Isabel March are literary reflections of Mr. and Mrs. Howells. In the chapter which follows, one catches glimpses of Howells himself talking with young writers in the office of* Harper's, *listening to sermons in New York churches, and contemplating the disparities between rich and poor in the* "huge, noisy, ugly, kindly city" *of his adoption. In this novel, which Howells tells us* "filled the *largest canvas I had ever allowed myself," we are introduced to a variety of characters, such as Colonel Woodburn, Alma Leighton, and Mr. Beaton, art-editor of* Every Other Week.]

First and last, the Marches did a good deal of travel on the Elevated roads, which, he said, gave you such glimpses of material aspects in the city as some violent invasion of others' lives might afford in human nature. Once, when the impulse of adventure was very strong in them, they went quite the length of the West side lines, and saw the city pushing its way by irregular advances into the country. Some spaces, probably held by the owners for that rise in value which the industry of others providentially gives to the land of the wise and good, it left vacant comparatively far down the road, and built up others at remoter points. It was a world of lofty apartment-houses beyond the Park, springing up in isolated blocks, with stretches of invaded rusticity between, and here and there an old country-seat standing dusty in its budding vines with the ground before it in rocky upheaval for city foundations. But wherever it went or wherever it paused, New York gave its peculiar stamp; and the adventurers were amused to find One Hundred and Twenty-fifth Street inchoately like Twenty-third Street and Fourteenth Street in its shops and shoppers. The butchers' shops and milliners' shops on the avenue might as well have been at Tenth as at One Hundredth Street.

The adventurers were not often so adventurous. They recognized that in their willingness to let their fancy range for them, and to let speculation do the work of inquiry, they were no longer young. Their point of view was singularly unchanged, and their impressions of New York remained the same that they had been fifteen years before: huge, noisy, ugly, kindly, it seemed to them now as it seemed then. The main difference was that they saw it more now as a life, and then they only regarded it as a spectacle; and March could not release himself from a sense of complicity with it, no matter what whimsical, or alien, or critical attitude he took. A sense of the striving and the suffering deeply possessed him; and this grew the more intense as he gained some knowledge of the forces at work—forces of pity, of destruction, of perdition, of salvation. He wandered about on Sunday not only through the streets, but into this tabernacle and that, as the spirit moved him, and listened to those who dealt with Christianity as a system of economics as well as a religion. He could not get his wife to go with him; she listened to his report of what he heard, and trembled; it all seemed fantastic and menacing. She lamented the literary peace, the intellectual refinement of the life they had left behind them; and he owned it was very pretty, but he said it was not life—it was death-in-life. She liked to hear him talk in that strain of virtuous self-denunciation, but she asked him, "Which of your prophets are you going to follow?" and he answered: "All—all! And a fresh one every Sunday." And so they got their laugh out of it at last, but with some sadness at heart, and with a dim consciousness that they had got their laugh out of too many things in life.

What really occupied and compassed his activities, in spite of his strenuous reveries of work beyond it, was his editorship. On its social side it had not fulfilled all the expectations which Fulkerson's radiant sketch of its duties and relations had caused him to form of it. Most of the contributions came from a distance; even the articles written in New York reached him through the post, and so far from having his valuable time, as they called it, consumed in interviews with his collaborators, he rarely saw any of them. The boy on the stairs, who was to fence him from importunate visitors, led a life of luxurious disoccupation, and whistled almost uninterruptedly. When any one came, March found himself embarrassed and a little anxious. The visitors were usually young men, terribly respectful, but cherishing, as he imagined, ideals and opinions chasmally different from his; and he felt in their presence something like an anachronism, something like a fraud. He tried to freshen up his sympathies on them, to get at what they were really thinking and feeling, and it was some time before he could understand that they were not really thinking and feeling anything of their own concerning their art, but were necessarily, in their quality of young, inexperienced men, mere acceptants of older men's thoughts and feelings, whether they were tremendously conservative, as some were, or tremendously progressive, as others were. Certain of them called themselves realists, certain romanticists; but none of them seemed to know what realism was, or what romanticism; they apparently supposed the difference a difference of material. March had imagined himself taking home to lunch or dinner the aspirants for editorial favor whom he liked, whether he liked their work or not; but this was not an easy matter. Those who were at all interesting seemed to have engagements and preoccupations; after two or three experiments with the bashfuller sort—those who had come to the metropolis with manuscripts in their hands, in the good literary tradition—he wondered whether he was otherwise like them when he was young like them. He could not flatter himself that he was not; and yet he had a hope that the world had grown worse since his time, which his wife encouraged.

Mrs. March was not eager to pursue the hospitalities which she had at first imagined essential to the literary prosperity of *Every Other Week;* her family sufficed her; she would willingly have seen no one out of it but the strangers at the weekly *table-d'hôte* dinner, or the audiences at the theatres. March's devotion to his work made him reluctant to delegate it to any one; and as the summer advanced, and the question of where to go grew more vexed, he showed a man's base willingness to shirk it for himself by not going anywhere. He asked his wife why she did not go somewhere with the children, and he joined her in a search for non-malarial regions on the map when she consented to entertain this notion. But when it came to the point she would not go; he offered to go with her then, and then she would not let him. She said she knew he would be anxious about his work; he protested that he could take it with him to any distance within a few hours, but she would not be persuaded. She would rather he stayed; the effect would be better with Mr. Fulkerson; they could make excursions, and they could all get off a week or two to the sea-shore near Boston—the only real sea-shore—in August. The excursions were practically confined to a single day at Coney Island; and once they got as far as Boston on the way to the sea-shore near Boston; that is, Mrs. March and the children went; an editorial exigency kept March at the last moment. The Boston streets seemed very queer and clean and empty to the children, and the buildings little; in the horse-cars the Boston faces seemed to arraign their mother with a down-drawn severity that made her feel very guilty. She knew that this was merely the Puritan mask, the cast of a dead civilization, which people of very amiable and tolerant minds were doomed to wear, and she sighed to think that less than a year of the heterogeneous gaiety of New York should have made her afraid of it. The sky seemed cold and gray; the east wind, which she had always thought so delicious in summer, cut her to the heart. She took her children up to the South End, and in the pretty square where they used to live they stood before their alienated house, and looked up at its close-shuttered windows. The tenants must have been away, but Mrs. March had not the courage to ring and make sure, though she had always promised herself that she would go all over the house when she came back, and see how they had used it; she could pretend a desire for something she wished to take away. She knew she could not bear it now; and the children did not seem eager. She did not push on to the sea-side; it would be forlorn there without their father; she was glad to go back to him in the immense, friendly homelessness of New York, and hold him answerable for the change, in her heart or her mind, which made its shapeless tumult a refuge and a consolation.

She found that he had been giving the cook a holiday, and dining about hither and thither with Fulkerson. Once he had dined with him at the widow's (as they always called Mrs. Leighton), and then had spent the evening there, and smoked with Fulkerson and Colonel Woodburn on the gallery overlooking the back yard. They were all spending the summer in New York. The widow had got so good an offer for her house at St. Barnaby for the summer that she could not refuse it; and the Woodburns found New York a watering-place of exemplary coolness after the burning Augusts and Septembers of Charlottesburg.

"You can stand it well enough in our climate, sir," the colonel explained, "till you come to the September heat, that sometimes runs well into October; and then you begin to lose your temper, sir. It's never quite so hot as it is in New York at times, but it's hot longer, sir." He alleged, as if something of the sort were necessary, the example of a famous South-western editor who spent all his summers in a New York hotel as the most luxurious retreat on the continent, consulting the weather forecasts, and running off on torrid days to the mountains or the sea, and then hurrying back at the promise of cooler weather. The colonel had not found it necessary to do this yet; and he had been reluctant to leave town, where he was working up a branch of the inquiry which had so long occupied him, in the libraries, and studying the great problem of labor and poverty as it continually presented itself to him in the streets. He said that he talked with all sorts of people, whom he found monstrously civil, if you took them in the right way; and he went everywhere in the city without fear and apparently without danger. March could not find out that he had ridden his hobby into the homes of want which he visited, or had proposed their enslavement to the inmates as a short and simple solution of the great question of their lives; he appeared to have contented himself with the collection of facts for the persuasion of the cultivated classes. It seemed to March a confirmation of this impression that the colonel should address his deductions from these facts so unsparingly to him; he listened with a respectful patience, for which Fulkerson afterward personally thanked him. Fulkerson said it was not often the colonel found such a good listener; generally nobody listened but Mrs. Leighton, who thought his ideas were shocking, but honored him for holding them so conscientiously. Fulkerson was glad that March, as the literary department, had treated the old gentleman so well, because there was an open feud between him and the art department. Beaton was outrageously rude, Fulkerson must say; though as for that, the old colonel seemed quite able to take care of himself, and gave Beaton an unqualified contempt in return for his unmannerliness. The worst of it was, it distressed the old lady so; she admired Beaton as much as she respected the colonel, and she admired Beaton, Fulkerson thought, rather more than Miss Leighton did; he asked March if he had noticed them together. March had noticed them, but without any definite impression except that Beaton seemed to give the whole evening to the girl. Afterward he recollected that he had fancied her rather harassed by his devotion, and it was this point that he wished to present for his wife's opinion.

"Girls often put on that air," she said. "It's one of their ways of teasing. But then, if the man was really very much in love, and she was only enough in love to be uncertain of herself, she might very well seem troubled. It would be a very serious question. Girls often don't know what to do in such a case."

"Yes," said March, "I've often been glad that I was not a girl, on that account. But I guess that on general principles Beaton is not more in love than she is. I couldn't imagine that young man being more in love with anybody, unless it was himself. He might be more in love with himself than any one else was."

"Well, he doesn't interest me a great deal, and I can't say Miss Leighton does, either. I think she can take care of herself. She has herself very well in hand."

"Why so censorious?" pleaded March. "I don't defend her for having herself in hand; but is it a fault?"

Mrs. March did not say. She asked, "And how does Mr. Fulkerson's affair get on?"

"His affair? You really think it *is* one? Well, I've fancied so myself, and I've had an idea of some time asking him; Fulkerson strikes one as truly domesticable, conjugable at heart; but I've waited for him to speak."

"I should think so."

"Yes. He's never opened on the subject yet. Do you know, I think Fulkerson has his moments of delicacy."

"Moments! He's *all* delicacy in regard to women."

"Well, perhaps so. There is nothing in them to rouse his advertising instincts."

Chapter IV

[*In the following chapter, Howells sets the stage for the final events. Beaton, the temperamental art-editor of* Every Other Week, *is philandering with Christine, the elder daughter of Dryfoos. Christine's dark character foreshadows the personal tragedy in store for her when Beaton's lack of interest in her becomes apparent. Her younger brother, Conrad, whom we meet in the office of* Every Other Week, *is unlike his two selfish and ignorant sisters. The idol of his rough old father, he nevertheless harbors humanitarian sympathies which anger his father when he understands them. After the dinner party for the staff of the magazine, when Lindau's views are declared, Dryfoos insists that Lindau be fired. When Conrad expresses sympathy for the strikers during the street-car strike which paralyses the city, Dryfoos slaps his son across the face. Soon afterwards, Conrad is killed in the strike, and his father, completely crushed by the turn of events, sells his magazine and returns to Pennsylvania. March becomes editor of* Every Other Week, *a position he still holds when we meet him, many years later, in* Their Silver Wedding Journey.]

The Dryfoos family stayed in town till August. Then the father went West again to look after his interests; and Mrs. Mandel took the two girls to one of the great hotels in Saratoga. Fulkerson said that he had never seen anything like Saratoga for fashion, and Mrs. Mandel remembered that in her own young ladyhood this was so for at least some weeks of the year. She had been too far withdrawn from fashion since her marriage to know whether it was still so or not. In this, as in so many other matters, the Dryfoos family helplessly relied upon Fulkerson, in spite of Dryfoos's angry determination that he should not run the family, and in spite of Christine's doubt of his omniscience; if he did not know everything, she was aware that he knew more than herself. She thought that they had a right to have him go with them to Saratoga, or at least go up and engage their rooms beforehand; but Fulkerson did not offer to do either, and she did not quite see her way to commanding his services. The young ladies took what Mela called splendid dresses with them; they sat in the park of tall, slim trees which the hotel's quadrangle enclosed, and listened to the music in the morning, or on the long piazza in the afternoon and looked at the driving in the street, or in the vast parlours by night, where all the other ladies were, and they felt that they were of the best there. But they knew nobody, and Mrs. Mandel was so particular that Mela was prevented from continuing the acquaintance even of the few young men who danced with her at the Saturday-night hops. They drove about, but they went to places without knowing why, except that the carriage man took them, and they had all the privileges of a proud exclusivism without desiring them. Once a motherly matron seemed to perceive their isolation, and made overtures to them, but then desisted, as if repelled by Christine's suspicion, or by Mela's too instant and hilarious good-fellowship, which expressed itself in hoarse laughter and in a flow of talk full of topical and syntactical freedom. From time to time she offered to bet Christine that if Mr. Fulkerson was only there they would have a good time; she wondered what they were all doing in New York, where she wished herself; she rallied her sister about Beaton, and asked her why she did not write and tell him to come up there.

Mela knew that Christine has expected Beaton to follow them. Some banter has passed between them to this effect; he said he should take them in on his way home to Syracuse. Christine would not have hesitated to write to him and remind him of his promise; but she had learned to distrust her literature with Beaton since he had laughed at the spelling in a scrap of writing which dropped out of her music-book one night. She believed that he would not have laughed if he had known it was hers; but she felt that she could hide better the deficiencies which were not committed to paper; she could manage with him in talking; she was too ignorant of her ignorance to recognize the mistakes she made then. Through her own passion she perceived that she had some kind of fascination for him; she was graceful, and she thought it must be that; she did not understand that there was a kind of beauty in her small, irregular features that piqued and haunted his artistic sense, and a look in her black eyes beyond her intelligence and intention. Once he sketched her as they sat together, and flattered the portrait without getting what he wanted in it; he said he must try her some time in colour; and he said things which, when she made Mela repeat them, could only mean that he admired her more than anybody else. He came fitfully, but he came often, and she rested content in a girl's indefiniteness concerning the affair; if her thought went beyond love-making to marriage, she believed that she could have him if she wanted him. Her father's money counted in this; she divined that Beaton was poor; but that made no difference; she would have enough for both; the money would have counted as an irresistible attraction if there had been no other.

The affair had gone on in spite of the sidelong looks of restless dislike with which Dryfoos regarded it; but now when Beaton did not come to Saratoga it necessarily dropped, and Christine's content with it. She bore the trial as long as she could; she used pride and resentment against it; but at last she could not bear it, and with Mela's help she wrote a letter, bantering Beaton on his stay in New York, and playfully boasting of Saratoga. It seemed to them both that it was a very bright letter, and would be sure to bring him; they would have had no scruple about sending it but for the doubt they had whether they had got some of the words right. Mela offered to bet Christine anything she dared that they were right, and she said, Send it anyway; it was no difference if they *were* wrong. But Christine could not endure to think of that laugh of Beaton's, and there remained only Mrs. Mandel as authority on the spelling. Christine dreaded her authority on other points, but Mela said she knew she would not interfere, and she undertook to get round her. Mrs. Mandel pronounced the spelling bad, and the taste worse; she forbade them to send the letter; and Mela failed to get round her, though she threatened, if Mrs. Mandel would not tell her how to spell the wrong words, that she would send the letter as it was; then Mrs. Mandel said that if Mr. Beaton appeared in Saratoga she would instantly take them both home. When Mela reported this result, Christine accused her of having mismanaged the whole business; she quarrelled with her, and they called each other names. Christine declared that she would not stay in Saratoga, and that if Mrs. Mandel did not go back to New York with her she should go alone. They returned the first week in September; but by that time Beaton had gone to see his people in Syracuse.

Conrad Dryfoos remained at home with his mother after his father went West. He had already taken such a vacation as he had been willing to allow himself, and had spent it on a charity farm near the city, where the fathers with whom he worked among the poor on the East side in the winter had sent some of their wards for the summer. It was not possible to keep his recreation a secret at the office, and Fulkerson found a pleasure in figuring the jolly time Brother Conrad must have teaching farm work among those paupers and potential reprobates. He invented details of his experience among them, and March could not always help joining in the laugh at Conrad's humorless helplessness under Fulkerson's burlesque denunciation of a summer outing spent in such dissipation.

They had time for a great deal of joking at the office during the season of leisure which penetrates in August to the very heart of business, and they all got on terms of greater intimacy if not greater friendliness than before. Fulkerson had not had so long to do with the advertising side of human nature without developing a vein of cynicism, of no great depth, perhaps, but broad, and underlying his whole point of view; he made light of Beaton's solemnity, as he made light of Conrad's humanity. The art editor, with abundant sarcasm, had no more humor than the publisher, and was an easy prey in the manager's hands; but when he had been led on by Fulkerson's flatteries to make some betrayal of egotism, he brooded over it till he had thought how to revenge himself in elaborate insult. For Beaton's talent Fulkerson never lost his admiration; but his joke was to encourage him to give himself airs of being the sole source of the magazine's prosperity. No bait of this sort was too obvious for Beaton to swallow; he could be caught with it as often as Fulkerson chose; though he was ordinarily suspicious as to the motives of people in saying things. With March he got on no better than at first. He seemed to be lying in wait for some encroachment of the literary department on the art department, and he met it now and then with anticipative reprisal. After these rebuffs, the editor delivered him over to the manager, who could turn Beaton's contrary-mindedness to account by asking the reverse of what he really wanted done. This was what Fulkerson said; the fact was that he did get on with Beaton; and March contented himself with musing upon the contradictions of a character at once so vain and so offensive, so fickle and so sullen, so conscious and so simple.

After the first jarring contact with Dryfoos, the editor ceased to feel the disagreeable fact of the old man's mastery of the financial situation. None of the chances which might have made it painful occurred; the control of the whole affair remained in Fulkerson's hands; before he went West again, Dryfoos had ceased to come about the office, as if, having once worn off the novelty of the sense of owning a literary periodical, he was no longer interested in it.

Yet it was a relief, somehow, when he left town, which he did not do without coming to take a formal leave of the editor at his office. He seemed willing to leave March with a better impression than he had hitherto troubled himself to make; he even said some civil things about the magazine, as if its success pleased him; and he spoke openly to March of his hope that his son would finally become interested in it to the exclusion of the hopes and purposes which divided them. It seemed to March that in the old man's warped and toughened heart he perceived a disappointed love for his son greater than for his other children; but this might have been fancy. Lindau came in with some copy while Dryfoos was there, and March introduced them. When Lindau went out, March explained to Dryfoos that he had lost his hand in the war; and he told him something of Lindau's career as he had known it. Dryfoos appeared greatly pleased that *Every Other Week* was giving Lindau work. He said that he had helped to enlist a good many fellows for the war, and had paid money to fill up the Moffitt County quota under the later calls for troops. He had never been an Abolitionist, but he had joined the Anti-Nebraska party in '55, and he had voted for Fremont and for every Republican President since then.

At his own house March saw more of Lindau than of any other contributor, but the old man seemed to think that he must transact all his business with March at his place of business. The transaction had some peculiarities which perhaps made this necessary. Lindau always expected to receive his money when he brought his copy, as an acknowledgment of the immediate right of the labourer to his hire; and he would not take it in a check because he did not approve of banks, and regarded the whole system of banking as the capitalistic manipulation of the people's money. He would receive his pay only from March's hand, because he wished to be understood as working for him, and honestly earning money honestly earned; and sometimes March inwardly winced a little at letting the old man share the increase of capital won by such speculation as Dryfoos's, but he shook off the feeling. As the summer advanced, and the artists and classes that employed Lindau as a model left town one after another, he gave largely of his increasing leisure to the people in the office of *Every Other Week*. It was pleasant for March to see the respect with which Conrad Dryfoos always used him, for the sake of his hurt and his gray beard. There was something delicate and fine in it, and there was nothing unkindly on Fulkerson's part in the hostilities which usually passed between himself and Lindau. Fulkerson bore himself reverently at times, too, but it was not in him to keep that up, especially when Lindau appeared with more beer aboard than, as Fulkerson said, he could manage ship-shape. On these occasions Fulkerson always tried to start him on the theme of the unduly rich; he made himself the champion of monopolies, and enjoyed the invectives which Lindau heaped upon him as a slave of capital; he said that it did him good.

One day, with the usual show of writhing under Lindau's scorn, he said, "Well, I understand that although you despise me now, Lindau—"

"I ton't desbise you," the old man broke in, his nostrils swelling and his eyes flaming with excitement, "I bity you."

"Well, it seems to come to the same thing in the end," said Fulkerson. "What I understand is that you pity me now as the slave of capital, but you would pity me a great deal more if I was the master of it."

"How you mean?"

"If I was rich."

"That would tebendt," said Lindau, trying to control himself. "If you hat inheritedt your money, you might pe innocent; but if you hat *mate* it, efery man that resbectedt himself would haf to ask *how* you mate it, and if you hat mate moch, he would know—"

"Hold on; hold on, now, Lindau! Ain't that rather un-American doctrine? We're all brought up, ain't we, to honour the man that made his money, and look down—or try to look down; sometimes it's difficult—on the fellow that his father left it to?"

The old man rose and struck his breast. "On-Amerigan!" he roared, and, as he went on, his accent grew more and more uncertain. "What iss Amerigan? Dere *iss* no Ameriga any more! You start here free and brafe, and you glaim for efery man de righdt to life, liperty, and de bursuit of habbiness. And where haf you entedt? No man that vorks vith his handts among you hass the liperty to bursue his habbiness. He iss the slafe of some richer man, some gompany, some gorporation, dat crindts him down to the least he can lif on, and that rops him of the marchin of his earnings that he might pe habby on. Oh, you Amerigans, you haf cot it down goldt, as you say! You ton't puy foters; you puy lechislatures and goncressmen; you puy gourts; you puy gombetitors; you pay infentors not to infent; you *aftertise*, and the gounting-room sees dat de editorial-room toesn't tink."

"Yes, we've got a little arrangement of that sort with March here," said Fulkerson.

"Oh, I am sawry," said the old man, contritely, "I meant noting bersonal. I ton't tink we are all cuilty or gorrubt, and efen among the rich there are goodt men. But gabidal"—his passion rose again—"where you find gabidal, millions of money that a man hass cot togeder in fife, ten, twenty years, you findt the smell of tears and ploodt! Dat iss what I say. And you cot to loog oudt for yourself when you meet a rich man whether you meet an honest man."

"Well," said Fulkerson, "I wish I was a subject of suspicion with you, Lindau. By the way," he added, "I understand that you think capital was at the bottom of the veto of that pension of yours."

"What bension? What feto?" The old man flamed up again. "No bension of mine was efer fetoedt. I renounce my bension, begause I would sgorn to dake money from a gofernment that I ton't peliefe in any more. Where you hear that story?"

"Well, I don't know," said Fulkerson, rather embarrassed. "It's common talk."

"It's a gommon lie, then! When the time gome dat dis iss a free gountry again, then I dake a bension again for my woundts; but I would *sdarfe* before I dake a bension now from a rebublic dat iss bought oap by monobolies, and ron by drusts and gompines, and railroadts adnt oil gompanies."

"Look out, Lindau," said Fulkerson. "You bite yourself mit dat dog some day." But when the old man, with a ferocious gesture of renunciation, whirled out of the place, he added: "I guess I went a little too far that time. I touched him on a sore place; I didn't mean to; I heard some talk about his pension being vetoed from Miss Leighton." He addressed these exculpations to March's grave face, and to the pitying deprecation in the eyes of Conrad Dryfoos, whom Lindau's roaring wrath had summoned to the door. "But I'll make it all right with him the next time he comes. I didn't know he was loaded, or I wouldn't have monkeyed with him."

"Lindau does himself injustice when he gets to talking in that way," said March. "I hate to hear him. He's as good an American as any of us; and it's only because he has too high an ideal of us—"

"Oh, go on! Rub it in—rub it in!" cried Fulkerson, clutching his hair in suffering, which was not altogether burlesque. "How did I know he had renounced his 'bension'? Why didn't you tell me?"

"I didn't know it myself. I only knew that he had none, and I didn't ask, for I had a notion that it might be a painful subject."

Fulkerson tried to turn it off lightly. "Well, he's a noble old fellow; pity he drinks." March would not smile, and Fulkerson broke out: "Dog on it! I'll make it up to the old fool the next time he comes. I don't like that dynamite talk of his; but any man that's given his hand to the country has got mine in his grip for good. Why, March! You don't suppose I wanted to hurt his feelings, do you?"

"Why, of course not, Fulkerson."

But they could not get away from a certain ruefulness for that time, and in the evening Fulkerson came round to March's to say that he had got Lindau's address from Conrad, and had looked him up at his lodgings.

"Well, there isn't so much bric-à-brac there, quite, as Mrs. Green left you; but I've made it all right with Lindau, as far as I'm concerned. I told him I didn't know when I spoke that way, and I honored him for sticking to his 'brinciples'; *I* don't believe in his 'brincibles'; and we wept on each other's necks—at least, he did. Dogged if he didn't kiss me before I knew what he was up to. He said I was his chenerous yong friendt, and he begged my barton if he had said anything to wound me. I tell you it was an affecting scene, March; and rats enough round in that old barracks where he lives to fit out a first-class case of *delirium tremens*. What does he stay there for? He's not obliged to?"

Lindau's reasons, as March repeated them, affected Fulkerson as deliciously comical; but after that he confined his pleasantries at the office to Beaton and Conrad Dryfoos or, as he said, he spent the rest of the summer in keeping Lindau smoothed up.

It is doubtful if Lindau altogether liked this as well. Perhaps he missed the occasions Fulkerson used to give him of bursting out against the millionaires; and he could not well go on denouncing as the slafe of gabidal a man who had behaved to him as Fulkerson had done, though Fulkerson's servile relations to capital had been in nowise changed by his nople gonduct.

Their relations continued to wear this irksome character of mutual forbearance; and when Dryfoos returned in October and Fulkerson revived the question of that dinner in celebration of the success of *Every Other Week*, he carried his complaisance to an extreme that alarmed March for the consequences.

A TRAVELER FROM ALTRURIA[1]

[The traveler from Altruria, Mr. Homos, is the guest of a popular novelist, at a summer hotel in New Hampshire. Mr. Twelvemough is rather embarrassed by his friend, who shows an inclination to relieve the waitresses of their heavy trays, and to help the expressman with his trunk. Worse still, he engages the other guests, the banker, the lawyer, the professor, the doctor, the minister, in friendly argument in which he quietly upholds the principles of a "good society," based on Christian ethics. Mr. Homos tells his listeners in the following speech, delivered at a "benefit" on the hotel lawn, that Altruria, too, passed through an Age of Accumulation, similar to that which now characterizes the United States. The speech, which brings A Traveler from Altruria to a close, is approved by the working people, headed by Reuben Camp, a young farmer, who gather to hear the "traveler;" the hotel guests, though they like Mr. Homos personally, are divided in their opinion. In the following two chapters may be found the essence of Howells' own form of Christian socialism.

Perhaps it was from these chapters that Howells preached on one occasion at Kittery Point, Maine, when the visiting minister failed to turn up, and Howells was asked to take his place in the pulpit. "I raced over to the Barnbury library, got the Trav. from Altruria, *and gave 'em a good dose of socialism."[2]]*

Chapter XI

"I could not give you a clear account of the present state of things in my country," the Altrurian began, "without first telling you something of our conditions before the time of our evolution. It seems to be the law of all life that nothing can come to fruition without dying and seeming to make an end. It must be sown in corruption before it can be raised in incorruption. The truth itself must perish to our senses before it can live to our souls; the Son of Man must suffer upon the cross before we can know the Son of God.

"It was so with His message to the world, which we received

---

[1] *A Traveler from Altruria* appeared for the first time in *The Cosmopolitan*, from November, 1892 to October, 1893. The following selection is from the last two chapters, as they were printed in the September and October issues of *The Cosmopolitan* of 1893.

[2] *Life in Letters*, II, 266. The library was in a converted barn.

in the old time as an ideal realized by the earliest Christians, who loved one another and who had all things common. The apostle cast away upon our heathen coasts won us with the story of this first Christian republic, and he established a commonwealth of peace and good-will among us in its likeness. That commonwealth perished, just as its prototype perished, or seemed to perish; and long ages of civic and economic warfare succeeded, when every man's hand was against his neighbor, and might was the rule that got itself called right. Religion ceased to be the hope of this world, and became the vague promise of the next. We descended into the valley of the shadow, and dwelt amid chaos for ages before we groped again into the light.

"The first glimmerings were few and indistinct, but men formed themselves about the luminous points here and there, and, when these broke and dispersed into lesser gleams, still men formed themselves about each of them. There arose a system of things better, indeed, than that darkness, but full of war and lust and greed, in which the weak rendered homage to the strong, and served them in the field and in the camp, and the strong in turn gave the weak protection against the other strong. It was a juggle in which the weak did not see that their safety was, after all, from themselves; but it was an image of peace, however false and fitful, and it endured for a time. It endured for a limited time, if we measure by the life of the race; it endured for an unlimited time if we measure by the lives of the men who were born and died while it endured.

"But that disorder, cruel and fierce and stupid, which endured because it sometimes masked itself as order, did at last pass away. Here and there one of the strong overpowered the rest; then the strong became fewer and fewer, and in their turn they all yielded to a supreme lord, and throughout the land there was one rule, as it was called then, or one misrule, as we should call it now. This rule, or this misrule, continued for ages more; and again, in the immortality of the race, men toiled and struggled, and died without the hope of better things.

"Then the time came when the long nightmare was burst

with the vision of a future in which all men were the law, and
not one man, or any less number of men than all.

"The poor dumb beast of humanity rose, and the throne
tumbled, and the sceptre was broken, and the crown rolled
away into that darkness of the past. We thought that heaven
had descended to us, and that liberty, equality, and fraternity
were ours. We could not see what should again alienate us from
one another, or how one brother could again oppress another.
With a free field and no favor we believed we should prosper on
together, and there would be peace and plenty for all. We had
the republic again after so many ages now, and the republic, as
we knew it in our dim annals, was brotherhood and universal
happiness. All but a very few, who prophesied evil of our lawless freedom, were wrapped in a delirium of hope. Men's minds
and men's hands were suddenly released to an activity unheard
of before. Invention followed invention; our rivers and seas
became the warp of commerce where the steam-sped shuttles
carried the woof of enterprise to and fro with tireless celerity.
Machines to save labor multiplied themselves as if they had been
procreative forces, and wares of every sort were produced with
incredible swiftness and cheapness. Money seemed to flow from
the ground; vast fortunes 'rose like an exhalation', as your
Milton says.

"At first we did not know that they were the breath of the
nethermost pits of hell, and that the love of money, which was
becoming universal with us, was filling the earth with the hate
of men. It was long before we came to realize that in the depths
of our steamships were those who fed the fires with their lives,
and that our mines from which we dug our wealth were the
graves of those who had died to the free light and air, without
finding the rest of death. We did not see that the machines for
saving labor were monsters that devoured women and children,
and wasted men at the bidding of the power which no man must
touch.

"That is, we thought we must not touch it, for it called itself
prosperity, and wealth, and the public good, and it said that it
gave bread, and it impudently bade the toiling myriads consider

what would become of them if it took away their means of wearing themselves out in its service. It demanded of the state absolute immunity and absolute impunity, the right to do its will
wherever and however it would, without question from the
people who were the final law. It had its way, and under its rule
we became the richest people under the sun. The Accumulation, as we called this power, because we feared to call it by its
true name, rewarded its own with gains of twenty, of a hundred,
of a thousand per cent., and to satisfy its need, to produce the
labor that operated its machines, there came into existence a
hapless race of men who bred their kind for its service, and
whose little ones were its prey almost from their cradles. Then
the infamy became too great, and the law, the voice of the people, so long guiltily silent, was lifted in behalf of those who had
no helper. The Accumulation came under control for the first
time, and could no longer work its slaves twenty hours a day
amid perils to life and limb from its machinery and in conditions
that forbade them decency and morality. The time of a hundred
and a thousand per cent. passed; but still the Accumulation demanded immunity and impunity, and, in spite of its conviction
of the enormities it had practised, it declared itself the only
means of civilization and progress. It began to give out that it
was timid, though its history was full of the boldest frauds and
crimes, and it threatened to withdraw itself if it were ruled or
even crossed; and again it had its way, and we seemed to prosper
more and more. The land was filled with cities where the rich
flaunted their splendor in palaces, and the poor swarmed in
squalid tenements. The country was drained of its life and
force, to feed the centres of commerce and industry. The whole
land was bound together with a network of iron roads that
linked the factories and founderies to the fields and mines, and
blasted the landscape with the enterprise that spoiled the lives of
men.

"Then, all at once, when its work seemed perfect and its
dominion sure, the Accumulation was stricken with consciousness of the lie always at its heart. It had hitherto cried out for a
free field and no favor, for unrestricted competition; but, in

truth, it had never prospered except as a monopoly. Whenever and wherever competition had play there had been nothing but disaster to the rival enterprises, till one rose over the rest. Then there was prosperity for that one.

"The Accumulation began to act upon its new consciousness. The iron roads united; the warring industries made peace, each kind under a single leadership. Monopoly, not competition, was seen to be the beneficent means of distributing the favors and blessings of the Accumulation to mankind. But, as before, there was alternately a glut and dearth of things, and it often happened that when starving men went ragged through the streets the storehouses were piled full of rotting harvests that the farmers toiled from dawn till dusk to grow, and the warehouses fed the moth with the stuffs that the operative had woven his life into at his loom. Then followed, with a blind and mad succession, a time of famine, when money could not buy the superabundance that vanished, none knew how or why.

"The money itself vanished from time to time, and disappeared into the vaults of the Accumulation, for no better reason than that for which it poured itself out at other times. Our theory was that the people, that is to say, the government of the people, made the people's money, but, as a matter of fact, the Accumulation made it and controlled it and juggled with it; and now you saw it, and now you did not see it. The government made gold coins, but the people had nothing but the paper money that the Accumulation made. But whether there was scarcity or plenty, the failures went on with a continuous ruin that nothing could check, while our larger economic life proceeded in a series of violent shocks, which we called financial panics, followed by long periods of exhaustion and recuperation. There was no law in our economy, but as the Accumulation had never cared for the nature of law, it did not trouble itself for its name in our order of things. It had always bought the law it needed for its own use, first through the voter at the polls in the more primitive days, and then, as civilization advanced, in the legislatures and the courts. But the corruption even of these methods was far surpassed when the era of consolidation came, and the necessity for statutes and verdicts and decisions became more stringent. Then we had such a burlesque of—"

"Look here!" a sharp, nasal voice snarled across the rich, full pipe of the Altrurian, and we all instantly looked there. The voice came from an old farmer, holding himself stiffly up, with his hands in his pockets and his lean frame bent toward the speaker. "When are you goin' to git to Altrury? We know all about Ameriky."

He sat down again, and it was a moment before the crowd caught on. Then a yell of delight and a roar of volleyed laughter went up from the lower classes, in which, I am sorry to say, my friend the banker joined, so far as the laughter was concerned. "Good! That's it! First-rate!" came from a hundred vulgar throats.

"Isn't it a perfect shame?" Mrs. Makely demanded. "I think some of you gentlemen ought to say something. What will Mr. Homos think of our civilization if we let such interruptions go unrebuked?"

She was sitting between the banker and myself, and her indignation made him laugh more and more. "Oh, it serves him right," he said. "Don't you see that he is hoist with his own petard? Let him alone. He's in the hands of his friends."

The Altrurian waited for the tumult to die away, and then he said, gently: "I don't understand."

The old farmer jerked himself to his feet again. "It's like this: I paid my dolla' to hear about a country where there wa'n't no co'perations, and no monop'lies, nor no buyin' up cou'ts; and I ain't agoin' to have no allegory shoved down my throat, instead of a true history, noways. I know all about how it is *here*. Fi'st, run their line through your backya'd, and then kill off your cattle, and keep kerryin' on it up from cou't to cou't, tell there ain't hide or hair of 'em left—".

"Oh, set down, set down! Let the man go on! He'll make it all right with you," one of the construction gang called out; but the farmer stood his ground, and I could hear him through the laughing and shouting, keep saying something, from time to time, about not wanting to pay no dolla' for no talk about co'perations and monop'lies that we had right under our own noses the whole while, and, you might say in your very bread-troughs; till, at last, I saw Reuben Camp make his way toward him, and, after an energetic expostulation, turn to leave him again.

Then he faltered out, "I guess it's all right," and dropped out of sight in the group he had risen from. I fancied his wife scolding him there, and all but shaking him in public.

"I should be very sorry," the Altrurian proceeded, "to have any one believe that I have not been giving you a bona fide account of conditions in my country before the evolution, when we first took the name of Altruria in our great, peaceful campaign against the Accumulation. As for offering you any allegory or travesty of your own conditions, I will simply say that I do not know them well enough to do so intelligently. But, whatever they are, God forbid that the likeness which you seem to recognize should ever go so far as the desperate state of things which we finally reached. I will not trouble you with details; in fact, I have been afraid that I had already treated of our affairs too abstractly; but, since your own experience furnishes you the means of seizing my meaning, I will go on as before.

"You will understand me when I explain that the Accumulation had not erected itself into the sovereignty with us unopposed. The workingmen who suffered most from its oppression had early begun to band themselves against it, with the instinct of self-preservation, first trade by trade and art by art, and then in congresses and federations of the trades and arts, until finally they enrolled themselves in one vast union, which included all the working-men whom their necessity or their interest did not leave on the side of the Accumulation. This beneficent and generous association of the weak for the sake of the weakest did not accomplish itself fully till the baleful instinct of the Accumulation had reduced the monopolies to one vast monopoly, till the stronger had devoured the weaker among its members, and the supreme agent stood at the head of our affairs, in everything but name, our imperial ruler. We had hugged so long the delusion of each man for himself that we had suffered all realty to be taken from us. The Accumulation owned the land as well as the mines under it and the shops over it; the Accumulation owned the seas and the ships that sailed the seas, and the fish that swam in their depths; it owned transportation and distribution, and the wares and products that were to be carried to and fro; and, by a logic irresistible and inexorable, the Accumulation *was*, and we were *not*.

"But the Accumulation, too, had forgotten something. It had found it so easy to buy legislatures and courts that it did not trouble itself about the polls. It left us the suffrage, and let us amuse ourselves with the periodical election of the political clay images which it manipulated and moulded to any shape and effect at its pleasure. The Accumulation knew that it was the sovereignty, whatever figure-head we called president or governor or mayor: we had other names for these officials, but I use their analogues for the sake of clearness, and I hope my good friend over there will not think I am still talking about America."

"No," the old farmer called back, without rising, "we hain't got there, quite, yit."

"No hurry," said a trainman. "All in good time. Go on!" he called to the Altrurian.

The Altrurian resumed:

"There had been, from the beginning, an almost ceaseless struggle between the Accumulation and the proletariate. The Accumulation always said that it was the best friend of the proletariate, and it denounced, through the press which it controlled, the proletarian leaders who taught that it was the enemy of the proletariate, and who stirred up strikes and tumults of all sorts, for higher wages and fewer hours. But the friend of the proletariate, whenever occasion served, treated the proletariate like a deadly enemy. In seasons of overproduction, as it was called, it locked the workmen out or laid them off, and left their families to starve, or ran light work, and claimed the credit of public benefactors for running at all. It sought every chance to reduce wages; it had laws passed to forbid or cripple the workmen in their strikes; and the judges convicted them of conspiracy, and wrested the statutes to their hurt, in cases where there had been no thought of embarrassing them, even among the legislators. God forbid that you should ever come to such a pass in America; but, if you ever should, God grant that you may find your way out as simply as we did at last, when freedom had perished in everything but name among us, and justice had become a mockery.

"The Accumulation had advanced so smoothly, so lightly, in all its steps to the supreme power, and had at last so thoroughly quelled the uprisings of the proletariate, that it forgot one thing: it forgot the despised and neglected suffrage. The ballot, because it had been so easy to annul its effect, had been left in the people's hands; and when, at last, the leaders of the proletariate ceased to counsel strikes, or any form of resistance to the Accumulation that could be tormented into the likeness of insurrection against the government, and began to urge them to attack it in the political way, the deluge that swept the Accumulation out of existence came trickling and creeping over the land. It appeared first in the country, a spring from the ground; then it gathered head in the villages; then it swelled to a torrent in the cities. I cannot stay to trace its course; but suddenly, one day, when the Accumulation's abuse of a certain power became too gross, it was voted out of that power. You will perhaps be interested to know that it was with the telegraphs that the rebellion against the Accumulation began, and the government was forced, by the overwhelming majority which the proletariate sent to our parliament, to assume a function which the Accumulation had impudently usurped. Then the transportation of smaller and more perishable wares—"

"Yes," a voice called—"express business. Go on!"

"Was legislated a function of the post-office," the Altrurian went on. "Then all transportation was taken into the hands of the political government, which had always been accused of great corruption in its administration, but which showed itself immaculately pure, compared with the Accumulation. The common ownership of mines necessarily followed, with an allotment of lands to any one who wished to live by tilling the land; but not a foot of the land was remitted to private hands for the purposes of selfish pleasure or the exclusion of any other from the landscape. As all business had been gathered into the grasp of the Accumulation, and the manufacture of everything they used and the production of everything that they ate was in the control of the Accumulation, its transfer to the government was the work of a single clause in the statute.

"The Accumulation, which had treated the first menaces of resistance with contempt, awoke to its peril too late. When it turned to wrest the suffrage from the proletariate, at the first election where it attempted to make head against them, it was simply snowed under, as your picturesque phrase is. The Accumulation had no voters, except the few men at its head and the creatures devoted to it by interest and ignorance. It seemed, at one moment, as if it would offer an armed resistance to the popular will, but, happily, that moment of madness passed. Our evolution was accomplished without a drop of bloodshed, and the first great political brotherhood, the commonwealth of Altruria, was founded.

"I wish that I had time to go into a study of some of the curious phases of the transformation from a civility in which the people lived *upon* each other to one in which they lived *for* each other. There is a famous passage in the inaugural message of our first Altrurian president, which compares the new civic consciousness with that of a disembodied spirit released to the life beyond this and freed from all the selfish cares and greeds of the flesh. But perhaps I shall give a sufficiently clear notion of the triumph of the change among us when I say that within half a decade after the fall of the old plutocratic oligarchy one of the chief directors of the Accumulation publicly expressed his gratitude to God that the Accumulation had passed away forever. You will realize the importance of such an expression in recalling the declarations some of your slave-holders have made since the civil war, that they would not have slavery restored for any earthly consideration.

"But now, after this preamble, which has been so much longer than I meant it to be, how shall I give you a sufficiently just conception of the existing Altruria, the actual state from which I come?"

"Yes," came the nasal of the old farmer, again, "that's what we are here fur. I wouldn't give a copper to know all you went through beforehand. It's too dumn like what we have been through ourselves, as fur as heard from."

A shout of laughter went up from most of the crowd, but the Altrurian did not seem to see any fun in it.

"Well," he resumed, "I will tell you, as well as I can, what Altruria is like, but, in the first place, you will have to cast out of your minds all images of civilization with which your experience has filled them. For a time, the shell of the old Accumulation remained for our social habitation, and we dwelt in the old competitive and monopolistic forms after the life had gone out of them. That is, we continued to live in populous cities, and we toiled to heap up riches for the moth to corrupt, and we slaved on in making utterly useless things, merely because we had the habit of making them to sell. For a while we made the old sham things, which pretended to be useful things and were worse than the confessedly useless things. I will give you an illustration from the trades, which you will all understand. The proletariate, in the competitive and monopolistic time, used to make a kind of shoes for the proletariate, or the women of the proletariate, which looked like fine shoes of the best quality. It took just as much work to make these shoes as to make the best fine shoes; but they were shams through and through. They wore out in a week, and the people called them, because they were bought fresh for every Sunday—"

"Sat'd'y night shoes!" screamed the old farmer. "I know 'em. My gals buy 'em. Half-dolla' a pai', and not wo'th the money."

"Well," said the Altrurian, "they were a cheat and a lie in every way, and under the new system it was not possible, when public attention was called to the fact, to continue the falsehood they embodied. As soon as the Saturday night shoes realized itself to the public conscience, an investigation began, and it was

found that the principle of the Saturday night shoe underlay
half our industries and made half the work that was done. Then
an immense reform took place. We renounced, in the most
solemn convocation of the whole economy, the principle of the
Saturday night shoe, and those who had spent their lives in
producing shams—"

"Yes," said the professor, rising from his seat near us and addressing the speaker, "I shall be very glad to know what became
of the worthy and industrious operatives who were thrown out
of employment by this explosion of economic virtue."

"Why," the Altrurian replied, "they were set to work making
honest shoes; and, as it took no more time to make a pair of
honest shoes, which lasted a year, than it took to make a pair of
shoes that lasted a week, the amount of labor in shoemaking was
at once enormously reduced."

"Yes," said the professor, "I understand that. What became
of the shoemakers?"

"They joined the vast army of other laborers who had been
employed, directly or indirectly, in the fabrication of fraudulent
wares. These shoemakers—lasters, button-holers, binders, and
so on—no longer wore themselves out over their machines.
One hour sufficed where twelve hours were needed before, and
the operatives were released to the happy labor of the fields,
where no one with us toils killingly, from dawn till dusk, but
does only as much work as is needed to keep the body in health.
We had a continent to refine and beautify; we had climates to
change and seasons to modify, a whole system of meteorology
to readjust, and the public works gave employment to the multi-
tudes emancipated from the soul-destroying service of shams.
I can scarcely give you a notion of the vastness of the improvements undertaken and carried through, or still in process of ac-
complishment. But a single one will, perhaps, afford a sufficient
illustration. Our southeast coast, from its vicinity to the pole,
had always suffered from a winter of antarctic rigor; but our
first president conceived the plan of cutting off a peninsula,
which kept the equatorial current from making in to our shores;
and the work was begun in his term, though the entire strip,

twenty miles in width and ninety-three in length, was not severed before the end of the first Altrurian decade. Since that time the whole region of our southeastern coast has enjoyed the climate of your Mediterranean countries.

"It was not only the makers of fraudulent things who were released to these useful and wholesome labors, but those who had spent themselves in contriving ugly and stupid and foolish things were set free to the public employment. The multitude of these monstrosities and iniquities was as great as that of the shams—"

Here I lost some words, for the professor leaned over and whispered to me: "He has got *that* out of William Morris. Depend upon it, the man is a humbug. He is not an Altrurian at all."

I confess that my heart misgave me; but I signalled the professor to be silent, and again gave the Altrurian—if he was an Altrurian—my whole attention.

Chapter XII

"And so," the Altrurian continued, "when the labor of the community was emancipated from the bondage of the false to the free service of the true, it was also, by an inevitable implication, dedicated to beauty and rescued from the old slavery to the ugly, the stupid, and the trivial. The thing that was honest and useful became, by the operation of a natural law, a beautiful thing. Once we had not time enough to make things beautiful, we were so overworked in making false and hideous things to sell; but now we had all the time there was, and a glad emulation arose among the trades and occupations to the end that everything done should be done finely as well as done honestly. The artist, the man of genius, who worked from the love of his work, became the normal man, and in the measure of his ability and of his calling each wrought in the spirit of the artist. We got back the pleasure of doing a thing beautifully, which was God's primal blessing upon all his working children, but which we had lost in the horrible days of our need and greed. There is not a working-man within the sound of my voice but has known this divine delight, and would gladly know it always if he only had the time. Well, now we had the time, the Evolution had given us the time, and in all Altruria there was not a furrow driven or a swath mown, not a hammer struck on house or on ship, not a stitch sewn or a stone laid, not a line written or a sheet printed, not a temple raised or an engine built, but it was done with an eye to beauty as well as to use.

"As soon as we were freed from the necessity of preying upon one another, we found that *there was no hurry.* The good work would wait to be well done; and one of the earliest effects of the Evolution was the disuse of the swift trains which had traversed the continent, night and day, that one man might overreach another, or make haste to undersell his rival, or seize some advantage of him, or plot some profit to his loss. Nine-tenths of the railroads, which in the old times had ruinously competed, and then, in the hands of the Accumulation, had been united to impoverish and oppress the people, fell into disuse. The commonwealth operated the few lines that were necessary for the collection of materials and the distribution of manufactures, and for pleasure travel and the affairs of state; but the roads that had been built to invest capital, or parallel other roads, or 'make work,' as it was called, or to develop resources, or boom localities, were suffered to fall into ruin; the rails were stripped from the landscape, which they had bound as with shackles, and the road-beds became highways for the use of kindly neighborhoods, or nature recovered them wholly and hid the memory of their former abuse in grass and flowers and wild vines. The ugly towns that they forced into being, as Frankenstein was fashioned, from the materials of the charnel, and that had no life in or from the good of the community, soon tumbled into decay. The administration used parts of them in the construction of the villages in which the Altrurians now mostly live; but generally these towns were built of materials so fraudulent, in form so vile, that it was judged best to burn them. In this way their sites were at once purified and obliterated.

"We had, of course, a great many large cities under the old

egoistic conditions, which increased and fattened upon the country, and fed their cancerous life with fresh infusions of its blood. We had several cities of half a million, and one of more than a million; we had a score of them with a population of a hundred thousand or more. We were very proud of them, and vaunted them as a proof of our unparalleled prosperity, though really they never were anything but congeries of millionaires and the wretched creatures who served them and supplied them. Of course, there was everywhere the appearance of enterprise and activity, but it meant final loss for the great mass of the business men, large and small, and final gain for the millionaires. These, and their parasites and necessary concomitants, dwelt together, the rich starving the poor and the poor plundering and misgoverning the rich; and it was the intolerable suffering in the cities that chiefly hastened the fall of the old Accumulation and the rise of the Commonwealth.

"Almost from the moment of the Evolution the competitive and monopolistic centres of population began to decline. In the clear light of the new order it was seen that they were not fit dwelling-places for men, either in the complicated and luxurious palaces where the rich fenced themselves from their kind, or in the vast tenements, towering height upon height, ten and twelve stories up, where the swarming poor festered in vice and sickness and famine. If I were to tell you of the fashion of those cities of our egoistic epoch, how the construction was one error from the first, and every correction of an error bred a new defect, I should make you weep, I should make you laugh. We let them fall to ruin as quickly as they would, and their sites are still so pestilential, after the lapse of centuries, that travelers are publicly guarded against them. Ravening beasts and poisonous reptiles lurk in those abodes of the riches and the poverty that are no longer known to our life. A part of one of the less malarial of the old cities, however, is maintained by the commonwealth in the form of its prosperity, and is studied by antiquarians for the instruction, and by moralists for the admonition, it affords. A section of a street is exposed, and you see the foundations of the houses; you see the filthy drains that belched into the common sewers, trapped and retrapped to keep the poison gases down; you see the sewers that rolled their loathsome tides under the streets, amidst a tangle of gas pipes, steam pipes, water pipes, telegraph wires, electric lighting wires, electric motorwires, and grip-cables; all without a plan, but makeshifts, expedients, devices, to repair and evade the fundamental mistake of having any such cities at all.

"There are now no cities in Altruria, in your meaning, but there are capitals, one for each of the Regions of our country, and one for the whole commonwealth. These capitals are for the transaction of public affairs, in which every citizen of Altruria is schooled, and they are the residences of the administrative officials, who are alternated every year, from the highest to the lowest. A public employment with us is of no greater honor or profit than any other, for with our absolute economic equality there can be no ambition, and there is no opportunity for one citizen to outshine another. But as the capitals are the centres of all the arts, which we consider the chief of our public affairs, they are oftenest frequented by poets, actors, painters, sculptors, musicians, and architects. We regard all artists, who are in a sort creators, as the human type which is likest the divine, and we try to conform our whole industrial life to the artistic temperament. Even in the labors of the field and shop, which are obligatory upon all, we study the inspiration of this temperament, and in the voluntary pursuits we allow it full control. Each, in these, follows his fancy as to what he shall do, and when he shall do it, or whether he shall do anything at all. In the capitals are the universities, theatres, galleries, museums, cathedrals, laboratories and conservatories, and the appliances of every art and science, as well as the administration buildings; and beauty as well as use is studied in every edifice. Our capitals are as clean and quiet and healthful as the country, and these advantages are secured simply by the elimination of the horse, an animal which we should be as much surprised to find in the streets of a town as the plesiosaurus or the pterodactyl. All transportation in the capitals, whether for pleasure or business, is by electricity, and swift electrical expresses connect the capital of each region with the villages which radiate from it to the cardinal points. These expresses run at the rate of a hundred and fifty miles an hour, and they enable the artist, the scientist, the literary man, of the remotest hamlet, to visit the capital (when he is not actually resident there in some public use) every day, after the hours of the obligatory industries; or, if he likes, he may remain there a whole week or fortnight, giving six hours a day instead of three to the obligatories, until the time is made up. In case of very evident merit, or for the purpose of allowing him to complete some work requiring continuous application, a vote of the local agents may release him from the obligatories indefinitely. Generally, however, our artists prefer not to ask this, but avail themselves of the stated means we have of allowing them to work at the obligatories, and get the needed exercise and variety of occupation in the immediate vicinity of the capital.

"We do not think it well to connect the hamlets on the different lines of radiation from the capital, except by the good country roads which traverse each region in every direction. The villages are mainly inhabited by those who prefer a rural life; they are farming villages; but in Altruria it can hardly be said that one man is more a farmer than another. We do not like to distinguish men by their callings; we do not speak of the poet This or the shoemaker That, for the poet may very likely be a shoemaker in the obligatories, and the shoemaker a poet in the voluntaries. If it can be said that one occupation is honored above another with us, it is that which we all share, and that is the cultivation of the earth. We believe that this, when not followed slavishly, or for gain, brings man into the closest relations to the Deity, through a grateful sense of the divine bounty, and that it not only awakens a natural piety in him, but that it endears to the worker that piece of soil which he tills, and so strengthens his love of home. The home is the very heart of the Altrurian system, and we do not think it well that people should be away from their homes very long or very often. In the competitive and monopolistic times men spent half their days in racing back and forth across our continent; families were scattered by the chase for fortune, and there was a perpetual paying and repaying of visits. One-half the income of those railroads which we let fall into disuse came from the ceaseless unrest. Now a man is born and lives and dies among his own kindred, and the sweet sense of neighborhood, of brotherhood, which blessed the golden age of the first Christian republic is ours again. Every year the people of each Region meet one another on Evolution day, in the regionic capital; once in four years they all visit the national capital. There is no danger of the decay of patriotism among us; our country is our mother, and we love her as it is impossible to love the step-mother that a competitive or monopolistic nation must be to its citizens.

"I can only touch upon this feature and that of our system as I chance to think of it. If any of you are curious about others, I shall be glad to answer questions as well as I can. We have, of course," the Altrurian proceeded, after a little indefinite pause, to let any speak who liked, "no sort of money. As the whole people control affairs, no man works for another, and no man pays another. Every one does his share of labor, and receives his share of food, clothing, and shelter, which is neither more nor less than another's. If you can imagine the justice and impartiality of a well-ordered family, you can conceive of the social and economic life of Altruria. We are, properly speaking, a family rather than a nation like yours.

"Of course, we are somewhat favored by our insular, or continental, position; but I do not know that we are more so than you are. Certainly, however, we are self-sufficing in a degree unknown to most European countries; and we have within our borders the materials of every comfort and the resources of every need. We have no commerce with the egoistic world, as we call that outside, and I believe that I am the first Altrurian to visit foreign countries avowedly in my national character, though we have always had emissaries living abroad incognito. I hope that I may say without offence that they find it a sorrowful exile, and that the reports of the egoistic world, with its wars, its bankruptcies, its civic commotions, and its social unhappiness, do not make us discontented with our own conditions.

Before the Evolution we had completed the round of your inventions and discoveries, impelled by the force that drives you on; and we have since disused most of them as idle and unfit. But we profit, now and then, by the advances you make in science, for we are passionately devoted to the study of the natural laws, open or occult, under which all men have their being. Occasionally an emissary returns with a sum of money, and explains to the students of the national university the processes by which it is lost and won; and at a certain time there was a movement for its introduction among us, not for its use as you know it, but for a species of counters in games of chance. It was considered, however, to contain an element of danger, and the scheme was discouraged.

"Nothing amuses and puzzles our people more than the accounts our emissaries give of the changes of fashion in the outside world, and of the ruin of soul and body which the love of dress often works. Our own dress, for men and for women, is studied, in one ideal of use and beauty, from the antique; caprice and vagary in it would be thought an effect of vulgar vanity. Nothing is worn that is not simple and honest in texture; we do not know whether a thing is cheap or dear, except as it is easy or hard to come by, and that which is hard to come by is forbidden as wasteful and foolish. The community builds the dwellings of the community, and these, too, are of a classic simplicity, though always beautiful and fit in form; the splendors of the arts are lavished upon the public edifices, which we all enjoy in common."

"Isn't this the greatest réchauffé of Utopia, New Atlantis, and City of the Sun that you ever imagined?" the professor whispered across me to the banker. "The man is a fraud, and a very bungling fraud at that."

"Well, you must expose him, when he gets through," the banker whispered back.

But the professor could not wait. He got upon his feet and called out: "May I ask the gentleman from Altruria a question?"

"Certainly," the Altrurian blandly assented.

"Make it short!" Reuben Camp's voice broke in, impatiently. "We didn't come here to listen to your questions."

The professor contemptuously ignored him. "I suppose you occasionally receive emissaries from, as well as send them to, the world outside?"

"Yes, now and then castaways land on our coasts, and ships out of their reckonings put in at our ports, for water or provision."

"And how are they pleased with your system?"

"Why, I cannot better answer than by saying that they mostly refuse to leave us."

"Ah, just as Bacon reports!" cried the professor.

"You mean in the New Altantis?" returned the Altrurian. "Yes; it is astonishing how well Bacon in that book, and Sir Thomas More in his Utopia, have divined certain phases of our civilization and polity."

"I think he rather *has* you, professor," the banker whispered, with a laugh.

"But all those inspired visionaries," the Altrurian continued, while the professor sat grimly silent, watching for another chance, "who have borne testimony of us in their dreams, conceived of states perfect without the discipline of a previous competitive condition. What I thought, however, might specially interest you Americans in Altruria is the fact that our economy was evolved from one so like that in which you actually have your being. I had even hoped you might feel that, in all these points of resemblance, America prophesies another Altruria. I know that to some of you all that I have told of my country will seem a baseless fabric, with no more foundation, in fact, than More's fairytale of another land where men dealt kindly and justly by one another, and dwelt, a whole nation, in the unity and equality of a family. But why should not a part of that fable have come true in our polity, as another part of it has come true in yours? When Sir Thomas More wrote that book, he noted with abhorrence the monstrous injustice of the fact that men were hanged for small thefts in England; and in the preliminary conversation between its characters he denounced the killing of men for any sort of thefts. Now you no longer put men to death for theft; you look back upon that cruel code of your mother England with an abhorrence as great as his own. We, for our part, who have realized the Utopian dream of brotherly equality, look back with the same abhorrence upon a state where some were rich and some poor, some taught and some untaught, some high and some low, and the hardest toil often failed to supply a sufficiency of the food which luxury wasted in its riots. That state seems as atrocious to us as the state which hanged a man for stealing a loaf of bread seems to you.

"But we do not regret the experience of competition and monopoly. They taught us some things in the operation of the industries. The labor-saving inventions which the Accumulation perverted to money-making we have restored to the use intended by their inventors and the Creator of their inventors. After serving the advantage of socializing the industries which the Accumulation effected for its own purposes, we continued the work in large mills and shops, in the interest of the workers, whom we wished to guard against the evil effects of solitude. But our mills and shops are beautiful as well as useful. They look like temples, and they are temples, dedicated to that sympathy between the divine and human which expresses itself in honest and exquisite workmanship. They rise amid leafy boscages beside the streams, which form their only power; for we have disused steam altogether, with all the offences to the eye and ear which its use brought into the world. Our life is so simple and our needs are so few that the hand-work of the primitive toilers could easily supply our wants; but machinery works so much more thoroughly and beautifully that we have in great measure retained it. Only, the machines that were once the workmen's enemies and masters are now their friends and servants.

"The farm-work, as well as the mill-work and the shop-work, is done by companies of workers; and there is nothing of that loneliness in our woods and fields which, I understand, is the cause of so much insanity among you. It is not good for man to be alone, was the first thought of his Creator when he considered him, and we act upon this truth in everything. The privacy of the family is sacredly guarded in essentials, but the social instinct is so highly developed with us that we like to eat together in large refectories, and we meet constantly to argue and dispute on questions of aesthetics and metaphysics. We do not, perhaps, read so many books as you do, for most of our reading, when not for special research, but for culture and entertainment, is done by public readers, to large groups of listeners. We have no social meetings which are not free to all; and we encourage joking and the friendly give and take of witty encounters."

"A little hint from Sparta," suggested the professor.

The banker leaned over to say to me, "From what I have seen of your friend when offered a piece of American humor, I should fancy the Altrurian article was altogether different. Upon the whole, I would rather not be present at one of their witty encounters, if I were obliged to stay it out."

The Altrurian had paused to drink a glass of water, and now he went on. "But we try, in everything that does not inconvenience or injure others, to let every one live the life he likes best. If a man prefers to dwell apart, and have his meals in private for himself alone or for his family, it is freely permitted; only, he must not expect to be served as in public, where service is one of the voluntaries; private service is not permitted; those wishing to live alone must wait upon themselves, cook their own food, and care for their own tables. Very few, however, wish to withdraw from the public life, for most of the discussions and debates take place at our midday meal, which falls at the end of the obligatory labors, and is prolonged indefinitely, or as long as people like to chat and joke or listen to the reading of some pleasant book.

"In Altruria *there is no hurry*, for no one wishes to outstrip another, or in any wise surpass him. We are all assured of enough, and are forbidden any and every sort of superfluity. If any one, after the obligatories, wishes to be entirely idle, he may be so, but I cannot now think of a single person without some voluntary occupation; doubtless there are such persons, but I do not know them. It used to be said, in the old times,

that 'it was human nature' to shirk and malinger and loaf, but
we have found that it is no such thing. We have found that it is
human nature to work cheerfully, willingly, eagerly, at the
tasks which all share for the supply of the common necessities.
In like manner we have found out that it is not human nature to
hoard and grudge, but that when the fear, and even the imagination, of want is taken away, it is human nature to give and to
help generously. We used to say, 'A man will lie, or a man will
cheat, in his own interest; that is human nature,' but that is no
longer human nature with us, perhaps because no man has any
interest to serve; he has only the interests of others to serve,
while others serve his. It is in no wise possible for the individual to separate his good from the common good; he is prosperous and happy only as all the rest are so; and therefore it is
not human nature with us for any one to lie in wait to betray,
another or seize an advantage. That would be ungentlemanly,
and in Altruria every man is a gentleman and every woman a
lady. If you will excuse me here for being so frank, I would like
to say something by way of illustration which may be offensive
if you take it personally."

He looked at our little group, as if he were addressing himself
more especially to us, and the banker called out jollily: "Go on!
I guess we can stand it," and "Go ahead!" came from all sides,
from all kinds of listeners.

"It is merely this: that as we look back at the old competitive
conditions we do not see how any man could be a gentleman in
them, since a gentleman must think first of others, and these
conditions *compelled* every man to think first of himself."

There was a silence broken by some conscious and hardy
laughter, while we each swallowed this pill as we could.

"What are competitive conditions?" Mrs. Makely demanded
of me.

"Well, ours are competitive conditions," I said.

"Very well, then," she returned, "I don't think Mr. Homos is
much of a gentleman to say such a thing to an American
audience. Or, wait a moment! Ask him if the same rule applies
to women."

I rose, strengthened by the resentment I felt, and said, "Do I understand that in your former competitive conditions it was also impossible for a woman to be a lady?"

The professor gave me an applausive nod as I sat down. "I envy you the chance of that little dig," he whispered.

The Altrurian was thoughtful a moment, and then he answered: "No, I should not say it was. From what we know historically of those conditions in our country, it appears that the great mass of women were not directly affected by them. They constituted an altruistic dominion of the egoistic empire, and except as they were tainted by social or worldly ambitions, it was possible for every woman to be a lady, even in competitive conditions. Her instincts were unselfish, and her first thoughts were nearly always of others."

Mrs. Makely jumped to her feet and clapped violently with her fan on the palm of her left hand. "Three cheers for Mr. Homos!" she shrieked, and all the women took up the cry, supported by all the natives and the construction gang. I fancied these fellows gave their support largely in a spirit of burlesque; but they gave it robustly, and from that time on, Mrs. Makely led the applause, and they roared in after her.

It is impossible to follow closely the course of the Altrurian's account of his country, which grew more and more incredible as he went on, and implied every insulting criticism of ours. Some one asked him about war in Altruria, and he said: "The very name of our country implies the absence of war. At the time of the Evolution our country bore to the rest of our continent the same relative proportion that your country bears to your continent. The egoistic nations to the north and the south of us entered into an offensive and defensive alliance to put down the new altruistic commonwealth, and declared war against us. Their forces were met at the frontier by our entire population in arms, and full of the martial spirit bred of the constant hostilities of the competitive and monopolistic epoch just ended. Negotiations began in the face of the imposing demonstration we made, and we were never afterward molested by our neighbors, who finally yielded to the spectacle of our civilization and united their political and social fate with ours. At present, our whole continent is Altrurian. For a long time we kept up a system of coast defences, but it is also a long time since we abandoned these; for it is a maxim with us that where every citizen's life is a pledge of the public safety, that country can never be in danger of foreign enemies.

"In this, as in all other things, we believe ourselves the true followers of Christ, whose doctrine we seek to make our life as He made it His. We have several forms of ritual, but no form of creed, and our religious differences may be said to be aesthetic and temperamental rather than theological and essential. We have no denominations, for we fear in this, as in other matters, to give names to things lest we should cling to the names instead of the things. We love the realities, and for this reason we look at the life of a man rather than his profession for proof that he is a religious man.

"I have been several times asked, during my sojourn among you, what are the sources of compassion, of sympathy, of humanity, of charity with us, if we have not only no want, or fear of want, but not even any economic inequality. I suppose this is because you are so constantly struck by the misery arising from economic inequality and want, or the fear of want, among yourselves, that you instinctively look in that direction. But have you ever seen sweeter compassion, tenderer sympathy, warmer humanity, heavenlier charity than that shown in the family where all are economically equal and no one can want while any other has to give? Altruria, I say again, is a family, and, as we are mortal, we are still subject to those nobler sorrows which God has appointed to men, and which are so different from the squalid accidents that they have made for themselves. Sickness and death call out the most angelic ministries of love; and those who wish to give themselves to others may do so without hinderance from those cares, and even those duties, resting upon men where each must look out first for himself and for his own. Oh, believe me, believe me, you can know nothing of the divine rapture of self-sacrifice while you must dread the sacrifice of another in it! You are not *free*, as we are, to do everything for others, for it is your *duty* to do rather for those of your own household!

"There is something," he continued, "which I hardly know how to speak of," and here we all began to prick our ears. I prepared myself as well as I could for another affront, though I shuddered when the banker hardily called out: "Don't hesitate to say anything you wish, Mr. Homos. I, for one, should like to hear you express yourself fully."

It was always the unexpected, certainly, that happened from the Altrurian. "It is merely this," he said. "Having come to live rightly upon earth, as we believe, or having at least ceased to deny God in our statutes and customs, the fear of death, as it once weighed upon us, has been lifted from our souls. The mystery of it has so far been taken away that we perceive it as something just and natural. Now that all unkindness has been banished from us, we can conceive of no such cruelty as death once seemed. If we do not know yet the full meaning of death, we know that the Creator of it and of us meant mercy and blessing by it. When one dies we grieve, but not as those without hope. We do not say that the dead have gone to a better place, and then selfishly bewail them, for we have the kingdom of heaven upon earth already, and we know that wherever they go they will be homesick for Altruria, and when we think of the years that may pass before we meet them again our hearts ache, as theirs must. But the presence of the risen Christ in our daily lives is our assurance that no one ceases to be, and that we shall see our dead again. I cannot explain this to you; I can only affirm it."

The Altrurian spoke very solemnly, and a reverent hush fell upon the assembly. It was broken by the voice of a woman wailing out: "Oh, do you suppose, if *we* lived so, we should feel so, too? That I should *know* my little girl was living?"

"Why not?" asked the Altrurian.

To my vast astonishment, the manufacturer, who sat the farthest from me in the same line with Mrs. Makely, the professor, and the banker, rose and asked, tremulously: "And have—have you had any direct communication with the other world?

Has any disembodied spirit returned to testify of the life beyond the grave?"

The professor nodded significantly across Mrs. Makely to me, and then frowned and shook his head. I asked her if she knew what he meant. "Why, didn't you know that spiritualism was that poor man's foible? He lost his son in a railroad accident, and ever since—"

She stopped and gave her attention to the Altrurian, who was replying to the manufacturer's question.

"We do not need any such testimony. Our life here makes us sure of the life there. At any rate, no externation of the supernatural, no objective miracle, has been wrought in our behalf. We have had faith to do what we prayed for, and the prescience of which I speak has been added unto us."

The manufacturer asked, as the bereaved mother had asked: "And if I lived so, should I feel so?"

Again the Altrurian answered: "Why not?"

The poor woman quavered: "Oh, I do believe it! I just *know* it must be true!"

The manufacturer shook his head sorrowfully and sat down, and remained there, looking at the ground.

"I am aware," the Altrurian went on, "that what I have said as to our realizing the kingdom of heaven on the earth must seem boastful and arrogant. That is what you pray for every day, but you do not believe it possible for God's will to be done on earth as it is done in heaven—that is, you do not if you are like the competitive and monopolistic people we once were. We once regarded that petition as a formula vaguely pleasing to the Deity, but we no more expected His kingdom to come than we expected Him to give us each day our daily bread; we knew that if we wanted something to eat we should have to hustle for it, and get there first; I use the slang of that far-off time, which, I confess, had a vulgar vigor.

"But now everything is changed, and the change has taken place chiefly from one cause, namely, the disuse of money. At first, it was thought that some sort of circulating medium *must* be used, that life could not be transacted without it. But life began to go on perfectly well, when each dwelt in the place assigned him, which was no better and no worse than any other; and when, after he had given his three hours a day to the obligatory labors, he had a right to his share of food, light, heat, and raiment; the voluntary labors, to which he gave much time or little, brought him no increase of those necessaries, but only credit and affection. We had always heard it said that the love of money was the root of all evil, but we had taken this for a saying, merely; now we realized it as an active, vital truth. As soon as money was abolished the power to purchase was gone, and even if there had been any means of buying beyond the daily needs, with overwork, the community had no power to sell to the individual. No man owned anything, but every man had the right to anything that he could use; when he could not use it, his right lapsed.

"With the expropriation of the individual the whole vast catalogue of crimes against property shrank to nothing. The thief could only steal from the community; but if he stole, what was he to do with his booty? It was still possible for a depredator to destroy, but few men's hate is so comprehensive as to include all other men, and when the individual could no longer hurt some other individual in his property, destruction ceased.

"All the many murders done from love of money, or of what money could buy, were at an end. Where there was no want, men no longer bartered their souls, or women their bodies, for the means to keep themselves alive. The vices vanished with the crimes, and the diseases almost as largely disappeared. People were no longer sickened by sloth and surfeit, or deformed and depleted by overwork and famine. They were wholesomely housed in healthful places, and they were clad fitly for their labor and fitly for their leisure; the caprices of vanity were not suffered to attaint the beauty of the national dress.

"With the stress of superfluous social and business duties, and the perpetual fear of want which all classes felt, more or less; with the tumult of the cities and the solitude of the country, insanity had increased among us till the whole land was dotted with asylums and the mad were numbered by hundreds of thousands. In every region they were an army, an awful army of anguish and despair. Now they have decreased to a number so small, and are of a type so mild, that we can hardly count insanity among our causes of unhappiness.

"We have totally eliminated chance from our economic life. There is still a chance that a man will be tall or short in Altruria, that he will be strong or weak, well or ill, gay or grave, happy or unhappy in love, but none that he will be rich or poor, busy or idle, live splendidly or meanly. These stupid and vulgar accidents of human contrivance cannot befall us; but I shall not be able to tell you just how or why, or to detail the process of eliminating chance. I may say, however, that it began with the nationalization of telegraphs, expresses, railroads, mines, and all large industries operated by stock companies. This at once struck a fatal blow at the speculation in values, real and unreal, and at the stock-exchange, or bourse; we had our own name for that gambler's paradise, or gambler's hell, whose baleful influence penetrated every branch of business.

"There were still business fluctuations as long as we had business, but they were on a smaller and smaller scale, and with the final lapse of business they necessarily vanished; all economic chance vanished. The founders of the common-wealth understood perfectly that business was the sterile activity of the function interposed between the demand and the supply; that it was nothing structural; and they intended its extinction, and expected it from the moment that money was abolished."

"This is all pretty tiresome," said the professor to our immediate party. "I don't see why we oblige ourselves to listen to that fellow's stuff. As if a civilized state could exist for a day without money or business!"

He went on to give his opinion of the Altrurian's pretended description, in a tone so audible that it attracted the notice of the nearest group of railroad hands, who were listening closely to Homos, and one of them sang out to the professor: "Can't you wait and let the first man finish?" and another yelled: "Put him out!" and then they all laughed, with a humorous perception of the impossibility of literally executing the suggestion.

By the time all was quiet again I heard the Altrurian saying: "As to our social life, I cannot describe it in detail, but I can give you some notion of its spirit. We make our pleasures civic and public as far as possible, and the ideal is inclusive and not exclusive. There are, of course, festivities which all cannot share, but our distribution into small communities favors the possibility of all doing so. Our daily life, however, is so largely social that we seldom meet by special invitation or engagement. When we do, it is with the perfect understanding that the assemblage confers no social distinction, but is for a momentary convenience. In fact, these occasions are rather avoided, recalling, as they do, the vapid and tedious entertainments of the competitive epoch, the receptions and balls and dinners of a semi-barbaric people striving for social prominence by shutting a certain number in and a certain number out, and overdressing, overfeeding, and overdrinking. Anything premeditated in the way of a pleasure we think stupid and mistaken; we like to meet suddenly, or on the spur of the moment, out-of-doors, if possible, and arrange a picnic or a dance or a play; and let people come and go without ceremony. No one is more host than guest; all are hosts and guests. People consort much according to their tastes—literary, musical, artistic, scientific, or mechanical—but these tastes are made approaches, not barriers; and we find out that we have many more tastes in common than was formerly supposed.

"But, after all, our life is serious, and no one among us is quite happy, in the general esteem, unless he has dedicated himself, in some special way, to the general good. Our ideal is not rights, but duties."

"Mazzini!" whispered the professor.

"The greatest distinction which any one can enjoy with us is to have found out some new and signal way of serving the community; and then it is not good form for him to seek recognition. The doing any fine thing is the purest pleasure it can give; applause flatters, but it hurts, too, and our benefactors, as we call them, have learned to shun it.

"We are still far from thinking our civilization perfect; but we are sure that our civic ideals are perfect. What we have already accomplished is to have given a whole continent perpetual peace; to have founded an economy in which there is no possibility of want; to have killed out political and social ambition; to have disused money and eliminated chance; to have realized the brotherhood of the race, and to have outlived the fear of death."

The Altrurian suddenly stopped with these words, and sat down. He had spoken a long time, and with a fullness which my report gives little notion of; but, though most of his cultivated listeners were weary, and a good many ladies had left their seats and gone back to the hotel, not one of the natives, or the work-people of any sort, had stirred; now they remained a moment motionless and silent before they rose from all parts of the field and shouted: "Go on! Don't stop! Tell us all about it!"

I saw Reuben Camp climb the shoulders of a big fellow near where the Altrurian had stood; he waved the crowd to silence with outspread arms. "He isn't going to say anything more; he's tired. But if any man don't think he's got his dollar's worth, let him walk up to the door and the ticket-agent will refund him his money."

The crowd laughed, and some one shouted: "Good for you, Reub!"

Camp continued: "But our friend here will shake the hand of any man, woman, or child that wants to speak to him; and you needn't wipe it on the grass first, either. He's a *man!* And I want to say that he's going to spend the next week with us, at my mother's house, and we shall be glad to have you call."

The crowd, the rustic and ruder part of it, cheered and cheered till the mountain echoes answered; then a railroader called for three times three, with a tiger, and got it. The guests of the hotel broke away and went toward the house, over the long shadows of the meadow. The lower classes pressed forward, on Camp's invitation.

"Well, did you ever hear a more disgusting rigmarole?" asked Mrs. Makely, as our little group halted indecisively about her.

"With all those imaginary commonwealths to draw upon, from Plato, through More, Bacon, and Campanella, down to Bellamy and Morris, he has constructed the shakiest effigy ever made of old clothes stuffed with straw," said the professor.

The manufacturer was silent. The banker said: "I don't know. He grappled pretty boldly with your insinuations. That frank declaration that Altruria was all these pretty soap-bubble worlds solidified was rather fine."

"It was splendid!" cried Mrs. Makely. The lawyer and the minister came toward us from where they had been sitting together. She called out to them: "Why in the world didn't one of your gentlemen get up and propose a vote of thanks?"

"The difficulty with me is," continued the banker, "that he has rendered Altruria incredible. I have no doubt that he is an Altrurian, but I doubt very much if he comes from anywhere in particular, and I find this quite a blow, for we had got Altruria nicely located on the map, and were beginning to get accounts of it in the newspapers."

"Yes, that is just exactly the way I feel about it," sighed Mrs. Makely. "But still, don't you think there ought to have been a vote of thanks, Mr. Bullion?"

"Why, certainly. The fellow was immensely amusing, and you must have got a lot of money by him. It was an oversight not to make him a formal acknowledgment of some kind. If we offered him money, he would have to leave it all behind him here when he went home to Altruria."

"Just as *we* do when we go to heaven," I suggested; the banker did not answer, and I instantly felt that in the presence of the minister my remark was out of taste.

"Well, then, don't you think," said Mrs. Makely, who had a leathery insensibility to everything but the purpose possessing her, "that we ought at least to go and say something to him personally?"

"Yes, I think we ought," said the banker, and we all walked up to where the Altrurian stood, still thickly surrounded by the lower classes, who were shaking hands with him and getting in a word with him now and then.

One of the construction gang said, carelessly: "No all-rail route to Altruria, I suppose?"

"No," answered Homos, "it's a far sea voyage."

"Well, I shouldn't mind working my passage, if you think they'd let me stay after I got there."

"Ah, you mustn't go to Altruria! You must let Altruria come to *you*," returned Homos, with that confounded smile of his that always won my heart.

"Yes," shouted Reuben Camp, whose thin face was red with excitement, "that's the word! Have Altruria right here, and right now!"

The old farmer, who had several times spoken, cackled out: "I didn't know, one while, when you was talk'n' about not havin' any money, but what some on us had had Altrury here for quite a spell, already. I don't pass more'n fifty dolla's through my hands, most years."

A laugh went up, and then, at sight of Mrs. Makely heading our little party, the people round Homos civilly made way for us. She rushed upon him, and seized his hand in both of hers; she dropped her fan, parasol, gloves, handkerchief, and vinaigrette in the grass to do so. "Oh, Mr. Homos," she fluted, and the tears came into her eyes, "it was beautiful, *beautiful*, every word of it! I sat in a perfect trance from beginning to end, and I felt that it was all as true as it was beautiful. People all around me were breathless with interest, and I don't know how I can ever thank you enough."

"Yes, indeed," the professor hastened to say, before the Altrurian could answer, and he beamed malignantly upon him through his spectacles while he spoke, "it was like some strange romance."

"I don't know that I should go so far as that," said the banker, in his turn, "but it certainly seemed too good to be true."

"Yes," the Altrurian responded, simply, but a little sadly; "now that I am away from it all, and in conditions so different, I sometimes had to ask myself, as I went on, if my whole life had not hitherto been a dream, and Altruria were not some blessed vision of the night."

"Then you know how to account for a feeling which I must acknowledge, too?" the lawyer asked, courteously. "But it was most interesting."

"The kingdom of God upon earth," said the minister—"it ought not to be incredible; but that, more than anything else you told us of, gave me pause."

"You, of all men?" returned the Altrurian, gently.

"Yes," said the minister, with a certain dejection, "when I remember what I have seen of men, when I reflect what human nature is, how can I believe that the kingdom of God will ever come upon the earth?"

"But in heaven, where He reigns, who is it does His will? The spirits of men?" pursued the Altrurian.

"Yes, but, conditioned as men are here—"

"But if they were conditioned as men are there?"

"Now, I can't let you two good people get into a theological dispute," Mrs. Makely pushed in. "Here is Mr. Twelvemough dying to shake hands with Mr. Homos and compliment his distinguished guest."

"Ah, Mr. Homos knows what I must have thought of his talk without my telling him," I began, skilfully. "But I am sorry that I am to lose my distinguished guest so soon."

Reuben Camp broke out: "That was my blunder, Mr. Twelvemough. Mr. Homos and I talked it over, conditionally, and I was not to speak of it till he had told you; but it slipped out in the excitement of the moment."

"Oh, it's all right," I said, and I shook hands cordially with both of them. "It will be the greatest possible advantage for Mr. Homos to see certain phases of American life at close range, and he couldn't possibly see them under better auspices than yours, Camp."

"Yes, I'm going to drive him through the hill country, after haying, and then I'm going to take him down and show him one of our big factory towns."

I believe this was done, but finally the Altrurian went on to New York, where he was to pass the winter. We parted friends;

I even offered him some introductions; but his acquaintance had become more and more difficult, and I was not sorry to part with him. That taste of his for low company was incurable, and I was glad that I was not to be responsible any longer for whatever strange thing he might do next. I think he remained very popular with the classes he most affected; a throng of natives, construction hands, and table-girls saw him off on his train; and he left large numbers of such admirers in our house and neighborhood, devout in the faith that there was such a commonwealth as Altruria, and that he was really an Altrurian. As for the more cultivated people who had met him, they continued of two minds upon both points.

CRITICAL ESSAYS

The following eight essays, written from 1882 to 1902, are landmarks in Howells' battle for realism. The first, entitled "Henry James, Jr.," traces the beginnings of a long literary friendship, in the course of which the critical position of both writers was defined. The second article, which we have entitled "The Smiling Aspects of American Life," has frequently been pointed to as proof of the accusation that Howells refused to look at the harsher side of society; actually Howells was merely defending the need for realism in American fiction. Since this country was then enjoying an age of peace and prosperity, Howells believed the scene to be more "smiling" than that described by Russian writers. The third essay, "Pernicious Fiction," is a defence of the realistic novel as opposed to the romantic tale, which lulls the reader to sleep "with idle lies about human nature and the social fabric." Here Howells gives his famous tests for a novel, which, he tells us, are "very plain and simple, and . . . perfectly infallible." The next two selections reflect another aspect of Howells' fight for realism, suggest how truly he gave "breadth" to literature in his position of author-critic, who had himself walked the "Main Travelled Road" of the Middle West. In the sixth selection of this collection, the reader may study the essential Tolstoyan concept, expressed in Que Faire, *which became a foundation stone of Howells' social thinking, that of the brotherhood of man based on shared work, which he incorporated in* Annie Kilburn. *The last two essays, written on the occasions of the deaths of Emile Zola and Frank Norris, show something of the source of Howells' realism and the influence it had on the younger generation of writers in this country. See Introduction, pp. cxxx–clxvii.*

HENRY JAMES, JR.*

The events of Mr. James's life—as we agree to understand events—may be told in a very few words. His race is Irish on his father's side and Scotch on his mother's, to which mingled strains the generalizer may attribute, if he likes, that union of vivid expression and dispassionate analysis which has characterized his work from the first. There are none of those early struggles with poverty, which render the lives of so many dis-

*Reprinted from *The Century*, XXV (November, 1882), 25–29. For a discussion of the relationship between James and Howells, see *Introduction*, pp. lxvii–lxix; lxxvii; clxvi–clxvii. A list of Howells' reviews of the works of James may be found in *A Bibliography of William Dean Howells*, by William M. Gibson and George Arms, New York, 1948.

tinguished Americans monotonous reading, to record in his
case: the cabin hearth-fire did not light him to the youthful
pursuit of literature; he had from the start all those advantages
which, when they go too far, become limitations.

He was born in New York city in the year 1843, and his first
lessons in life and letters were the best which the metropolis—
so small in the perspective diminishing to that date—could
afford. In his twelfth year his family went abroad, and after
some stay in England made a long sojourn in France and Switzerland. They returned to America in 1860, placing themselves
at Newport, and for a year or two Mr. James was at the Harvard
Law School, where, perhaps, he did not study a great deal of
law. His father removed from Newport to Cambridge in 1866,
and there Mr. James remained till he went abroad, three years
later, for the residence in England and Italy which, with infre-
quent visits home, has continued ever since.

It was during these three years of his Cambridge life that I
became acquainted with his work. He had already printed a
tale—"The Story of a Year"—in the "Atlantic Monthly," when
I was asked to be Mr. Fields's assistant in the management, and
it was my fortune to read Mr. James's second contribution in
manuscript. "Would you take it?" asked my chief. "Yes, and
all the stories you can get from the writer." One is much securer
of one's judgment at twenty-nine than, say, at forty-five; but
if this was a mistake of mine I am not yet old enough to regret it.
The story was called "Poor Richard," and it dealt with the
conscience of a man very much in love with a woman who loved
his rival. He told this rival a lie, which sent him away to his
death on the field,—in that day nearly every fictitious personage
had something to do with the war,—but Poor Richard's lie did
not win him his love. It still seems to me that the situation was
strongly and finely felt. One's pity went, as it should, with the
liar; but the whole story had a pathos which lingers in my mind
equally with a sense of the new literary qualities which gave me
such delight in it. I admired, as we must in all that Mr. James
has written, the finished workmanship in which there is no loss
of vigor; the luminous and uncommon use of words, the origi-

nality of phrase, the whole clear and beautiful style, which I confess I weakly liked the better for the occasional gallicisms remaining from an inveterate habit of French. Those who know the writings of Mr. Henry James will recognize the inherited felicity of diction which is so striking in the writings of Mr. Henry James, Jr. The son's diction is not so racy as the father's; it lacks its daring, but it is as fortunate and graphic; and I cannot give it greater praise than this, though it has, when he will, a splendor and state which is wholly its own.

Mr. James is now so universally recognized that I shall seem to be making an unwarrantable claim when I express my belief that the popularity of his stories was once largely confined to Mr. Fields's assistant. They had characteristics which forbade any editor to refuse them; and there are no anecdotes of thrice-rejected manuscripts finally printed to tell of him; his work was at once successful with all the magazines. But with the readers of "The Atlantic," of "Harper's," of "Lippincott's," of "The Galaxy," of "The Century," it was another affair. The flavor was so strange, that, with rare exceptions, they had to "learn to like" it. Probably few writers have in the same degree compelled the liking of their readers. He was reluctantly accepted, partly through a mistake as to his attitude—through the confusion of his point of view with his private opinion—in the reader's mind. This confusion caused the tears of rage which bedewed our continent in behalf of the "average American girl" supposed to be satirized in Daisy Miller, and prevented the perception of the fact that, so far as the average American girl was studied at all in Daisy Miller, her indestructible innocence, her invulnerable new-worldliness, had never been so delicately appreciated. It was so plain that Mr. James disliked her vulgar conditions, that the very people to whom he revealed her essential sweetness and light were furious that he should have seemed not to see what existed through him. In other words, they would have liked him better if he had been a worse artist—if he had been a little more confidential.

But that artistic impartiality which puzzled so many in the treatment of Daisy Miller is one of the qualities most valuable in the eyes of those who care how things are done, and I am not sure that it is not Mr. James's most characteristic quality. As "frost performs the effect of fire," this impartiality comes at last to the same result as sympathy. We may be quite sure that Mr. James does not like the peculiar phase of our civilization typified in Henrietta Stackpole; but he treats her with such exquisite justice that he lets *us* like her. It is an extreme case, but I confidently allege it in proof.

His impartiality is part of the reserve with which he works in most respects, and which at first glance makes us say that he is wanting in humor. But I feel pretty certain that Mr. James has not been able to disinherit himself to this degree. We Americans are terribly in earnest about making ourselves, individually and collectively; but I fancy that our prevailing mood in the face of all problems is that of an abiding faith which can afford to be funny. He has himself indicated that we have, as a nation, as a people, our joke, and every one of us is in the joke more or less. We may, some of us, dislike it extremely, disapprove it wholly, and even abhor it, but we are in the joke all the same, and no one of us is safe from becoming the great American humorist at any given moment. The danger is not apparent in Mr. James's case, and I confess that I read him with a relief in the comparative immunity that he affords from the national facetiousness. Many of his people are humorously imagined, or rather humorously *seen*, like Daisy Miller's mother, but these do not give a dominant color; the business in hand is commonly serious, and the droll people are subordinated. They abound, nevertheless, and many of them are perfectly new finds, like Mr. Tristram in "The American," the bill-paying father in the "Pension Beaurepas," the anxiously Europeanizing mother in the same story, the amusing little Madame de Belgarde, Henrietta Stackpole, and even Newman himself. But though Mr. James portrays the humorous in character, he is decidedly not on humorous terms with his reader; he ignores rather than recognizes the fact that they are both in the joke.

If we take him at all we must take him on his own ground, for clearly he will not come to ours. We must make concessions to him, not in this respect only, but in several others, chief among which is the motive for reading fiction. By example, at least, he teaches that it is the pursuit and not the end which should give us pleasure; for he often prefers to leave us to our own conjectures in regard to the fate of the people in whom he has interested us. There is no question, of course, but he could tell the story of Isabel in "The Portrait of a Lady" to the end, yet he does not tell it. We must agree, then, to take what seems a fragment instead of a whole, and to find, when we can, a name for this new kind in fiction. Evidently it is the character, not the fate, of his people which occupies him; when he has fully developed their character he leaves them to what destiny the reader pleases.

The analytic tendency seems to have increased with him as his work has gone on. Some of the earlier tales were very dramatic: "A Passionate Pilgrim," which I should rank above all his other short stories, and for certain rich poetical qualities, above everything else that he has done, is eminently dramatic. But I do not find much that I should call dramatic in "The Portrait of a Lady," while I do find in it an amount of analysis which I should call superabundance if it were not all such good literature. The novelist's main business is to possess his reader with a due conception of his characters and the situations in which they find themselves. If he does more or less than this he equally fails. I have sometimes thought that Mr. James's danger was to do more, but when I have been ready to declare this excess an error of his method I have hesitated. Could anything be superfluous that had given me so much pleasure as I read? Certainly from only one point of view, and this a rather narrow, technical one. It seems to me that an enlightened criticism will recognize in Mr. James's fiction a metaphysical genius working to aesthetic results, and will not be disposed to deny it any method it chooses to employ. No other novelist, except George Eliot, has dealt so largely in analysis of motive, has so fully explained and commented upon the springs of action in the persons of the drama, both before and after the facts. These novelists are more alike than any others in their processes, but with George Eliot an ethical purpose is dominant, and with Mr. James an artistic purpose. I do not know just how it should be stated of two such noble and generous types of character as Dorothea and Isabel Archer, but I think that we sympathize with the former in grand aims that chiefly concern others, and with the latter in beautiful dreams that primarily concern herself. Both are unselfish and devoted women, sublimely true to a mistaken ideal in their marriages; but, though they come to this common martyrdom, the original difference in them remains. Isabel has her great weaknesses, as Dorothea had, but these seem to me, on the whole, the most nobly imagined and the most nobly intentioned women in modern fiction; and I think Isabel is the more subtly divined of the two. If we speak of mere characterization, we must not fail to acknowledge the perfection of Gilbert Osmond. It was a profound stroke to make him an American by birth. No European could realize so fully in his own life the ideal of a European *dilettante* in all the meaning of that cheapened word; as no European could so deeply and tenderly feel the sweetness and loveliness of the English past as the sick American, Searle, in "The Passionate Pilgrim."

What is called the international novel is popularly dated from the publication of "Daisy Miller," though "Roderick Hudson" and "The American" had gone before; but it really began in the beautiful story which I have just named. Mr. James, who invented this species in fiction, first contrasted in the "Passionate Pilgrim" the New World and Old World moods, ideals, and prejudices, and he did it there with a richness of poetic effect which he has since never equalled. I own that I regret the loss of the poetry, but you cannot ask a man to keep on being a poet for you; it is hardly for him to choose; yet I compare rather discontentedly in my own mind such impassioned creations as Searle and the painter in "The Madonna of the Future" with "Daisy Miller," of whose slight, thin personality I also feel the indefinable charm, and of the tragedy of whose innocence I recognize the delicate pathos. Looking back to those early stories, where Mr. James stood at the dividing ways of the novel and the romance, I am sometimes sorry that he declared even superficially for the former. His best efforts seem to me those of romance; his best types have an ideal development, like Isabel and Claire Belgarde and Bessy Alden and poor Daisy and even Newman. But, doubtless, he has chosen wisely; perhaps the romance is an outworn form, and would not lend itself to the reproduction of even the ideality of modern life. I myself waver somewhat in my preference—if it is a preference—when I think of such people as Lord Warburton and the Touchetts, whom I take to be all decidedly of this world. The first of these especially interested me as a probable type of the English noble-man, who amiably accepts the existing situation with all its possibilities of political and social change, and insists not at all upon the surviving feudalities, but means to be a manly and simple gentleman in any event. An American is not able to pro-nounce as to the verity of the type; I only know that it seems probable and that it is charming. It makes one wish that it were in Mr. James's way to paint in some story the present phase of change in England. A titled personage is still mainly an incon-ceivable being to us; he is like a goblin or a fairy in a story-book. How does he comport himself in the face of all the changes and modifications that have taken place and that still impend? We can hardly imagine a lord taking his nobility seriously; it is some hint of the conditional frame of Lord Warburton's mind that makes him imaginable and delightful to us.

It is not my purpose here to review any of Mr. James's books; I like better to speak of his people than of the conduct of his novels, and I wish to recognize the fineness with which he has touched-in the pretty primness of Osmond's daughter and the mild devotedness of Mr. Rosier. A masterly hand is as often manifest in the treatment of such subordinate figures as in that of the principal persons, and Mr. James does them unerringly. This is felt in the more important character of Valentin Belgarde, a fascinating character in spite of its defects,—perhaps on account of them—and a sort of French Lord Warburton, but wittier, and not so good. "These are my ideas," says his sister-in-law, at the end of a number of inanities. "Ah, you call them ideas!" he returns, which is delicious and makes you love him.

He, too, has his moments of misgiving, apparently in regard to his nobility, and his acceptance of Newman on the basis of something like "manhood suffrage" is very charming. It is of course difficult for a remote plebeian to verify the pictures of legitimist society in "The American," but there is the probable suggestion in them of conditions and principles, and want of principles, of which we get glimpses in our travels abroad; at any rate, they reveal another and not impossible world, and it is fine to have Newman discover that the opinions and criticisms of our world are so absolutely valueless in that sphere that his knowledge of the infamous crime of the mother and brother of his betrothed will have no effect whatever upon them in their own circle if he explodes it there. This seems like aristocracy indeed! and one admires, almost respects, its survival in our day. But I always regretted that Newman's discovery seemed the precursor of his magnanimous resolution not to avenge himself; it weakened the effect of this, with which it had really nothing to do. Upon the whole, however, Newman is an adequate and satisfying representative of Americanism, with his generous matrimonial ambition, his vast good-nature, and his thorough good sense and right feeling. We must be very hard to please if we are not pleased with him. He is not the "cultivated American" who redeems us from time to time in the eyes of Europe; but he is unquestionably more national, and it is observable that his unaffected fellow-countrymen and women fare very well at Mr. James's hands always; it is the Europeanizing sort like the critical little Bostonian in the "Bundle of Letters," the ladies shocked at Daisy Miller, the mother in the "Pension Beaurepas" who goes about trying to be of the "native" world everywhere, Madame Merle and Gilbert Osmond, Miss Light and her mother, who have reason to complain, if any one has. Doubtless Mr. James does not mean to satirize such Americans, but it is interesting to note how they strike such a keen observer. We are certainly not allowed to like them, and the other sort find somehow a place in our affections along with his good Europeans. It is a little odd, by the way, that in all the printed talk about Mr. James—and there has been no end of it—his power of engaging your preference for certain of his people has been so little commented on. Perhaps it is because he makes no obvious appeal for them; but one likes such men as Lord Warburton, Newman, Valentin, the artistic brother in "The Europeans," and Ralph Touchett, and such women as Isabel, Claire Belgarde, Mrs. Tristram, and certain others, with a thoroughness that is one of the best testimonies to their vitality. This comes about through their own qualities, and is not affected by insinuation or by downright *petting*, such as we find in Dickens nearly always and in Thackeray too often.

The art of fiction has, in fact, become a finer art in our day than it was with Dickens and Thackeray. We could not suffer the confidential attitude of the latter now, nor the mannerism of the former, any more than we could endure the prolixity of Richardson or the coarseness of Fielding. These great men are of the past—they and their methods and interests; even Trollope and Reade are not of the present. The new school derives from Hawthorne and George Eliot rather than any others; but it studies human nature much more in its wonted aspects, and finds its ethical and dramatic examples in the operation of lighter but not really less vital motives. The moving accident is certainly not its trade; and it prefers to avoid all manner of dire catastrophes. It is largely influenced by French fiction in form; but it is the realism of Daudet rather than the realism of Zola that prevails with it, and it has a soul of its own which is above the business of recording the rather brutish pursuit of a woman by a man, which seems to be the chief end of the French novelist. This school, which is so largely of the future as well as the present, finds its chief exemplar in Mr. James; it is he who is shaping and directing American fiction, at least. It is the ambition of the younger contributors to write like him; he has his following more distinctly recognizable than that of any other English-writing novelist. Whether he will so far control this following as to decide the nature of the novel with us remains to be seen. Will the reader be content to accept a novel which is an analytic study rather than a story, which is apt to leave him arbiter of the destiny of the author's creations? Will he find his

account in the unflagging interest of their development? Mr.
James's growing popularity seems to suggest that this may be
the case; but the work of Mr. James's imitators will have much
to do with the final result.

In the meantime it is not surprising that he has his imitators.
Whatever exceptions we take to his methods or his results, we
cannot deny him a very great literary genius. To me there is a
perpetual delight in his way of saying things, and I cannot
wonder that younger men try to catch the trick of it. The
disappointing thing for them is that it is not a trick, but an
inherent virtue. His style is, upon the whole, better than that
of any other novelist I know; it is always easy, without being
trivial, and it is often stately, without being stiff; it gives a charm
to everything he writes; and he has written so much and in such
various directions, that we should be judging him very incom-
pletely if we considered him only as a novelist. His book of
European sketches must rank him with the most enlightened and
agreeable travelers; and it might be fitly supplemented from his
uncollected papers with a volume of American sketches. In his
essays on modern French writers he indicates his critical range
and grasp; but he scarcely does more, as his criticisms in "The
Atlantic" and "The Nation" and elsewhere could abundantly
testify.

There are indeed those who insist that criticism is his true
vocation, and are impatient of his devotion to fiction; but I suspect that these admirers are mistaken. A novelist he is not, after
the old fashion, or after any fashion but his own; yet since he has
finally made his public in his own way of story-telling—or call
it character-painting if you prefer,—it must be conceded that
he has chosen best for himself and his readers in choosing the
form of fiction for what he has to say. It is, after all, what a
writer has to say rather than what he has to tell that we care for
nowadays. In one manner or other the stories were all told long
ago; and now we want merely to know what the novelist thinks
about persons and situations. Mr. James gratifies this philosophic desire. If he sometimes forbears to tell us what he thinks
of the last state of his people, it is perhaps because that does not

interest him, and a large-minded criticism might well insist that it was childish to demand that it must interest him.

I am not sure that my criticism is sufficiently large-minded for this. I own that I like a finished story; but then also I like those which Mr. James seems not to finish. This is probably the position of most of his readers, who cannot very logically account for either preference. We can only make sure that we have here an annalist, or analyst, as we choose, who fascinates us from his first page to his last, whose narrative or whose comment may enter into any minuteness of detail without fatiguing us, and can only truly grieve us when it ceases.

THE SMILING ASPECTS OF AMERICAN LIFE*

M. Vogüé writes with perhaps too breathless a fervor, but his article is valuable for the light it casts upon the origins of Dostoïevsky's work, and its inspirations and motives. It was the natural expression of such a life and such conditions. But it is useful to observe that while *The Crime and the Punishment* may be read with the deepest sympathy and interest, and may enforce with unique power the lessons which it teaches, it is to be praised only in its place, and its message is to be received with allowances by readers exterior to the social and political circumstances in which it was conceived. It used to be one of the disadvantages of the practice of romance in America, which Hawthorne more or less whimsically lamented, that there were so few shadows and inequalities in our broad level of prosperity; and it is one of the reflections suggested by Dostoïevsky's book that whoever struck a note so profoundly tragic in American fiction would do a false and mistaken thing—as false and as mistaken in its way as dealing in American fiction with certain nudities which the Latin peoples seem to find edifying. Whatever their deserts, very few American novelists have been led out to be shot, or finally exiled to the rigors of a winter at Duluth; one might make Herr Most the hero of a labor-question romance with perfect impunity; and in a land where journeyman carpenters and plumbers strike for four dollars a day the sum of hunger and cold is certainly very small, and the wrong from class to class is almost inappreciable. We invite our novelists, therefore, to concern themselves with the more smiling aspects of life, which are the more American, and to seek the universal in the individual rather than the social interests. It is worth while, even at the risk of being called commonplace, to be true

*Harper's Magazine, LXXIII (Sept., 1886), 641-642. This essay, with few changes, was included in *Criticism and Fiction* (1891), Section XXI. For a further discussion of American society and criticism, see *Introduction*, pp. cxlv–cxlvii. A list of Howells' writing on Dostoevsky may be found in Gibson and Arms, *Bibliography*.

to our well-to-do actualities; the very passions themselves seem to be softened and modified by conditions which cannot be said to wrong any one, to cramp endeavor, or to cross lawful desire. Sin and suffering and shame there must always be in the world, we suppose, but we believe that in this new world of ours it is mainly from one to another one, and oftener still from one to one's self. We have death too in America, and a great deal of disagreeable and painful disease, which the multiplicity of our patent medicines does not seem to cure; but this is tragedy that comes in the very nature of things, and is not peculiarly American, as the large, cheerful average of health and success and happy life is. It will not do to boast, but it is well to be true to the facts, and to see that, apart from these purely mortal troubles, the race here enjoys conditions in which most of the ills that have darkened its annals may be averted by honest work and unselfish behavior.

It is only now and then, when some dark shadow of our shameful past appears, that we can believe there ever was a tragic element in our prosperity. Even then, when we read such an artlessly impressive sketch as Mrs. Sarah Bradford writes of Harriet Tubman—once famous as the Moses of her people—the self-freed bondwoman who led three hundred of her brethren out of slavery, and with a price set upon her head, risked her life and liberty nineteen times in this cause; even then it affects us like a tale

> "Of old, unhappy, far-off things,
> And battles long ago,"

and nothing within the date of actual history. We cannot realize that most of the men and women now living were once commanded by the law of the land to turn and hunt such fugitives back into slavery, and to deliver such an outlaw as Harriet over to her owner; that those who abetted such outlaws were sometimes mulcted to the last dollar of their substance in fines. We can hardly imagine such things now for the purposes of fiction; all troubles that now hurt and threaten us are as crumpled rose leaves in our couch. But we may nevertheless read Dostoïevsky, and especially our novelists may read him, to advantage, for in spite of his terrible picture of a soul's agony he is hopeful and wholesome, and teaches in every page patience, merciful judgment, humble helpfulness, and that brotherly responsibility, that duty of man to man, from which not even the Americans are emancipated.

PERNICIOUS FICTION*

It must have been a passage from Vernon Lee's *Baldwin*, claiming for the novel an indefinitely vast and subtle influence on modern character, which provoked the following suggestive letter from one of our readers:

"---, --- Co., Md., Sept. 18, 1886.
"Dear Sir,—With regard to article IV, in the Editor's Study in the September *Harper*, allow me to say that I have very grave doubts as to the whole list of magnificent things that you seem to think novels have done for the race, and can witness in myself many evil things which they have done for me. Whatever in my mental make-up is wild and visionary, whatever is untrue, whatever is injurious, I can trace to the perusal of some work of fiction. Worse than that, they beget such high-strung and supersensitive ideas of life that plain industry and plodding perseverance are despised, and matter-of-fact poverty, or everyday, commonplace distress, meets with no sympathy, if indeed noticed at all, by one who has wept over the impossibly accumulated sufferings of some gaudy hero or heroine.

"Hoping you will pardon the liberty I have taken in addressing you, I remain,

"Most respectfully yours,

. . . .

We are not sure that we have the controversy with the writer which he seems to suppose, and we should perhaps freely grant the mischievous effects which he says novel-reading has wrought upon him, if we were not afraid that he had possibly reviewed his own experience with something of the inaccuracy we find in his report of our opinions. By his confession he is himself proof that Vernon Lee is right in saying, "The modern human being has been largely fashioned by those who have

Harper's Magazine, LXXIV (April, 1887), 824-826. This essay, with few changes was included in *Criticism and Fiction* (1891), Section XVIII. For a discussion of Howells' view of the relation of morals to criticism, see *Introduction* pp. cxliv–cxlviii.

written about him, and most of all by the novelist," and there is nothing in what he urges to conflict with her claim that "the chief use of the novel" is "to make the shrewd and tolerant a little less shrewd and tolerant, and to make the generous and austere a little more skeptical and easy-going." If he will look more closely at these postulates, we think he will see that in the one she deals with the effect of the novel in the past, and in the other with its duty in the future. We still think that there "is sense if not final wisdom" in what she says, and we are quite willing to acknowledge something of each in our correspondent.

But novels are now so fully accepted by every one pretending to cultivated taste—and they really form the whole intellectual life of such immense numbers of people, without question of their influence, good or bad, upon the mind—that it is refreshing to have them frankly denounced, and to be invited to revise one's ideas and feelings in regard to them. A little honesty, or a great deal of honesty, in this quest will do the novel, as we hope yet to have it, and as we have already begun to have it, no harm; and for our own part we will confess that we believe fiction in the past to have been largely injurious, as we believe the stage play to be still almost wholly injurious, through its falsehood, its folly, its wantonness, and its aimlessness. It may be safely assumed that most of the novel-reading which people fancy is an intellectual pastime is the emptiest dissipation, hardly more related to thought or the wholesome exercise of the mental faculties than opium-eating; in either case the brain is drugged, and left weaker and crazier for the debauch. If this may be called the negative result of the fiction habit, the positive injury that most novels work is by no means so easily to be measured in the case of young men whose character they help so much to form or deform, and the women of all ages whom they keep so much in ignorance of the world they misrepresent. Grown men have little harm from them, but in the other cases, which are the vast majority, they hurt because they are not true—not because they are malevolent, but because they are idle lies about human nature and the social fabric, which it behooves us to know and to understand, that we may deal justly with ourselves and with one another. One need not go so far as our correspondent, and trace to the fiction habit "whatever is wild and visionary, whatever is untrue, whatever is injurious," in one's life; bad as the fiction habit is, it is probably not responsible for the whole sum of evil in its victims, and we believe that if the reader will use care in choosing from this fungus-growth with which the fields of literature teem every day, he may nourish himself as with the true mushroom, at no risk from the poisonous species.

The tests are very plain and simple, and they are perfectly infallible. If a novel flatters the passions, and exalts them above the principles, it is poisonous; it may not kill, but it will certainly injure; and this test will alone exclude an entire class of fiction, of which eminent examples will occur to all. Then the whole spawn of so-called un-moral romances, which imagine a world where the sins of sense are unvisited by the penalties following, swift or slow, but inexorably sure, in the real world, are deadly poison: these do kill. The novels that merely tickle our prejudices and lull our judgment, or that coddle our sensibilities, or pamper our gross appetite for the marvellous, are not so fatal, but they are innutritious, and clog the soul with unwholesome vapors of all kinds. No doubt they too help to weaken the mental fibre, and make their readers indifferent to "plodding perseverance and plain industry," and to "matter-of-fact poverty and commonplace distress."

Without taking them too seriously, it still must be owned that the "gaudy hero and heroine" are to blame for a great deal of harm in the world. That heroine long taught by example, if not precept, that Love, or the passion or fancy she mistook for it, was the chief interest of a life which is really concerned with a great many other things; that it was lasting in the way she knew it; that it was worthy of every sacrifice, and was altogether a finer thing than prudence, obedience, reason; that love alone was glorious and beautiful, and these were mean and ugly in comparison with it. More lately she has begun to idolize and illustrate Duty, and she is hardly less mischievous in this new rôle, opposing duty, as she did love, to prudence, obedience, and reason. The stock hero, whom, if we met him, we could not fail to see was a most deplorable person, has undoubtedly imposed himself upon the victims of the fiction habit as admirable. With him, too, love was and is the great affair, whether in its old romantic phase of chivalrous achievement or manifold suffering for love's sake, or its more recent development of the "virile," the bullying, and the brutal, or its still more recent agonies of self-sacrifice, as idle and useless as the moral experiences of the insane asylums. With his vain posturings and his ridiculous splendor he is really a painted barbarian, the prey of his passions, and his delusions, full of obsolete ideals, and the motives and ethics of a savage, which the guilty author of his being does his best—or his worst—in spite of his own light and knowledge, to foist upon the reader as something generous and noble. We are not merely bringing this charge against that sort of fiction which is beneath literature and outside of it, "the shoreless lakes of ditch-water," whose miasms fill the air below the empyrean where the great ones sit; but we are accusing the work of some of the most famous, who have, in this instance or in that, sinned against the truth, which can alone exalt and purify men. We do not say that they have constantly done so, or even commonly done so; but that they have done so at all marks them as of the past, to be read with the due historical allowance for their epoch and their conditions. For we believe that, while inferior writers will and must continue to imitate them in their foibles and their errors, no one hereafter will be able to achieve greatness who is false to humanity, either in its facts or its duties. The light of civilization has already broken even upon the novel, and no conscientious man can now set about painting an image of life without perpetual question of the verity of his work, and without feeling bound to distinguish so clearly that no reader of his may be misled, between what is right and what is wrong, what is noble and what is base, what is health and what is perdition, in the actions and the characters he portrays.

The fiction that aims merely to entertain—the fiction that is to serious fiction as the opéra bouffe, the ballet, and the pantomime are to the true drama—need not feel the burden of this obligation so deeply; but even such fiction will not be gay or trivial to any reader's hurt, and criticism will hold it to account if it passes from painting to teaching folly.

More and more not only the criticism which prints its opinions, but the infinitely vaster and powerfuler criticism which thinks and feels them merely, will make this demand. For our own part we confess that we do not care to judge any work of the imagination without first of all applying this test to it. We must ask ourselves before we ask anything else, Is it true?—true to the motives, the impulses, the principles that shape the life of actual men and women? This truth, which necessarily includes the highest morality and the highest artistry—this truth given, the book *cannot* be wicked and cannot be weak; and without it all graces of style and feats of invention and cunning of construction are so many superfluities of naughtiness. It is well for the truth to have all these, and shine in them, but for falsehood they are merely meretricious, the bedizenment of the wanton; they atone for nothing, they count for nothing. But in fact they come naturally of truth, and grace it without solicitation; they are added unto it. In the whole range of fiction we know of no *true* picture of life—that is, of human nature—which is not also a masterpiece of literature, full of divine and natural beauty. It may have no touch or tint of this special civilization or of that; it had *better* have this local color well ascertained; but the truth is deeper and finer than aspects, and if the book is true to what men and women know of one another's souls it will be true enough, and it will be great and beautiful. It is the conception of literature as something apart from life, superfinely aloof, which makes it really unimportant to the great mass of mankind, without a message or a meaning for them; and it is the notion that a novel may be false in its portrayal of causes and effects that makes literary art contemptible even to those whom it amuses, that forbids them to regard the novelist as a serious or right-minded person. If they do not in some moment of indignation cry out against all novels, as our correspondent does, they remain besotted in the fume of the delusions purveyed to them, with no higher feeling for the author than such maudlin affection as the *habitué* of an opium-joint perhaps knows for the attendant who fills his pipe with the drug.

BREADTH IN LITERATURE*

[A Southern critic] thinks it would be well if there were a school of Southern criticism for the censure of Southern literature; but at the same time he is disposed to defend this literature against a charge which we agree with him cannot lie against it alone. It has been called narrow, and he asks: "Is not the broadest of the new American fiction narrow, when compared, as it should be compared, with the authors of Russian fiction, French fiction, English fiction? Is there a living novelist of the North whose largest boundaries do not shrink to pitiful dimensions when put by the side of Tolstoï's, or Balzac's, or Thackeray's?"

We do not know certainly whether a Southerner thinks narrowness a defect of Northern fiction or not, but upon the supposition that he does so, we remind him that both Thackeray and Balzac are dead, and that our recent novelists might as well, for all purposes of argument, be compared with Cervantes and Le Sage. Moreover, Balzac is rather a narrow writer in each of his books, and if we are to grant him breadth we must take him in the whole group which he required to work out his *comédie humaine*. Each one of Mr. Henry James's books is as broad as any one of Balzac's; and we believe his *Princess Casamassima* is of a scope and variety quite unknown to them. Thackeray, to be sure, wandered through vast spaces, but his greatest work was concerned with the very narrow world of English society; his pictures of life outside of society were in the vein of caricature. As for Tolstoï, he is the incomparable; and no novelist of any time or any tongue can fairly be compared with him, as no dramatist can fairly be compared with Shakespeare. Nevertheless, if something of this sort is absolutely required, we will

Harper's Magazine, LXXV (Sept., 1887), 639-640. This essay, with few changes, became a part of *Criticism and Fiction* (1891), Section XXIII. For a discussion of Howells' remarks on sectionalism and realism, see *Introduction*, p. cxlvii, note 383.

instance Mr. J. W. De Forest, in his very inadequately named *Miss Ravenel's Conversion*,[1] as presenting an image of American life during the late rebellion, both North and South, at home and in the field, which does not "shrink to pitiful dimensions" even when "put by the side of Tolstoï's" *War and Peace;* it is an admirable novel, and spacious enough for the vast drama glimpsed in it. Mr. Cable's *Grandissimes*[2] is large enough to reflect a civilization; and Mr. Bishop, in *The Golden Justice* and *The House of a Merchant Prince*,[3] shows a feeling for amplitude in the whole design, as well as for close and careful work in the details.

The present English fiction is as narrow as our own; and if a Southerner had looked a little farther abroad he would have found that most modern fiction was narrow in a certain sense. In Italy he would have found the best men writing novels as brief and restricted in range as ours; in Spain the novels are intense and deep, and not spacious; the French school, with the exception of Zola, is narrow; the Norwegians are narrow; the Russians, except Tolstoï, are narrow, and the next greatest after him, Tourguénief, is the narrowest great novelist, as to mere dimensions, that ever lived, dealing nearly always with small groups, isolated and analyzed in the most American fashion. In fine, the charge of narrowness accuses the whole tendency of modern fiction as much as the American school. But we do not by any means allow that this superficial narrowness is a defect, while denying that it is a universal characteristic of our fiction; it is rather, for the present, a virtue. Indeed, we should call the present American work, North and South, thorough, rather than narrow. In one sense it is as broad as life, for each man is a microcosm, and the writer who is able to acquaint us intimately with half a dozen people, or the conditions of a neighborhood or a class, has done something which cannot in

[1] John William De Forest, *Miss Ravenel's Conversion from Secession to Loyalty*, (New York, 1867).

[2] George Washington Cable, *The Grandissimes, a Story of Creole Life*, (New York, 1880).

[3] William Henry Bishop, *The House of a Merchant Prince*, (New York, 1883). *The Golden Justice*, (New York, 1887).

any bad sense be called narrow; his breadth is vertical instead of lateral, that is all; and this depth is more desirable than horizontal expansion in a civilization like ours, where the differences are not of classes, but of types, and not of types either so much as of characters. A new method was necessary in dealing with the new conditions, and the new method is world-wide, because the whole world is more or less Americanized. Tolstoï is exceptionally voluminous among modern writers, even Russian writers; and it might be said that the *forte* of Tolstoï himself is not in his breadth sidewise, but in his breadth upward and downward. *The Death of Ivan Illitch* leaves as vast an impression on the reader's soul as any episode of *War and Peace*, which indeed can only be recalled in episodes, and not as a whole. In fine, we think that our writers may be safely counselled to continue their work in the modern way, because it is the best way yet known. If they make it true, it will be large, no matter what its superficies are; and it would be the greatest mistake to try to make it big. A big book is necessarily a group of episodes more or less loosely connected by a thread of narrative, and there seems no reason why this thread must always be supplied. Each episode may be quite distinct, or it may be one of a connected group; the final effect will be from the truth of each episode, not from the size of the group.

TOLSTOY'S CREED

Very likely [free trade] is not the true answer; but if it is a part of that truth, we have reason to be glad of it; and the remedy which it suggests, being public and political, is much easier of application than that proposed for the amelioration of human life by count Tolstoii in his latest work. *Que Faire*, he calls it; and he believes that the first thing we are to do for the other sinners and sufferers is to stop sinning and suffering ourselves. He tells us, with that terrible, unsparing honesty of his, how he tried to do good among the poor in Moscow, and how he failed to do any good, because he proposed a physical instead of a moral relief, a false instead of a real charity, while he grew more and more into conceit of himself as a fine fellow. He wished to live in idleness and ease, as he had always lived, and to rid himself of the tormenting consciousness of the misery all around him by feeding and clothing and sheltering it. But when he came to look closer into the life of the poor, even the poorest, he found that two-thirds of them were hard at work and happy; the other third suffered because they had lost the wholesome habit of work, and were corrupted by the desire to live, like the rich, in luxury and indolence; because, like the rich, they despised and hated labor. No rich man, therefore, could help them, because his life and aims were of a piece with theirs, while a great social gulf, forbidding all brotherly contact, was fixed between them. Therefore this singular Russian nobleman concludes that it is not for him to try to make the idle poor better than the idle rich by setting them at work, but that as one of the idle rich he must first make himself better than the idle poor by going to work with his own hands, by abolishing his own nobility, and by consorting with other men as if he were born the equal of all. It is the inexorable stress of this conclusion which

Harper's Magazine, LXXV (July, 1887), 316. For a discussion of Howells' appreciation of Tolstoy, and the relationship between *Annie Kilburn* and *Que Faire,* see *Introduction*, p. cxiv, note 289. A list of Howells' references to Tolstoy may be found in Gibson and Arms, *Bibliography*.

has forced him to leave the city, to forego his splendor in society and the sweets of his literary renown, to simplify his life, to go into the country, and to become literally a peasant and the companion of peasants. He, the greatest living writer, and incomparably the greatest writer of fiction who has ever lived, tells us that he finds this yoke easy and this burden light, that he is no longer weary or heavy laden with the sorrows of others or his share of their sins, but that he has been given rest by humble toil. It is a hard saying; but what if it should happen to be the truth? In that case, how many of us who have great possessions must go away exceeding sorrowful! Come, star-eyed Political Economy! come, Sociology, heavenly nymph! and soothe the ears tortured by this echo of Nazareth. Save us, sweet Evolution! Help, O Nebular Hypothesis! Art, Civilization, Literature, Culture! is there no escape from our brothers but in becoming more and more truly their brothers?

Count Tolstoii makes a very mortifying study of himself as an intending benefactor of the poor, and holds all the kindly well-to-do up to self-scorn in the picture. He found the poor caring for the poor out of their penury with a tenderness which the rich cannot know; he found a wretched prostitute foregoing her infamous trade, her means of life, that she might nurse a sick neighbor; he found an old woman denying herself that she might give food and shelter to a blind mendicant; he found a wretched tailor who had adopted an orphan into his large family of children. When he gave twenty kopecks to a beggar whom he met, the poor man with him gave three. But Count Tolstoii had an income of 600,000 rubles, and this poor man 150 rubles. He says that he ought to have given 3000 rubles to the beggar in order to have given his proportion. His wealth became not only ridiculous, but horrible, to him, for he realized that his income was wrung from the necessity of the wretched peasants. He saw cities as the sterile centres of the idleness and misery of the poor. He arraigned the present civil order as wrong, false, and unnatural; he sold all he had and gave it to the poor, and turned and followed Him. From his work-bench he sends this voice back into the world, to search the hearts of those who will hear, and to invite them to go and do likewise.

MAIN TRAVELLED ROADS

We must not be impatient of any writer who continues a short-story writer when he might freely become a novelist. Now that a writer can profitably do so, he may prefer to grow his fiction on the dwarf stock; he may plausibly contend that this was the original stock, and that the *novella* was a short story many ages before its name was appropriated by the standard variety, the duodecimo American, or the three-volume English; that Boccaccio was a world-wide celebrity five centuries before George Eliot was known to be a woman. To be sure, we might come back at him with the Greek romancers; we might ask him what he had to say to the interminable tales of Heliodorus and Longus, and the rest; and then not let him say.

But no such controversy is necessary to the enjoyment of the half-dozen volumes of short stories at hand, and we gladly postpone it till we have nothing to talk about. At present we have only too much to talk about in a book so robust and terribly serious as Mr. Hamlin Garland's volume called *Main-Travelled Roads*. That is what they call the highways in the part of the West that Mr. Garland comes from and writes about; and these stories are full of the bitter and burning dust, the foul and trampled slush of the common avenues of life: the life of the men who hopelessly and cheerlessly make the wealth that enriches the alien and the idler, and impoverishes the producer. If any one is still at a loss to account for that uprising of the farmers in the West, which is the translation of the Peasants' War into modern and republican terms, let him read *Main-Travelled Roads* and he will begin to understand, unless, indeed, Mr. Garland is painting the exceptional rather than the average. The stories are full of those gaunt, grim, sordid, pathetic, ferocious figures, whom our satirists find so easy to caricature as

Harper's Magazine, LXXXIII (Sept., 1891), 639–640. For a discussion of Howells' relationship with Hamlin Garland, see *Introduction*, p. cxxxvii. A list of Howells' writings on Garland may be found in Gibson and Arms, *Bibliography*.

Hayseeds, and whose blind groping for fairer conditions is so grotesque to the newspapers and so menacing to the politicians. They feel that something is wrong, and they know that the wrong is not theirs. The type caught in Mr. Garland's book is not pretty; it is ugly and often ridiculous; but it is heart-breaking in its rude despair. The story of a farm mortgage as it is told in the powerful sketch "Under the Lion's Paw" is a lesson in political economy, as well as a tragedy of the darkest cast. "The Return of the Private" is a satire of the keenest edge, as well as a tender and mournful idyl of the unknown soldier who comes back after the war with no blare of welcoming trumpets or flash of streaming flags, but foot-sore, heart-sore, with no stake in the country he has helped to make safe and rich but the poor man's chance to snatch an uncertain subsistence from the furrows he left for the battle-field. "Up the Coulée", however, is the story which most pitilessly of all accuses our vaunted conditions, wherein every man has the chance to rise above his brother and make himself richer than his fellows. It shows us once for all what the risen man may be, and portrays in his good-natured selfishness and indifference that favorite ideal of our system. The successful brother comes back to the old farmstead, prosperous, handsome, well dressed, and full of patronizing sentiment for his boyhood days there, and he cannot understand why his brother, whom hard work and corroding mortgages have eaten all the joy out of, gives him a grudging and surly welcome. It is a tremendous situation, and it is the allegory of the whole world's civilization: the upper dog and the under dog are everywhere, and the under dog nowhere likes it.

But the allegorical effects are not the primary intent of Mr. Garland's work: it is a work of art, first of all, and we think of fine art; though the material will strike many gentilities as coarse and common. In one of the stories, "Among the Corn Rows," there is a good deal of burly, broad-shouldered humor of a fresh and native kind; in "Mrs. Ripley's Trip" is a delicate touch, like that of Miss Wilkins; but Mr. Garland's touches are his own, here and elsewhere. He has a certain harshness and bluntness, an indifference to the more delicate charms of style;

and he has still to learn that though the thistle is full of an un-recognized poetry, the rose has a poetry too, that even over-praise cannot spoil. But he has a fine courage to leave a fact with the reader, ungarnished and unvarnished, which is almost the rarest trait in an Anglo-Saxon writer, so infantile and feeble is the custom of our art; and this attains tragical sublimity in the opening sketch, "A Branch Road," where the lover who has quarrelled with his betrothed comes back to find her mismated and miserable, such a farm wife as Mr. Garland has alone dared to draw, and tempts the broken-hearted drudge away from her loveless home. It is all morally wrong, but the author leaves you to say that yourself. He knows that his business was with those two people, their passions and their probabilities. He shows them such as the newspapers know them.

EMILE ZOLA*

In these times of electrical movement, the sort of construction in the moral world for which ages were once needed takes place almost simultaneously with the event to be adjusted in history, and as true a perspective forms itself as any in the past. A few weeks after the death of a poet of such great epical imagination, such great ethical force, as Émile Zola, we may see him as clearly and judge him as fairly as posterity alone was formerly supposed able to see and to judge the heroes that antedated it. The present is always holding in solution the elements of the future and the past, in fact; and whilst Zola still lived, in the moments of his highest activity, the love and hate, the intelligence and ignorance, of his motives and his work were as evident, and were as accurately the measure of progressive and retrogressive criticism, as they will be hereafter in any of the literary periods to come. There will never be criticism to appreciate him more justly, to depreciate him more unjustly, than that of his immediate contemporaries. There will never be a day when criticism will be of one mind about him, when he will no longer be a question, and will have become a conclusion.

A conclusion is an accomplished fact, something finally ended, something dead; and the extraordinary vitality of Zola, when he was doing the things most characteristic of him, forbids the notion of this in his case. Like every man who embodies an ideal, his individuality partook of what was imperishable in that ideal. Because he believed with his whole soul that fiction should be the representation, and in no measure the misrepresentation, of life, he will live as long as any history of literature survives. He will live as a question, a dispute, an affair of inextinguishable debate; for the two principles of the

*Reprinted by permission of Mildred Howells and John Mead Howells from *North American Review*, CLXXV (Nov. 1902), 587–596. For a discussion of Howells' interest in Zola and other European writers, see *Introduction*, p. cxlviii.

human mind, the love of the natural and the love of the unnatural, the real and the unreal, the truthful and the fanciful,
are inalienable and indestructible.

I

Zola embodied his ideal inadequately, as every man who embodies an ideal must. His realism was his creed, which he tried
to make his deed; but, before his fight was ended, and almost
before he began to forebode it a losing fight, he began to feel
and to say (for to feel, with that most virtuous and veracious
spirit, implied saying) that he was too much a romanticist by
birth and tradition, to exemplify realism in his work. He could
not be all to the cause he honored that other men were—men
like Flaubert and Maupassant, and Tourguenieff and Tolstoy,
and Galdós and Valdés—because his intellectual youth had been
nurtured on the milk of romanticism at the breast of his mother-
time. He grew up in the day when the great novelists and poets
were romanticists, and what he came to abhor he had first
adored. He was that pathetic paradox, a prophet who cannot
practise what he preaches, who cannot build his doctrine into
the edifice of a living faith.

Zola was none the less, but all the more, a poet in this. He
conceived of reality poetically and always saw his human docu-
ments, as he began early to call them, ranged in the form of an
epic poem. He fell below the greatest of the Russians, to whom
alone he was inferior, in imagining that the affairs of men group
themselves strongly about a central interest to which they constantly refer, and after whatever excursions definitely or defini-
tively return. He was not willingly an epic poet, perhaps, but
he was an epic poet, nevertheless; and the imperfection of his
realism began with the perfection of his form. Nature is sometimes dramatic, though never on the hard and fast terms of the
theatre, but she is almost never epic; and Zola was always epic.
One need only think over his books and his subjects to be convinced of this: "*L'Assommoir*" and drunkenness; "*Nana*" and
harlotry; "*Germinale*" and strikes; "*L'Argent*" and money get-

ting and losing in all its branches; "*Pot-Bouille*" and the cruel
squalor of poverty; "*La Terre*" and the life of the peasant;
"*Le Debâcle*" and the decay of imperialism. The largest of
these schemes does not extend beyond the periphery described
by the centrifugal whirl of its central motive, and the least of
the Rougon-Macquart series is of the same epicality as the
grandest. Each is bound to a thesis, but reality is bound to no
thesis. You cannot say where it begins or where it leaves off;
and it will not allow you to say precisely what its meaning or
argument is. For this reason, there are no such perfect pieces of
realism as the plays of Ibsen, which have all or each a thesis, but
do not hold themselves bound to prove it, or even fully to
state it; after these, for reality, come the novels of Tolstoy,
which are of a direction so profound because so patient of
aberration and exception.

We think of beauty as implicated in symmetry, but there are
distinctly two kinds of beauty: the symmetrical and the unsym-
metrical, the beauty of the temple and the beauty of the tree.
Life is no more symmetrical than a tree, and the effort of art to
give it balance and proportion is to make it as false in effect as
a tree clipped and trained to a certain shape. The Russians and
the Scandinavians alone seem to have risen to a consciousness of
this in their imaginative literature, though the English have
always unconsciously obeyed the law of our being in their
generally crude and involuntary formulations of it. In the
northern masters there is no appearance of what M. Ernest
Dupuy calls the joiner-work of the French fictionists; and there
is, in the process, no joiner-work in Zola, but the final effect is
joiner-work. It is a temple he builds, and not a tree he plants
and lets grow after he has planted the seed, and here he betrays
not only his French school but his Italian instinct.

In his form, Zola is classic, that is regular, symmetrical,
seeking the beauty of the temple rather than the beauty of the
tree. If the fight in his day had been the earlier fight between
classicism and romanticism, instead of romanticism and realism,
his nature and tradition would have ranged him on the side of
classicism, though, as in the later event, his feeling might have

been romantic. I think it has been the error of criticism not to take due account of his Italian origin, or to recognize that he was only half French, and that this half was his superficial half. At the bottom of his soul, though not perhaps at the bottom of his heart, he was Italian, and of the great race which in every science and every art seems to win the primacy when it will. The French, through the rhetoric of Napoleon III, imposed themselves on the imagination of the world as the representatives of the Latin race, but they are the least and the last of the Latins, and the Italians are the first. To his Italian origin Zola owed not only the moralistic scope of his literary ambition, but the depth and strength of his personal conscience, capable of the austere puritanism which underlies the so-called immoralities of his books, and incapable of the peculiar lubricity which we call French, possibly to distinguish it from the lubricity of other people rather than to declare it a thing solely French. In the face of all public and private corruptions, his soul is as Piagnone[1] as Savonarola's, and the vices of Arrabbiati, small and great, are always his test, upon which he preaches virtue.

II

Zola is to me so vast a theme that I can only hope here to touch his work at a point or two, leaving the proof of my sayings mostly to the honesty of the reader. It will not require so great an effort of his honesty now, as it once would, to own that

[1]Girolamo Savonarola (1452–1498) was a Dominican friar who undertook religious reform in the city of Florence. For his zeal his enemies finally burned him at the stake. The name Piagnoni (literally, snivelers; hence paid mourners, crapehangers) was given to the followers of Savonarola and carried the suggestion that they were hypocrites. Thirty years after the death of the Dominican fanatic, when certain preachers were attempting to continue his work, the name Piagnoni was given to the more moderate part of the popular faction of which the Arrabbiati (literally, the mad ones) constituted the extremist wing. These names arose again in the nineteenth century when, in an effort to harmonize religion and democracy, men like Césare Guasti saw in Savonarola their prophet. *Enciclopedia Italiana*, XXVII, 99. Howells here means to suggest that Zola, like Savonarola, was an austere moralist at heart in spite of the apparent immorality of his novels.

Zola's books, though often indecent, are never immoral, but always most terribly, most pitilessly moral. I am not saying now that they ought to be in every family library, or that they could be edifyingly committed to the hands of boys and girls; one of our first publishing houses is about to issue an edition even of the Bible "with those passages omitted which are usually skipped in reading aloud"; and it is always a question how much young people can be profitably allowed to know; how much they do know, they alone can tell. But as to the intention of Zola in his books, I have no doubt of its righteousness. His books may be, and I suppose they often are, indecent, but they are not immoral; they may disgust, but they will not deprave; only those already rotten can scent corruption in them, and these, I think may be deceived by effluvia from within themselves.

It is to the glory of the French realists that they broke, one and all, with the tradition of the French romanticists that vice was or might be something graceful, something poetic, something gay, brilliant, something superior almost, and at once boldly presented it in its true figure, its spiritual and social and physical squalor. Beginning with Flaubert in his "*Madame Bovary*," and passing through the whole line of their studies in morbid anatomy, as the "*Germinie Lacerteux*" of the Goncourts, as the "*Bel-Ami*" of Maupassant, and as all the books of Zola, you have portraits as veracious as those of the Russians, or those of Defoe, whom, indeed, more than any other master, Zola has made me think of in his frankness. Through his epicality he is Defoe's inferior, though much more than his equal in the range and implication of his work.

A whole world seems to stir in each of his books; and, though it is a world altogether bent for the time being upon one thing, as the actual world never is, every individual in it seems alive and true to the fact. M. Bruntière says Zola's characters are not true to the French fact; that his peasants, working-men, citizens, soldiers are not French, whatever else they may be; but this is merely M. Bruntière's word against Zola's word, and Zola had as good opportunities of knowing French life as M. Bruntière, whose aesthetics, as he betrays them in his instances, are of a flabbiness which does not impart conviction.[2] Word for word, I should take Zola's word as to the fact, not because I have the means of affirming him more reliable, but because I have rarely known the observant instinct of poets to fail, and because I believe that every reader will find in himself sufficient witness to the veracity of Zola's characterizations. These, if they are not true to the French fact, are true to the human fact; and I should say that in these the reality of Zola, unreal or ideal in his larger form, his epicality, vitally resided. His people live in the memory as entirely as any people who have ever lived; and, however devastating one's experience of them may be, it leaves no doubt of their having been.

III

It is not much to say of a work of literary art that it will survive as a record of the times it treats of, and I would not claim high value for Zola's fiction because it is such a true picture of the Second Empire in its decline; yet, beyond any other books I just now think of, his books have the quality that alone makes novels historical. That they include everything, that they do justice to all sides and phases of the period, it would be fatuous to expect, and ridiculous to demand. It is not their epical character alone that forbids this; it is the condition of every work of art, which must choose its point of view, and include only the things that fall within a certain scope. One of Zola's polemical delusions was to suppose that a fiction ought not to be selective, and that his own fictions were not selective, but portrayed the fact without choice and without limitation. The fact was that he was always choosing, and always limiting. Even a map chooses and limits, far more a picture. Yet this delusion of Zola's and its affirmation resulted in no end of misunderstanding. People said the noises of the streets, which he supposed himself to have given with graphophonic fulness and variety, were not music; and they were quite right. Zola, as far as his effects were voluntary, was not giving them music; he openly

[2] *Le Roman Naturalist* (1883).

loathed the sort of music they meant just as he openly loathed art, and asked to be regarded as a man of science rather than an artist. Yet, at the end of the ends, he was an artist and not a man of science. His hand was perpetually selecting his facts, and shaping them to one epical result, with an orchestral accompaniment, which, though reporting the rudest noises of the street, the vulgarest, the most offensive, was, in spite of him, so reporting them that the result was harmony.

Zola was an artist, and one of the very greatest, but even before and beyond that he was intensely a moralist, as only the moralists of our true and noble time have been. Not Tolstoy, not Ibsen himself, has more profoundly and indignantly felt the injustice of civilization, or more insistently shown the falsity of its fundamental pretensions. He did not make his books a polemic for one cause or another; he was far too wise and sane for that; but when he began to write them they became alive with his sense of what was wrong and false and bad. His tolerance is less than Tolstoy's, because his resignation is not so great; it is for the weak sinners and not for the strong, while Tolstoy's, with that transcendent vision of his race, pierces the bounds where the shows of strength and weakness cease and become of a solidarity of error in which they are one. But the ethics of his work, like Tolstoy's, were always carrying over into his life. He did not try to live poverty and privation and hard labor, as Tolstoy does; he surrounded himself with the graces and the luxuries which his honestly earned money enabled him to buy; but when an act of public and official atrocity[3] disturbed the working of his mind and revolted his nature, he could not rest again till he had done his best to right it.

---

[3] In 1893 Alfred Dreyfus was falsely condemned for giving military secrets to the Germans. On January 13, 1898, convinced that Captain Dreyfus had been framed by the military, Zola wrote an open letter to the newspaper *L'Aurore*, beginning with the words "J' accuse." Zola wished to be prosecuted by the government in order to have the whole case aired. He was tried in February, 1898, and a verdict imposing imprisonment and fine was brought against him. He appealed the case, however, and the verdict was quashed. In 1899 a second trial was held and Dreyfus was released and pardoned. Zola wrote his account of the case in "L' Affaire Dreyfus" (1901). Dreyfus was finally acquitted in 1906.

IV

The other day Zola died (by a casualty which one fancies he would have liked to employ in a novel, if he had thought of it),[4] and the man whom he had befriended at the risk of all he had in the world, his property, his liberty, his life itself, came to his funeral in disguise, risking again all that Zola had risked, to pay the last honors to his incomparable benefactor.

It was not the first time that a French literary man had devoted himself to the cause of the oppressed, and made it his personal affair, his charge, his inalienable trust. But Voltaire's championship of the persecuted Protestant had not the measure of Zola's championship of the persecuted Jew, though in both instances the courage and the persistence of the vindicator forced the reopening of the case and resulted in final justice.[5] It takes nothing from the heroism of Voltaire to recognize that it was not so great as the heroism of Zola, and it takes nothing from the heroism of Zola to recognize that it was effective in the only country of Europe where such a case as that of Dreyfus would have been reopened; where there was a public imagination generous enough to conceive of undoing an act of immense public cruelty. At first this imagination was dormant, and the French people conceived only of punishing the vindicator along with the victim, for daring to accuse their processes of injustice. Outrage, violence, and the peril of death greeted Zola from his fellow-citizens, and from the authorities ignominy, fine, and prison. But nothing silenced or deterred him, and, in the swift course of moral adjustment characteristic of our time, an innumerable multitude of those who were ready a few years ago to rend him in pieces joined in paying tribute to the greatness of his soul, at the grave which received his body already buried

[4]Zola was found dead in his Paris apartment on September 2, 1902. His death was caused by gas from a defective flue.

[5]In 1740 a Protestant, Jean-Pierre Espinasse, gave supper and a night's lodging to a Protestant minister, for which he was condemned to the galleys for life. Through Voltaire's efforts Espinasse was released in 1767. He returned to Switzerland and found his family living in poverty. After three years Voltaire succeeded in restoring to Espinasse a small portion of his property.

under an avalanche of flowers. The government has not been so prompt as the mob, but with the history of France in mind, remembering how official action has always responded to the national impulses in behalf of humanity and justice, one cannot believe that the representatives of the French people will long remain behind the French people in offering reparation to the memory of one of the greatest and most heroic of French citizens. It is a pity for the government that it did not take part in the obsequies of Zola; it would have been well for the army, which he was falsely supposed to have defamed, to have been present to testify of the real service and honor he had done it. But, in good time enough, the reparation will be official as well as popular, and when the monument to Zola, which has already risen in the hearts of his countrymen, shall embody itself in enduring marble or perennial bronze, the army will be there to join in its consecration.

V

There is no reason why criticism should affect an equal hesitation. Criticism no longer assumes to ascertain an author's place in literature. It is very well satisfied if it can say something suggestive concerning the nature and quality of his work, and it tries to say this with as little of the old air of finality as it can manage to hide its poverty in.

After the words of M. Chaumie at the funeral, "Zola's life work was dominated by anxiety for sincerity and truth, an anxiety inspired by his great feelings of pity and justice," there seems nothing left to do but to apply them to the examination of his literary work. They unlock the secret of his performance, if it is any longer a secret, and they afford its justification in all those respects where without them it could not be justified. The question of immorality has been set aside, and the indecency has been admitted, but it remains for us to realize that anxiety for sincerity and truth, springing from the sense of pity and justice, makes indecency a condition of portraying human nature so that it may look upon its image and be ashamed.

The moralist working imaginatively has always had to ask himself how far he might go in illustration of his thesis, and he has not hesitated, or if he has hesitated, he has not failed to go far, very far. Defoe went far, Richardson went far, Ibsen has gone far, Tolstoy has gone far, and if Zola went farther than any of these, still he did not go so far as the immoralists have gone in the portrayal of vicious things to allure where he wished to repel. There is really such a thing as high motive and such a thing as low motive, though the processes are often so bewilderingly alike in both cases. The processes may confound us, but there is no reason why we should be mistaken as to motive, and as to Zola's motive I do not think M. Chaumie was mistaken. As to his methods, they by no means always reflected his intentions. He fancied himself working like a scientist who has collected a vast number of specimens, and is deducing principles from them. But the fact is, he was always working like an artist, seizing every suggestion of experience and observation, turning it to the utmost account, piecing it out by his invention, building it up into a structure of fiction where its origin was lost to all but himself, and often even to himself. He supposed that he was recording and classifying, but he was creating and vivifying. Within the bounds of his epical scheme, which was always factitious, every person was so natural that his characters seemed like the characters of biography rather than of fiction. One does not remember them as one remembers the characters of most novelists. They had their being in a design which was meant to represent a state of things, to enforce an opinion of certain conditions; but they themselves were free agencies, bound by no allegiance to the general frame, and not apparently acting in behalf of the author, but only from their own individuality. At the moment of reading, they make the impression of an intense reality, and they remain real, but one recalls them as one recalls the people read of in last week's or last year's newspaper. What Zola did was less to import science and its methods into the region of fiction, than journalism and its methods; but in this he had his will only so far as his nature of artist would allow. He was no more a journalist than he was a scientist by nature; and, in spite of his intentions and in spite of his methods, he was essentially imaginative and involuntarily creative.

VI

To me his literary history is very pathetic. He was bred if not born in the worship of the romantic, but his native faith was not proof against his reason, as again his reason was not proof against his native faith. He preached a crusade against romanticism, and fought a long fight with it, only to realize at last that he was himself too romanticistic to succeed against it, and heroically to own his defeat. The hosts of romanticism swarmed back over him and his followers, and prevailed, as we see them still prevailing. It was the error of the realists whom Zola led, to suppose that people like truth in fiction better than falsehood; they do not; they like falsehood best; and if Zola had not been at heart a romanticist, he never would have cherished his long delusion, he never could have deceived with his vain hopes those whom he persuaded to be realistic, as he himself did not succeed in being.

He wished to be a sort of historiographer writing the annals of a family, and painting a period; but he was a poet, doing far more than this, and contributing to creative literature as great works of fiction as have been written in the epic form. He was a paradox on every side but one, and that was the human side, which he would himself have held far worthier than the literary side. On the human side, the civic side, he was what he wished to be, and not what any perversity of his elements made him. He heard one of those calls to supreme duty, which from time to time select one man and not another for the response which they require; and he rose to that duty with a grandeur which had all the simplicity possible to a man of French civilization. We may think that there was something a little too dramatic in the manner of his heroism, his martyry, and we may smile at certain turns of rhetoric in the immortal letter accusing the French nation of intolerable wrong, just as, in our smug Anglo-

Saxon conceit, we laughed at the procedure of the emotional courts which he compelled to take cognizance of the immense misdeed other courts had as emotionally committed. But the event, however indirectly and involuntarily, was justice which no other people in Europe would have done, and perhaps not any people of this more enlightened continent.

The success of Zola as a literary man has its imperfections, its phases of defeat, but his success as a humanist is without flaw. He triumphed as wholly and as finally as it has ever been given a man to triumph, and he made France triumph with him. By his hand, she added to the laurels she had won in the war of American Independence, in the wars of the Revolution for liberty and equality, in the campaigns for Italian Unity, the imperishable leaf of a national acknowledgment of national error.

FRANK NORRIS*

The projection which death gives the work of a man against the history of his time, is the doubtful gain we have to set against the recent loss of such authors as George Douglas, the Scotchman, who wrote "The House with the Green Shutters," and Frank Norris, the American, who wrote "McTeague" and "The Octopus," and other novels, antedating and postdating the first of these, and less clearly prophesying his future than the last. The gain is doubtful, because, though their work is now freed from the cloud of question which always involves the work of a living man in the mind of the general, if his work is good (if it is bad they give it no faltering welcome), its value was already apparent to those who judge from the certainty within themselves, and not from the uncertainty without. Every one in a way knows a thing to be good, but the most have not the courage to acknowledge it, in their sophistication with canons and criterions. The many, who in the tale of the criticism are not worth minding, are immensely unworthy of the test which death alone seems to put into their power. The few, who had the test before, were ready to own that Douglas's study of Scottish temperaments offered a hope of Scottish fiction freed the Scottish sentimentality which had kept it provincial; and that Norris's two mature novels, one personal and one social, imparted the assurance of an American fiction so largely commensurate with American circumstance as to liberate it from the casual and the occasional, in which it seemed lastingly trammelled. But the parallel between the two does not hold much farther. What Norris did, not merely what he dreamed of doing, was of vaster frame, and inclusive of imaginative intentions far beyond those of the only immediate contemporary

*Reprinted by permission of Mildred Howells and John Mead Howells from *North American Review*, CLXXV (Dec., 1902), 769–778. For a discussion of Howells' relation to Frank Norris and the younger writers of his generation, see *Introduction*, pp. cxxxviii; clxv. A list of Howells' writings on Norris may be found in Gibson and Arms, *Bibliography*.

to be matched with him, while it was of as fine and firm an intellectual quality, and of as intense and fusing an emotionality.

I

In several times and places, it has been my rare pleasure to bear witness to the excellence of what Norris had done, and the richness of his promise. The vitality of his work was so abundant, the pulse of health was so full and strong in it, that it is incredible it should not be persistent still. The grief with which we accept such a death as his is without the consolation that we feel when we can say of some one that his life was a struggle, and that he is well out of the unequal strife, as we might say when Stephen Crane died.[1] The physical slightness, if I may so suggest one characteristic of Crane's vibrant achievement, reflected the delicacy of energies that could be put forth only in nervous spurts, in impulses vivid and keen, but wanting in breadth and bulk of effect. Curiously enough, on the other hand, this very lyrical spirit, whose freedom was its life, was the absolute slave of reality. It was interesting to hear him defend what he had written, in obedience to his experience of things, against any change in the interest of convention. "No," he would contend, in behalf of the profanities of his people, "That is the way they *talk*. I have thought of that, and whether I ought to leave such things out, but if I do I am not giving the thing as I *know* it." He felt the constraint of those semi-savage natures, such as he depicted in "Maggie," and "George's Mother," and was forced through the fealty of his own nature to report them as they spoke no less than as they looked. When it came to "The Red Badge of Courage," where he took leave of these simple aesthetics, and lost himself in a whirl of wild guesses at the fact from the ground of insufficient witness, he made the failure which formed the break between his first and his second manner, though it was what the public counted a

[1]For a discussion of Howells' relationship to Stephen Crane, see *Introduction*, p. cxxxvii. A list of Howells' reviews of Crane may be found in Gibson and Arms, *Bibliography*.

success, with every reason to do so from the report of the sales.

The true Stephen Crane was the Stephen Crane of the earlier book; for "Maggie" remains the best thing he did. All he did was lyrical, but this was the aspect and accent as well as the spirit of the tragically squalid life he sang, while "The Red Badge of Courage," and the other things that followed it, were the throes of an art failing with material to which it could not render an absolute devotion from an absolute knowledge. He sang, but his voice erred up and down the scale, with occasional flashes of brilliant melody, which could not redeem the errors. New York was essentially his inspiration, the New York of suffering and baffled and beaten life, of inarticulate or blasphemous life; and away from it he was not at home, with any theme, or any sort of character. It was the pity of his fate that he must quit New York, first as a theme, and then as a habitat; for he rested nowhere else, and wrought with nothing else as with the lurid depths which he gave proof of knowing better than any one else. Every one is limited, and perhaps no one is more limited than another; only, the direction of the limitation is different in each. Perhaps George Douglas, if he had lived, would still have done nothing greater than "The House with the Green Shutters," and might have failed in the proportion of a larger range as Stephen Crane did. I am not going to say that either of these extraordinary talents was of narrower bound than Frank Norris; such measures are not of the map. But I am still less going to say that they were of finer quality because their achievement seems more poignant, through the sort of physical concentration which it has. Just as a whole unhappy world agonizes in the little space their stories circumscribe, so what is sharpest and subtlest in that anguish finds its like in the epical breadths of Norris's fiction.

II

At the other times when I so gladly owned the importance of this fiction, I frankly recognized what seemed to me the author's debt to an older master; and now, in trying to sum up my sense of it in an estimate to which his loss gives a sort of finality for me, I must own again that he seemed to derive his ideal of the novel from the novels of Zola. I cannot say that, if the novels of Zola had not been cast in the epic mould, the novels of Frank Norris would not have been epical. This is by no means certain; while it is, I think, certain that they owe nothing beyond the form to the master from whom he may have imagined it. Or they owe no more to him, essentially, than to the other masters of the time in which Norris lived out his life all too soon. It is not for nothing that any novelist is born in one age, and not another, unless we are to except that aoristic freak, the historical novelist; and by what Frank Norris wrote one might easily know what he had read. He had read, and had profited, with as much originality as any man may keep for himself, by his study of the great realists whose fiction has illustrated the latter part of the nineteenth century beyond any other time in the history of fiction; and if he seemed to have served his apprenticeship rather more to one of them than to another, this may be the effect of an inspiration not finally derived from that one. An Italian poet says that in Columbus "the instinct of the unknown continent burned"; and it may be that this young novelist, who had his instincts mostly so well intellectualized, was moved quite from within when he imagined treating American things in an epical relation as something most expressive of their actual relation. I am not so sure that this is so, but I am sure that he believed it so, and that neither in material nor in treatment are his novels Zolaesque, though their form is Zolaesque, in the fashion which Zola did not invent, though he stamped it so deeply with his nature and his name.

I may allow also that he was like Zola in his occasional indulgence of a helpless fondness for the romantic, but he quite transcended Zola in the rich strain of poetry coloring his thought, and the mysticism in which he now and then steeped his story. I do not care enough, however, for what is called originality in any writer to fatigue myself greatly in the effort to establish that of a writer who will avouch his fresh and vigorous powers to any one capable of feeling them. I prefer, in the presence of a large design left unfulfilled, to note the generous ideal, the ample purpose, forecast in the novel forming the first of the trilogy he imagined.

In one of those few meetings which seem, too late, as if they might have been so many, but which the New York conditions of overwork for all who work at all begrudge, I remember how he himself outlined his plan. The story of the Wheat was for him the allegory of the industrial and financial America which is the real America, and he had begun already to tell the first part of this story in the tragedy of the railroad-ridden farms of California, since published as "The Octopus." The second part, as he then designed, was to carry the tale to Chicago, where the distribution of the Wheat was to be the theme, as its production had already been the theme in the first. The last part was to find its scene in Europe, among the representative cities where the consumption of the Wheat was to form the motive. Norris believed himself peculiarly qualified for the work by the accidents of his life; for he was born in Chicago and had lived there till he was fifteen years old; then he had gone to California, and had grown up into the knowledge of the scene and action which he has portrayed so powerfully; later, he had acquainted himself with Europe, by long sojourn; and so he argued, with an enthusiasm tempered by a fine sense of his moral and artistic responsibility, that he had within himself the means of realizing the whole fact to the reader's imagination. He was aware that such a plan could be carried out only by years of ardent and patient study, and he expected to dedicate the best part of his strong young life to it.

III

Those who know "The Octopus" know how his work justified his faith in himself; but those who had known "McTeague" could not have doubted but he would do what he had undertaken, in the spirit of the undertaking. Norris did give the time and toil to the right documentation of his history. He went to California and renewed his vital knowledge of his scene; he was in California again, studying the course of the fact which was to bring him to Chicago, when death overtook him and ended his high emprise. But in the meantime he had given us "The Octopus," and before that he had given us "McTeague," books not all so unlike in their nature as their surfaces might suggest. Both are epical, though the one is pivoted on the common ambition of a coarse human animal, destined to prevail in a half-quackish triumph, and the other revolves about one of the largest interests of modern civilization. The author thought at first of calling "McTeague," as he told me, "The Golden Tooth," which would have been more significant of the irregular dentist's supremacy in the story, and the ideal which inspired him; but perhaps he felt a final impossibility in the name. Yet, the name is a mere mask; and when one opens the book, the mask falls, and the drama confronts us with as living a physiognomy as I have seen in fiction. There is a bad moment when the author is overcome by his lingering passion for the romantic, and indulges himself in a passage of rank melodrama; but even there he does nothing that denies the reality of his characters, and they are always of a reality so intense that one lives with them in the grotesquely shabby San Francisco street where, but for the final episode, the action passes.

What is good is good, it matters not what other things are better or worse; and I could ask nothing for Norris, in my sense of his admirable achievement, but a mind freed to criticism absolute and not relative. He is of his time, and, as I have said, his school is evident; and yet I think he has a right to make his appeal in "The Octopus" irrespective of the other great canvases beside which that picture must be put. One should dissociate it as far as possible from the work of his masters—we all have masters; the masters themselves had them—not because it is an imitation, and would suffer from the comparison, but because it is so essentially different, so boldly and frankly native, that one is in danger of blaming it for a want of conformity to models, rather than for too close a following. Yet this, again, does not say quite the right things, and what I feel, and wish others to feel, in regard to it, is the strong security of its most conscientious and instructed art. Here is nothing of experiment, of protest, of rebellion; the author does not break away from form in any sprawling endeavor for something newly or incomparably American, Californian, Western, but finds scope enough for his powers within the limits where the greatest fiction of our period "orbs about." The time, if there ever was one, for a prose Walt Whitman was past; and he perceived that the indigenous quality was to be imparted to his work by the use of fresh material, freshly felt, but used in the fashion and the form which a world-old art had evolved in its long endeavor.

"McTeague" was a personal epic, the Odyssey of a simple, semi-savage nature adventuring and experiencing along the low social levels which the story kept, and almost never rose or fell from. As I review it in the light of the first strong impressions, I must own it greater than I have ever yet acknowledged it, and I do this now with the regret which I hope the critic is apt to feel for not praising enough when praise could have helped most. I do not think my strictures of it were mistaken, for they related to the limits which certain facts of it would give it with the public, rather than to the ethical or aesthetic qualities which would establish it with the connoisseur. Yet, lest any reader of mine should be left without due sense of these, I wish now to affirm my strong sense of them, and to testify to the value which this extraordinary book has from its perfectly simple fidelity: from the truthfulness in which there is no self-doubt and no self-excuse.

IV

But, with all its power, "McTeague" is no such book as "The Octopus," which is the Iliad to its Odyssey.

It will not be suggesting too much for the story to say, that there is a kind of Homeric largeness in the play of the passions moving it. They are not autochthons, these Californians of the great Wheat farms, choking in the folds of the railroad, but Americans of more than one transplantation; yet there is something rankly earthy and elemental in them, which gives them the pathos of tormented Titans. It is hard to choose any of them as the type, as it is hard to choose any scene as the representative moment. It we choose Annixeter, growing out of an absolute, yet not gross, materiality, through the fire of a purifying love, into a kind of final spirituality, we think, with misgiving for our decision, of Magnus Derrick, the high, pure leader of the rebellion against the railroad, falling into ruin, moral and mental, through the use of the enemy's bad means for his good cause. Half a score of other figures, from either camp, crowd upon the fancy to contest the supreme interest, men figures, women figures; and, when it comes to choosing this episode or that as the supreme event, the confusion of the critic is even greater. If one were to instance the fight between the farmers and the sheriff's deputies, with the accompanying evictions, one must recall the tremendous passages of the train-robbery by the crazy victim of the railroad's treachery, taking his revenge in his hopeless extremity. Again, a half score of other scenes, other episodes rise from the remembered pages, and defy selection.

The story is not less but more epical, in being a strongly inter-wrought group of episodes. The play of an imagination fed by a rich consciousness of the mystical relations of nature and human nature, the body and the soul of earthly life, steeps the whole theme in an odor of common growth. It is as if the Wheat sprang out of the hearts of men, in the conception of the young poet who writes its Iliad, and who shows how it over-whelms their lives, and germinates anew from their deaths. His poem, of which the terms are naked prose, is a picture of the civilization, the society, the culture which is the efflorescence of the wheaten prosperity; and the social California, rank, crude, lusty, which he depicts is as convincing as the agricultural California, which is the ground of his work. It will be easily believed that in the handling nothing essential to the strong impression is blinked; but nothing, on the other hand, is forced in. The episode of Venamee and Angèle, with its hideous tragedy, and the long mystical epilogue ending almost in anti-climax, is the only passage which can be accused of irrelevance, and it is easier to bring than to prove this accusation.

As I write, and scarcely touch the living allegory here and there, it rises before me in its large inclusion, and makes me feel once more how little any analysis of a work of art can represent it. After all the critic must ask the reader to take his word for it that the thing is great, and entreat him to go see for himself: see, in this instance, the breadth and the fineness, the beauty and the dread, the baseness and the grandeur, the sensuality and the spirituality, working together for the effect of a novel unequalled for scope and for grasp in our fiction.

V

Fine work we have enough of and to spare in our fiction. No one can say it is wanting in subtlety of motive and delicate grace of form. But something still was lacking, something that was not merely the word but the deed of commensurateness. Perhaps, after all, those who have demanded Continentality of American literature had some reason in their folly. One thinks so, when one considers work like Norris's, and finds it so vast in scope while so fine and beautiful in detail. Hugeness was probably what those poor fellows were wanting when they asked for Continentality; and from any fit response that has come from them one might well fancy them dismayed and puzzled to have been given greatness instead. But Continentality he also gave them.

His last book is a fragment, a part of a greater work, but it is a mighty fragment, and it has its completeness. In any time but this, when the air is filled with the fizz and sputter of a thousand pin-wheels, the descent of such a massive aërolite as "The Octopus" would have stirred all men's wonder, but its light to most eyes appears to have seemed of one quality with those cheap explosives which all the publishing houses are setting off, and advertising as meteoric. If the time will still come for acknowledgment of its greatness, it will not be the time for him who put his heart and soul into it. That is the pity, but that in the human conditions is what cannot be helped. We are here to do something, we do not know why; we think it is for ourselves, but it is for almost anyone but ourselves. If it is great, some one else shall get the good of it, and the doer shall get the glory too late; if it is mean, the doer shall have the glory, but who shall have the good? This would not be so bad if there were life long enough for the processes of art; if the artist could outlive the doubt and the delay into which every great work of art seems necessarily to plunge the world anew, after all its experience of great work.

I am not saying, I hope, that Frank Norris had not his success, but only that he had not success enough, the success which he would have had if he had lived, and which will still be his too late. The two novels he has left behind him are sufficient for his fame, but though they have their completeness and their adequacy, one cannot help thinking of the series of their like that is now lost to us. It is Aladdin's palace, and yet,

> The unfinished window in Aladdin's tower
> Unfinished must remain.[1]

and we never can look upon it without an ache of longing and regret.

Personally, the young novelist gave one the impression of strength and courage that would hold out to all lengths. Health was in him always as it never was in that other rare talent of ours with whom I associate him in my sense of the irretrievable, the irreparable. I never met him but he made me feel that he could do it, the thing he meant to do, and do it robustly and quietly, without the tremor of "those electrical nerves" which imparted itself from the presence of Stephen Crane. With him my last talk of the right way and the true way of doing things was saddened by the confession of his belief that we were soon to be overwhelmed by the rising tide of romanticism, whose crazy rote he heard afar, and expected with the resignation which the sick experience with all things. But Norris heard nothing, or seemed to hear nothing, but the full music of his own aspiration, the rich diapason of purposes securely shaping themselves in performance.

[1]From Longfellow's poem *Hawthorne.*

Who shall inherit these, and carry forward work so instinct
with the Continent as his? Probably, no one; and yet good
work shall not fail us, manly work, great work. One need not
be overhopeful to be certain of this. Bad work, false, silly,
ludicrous work, we shall always have, for the most of those who
read are so, as well as the most of those who write; and yet there
shall be here and there one to see the varying sides of our manifold life truly and to say what he sees. When I think of Mr.
Brand Whitlock and his novel of "The Thirteenth District," [1]
which has embodied the very spirit of American politics as
American politicians know them in all Congressional districts;
when I think of the author of "The Spenders," [2] so wholly good
in one half that one forgets the other half is only half good;
when I think of such work as Mr. William Allen White's,[3] Mr.
Robert Herrick's,[4] Mr. Will Payne's[5]—all these among the
younger men—it is certainly not to despair because we shall
have no such work as Frank Norris's from them. They, and the
like of them, will do their good work as he did his.

---

[1] Brand Whitlock (1869–1934) was born in Urbana, Illinois. He became
a distinguished diplomat, who served as ambassador to Belgium before and
immediately after World War I. His novel *The Thirteenth District*, to
which Howells refers, had just been published when this essay was being
written.

[2] *The Spenders* (1902) was written by Harry Leon Wilson (1867–1939).

[3] William Allen White (1868–1944) had written *The Court of Boyville*
(1899) when Howells wrote this essay.

[4] Robert Herrick (1868–1938). See Howells' study "The Novels of
Robert Herrick," *North American Review*, CLXXXIX (June, 1909), 812–
820.

[5] William M. Payne (1858–1919) wrote *The Money Captain* in 1898.

ERRATA

Since the introduction and selections for the American Century Series edition of *Howells* were reprinted from the original plates of the American Writers Series edition, certain minor textual corrections in the introduction and selections have not been made.

INTRODUCTION

p. xviii, line 17: *First word should read* Forty

p. xx, footnote 10, line 10: Prairie de Vaches *should read* Prairie Des Vaches

   lines 16–17: *Through the Eye of a Needle* should read *Through the Eye of the Needle*

p. li, line 11: Old Manse *should read* Wayside

p. lx, footnote 148: 304–401 *should read* 364–401

p. lxv, line 6: 1866 *should read* 1869

p. lxxxiv, footnote 221, line 4: 1873 *should read* 1874

p. lxxxv, line 4: summer *should read* winter

p. lxxxvi, line 13: Englehardt *should read* Inglehart

   line 19: Ellie *should read* Effie

p. xc, footnote 236, line 14: Mrs. *Farrel* should read Mrs. *Farrell*

p. xcii, line 12: *Through the Eye of a Needle* should read *Through the Eye of the Needle*

p. xcviii, footnote 255, last line: Laurence *should read* Lawrence

p. ci, footnote 265, last line: Mrs. *Farrel* should read Mrs. *Farrell*

p. cv, footnote 273, line 3: *A Minister's Charge* should read *The Minister's Charge*

p. cxxiii, lines 2–3: *Through the Eye of a Needle* should read *Through the Eye of the Needle*

   footnote 313, line 5: five *should read* six

   footnote 313, line 21: *Line should read* Gronlund's *Co-operative Commonwealth.* Before he had read

SELECTIONS

p. 11, headnote line 7: Presiden *should read* President

p. 118, headnote line 7: Inglehardt *should read* Inglehart

p. 194, headnote line 8: Equity, New Hampshire, *should read* Maine, in order

p. 345, headnote last line: cxxxx–clxvii should read cxxxxi–clxvii

AI
A